IMPOSSIBLE SUBJECTS

POLITICS AND SOCIETY IN TWENTIETH-CENTURY AMERICA

Series Editors

WILLIAM CHAFE, GARY GERSTLE, LINDA GORDON, AND JULIAN ZELIZER

A list of titles in this series appears at the back of the book

Mae M. Ngai

IMPOSSIBLE SUBJECTS

ILLEGAL ALIENS AND THE
MAKING OF MODERN AMERICA

PRINCETON UNIVERSITY PRESS   PRINCETON AND OXFORD

First printing, 2004

Fourth printing and first paperback printing, 2005

New paperback edition, with a new foreword by the author, 2014

Paperback ISBN 978-0-691-16082-5

Library of Congress Control Number 2013957460

British Library Cataloging-in-Publication Data is available

This book has been composed in Minion Typeface Printed on acid-free paper. ∞

press.princeton.edu

Printed in the United States of America

10 9 8 7 6 5 4 3

To the memory of ————————————————————

Shih-hsun Ngai

and to
Hsueh-hwa Wang Ngai *and*
Michael S. Hing

It has always been easier, it always
will be easier, to think of someone as
a noncitizen than to
decide that he is a nonperson.

—ALEXANDER BICKEL, "Citizenship in the American Constitution"

Table of Contents

Figures and Illustrations

Tables

Acknowledgments _____

THIS BOOK has multiple histories. One is common to many first academic books: it began as a humble graduate school seminar paper, evolved into a dissertation, and then, with expansion and revision, finally matured into a book that one sends into the world with hopes that thoughtful people will find in it something useful. But it also has another genealogy, with origins not in the university but in family and community. As the daughter of Chinese immigrants, I grew up in a home where being Chinese and being American existed in tension, but not in contradiction. I later spent not a few years in New York's Chinatown community and labor movement as an activist and professional labor educator. In many ways my experience with immigrant workers and their struggles for legitimacy and equality motivated and sustained this study.

Nevertheless, this has been principally a project of historical scholarship, and I am indebted, first, to my teachers. At the State University of New York's Empire State College, the mecca of returning students, Robert Carey reintroduced me to reading history and suggested that I might think about going to graduate school. I thank my professors at Columbia University who taught me to read and write history: Elizabeth Blackmar, Alan Brinkley, Richard Bushman, Barbara J. Fields, Joshua Freeman, and Ira Katznelson. My biggest debt is to my advisor, Eric Foner, a great scholar, model teacher, and committed public intellectual, who took a chance by admitting a union organizer to the graduate program.

Many archivists and librarians eased my way through the labyrinths of archival research. I thank Robert Ellis at the National Archives in Washington; Waverly Lowell at the National Archives, Pacific regional branch, in San Francisco, California; Dr. Dorothy Cordova at the Filipino American National Historical Society in Seattle; Margo Gutíerrez at the Bensen Latin American Collection at the University of Texas-Austin; and the archivists and librarians at the Bancroft Library at the University of California-Berkeley; the National Archives at College Park, Maryland, and Northeast regional branch in New York City; the presidential libraries of Harry S. Truman, Lyndon Baines Johnson, and John F. Kennedy; the Herbert Lehman Library at Columbia University; the U.S. Library of Congress; the George Meany Memorial Archives in Silver Spring, Maryland; the Walter Reuther Labor and Urban History Archives at Wayne State University; and the Immigration History Research Center at the University of Minnesota.

I am especially grateful to the U.S. Immigration and Naturalization Service for granting me access to its subject files. As all historians know, it is a rare fortune to have the opportunity to consult previously unresearched records. This project would not have been possible without INS historian Marian Smith's commitment to the scholarly research of INS records. I am most grateful for her professionalism, patience, and good cheer during the months that I spent in her library and in response to the many queries I made during the years since. I thank Crystal Williams for her help with INS illustrations. Most (although not all) of the records I consulted at the INS central office have since been transferred to the National Archives in Washington (Record Group 85). At this writing much of the collection remains unprocessed, but researchers may request documents according to the information in my citations. Records that remain in the custody of the INS are so indicated.

Generous fellowships and grants supported additional research and writing of the book. I gratefully acknowledge the Social Science Research Council International Migration Program; New York University School of Law Samuel I. Goleib Fellowship in Legal History and NYU Asian Pacific American Studies; and the University of Chicago Division of Social Sciences.

I have benefited from support and constructive criticism from a wide circle of scholars in history, law, Asian American and Latino and Latina studies, and other fields. For reading all or parts of the penultimate draft of the manuscript I am grateful to Linda Bosniak, Gordon H. Chang, David L. Eng, Cindy Hahamovitch, Victoria Hattam, Matthew Jacobson, and Leti Volpp. Many people helped me by directing me to sources, reading drafts, correcting errors, and sharing their ideas and their own works in progress with me, and I thank them all: Jacqueline Bhabha, Beth Bates, Susan Carter, Gabriel J. Chin, Michael Dawson, Nicholas DeGenova, Mary Dudziak, Tami Friedman, Neil Gotanda, Ramón Gutiérrez, Charles Hawley, John Higham, Madeline Hsu, Erika Lee, Him Mark Lai, Adam McKeown, Rebecca McLennan, Nancy Morawetz, Gerald Neuman, Brian Niiya, Franklin Odo, Gary Y. Okihiro, Kunal Parker, Marc Simon Rodríguez, David Roediger, Teemu Ruskola, Lucy Salyer, George Sánchez, Dorothee Schneider, Paul A. Schor, Nayan Shah, Betty Lee Sung, Richard Sutch, John Kuo-wei Tchen, Christopher Tomlins, John Torpey, Dorothy Wang, Patrick Weil, Kevin Scott Wong, Kariann Yokota, Henry Yu, Michael Zakim, and Aristide Zolberg. I am saddened that Yuji Ichioka, who encouraged and advised me over the years, passed away before this book was published.

Colleagues in history and in other disciplines at the University of Chicago have become some of my closest interlocutors. For their intellectual generosity and collegiality I thank Danielle Allen, Leora Auslander, Kyeong-hee Choi, Cathy Cohen, Bruce Cumings, Prasenjit Duara, Norma Field, Michael Geyer, Friedrich Katz, Emilio Kouri, Tetsuo Najita, William Novak, Julie Saville, Saskia Sassen, and Amy Dru Stanley. I wish to especially thank Thomas Holt and George Chauncey for their mentorship and Kathleen Neils Conzen, chair of the Department of History, and Richard Saller, former dean of the

Division of Social Sciences and now provost of the university, for both intellectual and institutional support. I thank Aaron Shapiro, Deborah Cohen, Michael Stamm, and Michael Hing for research assistance.

I had the opportunity to present early versions of chapters at numerous workshops, seminars, and conferences. For their many suggestions I thank participants in the University of Chicago's Social History, Globalization, and Reproduction of Race and Racial Ideologies workshops; participants at annual meetings of the Law and Society Association, American Society for Legal History, Social Science History Association, and the Organization of American Historians; and participants at the American Bar Foundation seminar, New School Graduate Faculty seminar in political science, New York University workshop on the history of women and gender, New York University School of Law legal history colloquium, University of Illinois–Urbana–Champaign migration studies group, Newberry Library seminar on labor history, and New York–area Asian American women's writing group.

My editors at Princeton University Press have been tremendously supportive. I thank the editors of the Politics and Society in Twentieth-Century America series—William Chafe, Linda Gordon, Julian Zelizer, and especially Gary Gerstle, whose intellectual and editorial interventions made this an altogether better book. I thank my editor at Princeton, Brigitta van Rheinberg, who went to bat for this project at the earliest stage, and Gail Schmitt, who expertly managed the production process.

Finally, I thank professional colleagues, friends, and family members who each made a unique contribution to my ability to complete this project: Joseph McDermott, Bill Lynch, Jean Yonemura Wing, Eric Shtob and Sonia Collins, Stephen Brier and Teresa Karamanos, Carolyn Wong, May Ying Chen, Katie Quan, Alex Hing, Marion Thom, Kim Fellner and Alec Dubro, Eric Wakin and Michelle Barc, Tracy Lai and Stan Shikuma, Marc and Patty Favreau, Elizabeth Hegeman, John G. New, Chiu-hwa Wang, Janet Ngai and David Harris, John Ngai and Lisa Brunet. I dedicate this book to the memory of my father, Shih-hsun Ngai, and to my mother, Hsueh-hwa Wang Ngai, both exemplars of moral and academic integrity; and to my son, Michael Hing, who remains my joy and my inspiration.

I am grateful to everyone who helped make this a better book. All errors are mine.

Parts of this book were previously published and are reprinted here in revised or expanded form. Chapter 1 was published in abridged form as "The Architecture of Race in American Immigration Law: A Re-Examination of the Immigration Act of 1924" in *Journal of American History* 89 (1999), and appears here with permission of the editors. Chapter 2 was published as "The Strange Career of the Illegal Alien: Immigration Restriction and Deportation Policy in the United States, 1921–1965" in *Law and History Review* 21

(Spring 2003), and is reprinted with permission from University of Illinois Press. Chapter 3 is a revision of "From Colonial Subject to Undesirable Alien: Filipino Migration, Exclusion, and Repatriation" in *Re/Collecting Asian America: Essays in Cultural History*, ed. Josephine Lee, Imogene Lim, and Yuko Matsukawa (Temple University Press, 2002), and is printed with permission of the Press. Chapter 6 was published as "Legacies of Exclusion: Illegal Chinese Immigration During the Cold War Years" in *Journal of American Ethnic History* 18 (1998), and appears with permission of the editor.

Note on Language and Terminology

SOME READERS may object to my use of the term "illegal alien," because it carries pejorative connotations. To be sure, the phrase suggests a diminution of personhood and is particularly associated with racism towards Mexicans and other Latinos and Latinas.[1] I am sensitive to these renderings and I use the term not to reproduce racist stereotypes. To the contrary, the intention of this study is to locate the historical *origins* of those representations; to understand how, as Walter Lippmann described in 1922, words become "cue[s] for a whole train of ideas on which ultimately a vote of untold consequences may be based." Commenting on a 1920 survey in which New England college students said an alien was "a person hostile to this country," "a native of an unfriendly country," "an enemy from a foreign land," etc., Lippmann stated, "Yet the word alien is an unusually exact legal term, far more exact than words like sovereignty, independence, national honor, rights, defense, aggression, imperialism, capitalism, socialism, about which we so readily take sides 'for' or 'against.'"[2]

Following Lippmann, I use "alien" and "illegal alien" to refer to legal subjects. Alien, in its original and most general usage, refers to that which belongs to another person or place.[3] In American law, an alien is a person who is not a citizen. An illegal alien is an alien who is unlawfully present (e.g., an unauthorized border-crosser or visa-violator) or who otherwise commits a deportable offense (e.g., an alien convicted of a crime of moral turpitude, sometimes called a "criminal alien"). I sometimes refer to illegal aliens as undocumented migrants, in line with common contemporary usage, but it should also be understood that "undocumented" is a historically specific condition that is possible only when documents (most commonly a visa) are required for lawful admission, a requirement that was born under the modern regime of immigration restriction. Furthermore, not all illegal aliens are illegal because they lack documents; there are other types of unlawful presence and other grounds for deportation.

"Immigrant" is also a legal status that refers to an alien who comes for permanent settlement—a "legal permanent resident"—and who may be naturalized as a citizen. Not all migrants are immigrants. While the legal term for foreign students, temporary workers, visitors, and the like is "nonimmigrant," I prefer to use the more general term "migrant" because it does not privilege permanent settlement before other kinds of migration. Migrants participate variously in "one-way as well as repeated movements across nation-state boundaries . . . for permanent or shorter- and longer-term sojourns."[4]

Most often I refer to migrant groups in terms of their country or geographic region of origin: Mexican, Chinese, European, Asian. I distinguish migrants from U.S.-born or naturalized citizens when required by context. I use Japanese American and Chinese American as shorthand for all Japanese (or Chinese) in America. However, I do not use Mexican American in the same way, because the multigenerational/multistatus ethnic Mexican population under study here is better understood as a transnational or borderland community. I use Mexican American to refer to naturalized or native-born U.S. citizens of Mexican descent. I do not use Filipino American because for most of the period covered by this book, Filipinos and Filipinas were colonial subjects of the United States. On occasion I use terms that are outmoded or otherwise problematic if it makes sense in historical context (Negro, Asiatic, Oriental, Caucasian). Because all labels are constructs of some sort and for reasons of style, I have kept the use of scare quotes ("illegal alien," "Asiatic," etc.) to a minimum.

Chinese proper names and phrases are rendered in *pinyin*, save for public figures whose names are known by old-style romanization (e.g., Chiang Kaishek, Kuomintang), persons whose names include an American first name, and persons whose names appear in legal records in transliterated Cantonese. Japanese proper names are written with given name first, surname second.

The U.S. Immigration and Naturalization Service, the federal agency that is the subject of much of this study, has a long bureaucratic history. Congress created the Bureau of Immigration in 1891 and placed it in the Department of Commerce and Labor; when that department divided in 1913 the bureau remained in the Department of Labor. The Immigration Service was the field organization of the bureau; the Border Patrol, which Congress established in 1925, was a unit of the service. In 1932 the Bureau of Immigration and Bureau of Naturalization merged to become the Immigration and Naturalization Service (INS). In 1940 Congress moved the INS to the Department of Justice. I have tried to keep confusion over nomenclature to a minimum; in general I have referred to the agency by the name in use at the time of the period under discussion.

To protect their privacy I have used pseudonyms or initials when referring to individuals who appear in unpublished INS records (including transcripts of interrogations, reports of apprehensions, and records of confessions) and in field notes and correspondence in the Japanese Evacuation and Resettlement Study papers. Names of public officials and agency personnel have not been changed.

Foreword to the New Paperback Edition _____

THIS NEW EDITION of *Impossible Subjects* comes during a time of intensified public debate in the United States over unauthorized migration and immigration-policy reform. Existing and potential undocumented migrants continue to animate the central questions of immigration policy: legalization and the requirements of citizenship, border control and deportation, the labor market, family unity and separation. Indeed, many of the foundational issues of immigration restriction discussed in *Impossible Subjects* remain pertinent today. At the same time, the past ten years have seen some notable changes in American demography and politics, as well as in the field of immigration history. It seems appropriate to introduce new readers of *Impossible Subjects* by way of some comments on how the book fits into these changing landscapes of politics and scholarship.

I began researching and writing about the origins of illegal immigration to the U.S. as a dissertation topic in the mid-1990s. I found those origins in the restrictive immigration laws that Congress legislated in the 1920s and the border-control measures implemented thereafter. Positive domestic law, not race, culture, or bad character, produced "illegal aliens"—an insight that would not be so novel but for pervasive stereotyping of Mexicans and other Latinos and Latinas in twentieth-century American society. As I examined the history and contours of restriction, my thinking was influenced by recent scholarship on the historical nature of race and the nation, two categories of modern political life commonly thought to be natural and timeless. I believed that an analysis of the historical specificities of national and racial identities would offer new ways of thinking about immigration and citizenship. But if I was aware that I was pursuing a new line of inquiry, it is only in hindsight that I appreciate how much the greater intellectual terrain was shifting. Since the mid-1990s, the frameworks and methodologies guiding American immigration history have undergone a sea change. *Impossible Subjects* was influenced by, and helped constitute, that change.

The multidisciplinary field of migration studies has been at the forefront of the "transnational turn" that has swept the humanities and social sciences. Human migration, along with the circulation of commodities, currencies, and information, highlights the phenomenon of "globalization," a multivalent concept referring generally to the interconnectedness of the world in our time (defined by communications technology, supranational organization, neoliberal market policy, etc.). In a related vein, scholars have historicized the nation, in Benedict Anderson's famous phrase, as an "imagined community." With that insight also came recognition of nationalism's abiding influence on the practice of history. With much greater sensitivity to the construction of the American nation and the place of that nation in the world, scholars have critically reconceived immigration history in both domestic and global contexts. The normative assumptions that previously underlaid American immigration history—unidirectional migration, permanent settlement, and eventual inclusion, if not full assimilation and citizenship—have virtually collapsed in the face of alternate frameworks of analysis: transnationalism, diaspora, border-lands, colonialism and post-colonialism, hybridity. These concepts inform not only the study of contemporary immigration but also a reconsideration of earlier peri-ods, reshaping historical analysis. By showing that national boundaries have always been porous and that migration patterns have always been diverse, these histories establish a critical position against nationalist history. They also serve as a correc-tive to the tendency among social scientists to treat globalization as a new phenomenon.

Transnational migration histories emphasize ongoing influence and a mixture of politics and culture in both the sending and receiving nations, often supported by multiple migration patterns. Based on deep empirical research, often in non-Eng-lish language materials and in non-U.S. archival sources, this body of work reflects in part a transnational trend within the discipline of history itself: some of the best work on immigration to the United States has been done by scholars trained in non-U.S. fields of history. We now have really new portraits of migrants and trans-national communities in dynamic and fluid "regional worlds:" Atlantic, Pacific, western hemispheric. For example, transnational histories of Chinese and Mexican male labor migrations have shown the connections of "single" men to families and villages left behind and the changes in gender, family, and social relations wrought by migration in both sending and receiving communities. Empire, colonialism, and imperialism are now common thematics in migration studies. This scholarship helps us understand why, for example, Dominicans in the mid-twentieth century could say, "Yankee go home—and take me with you."[1]

Closely related to transnational histories but bearing a different analytic empha-sis are diasporic studies, which take the United States as one of many destinations from a region of origin and compare and contrast migration experiences across the world. Initially, diaspora referred to pre-modern and early-modern dispersals re-sulting from forced expulsions—Jewish, African, and Armenian—and their themes of banishment, alienation, and longings for home. In recent scholarship diaspora has assumed a more capacious meaning with regard to period and volition, em-bracing modern migrations driven by labor and trade, or by combinations of politi-cal exile and economic opportunity, in addition to the classical types. Transnational and disaporic methodologies each resituate the nation-state in global frameworks, but from different angles. Historian Kevin Kenny has sensibly urged combining the two in order to broaden our view beyond the single nation-state, while not losing the nation-state as a useful unit of analysis.[2]

A third type of transnational framing concerns "borderlands," especially the U.S.-Mexico borderlands. Older studies of the American southwest were concerned with the role of white settlement on the "frontier" in American national develop-ment; Chicano/a history shifted the focus on conquest and annexation. More recent borderlands scholarship has emphasized cross-cultural exchange and trade, con-flict, and change along shifting lines of power among indigenous peoples, Spanish and Mexicans and Anglo-Americans. Unlike transnational and diasporic histories that consider movement between multiple places at some distance from each other, borderlands history focuses on the dynamics of a single contact zone that overlaps the jurisdictions of neighboring nation-states. Here, two or more cultures meet, mix, and struggle, creating a hybrid social world across borders.[3]

The new immigration history is also characterized by new thinking on ethnicity and race. Implicit in the older literature on immigration (and in American history generally) was the notion that Euro-American immigrants possessed "ethnic" identities but had no meaningful relation to "race." Immigrants suffered from nativism, whereas race and racism were understood as questions of black-white ("American," not immigrant) relations. In general, the assimilation paradigm marginalized the question of race in immigration studies. If some groups (Asians, Latinos) seemed slow to assimilate, the reasons for their intractability were found in deep cultural difference (with the onus implicitly placed upon the immigrants), not in structures of racial subordination. Since the 1990s, critical studies of race and racism in Asian American, Latino/a, and labor and working class history emerged as powerful influences in United States history. Scholars have shown the sources that produced and reproduced racialized identities of Asians and Latinos (that is, the perception of permanent foreignness and inability to assimilate), as well as the processes by which European immigrants developed both national (American) and racial (white) identities. This body of scholarship has helped bridge the conceptual gap between race and ethnicity, bringing greater cohesion within the field of immigration history.[4]

These trends are all evident in *Impossible Subjects*, in its analysis of the production of racial knowledge and national identity, the construction of the border, and the influence of colonialism on migration policy. The book is not, strictly speaking, a transnational story; the focus is on the United States, on American law and its enforcement, and on migrants' experiences in America. But its approach is deeply influenced by the transnational imperative to regard the United States not in isolation but "in the world," as it is now common to say. Moreover, it takes a critical approach to nationalism in its historical analysis. American historical writing and political culture have a long and entrenched tradition of exceptionalism, including the idea that the United States was built upon the principle and practice of immigrant inclusion. Even if immigrants face obstacles along the way, it is believed that these obstacles are eventually overcome; Americans consider the path to full inclusion normative and evidence of the nation's democratic nature. In contrast, *Impossible Subjects* points out that illegal immigrants are a caste group that is categorically excluded from the national community. In contemporary political language, they live "in the shadows" and can never embark on the "path to citizenship." The undocumented are an increasingly large population in the United States (11.1 million at this writing). They are members of families that also include citizens and legal immigrants; they are part of communities, and they are a mainstay of low-skilled labor in agriculture, construction, and the service industries. In a liberal society that values the moral and legal equality of all persons, the undocumented are impossible subjects, persons whose presence is a social reality yet a legal impossibility. Their impossibility can be resolved in only one of two ways—legalization of status or expulsion. Moreover, the historical and contemporary association of Asians and Latino/as with illegal immigration and exclusion is also the grounds for their racialization as permanent outsiders. *Impossible Subjects* sought to explain how formal immigration status (or lack thereof) and the categories of restriction produced new racial knowledge and new ethno-racial identity formations in the interwar period.[5]

Some may concede these problems but consider them exceptions to an otherwise sound tradition of inclusion. *Impossible Subjects* argues that illegal immigration is not anomalous but inherent to the regime of immigration restriction. Nor is it a side channel to the main stream of the nation's history as a "nation of immigrants." In fact, that trope is a relatively recent invention, which emerged in the decades after World War II, when Euro-American ethnics, especially those whose forebears had immigrated in the early twentieth century, made their own claims of belonging. They celebrated their own rise to the middle class and political legitimacy and declared their experience typical of American history. The first two generations of immigration history scholarship canonized that view as a normative theory of immigration. But with historical distance we can now see that their success was the product of a specific moment in American history: the assimilation of the second generation of "new immigrants" in the post-World War II era was made possible by unprecedented American economic growth and global power, a steady decline in wealth inequality (1947–1974), and the generosity of the American welfare state, in particular, higher education and homeownership for World War II veterans.[6] The theme of universal inclusion and citizenship could be read back onto the eighteenth and nineteenth centuries only by bracketing the conquest of Native Americans, slavery, southwestern annexation, Asiatic exclusion, Jim Crow, and the acquisition of unincorporated territories (colonies). Indeed, the experience of the "new immigrants" at the turn of the twentieth century, as well as that generally of non-European migrants throughout American history, was marked by exploitation in a segmented labor market, political exclusion, social isolation, and nativist opposition. Even the Fourteenth Amendment's provision of birthright citizenship to all persons born in the United States, including the children of immigrants—the foundation for the second generation's access to the polity—has proved viable only under favorable conditions that are at once economic (expansion), demographic (concentration of voters), and political (foreign relations and domestic social movements). Perhaps, as historian David Gutiérrez suggests, immigration in the early twenty-first century, with its high incidence of labor exploitation and political exclusion, is the "new normal."[7]

From this angle, the prospects for democratic inclusion—now as in the past—are certainly not foreclosed, but must be understood not as organic or inevitable. Rather, they reside in conditions of possibility that are chiefly political, domestic and global. As I discuss in *Impossible Subjects*, illegal aliens have been able to legalize their status at certain moments—Europeans during the 1930s and 1940s, Chinese during the Cold War, Mexicans and others in the mid-1980s. In the two decades after World War II, Euro-Americans fought their own civil-rights battle to repeal the national origins quotas, finally succeeding in 1965 with passage of the Hart-Celler Act. Their triumph resulted from a constellation of political factors: the rise of Euro-American ethnics as important voting constituents in the urban industrial north; robust domestic-social movements (labor and civil rights); and the international embarrassment of discriminatory immigration quotas during the Cold War. But, if the abolition of national origins quotas in 1965 was an inclusionary reform, Hart-Celler was also an illiberal act because it continued the regime of numerical restriction and imposed it on the entire world, especially upon the countries of the Western Hemisphere, which previously had no numerical limitations. The global nature of restriction and the application of equal limits on all countries, regardless of size, need, or relationship to the United States, reflected the ethos of formal equality of the civil rights era. Ironically, it has been the single most important reason for unauthorized migration since 1965.[8] The Immigration and Control Act of 1986 legalized nearly three million undocumented immigrants, but because IRCA did not change the basic structures of restriction, unauthorized entry continued and in fact soared from 1990s to the late 2000s as part of the United States' long economic boom.

When *Impossible Subjects* was published in 2004, the prospects for the undocumented seemed dim. Ongoing economic expansion continued to draw unauthorized migrants, especially from Mexico and Central America, for work in low-skilled and low-waged jobs. But, at the same time, official and popular hostility against unauthorized migrants ran high. Since the mid-1990s the U.S.-Mexico border had undergone an unprecedented militarization. The numbers of apprehensions, detentions, and removals steadily increased into the new century. Between 2000 and 2005, over one thousand migrants died while trying to enter the country across the Arizona desert.[9] In December 2005, the U.S. House of Representatives passed an immigration bill that would have criminalized unauthorized migrants and anyone who assisted them, including humanitarian workers who left bottles of water in the desert.[10] The bill did not become law because it did not pass the Senate, but it ignited a new immigrant rights movement, led by immigrants themselves, legal and illegal. In May 2006, several million people participated in protests across the country, including hundreds of thousands in Los Angeles and Chicago and high school "walk outs" in several states, mobilized by Spanish-language radio, the Catholic Church, labor unions, student networks, and hometown associations. Their slogans expressed a politics of human and civil rights and the claims of belonging that come with living and working in America: "No human being is illegal," "We are America," and, presciently, "Today we march, tomorrow we vote."

Over the next several years three trends emerged that have altered the political landscape and created new possibilities for legalization and immigration-law reform. The first trend was the growth of the Latino/a population and its electoral power. In 2012, the Census Bureau estimated fifty-three million "Hispanics" in the U.S., 17 percent of the U.S. population. Moreover, contrary to stereotype, not all Latinos/as are undocumented. In fact, more than half are native born and nearly 75 percent of all Latino/as are U.S. citizens, either by native-birth or naturalization. Importantly, Latino/as comprise significant voting constituencies in states that previously voted Republican but tipped to Democratic in the 2008 and 2012 Presidential elections (Nevada, New Mexico, Colorado, Florida, Virginia, North Carolina [2008]).[11]

Second, a robust social movement of immigrant workers has emerged, sometimes allied with but also autonomous from, and occasionally in tension with, traditional organized labor. This movement has been building since the 1990s among Mexican, Central American, Chinese, Pakistani, and other immigrant workers. High-profile campaigns like "Justice for Janitors" to unionize Latino/a immigrant workers in Los Angeles overturned the conventional wisdom that immigrants could not be organized. Indeed, the opposite has proven true, that immigrants, including the unauthorized, are more likely to be receptive to unionizing efforts than native-born workers. Immigrant workers also have organized in community-based "worker centers," which are not unions but pursue similar goals of economic advancement. During the first decade of the century, worker centers grew prolifically among immigrant labor especially in areas where employers routinely flout wage and hour laws, such as day labor and garment sweatshops. The centers help workers sue for unpaid wages and more broadly advocate for economic justice. Immigrant workers, both legal and unauthorized and members of both unions and worker centers were a major force in the 2006 mass mobilizations for immigrant rights. In turn, the immigrant rights movement has further propelled labor organizing. Sociologist Ruth Milkman has aptly described the post-2006 immigrant rights movement as both a civil rights movement and a labor movement.[12]

Finally, there are the "dreamers." These are the nearly two million undocumented young adults, who came to the U.S. with their parents when they were young children; they essentially grew up as Americans but have no legal status.[13] The predicament of their impossibility is partially addressed by the Supreme Court's ruling in *Plyler v. Doe* (1982), which recognized the constitutional right of all children to public education regardless of immigration status. But *Plyler* also further exacerbates their predicament because although education brought greater social and cultural integration, they remain without lawful status. Upon graduating from high school they could not go to college or get a job, obtain a driver's license, open a bank account, or travel abroad—the common indices of becoming an adult that most Americans take for granted.

The activism of undocumented youth for access to higher education led to the introduction of the DREAM Act (Development, Relief and Education for Alien Minors) in the U.S. Congress in 2001. While federal legislation stalled over the next dozen years, fifteen state-level dream acts made unauthorized students eligible for in-state tuition fees at state universities.[14] Still lacking federal legislation in 2012, President Barack Obama established an administrative program of Deferred Action for Childhood Arrivals. DACA provided legalization (with authorization to work) for those younger than thirty years of age, who arrived before 2007 and before their sixteenth birthday, and who have a high school education.[15]

The student dreamers' movement, begun as a quest for education, by the late 2000s grew into a broader call for legalization and immigration law reform. By 2013, the movement had grown to seventy-five state and local dreamers' organizations and two nation-wide networks. Dream activists engage in legislative lobbying as well as radical acts of "coming out" and civil disobedience. They march under the sign, "undocumented, unafraid, and unapologetic." Like the second generation of Euro-American ethnics that sought to repeal the national origins quotas after World War II, the dream activists are also the acculturated children of immigrants. They took civics classes in high school and learned about the movements for female suffrage and black civil rights. Indeed the language of the "dream" and "coming out" resonate with both the civil rights and gay rights movements. Many of the dreamers have experience in high school and college student governments and organizations. They know, as dream activist-leader Gaby Pacheco explains, "how to navigate" politics and society.[16]

Trained in organizing, lobbying, and media skills, the dream activists have promoted a compelling message that highlights the injustice of their impossibility. They tell personal stories—stories of their dreams of becoming a teacher, or lawyer, or nurse; the high school valedictorian, who won a scholarship but could not go to college. They speak of the pain of watching a parent or sibling deported or their despair at facing a diminished future. They tell their stories because "we know the power of our narrative," explained Gaby Pacheco. The dreamers' identification as Americans, the innocence of their childhood migration, and their academic and civic achievements have elicited sympathy throughout American society. At the same time, Pacheco concedes that portraying the dreamers as deserving implicitly casts others—including their parents—as undeserving lawbreakers. They try to counter this by fighting for legalization for all unauthorized migrants. In fact, the dream activists' work has been crucial in swaying American public opinion to support legalization and a path to citizenship for all the undocumented.[17]

These trends of demography, electoral politics, and social activism burgeoned in the decade since *Impossible Subjects* was first published. Although I could not have predicted the specifics of how they would develop, they were foretold by general historical patterns—unauthorized entry as an invariable consequence of restrictive policy; the racial dynamics that regard some immigrants only for their labor and not as full persons and members of society; the role of immigrants themselves as social and political actors. I have been fortunate that *Impossible Subjects* has counted among its readers, college students, graduate students, and scholars; as well as immigrant-rights activists who are finding historical context and lessons for their own work. I hope they will all continue to find it useful. Many thanks to Princeton University Press and Brigitta van Rheinberg for this second edition. I am grateful for her support and loyalty over the years. I thank also my students, colleagues, friends, and family, and especially JGN, who continue to brighten my intellectual and personal life.

Washington, D.C.

NOTES

1. Parts of this foreword are drawn from my essay, "Immigration and Ethnic History," in *American History Now*, ed. Eric Foner and Lisa McGirr (American Historical Association and Temple University Press, 2011) and appear with the permission of the American Historical Association.

Quote from Jesse Hoffnung-Garskoff, A *Tale of Two Cities: Santo Domingo and New York after 1950* (Princeton 2008). Other exemplary works of transnational migration history include Alison Games, *Migration and the Origins of the English Atlantic World* (HUP 1999); Madeline Hsu, *Dreaming of Gold, Dreaming of Home: Transnationalism and Migration between the US and South China, 1882–1943* (Stanford 2000); Robert C. Smith, *Mexican New York: Transnational Lives of New Immigrants* (California 2006); Deborah Cohen, *Braceros: Migrant Citizens and Transnational Subjects in Post-war U.S. and Mexico* (UNC 2011); Eiichiro Azuma, *Between Two Empires: Race, History and Transnationalism in Japanese America* (Oxford 2005); Moon-Ho Jung, *Coolies and Cane: Race, Labor and Sugar in the Age of Emancipation* (Johns Hopkins 2006); Catherine Ceniza Choy, *Empire of Care: Nursing and Migration in Filipino American history* (Duke 2003).

2. Philip Kuhn, *Chinese among Others: Emigration in Modern Times* (Rowman and Littlefield 2008); Donna Gabaccia and Fraser Ottanelli, *Italian Workers of the World: Labor Migration and the Formation of Multethnic States* (Illinois 2001); Sandhya Shukla, *India Abroad: Diasporic Cultures of Postwar America and England* (Princeton 2003); Rebecca Kobrin, *Jewish Bialystock and its Diaspora* (Indiana 2010); Kevin Kenny, "Diaspora and Comparison: The Irish as a Case-Study," *Journal of American History* 90 (June 2003): 134–162.

3. Ramón Gutierrez, *When Jesus Came the Corn Mothers Went Away: Marriage, Sexuality and Power in New Mexico, 1500–1846* (Stanford 1991); James Brooks, *Captives and Cousins: Slavery, Kinship and Community in the Southwest Borderlands* (UNC 2002); Maria Montoya, *Translating Property: The Maxwell Land Grant and the Conflict over Land in the American West* (California 2002, Kansas 2005); Andrés Reséndez, *Changing National Identities at the Frontier: Texas and New Mexico, 1800–1850* (Cambridge 2005); Kelly Lytle Hernandez, *Migra!* (California 2010); Katherine Benton-Cohen, *Borderline Americans: Racial Division and Labor War in the Arizona Borderlands* (HUP 2009); Rachel St. John, *Line in the Sand: A History of the Western U.S.-Mexico Border* (Princeton 2012). On the formation of borderlands in the Pacific Northwest, Kornel Chang, *Pacific Connections: The Making of the U.S.-Canadian Borderlands* (California 2012).

4. David Roediger, *The Wages of Whiteness: Race and the Making of the American*

Working Class (Verso 1991); James Barrett and David Roediger,"'In-between Peoples': Race, Nationality, and the 'New Immigrant' working Class," *Journal of American Ethnic History* (Spring 1997): 3–47; David Gutiérrez, *Walls and Mirrors: Mexican Americans, Mexican Immigrants, and the Politics of Ethnicity* (California 1995); George Sánchez, *Becoming Mexican American: Ethnicity, Culture and Identity in Chicano Los Angeles, 1900–1945* (Oxford 1995); Lisa Lowe, *Immigrant Acts: On Asian American Cultural Politics* (Duke 1996); Matthew Jacobson, *Whiteness of a Different Color: European Immigrants and the Alchemy of Race* (Harvard 1998); John Kuo-wei Tchen, *New York Before Chinatown: Orientalism and the Shaping of American Culture 1776–1882* (Johns Hopkins 1999); Gary Gerstle, *American Crucible: Race and Nation in the Twentieth Century* (Princeton 2001); Thomas Guglielmo, *White on Arrival: Race, Color and Power in Chicago, 1890–1945* (Oxford 2003); Mary Ting Yi Lui, *The Chinatown Trunk Mystery: Murder, Miscegenation, and Other Dangerous Encounters in Turn of the Century New York* (Princeton 2005); Russell Kazal, *Becoming Old Stock: The Paradox of German American Identity* (Princeton 2004); Karen Leong, *The China Mystique: Pearl S. Buck, Anna May Wong, Mayling Soong, and the Transformation of American Orientalism* (California 2005); Victoria Hattam, *In the Shadow or Race: Jews, Latinos and Immigrant Politics in the U.S.* (Chicago 2007); Sarah Gualtieri, *Between Arab and White: Race and Ethnicity in the Early Syrian American Diaspora* (California 2009).

5. The undocumented population peaked at 12 million in 2007 then fell to 11.1 million in 2009 as a result of the U.S. economic recession; that number has remained stable since. Jeffrey Passel and D'Vera Cohen, "Unauthorized Immigrants: 11.1 in 2011," PEW Hispanic Research Center, Dec. 6, 2012, http://www.pewhispanic.org/2012/12/06/un-authorized-immigrants-11-1-million-in-2011/ (accessed Aug. 27, 2013). According to national polling data, 64 to 78 percent of Americans support legalization of status and a pathway to citizenship for the undocumented. http://www.pollingreport.com/immigration.htm (accessed Aug. 27, 2014).

6. Scholars have also shown that the assimilation of Euro-Americans, was more limited and slower than generally believed, with post-war benefits accruing to the latter birth cohorts of the second generation (born after 1920) or the third generation. Nancy Foner and Richard Alba, "The Second Generation from the Last Great Wave of Immigration: Setting the Record Straight" Migration Information Source, October 2006, www.Migrationinformation.org (last accessed Sept. 5, 2013); Joel Perlmann, *Italians then, Mexicans now* (Russell Sage 2005); Miriam Cohen, *Workshop to Office* (Cornell 1992).

7. David Gutiérrez, "The New Normal? Reflections on the Shifting Politics of the Immigration debate," *International Labor and Working Class History* 78 (Fall 2010), 118–122. On economic stagnation of Mexican Americans from 1965–2000, despite marked trends of acculturation (English-language acquisition and increased out-marriage), see Edward Telles and Vilma Ortiz, *Generations of Exclusion: Mexican Americans, Assimilation and Race* (Russell Sage 2008). Telles and Ortiz's findings implicate failing urban public schools and persistent segmentation in the labor market as key reasons for Mexican Americans' lack of socio-economic mobility in the late twentieth century.

8. Mae M. Ngai, "The Civil Rights Origins of Illegal Immigration," *International Labor and Working Class History* 78 (Fall 2010), 93–99.

9. For detailed analysis of border control and other mechanisms of enforcement from the 1990s to 2013 see Doris Meissner, Donald M. Kerwin, Muzaffar Chisti, and Clare Bergamon, *Immigration Enforcement: The Rise of a Formidable Machinery* (Migration Policy Institute 2013), http://www.nomoredeaths.org/information/deaths.html (last accessed Sept. 5, 2013). The cumulative total of deaths related to desert-border crossings between 2000 and 2013 is at least 2,666.

10. The Border Protection, Anti-terrorism, and Illegal Immigration Control Act of 2005 (H.R. 4437).

11. National Council of La Raza, "20 FAQ about Hispanics," http://www.nclr.org/index.php/about_us/faqs/most_frequently_asked_questions_about_hispanics_in_the_us/ (last accessed Sept. 5, 2013); Mark Hugo Lopez and Ana Gonzalez-Barrera, "Inside the Latino Electorate," Pew Hispanic Research Center, June 3, 2013, http://www.pewhispanic.org/2013/06/03/inside-the-2012-latino-electorate/ (last accessed Sept. 5, 2013).

12. Ruth Milkman, *LA Story: Immigrant Workers and the Future of the American Labor Movement* (Russell Sage, 2006); Jennifer Gordon, *Suburban Sweatshops: The Fight for Immigrant Rights* (Harvard 2005); Janice Fine, *Worker Centers: Organizing Communities at the Edge of the Dream* (Economic Policy Institute, 2006).

13. "Who and Where the Dreamers Are," Immigration Policy Institute, Oct. 2012, http://www.immigrationpolicy.org/just-facts/who-and-where-dreamers-are-revised-estimates (accessed Sept. 9, 2013) and Batalova, Hooker and Capps, "Deferred Action for Childhood Arrivals at the One-year Mark," MPI Issue Brief, August 2013, http://www.migrationpolicy.org/pubs/cirbrief-dacaatoneyear.pdf (accessed Sept. 9, 2013).

14. California, Texas, New York, Utah, Washington, Oklahoma, Illinois, Kansas, New Mexico, Nebraska, Maryland, Connecticut, Colorado, Minnesota, and Oregon. National Conference of State Legislatures, "Allow In-State Tuition for Undocumented Students," July 2013, http://www.ncsl.org/issues-research/educ/undocumented-student-tuition-state-action.aspx (accessed Sept. 9, 2013)

15. In the first year of DACA, 637,000 people applied, or 59 percent of the eligible population. Batalova et al, "Deferred Action for Childhood Arrivals at One-year Mark."

16. Author interview with Gaby Pacheco, Sept. 9, 2013, Washington, D.C. See also Walter Nicholls, *The DREAMers: How the Undocumented Youth Movement Transformed the Immigrant Rights Movement* (Stanford 2013); Hinda Seif, "Unapologetic and Unafraid: Immigrant Youth Come out of the Shadows," *New Directions in Childhood and Adolescent Development* 134 (2011): 59–75; René Galindo, "Embodying the Gap between National Inclusion and Exclusion: The Testimonios of Three Undocumented Students at a 2007 Congressional Hearing," 14 Harv. Lat. Law Rev. 377 (2011).

17. Pacheco interview. Polling data in 2012 and 2013 show 66 to 78 percent of respondents supporting some kind of legalization. http://www.pollingreport.com/immigration.htm (accessed Sept. 16, 2013)

IMPOSSIBLE SUBJECTS

Introduction

Illegal Aliens: A Problem of Law and History

IN 2001 THE UNITED STATES Immigration and Naturalization Service ordered Rosario Hernandez of Garland, Texas, deported to his native Mexico. Hernandez, a 39-year-old construction worker, had immigrated to Texas from Guadalajara, Mexico, when he was a teenager. His removal was ordered on grounds that he had been convicted three times for driving while intoxicated—twice nearly twenty years ago and once ten years later. After the third conviction Hernandez served five weekends in jail, joined Alcoholics Anonymous, and gave up drinking. However, according to laws passed by Congress in 1996 the multiple convictions amounted to an "aggravated felony" and made his removal mandatory, not subject to review by a judge. Hernandez considered the deportation unfair: "I already paid for my mistakes," he said, "How can they punish somebody two times for the same thing?"

Hernandez is married to a U.S. citizen and has two children, who are also American citizens. His wife Renee said, "I respect him for admitting to his mistakes and changing his life. What people don't realize is that this was a surprise attack on my life, as well. We have a baby here whose whole person is forming. He changes every day, and you want both parents to be a part of that." Hernandez's older son, Adrian, asks, "Where is my daddy going to be?"[1]

When I read Hernandez's story I was struck by its resemblance to another story that I had come across while researching this book. In the early 1930s the INS ordered Mrs. Lillian Joann Flake, a longtime resident of Chicago, deported to her native Canada. Like Hernandez, Flake was married to an American citizen and had a daughter, also a citizen. She had a record of theft and shoplifting, which the INS considered "crimes of moral turpitude." Flake's deportation was canceled by an act of grace by Secretary of Labor Frances Perkins. The 1996 laws, however, explicitly deny administrative relief in cases like Hernandez's.[2]

Then, as now, legal reformers and immigrant advocates publicized deportation stories like these in order to call attention to what they believed was a problem in American immigration policy. Reformers argued that the nation's sovereign right to determine the conditions under which foreigners enter and remain in the country runs into trouble when the government expels people who have acquired families and property in the United States. They found cases like Hernandez's and Flake's compelling because embedded in their narratives were normative judgments that esteem the immigrant's integration into society and the sanctity of the family. Deportation, which devalues assimilation—indeed cancels it—and separates families, seemed draconian punishment for crimes of drunk driving and petty theft. In Flake's time, reformers wrote almost exclusively about deportation cases involving Europeans and paid scant attention, if any, to the deportation of Mexican or Chinese criminal aliens. Nowadays, however, non-European cases like Hernandez's also receive public sympathy, especially when they involve rehabilitated criminals who are longtime permanent residents with families. This shift reflects the increase in the number of immigrants from the third world over the last quarter century and contemporary multicultural sensibilities.

We ought not rush to the conclusion, however, that race no longer operates in either the practice or representation of deportation. Then, as now, few reformers advocated for those aliens who entered the country by crossing the border without authorization. That preoccupation has focused on the United States–Mexico border and therefore on illegal immigrants from Mexico and Central America, suggesting that race and illegal status remain closely related.

But we might ask, first, what it is about the violation of the nation's sovereign space that produces a different kind of illegal alien and a different valuation of the claims that he or she can make on society? Unauthorized entry, the most common form of illegal immigration since the 1920s, remains vexing for both state and society. Undocumented immigrants are at once welcome and unwelcome: they are woven into the economic fabric of the nation, but as labor that is cheap and disposable. Employed in western and southwestern agriculture during the middle decades of the twentieth century, today illegal immigrants work in every region of the United States, and not only as farmworkers. They also work in poultry factories, in the kitchens of restaurants, on urban and suburban construction crews, and in the homes of middle-class Americans. Marginalized by their position in the lower strata of the workforce and even more so by their exclusion from the polity, illegal aliens might be understood as a caste, unambiguously situated outside the boundaries of formal membership and social legitimacy.

At the same time, illegal immigrants are also members of ethno-racial communities; they often inhabit the same social spaces as their co-ethnics and, in many cases, are members of "mixed status" families. Their accretion engenders paradoxical effects. On the one hand, the presence of large illegal populations in Asian and Latino communities has historically contributed to the construction of those communities as illegitimate, criminal, and unassimilable. Indeed, the association of these minority groups as unassimilable foreigners has led to the creation of "alien citizens"—persons who are American citizens by virtue of their birth in the United States but who are presumed to be foreign by the mainstream of American culture and, at times, by the state.

On the other hand, ethno-racial minority groups pursue social inclusion, making claims of belonging and engaging with society, irrespective of formal status. Latino studies scholars Williams Flores and Rena Benmayor, for example, argue that the mobilization of "cultural citizenship" by subordinate ethnic groups is "redressive" and contributes to a multicultural society. From another angle, a nonjuridical concept of membership suggests the production of collectivities that are not national but transnational, sited in borderlands or in diaspora.³ The liabilities of illegal alienage and alien citizenship may thus be at least partially offset through individual and collective agency, within and across nation-state boundaries.

This book addresses these and other issues by charting the historical origins of the "illegal alien" in American law and society and the emergence of illegal immigration as the central problem in U.S. immigration policy in the twentieth century. It examines the statutory structures, judicial genealogies, and administrative enforcement of restrictive immigration policy that began in the United States after World War I. Restriction not only marked a new regime in the nation's immigration policy; I argue that it was also deeply implicated in the development of twentieth-century American ideas and practices about citizenship, race, and the nation-state.

I focus on the years 1924 to 1965, which mark the tenure of the national origins quota system put into place by the Johnson-Reed Immigration Act of 1924.⁴ The Johnson-Reed Act was certainly not the nation's first restrictive immigration law. The exclusion of Chinese, other Asians, and various classes of undesirable aliens (paupers, criminals, anarchists, and the like) in the late nineteenth and early twentieth centuries signaled the beginnings of a legal edifice of restriction. But the 1924 act was the nation's first *comprehensive* restriction law. It established for the first time *numerical limits* on immigration and a *global* racial and national hierarchy that favored some immigrants over others. The regime of immigration restriction remapped the nation in two important ways. First, it drew a new ethnic and racial map based on new categories and hierarchies of difference. Second, and in a different register, it articulated a new sense of territoriality, which was marked by unprecedented awareness and state surveillance of the nation's contiguous land borders.

Most of the scholarship about immigration to the United States focuses on the period before 1924, the era of open immigration from Europe, and the period since 1965, when the national origins quota system was abolished and immigration from the third world increased. Thus, at one level, this study is an attempt to address a gap in the historiography of American immigration. Although Americans long ago concluded that the national origins quota system was an illiberal policy that blighted the nation's democratic tradition, we still know little about *how* that restriction actually worked, how the nation was racially and spatially reimagined. To be sure, historians have studied the consequence of the *absence* of immigration during these decades. Most im-

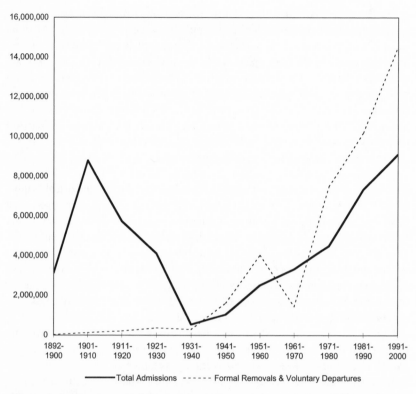

Aliens admitted and expelled, by decade, 1890–2000. (Source: U.S.-INS, *2000 Statistical Yearbook.*)

portant, the cutoff of European immigration created conditions for the second generation of those immigrants who had come to the United States from the 1890s to World War I to more readily assimilate into American society. The loosening of these ethnic groups' ties to their homelands facilitated that process, as did the spread of American popular culture and consumerism, industrial-class formation and organization, and the nationally unifying experience of World War II.[5]

But restriction meant much more than fewer people entering the country; it also invariably generated illegal immigration and introduced that problem into the internal spaces of the nation. Immigration restriction produced the illegal alien as a *new legal and political subject,* whose inclusion within the nation was simultaneously a social reality and a legal impossibility—a subject barred from citizenship and without rights. Moreover, the need of state authorities to identify and distinguish between citizens, lawfully resident immigrants, and illegal aliens posed enforcement, political, and constitutional problems for the modern state. The illegal alien is thus an "impossible subject," a person who cannot be and a problem that cannot be solved.

Even as Congress abolished quotas based on national origin in 1965, it preserved the principle of numerically limiting immigration and, in fact, extended it to cover the entire globe. Americans remain committed to the principle of numerical restriction to the present day. The controversies over immigration policy taking place at the beginning of the twenty-first century center on whether immigrants contribute positively or deleteriously to the nation's economy and culture, but there is virtually no political support for open or numerically unrestricted immigration. If the principle of immigration restriction has become an unquestioned assumption of contemporary politics, we need to ask how it got to be that way and to consider its place in the historical construction of the nation.

Immigration and Citizenship

Immigration policy is constitutive of Americans' understanding of national membership and citizenship, drawing lines of inclusion and exclusion that articulate a desired composition—imagined if not necessarily realized—of the nation. The concept is manifest in the titles of books on U.S. immigration policy: *The Face of the Nation, Making Americans, A Nation by Design.*[6] In the United States immigration has always been understood as a path that leads to citizenship, as sociologist Rogers Brubaker has noted: "Admission to citizenship is viewed as the normal sequel to admission for settlement." Chinese exclusion, the exception that proves the rule, was another means by which the nation defined itself.[7]

The telos of immigrant settlement, assimilation, and citizenship has been an enduring narrative of American history, but it has not always been the reality of migrants' desires or their experiences and interactions with American society and state. The myth of "immigrant America" derives its power in large part from the labor that it performs for American exceptionalism. As political theorist Bonnie Honig argues, the myth "shores up the national narrative of liberal consensual citizenship, allowing a disaffected citizenry to experience its regime as choiceworthy, to see it through the eyes of still-enchanted newcomers whose choice to come here . . . reenact[s] liberalism's . . . fictive foundation in individual acts of uncoerced consent."[8]

Yet if the iconic immigrant serves exceptionalist political culture, that narrative is legally grounded in a relatively easy process of naturalization (five years residence with no criminal record) and in the principle of *jus soli*, which confers citizenship upon all those born on U.S. soil and, therefore, to the American-born children of immigrants. Moreover, in matters other than the admission and expulsion of aliens, the Constitution protects all persons, not just citizens. Aliens do not enjoy all the privileges of citizenship—notably the franchise—but outside the immigration domain, and in civil society generally, they have the same rights as citizens to equal protection under the Fourteenth Amendment.[9] The capaciousness of the Constitution in this regard is not unproblematic: critics have argued that aliens' lack of substantive rights in matters of immigration compromises their rights while they are present. Legal and political theorists also dispute the implications of the Constitution's protection of aliens. While some cite it as evidence of the nation's inclusive traditions, others worry that the extension of so many rights to aliens diminishes the value of citizenship.[10]

Nevertheless, the line between alien and citizen is soft. At least in principle, access to naturalization ensures that the condition of alienage, with its limited rights, is temporary. This principle is important because it recognizes the moral and political imperative of equality that is central to liberal democracy.[11] Yet the promise of citizenship applies only to the *legal* alien, the lawfully present immigrant. The *illegal* immigrant has no right to be present, let alone embark on the path to citizenship. The illegal alien crosses a territorial boundary, but, once inside the nation, he or she stands at another juridical boundary. It is here, I suggest, that we might paradoxically locate the outermost point of exclusion from national membership.

Some readers might find this unproblematic, for, after all, the nation *is* bounded and exclusion from citizenship would seem a logical consequence of illegal immigration. But, as this book aims to show, illegal alienage is not a natural or fixed condition but the product of positive law; it is contingent and at times it is unstable. The line between legal and illegal status can be crossed in both directions. An illegal alien can, under certain conditions, adjust his or her status and become legal and hence eligible for citizenship. And legal aliens who violate certain laws can become illegal and hence expelled and, in some cases, forever barred from reentry and the possibility of citizenship. I suggest that shifts in the boundary between legal and illegal status might tell us a lot about how the nation has imagined and constructed itself over time.

This line of inquiry intervenes in a burgeoning field of citizenship studies. Legal scholar Linda Bosniak has observed that recent scholarship largely concerns not citizenship as formal membership in the nation-state but issues of substantive citizenship, such as civic virtue and group identities in a multicultural society. Many scholars presume that as a formal status category, universal liberal citizenship in the United States has been achieved, that its historical exclusions based on race and gender have been overcome, and that the challenge, now, is to go beyond passive citizenship to normative definitions of active citizenship.[12] However, the presence of aliens within the national community suggests that "citizenship's threshold and its substantive character are, in fact, deeply interwoven." Illegal aliens, who comprise a caste that lives and works outside of citizenship, pose an even greater predicament and challenge for liberal democratic society.[13]

Immigration Policy and the Production of Racial Knowledge

A second, related theme of this book concerns how restrictive immigration laws produced new categories of racial difference. The construction of racial hierarchies has been, of course, an ongoing project in American history since the colonial period. If we understand that race is not a biological fact but a socially constructed category of difference, it should also be emphasized that, as Paul Gilroy states, "there is no racism in general."[14] Race is always historically specific. At times, a confluence of economic, social, cultural, and political factors has impelled major shifts in society's understanding (and construction) of race and its constitutive role in national identity formation. The Civil War was obviously one of those times; the present multicultural moment is another. I argue that the 1920s was also an extraordinary time when immigration policy realigned and hardened racial categories in the law.

The national origins quota system classified Europeans as nationalities and assigned quotas in a hierarchy of desirability, but at the same time the law deemed all Europeans to be part of a white race, distinct from those considered to be not white. Euro-American identities turned both on ethnicity—that is, a nationality-based cultural identity that is defined as capable of transformation and assimilation—and on a racial identity defined by whiteness.

The 1924 Johnson-Reed Act also excluded from immigration Chinese, Japanese, Indians, and other Asians on grounds that they were racially ineligible for naturalized citizenship, a condition that was declared by the Supreme Court in the early 1920s.[15] These developments resolved the legal ambiguities and conflicts over the racial status of Asians that had vexed the law since their arrival in the mid-nineteenth century. They also simultaneously solidified the legal boundaries of the "white race."[16]

The immigration laws during the 1920s did not assign numerical quotas to Mexicans, but the enforcement provisions of restriction—notably visa requirements and border-control policies—profoundly affected Mexicans, making them the single largest group of illegal aliens by the late 1920s. The actual and imagined association of Mexicans with illegal immigration was part of an emergent Mexican "race problem," which also witnessed the application of Jim Crow segregation laws to Mexicans in the Southwest, especially in Texas, and, at the federal level, the creation of "Mexican" as a separate racial category in the census.[17]

Thus, unlike Euro-Americans, whose ethnic and racial identities became uncoupled during the 1920s, Asians' and Mexicans' ethnic and racial identities remained conjoined. The legal racialization of these ethnic groups' national origin cast them as permanently foreign and unassimilable to the nation. I argue that these racial formations produced "alien citizens"—Asian Americans and Mexican Americans born in the United States with formal U.S. citizenship but who remained alien in the eyes of the nation.

Alien citizenship was not a new phenomenon, nor was it just the consequence of immigration legislation. Indeed, alien citizenship flowed directly from the histories of conquest, colonialism, and semicolonialism that constituted the United States' relations with Mexico and in Asia. Those histories indelibly stamped the social experiences and subordination of Mexicans and Asians with racisms that were, as cultural critic Lisa Lowe described, the "material trace of history." For Chinese and other Asians, alien citizenship was the invariable consequence of racial exclusion from immigration and naturalized citizenship. For Mexicans, the concept of alien citizenship captured the condition of being a foreigner in one's former native land. The immigration experiences and racial formations of Asians and Mexicans in twentieth-century America cannot be understood apart from these legacies of conquest and colonialism.[18]

In one sense alien citizenship spoke to a condition of racial otherness, a badge of foreignness that could not be shed. But alien citizenship was not only a racial metaphor. While not strictly a legal term, the concept underwrote both formal and informal structures of racial discrimination and was at the core of major, official race policies, notably the repatriation of 400,000 persons of Mexican descent during the Great Depression (of which half were estimated to be U.S. citizens) and the internment of 120,000 persons of Japanese ancestry during World War II (two-thirds of them citizens).[19]

The racial formations of Asians and Mexicans in the 1920s were particularly significant because they modified a racial map of the nation that had been marked principally by the contours of white and black and that had denoted race as a sectional problem. But that changed with the Great Migration of African Americans, and to a lesser extent, Mexicans, to northern cities during the World War I era. Immigration law was part of an emergent race policy that was broader, more comprehensive, and national in scope. In addition to immigration law, that policy involved the legal justification for de facto segregation in the North and the completion of the legal process of forced assimilation of American Indians.[20]

In this period the concept of race itself also changed, from late-nineteenth-century race science, which centered on physiognomic difference and hierarchy, to twentieth-century racial ideas that linked race to both physiognomy and nationality. Modern racial ideology depended increasingly on the idea of complex cultural, national, and physical *difference* more than on simple biological hierarchy.[21]

The system of racial classification and regulation that emerged in the

1920s should be seen in the context of a longer historical process of legal configuring within the national state, which had struggled since the late nineteenth century to find a racial logic capable of circumventing the imperative of equality established by the Fourteenth Amendment. That process involved a double move. On the one hand the law separated public and private spheres, prohibiting racial discrimination by the state but permitting it in private relations. On the other hand Congress and the courts sneaked racial distinctions into public policy through doctrinal rationalizations like "separate but equal."[22] During the 1920s the legal traditions that had justified racial discrimination against African Americans were extended to other ethnoracial groups in immigration law through the use of euphemism ("aliens ineligible to citizenship") and the invention of new categories of identity ("national origins").

Nationalism and Sovereignty

Immigration policy not only speaks to the nation's vision of itself, it also signals its position in the world and its relationships with other nation-states. At one level this means that foreign policy invariably becomes implicated in the formulation of immigration policy. It suggests as well a need to critique American exceptionalism and U.S.-centric history. Recent literature on nations and nationalism has shown us not only that nations are, in Benedict Anderson's famous phrase, historically produced "imagined communities." It has also revealed the powerful influence that nationalism has had on the writing of history.[23]

What does it mean to rethink American immigration history in the context of global developments and structures? At one level, transnational and diasporic approaches remap migration patterns and experiences, yielding new insights. For example, the nineteenth-century migration of labor from capitalism's rural peripheries to its industrializing centers has traditionally focused on the Atlantic world, both within Europe and from Europe to North America. Scholars are now examining the Pacific world as part of the same global movement, from which vantage point one can compare and contrast immigration policies in the English settler nations of North America (the United States and Canada) and Australia within the same general frame.[24]

A global framework also helps us put the advent of immigration restriction in the United States into broader historical perspective. We have understood this juncture mainly in terms of the domestic politics of eugenics and nativism during the World War I era.[25] But the Great War was the turning point not just for United States immigration policy; it marked a seminal change in the world order. The war simultaneously destabilized and entrenched nation-state boundaries, ushering in an interstate system based on Westphalian sovereignty, which sanctified the integrity of the territorial nation-state and the principle that no nation can interfere in the affairs of another. Yet the interstate system, aimed at achieving order and peace, was based on "crustacean" borders. That changed, among other things, how nation-states regulated migration. Rigid border controls, passports, and state restrictions on entry and exit became the norms for governing emigration and immigration. It was, as political scientist Aristide Zolberg describes, a new, "hypernationalist" regime of immigration restriction. When Congress legislated restriction in the United States, with its emphasis on territoriality, border control, and documents, it acted as part of this global trend.[26]

World War I also created the problem of millions of people *without* national citizenship: war refugees and stateless persons, as well as those denationalized by European governments after the war on grounds of their "enemy origin." The concept of inalienable individual rights, central to European political philosophy, was shown to inhere not in human personage, after all, but in the *citizen*, as rights were only meaningful as they were recognized and guaranteed by the nation-state. The World War I refugee crisis demonstrated that loss of citizenship meant a loss of rights; as Hannah Arendt famously wrote, it signaled the "end of the rights of man." Writing at about the same time as Arendt, U.S. Supreme Court chief justice Earl Warren similarly stated in a denationalization case, "Citizenship *is* man's basic right, for it is nothing less than the right to have rights."[27] It seems no accident that illegal aliens also emerged in the wake of World War I, produced by hypernationalist immigration controls and in the same juridical no-man's-land as refugees and the stateless. Indeed, the rush after World War I to legislate restriction in Congress, while argued in the domestic political language of racial nativism, was a direct response to the specter of millions of destitute European war refugees seeking entry into the United States.

Finally, a globalist perspective implies a critique of nationalism—the ideology that privileges the perceived interests of the nation over and against the interests of others. It suggests a need to dislodge, through critical analysis, the colonialist and superpower nations from their self-claimed positions at the center of world history. Dipesh Chakrabarty spoke to this imperative in another context with a call to "provincialize Europe." In the immigration context this means understanding the forces and relations of power that generate migration between nations. Particularly in the decades since World War II, migration to the United States has been the product of specific economic, colonial, political, military, and/or ideological ties between the United States and other countries (Mexico, South Korea, Cuba, the Philippines, El Salvador, to name a few) as well as of war (Vietnam). Saskia Sassen reminds us that migration is an "embedded," "temporally and spatially bounded" process that crosses these kinds of "bridges" between sending and receiving nations. It is not, as conventional thinking suggests, a unidirectional phenomenon, in which the hapless poor of the world clamor at the gates of putatively disinterested wealthier nations.[28]

We remain blind to this insight in large part because our understanding of immigration has been powerfully influenced by nationalism. Americans want to believe that immigration to the United States proves the universality of the nation's liberal democratic principles; we resist examining the role that American world power has played in the global structures of migration. We like to believe that our immigration policy is generous, but we also resent the demands made upon us by others and we think we owe outsiders nothing.

Indeed, nationalism's ultimate defense is sovereignty—the nation's self-proclaimed, absolute right to determine its own membership, a right believed to inhere in the nation-state's very existence, in its "right of self-preservation."[29] The doctrine appeared in international law in the eighteenth century and explicitly in American immigration law in the late nineteenth century when the Supreme Court established that the regulation of immigration was incident to the nation's control over foreign affairs and gave Congress plenary, or absolute, power over it.[30]

By situating regulation over immigration under the rubric of state relations, the Court presumed that migrants were agents, or potential agents, of foreign states. Referring to the undesirable Chinese in 1893, the Court explained,

> If . . . the government of the United States, through its legislative department, considers the presence of foreigners of a different race in this country . . . to be dangerous to its peace and security, their exclusion is not to be stayed because at the time there are no actual hostilities with the nation of which the foreigners are subject. The existence of war would render the necessity of the proceeding only more obvious and pressing.[31]

But are migrants really proxies for foreign troops? In truth, immigrants have historically pursued not the political interests of states but individual and family improvement. Even when politically motivated, migration is more often a matter of escape than one of conquest. Scholars and policymakers thus distinguish between economic migrants and asylum-seekers. To be sure, some nation-states have promoted, even subsidized, emigration for purposes of colonization or population and social control. In the nineteenth century, transnational migration became increasingly associated with international politics, as part of the development of a global order of competitive nation-states. States also began to assume responsibility for the safety of their nationals living abroad. Late-nineteenth-century American immigration doctrine indexed these general trends. At the same time, the Supreme Court's association of migration with foreign state interests in the Chinese exclusion cases contained a double irony, for the English had colonized the eastern seaboard of North America with royal charters and the Chinese had left Guangdong Province for California in violation of the imperial ban against emigration.[32]

The notion that migrants pose a potential threat of foreign invasion has become a familiar provocation in nationalist discourses. But immigrants have always been but a small percentage of the receiving country's total population, never approaching anything that could be considered an actual invasion. The association of immigration control with the state's authority to wage war reveals that sovereignty is not merely a claim to national rights but a theory of power.[33]

The centrality of sovereignty in immigration policy has had important consequences. For one, it has allowed Congress to create, as even the Supreme Court described, "rules that would be unacceptable if applied to citizens." Second, it has marginalized or erased other issues from consideration in policy formation, such as human rights and the global distribution of wealth.[34] Political theorists and other scholars have debated whether liberalism's commitment to the irreducible equal worth of all human beings can accommodate nationalism's presumed right to exclude. As K. Anthony Appiah wrote, dividing humanity into nation-states means that "all individuals in the world are obliged, whether they like it or not, to accept the political arrangements of their birthplace, however repugnant those arrangements are to their principles or ambitions—unless they can persuade somebody else to let them in."[35]

The task of this book, however, is not to resolve this foundational problem. Its more modest goal is to detach sovereignty and its master, the nation-state, from their claims of transcendence and to critique them as products of history. I do not dispute that the principle of sovereignty will continue to operate in immigration law as long as we live in a world of nation-states. But, the sovereign right to determine membership need not be unconditional. I suggest that a historical perspective might show us how sovereignty's content and relationship to other legal and moral norms are contingent—and, therefore, also subject to change.[36]

As a sociolegal history, *Impossible Subjects* proceeds from the contention that law not only reflects society but constitutes it as well, that law normalizes and naturalizes social relations and helps to "structure the most routine practices of social life."[37] I examine law and policy at three levels: in the legislative and political discourses of restriction; in judicial decisions that sought to square competing demands of sovereignty and individual rights; and in the practical articulation of the law, the everyday meanings and consequences of law that are produced by the bureaucratic state's interactions with migrants and with other social actors.

The book begins with an analysis of the regime of immigration restriction that emerged in the 1920s. In part I, "The Regime of Quotas and Papers," I discuss the two principal features of restriction: first, the invention and codification of new racial concepts—"national origins" and "racial ineligibility to citizenship"—and second, the articulation of a new nation-state territoriality based on border control and deportation policy. I show how, considered together, these features of restriction put European and non-European immigrant groups on different trajectories of racial formation, with different prospects for full membership in the nation.

The middle chapters of the book, in parts II and III, investigate how the regime of immigration restriction and control operated with regard to particular ethno-racial groups. I examine the experiences of Filipinos, Mexicans, Japanese, and Chinese, who variously comprised illegal aliens, alien citizens, colonial subjects, and foreign contract-workers—all liminal status categories that existed outside the normative teleology of immigration, that is, legal admission, permanent-resident status, and citizenship. I argue that the adjudication of these groups' legal status not only directly underwrote their particular social experiences but also profoundly shaped the general character of American immigration, citizenship, and the state in the twentieth century.

Part II, "Migrants at the Margins of Law and Nation," examines the role of racialized foreign labor—Filipinos and Mexicans—in the political and cultural economies of the United States West and Southwest. I argue that the region's industrial agriculture practiced a kind of "imported colonialism," which created a migratory agricultural proletariat outside the polity. Imported colonialism also challenged cultural and political norms across a broad spectrum, from the proprieties of interracial sex to nation-bounded definitions of the working class.

Part III, "War, Nationalism, and Alien Citizenship," considers the trajectory of Asian Americans' citizenship during World War II and the Cold War, when Japanese American and Chinese American citizenship experienced numerous shifts according to shifting exigencies of United States foreign policy in East Asia. In these chapters I examine the wartime internment of Japanese Americans and the postwar resolution of arguably the most important legacy of Chinese exclusion, the "paper son" problem (citizenship based on fraudulent claims). I argue that these were crucibles in which Asiatic alien citizenship was first reproduced and then later resolved under conditions of coercive assimilation and nationalism.

Part IV, "Pluralism and Nationalism in Post–World War II Immigration Reform," analyzes the movement to reform immigration policy from the end of World War II to 1965, when Congress passed the Hart-Celler Act. Here I examine how that celebrated reform of immigration law both changed *and* sustained the regime of immigration restriction. I complicate the conventional view that the Hart-Celler Act was a liberal reform by placing the pluralist politics of reform in the context of post–World War II geopolitical

and economic nationalisms. I show how the 1965 reforms invariably reproduced—at ever higher levels—illegal immigration and made it the central
problem that has preoccupied American immigration policy throughout the
late twentieth century and into the twenty-first.

The interactions, conflicts, and negotiations between migrants, the state,
and society that animate the history in this book, I argue, are integral to the
historical processes that define and redefine the nation. I do not believe that
immigrants are external to the nation but that, as Homi Bhabha wrote, "the
migrants, the minorities, the diasporic come to change the history of the
nation."[38]

Part I

THE REGIME OF QUOTAS AND PAPERS

THE JOHNSON-REED Immigration Act of 1924 marked both the end of one era, that of open immigration from Europe, and the beginning of a new one, the era of immigration restriction. The law placed numerical limits on immigration and established a quota system that classified the world's population according to nationality and race, ranking them in a hierarchy of desirability for admission into the United States. Paradoxically, the quota system, while closing America's gates to the "undesirable races" of southern and eastern Europe, redrew the color line around Europe instead of through it. Restriction also demanded a system of visa controls to track the allocation of quotas and border surveillance to ensure that only persons with the proper documents entered the country. The new regime had two major consequences: it remapped the ethno-racial contours of the nation and generated illegal immigration as the central problem in immigration law.

The following two chapters analyze these key characteristics of restriction by examining the statutory architecture and administrative enforcement of the Johnson-Reed Act. Chapter 1 addresses the law's system of quotas based on "national origin" and the marking of racial boundaries of citizenship. Chapter 2 examines restriction's emphasis on territoriality and the production of illegal aliens, as expressed in the formulation of deportation policy and in the creation of the Border Patrol. But first it will be useful to briefly review the historical trajectory of immigration policy that preceded restriction.

From Regulation to Restriction

Before the 1920s immigration into United States was numerically unrestricted, reflecting a tradition of laissez-faire labor mobility that dated to the colonial period. Freedom of movement was a right acquired in Europe and North America with the emergence of capitalism, as peasants became unshackled from their places of birth and servants from the authority of their masters. The French Revolution, for example, heralded freedom of movement in the Declaration of the Rights of Man and Citizen.[1] From the seventeenth to the nineteenth century the free global movement of labor was essential to economic development in the New World. This was the case even if many of the laborers themselves were not free but, rather, were enslaved or indentured. That process reached its apogee in the second half of the nineteenth century, as people the world over moved from capitalism's rural peripheries to its industrializing centers. Thus, until the late nineteenth century in the United States, immigration was encouraged and virtually unfettered.

State control of migration was considered either a matter of local police powers (vagrancy, dependency, etc.) or a matter of commerce.[2]

The major exception to the rule of open immigration was Chinese exclusion. Like their European counterparts, Chinese laborers migrated to the United States in the nineteenth century to participate in the nation's industrial expansion. Their migration was part of the making of the Pacific world, part of a succession of Asian peoples that provided labor for Euro-American settler societies in Hawai'i, Australia, and western Canada, as well as the western United States. But nineteenth-century Asiatic migration was also born of European colonial penetration of East Asia and of India; and on the United States Pacific Coast, Asian migrants collided with the racial imperatives of American manifest destiny, the ideology of continental expansion that had declared the West the domain of Anglo-Saxon civilization. After Congress legislated Chinese exclusion in 1882, Japanese and other Asians immigrated to replace Chinese labor but became new targets of exclusion. A diplomatic agreement between the United States and Japan in 1907 curbed Japanese immigration and the Immigration Act of 1917 excluded Asian Indians and all other native inhabitants of a "barred Asiatic zone" that ran from Afghanistan to the Pacific. The Chinese exclusion law and federal courts also declared Asians racially ineligible for naturalization. Exclusion made Asians into permanent foreigners and guaranteed they would be but a small, marginalized population in America for nearly one hundred years.[3]

Chinese exclusion was also significant because it occasioned the United States Supreme Court to articulate the principle that control over immigration was a matter of national sovereignty. Believing immigration to be a potential form of "foreign aggression and encroachment," the Court gave Congress absolute control over it as part of its authority over foreign relations. It ruled that aliens enter and remain in the United States only with "the license, permission, and sufferance of Congress."[4]

Notwithstanding Congress's absolute power over matters of admission and expulsion, as a practical matter mass immigration from Europe faced few legal impediments in the late nineteenth and early twentieth century. The first federal immigration laws established qualitative criteria for selective or individual exclusion that expressed normative definitions of social desirability—those not welcome included criminals, prostitutes, paupers, the diseased, and anarchists, as well as Chinese laborers.[5]

Despite the growing list of excludable categories, the Immigration Service excluded only 1 percent of the 25 million immigrants from Europe who arrived in the United States from 1880 to World War I. The unskilled workers who entered during those years from eastern and southern Europe provided the labor for the nation's industrialization and for building the infrastructure of cities. They shoveled pig iron in steel mills, sewed shirtwaists, and dug tunnels for sewer and subway lines. At the same time, however, demands for restricting European immigration emerged among native-born white Americans, who associated immigrants with the spread of urban slums and class conflict. New England elites as well as native-born craft workers considered the new immigrants to be unassimilable backward peasants from the "degraded races" of Europe, incapable of self-government. The American Protective Association, formed in 1887, was anti-immigration and anti-Catholic, and boasted 2.5 million members at its peak in the mid-1890s.[6]

During and immediately after World War I a confluence of political and economic trends impelled the legislation of immigration restriction. First, wartime nationalism produced a feverish sentiment against presumably disloyal "hyphenated Americans." While war nationalism aimed principally at German Americans, it provided a popular basis of support for the restrictionist movement against eastern and southern Europeans. In 1917 Congress passed the most stringent immigration law to date, which included a provision that made literacy a requirement for admission. The literacy test was aimed specifically at curtailing immigration from eastern and southern Europe. Congress had passed such a requirement four times since the 1890s, but Presidents Cleveland, Taft, and Wilson had vetoed it, believing it was contrary to the principle of individual selection. Congress finally passed it in 1917 only by overriding Wilson's second veto. A strong antiradical current also ran through postwar nativism, which associated Jews with Bolshevism and Italians with anarchism.[8]

Second, in the economic realm, by 1920 the country simply no longer needed the same levels of mass immigration. The phenomenal growth of the American economy in the decades before and after the turn of the century had been achieved principally through continuous additions of labor. By the 1920s industrial capitalism had matured to the point where economic growth could come more from technological advances in mass production than from a continued expansion of the manufacturing workforce.[9] (The exception was in agriculture, which, as we will see, had important consequences for immigration policy).

Finally, the international system that emerged with World War I gave primacy to the territorial integrity of the nation-state, which raised the borders between nations. For example, the introduction of passport controls in Europe and the United States, begun as emergency war measures, became, without exception, the norm in regulating international migration. In the United States, the Immigration Act of 1924 would require not only passports (documentary evidence of national identity) but also visas (documentary proof of permission to enter) for admission into the country.[10]

After World War I immigration began to pick up again. Nativist pressed alarm that the literacy test did little to stem the flow. The li in Europe had increased since the 1890s, and the test, which i nizing a few words in one's native language on flash car barrier to immigration. By the end of 1920 immigration neared prewar levels, and Ellis Island was again teeming with immigrants.

A crisis atmosphere surrounded discussion of immigration in Congress in 1920–21. The American Legion, the American Federation of Labor, and the patriotic orders warned that "hordes" of impoverished people fleeing war-torn Europe were on the way, their migration facilitated by a drop in the cost of transoceanic travel.[11] Congressman Albert Johnson of Washington, chair of the House immigration committee and an avowed restrictionist, called for an immediate, two-year suspension of immigration lest the nation be inundated with a flood of undesirable aliens. Johnson cited reports from American consular officials in Europe as evidence of looming danger. The consul in Warsaw estimated there were 100,000 to 350,000 "Polish subjects of the Hebrew race" with relatives in America anxious to emigrate immediately. The report from Italy described a large proportion of emigrants from Catania as peasants "small in stature and low in intelligence"; in Florence the consul considered the emigrant population to be "honeycombed" with socialist ideas. Johnson believed that only by barring them altogether would it be possible to keep subversives out of the United States.[12]

Support for restriction in Congress became overwhelming. Not all supporters were 100-percent Americanists, but few could resist the combination of nativism, job scarcity, and anti-Bolshevism that fueled the politics of restriction. In May 1921, Congress passed an emergency measure that restricted immigration to 355,000 a year, set a quota for each European country at 3 percent of the number of foreign-born of that nationality residing in the United States in 1910, and gave fourteen months to devise a permanent policy.[13]

Chapter One

The Johnson-Reed Act of 1924 and the Reconstruction of Race in Immigration Law

> Each upthrust of nativism left a mark on American
> thought and society. . . . [T]he anti-foreign wave
> that flowed without pause for two decades in the
> early twentieth century . . . must stand alone in its
> persistence, in its complexity, and in the
> massiveness of its institutional deposit. . . . [T]he
> country would never be the same again, either in
> its social structure or in its habits of mind.
>   —JOHN HIGHAM[1]

ALTHOUGH Congress legislated the first numerical restrictions in 1921, it would be nearly a decade before permanent immigration quotas were implemented. The intervening years were filled with contention and difficulty as Congress debated the design of a new system. All were keenly aware of the stakes: the new order would codify certain values and judgments about the sources of immigration, the desired makeup of the nation, and the requirements of citizenship.

The nativists who had led the drive for restriction believed there were serious flaws in the 3-percent quotas that were established in 1921. The law set the quotas according to the 1910 census because data from the 1920 census was not fully compiled at the time. Using 1910 as the base, the southern and eastern European countries received 45 percent of the quotas and the northern and western European countries received 55 percent. Although the quotas reduced southern and eastern European immigration by 20 percent from prewar levels, nativists believed it was still unacceptably high. They argued for a 2-percent quota based on the 1890 census. That was when, they argued, the sources of European immigration shifted, altering the racial homogeneity of the nation. The 1890 formula reduced the level of immigration to 155,000 per year and reduced the proportion of southern and eastern European immigration to a mere 15 percent of the total.[2]

But, the 1890 formula was crudely discriminatory and therefore vulnerable to criticism. Opponents of the bill pointed out that using the 1920 census figures, the most up-to-date, was conceptually more sound, but since that gave even greater weight to the newer immigrants, it defeated the whole purpose of the quotas as far as the nativists were concerned. Proponents of restriction thus labored to devise a plan that would discriminate without appearing to do so. W. W. Husband, the commissioner general of immigration, advocated a plan to set quotas according to the rate at which each immigrant group became citizens. Naturalization was an indication of assimilation, Husband contended. Moreover, he believed that some nationalities "naturally" sought American citizenship, while others did not. Husband argued for disfavoring the immigration of those groups that resisted assimilation, rather than "advertising and going out into the highways and byways and dragging people into Americanization. . . . [W]hen you try to change [a man] by a hothouse process it does not work," he said. Not surprisingly, Husband found that the rate of naturalization was 67 percent among northern and western Europeans and 32 percent among southern and eastern Europeans.[3]

Another proposal was introduced by David Reed, the Republican from Pennsylvania and chair of the Senate immigration committee, and John Trevor, a leading restrictionist and head of an immigration-restriction coalition of patriotic orders and societies. Trevor, a New York lawyer, sat on the board of the American Museum of Natural History and was an associate of Madison Grant, author of the best-selling tract *The Passing of the Great Race.* In March 1924 Trevor submitted a proposal for quotas based on "national origin" to the Senate immigration committee. Like other restrictionists, Trevor warned that the new immigration threatened to lower the standard of living and dilute the "basic strain" of the American population. But Trevor turned the debate on its head by arguing that the quotas enacted in 1921 discriminated against native-born Americans and northwestern Europeans. Those quotas were based on the number of foreign born in the population, leaving "native stock" Americans out of the equation. As a result, the 1921 act admitted immigrants from southern and eastern Europe on a "basis of substantial equality with that admitted from the older sources of supply," discriminating against "those who have arrived at an earlier date and thereby contributed more to the advancement of the Nation." To be truly fair, Trevor argued, the national origins of the *entire* population should be used as the basis for calculating the quotas. He calculated an apportionment of national origins quotas based on the nation's population in 1920, which gave 16 percent of the total to southern and eastern Europe and 84 percent to northern and western Europe. The quotas were nearly identical to those calculated at 2 percent of the foreign-born population in 1890, yet could be declared nondiscriminatory because they gave fair representation to each of the nation's "racial strains."[4]

In May, Congress passed an immigration act based on Trevor's concept of national origins quotas.[5] It restricted immigration to 155,000 a year, established temporary quotas based on 2 percent of the foreign-born population in 1890, and mandated the secretaries of labor, state, and commerce to determine quotas on the basis of national origins by 1927. The law also excluded from immigration all persons ineligible to citizenship, a euphemism for Japanese exclusion. Finally, Congress placed no numerical restrictions on immigration from countries of the Western Hemisphere, in deference to the need for labor in southwestern agriculture and American diplomatic and trade interests with Canada and Mexico.

Taken together, these three components of the Immigration Act of 1924 constructed a vision of the American nation that embodied certain hierarchies of race and nationality. At its core, the law served contemporary prejudices among white Protestant Americans from northern European backgrounds and their desire to maintain social and political dominance. Those prejudices had informed the restrictionist movement since the late nineteenth century. But the nativism that impelled the passage of the act of 1924 articulated a new kind of thinking, in which the cultural nationalism of the late nineteenth century had transformed into a nationalism based on race.

In the eighteenth and early nineteenth century, "race" and "nation" were loosely conflated in intellectual discourse and in the public imagination. Race indicated physical markers of difference (especially color) but also often simultaneously referred to culture—commonalties of language, customs, and experience. *Race, people,* and *nation* often referred to the same idea. In the mid- and late nineteenth century, physical anthropology gave rise to "scientific" classifications that treated race as a distinctly biological concept. Social Darwinists believed civilization evolved to higher levels as a result of race competition and the survival of the fittest. Many, including Herbert Spencer and John Fiske, also held neo-Lamarckian views that cultural characteristics and behaviors acquired from the environment were inheritable. Of course, neo-Lamarckianism was two-faced, as it could both claim the inheritability of socially degenerate behavior and provide opportunity for race improvement. Thus, some social evolutionists believed that immigrants from the "backward" peoples or races of Europe might eventually become Americanized.[6]

The nativism of the late nineteenth and early twentieth century comprised a cultural nationalism in which cultural homogeneity more than race superiority was the principal concern. Restrictionists did not entirely discount the possibility of assimilation but complained that the high volume of immigration congested the melting pot, creating "alien indigestion." But by World War I, restrictionists spoke increasingly of "racial indigestion" and rejected the idea of the melting pot altogether. The shift in thinking evidenced the influence of eugenics, which had grown after the rediscovery of Mendelian genetics in the early twentieth century disproved Lamarckianism and severed environment from biology.[7]

The eugenicists were strict biological determinists who believed that intelligence, morality, and other social characteristics were permanently fixed in race. They believed racial boundaries were impermeable and that assimilation was impossible. In its most radical articulation, eugenics espoused social policy that advocated race breeding and opposed social reform because, as Charles Davenport, the founder of the Galton Society, said, the latter "tends to ultimately degrade the race by causing an increased survival of the unfit."[8] Witnesses who testified at congressional hearings frequently invoked race theories alleging the superiority of "Nordics" over the "Alpine" and "Mediterranean" races of southern and eastern Europe and warned that race-mixing created unstable "mongrel" races. During the 1920s the House committee retained a scientific expert, Harry H. Laughlin, the director of the Eugenics Institute at Cold Spring Harbor, New York, the research arm of the Galton Society. Laughlin supplied Albert Johnson with copious amounts of data on "degeneracy" and "social inadequacy" (crime, insanity, feeblemindedness) showing the alleged racial inferiority and unassimiability of southern and eastern Europeans. Laughlin also cited the psychologist Robert Yerkes's intelligence tests conducted among soldiers during World War I as evidence of racial hierarchy. The army tests shocked contemporaries because they purported to show that the average white American male had the mental age of 13 (a score of 12 ranked as "moron"). Eugenicists seized upon Yerkes's study because it appeared to vindicate their innatist theory of intelligence: the tests indicated low intelligence among African Americans (10.4), and ranked Poles, Italians, and Russians barely higher (10.7 to 11.3).[9]

To the extent that historians have focused their attention on the legislative process leading to the 1924 act, the race-nativism of men like Madison Grant, Harry Laughlin, and John Trevor has dominated the story of the law. No doubt, scientific racism clarified and justified fears about immigration that were broadly based, and also enabled the descendents of the old immigration to redeem themselves while attacking the new immigrants.[10] But if the language of eugenics dominated the political discourse on immigration, it alone did not define the national origins quota system. Placing the eugenics movement in the foreground of the story of the Johnson-Reed Act has obscured from view other racial constructions that took place in the formulation of immigration restriction, some of which have turned out to be more enduring in twentieth-century racial ideology.

In fact, the national origins quota system involved a complex and subtle process in which race and nationality disaggregated and realigned in new and uneven ways. At one level, the new immigration law differentiated Europeans according to nationality and ranked them in a hierarchy of desirability. At another level, the law constructed a white American race, in which persons of European descent shared a common whiteness distinct from those deemed to be not white. In the construction of that whiteness, the legal boundaries of both white and nonwhite acquired sharper definition. Thus, paradoxically, as scientific racism weakened as an explanation for Euro-American social development, hereditarianism hardened as a rationale for the backwardness and unassimiability of the nonwhite races. Moreover, the idea of racial "difference" began to supplant that of racial superiority as the basis for exclusionary policies. Lothrop Stoddard, a leading race-nativist who explicitly advocated for white supremacy in *The Rising Tide of Color* in 1920, argued in 1927, "When we discuss immigration we had better stop theorizing about superiors and inferiors and get down to the bedrock of *difference*."[11]

The Invention of National Origins

It was one thing for David Reed and John Trevor to convince Congress that a system of quotas based on "national origins" was a conceptually sound and nondiscriminatory way to align immigration with the composition of the American people. But it was quite another matter to actually design that system—to define the "national origins" of the American people and to calculate the proportion of each group to the total population.

The Johnson-Reed Act mandated the formation of a committee under the Departments of Commerce, Labor, and State to allocate quotas by 1927. Dr. Joseph A. Hill, an eminent statistician with a thirty-year tenure at the Bureau of Census, chaired the Quota Board, as the committee was known. Computing the national origins quotas was arguably the most difficult challenge of Hill's career: Congress would reject reports submitted by the Quota Board and postpone implementation of the quotas twice before finally approving a third report in 1929.

Indeed, the project was marked by doubt from the beginning. The law required quotas to be allocated to countries—sovereign nation-states recognized by the United States—in the same proportion that the American people traced their origins to those geographical areas, through immigration or the immigration of their forebears. Census and immigration records, upon which the Quota Board relied, however, were woefully incomplete. The census of 1790, the nation's first, did not include information about national origin or ancestry. The census did not differentiate the foreign-born until 1850 and did not differentiate the parental nativity of the native-born until 1890. Immigration was unrecorded before 1820, and not classified according to national origin until 1899, when the Immigration Service began designating immigrants by "race or people." Emigration was not recorded at all until 1907 and not recorded according to nationality until 1909. To complicate things further, many boundaries in Europe changed after World War I, requiring a translation of political geography to reattribute origins and allocate quotas according to the world in 1920.[12]

Before the Quota Board could address the data (or lack of it), it had to conceptualize the categories that comprised the national origins quota system. "National origin," "native stock," "nationality," and other categories were not natural units of classification; they were constructed according to certain social values and political judgments. For example, "native stock" did not refer to persons born in the United States but to persons who descended from the white population of the United States at the time of the nation's founding. The board defined the "immigrant stock" population as all persons who entered the United States after 1790 and their progeny.[13]

The law defined "nationality," the central concept of the quota system, according to country of birth.[14] Although the statute made no explicit reference to race, race entered the calculus and subverted the concept of nationality in myriad ways. Ironically, nationality did not mean "country of birth" as far as defining the American nationality was concerned. The law excluded nonwhite people residing in the United States in 1920 from the population universe governing the quotas. The law stipulated that " 'inhabitants in continental United States in 1920' does not include (1) immigrants from the [Western Hemisphere] or their descendants, (2) aliens ineligible for citizenship or their descendants, (3) the descendants of slave immigrants, or (4) the descendants of the American aborigines."[15]

The Quota Board applied that provision according to race categories in the 1920 census: "white," "black," "mulatto," "Indian," "Chinese," "Japanese," and "Hindu."[16] It discounted from the population all blacks and mulattos, eliding the difference between the "descendants of slave immigrants" and the descendants of free Negroes and voluntary immigrants from Africa.[17] It discounted all Chinese, Japanese, and South Asians as persons "ineligible to citizenship," including those with American citizenship by native-birth. The provision also excluded the Territories of Hawai'i, Puerto Rico, and Alaska, which American immigration law governed and whose natives were United States citizens.[18] In other words, to the extent that the "inhabitants of the continental United States in 1920" constituted a legal representation of the American nation, the law excised all nonwhite, non-European peoples from that vision, erasing them from the American nationality.

On a practical level, eliminating nonwhite peoples from the formula resulted in larger quotas for European countries and smaller ones for other countries. For example, African Americans comprised 9 percent of the United States population in 1920; if they had been counted, and their "national origins" in Africa considered, 9 percent of the quota would have been allocated to African nations, resulting in 13,500 fewer slots for Europe.

Race altered the meaning of nationality in other ways as well. Formally the quota system encompassed all countries in the world, except for those of the Western Hemisphere. China, Japan, India, and Siam each received the minimum quota of one hundred; but the law excluded the native citizens of those countries from immigration because they were deemed to be racially ineligible to citizenship. Congress thus created the oddity of immigration quotas for non-Chinese persons of China, non-Japanese persons of Japan, non-Indian persons of India, and so on. With regard to the independent African nations, Ethiopia, Liberia, and South Africa received quotas of one hundred each, amounting to a concession of two hundred immigration slots for black Africans. European mandates and protectorates in Africa, the Near East and Far East—for example, Tanganyika, Cameroon, Palestine, New Guinea— each had their own quotas, which in practice served to increase the quotas of Great Britain, France, and Belgium, the nations with the largest colonial empires (table 1.1).

Thus, while the national origins quota system intended principally to restrict immigration from southern and eastern Europe and used the notion of national origins to justify discrimination against immigrations from those nations, it did more than divide Europe. It also divided Europe from the non-European world. It defined the world formally in terms of country and nationality but also in terms of race. The quota system distinguished persons of the "colored races" from "white" persons from "white" countries. The new taxonomy was starkly represented in a table of the population of the United States published in 1924, in which the column "country of birth" listed fifty-three countries (Australia to Yugoslavia) and five "colored races" (black, mulatto, Chinese, Japanese, Indians).[19] In this presentation, white Americans and immigrants from Europe have "national origins," that is, they may be identified by the country of their birth or their ancestors' birth. But, the "colored races" were imagined as having *no country of origin*. They lay outside the concept of nationality and, therefore, citizenship. They were not even bona fide immigrants.

Thus the national origins quota system proceeded from the conviction that the American nation was, and should remain, a white nation descended from Europe. If Congress did not go so far as to sponsor race breeding, it did seek to transform immigration law into an instrument of mass racial engineering. "The stream that feeds the reservoir should have the same composition as the contents of the reservoir itself," Hill said. "Acceptance of that idea doesn't necessarily imply a belief that the composition of the American people can not be improved, but it does probably imply a conviction . . . that it is not likely to be improved by unregulated immigration but rather the contrary."[20]

Like most of their contemporaries, members of Congress and the Quota Board treated race as self-evident of differences that were presumed to be natural. Few, if any, doubted the Census Bureau's categories of race as any-

TABLE 1.1

Immigration Quotas Based on National Origin (annual quota for each fiscal year
beginning July 1, 1929)

Country or Area	Quota
Afghanistan*	100
Albania	100
Andorra	100
Arabian peninsula	100
Armenia	100
Australia (including Tasmania, Papua, islands pertaining to Australia)	100
Austria	1,413
Belgium	1,304
Bhutan*	100
Bulgaria	100
Cameroon (British mandate)	100
Cameroon (French mandate)	100
China*	100
Czechoslovakia	2,874
Danzig, Free City of	100
Denmark	1,181
Egypt	100
Estonia	116
Ethiopia (Abyssinia)	100
Finland	569
France	3,086
Germany	25,957
Great Britain and Northern Ireland	65,721
Greece	307
Hungary	869
Iceland	100
India*	100
Iraq (Mesopotamia)	100
Irish Free State	17,853
Italy	5,802
Japan*	100
Latvia	236
Liberia	100
Liechtenstein	100
Monaco	100
Morocco (French & Spanish Zones and Tangier)	100
Muscat (Oman)*	100
Nauru (British mandate)	100
Nepal*	100
Netherlands	3,153
New Zealand	100

nordics [Germany / Great Britain and Northern Ireland / Greece] (handwritten annotation)

TABLE 1.1 *Continued*

Country or Area	Quota
Norway	2,377
New Guinea, Territory of (including appertaining islands) (Australian mandate)*	100
Palestine (with Trans-Jordan) (British mandate)	100
Persia	100
Poland	6,524
Portugal	440
Ruanda and Urundi (Belgian mandate)	100
Rumania	295
Russia, European and Asiatic	2,784
Samoa, Western (mandate of New Zealand)	100
San Marino	100
Siam*	100
South Africa, Union of	100
South West Africa (mandate of Union of South Africa)	100
Spain	252
Sweden	3,314
Switzerland	1,707
Syria and the Lebanon (French mandate)	123
Tanganyika (British mandate)	100
Togoland (British mandate)	100
Turkey	226
Yap and other Pacific islands under Japanese mandate*	100
Yugoslavia	845

Source: *Proclamation by the President of the United States*, March 22, 1929 (Washington, D.C., 1929).

*Quotas for these countries available only for persons born within the respective countries who are eligible to citizenship in the United States and admissible under the immigration laws of the United States.

thing other than objective divisions of an objective reality, even though the census's racial categories were far from static. Such confidence evinced the strength of race-thinking generally as well as the Progressive faith in science, in this case, the sciences of demography and statistics. Indeed, few people doubted the census at all. Census data carried the weight of official statistics; its power lay in its formalization of racial categories. The census gave the quotas an imprimatur that was nearly unimpeachable and was invoked with remarkable authority, as when, during the floor debate in the House in 1924, Congressman William Vaile retorted to an opponent of the national origins principle, "Then the gentleman does not agree with the Census!"[21]

Demography, and the census itself, far from being the simple quantification of a material reality, grew in the late nineteenth and early twentieth

century as a language of interpreting the social world. Census officials like
Francis Amasa Walker and Richmond Mayo Smith took the census beyond
its Constitutional function as an instrument of apportionment. As historian
Margo Anderson observed, the classifications created for defining urban and
rural populations, social and economic classes, and racial groups created a
vocabulary for public discourse on the great social changes taking place in
America at the time—industrialization, urban growth, and, of course, immigration.[22] In fact, the census was the favored form of scientific evidence cited
by restrictionists and nativists during this period.

That practice actually began with census officials. Francis Walker, the superintendent of the 1870 and 1880 censuses, was president of MIT and a
brilliant scholar in the new field of statistics. He was also an ardent nativist
and Social Darwinist who believed immigrants from Italy, Hungary, Austria,
and Russia were "vast masses of peasantry, degraded below our utmost con-
ceptions . . . beaten men from beaten races, representing the worst failures in
the struggle for existence."[23] Walker was a leading member of the Immigration Restriction League during the 1890s. Analyzing census data, Walker developed the theory that immigration retarded the natural birthrate of Americans, which he lauded as the highest in the world and as evidence of the
nation's greatness. Because immigrants crowded native-born Americans from
unskilled jobs, Walker theorized, the latter adjusted to their limited job opportunities by having fewer children. He considered immigration a "shock"
to the principle of natural population increase.[24]

The causal link in this theory rested on the assumption that the nation
possessed a natural character and teleology, to which immigration was external and unnatural. Those assumptions resonated with conventional views
about America's providential mission, Manifest Destiny, and the general
march of progress. Yet, they were rooted in the profoundly conservative
viewpoint that the composition of the American nation should never change.
Few people during the 1920s understood, much less accepted, Horace Kallen's view that the English had settled the North American Atlantic seaboard
not as a divine mission but as an accident of history.[25]

Walker's assumptions regarding "natural" population increase also involved a bit of sophistry. In 1873 Walker criticized that theory as Elkanan
Watson had postulated it in the early nineteenth century. Noting that the
population of the United States had increased by about one-third during
each of the two decades following the 1790 census, Watson made projections
for population increases up to 1900 based on the same, extraordinary rate of
growth. Francis Walker disagreed, stating, "Geometric progression is rarely
attained, in human affairs." Yet in the 1890s Walker resuscitated Watson's
theory to support the restrictionist agenda. As Walker developed the theory
that immigration negatively affected population growth, he credited Watson's

projections as evidence of America's high natural rate of growth and simply ignored the criticisms he had made twenty years before.[26]

Francis Walker's theory of the declining native birthrate and the census data upon which it was based became the foundation for the restrictionists' claim that immigration threatened to overwhelm the American nation. It anchored Madison Grant's famous thesis that the great Nordic race was in danger of extinction. Paraphrasing Walker, Grant warned that upward mobility on the part of native workers was a form of race suicide. "A race that refuses to do manual work and seeks 'white collar' jobs," he said, "is doomed through its falling birth rate to replacement by the lower races or classes. In other words, the introduction of immigrants as lowly laborers means a replacement of race." Similarly, a 1922 publication by the Commonwealth Club of California on "Immigration and Population" carried the subtitle, "The Census Returns Prove That Immigration in the Past Century Did Not Increase the Population, but Merely Replaced One Race Stock by Another."[27]

Like Francis Walker, Joseph Hill also came from an elite, old-line New England family. The son of a minister and a cousin of Henry Adams, he graduated from Exeter and Harvard (as did his father and grandfather) and received his Ph.D. at Halle, Germany. Although Hill began his tenure at the Census Bureau in 1899, two years after Walker's death, he held many of the same views. In 1910 Hill contributed two monographs to the Dillingham Commission's study of immigration, using previously unpublished and untabulated census data, which were of great importance to the restrictionist movement. The first study analyzed occupational distribution by nativity; the second determined differentials in fecundity between the foreign-born, the native-born of foreign-born parents, and native-born of native parents. Not coincidentally, these studies provided additional empirical evidence to Francis Walker's theory of the retarded native birthrate.[28]

Like other scientists and social scientists that believed in racial difference, Hill strove for ever more precise categories of classification and comparisons of type. He added new questions to the census in 1910 and 1920 that were aimed at elucidating differences in race and nationality in increasing detail. Hill restored the "mulatto" race category (which had been eliminated in the 1900 census) and added questions to ascertain literacy, ability to speak English, mother tongue, number of children born and living, and length of time in the United States. He was particularly interested in creating indices to gauge assimilation and presenting data in tables that made racial comparisons convenient.[29]

In a sense, demographic data was to twentieth-century racists what craniometric data had been to race scientists during the nineteenth. Like the phrenologists who preceded them, the eugenicists worked backward from classifications they defined a priori and declared a causal relationship between the data and race. Instead of measuring skulls, they counted inmates in state institutions. If statistics showed that immigrants were less healthy, less educated, and poorer than native-born Americans, the data were deemed to be evidence of the immigrants' inferior physical constitution, intelligence, and ambition.

Unlike Francis Walker, Joseph Hill did not aggressively campaign for restriction. He endorsed the national origins principle in a restrained way and otherwise scrupulously avoided taking political positions. Yet, like all scientists, he brought his own political views and values to his work—to the questions he asked, to the ways in which he classified data, and to the interpretations he drew from the data. In Hill's case, those politics had guided a proliferation of census data on the foreign born that served the nativist movement.[30]

That is not to say that Hill's work was unscientific or unprofessional. To the contrary, he was a serious professional, who worked according to the established methods and disciplinary requirements of his field. As Nancy Stepan has pointed out, scientific racism's power lay, in large part, in its adherence to scientific methodology and disciplinary standards. If race science were merely "pseudo-science" it would have had far less currency.[31]

In fact, Hill agonized over the methodological problems in determining national origins. One of the most serious problems he confronted was the lack of reliable information about the national origins of the white, native-stock population. Hill deduced that roughly half of the white population in 1920 comprised descendants from the original colonial population, but the census of 1790 did not record data on place of birth. A study conducted by the Census Bureau in 1909, "A Century of Population Growth," classified the population of 1790 according to country of origin by analyzing the surnames of the heads of households recorded in the census. The study found 87 percent of the population to be English. Independent scholars believed the report was inaccurate, however, because it failed to take into account that some names were common to more than one country and that many Irish and German names had been Anglicized. It omitted Scandinavians from the national composition altogether. Hill also believed the report was "of questionable value."[32]

Nevertheless, Hill decided to use "A Century of Population Growth" because no other data existed. But Irish, German, and Scandinavian American groups criticized the report and lobbied Congress that the calculations in the Quota Board's first report slighted their populations.[33] Hill realized that the flawed report endangered the credibility of the entire exercise. With the help of a $10,000 grant from the American Council of Learned Societies, Hill enlisted Howard Barker, a genealogist, and Marcus Hansen, an immigration historian, to determine the national origins of the white population in 1790.

Their conclusions, based on a more sophisticated method of analyzing surnames and reported to the Quota Board in 1928, adjusted the allocations of origins of the colonial stock considerably. Great Britain and Northern Ireland's share fell from 82 percent to 67 percent of the total, reducing its quota by ten thousand.[34]

Assuming for the moment that Barker and Hansen discerned the national origins of the population at 1790 with a fair degree of accuracy, determining the national origins of the American population from that base by following their descendants forward in time from 1790 to 1920 was an entirely different matter. The basic methodology employed by the Quota Board assumed an analysis of the population in terms of numerical equivalents, not actual persons. Hill explained that the Quota Board could not "classify people into so many distinct groups of individual persons, each group representing the number of individual persons descending from a particular country." He continued,

> Even if we had complete genealogical records that would not be possible because there has been a great mixture of nationalities through inter-marriage since this country was first settled. So when the law speaks of the number of inhabitants having a particular national origin, the inhabitant must be looked upon as a unit of measure rather than a distinct person. That is to say, if we have, for example, four people each of whom had three English grandparents and one German grandparent, we have the equivalent of three English inhabitants and one German inhabitant.[35]

Herein lay the fundamental problem of the whole project: its methodology assumed that national identities were immutable and transhistorical, passed down through generations without change. The Quota Board assumed that even if nationalities combined through intermarriage, they did not mix but remained discrete, unalloyed parts in descendants that could be tallied as fractional equivalents. The board's view of national origin drew from the concept of race defined by bloodline and blood quantum, which was available in the established definition of Negro. Rather than apply the "one-drop of blood" rule, however, the board conceived of intermarriage between European nationalities in Mendelian terms. But is a person with three English grandparents and one German grandparent really the numerical equivalent of her ancestors? Or does that person perhaps develop a different identity that is neither English nor German but one that is syncretic, produced from cultural interchanges among families and communities and by the contingencies of her own time and place? By reifying national origin, Congress and the Quota Board anticipated the term "ethnicity," inventing it, so to speak, as Werner Sollors said, with the pretense of being "eternal and essential," when in fact it is "pliable and unstable." Sollors's view of ethnicity as a "pseudo-historical explanation" triggered by "the specificity of power relations at a given historical moment" fits well the notion of immigration quotas based on national origin.[36]

At the same time, the Quota Board ignored intermarriage between Euro-Americans and African Americans and Native American Indians, never problematizing the effect of miscegenation on the "origins" of the white population. Thus, even as the board proceeded from an assumption that all bloodlines were inviolate, it conceptualized national origin and race in fundamentally different ways.[37]

Even when considered on its own terms, the task of calculating national origins was beset by methodological problems. The Quota Board had to make a number of assumptions in order to fill the gaps in the data. Hill acknowledged that his computations involved "rather arbitrary assumptions," some of which did "violence to the facts." Most serious—and surprising, in light of Hill's longstanding interest in immigrant fecundity—of these was his decision to apply the same rate of natural increase to all national groups. Hill also weighted the population figures for each decade, giving each earlier decade greater numerical importance than the succeeding one, to allow for a larger proportion of descendants from earlier immigrants. The net result of these assumptions tilted the numbers towards the northern European nationalities.[38]

Even Hill expressed concern that the entire exercise rested on so many assumptions that the conclusions might not be viable. Ultimately, he rationalized that errors in the process would not significantly effect the outcome. Because the quotas represented a ratio of one quota slot to 600 people, Hill said, a deviation of 60,000 in the population of any nationality would alter that nationality's quota by only 100.[39]

As Hill prepared the Quota Board's third report in 1928 and early 1929, the political atmosphere was contentious and the implementation of the quotas—already twice postponed by Congress—remained in doubt. In 1928 criticism over the hardships wrought by restriction mounted: YMCAs, church congregations, and the League of Women Voters petitioned Congress to admit families who were unable to join men who had immigrated before 1924 because their quotas were oversubscribed.[40]

Political controversy intensified in the fall of 1928 when Herbert Hoover campaigned for president on a platform opposing national origins as a basis for the quota system. As secretary of commerce, Hoover had signed off on the Quota Board's first two reports. But, as criticism of national origins grew, legislation repealing the quotas gained support in Congress. Worried about losing political support among German and Scandinavian American voters in traditionally Republican midwestern states, Hoover claimed that national origins quotas were impossible to determine "accurately and without hardship." Observers noted that Hoover's Democratic rival, Al Smith, opposed the quotas in the North while favoring them before Southern audiences.[41]

In February 1929 the nativist lobby stepped up its own efforts, mobilizing mass petitions to Congress from the American Legion, the Grange, and the Daughters of the American Revolution. On behalf of the patriotic societies, John Trevor and Demerest Lloyd took out a series of advertisements in the *Washington Post* defending the "national origins basis . . . [as] the only one which does not discriminate for or against any [nation]" and exhorting members of Congress to stand firm against the efforts of "hyphenates" who would "play politics with the nation's blood stream."[42]

Critics continued to lobby Congress that the national origins quotas were "inspired by bigotry" and based on a method that "must be carried out by deductions, conjecture, assumptions, guesswork, and arbitrary means." Hill knew that the political opponents of national origins quotas would seek another postponement in order to work for the law's repeal. Congress had accepted the principle of national origins as fair and nondiscriminatory, but the claim to fairness would evaporate if the quotas could not be accurately determined.[43]

Hill presented the Quota Board's third report to the Senate immigration committee in February 1929. Although the first two postponements were valuable, Hill testified, "The present computations are as near as we can get on this matter of determining the national origins, practically." S. W. Boggs, the State Department's geographer and secretary of the Quota Board, similarly told the Senate committee that the "whole quota is affected by [an] element of error" but that the "results are practically as good as they can be made." Another postponement, he added, would not make any "material change" in the quotas.[44]

Hill and Boggs survived the hearings; two weeks later the secretaries of labor, state, and commerce submitted the Quota Board's report to the president. The secretaries, however, issued a caveat that they "neither individually nor collectively are expressing any opinion on the merits or demerits of this system of arriving at the quotas." A more honest inquiry into the matter by the Quota Board might have concluded that determining the national origins of the American people was theoretically suspect and methodologically impossible. But relentless lobbying by the restrictionists and the pedigree of the quotas' authors overcame all obstacles and doubts. In the end Congress and the president accepted the Quota Board's calculations. And, once promulgated by the president, the "national origins" of the American people, and the racial hierarchies embedded in them, assumed the mantle of fact and the prestige of law.[45]

Lawmakers had invoked anthropology and scientific racism to create an immigration system based on national origins, but that had only gone as far as establishing a general ideological framework. It fell to civil servants in the executive branch to translate that ideology into actual categories of identity for purposes of regulating immigration and immigrants. Indeed, the enumeration and classification of the population *enabled* such regulation. As historian Vicente Rafael has pointed out, the value of such population schedules to the modern state lay in their "render[ing] visible the entire field of [state] intervention." Thus the invention of national origins was not only an ideological project; it was also one of state building.[46]

Sociologist John Torpey points out that nationality is a legal fact that, to be implemented in practice, must be codified and not merely imagined. While "citizen" is defined as an abstract, universal subject, the citizenry is not an abstraction but, in fact, a collection of identifiable corporeal bodies. As Partha Chaterjee has written, the modern nation-state is a "single, determinate, demographically enumerable form." This is part of the "logic of the modern regime of power," which pushes "the processes of government in the direction of administration and the normalization of its objects of rule."[47]

The national origins quota system created categories of difference that turned on both national origins and race, reclassifying Americans as racialized subjects simultaneously along both axes. That racial representation of the American nation, formalized in immigration quotas, reproduced itself through the further deployment of official data. The process of legitimation was evident in Joseph Hill's last monograph, "Composition of the American Population by Race and Country of Origin," written in 1936. Hill's analysis derived from the racial constructions embedded in immigration policy as it had evolved during the 1920s. It also reflected the distance Hill had traveled in his own thinking. After noting that "the population of the United States . . . is almost 90 percent white and almost 10 percent Negro," and that 68.9 percent of the "total white stock" in the United States derived from Great Britain and Northern Ireland, the Irish Free Republic, and Germany, Hill mused about the future of the "composite American." He speculated that if immigration were to be completely cut off, the foreign-born element of the population would disappear within seventy-five to one hundred years. Perhaps after another seventy-five years, the native population of foreign parentage would disappear. "[T]he white population would then be 100 percent native white of native parentage," he said. "Its composition by country of origin would not differ greatly from that of the present white population, but with the intermingling of national or racial stocks in the melting pot it would be a more homogeneous population. Few persons could then boast of unmixed descent from any single country or people."[48]

Joseph Hill readily assumed that the "composite American" would be white. The colored races had no place in his vision of the American nation, whether through intermarriage or by inclusion in a pluralist society. But if the elision of "American" and "white" was a predictable articulation of con-

temporary race thinking, Hill's assertion of a white American race represented an evolution in race ideology. Hill had rehabilitated the old trope of
the melting pot, but with a new twist. Traditionally, the idea of the melting
pot was based on cultural assimilation, the Americanization of immigrants
from diverse European backgrounds through education, work, and social
advancement. Nativists rejected that idea in the 1910s and the years immediately after World War I in favor of theories that emphasized race purity.
Congress and the Quota Board invented national origins that paradoxically
upheld both the inviolate nature of racial bloodlines and the amalgamation
of the descendents of European nationalities into a single white American
race. Hill presciently imagined that one consequence of restricting European
immigration would be the evolution of white Americans.

Asians and the Rule of Racial Unassimilability

The system of quotas based on national origin was the first major pillar of
the Immigration Act of 1924. The second provided for the exclusion of persons ineligible to citizenship. By one account, the provision barred half the
world's population from entering the United States.[49]

Ineligibility to citizenship and exclusion applied to the peoples of all the
nations of East and South Asia. Nearly all Asians had already been excluded
from immigration, either by the Chinese exclusion laws[50] or by the "barred
Asiatic zone" that Congress created in 1917. The barred zone encompassed
the entire area from Afghanistan to the Pacific, save for Japan, which the
State Department wished not to offend, and the Philippines, a United States
territory.[51] In 1907 the Japanese government agreed to prevent laborers from
emigrating to the United States, but nativists complained that the diplomatic
agreement was ineffective. The exclusion of persons ineligible to citizenship
in 1924 achieved statutory Japanese exclusion and completed Asiatic exclusion, thereby constituting "Asian" as a peculiarly American racial category.
Moreover, it codified the principle of racial exclusion into the main body of
American immigration and naturalization law.[52]

Two major elements of twentieth-century American racial ideology evolved
from the genealogy of the racial requirement to citizenship: the legal definition of "white" and the rule of racial unassimilability. The origins of these
concepts lay in the Nationality Act of 1790, which granted the right to naturalized citizenship to "free white persons" of good moral character. However,
that idea—including the legal boundaries of "white"—was contested
throughout the nineteenth century with regard to the citizenship status of
Native American Indians and African Americans and later with regard to the
eligibility of Asians to citizenship. The resolution of the latter in the early
1920s constituted the perfection of racial doctrine in citizenship law, which

remained in effect until 1952 when the McCarran-Walter Act abolished all racial requirements to citizenship.[53]

After the Civil War and the passage of the Fourteenth Amendment, Congress amended the Nationality Act to extend the right to naturalize to "persons of African nativity or descent." It defeated Charles Sumner's proposal that all references to race be stricken from the requisites of citizenship; in 1870 white Californians already viewed Chinese immigration with hostility. As it was, granting the right to naturalization to persons of African nativity was a gratuitous gesture to the former slaves. No one seriously believed that "the [N]egroes of Africa [would] emigrate," a federal judge explained in 1880, ". . . while the Indian and the Chinaman were in our midst, and at our doors and only too willing to assume the mantle of American sovereignty."[54]

Congress thus retained the language of race in the Nationality Act of 1870, encoding racial prerequisites to citizenship according to the familiar black-white categories of American race relations. European immigrants fit into that construction as white persons: between 1907 and 1924, nearly 1.5 million immigrants, nearly all from European countries, became American citizens.[55] The Chinese Exclusion Act of 1882 included a provision that made Chinese ineligible to citizenship, but that remained outside the main body of naturalization law. Japanese, Asian Indians, Armenians, Syrians, Mexicans, and other peoples that immigrated into the United States in the early twentieth century thus posed a challenge to the race categories in citizenship law. Where did they stand in relation to the black-white paradigm? To a great extent, black and white had been defined in terms of each other. As Takao Ozawa observed, "White persons, as construed by the Supreme Court of the United States and the state courts, means a person without Negro blood."[56] Through the struggles between Asian and other immigrants and the government over their rights to citizenship, the legal boundaries between white and not-white clarified and hardened.

Between 1887 and 1923 the federal courts heard twenty-five cases in which the racial status of immigrants seeking citizenship was contested, culminating in two Supreme Court decisions, *Takao Ozawa v. U.S.* (1922) and *U.S. v. Bhagat Singh Thind* (1923).[57] By ruling that Japanese and Asian Indians were racially ineligible to citizenship, the two decisions cast Japanese and Asian Indians with Chinese as unassimilable aliens and helped constitute the racial category "Asian." The joining of Japanese and Asian Indians with Chinese was not preordained, however, but was the culmination of three decades of social, political, and judicial struggle over their status in America.

Since the 1890s, both the Japanese government and Japanese immigrants had worked to distinguish Japanese in America from Chinese and the latter's fate as a despised and excluded race. Japanese immigrant associations advocated for adopting the Western style of dress and learning English, believing that Chinese immigrants set themselves apart by retaining traditional customs. Kyutaro Abiko, publisher of the *Nichibei Shimbun* and a wealthy labor contractor and landowner, led a movement for permanent settlement, family immigration, and assimilation. He urged Japanese to take up farming and, in the cities, small businesses, in order to establish economic roots and independence. In northern and central California Japanese bought land, formed partnerships to purchase acreage, and entered share- and cash-lease agreements with Anglo-American landowners, who, facing a shortage in farm labor, were eager to contract with them. In less than a decade Japanese agricultural land holdings in California grew nearly fivefold, from 61,858 acres in 1905 to 281,687 acres in 1913.[58]

By deciding to become yeoman farmers, Japanese immigrants embraced the quintessential requirement for American liberty and civic virtue, but nativists rejected their endeavors as a foreign conspiracy to take California from white people. United States senator James Phelan, formerly the mayor of San Francisco and for thirty years a leading California exclusionist, claimed Japanese land colonies in Merced County "destroyed the area for white settlement and the desirable element."[59]

Anti-Japanese sentiment on the Pacific Coast clashed with American geopolitical interests in the Far East, which desired friendly relations with Japan. By the beginning of the century Japan had established itself as an imperialist power with colonial possessions, a powerful navy, treaty alliances with Western nations, and economic privileges on the northeast Asian mainland. In 1905, when the San Francisco School Board segregated Japanese from white children, the incident quickly evolved into a diplomatic crisis between Japan and the United States. President Theodore Roosevelt, calling the segregation of Japanese "a wicked absurdity," sent Secretary of Labor and Commerce Victor Metcalf to San Francisco to intervene in the situation, and he authorized Secretary of State Elihu Root to "use the armed forces of the United States to protect the Japanese . . . if they are menaced by mobs." Roosevelt opposed statutory exclusion but pursued immigration restriction through administrative and diplomatic means.[60] In 1907 he issued an executive order that barred immigration from Hawai'i to the mainland, effectively eliminating one major source of Japanese immigration. Later that year Japan and the United States negotiated the "Gentleman's Agreement," in which Japan agreed to voluntarily restrict emigration by refusing passports to laborers. The agreement fell short of the wishes of both Japanese immigrants and California nativists, but it served both nations' official interests. It predicated the Root-Takahira Agreement of 1908, in which Japan and the United States pledged to respect their respective interests in Korea and the Philippines, and the U.S.-Japan Treaty of Navigation and Commerce of 1911.[61]

Unable to legislate Japanese exclusion, nativists on the Pacific Coast used the concept of ineligibility to citizenship, which they presumed applied to Japanese on the basis of a federal court ruling in 1894.[62] In 1913 California passed the Alien Land Law, proscribing agricultural land ownership by persons ineligible to citizenship. The *Nichibei Shinbum* called the law the "height of discriminatory treatment," according Japanese "worse treatment than people of third-rate southern and eastern European nations living in the United States." In 1921 Washington state passed a similar land law; other laws in western states barred aliens ineligible to citizenship from obtaining licensure in law, pharmacy, teaching, realty, and other professions.[63]

Hostility toward Japanese echoed the racism of economic entitlement that had fueled the anti-Chinese movement in the late nineteenth century, but also evinced anxiety over Japan's standing as a world power. Contemporary literature compared Japanese to the Prussian Hollenzollerns, calling Japan "one of the most turbulent and disturbing" world powers, and expressed particular alarm at the buildup of Japan's navy.[64] Japan's teleologic rationale for expansion especially disconcerted Anglo-Americans. The latter believed civilization marched only in one direction—westward—but Japanese saw two cultural impulses emanating from the original seat of civilization in Persia and Armenia, one to the east and one to the west. Japan, a young nation, was free to take the best of Europe and the best of Asia: according to one Japanese writer, "At her touch the circuit is completed, and the healthy fluid shall overflow the earth."[65]

With Japan competing with Western nations on modern, imperialist terms, nativists could hardly say Japanese were the same as the backward Chinese. Sensitive to Japanese power and American diplomatic interests, nativists shunned allegations of racial inferiority. The unctuous James Phelan is perhaps most remembered for the crude utterance "a Jap [is] a Jap," but he also said, "Personally we have nothing against the Japanese, but as they will not assimilate with us and their social life is so different from ours, let them keep at a respectful distance."[66] Similarly, California governor William Stephens acknowledged the Pacific was quickly becoming "one of the most important highways of commerce on this earth. Amity and concord and that interchange of material goods as well as ideas, which such facilities offer, will inevitably take place to the benefit of both continents. But that our white race will readily intermix with the yellows strains of Asia, and that out of this interrelationship shall be born a new composite human being is manifestly impossible."[67]

Foreign policy also influenced American legal posture toward Asian Indian immigration. In that case, immigration policy turned in large part on American relations with Great Britain and the evolution of Asiatic exclusion within the British Empire. Asian Indians first entered the United States in significant numbers in 1906–1909, after a racist movement in British Columbia drove them out of work and wrested an agreement from the British to halt Indian immigration to Canada. In the western United States, Asian Indians met an atmosphere already hostile to Chinese and Japanese, but their status as British subjects made it possible that they might be protected from racial attacks. The first race riot against Asian Indians, in Bellingham, Washington, in the summer of 1907—a three-day-long rampage of five hundred white sawmill workers that drove Indian workers out of town—prompted an inquiry from the British ambassador to the United States. But the British had their own reasons for discouraging Indian immigration into the United States. They worried that Indians would find sympathy for Indian self-government among anti-imperialists in the United States. They had already retreated from upholding the rights of their Indian subjects within the British Empire, acquiescing to demands by the "white Canada" movement as well as white settlers in Natal, the Transvaal, and Australia to exclude Indians from their corners of the dominion. Thus the British ambassador did little more than register a pro forma complaint after the Bellingham riot. The Roosevelt administration considered the status of Asian Indians important only as it affected American relations with Great Britain and Japan. As long as the British turned a blind eye, the administration hoped to use Indian exclusion to pressure Japan for Japanese exclusion.[68]

The right to naturalization became the principal grounds upon which Japanese and Indian immigrants fought for their rights in America. As early as the first decade of the century the Bureau of Naturalization informed clerks of court that they should warn petitioners who appeared to be not-white that the courts might deny their applications for citizenship. In 1906 Charles Bonaparte, the United States attorney general, specifically held Japanese to be ineligible and instructed clerks of court to refuse Japanese petitions. Asian Indians, as British subjects, may have been eligible to citizenship under an 1870 agreement of reciprocity between the United States and England, but in 1907 Bonaparte stated flatly, "Under no construction of the law can natives of British India be regarded as white persons." Despite these instructions, during the 1900s and 1910s several hundred Japanese and South Asian Indians became naturalized citizens.[69]

Immigrants who were denied citizenship on grounds of racial ineligibility repaired to the federal courts for redress. Sometimes the United States litigated against immigrants who they believed had been improperly naturalized by the local courts. In each case, the court's decision turned on whether the petitioner could be considered a "white person" within the meaning of the statute. The possibility that the petitioners might be legally defined as black was never considered, notwithstanding legal and social precedence that treated Asians akin to black people. In the early twentieth century, however, no one seeking naturalized citizenship appealed to the courts claiming legal status as a black person, owing to the geographic emphasis of the law's language ("persons of African nativity or descent") as well as the social stigma and unequal status associated with blackness.[70]

Immigrants who were denied citizenship on account of race took grave offense. Racial ineligibility not only implied a status of innate inferiority but also contradicted the democratic premises of citizenship in the American nation. During the Progressive era, assimilative practices emphasized Americanizing immigrants through teaching the English language, the work ethic, the Constitution, and other democratic values. If Europeans could become Americans through education, why could not others? Moreover, in 1918 Congress had granted "any alien" who served during the First World War the right to naturalize without first making a declaration of intent and without proof of five years' residence, suggesting that loyalty—especially in its ultimate test—qualified one to citizenship. The lower courts naturalized some Japanese, Asian Indians, and Filipinos on that basis.[71]

Takao Ozawa argued his case for citizenship on grounds of his impeccable moral character, his assimilation to American society, and his wholehearted embrace of American political ideals. He had emigrated from Japan as a child in 1894, graduated from high school in Berkeley, California, and attended the University of California. He moved to Honolulu in 1906, married, and had two children, whom he sent to American church and school. He worked for an American company, spoke English fluently, and did not drink, smoke, or play cards. "In name, General Benedict Arnold was an American, but at heart he was a traitor. In name, I am not an American, but at heart I am a true American," said Ozawa in his brief to the court.[72]

Bhagat Singh Thind similarly argued that he was "willing and eager to undertake the responsibilities of citizenship, having shown my eagerness by buying Liberty bonds to help carry on America's part in the war and by enlisting in the fighting forces of the country." Thind wrote his brief from Camp Lewis, Washington, where he was stationed with the United States Army. He was a veteran of the world war who had come to the United States from the Punjab in 1913. He was a democrat who supported Indian self-rule. In federal court, District Judge Charles Wolverton upheld Thind's naturalization, citing witnesses who were "most favorably impressed with his deportment, and manifestly believe in his attachment to the principles of this government."[73]

Ozawa and Thind thus argued their claims on the principle of consensual citizenship, but that principle was always a double-edged sword, for the idea of a social compact required consent by both the individual *and* the community. It implied liberal, inclusive possibilities, but it also justified racism and exclusion. The exclusionary side of consent was articulated most forcefully in the Supreme Court's *Dred Scott* decision. The ideological foundation of Chief Justice Taney's infamous statement that Negroes had no rights that white people were bound to respect lay in the idea that the former were not party to the social contract embodied in the Constitution. Similarly, in the mid-nineteenth century, American nationalism revived the mythology of Anglo-Saxonism, ascribing a racial origin to (and thus exclusive ownership of) the democratic foundations of the nation.[74]

The racial tensions within the basic doctrine of citizenship complicated the matter of immigrants' rights to naturalize. Since the principle of consensual citizenship was not absolute, the courts felt no compulsion to rule on the propriety of race as a condition of citizenship. Indeed, despite the Fourteenth Amendment, whiteness was already a condition of *full* citizenship; by the turn of the century African Americans had been forced into second-class status by disfranchisement, lynching, and Jim Crow segregation. Kelly Miller, a professor at Howard University, wrote in the *Nation* in 1924 that the racial requirement to citizenship was "the most curious inconsistency to be found in American law. The race most deeply despised is a yoke-fellow in privilege when it comes to citizenship eligibility," notwithstanding, of course, that "in apportioning the privileges and advantages of citizenship the Negro is set apart in a separate class" by state laws. Miller advocated for eliminating all racial distinctions from the law. Nativists and exclusionists drew the opposite conclusion. They commonly held that the low social status of the Negro was proof that granting citizenship to the freed slaves had been a mistake; the same mistake should not be repeated by granting citizenship to Asiatics.[75] Thus, the racial prerequisite cases would decide on which side of America's *herrenvolk* democracy Asians and other non-Europeans would fall.

Ozawa, Thind, and other immigrants seeking naturalization did not challenge the constitutionality of the racial prerequisite. They made their claims on grounds of their adherence to American ideals, but they also argued that, within the terms of the law, they were white and therefore also racially eligible to citizenship. Their arguments were thus contradictory, reflecting both democratic sentiments and strategic decisions to argue according to the law and not against its discriminatory nature.

Ironically, the few petitioners who successfully litigated their status as white persons did so with the aid of scientific race theories. In 1909 a federal court in Georgia ruled that George Najour, a Syrian, was eligible to citizenship. District Judge Newman stated that "free white person" referred to race, not color. "Fair or dark complexion should not be able to control" race, he said. Judge Newman cited A. H. Keane's *The World's People*, which divided the world's people into four categories: the "Negro or black, in the Sudan, South Africa, and Oceania (Australasia); Mongol or yellow, in Central, North, and East Asia; Amerinds (red or brown) in the New World; and Caucasians (white and also dark), in North Africa, Europe, Irania, India, Western Asia, and Polynesia" and noted that Keane "unhesitatingly place[d] the Syrians in the Caucasian or white division."[76]

Using similar logic, federal courts admitted Syrians, Armenians, and Asian Indians to citizenship as white persons in seven cases between 1909 and 1923. In each case the court interpreted whiteness to mean something more than just color and bowed to anthropologic and ethnologic definitions of race. Not all the courts agreed; most ruled against the petitioners' claim to whiteness, usually relying on "common knowledge" definitions of race. During the 1910s "white" and "Caucasian" became increasingly antagonistic concepts in judicial argument.[77]

Takao Ozawa cited anthropology and ethnology that identified Japanese as Caucasian or white. Although the Japanese had mixed with the Mongolian and Malay races, their "dominant strains are 'white persons,' speaking an Aryan tongue and having Caucasian root stock." That was why, Ozawa said, "the uncovered part of the [Japanese] body [is] white," and, moreover, why Japanese possess a "mental alertness, a quality of mind in which they differ from other Asiatics and resemble the Europeans and the inhabitants of North America, above the Mexican line." Racially, Japanese are "a superior class, fit for citizenship."[78]

Moreover, Ozawa argued, Japanese were quite assimilable. The rest of Asia was hopelessly backward, but Japan had imbibed Western values and made the transition to modernity. The Japanese race was highly adaptable, having absorbed, centuries ago, elements of ancient Chinese culture (when it was great) and, more recently, the modern ways introduced after Commodore Matthew Perry opened Japan to the West. Ozawa understood the profound irony of his historical predicament. "It is preposterous to claim that a nation, which has shown itself to have the greatest capacity for adaptation, against whom the severest criticism is that they are imitators, is not capable of adjusting itself to our civilization," he said.[79]

Once establishing his racial pedigree, however, Ozawa betrayed a democratic impulse, saying that race should not determine citizenship. "The preservation of a conventional racial type is a matter of aesthetics," he said. "What really counts in humanity is home influence and education, and where the ideals are high, racial type is of little moment."[80]

The Supreme Court grappled with the inconsistencies in racial taxonomies. It acknowledged that color as an indicator of race was insufficient, given the "overlapping of races and a gradual merging of one into the other, without any practical line of separation." Despite the impossibility of determining clear racial types, the Court resisted the logical conclusion that no scientific grounds for race existed. The Court sidestepped the problem by simply asserting that white and Caucasian were one and the same. Since an "almost unbroken line of decisions in federal and state courts . . . held that 'white person' meant to indicate only a person of what is popularly known as the Caucasian race," the Court said, Japanese cannot be Caucasian because they are not white.[81]

In *Ozawa* one senses the Court struggling to reconcile race as a popular concept, as scientific classification, and as judicial and congressional precedent. The Court tried to invoke science to its advantage but foundered when confronted with scientific theories of race. *Ozawa* elided the differences between common understanding and scientific evidence, as in its phrase "popularly known as Caucasian." Thus, *Ozawa* settled the issue of Japanese ineligibility to citizenship, but it did not clearly resolve the problem of racial definition. In *Ozawa* the Court made the prescient comment that the racial prerequisite to citizenship was "part of our history."[82] Three months later, when the Supreme Court ruled on Bhagat Singh Thind's petition for citizenship, the Court found its grounding in history.

Thind argued his eligibility to citizenship as a white person based on his Aryan and Caucasian roots. "Speaking literally, color cannot be the only test of the white or Caucasian race; strictly speaking no one is white. . . . [T]he true test of race is blood or descent," he said. Citing anthropological experts at length, Thind noted that the Aryans of India have physical features "about the same" as the modern Englishman or German. They are a "tall, long-headed race with distinct European features, and their color on the average is not as dark as the Portuguese or Spanish and is lighter than the Moor." Because marrying outside of caste in India is strictly forbidden, Thind argued that he was a "pure Aryan."[83]

The government conceded that Thind might be a "border line case," ethnologically speaking, but averred that the meaning of the statute was clear that "Hindus" are excluded from "white persons." It rejected Thind's claim to whiteness as ridiculous: "In the popular conception he is an alien to the white race and part of the 'white man's burden'. . . . Whatever may be the white man's burden, the Hindu does not share it, rather he imposes it."[84]

The Court clarified the meaning of *Ozawa*, saying, "Caucasian is a conventional word of much flexibility. . . . The word [Caucasian] by common usage has acquired a popular meaning, not clearly defined to be sure, but sufficiently so to enable us to say that its popular as distinguished from its scientific application is of appreciably narrower scope. . . . The words of the statute are to be interpreted in accordance with the common man from whose vocabulary they were taken." What mattered, said the Court, was the racial designation of "living persons *now* possessing in common the requisite characteristics," not in the "dim reaches of antiquity."[85]

In *Thind* the Court dismissed science altogether. The term "Caucasian," it said, "under scientific manipulation, has come to include far more than the unscientific mind suspects." Noting Keane's classification of not only Indians but also Polynesians and the Hamites of Africa as Caucasians, the Court commented dryly, "We venture to think that the average well-informed white American would learn with some degree of astonishment that the race to which he belongs is made up of such heterogeneous elements." Moreover, scientific authorities disagreed irreconcilably over the proper racial division: Blumenbach has five races; Keane, four; Deniker, twenty-nine. In any case, the original framers of the law "used familiar words of speech [intending] to include only the type of man whom they knew as white . . . [those] from the British Isles and northwestern Europe . . . bone of their bone and flesh of their flesh, and their kind whom they must have had affirmatively in mind."

Furthermore, the Court maintained, the meaning of white readily expanded to accommodate immigrants from "Eastern, Southern, and Mid-Europe, among them Slavs and the dark-eyed, swarthy people of Alpine and Mediterranean stock." These immigrants were "received as unquestionably akin to those already here and readily amalgamated with them."[86]

Scientific racism had developed in the nineteenth century not as an innocent or neutral query of the natural world but as an effort to prove race and racial difference by men committed to racial prejudice. When science failed in its purpose, the Court disposed of science. The Court doubted the etymology of "Caucasian" and the efficacy of racial classification generally but, as Ian Haney López points out, "it did so not to challenge the construction of racial beliefs, but to entrench them even further. . . . The Court stanched the collapsing parameters of whiteness by shifting judicial determinations of race off of the crumbling parapet of physical difference and onto the relatively solid earthwork of social prejudice."[87] The Court's edict—"What we now hold is that the words 'free white persons' are words of common speech, to be interpreted with the understanding of the common man"— amounted to a concession to the socially constructed nature of race.[88] Moreover, its acknowledgment of the assimilability of eastern and southern Europeans and its insistence on the unassimilability of Asians rendered a double meaning to assimilation. For Europeans, assimilation was a matter of socialization and citizenship its ultimate reward. Asians, no matter how committed to American ideals or practiced in American customs, remained racially unassimilable and, therefore, forever ineligible to citizenship.[89]

The *Ozawa* and *Thind* rulings completed the legal construction of the "Asiatic" as a racial category. Although the decisions applied to Japanese and South Asians, respectively, the Court made a leap in racial logic to apply the rule of ineligibility to Koreans, Thai, Vietnamese, Indonesians, and other peoples of Asian countries who represented discrete ethnic groups and, anthropologically speaking, different racial groups. The Court used retroactive reasoning to conclude that the natives of all Asian countries were racially ineligible to citizenship. In the last paragraph of *Thind*, the Court wrote:

> It is not without significance in this connection that Congress, by the [Immigration] Act of 1917 . . . has now excluded from admission into this country all natives of Asia within designated limits of latitude and longitude, including the whole of India. This not only constitutes conclusive evidence of the congressional attitude of opposition to Asiatic immigration generally, but is persuasive of a similar attitude towards Asiatic naturalization as well, since it is not likely that Congress would be willing to accept as citizens a class of persons whom it rejects as immigrants.[90]

In 1923, on the heels of *Ozawa* and *Thind*, the Court issued four rulings upholding California and Washington state laws proscribing agricultural land ownership by aliens ineligible to citizenship. Those laws had been passed in the 1910s to drive Japanese and other Asians from farming. In *Terrace v. Thompson*, the Court held that the alien land laws fell within the states' police powers to protect the public interest. The Court did not address whether Japanese or other Asians were eligible to citizenship. That had already been decided—indeed, naturalized—by *Ozawa* and *Thind*. The Court contended, moreover, that the alien land laws did not discriminate against Japanese because the laws applied to *all* aliens ineligible to citizenship, eliding the racial foundation of the concept. The Court held that it was logical and necessary to distinguish between citizens and aliens when considering land ownership, claiming, "[P]erfect uniformity of treatment of all persons is neither practical nor desirable. . . . [C]lassification of persons is constantly necessary [and] must therefore obtain in and determine legislation." The Court asserted, "One who is not a citizen and cannot become one lacks an interest in, and the power to effectually work for the welfare of the state, and so lacking, the state may rightfully deny him the right to own or lease land estate within its boundaries. If one incapable of citizenship may lease or own real estate, it is within the realm of possibility that every foot of land within the state may pass to the ownership of non-citizens." In this way the Court both refined and obscured the racial logic embedded in the concept of ineligibility to citizenship, rendering invisible its premise of racial unassimilability.[91]

Together, the naturalization and land cases solidified the concept "ineligible to citizenship." Armed with the concept, California nativists reinvigorated their efforts for statutory Japanese exclusion. The timing was to their advantage: the U.S.-Japan Treaty of Commerce and Navigation expired that year and Congress was considering immigration legislation. While national attention focused on restricting immigration from Europe, the leading California exclusionists formed the California Joint Immigration Committee (CJIC) to press for Japanese exclusion. The CJIC, a successor organization to the Asiatic Exclusion League, was an alliance of the American Legion, the California State Federation of Labor, the Grange, and the Native Sons of the Golden West. It mounted an aggressive propaganda and lobbying campaign headed by V. S. McClatchy, the co-owner of the *Sacramento Bee* and one of California's most virulent racists, and worked in concert with former California officials now in the U.S. Senate, James Phelan and former governor Hiram Johnson. The CJIC made for a formidable pressure group.[92]

The exclusion rhetoric of the CJIC and others carefully promoted unassimilability based on racial difference, not inequality, although their racial animus was evident. The Japanese are the "most unassimilable and most dangerous because they have no idea, and no intention, of assimilation," McClatchy testified to the Senate. The American Legion asserted that because Japanese "can never become an integral part of the American national stock through blood fusion," they will "remain among us a race apart."[93] The nativist argument treated ineligibility to citizenship as a natural condition, a racial characteristic of Japanese, instead of the legal construction that it was.

The exclusionists faced significant opposition from American business interests in Japan and the Pacific generally as well as from powerful religious organizations like the Federal Council of Churches and the Protestant missions. By the 1920s Japan counted many sympathizers among American elites, including progressivist attorney George Wickersham, who argued Ozawa's case before the Supreme Court, and religious leader Sidney Gulick, who founded the National Committee on American-Japanese Relations. On behalf of the committee, Wickersham proposed a new treaty to replace the Gentleman's Agreement that would place more rigid restrictions on immigration but confer the privilege of citizenship on all who personally qualified.[94]

The most important opposition to exclusion came from the State Department, because Japan strongly protested the exclusion clause in the immigration bill. Japanese Ambassador Masanao Hanihara told Secretary of State Charles Evan Hughes that Japan was willing to renegotiate the Gentleman's Agreement, but that it would not countenance discriminatory treatment:

> [I]t is not the intention of the Japanese Government to question the sovereign right of any country to regulate immigration into its own territories. Nor is it their desire to send their nationals to the countries where they are not wanted. . . . To Japan the question is not one of expediency, but of principle. To her the mere fact that a few hundreds or thousands of her nationals will or will not be admitted into the domains of other countries is immaterial. . . . The important question is whether Japan as a nation is or is not entitled to the proper respect and consideration of other nations.[95]

Hughes told the Senate committee that the administration wished to avoid "resentment and difficulties, which will arise from statutory exclusion." The secretary advocated for a small quota for Japan and continued observance of the Gentleman's Agreement.[96] The House immigration committee was dominated by restrictionists: its chair, Albert Johnson, was a staunch nativist who had cut his political teeth in the anti–Asian Indian agitation and riots in the state of Washington in the early 1900s.[97] But, under pressure from the administration, the House committee divided and the Senate committee supported a quota for Japan. The opposition to Japanese exclusion was significant but, like their counterparts advocating for quotas based on national origin, the Californians lobbied intensely and relentlessly. The political tide turned to their favor when Henry Cabot Lodge made an incendiary speech on the Senate floor, claiming that Hanihara's letter to Hughes, which expressed concern that passage of an exclusion law would have "grave consequences" for U.S.-Japanese relations, was a "veiled threat" against the United States. David Reed, the senator from Pennsylvania and the leading supporter for a Japanese quota, threw his support to exclusion. The rest of the Senate followed.[98]

Japan considered the Immigration Act of 1924 cause for national humiliation. In retaliation, it imposed a 100 percent tariff on goods imported in any quantity from America, like preserved fruits and cotton and woolen goods. Within a year American traders in Japan reported that exclusion had virtually ruined their businesses. Japan also appealed to the League of Nations and continued to raise the issue of racial equality in international forums. The exclusionists celebrated the passage of the immigration law in 1924 but McClatchy noted, "Japan is no ordinary adversary." In fact, support for a Japanese quota continued throughout the late 1920s and early 1930s.[99]

Japanese immigrants felt thoroughly dejected by the 1924 immigration act, which foredoomed them to permanent disfranchisement and social subordination. Their only hope lay in the Nisei, the second generation. Some Japanese considered moving to Mexico or other states, but immigrant leaders discouraged relocation. They considered California "heaven" in terms of agricultural production. "The foundation of race development must rest on agriculture," said the *Shin Sekai*. "The Alien Land Law will be a *dead letter* as the second generation comes of age."[100]

Asian Indians had already been excluded from immigration by the barred zone created in 1917. But *Thind* sealed their fate as unassimilable Asians in the United States. A small minority group with no national government to speak on their behalf, Indians became targets of legal vengeance. In the wake of *Thind*, California attorney general U. S. Webb instituted proceedings to revoke Indian land purchases. The United States Justice Department went to court to denaturalize Asian Indians on the grounds that they had obtained citizenship by fraudulent means. Between 1923 and 1927 the federal courts cancelled the naturalization certificates of sixty-five Asian Indians.[101] An attempt to pass a resolution in Congress ratifying and confirming all naturalizations granted to Indians before 1923, initiated with the support of Supreme Court chief justice Taft and the Labor Department was quashed by Albert Johnson and the CJIC. Although W. W. Husband of the Labor Department told the Senate immigration committee that that "the admission of a few Hindus would not at all break down the rule of rigid exclusion," McClatchy understood that every breach in the wall of exclusion had the potential for widening. The CJIC worried that confirming the naturalization of Indians held implications for Japanese and Chinese who entered the armed forces and Japanese who had been naturalized in Hawai'i.[102]

Despite the tortured judicial genealogy of the racial-prerequisite cases, ineligibility to citizenship, like national origins, acquired an aura of fact once declared by the Supreme Court and Congress. It became an indication of a natural condition, a badge of racial difference and the unassimilability of Asian peoples in America.

Race, Citizenship, and Conquest

The Immigration Act of 1924 exempted Mexico and other countries of the Western Hemisphere from numerical quotas. Mexicans were also not excluded from immigration on grounds of racial ineligibility to citizenship because, for purposes of naturalization, and therefore for immigration, the law deemed Mexicans to be white. Thus, under the act of 1924, Mexican immigration policy differed fundamentally from both European and Asiatic policies.

Both agricultural labor needs in the Southwest and American foreign policy interests in the Western Hemisphere impeded the restriction of Mexican immigration. The cutoff of Asian and European immigration created a special need for farm labor in California; growers there and in Texas lauded Mexican labor in part because they believed Mexicans would not settle permanently in the United States. Foreign policy considerations also weighed heavily against Mexican restriction. Senator David Reed, the cocreator of the national origins principle and sponsor of the Immigration Act of 1924, opposed quotas in the Americas on grounds of the tradition of Pan-Americanism. Some elected officials sympathized with the idea of restricting Mexican immigration but did not see how, in fairness, Congress could impose quotas on Mexico and not Canada. Thus the Senate defeated proposals to put the Western Hemisphere under the quota system in 1924 by a vote of sixty to twelve.[103]

The history of the Southwest as former Mexican territory, annexed by the United States as a result of the Mexican-American War, further complicated the meanings of nationality and citizenship. Euro-Americans never considered Mexicans their racial equals. Manifest Destiny touted the Anglo-Saxon, and during the Mexican-American War, expansionists wanted to take all of Mexico but abandoned the idea because they did not want to bring a populous colored race into the nation. Americans also looked upon the Mexicans as a mixed or impure race, comprising Indian and Spanish blood, and hence with even greater racial suspicion.[104]

Yet, paradoxically, conquest facilitated the racialization of Mexicans in the United States as "white." In order for the United States to exercise sovereignty over the annexed territory it had to have jurisdiction over all the inhabitants. That was accomplished in the Treaty of Guadalupe Hidalgo, which specified the terms of Mexico's defeat in 1848. In addition to giving Mexico's northern half to the United States, the treaty stipulated that all inhabitants in the ceded territory who did not announce their intention to remain Mexican citizens or leave the territory in one year would automatically become citizens of the United States. Carey McWilliams estimated that fewer than two thousand of the seventy-five thousand Mexican nationals in the ceded territory remained Mexican citizens under that provision. American citizenship in this instance was not consensual, either in terms of traditional liberal ideology or by individual assent. Rather, it indicated Mexicans' new status as a conquered population.[105]

The practice of ascriptive citizenship was actually established before the Mexican-American War, in earlier stages of white American settlement in the Southwest. When Texas declared independence from Mexico in 1836, the Texas constitution recognized Mexicans as citizens of the republic. In 1845, when Texas joined the Union, Congress passed a joint resolution that recognized all the citizens of the former republic as citizens of the United States.[106]

When they conferred citizenship upon Mexicans en masse, Americans were aware that the right to naturalization applied only to free white persons. The California constitutional convention of 1849 formally granted Mexicans the same citizenship rights as white persons. Delegates commented that "a small amount of Indian blood" was acceptable, as was suffrage for Mexicans, as long as Negroes and Indians were not admitted to the polity. Anticipating Baghat Singh Thind's arguments before the Supreme Court, a *Californio ranchero* delegate from Santa Barbara, Don Pablo de la Guerra, told the convention that the "true significance of the word 'White'" lay in ancestry and social standing, not skin color. "Many citizens of California have received from nature a very dark skin," said de la Guerra. "Nevertheless, there are among them men who have heretofore been allowed to vote and . . . to fill the highest public offices. It would be very unjust to deprive them of the privilege of citizens merely because nature had not made them white."[107]

De la Guerra's perspective was not unusual. At the time of annexation Euro-Americans in the Southwest generally interacted with the native *Californios*, *Tejanos*, and *Nuevo Mexicanos* of the region more on the basis of class than race. Anglo settlers intermarried with the native upper-class elite, who owned most of the land and occupied the center of the seigniorial order. Many of them descended from the first Spanish settlements and missions in the northern borderlands during the seventeenth century. Yet, the white skin and Castillian blood of the native ranchero class may have been more apocryphal than real, a later invention by the Mexican American middle class striving to distance itself from the racial opprobrium associated with "Mexican" that emerged in the Southwest after World War I.[108] During the late eighteenth century Indians and *gente de razón* of the California missions both polarized and amalgamated, as the conscription of Indians for labor also included conversion and, to some extent, intermarriage.[109] As the proceedings of the California constitutional convention suggest, Mexicans in the southwest at the time of conquest were already a *mestizo* population.

Intermarriage between white Americans and the native ranchero elite implied a degree of racial acceptance between the upper classes. But it also took place in context of Euro-American manifest destiny, which informed nearly all Anglo-Mexican relations. Most mixed marriages took place between Anglo men and the daughters of rancheros, giving the former access to land held by the latter's families and facilitating the process of dispossession. Indeed, white Americans consolidated annexation through armed violence, land thievery, and the imposition of American political institutions, as well as through intermarriage.[110] By 1910 the ranchero class had been virtually eliminated by the breakup of its land grants and the region's economic transformation to commercial agriculture that was wrought by the completion of the railroad, the invention of refrigerated freight cars, and the irrigation of south Texas and southern California.[111]

During the first two decades of the twentieth century not one, but two major streams of migration fed that transformation: laborers from the interior of Mexico, pushed from the land by the Mexican Revolution of 1910–1920,[112] and white farmers and businessmen from the southern and midwestern United States. The number of Mexicans enumerated in the census grew from 224,275 in 1910 to 651,596 in 1920.[113] The displaced native elite had been reduced to a feeble Mexican American middle class derisively called *los tuvos* (the has-beens); southwestern society now divided between growing populations of white property owners and skilled workers on the one hand and landless Mexican agricultural laborers on the other. Mexican immigration into the United States peaked in the mid-1920s and continued at high levels through the end of the decade, meeting labor demands not only in southwestern agriculture and mining but in the Midwest and North as well, owing to the cutoff of European immigration. The rapidly changing environment produced new class relations thickly overlaid with race.[114]

In the context of socioeconomic changes in the Southwest and the nativist climate in national politics, calls for restricting Mexican immigration grew. Throughout the late 1920s, in hearings on legislation proposed by John Box, the congressman from east Texas, immigration quotas for Mexico and other countries of the Western Hemisphere were debated. Although the large cotton and fruit growers who relied on Mexican labor opposed restriction, white small farmers squeezed by agribusiness and the urban middle class concerned about the emerging "Mexican problem" clamored against Mexican immigration.[115] An editorial in the *Saturday Evening Post* typified the temper of the time, combining traditional assumptions about race, immigrant fecundity, and job competition: "How much longer [are] we going to defer putting the Mexican Indian under the quota law we have established for Europe," the *Post* asked. "Mexican laborers often have nine children, or even more. At the nine-child rate, any of these Mexicans who are coming in by the trainload might be expected to average 729 great grandchildren. . . . No temporary considerations of expediency should carry the smallest weight in preventing the proper economic protection of our own flesh and blood."[116]

Anti-Mexican rhetoric invariably focused on allegations of ignorance, filth, indolence, and criminality. Government agencies in California like the state Department of Public Health, the state Commission of Immigration and Housing, and the Los Angeles County Department of Outdoor Relief released official reports filled with statistics on the high rate of social degeneracy among Mexicans, often introduced with calls for immigration restriction. The president of the Commission of Immigration and Housing, Edward Hanna, cited statistics showing that "Mexicans as a general rule become a public charge under slight provocation." He alleged that Mexicans "are very low mentally and are generally unhealthy," attributing their difficulties to race, as they "are for the most part Indians."[117]

Edythe Tate Thompson, chief of the state Tuberculosis Bureau, wrote in the preface to the bureau's report on Mexicans in the Los Angeles County Hospital that the study aimed to refute the claim that Mexicans are "cheap" and noted the need for a quota on Mexican immigration. Thompson was an ardent restrictionist who corresponded frequently with Albert Johnson and distributed the tuberculosis report widely. Statistics from Thompson's report and similar studies became common citations in testimonies, publications, and editorials as evidence of the need for restriction.[118]

In addition to their demands for a quota on Mexican immigration the CJIC also called for excluding Mexicans on grounds of racial ineligibility to citizenship. But the Labor Department concluded there was no basis to pursue such a policy, citing a long list of treaties, conventions, acts of Congress, and court decisions.[119] The most notable ruling in the judicial record was *In re Rodriguez*, which in 1897 upheld the right of a Mexican immigrant to naturalize. Ricardo Rodriguez, a thirty-seven-year-old native of Mexico who lived in San Antonio for ten years, petitioned to become a citizen in Bexar County. At the hearing of Rodriguez's application, two attorneys of the court contested his eligibility on grounds that "he is not a white person, nor an African, nor of African descent." In District Court, Judge Maxey noted that "as to color, he may be classed with the copper-colored or red men. He has dark eyes, straight black hair, and high cheek bones," but concluded that because he "knows nothing of the Aztecs or Toltecs, [h]e is not an Indian."[120]

The court also tried to ascertain Rodriguez's understanding of and support for the Constitution. Rodriguez could not explain the principles of the Constitution, but the judge attributed his seeming ignorance to his illiteracy and accepted testimony by a white acquaintance of Rodriguez, who said, "I know the man. I know that he is a good man, and know, . . . whatever the principles of the Constitution might be, that he would uphold them if he knew what they were." The witness said Rodriguez was peaceable, honest and hardworking, of good moral character, and law-abiding "to a remarkable degree."[121]

Judge Maxey conceded, "If the strict scientific classification of the anthropologist should be adopted, [Rodriguez] would probably not be classed as white." However, the constitution of the Texas Republic, the Treaty of Guadalupe Hidalgo, the Gadsden Treaty, and other agreements between the United States and Mexico either "affirmatively confer[red] the rights of citizenship upon Mexicans, or tacitly recognize[d] in them the right of individual naturalization." Noting that such agreements covered "all Mexicans, without discrimination as to color," Judge Maxey concluded that Rodriguez was "embraced within the spirit and intent of our laws upon naturalization."[122]

In re Rodriguez was significant because it recognized rights established by treaty over the narrow racial requirements in the law. By privileging Mexicans' nationality over their race, even as a conquered nationality, the court staved the Mexicans' formal racialization to an extent. The ruling also anticipated Ozawa and Thind by acknowledging the subjectivity of racial identification. Despite the judge's perception that Rodriguez was probably Indian (or, at least, not white) based on ocular examination, the court bowed to Rodriguez's own claim that he was not Indian, Spanish, or African. Indeed, upon questioning, Rodriguez said he did not know "where [his] race came from": his parents told him he was Mexican and he considered himself a "pure blooded Mexican." Rodriguez may have lacked schooling, but he understood his nationality.[123]

Secretary of Labor James Davis also recognized that the problem of self-identification impeded race-based immigration policy. Davis advised Johnson, "The Mexican people are of such a mixed stock and individuals have such a limited knowledge of their racial composition that it would be impossible for the most learned and experienced ethnologist or anthropologist to classify or determine their racial origin. Thus, making an effort to exclude them from admission or citizenship because of their racial status is practically impossible."[124]

Mexicans were thus deemed to be white for purposes of naturalization, an unintended consequence of conquest. Their legal whiteness was contingent and unstable, however. It did not preclude the Census Bureau from enumerating Mexicans as a separate race in 1930, albeit with an imprecise definition of the Mexican race as "persons who were born in Mexico and are not definitely white, Negro, Indian, Chinese, or Japanese."[125] But it did preclude Mexican exclusion by the rule of racial ineligibility. With legislative means of exclusion deemed inappropriate or inapplicable, the State Department moved in 1929 to restrict Mexican immigration through administrative means. The United States consuls in Mexico began to strictly enforce existing provisions of the immigration law to deny visas to prospective immigrants.

Consular officials used the ban on contract labor, the literacy test, and the provision excluding persons "likely to become a public charge" to refuse visas. The policy had an immediate effect. During the first ten months of fiscal year 1930, the United States issued only 11,023 visas to Mexicans. The department estimated that immigration for 1930–31 would be only 13,000, compared to an average annual rate of immigration of 58,747 over the previous five years—a decrease of 76.7 percent.[126]

The decrease, however, referred only to legal immigration. Mexicans continued to enter the United States by crossing the border at unofficial points and avoiding immigration inspection. That in itself was not new: migration across the border, both to and from the United States, had had an informal, unregulated character from the late nineteenth century to World War I. Increases in the head tax in 1917 and 1924 impelled increasing numbers of Mexicans to cross the border without official inspection. By the late 1920s the difference between legal and illegal immigration hardened, just as Mexican immigrants had emerged as a race problem in the Southwest. As we shall see in the next chapter, Mexicans would become racialized aliens in the United States in large part by their illegal presence in the region that was once Mexico.

Chapter Two

Deportation Policy and the Making and Unmaking of Illegal Aliens

> [D]eportation is . . . exile, a dreadful punishment,
> abandoned by the common consent of all civilized
> peoples. . . . That our reasonable efforts to rid
> ourselves of unassimilable immigrants should in
> execution be attended by such a cruel and
> barbarous result would be a national reproach.
> —JUDGE LEARNED HAND, 1929[1]

IN JANUARY 1930, officials of the Bureau of Immigration testified about the Border Patrol before a closed session of the House immigration committee. Henry Hull, the commissioner general of immigration, explained that the Border Patrol did not operate "on the border line" but as far as one hundred miles "back of the line." The Border Patrol, he said, was "a scouting organization and a pursuit organization." Officers operate on roads "without warrants and wherever they find an alien they stop him. If he is illegally in the country, they take him to unit headquarters."[2]

George Harris, the assistant commissioner general, added that Congress had authorized the Border Patrol to arrest aliens without warrant in 1925. It is true, Harris said, that the law provided for arrest without warrant when an alien "enters in the presence or view . . . of the officer, but this does not necessarily mean that the officer must see the alien at the exact moment that he crosses the border into the United States. Entry is a continuing offense and is not completed until the alien . . . reaches his interior destination."[3]

Members of the House committee expressed concern that the Border Patrol, which was not a criminal law enforcement agency and had no statutory authority to execute search warrants, had defined its jurisdiction not just at the border but far into the nation's interior—easily one or two hundred miles but, theoretically, the entire interior. If, as Hull said, "wherever [officers] find an alien, they stop him," how did the officers know the difference between an alien and a citizen? Indeed, what did it mean that Border Patrol officers could stop, interrogate, and search without a warrant anyone, anywhere, in the United States?

Yet if Congress was uneasy about the Border Patrol's reach, it had nearly assured such an outcome when it passed the Immigration Acts of 1921 and 1924, which for the first time imposed numerical restrictions on immigration. Because illegal entry is a concomitant of restrictive immigration policy, the quota laws stimulated the production of illegal aliens and introduced that problem into the internal spaces of the nation. Although unlawful entry had always resulted from exclusion, in the 1920s illegal immigration achieved mass proportions and deportation assumed a central place in immigration policy. The nature and demands of restriction raised a range of problems for the modern state, which were at once administrative (how should restriction be enforced?), juridical (how is sovereignty defined?), and constitutional (do illegal aliens have rights?).

These questions had been answered with relative ease in the late nineteenth century, when illegal aliens comprised Chinese and other marginalized persons (criminals, the insane, prostitutes, etc.), to the effect that aliens could be summarily expelled from the United States. Upholding Chinese exclusion, the Supreme Court in the 1880s and 1890s located Congress's power to regulate immigration outside of the Constitution, in the nation's sovereignty, which power it deemed was absolute. In the era of numerical restriction, the exercise of this sovereign power over immigrants, especially those illegally present, gave rise to complex and troubling issues.[4]

This chapter examines the advent of mass illegal immigration and deportation policy under the Immigration Act of 1924. It argues that numerical restriction created a new class of persons within the national body—illegal aliens—whose inclusion in the nation was at once a social reality and a legal impossibility. This contradiction challenged received notions of sovereignty and democracy in several ways. First, the increase in the number of illegal entries created a new emphasis on control of the nation's contiguous land borders, which emphasis had not existed before. This new articulation of state territoriality reconstructed national borders and national space in ways that were both highly visible and problematic. At the same time, as suggested above, the notion of border control obscured the policy's unavoidable slippage into the interior.

Second, the application of the deportation laws gave rise to an oppositional political and legal discourse, which imagined deserving and undeserving illegal immigrants and, concomitantly, just and unjust deportations. These categories were constructed out of modern ideas about social desirability, in particular with regard to crime and sexual morality, and values that esteemed family preservation. Critics argued that deportation was unjust in cases where it separated families or exacted other hardships that were out of proportion to the offense committed. As a result, during the 1930s deportation policy became the object of legal reform to allow for administrative discretion in deportation cases. Just as restriction and deportation "made" illegal aliens, administrative discretion "unmade" illegal aliens.

Taken together, these trends redefined the normative basis of social desirability and inclusion in the nation. That process had an important racial dimension, as the application and reform of deportation policy had disparate effects on Europeans and Canadians, on the one hand, and Mexicans, on the other hand. But, the disparity was not simply the result of existing racism. Rather, the processes of territorial redefinition and administrative enforcement informed divergent paths of immigrant racialization. Europeans and Canadians tended to be disassociated from the real and imagined category of illegal alien, which facilitated their national and racial assimilation as white American citizens. In contrast, Mexicans emerged as iconic illegal aliens. Illegal status became constitutive of a racialized Mexican identity and of Mexicans' exclusion from the national community and polity.

Deportation Policy and the Making of Illegal Aliens

The illegal immigrant cannot be constituted without deportation—the possibility or threat of deportation, if not the fact. The possibility derives from the actual existence of state machinery to apprehend and deport illegal aliens. The threat remains in the temporal and spatial "lag" that exists between the act of unlawful entry and apprehension or deportation (if, in fact, the illegal alien is ever caught). The many effects of the lag include the psychological and cultural problems associated with "passing" or "living a lie," community vulnerability and isolation, and the use of undocumented workers as a highly exploited or reserve labor force. Examining the policy and practice of deportation provides us not only with an understanding of how illegal immigration is constituted but also a point of entry into the experience of illegal immigrants, which, by its nature, remains largely invisible to the mainstream of society.[5]

Deportation was not invented in the 1920s, but it was then that it came of age. In a sense, legal provisions for the deportation of unwanted immigrants existed in America since colonial times, the principle having been derived from the English poor laws. A 1794 Massachusetts law, for example, called for the return of paupers from towns to the towns from where they came, or "to any other State, or to any place beyond sea, where he belongs." The expense of transatlantic removal, however, meant that deportations to Europe rarely took place, if at all. The Alien and Sedition Laws (1798–1801) provided for the exclusion and expulsion of aliens on political grounds. But Americans quickly rejected the principle of political removal during peacetime, and the nation operated without federal regulation of immigration for the better part of the nineteenth century. Unfettered migration was crucial for the settlement and industrialization of America, even if the laboring migrants themselves were not always free.[6]

Congress legislated the first federal restrictions on entry in 1875 when it banned persons convicted of "crimes involving moral turpitude" and prostitutes (a provision aimed at barring Chinese women from entry). During the 1880s the number of excludable classes grew to comprise the mentally retarded, contract laborers, persons with "dangerous and loathsome contagious disease," paupers, polygamists, and the "feebleminded" and "insane," as well as Chinese laborers. The litany of excludable classes articulated concern over the admission of real and potential public charges as well as late-nineteenth-century beliefs, derived from Social Darwinism and criminal anthropology, that the national body had to be protected from the contaminants of social degeneracy.[7]

Still, the nation's borders were "soft" and, for the most part, unguarded. Inspection at arrival sought to identify excludable persons and to deny them admission, but little could be done if they evaded detection and entered the country. Subsequent discovery was commonly the result of being hospitalized or imprisoned, yet no federal law existed mandating the removal of alien public charges from the country. It was not until 1891 that Congress authorized the deportation of aliens who within one year of arrival became public charges from causes existing prior to landing, at the expense of the steamship company that originally brought them. Congress otherwise established no mechanism and appropriated no funds for deportation.[8]

Congress gradually extended the statute of limitations on deportation. The Immigration Act of 1917 added six excludable categories and harsher sanctions, extended the period of deportability to five years, removed all time limits for aliens in certain classes, and for the first time appropriated funds for enforcement. The new, harsh law was applied to immigrant anarchists and communists in a sweep of postwar vengeance against radicalism and labor militancy, culminating in the Palmer Raids in the winter of 1919–1920, in which authorities arrested ten thousand alleged anarchists and ultimately deported some five hundred.[9]

The Red Scare notwithstanding, few people were actually excluded or deported before the 1920s. Between 1892 and 1907 the Immigration Service deported only a few hundred aliens a year and between 1908 and 1920 an average of two or three thousand a year—mostly aliens removed from asylums, hospitals, and jails. Deportation appears even less significant when one considers that some one million people a year entered the country in the decade preceding World War I. Congress and the Immigration Service conceived of and executed deportation as an adjunct to the "general process of exclusion," a correction to the improper admission of excludable aliens.[10] Perhaps most important, mere entry without inspection was insufficient grounds for deportation. The statute of limitations on deportation was consistent with the general philosophy of the melting pot: it seemed unconscionable to expel immigrants after they had settled in the country and had begun to assimilate.

The passage of the quota laws marked a turn in both the volume and nature of unlawful entry and in the philosophy and practice of deportation. In general, of course, legislators write laws to include sanctions against their violation. But Congress evinced a wholly different approach toward deportation in the act of 1924 than it had taken previously. The new law eliminated the statute of limitations on deportation for nearly all forms of unlawful entry and provided for the deportation at any time of any person entering after July 1, 1924, without a valid visa or without inspection.[11]

In addition, Congress for the first time legislated a serious enforcement mechanism against unlawful entry by creating a land Border Patrol. In 1929 Congress made unlawful entry a misdemeanor, punishable by one year of imprisonment or a $1,000 fine, or both, and made a second unlawful entry a felony, punishable by two years imprisonment or a $2,000 fine, or both. Deportation thus amounted to permanent banishment under threat of felony prosecution.[12]

The criminalization of unauthorized entry marked a radical departure from previous immigration policy, which deemed deportation to be a civil, or administrative, procedure. That policy deprived aliens in deportation proceedings rights protected by the Fourth and Fifth Amendments, but it also protected deportees from criminal punishment.[13] The 1929 law made illegal entry a separate criminal offense. In effect, illegal immigrants inherited the worst of both propositions: they were subject to both deportation, under which proceedings they still lacked constitutional protections, and separate criminal prosecution and punishment. Criminal conviction also made future reentry impossible.[14]

The Immigration Act of 1924 and its attendant enforcement mechanisms spurred a dramatic increase in the number of deportations. A contemporary observed that the "extensive use of the power to expel" began in 1925 and that deportation quickly became "one of the chief activities of the Immigration Service in some . . . districts." By 1928 the bureau was exhausting its funds for deportations long before the fiscal year ended. Carl Robe White, the assistant secretary of labor, told the House immigration committee that the department needed an annual budget of $10 million for deportations, more than ten times the appropriation for the previous year.[15]

In order to make expulsion more efficient, in 1927 the Immigration Service allowed illegal aliens without criminal records to depart voluntarily, thereby avoiding the time and expense of instituting formal deportation proceedings. The number of aliens expelled from the country rose from 2,762 in 1920 to 9,495 in 1925 and to 38,796 in 1929.[16] The Immigration Service continued to deport public charges delivered to it by state institutions. But "aliens without proper visa" rapidly became the largest single class of deportees, representing over half the total number of formal deportations and the overwhelming majority of voluntary departures by the late 1920s.[17]

This shift in the principal categories of deportation engendered new ways of thinking about illegal immigration. Legal and illegal status became, in effect, abstract constructions, having less to do with experience than with numbers and paper. One's legal status now rested on being in the right place in the queue—if a country has a quota of N, immigrant N is legal but immigrant $N + 1$ is illegal[18]—and having the proper documentation, the prized "proper visa." These were not absolute, of course, as preference categories privileged certain family relations, and qualitative indices for exclusion remained in force. However, the qualitative aspects of admission were rendered less visible as they were absorbed by the visa application process, which after 1924 took place at United States consular offices abroad. In addition to overseeing the distribution of quota slots, U.S. consuls determined the desirability of both quota and nonquota prospective migrants according to the submission of a "dossier," questionnaire and interview, and medical certification.[19] In 1924 the Immigration Service terminated line inspection at Ellis Island because medical exclusions were determined abroad. Thus, upon arrival, immigrants' visas were inspected, not their bodies. The system shifted to a different, more abstract register, which privileged formal status over all else. It is this system that gave birth to what we today call the "undocumented immigrant."

The illegal alien that is abstractly defined is something of a specter, a body stripped of individual personage. The mere idea that persons without formal legal status resided in the nation engendered images of great danger. In 1925 the Immigration Service reported with some alarm that 1.4 million immigrants—20 percent of those who had entered the country before 1921—might already be living illegally in the United States. The service conceded that these immigrants had lawfully entered the country, but because it had no record of their admission, it considered them illegal. It warned further about those who entered without authorization after the quota laws were passed:

> [I]t is quite possible that there is an even greater number of aliens in the country whose legal presence here could not be established. No estimate could be made as to the number of smuggled aliens who have been unlawfully introduced into the country since the quota restrictions of 1921, nor of those who may have entered under the guise of seamen. The figures presented are worthy of very serious thought, especially when it is considered that there is such a great percentage of our population . . . whose *first act* upon reaching our shores was to break our laws by entering in a clandestine manner—all of which serves to emphasize the potential source of trouble, not to say menace, that such a situation suggests.[20]

Positive law thus constituted undocumented immigrants as criminals, both fulfilling and fueling nativist discourse. Once nativism succeeded in legislating restriction, anti-alien animus shifted its focus to the interior of the nation and the goal of expelling immigrants living illegally in the country. The *Los Angeles Evening Express* alleged there were "several million foreigners" in the country who had "no right to be here." Nativists like Madison Grant, recognizing that deportation was "of great importance," also advocated alien registration "as a necessary prelude to deport on a large scale." Critics predicted, "If every man who wears a beard and reads a foreign newspaper is to be suspected unless he can produce either an identification card or naturalization papers, we shall have more confusion and bungling than ever."[21]

Prohibition supplied an important cache of criminal tropes, the language of smuggling directly yoking illegal immigration to liquor-running. The California Joint Immigration Committee described illegal aliens as "vicious and criminal," comprising "bootleggers, gangsters, and racketeers of large cities."[22] Similarly, Edwin Reeves, a Border Patrol officer in El Paso during the 1920s, recalled, "Every fellow you caught with a load of liquor on his back . . . was a wetback." The *National Republic* claimed that two million aliens intent upon illegally entering the United States were massed in Canada, Mexico, and Cuba, on the "waiting lists" of smugglers.[23]

In this story, aliens were not only subjects—that is, the smugglers—they were also the objects, the human goods illegally trafficked across the border. In 1927 the Immigration Bureau reported that the "bootlegging of aliens" was "a lucratively attractive field of endeavor for the lawlessly inclined . . . [that] has grown to be an industry second in importance only to the bootlegging of liquor." It emphasized, "The bootlegged alien is by all odds the *least* desirable. Whatever else may be said of him: whether he be diseased or not, whether he holds views inimical to our institutions, *he at best is a law violator from the outset.*"[24] This view that the undocumented immigrant was the least desirable alien of all denotes a new imagining of the nation, which situated the principle of national sovereignty in the foreground. It made state territoriality—not labor needs, not family unification, not freedom from persecution, not assimilation—the engine of immigration policy.

Territoriality was highly unstable, however, precisely because restriction had created illegal immigrants *within* the national body. This was not an entirely new phenomenon—it had existed since Chinese exclusion—but important consequences resulted from the different nature and scale of illegal immigration in the late 1920s. Illegal immigrants now comprised all nationalities and ethnic groups. They were numerous, perhaps even innumerable, and were diffused throughout the nation, particularly in large cities. An illegal immigrant might now be anyone's neighbor or coworker, possibly one's spouse or parent. Her illegal status might not be known to her social acquaintances and personal intimates. She might not even be aware of her own illegal status, particularly if it resulted from a technical violation of the law. She might, in fact, be a responsible member of society (employed, taxpaying, and notwithstanding her illegal status, law-abiding). Even if she were indigent or uneducated, she might have a family, social ties in a community, and interact with others in ways that arguably established her as a member of society.

The problem of differentiating illegal immigrants from citizens and legal immigrants signaled the danger that restrictionists had imagined—in their view, illegal aliens were an invisible enemy in America's midst. Yet their proposed solutions, such as compulsory alien registration and mass deportations, were problematic exactly because undocumented immigrants *were* so like other Americans. During the interwar period a majority of political opinion opposed alien registration on grounds that it threatened Americans' perceived rights of free movement, association, and privacy.[25] The Immigration Service had traditionally "never made any considerable attempt . . . to go out and look for aliens unlawfully in the country" and through the late 1920s remained reluctant to conduct mass raids, particularly in the North.[26] The problem of differentiation revealed a discontinuity between illegal immigration as an abstract general problem, a "scare" discourse used at times to great political effect, and illegal immigrants who were real people known in the community, people who committed no substantive wrongs.

Yet, if illegal aliens were so like other Americans, the racial and ethnic diversity of the American population further complicated the problem of differentiation. We might anticipate that illegal aliens from Europe and Canada were perceived and treated differently from those of Mexican or Asian origin.[27] In fact, the racial dimensions of deportation policy were not merely expressions of existing racial prejudice. Rather, they derived from processes of territoriality and administrative enforcement that were not in the first instance motivated or defined by race.

We might approach this problem by considering the problem of defining and controlling the border and by returning to Commissioner Hull's testimony that the Border Patrol did not operate "on the border line" but "back of the line." Contemporaries understood the distinction, if not the full implications. Writing about the Border Patrol in the Southwest, one author described apprehending aliens "at some distance back from the International Line" a "man-sized job." She explained, "To capture an alien who is in the act of crawling through a hole in the fence between Arizona and Mexico is easy compared with apprehending and deporting him after he is hidden in the interior, among others of his own race who are legally in this country."[28] The Border Patrol's capacious definition of its jurisdiction illustrates the nation's borders (the point of exclusion) collapsing into and becoming indistinguishable from the interior (the space of inclusion). But this is not to say that the border was eliminated. Policies of restriction and deportation reconstructed and raised the borders, even as they destabilized them. History and policy also constructed the U.S.-Mexican and U.S.-Canadian borders differently. The processes of defining and policing the border both encoded and generated racial ideas and practices which, in turn, produced different racialized spaces internal to the nation.

The Border and the Border Patrol

Before the 1920s the Immigration Service paid little attention to the nation's land borders because the overwhelming majority of immigrants entering the United States landed at Ellis Island and other seaports. The flow of immigrants into the country had been not only welcome but had been focused at fixed points that rendered land borders invisible. One immigration director described the situation as "equivalent to a circle with locked doors with no connecting wall between them."[29] A small force of the Customs Service and the Chinese Division of the Immigration Service jointly patrolled the Mexican and Canadian borders against illegal entry by Chinese. The Chinese patrol inspector, assigned to horseback detail or inspecting freight cars, occupied the loneliest and bottommost position in the hierarchy of the service.[30]

Immigration inspectors ignored Mexicans coming into the southwestern United States during the 1900s and 1910s to work in railroad construction, mining, and agriculture. The Immigration Bureau did not seriously consider Mexican immigration within its purview, but rather as something that was "regulated by labor market demands in [the southwestern] border states." The bureau also described the Southwest as the "natural habitat" of Mexicans, acknowledging, albeit strangely, Mexicans' claims of belonging in an area that had once been part of Mexico. The Immigration Act of 1917 doubled the head tax and imposed a literacy test, erecting the first barriers to entry, but unlawful entry was limited, as the Labor Department exempted Mexicans from the requirements during the war. It was not until 1919 that Mexicans entering the United States were required to apply for admission at lawfully designated ports of entry."[31]

Before World War I the U.S.-Canada border was also soft. In some ways it was not unlike the Mexican border: vast stretches of the northern border area were sparsely populated, economically undeveloped, and intemperate for many months of the year. As in the case of the Mexican border, the first inspection policies instituted along the Canadian border in the 1890s were aimed not to restrict Canadians but to deter Chinese and Europeans of the excludable classes who sought entry into the United States through the unguarded back door. Throughout the nineteenth century, Canadians circulated freely into the United States: Canadian farmers participated in the settlement of the American West, which movement preceded expansion to the Canadian West; and industry and manufacturing in Michigan and New England drew labor from Canada as well as from Europe.[32] But Canadians assumed a different economic relationship to the United States than did Mexicans. Except for

2.1 U.S. Immigration Service station, Brownsville, c. 1920s. (By permission of the Robert Runyon Photograph Collection E/VN03947, Center for American History, University of Texas at Austin.)

2.2 In 1960 the U.S.-Mexico and U.S.-Canada borders were marked by over two hundred official ports of entry, some of which were like this INS border inspection station at Antelope Wells, New Mexico. (Courtesy of U.S.-INS Historical Reference Library.)

French Canadians, who played an important role in New England lumbering and manufacturing, Canadians did not comprise a major source of unskilled labor for American industry. In large part this was because Canada itself suffered a labor shortage and relied on immigrant labor for its own economic development. For example, in the early twentieth century the sugar beet industry on both sides of the border—in Michigan, Wisconsin, and southern Ontario—recruited European agricultural laborers. After 1924, when European immigration to the United States declined, American sugar beet growers resorted not to Canadian labor but to Mexican and, secondarily, to Filipino labor.[33]

If both the Mexican and Canadian borders were soft until World War I, the passage of the quota laws in 1921 and 1924 threw the nation's contiguous land borders into sharp relief for immigration authorities. Although the majority of immigrants from Europe continued to land at seaports, contemporaries imagined that illegal aliens would overrun the land borders. One writer, believing that "the tide of immigration now beats upon the land borders—not upon the sea coasts—of the United States," asked, "Can these long borders ever be adequately patrolled?"[34]

Indeed, illegal European immigrants entered the United States across both borders. Belgian, Dutch, Swiss, Russian, Bulgarian, Italian, and Polish immigrants enlisted in agricultural labor programs in the Canadian west, only to arrive in Canada and immediately attempt entry into the United States, at points from Ontario to Manitoba. An investigation by the Federal Bureau of Investigation in 1925 reported that "thousands" of immigrants, "mostly late arrivals from Europe," were "coming [into Canada] as fast as they can get the money to pay the smugglers." The most heavily traveled route for illegal European immigration was through Mexico. The commissioner general of immigration noted, "Long established routes from southern Europe to Mexican ports and overland to the Texas border, formerly patronized almost exclusively by diseased and criminal aliens, are now resorted to by large numbers of Europeans who cannot gain legal admission because of passport difficulties, illiteracy, or the quota law."[35]

By the late 1920s surreptitious entry into the United States by Europeans declined. The threat of apprehension and deportation was a deterrent but alternate legal methods also existed for circumventing the quota laws. Europeans could go to Canada and be admitted to United States legally after they had resided in Canada for five years. The evidence suggests that this was a popular strategy: the proportion of lawful admissions from Canada of persons not born in Canada increased from 20 percent in 1925 to over 50 percent in the early 1930s.[36] And, as European immigrants in the United States became naturalized citizens, they could bring relatives over legally as nonquota immigrants. In 1927 over 60 percent of the nonquota immigrants admitted to the United States were from Italy, with the next largest groups coming from Poland, Czechoslovakia, and Greece.[37]

This is not to say that illegal immigration of Europeans and Canadians stopped. The Immigration Service continued to deport illegal aliens to Europe and to Canada—deportations remained fairly constant at six thousand to eight thousand a year through the early thirties. But the number of persons deported for surreptitious entry declined, whereas the number deported for overstaying temporary visas increased.[38] In general, the Immigration Service was more concerned with the bureaucratic burden of processing the high volume of legal traffic crossing the U.S.-Canada border in both directions. It also relied on the 1894 agreement between the United States and Canada that made Canadian rail carriers responsible for checking the status of passengers traveling to the United States, for deterring illegal entry from Canada.[39]

The service's work on the Canadian border contrasted to what the commissioner general described as the "high pitch" of its work along the U.S.-Mexico border.[40] During the late twenties the number of illegal Mexican immigrants deported across the southern border skyrocketed—from 1,751 expulsions to 1925 to over 15,000 in 1929.[41] Deportations for entry without a proper visa accounted for most of the increase. Although Mexicans did not face quota restrictions, they nevertheless faced myriad entry requirements, such as the head tax and visa fee, which impelled many to avoid formal admission and inspection.

Mexicans coming to the United States encountered a new kind of border. Notwithstanding the lax immigration procedures before World War I, the United States–Mexico border had had a long history of contestation. Born of war and annexation, it was contested, literally from its first imagination, by the Mexican and American surveyors charged with drawing the boundary after the Mexican-American War. Consolidating American sovereignty in the conquered territory was a protracted process, as armed skirmishes and rebellion along the border attended the appropriation of property and the imposition of American political institutions. After a decade of instability wrought by the Mexican Revolution and World War I, the border as a political marker became basically settled.[42]

During the 1920s, immigration policy rearticulated the U.S.-Mexico border as a cultural and racial boundary, as a creator of illegal immigration. Federal officials self-consciously understood their task as creating a barrier where, in a practical sense, none had existed before. The service instituted new policies—new inspection procedures and the formation of the Border Patrol—that accentuated the difference between the two countries. As historian George Sánchez described, crossing the border became "a momentous occasion, a break from the past . . . a painful and abrupt event permeated by an atmosphere of racism and control—an event that clearly demarcated one society from another."[43]

Inspection at the Mexican border involved a degrading procedure of bathing, delousing, medical-line inspection, and interrogation. The baths were new and unique to Mexican immigrants, requiring them to be inspected while naked, have their hair shorn, and have their clothing and baggage fumigated. Line inspection, modeled after the practice formerly used at Ellis Island, required immigrants to walk in single file past a medical officer.[44] These procedures were particularly humiliating, even gratuitous, in light of the fact that the Immigration Act of 1924 required prospective immigrants to present a medical certificate to the U.S. consul when applying for a visa, that is, before travel to the United States. Line inspection at Ellis Island was eliminated after 1924, and at El Paso the service exempted all Europeans and Mexicans arriving by first class rail from line inspection, the baths, and the literacy test. Racial presumptions about Mexican laborers, not law, dictated the procedures at the Mexican border.

More than anything else, the formation of the Border Patrol raised the border. In the Mexican border district, the Immigration Service first recruited patrol officers from the civil-service railway postal clerk registers, but that proved to be a mistake, as they were generally unqualified and the service quickly exhausted the register.[45] Receiving a temporary reprieve from civil service requirements, the Immigration Service hired former cowboys, skilled workers, and small ranchers as its first patrol officers. Almost all were young, many had military experience, and not a few were associated with the Ku Klux Klan. "Dogie" Wright was a typical recruit. The son of a Texas Ranger, Wright had also been a ranger and a deputy United States marshal before he joined the Border Patrol in 1925. Some patrolmen, according to Clifford Perkins, the first Border Patrol inspector in charge in El Paso, "were a little too quick with a gun, or given to drinking too much, too often"; many emulated the "rough but effective methods of the Texas Rangers." Of thirty-four patrol inspectors in the El Paso district in 1927, only one was Mexican American. Pedro (Pete) Torres, a native of New Mexico, had a reputation as an "extremely valuable man on the river, for he thought like a Mexican and looked like one" and could "roam through Mexican neighborhoods without arousing suspicion." Torres had "no nerves at all," according to Perkins. "He may have been a little quick on the trigger, but his actions in every shooting match during which smugglers were killed always proved justified by the circumstances."[46]

Officials labored to create a professional enforcement arm of the Immigration Service out of such material. Perkins recalled a training program comprising weekly lectures on investigative procedures, but training mostly took place on the job. Edwin Reeves said, "They just give you a .45 single action revolver with a web belt—and that was it." A civil service exam was soon

2.3 The first Border Patrol of the U.S. Immigration Service, El Paso, Texas, 1925. (Courtesy of U.S.-INS Historical Reference Library.)

instituted, which included math, writing an English essay, and demonstrating knowledge of Spanish "as spoken along the Mexican border." During the late 1920s turnover continued to average 25 percent within the first six months. A lack of professionalism plagued the force. In the El Paso district, drinking on the job, reading and socializing with friends while on duty, reckless driving, rumor-mongering, and accepting gratuities from aliens were common problems.[47]

More important, the Border Patrol's work assumed the character of criminal pursuit and apprehension, although officially it was charged with enforcing civil, not criminal, laws and was not trained as a criminal enforcement agency. As discussed above, the service interpreted its authorization to apprehend illegal aliens without warrant to apply to anywhere within the interior of the nation. It also seized goods it believed were "obviously contraband or smuggled," a practice that the commissioner general acknowledged had dubious legal sanction. During the Border Patrol's first five years of service, fifteen officers were killed in the line of duty, twelve in the Mexican border districts.[48]

As Border Patrol officers zealously pursued illegal aliens, smugglers, and criminals, the Immigration Service received complaints from white Americans who were interrogated by discourteous patrolmen or arrested without warrant. One citizen protested that the Border Patrol "enacted the role of Jesse James" on public highways. In 1929, in response to such adverse criticism, the service discontinued the "promiscuous halting of traffic" in the border area, acknowledging that it was "dangerous and probably illegal." A national conference of immigration commissioners and district directors held the same year devoted considerable attention to the conduct of Border Patrol officers and inspectors, including issues of lack of civility toward immigrants, bribery, and covering up misconduct. Official policy deemed "courtesy and consideration," "good morning and a smile," and "I'm sorry" as the "least expensive and perhaps the most useful" of the service's tools.[49]

Thus patrolmen were trained to act with civility, courtesy, and formality when dealing with Anglo citizens, ranch owners, immigrants arriving from Europe, and "high class people com[ing] in as tourists" from Canada. But the quasi- and extra-legal practices associated with rancher vigilantism and the Texas Rangers suited the needs of the Border Patrol in the Southwest, particularly when it involved patrolling large expanses of uninhabited territory far removed from Washington's bureaucratic oversight.[50] The Border Patrol functioned within an environment of increased racial hostility against Mexicans; indeed, its activities helped constitute that environment by aggressively apprehending and deporting increasing numbers of Mexicans. The Border Patrol interrogated Mexican laborers on roads and in towns, and it was not uncommon for "sweeps" to apprehend several hundred immigrants at a time. By the early 1930s the Immigration Service was apprehending nearly five times as many suspected illegal aliens in the Mexican border area as it did in the Canadian border area. The Los Angeles newspaper *La Opinión* believed the aggressive deportation policy would "de-Mexicanize southern California."[51]

Moreover, many Mexicans entered the United States through a variety of means that were not illegal but comprised irregular, unstable categories of lawful admission, making it more difficult to distinguish between those who were lawfully in the country and those who were not. Mexicans living in Mexican border towns who commuted into the United States to work on a daily or weekly basis constituted one category of irregular entry. The service counted these commuters as immigrants and collected a one-time head tax from them. It also required them to report to the immigration station once a week for bathing, a hated requirement that gave rise to a local black market in bathing certificates.[52]

Many other Mexicans entered legally as "temporary visitors" to work for an agricultural season and then returned to Mexico. According to one estimate, 20 to 30 percent of legal Mexican entrants during the 1920s and 1930s were classified as nonimmigrants—that is, as nonresident aliens intending to stay from six months to a year. The Immigration Service did not require a passport or visa for such entry from Canada, Mexico, or Cuba, as part of a reciprocal arrangement with those countries. That policy served Americans with business in neighboring countries but was also available to seasonal laborers working in the United States. One had only to pay a refundable head tax; if one failed to depart within the time limit, one became illegal.[53] Immigration policy had thus constructed classifications of entry that supported local and regional labor markets but that were also perceived as opportunities for illegal immigration. The instability of these immigration categories led officials to cast additional doubt and suspicion on Mexican immigrants.

It was ironic that Mexicans became so associated with illegal immigration because, unlike Europeans, they were not subject to numerical quotas and, unlike Asiatics, they were not excluded as racially ineligible to citizenship. But as numerical restriction assumed primacy in immigration policy, its enforcement aspects—inspection procedures, deportation, the Border Patrol, criminal prosecution, and irregular categories of immigration—created many thousands of illegal Mexican immigrants. The undocumented Mexican laborer who crossed the border to work in the burgeoning industry of commercial agriculture emerged as the prototypical illegal alien.

Mexican immigration abated during the 1930s, owing to the policies of deportation and administrative exclusion, as well as a lack of employment in the United States caused by the Depression. As economic insecurities among Euro-Americans inflamed racial hostility toward Mexicans, efforts to deport and repatriate the latter to Mexico grew. The movement did not distinguish between legal immigrants, illegal immigrants, and American citizens. Mexican Americans and immigrants alike reaped the consequences of racialized foreignness that had been constructed throughout the 1920s.

In addition to the deportation of illegal aliens by the INS, local and state authorities acted in myriad ways during the Depression to restrict the movement of Mexicans and Mexican Americans and to expel them from the country. California towns passed settlement laws that restricted relief to residents in order to deny welfare to unemployed migrant workers. Many towns, including the city of Los Angeles, deployed police at so-called "bum blockades" to keep indigent migrants from entering. In 1936 the governor of Colorado proclaimed martial law in the state's southern counties, giving officers of the Southern Colorado Military District instructions to turn back Mexican workers attempting to enter the state on alleged labor contracts.[54] In El Paso, Anglos demanded that the International Bridge be closed from 6:00 P.M. to 10:00 A.M. in order to keep local commuters from Juárez from going to work in El Paso. Local relief agencies, wanting "something done" about Mexicans on their rolls, reported lists of Mexicans to immigration authorities for deportation, including citizens and legal residents.[55]

Owing to its bureaucratic mandate, the INS understood the importance of distinguishing between Mexican Americans and immigrants. Notwithstanding the summary character of deportation proceedings, the INS could not actually deport Mexicans who could document their legal residence or American citizenship. After a public outcry against alleged illegal Mexican workers at the Isabella Sugar Company in Michigan in 1935, an Immigration Service investigation of two hundred workers revealed that none were in the country illegally and that 60 percent were born in Texas.[56] The Denver district director of the Immigration Service reported only a handful of deportable aliens among the hundreds of Mexicans apprehended by the military in southern Colorado; moreover, he said, his local inspectors were not eager to "hunt, apprehend and deport" Mexicans, whom they knew were mostly longtime residents who had settled in the area after working on the railroads during World War I. The service responded similarly to the Morrill County, Nebraska, Relief Committee that many of the Mexicans it reported to the service were American citizens. It noted as well that aliens who were "victims of the general economic depression" were not removable simply because they received public relief.[57]

These finer points of law did not abate sentiments to rid the country of the Mexican problem. Voluntary repatriation remained the only method of removing large numbers of Mexicans from the country. While the immigration statutes allowed for voluntary repatriation of indigent aliens at federal expense within three years of entry, municipal and state authorities had freer rein to expel unwanted Mexicans from their jurisdictions. They also had the cooperation of the Mexican government, which welcomed repatriation as a return of its citizens home and made efforts to resettle the returnees. The first major repatriation occurred, in fact, not during the Great Depression but in the post–World War I economic recession, in a program sponsored by the Mexican government. The Mexican *Secretaria de Relaciones Exteriores* established a department of repatriations, which administered the program through the network of Mexican consuls in the United States. Between 1920 and 1923, the program repatriated some 100,000 Mexicans with "free return transportation to the Mexican interior and subsistence."[58]

That project was dwarfed by the repatriations of the Great Depression. Led by the Los Angeles county relief agencies, local authorities throughout the Southwest and Midwest repatriated over 400,000 Mexicans during the early 1930s.[59] Authorities calculated that it cost less to transport a Mexican family to the border than it did to keep them on relief. Frank Shaw, a Los Angeles County supervisor, estimated that county-sponsored removal of 10,000 indigent cases a year would save the county $2.4 million. Thus the county welfare bureaus organized and sent trainloads of Mexicans to the border, where the Mexican government received them. An estimated 60 percent were children or American citizens by native birth; a contemporary observed that the "vast majority" spoke English and that many had been in the United States for at least ten years.[60]

Although the Immigration Service neither organized nor funded these repatriations, it encouraged repatriation by generating an atmosphere of fear of deportation. In early 1931 the service undertook a deportation drive in southern California that local authorities publicized widely as a "scare head" campaign. On February 26, authorities raided *La Placita*, the plaza at the center of the Mexican *colonía* in downtown Los Angeles. Police and immigration officers raided the park at midday, lined up some four hundred people, and demanded to see passports or other evidence of legal entry and residence. The service detained some thirty Mexicans and five Chinese for further questioning. Similar tactics were deployed in other towns and cities. A witness described an immigration raid in San Fernando on Ash Wednesday as "the day of judgment. . . . [The] deputy sheriffs arrived in late afternoon when the men were returning home from working in the lemon groves. They started arresting people. . . . The deputies rode around the neighborhood with their sirens wailing and advising people to surrender themselves to the authorities. They barricaded all the exits to the *colonía* so that no one could escape."[61]

Charles Visel, head of the Los Angeles Citizens Committee on the Coordination of Unemployment Relief, acknowledged the Immigration Service's "efficiency, aggressiveness, [and] resourcefulness" in deporting Mexicans from the city. "The exodus of aliens deportable and otherwise who have been scared out of the community has undoubtedly left many jobs which have been taken up by other persons (not deportable) and citizens of the U.S. and our municipality," he said.[62] Indeed, many Mexicans voluntarily left the country, induced by the atmosphere of growing racial animus. The first wave of repatriates, in fact, were not destitute Mexicans sent by relief bureaus but comprised Mexicans of modest means who decided to leave before things got worse.[63]

The repatriation movement, then, comprised voluntary departures, formal deportations by the INS, and organized repatriations by local welfare bureaus. Some agencies tried to depict repatriation as an act of benevolence— repatriates left Detroit amidst great fanfare, with Diego Rivera and Frieda Kahlo wishing them well at the train station[64]—but most departed with apprehension and bitterness. Many were directly pressured into leaving by relief workers. The Detroit Department of Public Assistance denied cash relief to Mexicans, giving out meal tickets to cafeterias instead, which caused Mexicans public humiliation. Relief workers pressured Mexicans with American citizenship to repatriate, citing the dependency of their families.[65] By 1933 most people who had been inclined to leave had done so. News of difficult conditions in Mexico had filtered back to the United States; moreover, federal New Deal programs afforded additional relief for the unemployed. Repatriates who tried to return to the United States found they were ineligible for reentry because they had been public charges. With Mexicans less responsive to the invitation to repatriate, welfare officials resorted to "abuse and manipulation . . . [and] harassment in allocating relief."[66]

Despite the evident distress experienced by the repatriates and the questionable legality of "repatriating" Mexican Americans with United States citizenship, few objected to the project. In the late 1920s the fledgling Mexican American civil rights movement had supported the Box Bill, on grounds that unchecked Mexican immigration depressed wages and living standards in the Southwest and invited racial antipathy from the Anglo-American population. A member of the League of United Latin American Citizens (LULAC) in south Texas explained to Paul Taylor that he sympathized with the plight of immigrant laborers but added, "We are handicapped by the steady flow of immigration of the laboring peon class. The native-born don't get a chance. . . . We have not been able to convince some people that there is a difference between us [and Mexican immigrants]."[67] LULAC's position was indicative of Mexican Americans' ambivalence towards the recent immigrant population, which by the mid-1920s outnumbered native-born Mexican Americans. In 1930 only 18.6 percent of the "Mexican" population in the United States were native-born of native-born parents, that is, of the third generation or greater. Historian David Gutiérrez has noted that "the unprecedented influx of Mexicans from Mexico raised some confusing questions about what now defined a Mexican in the United States."[68]

Many Mexican Americans felt both pride in their cultural heritage and resentment at being associated with the pejorative "Mexican," which cast them as foreigners and social inferiors. Those in the middle classes, in particular, insisted on being called Latin Americans or Spanish Americans to distinguish their American citizenship and to make a claim to whiteness. "As a matter of absolute record, it was the Latin American who first braved and tamed the Texas wilderness. They were the first white race to inhabit this vast empire of ours," stated the *LULAC News*. LULAC, which allowed only American citizens as members, advocated for school desegregation, sponsored hygienic campaigns, and encouraged rapid assimilation into American culture.[69] Even as LULAC insisted on its American-ness, however, its views were not necessarily anti-Mexican and sometimes even dovetailed with Mexican nationalist sentiments. Many believed it was also in the best interests of Mexico to limit immigration. The Mexican government estimated that during the 1920s one-eighth of Mexico's total population emigrated to the United States, causing labor shortages in some areas of the Mexican interior.[70]

The lone voices of protest against repatriation came from supporters of agribusiness. Dr. George Clements, the director of the agricultural division of the Los Angeles Chamber of Commerce, and James Batten, a Claremont College professor, both criticized the county for giving immigrants false information to encourage their departure. Batten warned, "In depleting the supply [of Mexican labor] we may be riding for a fall. . . . White men are doing work today that they will not do when other work is available."[71]

A final episode in repatriation took place in 1939–1940. At the request of the Mexican government, the INS transported over 1,200 Mexicans from throughout Texas—mostly families and approximately half American citizens—to the border at Brownsville. The INS organized twenty-eight contingents, comprised almost entirely of families with American-born children. As with some of the earlier repatriations, the Mexican government arranged for the families to resettle on small agricultural holdings, although these projects were often unsuccessful.[72]

Nearly 20 percent of the Mexican population in the United States returned to Mexico during the early years of the Depression. The repatriation of Mexicans was a racial expulsion program exceeded in scale only by the Native American Indian removals of the nineteenth century. But with a population of over 1.4 million, Mexicans were too numerous to be completely removed; moreover, their labor was still needed for farming, mining, and railway maintenance work throughout the Southwest. In fact, work was sometimes the preferred alternative to both repatriation and relief. From August to October 1935, the California Relief Administration and the federal Works Progress Administration denied relief to seventy-five thousand Mexican workers in order to force them to work the harvests in southern California. Similarly, state authorities forced men on relief in Sonoma County to pick hops for 75¢ a day and to live in "miserable impoverished shelters." Repatriation also sometimes served as an antidote to labor militancy. Authorities attempted to quell the 1933 berry-pickers' strike in El Monte, California, by sending informants to identify the "troublemakers," whom they then repatriated.[73] Repatriation thus saved local welfare bureaus millions of dollars, temporarily alleviated the labor market of surplus, provided a solution for Anglo-Americans who blamed Mexicans for their economic woes, and, at least in the short term, reduced the base of labor militancy.

Administrative Law Reform and the Unmaking of Illegal Aliens

At the same time that Mexicans and Mexican Americans were being deported and repatriated during the late 1920s and early 1930s, the volume of deportations of European immigrants also increased. These illegal aliens comprised unauthorized border-crossers, visa violators, and those who entered lawfully but committed a deportable offense subsequent to entry. Many had already settled in the country and acquired jobs, property, and families. Unlike Mexicans, these Europeans were accepted as members of society. But if their inclusion in the nation was a social reality, it was also a legal impossibility. Resolving that contradiction by means of deportation caused hardship and suffering to these immigrants and their families. It struck many as simply unjust.

Testifying before Congress in 1934, Nicholas Grisanti of the Federation of Italian Societies in Buffalo, New York, cited a typical case of an unjust deportation. An Italian immigrant lived most of his life in Buffalo. He was married with three small children and was gainfully employed. But, Grisanti explained, "at some previous year he had taken as a boy a half bag of coal from the railroad tracks to help keep his family warm," for which crime he was convicted and given a suspended sentence. Years later, he went to Canada for a summer vacation. The Immigration Service considered his return a "new entry" and ordered him deported, on grounds that he had been convicted of a crime involving moral turpitude before "time of entry." His deportation was thwarted after a public outcry led acting New York Governor Herbert Lehman to pardon the "little offense."[74]

In a sense, the protest against unjust deportations stemmed from the fact that European and Canadian immigrants had come face-to-face with a system that had historically evolved to justify arbitrary and summary treatment of Chinese and other Asian immigrants. It seemed that the warning sounded by Justice Brewer's dissent in *Fong Yue Ting* had come true. Justice Brewer had acknowledged that the absolute power of the state to expel unwanted aliens was "directed only against the obnoxious Chinese, but," he asked, "if the power exists, who shall say it will not be exercised tomorrow against other classes and other people?"[75]

Indeed, as early as 1920, in the aftermath of the Palmer raids, legal scholars noted that alleged anarchists in deportation proceedings were deprived of their civil liberties according to the "methods applied in the Chinese deportation cases."[76] After 1924 not only anarchists but Europeans who unlawfully entered the country also were caught in the legal machinery designed for the "obnoxious Chinese."

Thus during the late 1920s and early 1930s a critique of deportation policy emerged among social welfare advocates and legal reformers. These reformers did not directly challenge deportation as a prerogative of the nation's sovereign power. But they did search for ways to reconcile conflicting imperatives of national sovereignty and individual rights. During the early 1930s several legal studies called for administrative law reform in deportation. These included *Deportation of Aliens from the U.S. to Europe*, by Jane Perry Clark, a Barnard political scientist, published in 1931; a report on deportation by the National Commission on Law Observance and Enforcement (Wickersham Commission), issued in 1931; and *Administrative Control of Aliens: A Study in Administrative Law and Procedures*, by William Van Vleck, dean of George Washington University Law School, published in 1932 for the Commonwealth Fund. All three studies based their findings on an examination of actual deportation cases and other administrative records of the Immigration Service.[77] Although the latter two concerned general policy and did not limit their studies to deportations of any particular ethno-racial group, all three were generally motivated by the Immigration Service's treatment of European and Canadian immigrants.

Clark, Van Vleck, and the Wickersham Commission came to essentially the same two general conclusions. First, they believed deportation policy was applied in arbitrary and unnecessarily harsh ways, resulting in great personal hardship to individuals and in the separation of families, with no social benefit. Second, in terms of procedure, they concluded that deportation policy frequently operated in the breach of established traditions of Anglo-American jurisprudence, especially those concerning judicial review and due process. As Lucy Salyer has shown, during the late nineteenth and early twentieth century the federal courts generally upheld the summary character of immigration proceedings, notwithstanding the principle established by the Supreme Court in 1903 in the *Japanese Immigrant Case* that aliens in immigration proceedings had rights derived from "fundamental principles that inhere in due process of law." By the 1920s aliens had won only a few procedural rights, among them the right to an administrative hearing and the right to counsel. But critics found even these gravely lacking or undermined by the lack of other procedural safeguards, and cited a broad range of abuses. The Wickersham Commission noted the danger at hand: "The very investigations to see whether suspected persons are subject to deportation, by their nature, involve possible interference of the gravest kind with the rights of personal liberty. . . . These investigations are not public, and they often involve American citizens."[78]

Specifically, critics charged, aliens were often "forcibly detained." The Boards of Special Inquiry, which conducted formal deportation hearings, were often one-man tribunals, with the immigration inspector often appearing simultaneously as arresting officer, prosecutor, and judge.[79] The boards operated without rules of evidence, readily admitting hearsay, opinion, anonymous letters, and "confidential information." The alien also bore the burden of proof "to show cause . . . why he should not be deported." One study found that only one-sixth of aliens in deportation proceedings had legal representation, "ranging from one or two percent along the Mexican border to about 20 percent in New York City."[80]

Moreover, the Immigration Service interpreted the statute in ways that grossly stretched the law's meaning in order to justify grounds for deportation. The greatest abuse surrounded the application of the provision "liable to become a public charge at time of entry" (or "LPC"), which, Clark said, was "shaken on deportation cases as though with a large pepper shaker." The service deported immigrants who committed minor crimes or violated norms of sexual morality, such as bearing children out of wedlock, that were not deportable offenses, on grounds that they were "LPC before entry." In other words, the Immigration Service considered lapses or misfortune subsequent to entry to be the teleological outcome of a prior condition, which it adduced by way of retroactive judgment.[81]

Finally, immigrants under warrants of deportation had few avenues of

appeal. The Labor Department's Board of Review, which made recommendations to the secretary of labor, had no statutory authority. Judicial review was
extremely rare, as the federal courts historically practiced great restraint in
immigration cases, having progressively narrowed the grounds for judicial
review in Chinese exclusion cases over the years. During the late 1920s and
1930s the courts heard fewer than three hundred writs of habeas corpus in
deportation cases and found nearly 70 percent of them in favor of the Immigration Service.[82]

The legal critique of deportation policy evinced the preoccupations of legal realism during the years between the two world wars: a rejection of cate-
gorical thinking and a desire to transform differences of kind into differences
of degree; the privileging of experience over formal logic; and, consequently,
a belief in the need for discretionary authority in the emerging regulatory
state. According to the legal critics, deportation policy seemed to be a problem of law gone amok, emanating perhaps less from politics than from the
administration of law based on rigid categories without room for discretion
or experience. Because the main thrust of the criticisms concerned problems
in procedure and enforcement, administrative law reform provided an alternative, less contentious route for reforming deportation policy than the more
overtly political tack taken by liberal social welfare and immigration advocates. The latter had few friends in Congress during the Depression, when
work was scarce and there were renewed calls for restriction and deportations. In fact, the gaze of administrative law reformers was aimed not so
much at Congress as it was toward the judiciary, where they believed progress might be made in more clearly defining the limits of executive power in
matters of deportation.[83]

Yet embedded in the arguments for administrative law reform was a powerful political critique. That critique challenged the eugenical premises of
immigration policy, that is, the idea that social undesirability derived from
innate character deficiencies, which were perceived to be rooted biologically
in race, gender, or "bad blood." In a sense, administrative law reform was a
stalking horse for a broader cultural challenge to nativist politics, challenging, in particular, late-nineteenth- and early-twentieth-century theories about
social degeneracy and, more specifically, ideas about gender roles, sexual morality, and crime. These normative standards of social desirability and moral
fitness for citizenship continued to define the qualitative standards for immigrant admission and deportation in the Immigration Act of 1924, even as
they were eclipsed by the law's new emphasis on numerical restriction. In the
late 1920s and 1930s legal critics challenged the application of these qualitative standards in deportation cases.

The trend may be discerned from a reading of William Van Vleck's treatise
Administrative Control of Aliens. The treatise followed several lines of criticism that challenged traditional ideas about female dependency and sexual

morality. Van Vleck cited several cases in which the Immigration Service had ordered women deported as LPC because they were without male support, even though the women were employed and self-supporting. In one case, the service deported a woman whose husband became ill with tuberculosis fourteen months after they arrived in the United States on the grounds that she was dependent on her husband—even though she was employed. Van Vleck cited other cases of single mothers supporting their children or living with other relatives, recognizing that the family was a diverse institution that included female-headed households and extended families.[84]

Van Vleck also opposed the state assuming the role of sex police, stating, "[T]here appears from time to time evidence of a tendency on the part of some of the immigration officers to regard themselves as charged with the duty and the authority of exercising a general supervision of conduct and morals over our alien population." He evinced unease at the deportation of aliens on grounds of fornication, adultery, lewd and lascivious carriage, and other sexual activities. In some of these cases aliens were deported because state laws considered their transgressions to be crimes of moral turpitude; others were judged as LPC at time of entry.[85]

In line with modern thinking that considered crime environmentally, Van Vleck considered adultery and other moral transgressions to be social problems, not indications of deficiencies in character. He criticized as flawed reasoning the conclusion that "violations of the code as to sex morals before entry" were evidence of "'criminal tendencies' or signs of a 'weak moral nature'" that rendered them LPC at time of entry. He cited as an example the case of a young immigrant woman who had two illegitimate children during the first two years of residence in the United States. He said, "Evidence in the record tend[s] to show that before her entry . . . she had been well behaved and had lived quietly with her mother," and he cited the examining inspector in the case as asserting that the woman's morals "were entirely controlled by outside forces."[86]

At another level, the issue of sexual morality was linked to notions about family privacy, as deportation cases involving aliens accused of adultery and other crimes of immorality came to the attention of authorities almost always because they were reported by angry relatives or jealous suitors. In a turn from Progressive-era thinking that advocated state intervention in the family, Van Vleck deplored the use of LPC in cases of family disputes leading to unproved allegations and accusations by angry spouses, parents, or relatives.[87] (These cases also indicate the heightened sensitivity among immigrants that individuals could use the power of the state to intervene in personal disputes—"calling Immigration," as it were.)

The idea of the family's privacy was connected to its sanctity. One of the most tragic consequences of deportation, Van Vleck argued, was the separation of families. He pointed out, "If [the deported alien] is a poor man his wife and children have not the money to follow him. Even if they have the money and do follow him, this may mean the expatriation of American citizens." Similarly, Max Kohler, a former assistant attorney general who represented many immigrants, invoked the Supreme Court's 1923 ruling in *Meyer v. Nebraska* to oppose the separation of family by immigration restrictions. In *Meyer* the Court claimed that the scope of individual liberty included the right of individuals "to marry, establish a home and bring up children" without interference from the state, anticipating the Supreme Court's decision decades later that located in *Meyer* the precedent for defining privacy to be a fundamental right.[88]

While Kohler posited family unity in fundamental terms of personal liberty, most reformers constructed a more conditional context for family rights. They utilized a cost-benefit analysis that weighed violations of the immigration law that were technical or not substantively harmful to the public good against family separation that resulted either in the forced expatriation of dependents (often United States citizens) or in leaving them without support, making them public charges. The proverbial poor man's theft of a loaf of bread or sack of coal became a favorite of reform discourse. In this telling, family trumped both the original crime and the looming deportation. The family here was cast in the traditional patriarchal mode, in which the male head of household is heroic because he breaks the law and risks imprisonment for his family's welfare. But Van Vleck also narrated unmarried women with children as legitimate families that were worthy of preservation. And, if the trope of stealing to feed one's family ranked loyalty to one's family above one's obligation to the state, Van Vleck extended the idea of loyalty to protect family members who suffered from moral lapses.

Van Vleck's views were not isolated but articulated a trend among legal scholars and in the federal courts as well. In 1931 the *Yale Law Journal* noted a trend in the federal Circuit Courts of Appeal recognizing the severe consequences of restricting judicial review in matters of exclusion and expulsion. These cases suggested the need for "a more exacting construction of the due process rights of an alien and a more restricted construction of the statutory grounds upon which deportation orders may be based." The journal noted that courts were throwing out LPC cases that were "obviously grotesque." In one case the court overturned an order to deport a self-supporting Swedish woman living in California on grounds of a misdemeanor involving "moral turpitude," in this case cohabitation, and LPC. In a remarkable recognition of gender equality, the court said that "as to her lapses [from virtue] not amounting to prostitution, the petitioner stands exactly in the same position before the court as would a man who was similarly charged. . . . [The] petitioner then may not be excluded on this ground, unless the paramour, if an alien, could be excluded under the same circumstances." By the early 1930s the Immigration Service tempered its use of LPC. The trend benefited Europeans and Canadians, who had comprised the vast majority of LPC deportation cases. The deportation of Europeans and Canadians as LPC dropped from a high of nearly two thousand in 1924 to fewer than five hundred in 1932.[89]

During this period the courts made other refinements in deportation law. They clarified that conviction of a crime "before entry" referred to crimes committed outside the United States before the immigrant's first entry into the country. Other cases eliminated criminal misconduct from the public-charge category according to Judge Learned Hand's reasoning that public charge suggested "dependency not delinquency" and that LPC should not be used to deport people for petty crimes that were not deportable offenses. Echoing Justice Brewer's dissent in Fong Yue Ting, Judge Hand likened deportation to exile, "a dreadful punishment, abandoned by the common consent of all civilized people."[90]

The appeal to prevent family separation was particularly effective in areas where European immigrants were numerous and had some political influence. In New York many convicted felons received executive pardons after they served their prison terms in order to prevent their deportation, including the Italian man in Buffalo who stole a half sack of coal when he was a boy. Governor Herbert Lehman granted 110 such pardons during his tenure.[91]

Although executive pardons and federal court rulings addressed some of the problems in deportation policy, these fell short of clarifying a uniform national policy. In the early 1930s the Immigration Service remained resistant to the idea that it should relieve aliens' families of hardship, citing its "plain duty of ridding the country of those uninvited guests who have 'crashed the gate.'" As for the "alleged hardship to the alien . . . or to his family," the service pointed out the primacy of "the hardships inflicted upon the American citizen and lawfully resident and law-abiding alien in their exposure to the competition in employment of opportunities of bootlegged aliens."[92]

In 1933 and 1934 liberals adopted a new legislative strategy for immigration reform, which proceeded simultaneously along two tracks: one that proposed to impose yet harsher sanctions on criminals and one that proposed to prevent family separation in cases that were "exceptionally meritorious." Legislation introduced in 1933 and 1934 linked the two issues within a single bill. This strategy gave reformers political cover by demonstrating their commitment to restriction and against criminals while arguing for compassion for "relatively harmless and deserving people."[93]

Just who were the criminals and who were the deserving, however, was under realignment. Since the Progressive era, relativism and environmentalism had grown increasingly influential in thinking about criminal and moral deviance. There was also broader social support for the idea that people who made mistakes could be reformed. Speaking against the 1929 law that forever barred readmission after deportation, Jane Addams pointed out, "To make an old mistake indelible—to lay a dead hand on the future, is always of doubtful value." Thus petty crimes and sexual transgressions, once deemed evidence of innate character deficiency, could now be considered "more or less innocent [offenses] against the immigration law," falling below the bar set for deportation. Deportation for minor offenses was now considered punitive and unjust.[94]

The discourse on unjust deportation referred mostly to European immigrants and only occasionally to Mexicans. Ethnic Mexicans in the United States voiced the same concerns as did Europeans; for example, the Los Angeles Spanish-language newspaper *La Opinión* criticized the deportation of Mexicans who had ten years of residence in the United States, businesses, and families.[95] But Mexicans remained marginalized from the mainstream of immigration discourse. Among Euro-American reformers, references to immigrants of good moral character were usually not racially explicit, but by definition such immigrants were unlikely to be Mexican because "Mexican" had been constructed as a negative racial category. More important, reformers did not call for leniency in cases of unlawful entry, because this was a core component of the system based on numerical restriction, *which none of them directly opposed*. In contrast to environmentalist and relativist notions of crime, the idea of transgressing the nation's sovereign space stood out as an absolute offense. Thus while European immigrants with criminal records could be constructed as "deserving," Mexicans who were apprehended without proper documents had little chance of escaping either the stigma of criminalization or the fate of deportation.

Legislative and administrative reforms operated in ways that fueled racial disparity in deportation practices. In 1929 Congress passed the Registry Act, which legalized the status of "honest law-abiding alien[s] who may be in the country under some merely technical irregularity." The law allowed immigrants to register as permanent residents for a fee of $20 if they could show they resided in the country continuously since 1921 and were of good moral character. The law did not formally favor Europeans over Mexicans. But of the 115,000 immigrants who registered their prior entries into the country between 1930 and 1940, 80 percent were European or Canadian. According to Berkeley economist Paul S. Taylor, many Mexicans qualified for an adjustment of status under the Registry Act but few knew about it, understood it, or could afford the fee.[96]

During the 1930s and 1940s the Labor Department instituted a series of reforms that addressed, albeit in limited ways, questions of due process in deportation proceedings and established administrative mechanisms whereby certain illegal aliens—mostly Europeans—could legalize their status. Immigration and administrative law reformers welcomed the administration of Franklin D. Roosevelt in 1933. Roosevelt's secretary of labor, Frances Perkins, was a New York Progressive-era reformer, and the new head of the INS, Daniel W. MacCormack, was the first immigration commissioner who did not come directly from organized labor. Perkins and MacCormack took seriously the criticisms that had been mounting against the Immigration Service's practices. The secretary noted that "much of the odium which has attached to the Service has been due to the policies and methods followed in connection with deportations and removals."[97]

Perkins also appointed a civilian panel to investigate the practices of the INS. The Ellis Island Committee included northern urban elites noted for their charitable work among immigrants, like Mrs. E. Marshall Field and Mrs. Vincent Astor, and immigrant advocates, such as Max Kohler and Read Lewis of the Foreign Language Information Service. The committee's report, issued in March 1934, echoed the criticisms made by Van Vleck and the Wickersham Commission. In particular, it emphasized the need for administrative discretion to not deport in cases "deemed to involve extraordinary hardship, such as where deportation would involve the disruption of a family."[98]

In 1934 Perkins and MacCormack instituted a series of administrative reforms at the INS. One line of reform concerned procedures and due process. The INS discontinued the practice of arresting suspected aliens without warrant at places removed from the actual time and place of entry. It also mandated that the same officer could not conduct the preliminary examination and the final hearing.[99]

MacCormack also undertook a campaign to raise the professional level of INS personnel. In 1934 and 1935 he conducted two "lecture courses of study" for all INS employees. The stated reason for the lecture series was to facilitate the consolidation of the Bureau of Immigration and the Bureau of Naturalization into the INS in 1932. But MacCormack clearly placed the education work in a broader context of reform. In his inaugural lecture, the commissioner general stated, "Almost every department of the Government has some human problems. Our Service is one whose every problem is human—whose every act and decision affects the lives and welfare of human beings. We must, therefore, ever strive for that most difficult ideal—technical accuracy informed by justice and by humanity." He urged INS officers to perform their duties "efficiently, but at the same time humanely and in the spirit of helpfulness rather than persecution." Lecture topics included bureaucratic administration and procedures, including how to file paper work and conduct legal research, and key aspects of immigration and naturalization law, such as visa procedures, deportation policy, naturalization requirements, Chinese exclusion, and immigration from the insular territories. Specialists first delivered lectures to staff at INS headquarters; the lectures were then printed and sent to the field, where district directors delivered them to their subordinates. The series at central office followed a rigorous weekly schedule that included sessions on Christmas Eve and New Year's Eve.[100]

A third type of reform concerned the use of administrative discretion to grant relief from deportation for aliens for whom deportation would cause hardship. At one level, MacCormack undertook an intense effort to lobby Congress to pass legislation that provided for discretionary relief from deportation in "meritorious" cases. He stated, the "[The immigration laws] are so rigid that at times they defeat their purpose and . . . sometimes result in extreme hardship and injustice both to the alien and to the innocent relatives of the alien." Giving discretionary relief was not a question of "sentimentality," MacCormack said, but necessary to prevent the creation of public charges.[101] MacCormack believed, moreover, that "illegal entry in itself is not a criterion on character." To the contrary, he said, "the mother who braces the hardship and danger frequently involved in an illegal entry for purpose of rejoining her children cannot be held by that sole act to be a person of bad character."[102]

But Congressional action would be slow in coming. Although Democrats now controlled Congress, the party's southern wing served as a conservative block against reform in immigration matters. In the context of economic emergency posed by the Depression, immigration reform was not high on Roosevelt's list of legislative priorities. Without statutory reform, Perkins and MacCormack creatively used provisions of existing law to suspend deportations and to legalize the status of certain illegal immigrants in hardship cases. This involved a two-step procedure whereby the secretary granted the illegal alien a waiver from deportation and allowed him or her to depart to Canada and to reenter the United States as a legal permanent resident.

The secretary granted waivers by invoking an obscure clause of the Immigration Act of 1917, the Seventh Proviso to Section 3, which stipulated that "aliens returning after a temporary absence to an unrelinquished United States domicile of seven consecutive years may be admitted in the discretion of the Attorney General and under such conditions as he may prescribe." Congress intended the Seventh Proviso as a hardship measure for aliens "who have lived here for a long time" who were temporarily out of the country when the Immigration Act of 1917 was passed and who, for reasons often technical in nature, were excludable upon their return. Perkins's innovation was to use the concept "returning after a temporary absence" to apply to aliens who had not yet departed and to include in its scope illegal aliens.[103] By invoking the Seventh Proviso to waive deportations Perkins reverted to the central principle of pre-1924 immigration policy inherent in the statute of limitations on deportation, the idea that immigrants who have settled in the country should not be expelled.[104]

The process of readjustment of status was known as the "pre-examination" procedure. Since 1933 the INS had granted letters to legal aliens going to Canada for short visits assuring them of reentry, provided that they were first examined and found admissible by immigration inspectors. It began as a gesture of courtesy that allowed legal aliens departing temporarily to avoid the necessity of applying for a formal reentry permit. The Canadian authorities also required written assurance that the visitors would not remain in Canada. The practice became known in INS parlance as "pre-examination"—that is, inspection for readmission before departure.[105]

In 1935 pre-examination was extended to illegal immigrants to facilitate their legalization. A formal agreement between the U.S. Department of State and Immigration Service and their Canadian counterparts detailed procedures whereby an immigrant in the United States without a visa could be "pre-examined" for legal admission, leave the country as a "voluntary departure," proceed to the nearest American consul in Canada, obtain a visa for permanent residence, and reenter the United States formally as a legal admission.[106]

The INS thus suspended state territoriality in order to unmake the illegal status of certain immigrants. Although the whole procedure was a bureaucratic arrangement, the INS and State Department would not simply issue new documents granting an alien's legal status. The alien had to cooperate by physically leaving and reentering the country, to enact a voluntary departure and a legal admission. Some aliens failed to understand the necessity of the performance (or could not afford to make the trip to Canada) and wondered why, if it was willing to adjust their status, the INS would not simply leave them alone.[107]

The pre-examination program was an ad hoc procedure that officials made up as they went along, both broadening and narrowing its scope. Eventually it was routinized and written into the Code of Federal Regulations.[108] It was initially meant for immigrants who had a U.S.-citizen spouse or children and whose illegal status resulted from technical error. This was an uncontroversial political calculus in which preventing hardship for citizens easily trumped deportation for trivial causes. But "hardship" proved to be an elastic concept, another version of the notion of "deserving." It was quickly extended to certain types of criminal cases, or, more precisely, to certain criminals. A typical case involved Mrs. Lillian Joann Flake, who was charged with theft in 1918 and 1922 and larceny (shoplifting) in 1930. A native Canadian, she lived in the United States for more than seventeen years and had a husband and daughter in Chicago. In another case, the INS argued on behalf of Carlos Reali, an Italian, "in view of the fact that the alien is married to a native of the United States and that there are three American-born children." His record, added the INS, was good, notwithstanding his acquiring a visa by fraud and perjury in 1924. The INS vacated Flake's, Reali's, and hundreds of others' orders of deportation, allowing them to depart the country voluntarily and obtain a legal visa for readmission.[109]

Restrictionists in Congress criticized the secretary for "granting waivers to lawbreakers" and "exerting unusual efforts to protect and keep within our

borders hundreds of deportable foreigners branded as criminals." One angry
senator counted 119 such cases in 1937 and a congressman cited nearly 700
cases in 1940. Perkins defended the practice, stating that in most cases the
crimes committed "amounted only to violations of law committed many
years ago and were counterbalanced by long periods of good moral conduct
and useful service in the community."[110]

In 1940, when Congress moved the INS from the Department of Labor to
the Department of Justice, the INS continued pre-examination program. Defending the use of the Seventh Proviso in 1943 the attorney general stated
that the "American sense of justice and fair play" ought to "respect [the
alien's] rehabilitation and not to brand and treat him as a criminal perpetu-
ally." Although the attorney general claimed that the INS did not grant
waivers to criminals convicted of serious offenses, in fact Seventh Proviso
and pre-examination cases included those involving fraudulent naturalization, larceny, bigamy, rape, even manslaughter. The only cases that were denied relief appear to be those involving alleged anarchists and smugglers.[111]

"Hardship" also extended beyond cases involving aliens with a U.S.-citizen
spouse or child. By the early 1940s suspension of deportation and pre-examination were available to aliens with a legally resident alien relative, those
with long-term residence in the United States, and "exceptionally meritorious" cases, the latter constituting a general loophole.[112] The expanding
grounds for eligibility suggest a policy grounded in the idea that what mattered most was not the immigrant's formal status but his or her presence and
ties in the community. This was a remarkable acknowledgement that undercut the premises of restriction and territoriality.

Significantly, however, the privilege of pre-examination became restricted
to European immigrants. Asiatics did not qualify, because they were categorically excluded from immigration on grounds of racial ineligibility.[113]
Mexicans were not initially excluded. After MacCormack formalized the pre-
examination procedure, INS El Paso district director Grover Wilmoth implemented the procedure for Mexican hardship cases, but in 1938 he became
stonewalled by the American consul in Juárez, William Blocker, who argued
that those applying for visas at Juárez "were of the laboring class, some of
them actually on relief." They should, he said, "unquestionably" be denied
visas. In fact the INS Board of Special Inquiry had ruled in Canadian pre-
examination cases that receipt of relief during the Depression, when no work
was available, was not evidence of LPC. Blocker deliberately slowed the work
of processing visas for Mexican pre-examination cases to only a handful a
month in order to frustrate Wilmoth's efforts to grant relief to Mexican
cases.[114]

I found no evidence that Wilmoth's higher-ups in the INS argued with the
State Department for a fair application of the policy; rather, the INS seems
to have quickly scuttled the program for Mexicans.[115] It clarified that the

"general pre-examination procedure is limited to certain aliens—relatives of US citizens—desiring to proceed to *Canada*." Later documents conspicuously referred to the program as the "Canadian pre-examination procedure." Thus, initially, Mexicans were excluded not explicitly but by a lack of propinquity, by their distance from Canada, where physical departure and reentry were performed. In 1945 the INS explicitly restricted pre-examination to "other than a citizen of Canada, Mexico, or any of the islands adjacent to the United States." This policy appeared to be race-neutral in that it applied to all countries with contiguous borders to the United States, but in fact it was meant to categorically deny relief to Mexican and Caribbean migrants. Because pre-examination involved permission for temporary entry into Canada to acquire the U.S. visa, it was irrelevant to Canadians, who did not need special permission to enter Canada.[116]

The racism of the policy was profound, for it denied, a priori, that deportation could cause hardship for the families of non-Europeans. In stressing family values, moreover, the policy recognized only one kind of family, the intact nuclear family residing in the United States, and ignored transnational families. It failed to recognize that many undocumented male migrants who came to the United States alone in fact maintained family households in their home country and that migration-remittance was another kind of strategy for family subsistence.

For Europeans, however, the policy was clearly a boon. In fact, pre-examination became an official and routine procedure for adjusting the status of Europeans who were not legally present in the United States. By the early 1940s pre-examination was used to help adjust the status of refugees from European fascism who had entered the United States in the 1930s by way of tourist or visitor visas.[117] Pre-examination continued with only two brief interruptions until the practice was terminated in 1958. The data indicate that between 1935 and 1959 the INS processed nearly 58,000 pre-examination cases and granted approval in the vast majority of them.[118]

Apart from pre-examination, the INS began to suspend orders of deportation after 1940, when Congress gave the attorney general authority to grant discretionary relief as part of the Alien Registration Act. Discretionary relief appears to be a concession granted in exchange for alien registration, which had been long opposed but passed as a wartime measure. The 1940 law allowed for the suspension of deportation in cases involving aliens of good moral character if deportation would result in "serious economic detriment" to the alien's immediate family. It excluded alien anarchists, convicted narcotics dealers, and the "immoral classes," the latter comprising prostitutes and the mentally ill. "Good moral character" was not precluded by having a criminal record, but referred to "reputation which will pass muster with the average man [that] need not rise above the level of the common mass of people."[119]

The INS suspended the deportations of several thousand aliens a year from 1941 through the late 1950s. An internal Justice Department study of 389 randomly selected cases conducted in 1943 revealed that 45.8 percent involved seamen, 18.3 percent involved visitors (visa overstays), and 10.5 percent involved border-crossers. The overwhelming majority (73 percent) was of European origin (mostly German and Italian). Only 8 percent of the cases involved Mexicans.[120]

As for alien registration, the 1940 law required fingerprinting and yearly registration of all aliens resident in the United States. While clearly a wartime measure, the INS took pains to reassure immigrants that their loyalty was not under question, calling registration an "inventory" or a measure of prudence dictated by national security. This was, perhaps, aimed at securing the cooperation of the nation's four million foreign-born residents. But the nativism that had fueled earlier demands for compulsory alien registration was now displaced by more pluralist views. Speaking in Los Angeles in August 1940, Assistant Secretary of Labor Marshall Dimock explained alien registration as part of the nation's "defense program" but emphasized that national unity was the key to the nation's security. Americans must be vigilant "to discourage any tendency toward setting a particular group from others" based on differences of religion, color, economic status, or alienage. The "blue-eyed, flaxen-haired farmer from Wisconsin, Minnesota, and the Dakotas," he said, "who in scores of cases have lived here most of their lives but who for one reason or another are not technically Americans . . . are as good Americans as we are." And, in what was becoming a familiar rhetorical move, Dimock underscored his call to embrace these noncitizens with a call for vigilance against undesirables. "Our immigration laws are being enforced as vigilantly as possible," he said. "We are constantly tightening up our border defenses against undesirable aliens; we have strengthened our deportation machinery; and in cooperation with other designated agencies we have armed ourselves to cope with subversive activities."[121]

In general, despite various reforms, change was limited and slow. Discretionary relief from deportation became incorporated into immigration law in the Immigration and Naturalization Act of 1952.[122] But throughout the 1950s and early 1960s almost no progress was made in matters of due process and judicial review. The INS exempted itself from the Administrative Procedures Act (APA), which Congress passed in 1946. The Supreme Court ruled in 1950 (*Wong Yang Sung v. McGrath*) that deportation proceedings were of a judicial character requiring a fair hearing and ordered the INS to adhere to the terms of the APA, notably the separation of functions, that is, that the investigating inspector (prosecutor) cannot be the hearing officer (judge). The INS reported a drop in the number of deportations of illegal Mexican immigrants from 16,903 in 1949 to 3,319 in 1950 as a result of the *Sung* decision. But Congress acted quickly to nullify *Sung* and to restore the

INS's ability to deport efficiently by granting the INS statutory exemption to the APA. Indeed, if during the New Deal and World War II immigration officials showed an interest in administrative reform in areas of due process, their successors were generally impervious to it.[123]

Numerical restriction legislated in the 1920s displaced qualitative reasons for inclusion and exclusion with criteria that were at once more abstract and arbitrary—the quota slot and the proper visa. Previously, territoriality had been exercised to exclude people not deemed fit to be part of the nation. In the 1920s qualitative norms of desirability remained in the law as grounds for inclusion and expulsion, but, as we have seen, they were employed in deportation cases less often than was the rule of documentation and, moreover, they were applied irregularly and with considerable discretion. As qualitative norms receded in importance, territoriality—defining and policing the national space—became both the means and the ends of immigration policy.

However, Americans increasingly believed that deportation, initially imagined for the despised and dangerous classes, was undemocratic and unjust when applied to ordinary immigrants with homes and families in the United States. Hence during the 1930s and early 1940s statutory and administrative reforms attempted to ease the tension between sovereignty and democracy that immigration policy had created. Family values and environmentalist views of delinquency and morality paved the way for reform, while race directed its reach.

Thus it became possible to unmake the illegality of Italian, Polish, and other European illegal immigrants through the power of administrative discretion. Of course, not all illegal European immigrants were legalized, but a rough estimation suggests that between 1925 and 1965 some 200,000 illegal European immigrants who were construed as deserving successfully legalized their status under the Registry Act, through pre-examination, or by suspension of deportation. The formal recognition of their inclusion in the nation created the requisite minimum foundation for acquiring citizenship and contributed to a broader reformation of racial identity taking place, a process that reconstructed the "lower races of Europe" into white ethnic Americans.[124]

By contrast, walking (or wading) across the border emerged as the quintessential act of illegal immigration, the outermost point in a relativist ordering of illegal immigration. The method of Mexicans' illegal entry could thus be perceived as "criminal" and Mexican immigrants as undeserving of relief. Combined with the construction of Mexicans as migratory agricultural laborers (both legal and illegal) in the 1940s and 1950s, that perception gave powerful sway to the notion that Mexicans had no rightful presence on United States territory, no rightful claim of belonging.

The basic principle of immigration law doctrine that privileged Congress's plenary power over the individual rights of immigrants remained intact. The contradiction between sovereignty and individual rights was resolved only to the extent that the power of administrative discretion made narrow exceptions of the sovereign rule. That European and Canadian immigrants had far greater access to discretionary relief meant that they could, as legal aliens, more readily enjoy the rights that the Constitution afforded all persons. The unlikelihood that Mexicans would receive relief tended to confine them to the domain of immigration law, where sovereignty, not the Constitution, ruled. Indeed, in the context of immigration law that foregrounded territoriality and border control, and in the hands of immigration officials operating within the contingencies of contemporary politics and social prejudices, the exercise of administrative discretion served to racialize the specter of the illegal alien.

Part II ——————————————————————————

MIGRANTS AT THE MARGINS
OF LAW AND NATION

THE JOHNSON-REED Immigration Act of 1924 was motivated primarily by political concerns over the country's ethnic and racial composition, but economic factors were still relevant. The business and manufacturing class did not oppose immigration restriction. American industry had matured sufficiently by the 1920s such that economic growth no longer came from a sheer expansion in capacity but from increases in productivity that were made possible by technological advances and refinements in industrial discipline.

But if by the 1920s the size of the industrial workforce had stabilized, the situation in agriculture was quite different. During this time, commercial agriculture burgeoned, particularly in California and Texas. In the early decades of the century, irrigation technology, the completion of regional railroad lines, and the invention of the refrigerated railroad car had promoted the development of large-scale production of fruits and vegetables for consumption in the nation's cities. After World War I, agribusiness was poised for take-off, but the decline in immigration caused by restrictive legislation posed the threat of a labor shortage.

Industrial agriculture in the West and Southwest was a special genre of American farming. But it was not its commercial nature that set it apart. Farming in the United States had long been a commercial enterprise. As Richard Hofstadter pointed out, by the mid-nineteenth century the yeoman farmer had metamorphosed into a businessman, who esteemed not land but "land values." The mechanization of agriculture in the 1920s, which accelerated existing trends towards large-scale production and land consolidation, began to drive small farmers from the land. Still, family-owned and operated farms endured in midwestern and plains states well into the twentieth century, even if they were in heavy debt to the banks and often struggled at the brink of tenancy.[1]

In the West, however, there were few family farms. The monopolization of land had occurred quickly in the nineteenth century, along with white settlement. (Ironically, by the early twentieth century Japanese comprised many of the family farmers in California.) Moreover, while the production of wheat and other grains became mechanized, fruit and vegetable production in the West and Southwest (like cotton in the South), was not. Western agriculture was industrial farming that desired a new kind of farm labor that which was cheap, plentiful, and seasonal. That is to say, large-scale commercial farming required a migratory agricultural proletariat. Native white Americans and recent European immigrants were not categorically opposed to such work, but higher wages could be found in industry. Just as important, perhaps, whites viewed farm labor as degraded, owing to its association with Asiatics. But if Chinese, Japanese, and Indian migrants had successively supplied the mainstay of agricultural labor on the Pacific Coast from the late nineteenth century to the 1910s, the Johnson-Reed Act of 1924 cut off Asiatic immigration entirely. Who would work in the factories in the field?[2]

Imported Colonialism

The following two chapters address the recruitment of Filipino colonial subjects and Mexican migrants, including undocumented workers and imported contract laborers, to meet the labor needs of western agriculture. Mexican and Filipino migrants entered the United States through "loopholes" in an otherwise globally restrictive immigration policy. Mexican immigration was not numerically restricted because the law exempted the countries of the Western Hemisphere from quotas. Filipinos were colonial subjects of the United States, not aliens, and therefore not under the jurisdiction of the immigration laws.

At another level the use of Mexican and Filipino migrants as migratory farm laborers fit the historical legacies of Manifest Destiny and conquest in the West and Southwest. Western expansion in the mid-nineteenth century had been justified on grounds of Anglo-Saxon superiority and the region's economic development had always been highly racialized. In the 1920s Mexican and Filipino migrations betrayed a racialized, colonial character. In the latter case the colonial relationship was explicit, as the Philippines were an American colonial possession. As colonial subjects, Filipinos had had a history of labor migration within the territorial jurisdiction of the United States. During the first decade of the twentieth century, sugar plantation owners in Hawai'i recruited Filipino workers as an answer to Japanese labor militancy on the islands. During the 1920s Filipinos migrated—from both Hawai'i and directly from the Philippines—to California, the Pacific Northwest, and Alaska, for work in agriculture and fish canning. But a colonial labor force in the colonies was one thing; importing colonial subjects directly into the metropolis was another.

Mainstream American politics had rationalized the colonial possession of the Philippines as a benevolent project that would civilize the backward Filipinos, but that mythology turned into a social crisis when real Filipinos showed up in California in the late 1920s. White Americans would not tolerate the presence of acculturated Filipinos who demanded wage and social equality. The young, male Filipino workers who frequented dance halls and dated white women incurred their special wrath. The idea of sexual intimacy between white women and brown-skinned colonial subjects was so incendiary that it produced race riots and legal measures that excluded and expelled Filipinos from the continental United States.

Mexican migrants proved to be a better source of foreign labor for western and southwestern agriculture. In part this reflected Mexico's proximity to the United States and growers' belief that Mexicans returned to Mexico after each harvest season. But this was only partly the case; in fact, Mexicans comprised a transnational labor force that included seasonal migrants as well as immigrants and U.S.-born Mexican Americans. The agricultural labor market and immigration laws worked in tandem to create a kind of imported colonialism, which constructed Mexicans working in the United States as a foreign race and justified their exclusion from the polity. Exclusion had various forms: Jim Crow–type laws in Texas, which segregated and disfranchised Mexican American citizens; restrictive immigration laws, which produced Mexican illegal aliens; and a state-sponsored contract labor program, the bracero program, which imported nearly four million Mexican workers on temporary contracts from World War II to the early 1960s.

These colonial-like practices took place in the context of the history of the Southwest as ceded territory from Mexico and the United States' economic penetration of Mexico in the late nineteenth and twentieth centuries. Yet Mexican labor migration operated officially within the framework of immigration laws and state relations between independent sovereign nations. These modern modalities were perhaps more suitable for achieving colonial-like relations with Mexican migrant workers because they obscured the contradictions in American democracy that official colonialism in the Philippines had made uncomfortably plain.[3]

Chapter Three

From Colonial Subject to Undesirable Alien: Filipino Migration in the Invisible Empire

[I]n many ways it was a crime to be a Filipino in
California. I came to know that the public streets
were not free to my people: we were stopped each
time these vigilant patrolmen saw us driving a car.
We were suspect each time we were seen with a
white woman. And perhaps it was this narrowing of
our life into an island, into a filthy segment of
American society, that had driven [some] Filipinos
inward . . . 'Please God, don't change me in
America!' I said to myself.
—Carlos Bulosan[1]

ON FEBRUARY 6, 1937, Carlos Rodesillas, a 36-year-old Filipino from Stockton, California, and his two children, three and six years old, sailed out of San Francisco Bay on the S.S. *Hoover.* They landed at Manila and then traveled to Rodesillas's hometown in Iloilo Province on Panay, an island at the middle of the Philippine archipelago in the Visayan Sea.[2] The Rodesillases were among some two thousand Filipinos who returned to the Philippines during the late 1930s under a federal repatriation program for indigent Filipinos. Congress authorized the program in 1935, shortly after it passed the Tydings-McDuffie Act, which established the Philippines as a commonwealth and set a ten-year transition period to full independence.[3] The federal government sponsored Rodesillas's voyage home; the California Emergency Relief Association paid passage of the children, who, owing to their birth in the United States, were American citizens.

When Rodesillas first migrated to the United States, he was neither an American citizen nor an alien. Rather, he was a "national," a colonial subject who owed allegiance to the American flag and who could, concomitantly, travel freely within the territorial domain of the United States. He departed California as an alien, his alienage a badge of the Philippines' new status. For when the United States decided to relinquish its colonial claim to the Philippines, it simultaneously repudiated the right of Filipinos to enter and live in America. The Tydings-McDuffie Act declared that for purposes of immigration "the Philippines shall be considered a foreign country" and set an annual quota from the islands of fifty, the lowest of any in the world.[4]

Filipino migration and racial formation differed from most other migration experiences, owing to the Philippines' status as a United States territory. In a sense, Filipino migrants were the corporeality of contradictions that existed in American colonial policy and practice. When Filipino laborers began entering the mainland United States in large numbers during the mid-1920s, they forced Americans to confront their colonial subjects, the objects of their tutelage and uplift. The arrival of Filipino immigrants in the imperial metropole rendered visible the colonialism that Americans had tried to make invisible through the myths of historical accident and benevolence. Filipino migration lay bare contradictions between the insular policy of benevolent assimilation and the immigration policy of Asiatic exclusion, which had fully matured by the 1920s, and domestic racism generally. These contradictions unfolded in a wave of race riots and labor conflicts that swept California and the Pacific Northwest, leading to decolonization, exclusion, and repatriation in the 1930s. This chapter examines the experience of Filipino migration and exclusion, and the process by which Filipinos transformed from colonial subjects to undesirable aliens.

Benevolent Assimilation

The United States acquired the Philippine Islands, along with Puerto Rico and Guam, as a result of its victory in the Spanish-American War in 1898. The acquisition of these territories posed a challenge for Americans' beliefs in democracy and self-government, ideals that were rooted in the nation's birth and in the rationale for its existence. To be sure, the territories were neither the first instance of American conquest nor the nation's first extraterritorial acquisitions. Guided by the doctrine of Manifest Destiny, the United States went to war with Mexico in 1848, wresting the latter's northern half in order to complete America's continental expansion. The United States purchased Alaska from Russia in 1867 and annexed Hawai'i in 1898, prior to and independently of the Spanish-American War. But these territories were all incorporated into the United States according to the model of continental expansion that was first established by the Northwest Ordinance in 1787. That is, they were considered future states.[5]

Although Alaska and Hawai'i were not contiguous to the continental United States, Americans employed some creative thinking to justify their inclusion in the nation. Alaska was imagined as a space devoid of people, ready for white settlement, much like the American West. Proponents of Alaskan annexation also believed the territory would act as a sort of rearguard pressure that would impel Canada to join the United States. The overthrow of the Hawai'ian monarchy and the establishment of the Republic of Hawai'i by expatriate American sugar planters in 1895 engendered a view of Hawai'i as a nation compatible with American politics and society, as long as its Asiatic population was kept outside the bounds of citizenship. Some also argued that Hawai'i was located at the nation's "natural defense perimeter." Henry Cabot Lodge called the mainland the "citadel" and Hawai'i "a necessary outwork . . . which ought to belong to us."[6]

But statehood was utterly unthinkable for the territories acquired from Spain. They were densely populated by non-European peoples whom Americans considered to be backward, alien races: as the Filipino nationalist leader Manuel Roxas would later remark, statehood would have resulted in fifty Filipino representatives in Congress.[7] Americans also considered the islands climactically inhospitable to white settlement, and, in the case of the Philippines, at such great distance from the United States as to make statehood even more problematic. The American acquisition of the former Spanish colonies thus required a break with the tradition of incorporation and its promise of statehood. It meant expanding American sovereignty over territories with permanently unequal status; that is to say, it meant establishing colonies. Americans divided sharply on the issue during the Senate's debate over the Treaty of Paris. A significant faction of anti-imperialists opposed possession of the territories because they would not violate the democratic principle of incorporation, but neither would they support the incorporation of backward colored races into the nation.

If colonialism seemed to contradict American ideals, new rationales for foreign expansion had gained widespread currency during the 1880s and 1890s. Expansionists believed that the nation's prosperity and stability depended on the establishment of new markets for surplus goods and for relieving domestic tensions, which they believed were caused by industrialization, urbanization, and the closing of the frontier. Social Darwinism and Anglo-Saxonism suffused the new imperialist thinking. The Reverend Josiah Strong posited expansion to the Pacific as part of an inexorable westward march of Christian civilization. Brooks Adams and Alfred Thayer Mahan applied the concept of "survival of the fittest" to the international competition of nations and, importantly, added a martial element to the evolutionist vision, boldly acknowledging that military might was necessary to ensure the nation's commercial eminence.[8]

During the Senate debate over the Treaty of Paris, the theme of "duty" to protect and civilize Filipinos and Puerto Ricans emerged to give moral justification to the annexationists' second, more plainly materialist theme of economic advantage. The combination of the two was powerful, as it promoted the nation's glory, seen primarily as global commercial conquest, within familiar democratic principles. Jacob Gould Schurman, who headed the first American commission in the Philippines (1899–1900), went as far as to consider commercial opportunity only a coincident benefit to annexation. Trade was not, he said, a "justifiable motive for originally taking the Archipelago": the sole object to be considered in the administration of the Philippines was the welfare of the natives. Economic development was promoted as modernizing progress, even as "economic emancipation." Thus Americans believed that their imperialist venture was noble in purpose, unlike Old World colonialism. The most militant expansionists denied it was imperialist at all. Roosevelt refused the label; Senator Alfred Beveridge, Jr., declared expansion was "for the Greater Republic, not for Imperialism." These extraordinary denials were not necessarily insincere but evinced what Stuart Creighton Miller has described as an "exaggerated sense of innocence produced by a kind of 'immaculate conception' view of this country's origins."[9]

Central to the colonial project was the belief that the new territories were inhabited by backward races incapable of self-rule. Americans saw Filipinos as a motley colored race comprising innumerable uncivilized tribes. While it was common to view all non-European peoples as backward, casting Filipinos as "tribal" was essential because it denied them the status of nationhood. "Denationalizing" the Philippines justified annexation and cast the American mission as benevolence—the United States had not denied national self-determination because no nation existed. Thus when President McKinley declared American sovereignty throughout the Philippines on December 21, 1899, he found no contradiction in announcing the United States' commitment to individual freedom for Filipinos but not their national freedom. "We come not as invaders or conquerors," McKinley said, "but as friends, to protect the natives in their homes, in their employments, and in their personal and religious rights. . . . [T]he mission of the United States is one of benevolent assimilation." He also stated that those who "cooperate" with the United States "will receive the reward of its support and protection. All others will be brought within the lawful rule we have assumed, with firmness if need be."[10]

McKinley's threat to use "firmness" was an understatement. When Spain transferred title to the islands to the United States, it occupied only Manila. The rest of Luzon, and most of the archipelago, was under control of Filipino nationalists, who had overthrown Spanish colonial rule in 1896 and had established an independent republic in 1898. Denationalizing the Philippines was thus not only a discursive project but a military operation as well: benevolent assimilation had to be imposed by armed force. The United States deployed over 125,000 troops—two-thirds of the American army—to bring the islands under American sovereignty. Although largely forgotten, the Philippine-American War (1899–1902) was longer and bloodier than the Spanish-American War that preceded it. The United States vastly underestimated the Filipinos, who waged a tenacious guerilla war until they were ultimately defeated by the superior military force of the United States. The war was especially brutal; over 4,200 Americans were killed and some 2,800 were wounded. More than 20,000 Filipinos died in the fighting and another 200,000 died from famine or disease.[11]

Even before the war was over, the Supreme Court established, in a series of cases in 1901, the legal grounds for the United States' possession of colonies. Known collectively as the *Insular Cases*,[12] the Court's rulings invented a new legal category called "unincorporated territory," which alleviated the United States from the promise, assumed in the Northwest Ordinance and by historical practice, of eventual statehood and, with it, equal status and full citizenship rights to its inhabitants.

The *Insular Cases* were prompted by controversy over whether or not goods imported from the territories into the United States were subject to tariffs. This was an important question for business and trade, but it also begged the larger question of whether or not the Constitution applied *ex propio vigore*, or of its own force, to unincorporated territories. Contemporaries paraphrased the problem as whether or not the Constitution followed the flag. The Court made the innovative claim that the territories acquired from Spain belonged to, but were not part of, the United States. As Justice Edward Douglass White formulated in *Downes v. Bidwell*: "[W]hilst in an international sense Porto Rico was not a foreign country, since it was subject to the sovereignty of and was owned by the United States, it was foreign to the United States in a domestic sense, because the island had not been incorporated into the United States, but was merely appurtenant thereto as a possession."[13]

The Court ruled that Congress had the discretion to determine the status of territories, to decide if they were to be incorporated or not, and to decide what provisions of the Constitution extended to which territories. The *Insular Cases* provided that Congress held plenary power over the governance of territories, which emanated from the Territorial Clause of the Constitution and the nation's sovereign right to make war and to make treaties. As in immigration doctrine, the Court invoked national sovereignty to justify granting limited rights to the United States' colonial subjects.[14]

American colonial policy also declared a new legal status for the inhabitants of the unincorporated territories—the "U.S. national." Nationals occupied a liminal status that was neither citizen nor alien. They owed allegiance to the United States but did not have the rights of citizens, most notably the rights of representation and trial by jury. Congress granted U.S. citizenship to Puerto Ricans in 1917, but this was a second class of citizenship, still without the right of representation, and, moreover, subject to revocation by Congress.[15]

Nationals did have one important right: freedom of movement within the territorial jurisdiction of the United States. The prospect of Filipinos migrating to the continental United States had been an issue during the debates over the Treaty of Paris, as anti-imperialists feared that keeping the Philippines would introduce another "race problem" into American society and erode the barriers to Oriental immigration.[16] Annexationists dismissed their concerns. Senator Albert Beveridge, Jr., said, "It is not proposed to make them citizens. Those who see disaster in every forward step of the Republic prophesy that Philippine labor will overrun our country or starve our workingmen. But the Javanese have not so overrun Holland . . . and India's millions of surplus labor have not so overrun England. Whips of scorpions could not lash the Filipinos to this land of fervid enterprise, sleepless industry, and rigid order." Whitelaw Reid, editor of the *New York Herald Tribune*, stated similarly: "It is a bugbear that the Filipinos would be citizens of the United States, and would therefore have the same rights of free travel and free entry of their own manufactures with our citizens. The treaty did not make them citizens of the United States at all, and they will never be."[17] But Beveridge and Reid's confidence was misplaced. Filipinos were not citizens, but as nationals they could not, at least legally, be prohibited from traveling to the mainland United States.

The Problem of the Migrating Filipino National

Filipinos did not migrate to imperialism's metropolitan center in significant numbers until the middle of the 1920s. During the first decades of American rule, the territorial government sponsored several hundred students from elite families for university training in the United States. They studied medicine, law, higher education, and politics. By World War I most of these scholarship students, or *pensionados*, returned to the Philippines and assumed positions in the nation-building project.[18]

Filipino leaders discouraged the emigration of laborers. They believed their labor was needed for domestic industry and agriculture. American sugar interests in the Philippines supported this view. Beginning in 1910, however, Filipinos began migrating to Hawai'i, where the sugar industry suffered from serious labor problems. The curtailment of Japanese immigration by the Gentleman's Agreement in 1908 severely affected the labor supply. Japanese plantation workers in Hawai'i were also becoming increasingly militant, and strikes were common during the 1900s. In 1909 a strike in Oahu shut down six of the island's major plantations.[19] Seeking an alternative source of workers, the Hawai'i Sugar Planters Association began intensive labor recruitment in the Philippines. Between 1907 and 1919 over 24,000 Filipinos went to Hawai'i. Another 48,000 emigrated between 1920 and 1929. In 1915 the Philippine legislature passed a law regulating labor recruitment and emigration, requiring recruiters to be licensed and Hawai'ian employers to sign individual three-year contracts with Filipino workers and to subsidize round-trip passage. The Philippine government also stationed a labor commissioner in Hawai'i to monitor the Filipinos' sojourn there.[20]

During World War I employers on the mainland sought Filipino labor. In 1917 shipbuilders in San Francisco and Philadelphia sought to import Filipino carpenters, machinists, and coopersmiths from Manila. Raisin and other vineyardists in northern California similarly sought labor from the Philippines. Growers from California and Hawai'i complained that the territorial government placed "obstacles" in the way of labor agents working on their behalf. Brigadier General Frank MacIntyre, the chief of the Bureau of Insular Affairs, responded, "It has never been the policy of the Philippine government to encourage the deportation of labor."[21]

Nevertheless, emigration to the mainland slowly increased during the 1910s. The 1920 census counted 5,603 Filipinos residing on the mainland, mostly on the West Coast. Many were self-supporting students from the middle classes—the first generation educated in the American school system in the Philippines—who had followed in the wake of the pensionados. Other immigrants were laborers who had worked in Hawai'i and ventured to the mainland when their contracts expired. Both students and laborers found employment in the Alaskan salmon canneries and in agriculture in California, Oregon, and Washington. The post–World War I recession, however, left many Filipinos destitute. In March 1921 the Philippino Council of Seattle held a mass meeting. The participants described the situation in desperate terms: they estimated there were some one hundred Filipinos homeless, with many others dependent on charity. They petitioned the Philippine government for financial relief and requested that the United States Employment Service establish a special department to help Filipinos find work.[22] Francisco Varona, the Philippine labor commissioner at Hawai'i, investigated the conditions of Filipinos on the mainland for Governor General Leonard Wood's office. He supported the idea of a Filipino employment service. Although there was a high rate of unemployment on the Pacific Coast, Washington and California agreed to establish Filipino employment services because they believed only a limited number of jobs suited Filipinos, "on account of their physique." Varona also recommended using Army transport to send indigent Filipinos who wished to return to the Philippines. Very few Filipinos intended to return to the Philippines or Hawai'i, however. Varona encouraged Filipinos to form local "councils" that would "at least keep them from general demoralization." He also tried to dissuade Filipinos in Hawai'i from coming to the United States. In an open letter published in the Filipino press in Honolulu, he stated that hundreds of Filipinos in California and Seattle were jobless, as well as millions of white American workers. The Alaskan canneries were practically closed, he said. Varona urged Filipinos in Hawai'i to return home to the Philippines.[23]

In September 1924, the territorial government placed an announcement in the *Philippine Islands Free Press* stating: "Young Filipinos intending to go to the U.S. to work their way through college are advised by the Governor General to stay at home. According to information received this week from the Bureau of Insular Affairs, many Filipino students on the Pacific coast are at present unemployed. Unless the student has sufficient funds to reach the Middle West or East where the chances of getting employment are better, he should not venture to the U.S. these days."[24]

Despite official efforts to discourage Filipinos from traveling to the United States, migration increased dramatically in the late 1920s. After Congress passed the Immigration Act of 1924, western agriculture turned to Filipinos and Mexicans to replace Japanese farm labor. Between 1920 and 1929 some 14,000 Filipinos migrated from Hawai'i to the mainland, 10,000 of them in the latter half of the decade. Another 37,600 came directly from the Philippines. By 1930 there were some 56,000 Filipinos on the West Coast, more than ten times the number counted in the 1920 census.[25] They were overwhelmingly young, single men. Nearly 85 percent of the Filipinos arriving in California during the 1920s were under thirty years of age, 93 percent were male, and 77 percent were single. In San Francisco and Los Angeles, Filipinos found employment as domestics and in hotels and restaurants as bellmen, cooks, dishwashers, and janitors.

Most, however, were migrant laborers who followed the harvest or canning seasons, usually finding work from Filipino labor contractors. They worked in agriculture, cutting asparagus, picking fruit and hops, thinning lettuce, and topping beets; and in lumber mills and canneries in California and the Pacific Northwest. The other major artery in the migrant circuit reached Alaska, where many Filipinos worked on summer contracts in the salmon canneries. There they did the hardest and dirtiest work, such as hauling or cleaning fish. Filipinos were contracted at $250 or more for a four-month season, most of which disappeared in deductions the companies and contractors made for food and supplies or in gambling.[26]

For example, a laborer who came in 1926 recalled working in Washington, Sacramento, and Clarksburg. Moving with a small group of friends, he said, "We always found jobs by staying in town until we hear of somebody looking for men to go to work. Right away we'd ask if we could go with them."[27] Similarly, Trinidad Rojo, who would become the editor of the *Salinas Philippines Mail*, graduated from an American-style high school in Ilocos Sur and came to the United States in 1926, when he was twenty-four years old. Rojo considered his experience to be typical of self-supporting Filipino students: after arriving in Seattle he worked as a houseboy, then he worked in Alaska for two months, then he picked hops in Moxee City, near Yakima. Once he began studying at the University of Washington, he worked as a houseboy during the school year and in the Alaskan canneries during the summer.[28]

In California, Filipinos, along with Mexicans, became the mainstay of mi-

3.1 Filipinos were the mainstay of asparagus, lettuce, and other crops in California in the 1930s. (Reprinted, by permission, from Jesse Quinsaat, in *Letters in Exile: An Introductory Reader on the History of Pilipinos in America*, Los Angeles, 1976.)

gratory agricultural labor. By 1930 Filipinos comprised 80 percent of the asparagus workforce in the Sacramento River delta region and a major share of the lettuce workforce in the San Joaquin Valley. Living conditions in Filipino labor camps were poor. Although they were noted for their cleanliness, bunkhouses and cabins were of poor construction and severely overcrowded.[29]

During the winter, when there was no work, Filipino laborers repaired to the cities. In the early 1930s the Filipino population in Seattle numbered only a few hundred during the summer but over three thousand during the winter. For young men seeking education and adventure in America, life was difficult and often lonely. Many regularly sent remittances home. Not a few returned with a college degree or with enough money to buy a piece of land but—as in most immigrant experiences—the majority never did.[30]

Racial violence against Filipinos took place as early as 1926 in Stockton, California. In 1928 in Dinuba, in central California, a gang of white youths attacked Filipino laborers in the company of local white girls. In November 1927 a group of whites expelled Filipino laborers from the Yakima Valley in Washington. An apple grower who had hired eleven Filipino workers brought them to the Sunnyside jail for "safekeeping" after he learned that whites were "en route" to his ranch to "deport" Filipinos. An estimated five hundred Filipino workers left the area that month after white residents threatened to attack them.[31]

The following year saw more violence in central Washington. In September 1928, white mobs drove three hundred Filipinos from Wenatchee. A "committee of citizens" met two buses transporting Filipinos to apple growers in Cashmere and "escorted" them out of the valley. Filipinos already working in Cashmere wired Pedro Guevara, the resident commissioner representing the Philippine government in Washington, D.C., that they could not leave the area because they had no funds and that local authorities ignored their appeals for protection. In October, Filipinos reported to Guevara that eight men in Yakima were mobbed. These first incidents of anti-Filipino violence were strikingly similar to the riots that drove Asian Indians out of the state's small lumber and farming towns in 1907–1909.[32]

The eruption of anti-Filipino violence took some people, including officials at the Bureau of Insular Affairs, by surprise. It seemed that throughout the twenties most white Americans had barely noticed Filipinos. Bruno Lasker, who studied the Filipino problem in 1930, could not recall a single article on Filipino migration in a popular periodical prior to 1928. Before 1929, he added, none of the national organizations concerned with immigration or social welfare showed interest in Filipinos. The Philippine colonial project had long faded from the public's attention; both the pensionados and post–World War I migrants who came to the mainland were largely invisible to white Americans. Lasker believed that Filipinos who had arrived in the early 1920s, "students and workers, boys and men . . . for the most part full of hope and ambition, accustomed to meet life's hardships as they come, trustful—perhaps a little childlike in their simplicity . . . made a good impression [on Americans]. They were not, of course, particularly noticed so long as their number remained small."[33]

Besides the rapid growth of the Filipino population on the West Coast in the late 1920s, however, the reasons for anti-Filipino hostility were less clear. Authorities worried that they knew very little about Filipinos. They did not even know how many Filipinos were in the country. In 1928–1929 the California Department of Labor, the Bureau of Insular Affairs, and the American Council of the Institute of Pacific Relations each commissioned studies to gather facts about Filipino population on the mainland and to adduce the causes of anti-Filipino feeling.

Contemporaries quickly came to the conclusion that job competition was the chief cause of conflict.[34] Yet that conclusion was not supported by the actual patterns of employment and racial conflict. The majority of Filipinos worked in agriculture as migrant farmworkers. If Filipinos competed with other ethnic groups for farm work, it was not with whites but with Mexicans and, to a lesser extent, with Japanese, South Asians, and Koreans: one contemporary described the competition among migrant workers of color during the late 1920s as "cut-throat."[35] By the 1920s there were few native white Americans in California agriculture, especially in fieldwork; most whites had jobs in packing sheds or as ranch foremen. During the middle and late 1920s, when commercial agriculture burgeoned in California, employers often sought white labor but found it scarce. "Whites won't turn a hand to menial labor during good times," stated a manager of an employment agency in the Imperial Valley.

White farm laborers were often itinerants from other states. Some regularly worked the migrant circuit, mainly picking and packing fruit, but others, according to a labor specialist in the San Joaquin Valley, worked only a few days or a week at a time—"enough to buy gasoline and move on." Growers gave them the "best picking fields" and separate camps "away from foreign labor," but such privileged treatment was not always enough to instill loyalty in the workers. They "leave and even take the tents with them," said one farmer. Growers also complained that whites made poor workers. They said whites worked too slowly and could not pack fruit properly. Turnover was high. They were difficult to supervise. "You can't tell a white boy anything," said one farmer.[36]

Nor did Filipinos compete with white labor in manufacturing or in other urban industries. Filipino employment in hotels and restaurants in Los Angeles and other cities was confined to menial occupations, such as kitchen workers, dishwashers, pot washers, janitors, housemen, and elevator operators. Here, the established workforce comprised African Americans and white women. These workers may have resented the entrance of Filipinos into hotel and domestic occupations, but they were neither the constituency of organized labor nor the active participants in anti-Filipino riots, which took place in rural areas.[37]

In 1928 the California Building Trades Council charged that Filipinos were "forcing their way into the building industry, many of them working as engineers, painters, electricians, carpenters' helpers, and laborers." This claim was also largely unsubstantiated. According to Lasker, Filipinos were confined to unskilled construction jobs and did not compete with white skilled workers. In general, Lasker said, Filipinos were excluded from industrial employment. The few exceptions were in sawmills and box factories. But here, too, Filipinos were hired in unskilled jobs or for seasonal work. In Oregon, Filipinos worked in sawmills only as temporary extra hands.

Moreover, although labor unions complained that Filipinos undercut the wages of white workers, they did not support Filipino workers' struggles against wage discrimination. For example, in 1927 a Stockton box company hired Filipinos at 35¢ an hour when the wage for common labor had previously been 40¢. When they learned that they were paid at a lower rate, the Filipino workers walked out on strike. However, the union that represented skilled workers was prohibited by its constitution to allow Oriental membership, and the skilled white workers in the factory did not join the strike. In another instance, Filipino sawmill workers in Montesano, Washington, struck successfully for higher wages in 1924. Roman Simbe, a leader of the Filipino club that led the strike, recalled, "We shut down one mill, and then another mill. . . . Filipinos alone put up the strike. We shut [the company] down."[38]

Filipino farm laborers also demanded wage equality. In 1928 asparagus workers in the Stockton area elected representatives, who petitioned the asparagus growers with their demands. "Filipino workers intended and always do intend to uphold and EMULATE the STANDARD OF AMERICAN WAGES," they stated. In 1930, Filipino lettuce workers in Salinas struck to protest a wage reduction from 40¢ an hour, the traditional rate, to 35¢. During the late 1920s ethnic labor organizations formed in areas of Filipino concentration throughout California, north of the San Joaquin Valley, in coastal areas from Santa Barbara to Monterey, and in the Imperial Valley. These unions were sometimes organized by Filipino labor contractors, with whom growers negotiated wage rates and other conditions of work.[39]

Filipinos were sensitive to the charge that they undermined whites as cheap labor and believed that by refusing to work for lower wages they might diffuse the hostility against them. The asparagus workers noted that only by "emulating" American wage standards could Filipinos "prove themselves loyal and true to the American most precious TRADITION, thereby becoming [the] most desirable types of people required to remain and live in this country, beyond reproach." Indeed, while the growers who hired Filipino labor praised them for being good workers—they considered Filipinos to be dependable, fast, and physically suited for stoop labor, and found dealing with labor contractors convenient—they also complained that Filipino workers refused to work for less than 40¢ an hour.[40]

Despite Filipinos' efforts for wage equality, anti-Filipino sentiment found violent expression. During the fall and winter of 1929–1930 at least thirty incidents of racial violence against Filipinos took place on the Pacific Coast, including two large-scale race riots and several firebombings.[41] Contemporary observers almost always described the perpetrators as "itinerants," "hoodlums," or "loafers." The first major riot took place in Exeter, in the San Joaquin Valley, in October 1929. Itinerant Italian workers harassed and attacked Filipinos at a local carnival, the latter having brought local white girls to the fair as their dates. For several weeks white men molested or provoked fights with Filipinos on the streets of the town, attacking them with clubs and slingshots made with wire. At the end of the month a mob of two to three hundred whites visited every ranch in the area where Filipinos were employed, demanding their dismissal and destroying the Filipinos' and the growers' property. They destroyed thirty thousand trays of fruit at one ranch and burned a barn and ten tons of hay at another. The sheriff did little to stop the rampage: evidence that later surfaced suggested that he had joined in with, if not led, the vigilantes. Throughout the fall, crudely written signs appeared in Santa Clara and Mountain View: "get rid of all Filipinos or we'll burn this town down" and "work no Filipinos or we'll destroy your crop and you too."[42] In the San Joaquin Valley, a Filipino labor camp in Dinuba was firebombed. Similarly, in Arvin, a "committee" of "loafers" presented growers with warnings and petitions and fired shots at the Filipino laborers' bunkhouses. Filipino labor contractors in the valley insisted on carrying guns in the fields to protect their men.[43]

Yet, curiously, despite the agitation against Filipino employment, the white laborers who attacked Filipino farmworkers often did not actually want the jobs in question. Nor did the trouble appear to derive from anxieties caused by the Depression, which had just begun. Through the late 1920s a labor shortage existed in California agriculture, and whites in rural areas generally had no trouble getting work, despite their reputation for being difficult and unreliable, and the 1929 harvest season was no different. E. J. Firebraugh, whose ranch in Exeter was destroyed by rioters, said, "Nobody [was] suffering for jobs when trouble occurred. Plenty of work doesn't eliminate the possibility of trouble."[44]

A more complicated set of problems, then, seems to have existed. At one level, the riots did express anxiety among whites over job competition, even if it was more imaginary than it was real. White migrant farmworkers who had traditionally worked the fig and apple harvests in Pajaro Valley regarded the increase in the number of Filipinos in the adjoining Salinas Valley's lettuce fields with apprehension and suspicion. The Filipino newspaper the *Torch* pointed out, "The lettuce is a new product in the Salinas Valley. No white men thinned lettuce before the Filipinos. Work in the lettuce fields is very hard."[45] Once the Depression started, Filipinos became the target of resentment among unemployed white workers, for whom Asiatics were familiar and convenient scapegoats, even if they did not want the same work.

Thus competition between Filipino and white Americans over jobs and wages existed but was not typical of their respective positions in the labor market. Wages did constitute a site of conflict, but the conflict was driven by Filipinos' *resistance* to being used as cheap labor. Yet the charge that Filipinos threatened white American workers' jobs and wages was ubiquitous. It was repeated not only by nativists like Paul Scharrenberg and V. S. McClatchy but by journalists and scholars who were sympathetic to Filipinos. Lasker, whose careful study identified specific and limited areas of ethnic job displacement, believed economic competition provided the "background" for anti-Filipino hostility among whites even where there was no direct competition. He also believed that organized labor's support for restrictive immigration on economic grounds was "easily understandable," even though his own research concluded that Filipinos did not threaten the jobs of white union men.[46] Lasker did not explain this puzzle; in a sense, his thinking was part of it.

The *perception* of widespread job competition was, in fact, fueled by long-standing racial animus towards Asiatics. The central element of this hostility was the ideology of white entitlement to the resources of the West. That outlook overdetermined race relations and created the problem, both real and imagined, of economic displacement. Filipinos were greeted by a tradition of anti-Oriental racism that was eighty years in the making. By the 1920s, anti-Asiatic politics had fully matured on the West Coast, especially in California, where exclusion had become a staple of the urban and middle-class Progressivist strain of the Democratic Party.[47] When nativists called Filipinos the "third invasion" from the Orient, they placed the problem within a discourse that held maximum political purchase.

The Social Maladjustment of a "Womanless Group"

But at another level, the anti-Filipino riots evinced dynamics quite different from those that had fueled previous movements for Asiatic exclusion. In fact, Orientalist tropes did not easily apply to Filipinos. Filipinos could not be considered heathen or steeped in ancient traditionalism: they were Christians; they went to American schools and spoke English; they wore Western-style clothes; they were familiar with American popular culture. If nativists believed Chinese and Japanese were unassimilable because they were radically *different* from Euro-Americans, both racially and culturally, they were discomfited precisely by the extent of Filipinos' Americanization. For Filipinos, of course, the conflicting impulses of nationalism and assimilation were inherent to the colonized identity. The Anglo-American mentality con-

tained a version of the same contradiction. In a sense, the reaction of white
Americans to the acculturation of Filipinos was similar to the unsettled response of nineteenth-century Americans to acculturated Native Americans,
or that of the English to their anglicized colonial subjects of India, whose
partial resemblance threatened to mock, even as it mimicked.[48]

Unlike the English, however, white Americans had available to them an
avenue for denying the acculturation of their brown-skinned imitators. Because American culture was racially segregated as well as hybrid, white
Americans could deny the "American-ness" of Filipinos by ascribing to them
attributes that derived from racial representations of African Americans, especially those that depicted black men as sexually aggressive. In fact, this idea
neatly bridged the construction of Filipinos as backward savage tribes in the
Philippines and the appearance of contemporary, acculturated Filipinos in
the United States.

The identification of Filipinos with Negroes was not new. During the Philippine-American War, American soldiers commonly referred to Filipinos as
"niggers," which was a familiar epithet that was applicable to all uncivilized,
dark-skinned peoples. The racial icon assumed a gendered dimension as
early as 1904 when, at the Louisiana Purchase Exposition, a group of white
Marines assaulted uniformed Philippine Scouts—the "most advanced Filipinos"—whom a group of white schoolteachers from St. Louis had offered
to escort through the fairgrounds.[49]

By the late 1920s the most common complaint against Filipinos, in addition to their alleged displacement of white labor, was that they fancied white
women. Filipino men, it was said, spent all their wages on flashy clothes,
cheap entertainment, and white women, whom they met at taxi dance halls.
The halls were establishments where a ten-minute dance with a girl cost ten
cents. Popular during the Progressive era, the dance hall was a zone of commercialized and sexualized leisure, which catered to men of all ethnic groups
and was targeted by social reformers as the moral ruin of the young female
employees. In rural California towns, the women who worked in the dance
halls were Polish-Americans and from other eastern European ethnic groups.
By the late 1920s the taxi dance hall had become associated with the "Filipino problem," the physical and metaphorical site for Filipinos' sudden visi-
bility as a social and sexual menace to white society.[50]

The notion that Filipino men were oversexed was commonplace. Their
sexuality was linked to their primitive development: references to Filipinos'
"childlike" nature undergirded claims of both labor docility and sexual pro-
miscuity. This construction of Filipinos' sexuality was not limited to the
eugenicists and anti-Asiatic exclusion lobby. It was shared by progressivists
and liberals. For example, David Barrows, president of the University of California and the first superintendent of education in the Philippines, said the
Filipinos' "vices are almost entirely based on sexual passion." Barrows ex-

plained that Filipinos "in most cases, [were] only a few years removed from the even, placid life of a primitive native barrio." Even the liberal Carey McWilliams was susceptible to the influence of racial stereotyping. In his pluralist tract *Brothers under the Skin*, McWilliams wrote that Filipinos' "sexual experiences are, indeed, fantastic."[51]

While the sexual representation of both Filipino and African American men was constructed on notions of racial primitiveness, there were some important differences. Most important, antagonism toward Filipino male sexuality was bound up in social anxieties about the homosocial nature of the Filipino workforce. These anxieties were filtered through and legitimated by modern sociology. The Filipino "race problem" was a minor cottage industry in sociology during the 1930s, with many studies conducted by Emory Bogardus at the University of Southern California and his students, many of whom were Filipinos. Bogardus had been trained by Robert E. Park at the University of Chicago. Perhaps the most common theme in the sociological literature was that the abnormal sex ratio among Filipinos in the United States led to "social and psychological maladjustment," which in turn led to "moral problems." Constantly on the move, following the harvest season, these young single men lacked both family life and a stable community. More than anything, it was argued, they lacked moral supervision. In this context, one writer said, young Filipinos "went beserk by spending lavishly on the dance halls, dating blondes, and getting mixed up with fist fights that occasionally resulted [in] assaults and murder," all behaviors that violated the Filipino community's "Christian ideals."[52]

The argument proceeded to connect Filipinos' deviation from heterosexual family and social relations to race-mixing and race conflict. One sociologist said that being a "womanless group . . . explain[ed] [Filipinos'] tendency to associate with white women . . . [and led to] strained relations between the two races." He cited a white employer of Filipinos who said "he would have nothing against them if they did not display so much interest in American women," that is, white women.[53]

Filipinos' "womanlessness" thus became associated with the specter of race-mixing. But if Filipinos frequented the dance halls, relatively few Filipinos married white women. A sociologist found that Filipino out-marriage occurred most often with Mexicans, and then with "mulattos." These unions were relatively successful, he argued, because the partners shared similar religious beliefs, occupational status, and "color proximity." Marriage to American, that is, white women had the least success, on account of cultural differences.[54]

At another level, the critique of Filipino male sexuality associated their homosocial condition with a lack of masculinity. This was a shift from early and mid-nineteenth-century mythologies of the homosocial culture of the western frontier—a world inhabited by manly adventurers, sailors, forty-

3.2 Filipino migrant workers who dated white women incurred the wrath of white Americans. Here, a beach party in California, c. 1930. (Reprinted, by permission, from Quinsaat, *Letters in Exile.*)

niners, Indian-fighters, construction and railroad workers, and traders who cleared the way for settlement by civilized society. The only women in that world were barmaids and prostitutes. As Robert Lee has described, by the 1870s the "predominantly male homosocial culture of the West began to be displaced by the Victorian cult of domesticity [and] the white bourgeois family." The presence of an all-male Asiatic workforce on the Pacific Coast threatened the emerging social order founded upon the "racially exclusive, presumptively heterosexual, nuclear family." Since the time of anti-Chinese movement in the late nineteenth century, the Oriental threat was cast as an "ambiguous, inscrutable, and hermophridatic" sexuality, a "third sex."[55]

In the 1920s and 1930s, contemporaries described Filipinos in similar terms: as feminized males, not homosexual yet not fully heterosexual either. A social worker in southern California said, "[Filipinos are] very emotional. Women are their weakness. Filipinos are easy prey for women who can pick up any Filipino on the street. . . . Filipinos are too sentimental for words." Another said, "The boys are peacocks. . . . they won't save money and they strut." A sociologist said Filipinos were influenced by the romance stories promoted in American movies and movie magazines.[56]

These racialized sexual representations of Filipino men and fears of race-mixing fueled the anti-Filipino riots in Watsonville, California, in January 1930. Local white youths and Filipino laborers had clashed and fought on the streets on numerous occasions in the late 1920s. As in other towns, the conflicts usually involved Filipinos dating whites, including teenaged girls from local families. In early January 1930, at the urging of Judge D. W. Rohrback, the Northern Monterey County Chamber of Commerce passed a resolution calling for the exclusion of Filipinos from the area. In an interview in the *Watsonville Evening Pajaronian*, the judge declared that Filipinos were "little brown men attired like Solomon in all his glory, strutting like peacocks and endeavoring to attract the eyes of young American and Mexican girls." He believed that the worst part about the Filipino was "his mixing with young white girls from thirteen to seventeen. He gives them silk underwear and makes them pregnant and crowds whites out of jobs in the bargain." Filipinos, the judge added, were "just ten years removed from a bolo and breechcloth. . . . Fifteen of them will live in one room and content themselves with squatting on the floor eating rice and fish."[57]

The judge's language offended the Filipino community. The Filipino Federation of America in Stockton held a mass meeting of three thousand people. The meeting passed a resolution stating that the judge's "malicious and very sweeping [charges] deeply wounded the feeling of all Filipinos; such criticisms phrased in a gross and insulting language being false, unjust and personal in nature." They resolved that Filipinos in the region would "present a solid front for a most vigorous protest" and "show . . . that the Filipinos have self-respect and [are] endowed with humane attributes enjoyed by other people." Finally, they appealed to their "home government, through the Philippine legislature [and] the resident commissioner in Washington . . . [to] use all just and honorable means by appropriate legislative measures for the preservation of mutual trust and confidence of the people concerned." Other Filipinos more plainly asserted their rights to social equality. The Filipino press in Stockton defended the right of Filipinos to date local women. Angenor Cruz, a Filipino businessman, asserted that the taxi dance hall served a legitimate social purpose, owing to the absence of Filipino women in America; moreover, he said, Filipino men were "much more considerate and respectful toward American girls than the Americans are themselves."[58]

A newly opened Filipino taxi dance hall on the outskirts of Watsonville, organized as a private club by Cruz and other entrepreneurial Filipinos, became the target of vigilante wrath. Beginning on January 19 large crowds— from two hundred to eight hundred people—gathered outside the hall every night for a week, threatening to lynch the Filipinos inside. By day, gangs of local white youth stalked and assaulted Filipinos throughout the area, throwing some into the river, tearing the clothes from others, and throwing rocks and firing rifle shots at Filipinos in cars and at labor camps. On January 22 some four hundred whites attacked the club, where they beat a number of Filipinos, and then drove to a local ranch and fired upon the bunkhouse. One shot killed Fermin Tobera, a twenty-two-year-old lettuce picker, as he lay sleeping. The local white press had dismissed the disturbances as a "Roman holiday," but when the rioting achieved fatal results, the sheriff deputized members of the local American Legion to diffuse the mobs roaming the valley. The authorities arrested eight white youths who had rioted at another ranch but did not investigate or prosecute the murder of Fermin Tobera. On February 2 over a thousand Filipinos gathered in Los Angeles to protest Tobera's murder. The same day was declared a National Day of Humiliation in the Philippines to mark the arrival of the young worker's body in Manila.[59]

Violence against Filipinos in California and the Pacific Northwest continued. The Filipino Federation in Stockton was firebombed. In August two workers identified as Italian and Slavic and wielding jack handles chased Filipinos through the streets of Watsonville, and a rash of rioting and night-riding erupted throughout central California, in Delano, Arvin, Rheedley, Yuba, Marysville, and Bakersfield. Judge Sylvain Lazarus of San Francisco denounced Filipinos as "a race scarcely more than savages." In San Francisco and El Centro, authorities issued orders to police to arrest any Filipino seen in the company of a white girl. The press reported incidents of racial violence against Filipinos in Washington, Chicago, and Florida.[60]

Yet while outrage and alarm at the spread of violence pervaded the Filipino community, Filipinos did not all agree on the source of the problem or the solution. The Rizal Club and Filipino Christian League in Stockton called for the dance halls to be closed. These Filipino elites believed the young men who frequented the dance halls were an unrepresentative minority that invited racial hostility toward the entire community. Comparing Filipinos to other migrant groups in rural California, Felix Zamora said Filipinos were "wild," whereas Japanese and Mexicans were "family oriented" and wanted to maintain "their way of living." Others blamed the taxi dance hall girls for exploiting young Filipinos and adopted a protective stance toward "our boys," who, they believed, were lonely and impressionable, easily seduced by girls with "loose morals" and little education.[61]

Filipinos deemed both taxi dance hall girls and itinerant European laborers to be their social inferiors, evincing class bias as well as the belief that
they were more Americanized than European immigrants. Hazel Simbe, for
example, resented the Croatians who "drove all the Filipinos out" of Aberdeen, Washington, in 1931. "They couldn't even speak English, a lot of
them," she recalled. "The Filipinos could all speak English." This sense of
superiority contained a bitterness over the failure of Americans to recognize
the success of benevolent assimilation, but that bitterness, paradoxically, was
nationalist in its thrust. The journalist Jose Bulatao compared Filipino men
in the United States who "take care of their families and will never become
social burdens" to the "American soldiers, going to our country, [where]
they marry our women and then leave their children to be cared for by our
government—thousands, tens of thousands of fatherless children are left by
the Americans of cultured mentality. . . . And our people are still jungle folk
and of Primitive Moral Code?" Bulatao also believed it was regrettable that
Filipino men associated with "white women of low breed," but he asserted
that Filipinos had the right to do so and that such relationships were understandable because "it is only natural that the demands should be supplied by
any means from anywhere."[62] The conflict over interracial marriage played
out in the legal arena as well. Using law to police sexual relations between
Filipinos and whites was difficult because the racial classification of Filipinos
was legally ambiguous. California's antimiscegenation statutes, which were
written in the nineteenth century, prohibited marriage between "white persons" and "negroes, mulattoes, and Mongolians." During the 1920s, U.S.
Webb, the state attorney general, argued that Filipinos were "Mongolian,"
and some county clerks refused to issue marriage licenses to Filipino-white
couples. But the courts often disagreed, citing ethnologists that classified Filipinos as being of the "brown" or "Malay race," and not of the "yellow race."
In 1933, the Los Angeles Superior Court ruled that Salvador Roldan was
"Malay," not a "Mongolian," allowing his marriage to Marjorie Rogers, a
"Caucasian." But the court, undoubtedly aware of the race riots attending
the Pacific Coast, noted that it ruled only on the law and urged the legislature to align the law with contemporary "common thought." Later that year
the legislature amended the antimiscegenation law to explicitly include
"members of the Malay race" within its scope. It also retroactively voided
and made illegal all previous Filipino-white marriages, a particularly vindic-
tive measure that echoed Attorney General Webb's revocation of South Asians'
naturalized citizenship after the *Thind* decision in 1923.[63]

Thus anti-Filipino hostility was a site where ideas about gender, sexuality,
class, and colonialism intersected in violent ways and, moreover, informed
the construction of the racial identity of both European and Filipino migrants. That process gave immigrant workers from southern and eastern European a purchase on whiteness, which was part of their own Americanization. By contrast, Filipinos were denied their American acculturation and

reclassified into an identity that combined racial representations of Negroes and Orientals. Anti-Filipino racism was animated by the construction of Filipino sexuality as physically base and socially dangerous. That construction served the desire to strip Filipinos of their American-ness and to overturn benevolent assimilation—the colonial policy that had, ironically, led Filipinos to demand wage and social equality in the United States.

Decolonization and Exclusion

Racial violence at the grassroots level provided empirical evidence for the national nativist lobby's efforts to pass legislation excluding Filipinos from the United States. The California Joint Immigration Committee, American Federation of Labor, and the American Legion passed resolutions for Filipino exclusion at their conventions in 1927, 1928, and 1929. The American Coalition, the national umbrella organization of the patriotic societies, which had led the lobby for immigration quotas based on national origin during the early 1920s, gave full backing to the demand for Filipino exclusion.[64]

In 1928 and 1929 Congressman Richard Welch of San Jose, California, introduced into the House legislation that would declare Filipinos "aliens" and, on that basis, exclude them from the United States.[65] The constitutionality of the Welch bill was questionable, however, because by treaty Filipinos were not aliens. Filipinos owed allegiance to the United States and as wards of the United States they were entitled to its protection. Welch argued that while the United States got the Philippines through war, "our duty to them is political. . . . [I]mmigration and the mixing of races and the movements of people are entirely a different proposition." McClatchy similarly argued that colonial status was not an issue because Filipinos were racially ineligible to citizenship and therefore excludable under the terms of the Johnson-Reed Act. Proponents of this argument pointed out that citizens of the Philippines of Chinese descent were excludable under terms of the Chinese Exclusion Act in 1904. Therefore, the argument went, the right of citizens of the Philippines to freely enter the United States was limited to those racially eligible to American citizenship.[66]

It was a weak argument, for such a policy would have excluded virtually all citizens of the Philippines, making freedom of movement an obvious mockery. Although Filipino exclusion had been adopted by the national nativist lobby, the issue continued to be perceived in Washington as a strident regional interest that ran counter to the nation's constitutional principles and standing in the international community. This was evident at the House hearings on the Welch bill. Samuel Dickstein, chair of the House immigration committee, was clearly offended by Welch's proposed legislation, calling it "the first bill of its character, which deals with a race of people under the

American flag, that I have ever seen before." Brig. General F. LeJ. Parker, chief of the Bureau of Insular Affairs of the War Department, testified that the "matter is not one of immigration but of being fair, honest, and treating justly the loyal men" who volunteered to fight in the world war. Parker, who noted that the Philippine government had long maintained a policy of discouraging emigration, sought a solution to the problem of race on the mainland short of altering the islands' status. Secretary of State Henry Stimson emphasized that American trade in Asia depended upon public opinion: "Our reputation in the Orient will depend on fair dealing and good will, and nothing will be judged more sharply than the way in which we have kept our promises to the Filipino people thirty years ago when we said we would govern in their interest and in our interest."[67]

In order to overcome these obstacles, the movement for exclusion began to identify its interest with Philippine independence.[68] The exclusionists were not, of course, motivated by a desire for freedom for the Philippines; rather, they sought to free the United States of the Philippines and, with it, the Filipino problem. Whatever economic benefits accrued from the insular possession, they were not, in the exclusionists' eyes, worth the price of another Asiatic invasion of the mainland. In fact, neither the eugenicists nor organized labor held much respect for American interests in the Philippines. They believed the sugar industrialists were but the latest incarnation of a long line of monopolists who used cheap labor to undermine American standards.

The American Federation of Labor made independence for the Philippine Islands a priority on its political agenda. As it did, it took care to avoid overtly racial claims, emphasizing instead economic arguments, notwithstanding their dubious grounding in fact. Welch, too, insisted "we have no racial prejudices" but that Americans suffered a loss of jobs to cheap Filipino and Mexican labor. Attorney General U. S. Webb, a close associate of the CJIC, argued for exclusion on grounds of unassimilability and difference but emphasized that these meant no suggestion of inferiority. Webb evinced an updated version of Manifest Destiny that asserted white entitlement but denied claims to racial superiority. He said, "This Government as founded . . . was then a Government of and for the white race, and it was, I think, with the thought and hope of its founders that it would continue to be the Government of the whites." Webb did not blame others for wanting to come to America, but, he said, "We thank God that only we, the white people, found it first and we want to be protected in our enjoyment of it." The CJIC was the most outspoken about the undesirability of Filipinos and made no effort to soft-pedal their allegations of unassimilability, racial instability, and the "sex problem." Morally, said McClatchy, Filipinos were the "worst form of Orientals," because of the "criminal nature in which we find them engaged . . . in the delinquency of young girls."[69] In the Senate, Millard Tydings of

Maryland, who believed it was illogical to exclude Chinese and Japanese but not Filipinos, invoked the spectre of more race riots to support Philippine independence. Senator Hawes suggested that independence would be a "constructive settlement of the whole problem" before exclusionist sentiment grew too strong.[70]

The nativists' entrance into the political debate over Philippine independence brought that struggle to a head. This was a relief to many. Although the issue of Philippine colonialism had faded from public discourse—it having successfully been rendered benevolent—low-intensity conflict and uncertainty over the islands' future status unsettled Congress throughout the 1910s and 1920s. In 1916 Filipino leaders succeeded in inserting a general commitment to Philippine independence, but with no date or plan for achieving it, into the preamble of the Jones Act. During the 1920s, under the regime of Governor General Francis Harrison, a policy of rapid Filipinization brought the proportion of Filipinos in the Philippine civil service to 90 percent, up from just half in 1903. By 1930, thirty thousand Filipino teachers and only 293 Americans taught in the islands' American public school system.[71] As United States colonialism constructed itself towards a neocolonialist model— in which hegemony rests on economic dominance and not direct political rule—American elites became more receptive to a political divestiture of the islands. Although Americans with landed investments and commercial business in the Philippines benefited from the terms of bidirectional free trade dictated by the 1909 Payne-Aldrich Act, independence became increasingly preferable to continued uncertainty over the Philippines' status; statehood, of course, was not an option. Other business interests, such as western sugar-beet companies, northern dairymen, and southern cotton-planters, sought to throw the Philippines over the American tariff wall, especially after the onset of the Depression, when easy scapegoats and quick solutions were sought.[72] Finally, unlike Cuba, the Philippines' importance to the United States was more strategic than it was commercial. It became increasingly apparent that Washington would maintain a military presence after decolonization (under the guise of protecting the islands from foreign aggression); indeed, this was central to the evolving neocolonialist model.[73] Thus when the nativist lobby entered the political fray in the early 1930s, it threw its political weight behind a trend that had been gathering momentum for some years.

Ironically, some Philippine political leaders viewed the accelerated pace toward independence with alarm. Since 1908, when the Federalist Party dropped its plank for statehood, independence had been the common denominator across the entire Filipino political spectrum. The issue was not if, but when. Filipino politicians had historically risen on the strength of nationalist and anti-American rhetoric, but they and their constituency, the *mestizo* landowning elite that grew wealthy from exporting duty-free agricultural products to the United States, were far less sanguine about actualizing national independence. During the debates over the Jones Act, for example, moderate leaders, including Manuel Quezon, advocated home rule, not full independence. As late as 1929, General Aguinaldo, long past his glory days as leader of the Philippine Revolution, believed the Filipino people were not yet ready for democratic self-rule. However, by the late 1920s most Filipino political leaders publicly called for immediate and complete independence. Quezon, now president of the Philippine Senate, stated he would trade the protective American tariff for freedom—"Let Filipinos be poor and forever poor but independent," he declared—although privately he and others were more hesitant. The Philippine press was more openly divided. The *Herald*, for example, editorialized that "immediate independence is a mere slogan, an ideal" that, if actualized, "would mean economic disaster."[74] But among the Filipino polity, political momentum was for independence. In February 1930 an "independence congress" of two thousand Filipino delegates convened in Manila. Filipinos in the United States, who experienced the most acute racial and cultural contradictions of benevolent assimilation, advocated immediate independence. The Filipino Federation of America declared itself "100 percent" for independence.[75]

In 1932 Congress passed the Hare-Hawes-Cutting Act over President Hoover's veto, providing for the immediate establishment of a Philippine commonwealth and a ten-year transition period to independence. The United States would retain the right to military bases on the islands after full independence. The act also imposed tariffs on Philippine imports into the United States but allowed American goods to continue to flow freely into the Philippines. The *Stockton Three Stars*, stung by the unequal terms of the act, postulated that independence was but a scheme to "kick out . . . Philippine sugar and immigration from this country."[76] Quezon opposed the bill as unjust and went to Washington seeking its modification, since the measure required ratification by the Philippine legislature. The renegotiated act, the Philippines Independence Act of 1934, also known as the Tydings-McDuffie Act, left open the question of American military bases after independence, but in most other respects it was similar to the Hare Act, setting a ten-year transition period during which executive powers would be increasingly assumed by the Philippine government and a republican constitution drawn.[77]

Independence, under commonwealth status, reproduced many features of the colonial relationship. Citizens of the Philippine Commonwealth continued to owe allegiance to the United States, yet the act declared that "citizens of the Philippine Islands who are not citizens of the United States shall be considered as if they are aliens" and that "for such purposes the Philippine Islands shall be considered a separate country" with an annual immigration quota of fifty. Because the minimum quota for all countries under the Immigration Act of 1924 was one hundred, the Philippine quota was a gratuitous gesture meant to degrade Filipinos to a status something short of nationhood, their American tutelage placing them just barely above the fully ex-cludable Asiatic races.

Moreover, the act granted American citizens continued unrestricted and unlimited entry into the Philippines, as well as the rights and privileges of Filipino citizens of the Philippines, without the necessity of naturalization. Bidirectional free trade was replaced by a one-sided agreement, which sub-jected Filipino products to the same tariff schedules that applied to all other countries yet which granted American capital and products continued free access to the Philippine market.

Finally, the Tydings-McDuffie Act deemed Filipinos living in the United States who arrived before May 1, 1934, to be aliens but not subject to depor-tation for any act or condition that existed prior to that date. They were, however, subject to deportation for deportable acts committed after May 1, 1934. The *Salinas Philippines Mail* called the Tydings-McDuffie Act "a bait to entrap us. . . . It restricts our liberty of action. We cannot send our products [into] American markets. We cannot come to the United States. We must stay home and slave to pay off principal and interest on bonds held by foreign capitalists."[78] Indeed, with independence at least a decade away and by losing the protection of the tariff and the right to enter the United States without restriction, Filipinos would seem to have been handed a poor bargain.

Repatriation and the Return to Invisibility

Decolonization required one additional measure. The catalysts of the crisis that led to independence—the Filipino laborers who arrived in large num-bers in the continental United States, bringing American colonial policy home, so to speak—remained a problem to be solved. It would not be enough to restrict future immigration to fifty a year. Race conflict, labor militancy, and sexual anxiety continued to attend the Filipino presence on the Pacific Coast; in particular, Filipino labor organizing in California agri-culture and in the Alaska canning industry intensified during the mid-1930s.[79]

The "voluntary" repatriation of hundreds of thousands of Mexicans dur-ing the early years of the Depression suggested a method of ridding the country of the remaining Filipino population. In fact, proposals to repatriate Filipinos emerged in the early 1930s, before Philippine independence was enacted. As with the entire colonial experience, proponents of repatriation expressed benevolent intentions to assist Filipinos who had become jobless and homeless during the Depression. During the early 1930s, concerned Fili-pinos inquired of the possibility of government-assisted repatriation.[80] In 1933 the House passed two resolutions sponsored by Samuel Dickstein sup-porting the repatriation of indigent Filipinos at federal expense. Dickstein considered repatriation a "national emergency," which justified use of army and navy transport to "secure relief to communities in the United States by removing from them the unemployed Filipinos residing therein who have become a serious economic problem to these cities, these communities, and, in fact, to the several States." The Philippine resident commissioner in Washington, Camilo Osias, supported the idea. Dickstein optimistically predicted that twenty thousand to thirty thousand Filipinos—nearly half the population in the United States—would avail themselves of the benefit, if offered. However, legislation failed to pass because it was unclear if repatriates—who remained United States nationals—would be able to reenter the United States.[81]

In 1935, on the heels of the passage of the Tydings-McDuffie Act, Richard Welch introduced new legislation to repatriate Filipinos. The Welch bill explicitly provided that Filipinos would be virtually unable to reenter the United States. Section 4 of the act read, "No Filipino who receives the benefits of this Act shall be entitled to return to the continental United States except as a quota immigrant under the provisions of [the Tydings-McDuffie Act]." The Immigration and Naturalization Service, which was charged with administering the repatriation program, estimated that ten thousand to fifteen thousand Filipinos might "avail themselves of the privilege of returning to Manila"—fewer than Dickstein had speculated, but still nearly a quarter of the population. Congress appropriated $100,000 to the program, far less than Welch and the INS deemed necessary to ship the large numbers of people that they intended. Informed by the War and Navy Departments that military transport was unavailable for repatriation purposes, the INS proceeded to negotiate steerage rates with Pacific Coast steamship companies.[82]

The man at the center of the West Coast operation was Edward Cahill, the San Francisco district commissioner of the INS. Cahill was an ambitious bureaucrat who saw in the repatriation program an opportunity to advance his position and the cause of Asiatic exclusion. He claimed credit for conceiving the idea for a repatriation program—considering it "my brainchild"—and suggesting it to Welch. During the lifetime of the program, he remained constantly and aggressively involved in efforts to promote, expand, and extend it. He was keen to the effects of public relations and sought to use the press to the advantage of the program. Cahill recommended "working with the right leaders, both Filipino and American," placing advertisements in local newspapers, and sending INS representatives to agricultural areas to recruit repatriates. He understood that the INS should avoid any "word or thought of deportation." In the event that voluntary departure "slows up and we need an inducement to satisfy the vanity," he fancifully thought "some arrangement might be worked out with our western universities to give a thirty-day course in agriculture, with a certificate for those who finish the course, so they could return to the homeland displaying an emblem to denote the benefit they derived from their stay in the United

States." The INS issued press releases to Filipino newspapers and posted translations of the act in pool halls, restaurants, and other sites frequented by Filipinos. The service also sent letters to Filipino community organizations, asking them to publicize the repatriation program among their members.[83]

Despite these efforts, Filipinos were slow to sign up. Cahill blamed a negative propaganda campaign by unnamed agricultural interests who he alleged sought to exploit Filipino cheap labor. He lamented that without more aggressive INS outreach, Filipinos would remain ignorant of the provisions and benefits of repatriation. In reality, however, Filipinos in the United States, who were passionate about political debate and remained well informed about Philippine-American politics, were more skeptical than ignorant of the repatriation program's ostensible benefits. The *Los Angeles Philippine Herald Tribune* acknowledged there was a "whispering campaign" discouraging repatriation, but noted that for Filipinos in America, "shorn of wealth they have earned and acquired; equipped with experiences they could not utilize in their own country; possessed of education but no place to fit in; would not these facts explain why the repatriation act has all the earmarks of glaring failure?" Similarly, the *Los Angeles Times* reported that Filipinos believed that returning home as paupers they would be disgraced. A Filipino on relief at the Los Angeles County Welfare Office told an interviewer, "I would prefer to stay in America. I would rather go hungry and die here than go home with an empty hand." Although critics faulted Filipinos' prideful nature, Francisco Varona, former labor commissioner to Hawai'i, believed the problem was not so much pride as it was fear. Filipinos, he said, would "like to return to the islands and follow their trade or practice their profession. But the Filipinos in the United States seemed afraid. They dread the thought of returning home because they fear they may not be able to get work."[84]

By the end of the first fiscal year of the program, only 157 Filipinos had repatriated under the auspices of the INS. Welch succeeded in getting Congress to extend the program another year and to reappropriate the unspent monies. A vigorous effort resulted in 585 repatriations during fiscal year 1937. However, by this time economic conditions had begun to improve, so that Filipinos became more hopeful that their luck in the United States would change, and the repatriations continued at a moderate pace. In all, Congress extended the repatriation act three times, allowing it to finally expire in 1940, and allocated a total of $250,000 to the project. From the first sailing in April 1936 to the last in July 1941, a total of 2,064 Filipino nationals returned to the Philippines.[85]

Who were the repatriates? According to data compiled from the manifests of 1,259 passengers who departed from 1936 to 1939, the overwhelming number of repatriates came from California, reflecting Cahill's efforts. Eight percent came from Seattle and the Pacific Northwest. Another 10 percent were brought from other parts of the country by the INS via the service's scheduled transcontinental "deportation parties." Ninety-five percent of the repatriates were men. The average age was thirty-five, somewhat older than the general Filipino population in the United States. Twenty-one percent of the men were married; most had wives and families in the Philippines. Of couples traveling together, approximately one-quarter were Filipino-American marriages. Over two hundred children returned to the Philippines with their parents.[86]

Judging by their baggage, many repatriates do not appear to have been indigent, especially in the earlier sailings. For example, of the 126 passengers sailing out of San Francisco on the SS *Chaumont* on November 9, 1936, forty-three listed special baggage, including numerous violins, guitars, tennis rackets, typewriters, phonographs, radios, briefcases, boxes of books, bicycles, framed pictures, and the like. Families on the *Chaumont* and other ships brought household furnishings, including cribs, washing machines, dishes, and sewing machines. This suggests that Filipinos who chose to return to the Philippines during the earlier phases of the program were not desperately poor but, rather, were inclined to return home and took advantage of the free transportation. It also offers a glimpse at the rich cultural life of Filipino laborers, students, and student-laborers in the United States.[87]

The desire of Filipino men to repatriate with wives and children who were citizens of the United States posed a problem for the authorities. The legislation provided transportation only for natives of the Philippines. In California, the State Emergency Relief Administration (SERA), which had subsidized a substantial portion of the repatriation of Mexicans during the early 1930s, was a logical source to provide passage for family members, especially the American-citizen children.[88] However, in October 1935 the governor of the Philippines lodged a strong protest at the repatriation of American-born wives and children. He believed such families were destitute and would become public charges in the Philippines, and he threatened to return them to the United States. By March 1936 the Philippine government softened its position, at least towards the American-born children of Filipinos.[89]

The "white wives," however, remained a problem. The Philippine government frowned upon their migration, citing their likely indigence, but in truth American women were not welcome in Philippine society, which considered them outsiders and of low class. The INS tried to discourage them from traveling to the Philippines by emphasizing the lack of any federal appropriation for their transportation expenses. Yet, as Cahill acknowledged, there was "no way that we can prevent anyone from buying a ticket to go to Manila, and if the white wife of a Filipino purchases a ticket, there is nothing to prevent her from traveling on the same ship with her husband."[90]

In addition to these Filipino workers and their families, the INS repatriated nearly a hundred Filipinos from state prisons, asylums, and hospitals. As early as August 1935, less than a month after the repatriation act was enacted, the California Board of Prison Terms and Paroles informed the INS that it had 185 Filipinos incarcerated in the state's prisons who they wished to repatriate. The INS district commissioner believed repatriation might "reliev[e] overcrowded conditions of the penal institutions." In October 1935 the INS began to develop plans to facilitate the removal of Filipinos from state institutions. An INS official advised prison authorities, "Favorable consideration will be given to properly supported applications filed by Filipino convicts incarcerated in jails and prisons, presuming that the state authorities will commute the sentences . . . [and that] the action taken by the Filipino to be repatriated is entirely voluntary." At first, the INS repatriated criminals and the insane on separate ships, apart from the general repatriate population, but by 1938 it was sending small groups of inmates with regular sailings. These included convicts, the insane, and persons with leprosy, tuberculosis and other illnesses.[91]

The inclusion of inmates from state institutions in the repatriation program reflected the historical practice of the INS and state authorities in matters of deportation and indicated the extent to which officials conflated repatriation and deportation. If the country could be rid of Filipinos, so too would the institutions be relieved of the burden they imposed. The practice provoked an angry letter from Paul McNutt, the United States high commissioner in the Philippines, to Frank Merriam, the governor of California. "I vigorously protest the action of the California State Board of Parole making the Philippine Islands a dumping ground for parole prisoners," he wrote. "The parole of a prisoner to another jurisdiction under the United States flag without the consent of the authorities concerned and without proper supervision is indefensible."[92]

Repatriates complained that the INS treated them poorly, like deportees or criminals. Cahill sent INS officers and guards with each sailing to keep order and to make sure that the ships' managers adhered to a strict food budget. In 1937 sixty of the ninety-nine repatriates aboard the SS *President Jackson* petitioned the authorities for better food and conditions. They protested that they were not allowed to leave the ship when it stopped at ports. A repatriate wrote to the *Philippines Mail*, "The repatriation is supposed to be a Santa Claus gift to Filipinos who want to go home, but have not the money for fare. But in view of the shabby, shameful and almost inhuman treatment we received, the administration of the Repatriation Act reminds us of a CROCODILE's affection and caresses."[93]

We know little of what happened to the repatriates once they arrived in the Philippines. In 1938 the *Philippines Free Press* reported that repatriated paroled convicts were involved in numerous crimes in Manila and elsewhere in the provinces, but there is little evidence on the experiences of the mass of repatriates. A study of Filipinos who returned to the Philippines during the early 1930s, before the INS program, concluded that a readjustment period of two to three years was common. Some bought and improved land; others opened small stores or businesses of their own. Of the "better class" of Filipinos, those educated in the United States easily found employment as teachers and in other urban professions. Others tried to improve social conditions in their hometowns but often encountered conflicts owing to their "American ways" and "hyperaggressiveness."[94] We might speculate that these patterns were repeated with the INS repatriates, since they came from the same general population of Filipinos in the United States, although economic conditions in the Philippine Islands during the mid- and late-1930s remained depressed.

If the purpose of repatriation was to resolve the contradiction of benevolent assimilation by ridding the country of Filipino laborers and the Filipino problem, the INS program was only partially successful. Certainly, tens of thousands of Filipinos did not repatriate, as Cahill and Welch had hoped. While some two thousand Filipinos took advantage of the opportunity to return home, many others chose not to go, for reasons involving pride, uncertainty about employment prospects, or simply because they preferred to remain in the United States. Unlike the Mexican repatriation program, which was unofficial and did not, at least theoretically, bar repatriates from reentering the country, the Filipino repatriation act explicitly prohibited Filipino repatriates from returning to America. In a sense, Filipinos' lack of participation and support for the repatriation program constituted an act of resistance against efforts to expel them from the United States.

The Filipino problem that exploded on the West Coast during the late 1920s and early 1930s subsided by the late 1930s. As the economy improved, and especially after the start of World War II, rural whites in California moved to industrial jobs in urban areas. Also, young Filipino men became a little older, and in any event mixed marriages were less common after California amended its antimiscegenation law to include Filipinos. The generation of laboring men that had come to the United States during the 1920s settled, for the most part, into homosocial "Little Manilas" at the margins of Chinatown communities. Labor militancy among Filipino cannery and agricultural workers continued throughout the 1930s, and Filipino trade unionists became important figures in the Pacific Coast labor movement, affiliating with both AFL and CIO unions.[95]

World War II overshadowed the commonwealth status of the islands and the transition period to independence, as the Philippines and the United States were allies in a crucial theater of the Pacific war. The American liberation of the Philippines from Japan served to further ennoble the United States as the protector of the Filipino people. After the war, the Philippines achieved full independence, and the United States, in recognition of the role Filipinos played in the war, made Filipinos eligible to naturalized citizenship.[96]

Yet, even as Filipinos remaining in the United States carved out a place in the lower ranks of the working class and in small middle-class enclaves, they seemed to return to a state of invisibility. If the repatriation program had limited numerical success, the cultural impact of the project—and the broader movement for decolonization and exclusion within which it was embedded—was more far-reaching. It restored benevolent assimilation to the status of myth, disembodied and abstracted from its putative beneficiaries. It was as though the entire experience of Filipino migration during the first half of the century was willfully forgotten by a public determined to erase the colonial past from the American imagination.

Chapter Four

Braceros, "Wetbacks," and the National Boundaries of Class

Let us go to the United States
To earn good salaries,
Because the Big-Footed people
Need workers
   —*Mexican corrido*, "Advice to the Northerners"[1]

He no gotta country, he no gotta flag
He no gotta voice
all got is the han'
To work like the burro; he no gotta lan' . . .
—AMÉRICO PAREDES[2]

IN 1958 the U.S. Supreme Court upheld the government's revocation of Clemente Martínez Pérez's citizenship. Martínez, who was born in El Paso, Texas, and therefore an American citizen by native birth, lost his citizenship because he had voted in an election in Mexico and failed to report for U.S. military service during World War II, both of which acts were grounds for citizenship revocation under the Nationality Act of 1940.[3] Dissenting in the case, Chief Justice Earl Warren wrote, "Citizenship *is* man's basic right, because it is nothing less than the right to have rights." But, it would not be until 1967, during the rights revolution in law, that the Supreme Court would rule that citizenship was inviolable and not subject to compulsory revocation by the state.[4]

Clemente Martínez's case is of interest not only because it is part of the history of legal conflict over the boundaries and terms of American citizenship.[5] It also opens a window on the heterogeneous and transnational character of the Mexican/American political subject. Martínez was a U.S. citizen, but not only had he voted in a Mexican election, suggesting an assumption of Mexican citizenship (although there is no evidence that he naturalized as a Mexican citizen), he also inhabited additional legal-status categories as a *bracero*, that is, a Mexican national contracted to work in the United States, and an illegal alien.

Born in 1909 in El Paso, Martínez was taken back to Mexico by his parents in 1919 or 1920. He married and had children and lived in Mexico without interruption until 1943. During World War II Martínez entered the United States twice, as a Mexican-national contract worker under the wartime Migrant Labor Agreement between the United States and Mexico, commonly known as the bracero program. On both occasions he worked as a railroad laborer and returned to Mexico upon the completion of his contract. In 1947 Martínez tried to enter the United States as a U.S. citizen, claiming his birth in Texas, but because he admitted to avoiding military service and voting in a Mexican election, the INS excluded him on grounds that he had expatriated himself. In 1952 he entered the United States, this time claiming he was a Mexican national in order to get a berth as an agricultural worker in the bracero program. A year later, in San Francisco, the INS ordered Martínez deported on grounds that he was an "undesirable alien." From the Court's recounting of his case, Martínez had "surrendered himself" to immigration authorities.[6] This suggests that he was not a typical bracero who "skipped" his contract and was subsequently apprehended by the INS, but that he had perhaps deliberately presented himself to the INS in order to get a hearing, hoping to regain his U.S. citizenship. He might have planned to bring his family to the United States to join him. But if that were the case, his strategy backfired. A federal court rejected Martínez's claim that he could not be deported because he was a native-born citizen of the United States, ruling that he was not a citizen.[7] With the outcome of the Supreme Court's ruling, Martínez was deported to Mexico, even though he never actually possessed legal status as a Mexican citizen, notwithstanding his three-time participation in the bracero program.[8]

Clemente Martínez's career and shifting fortunes as an American citizen, a Mexican bracero worker, an illegal alien, and a deported Mexican national might be read as a small treatise on the hybrid and ambiguous legal identities of ethnic Mexicans living in the border region. These identities were shaped and reshaped as they were buffeted between the transnational social realities of cross-border migration, life, and work, and the legal demands of nation-states, which resist transnational experiences. Martínez's story also suggests that citizenship was both an abstract concept imposed from above by the state and a utilitarian instrument of migrant agency.

This chapter examines the legal production and state policing of a transnational Mexican labor force during the middle decades of the twentieth century, which formed the context of Clemente Martínez's story. It argues that immigration law and practices were central in shaping the modern political economy of the Southwest, one based on commercial agriculture, migratory farm labor, and the exclusion of Mexican migrants and Mexican Americans from the mainstream of American society. In particular, immigration policies helped create a Mexican migratory agricultural proletariat, a racialized, transnational workforce comprising various legal status categories across the U.S.-Mexico boundary—Mexican Americans, legal immigrants, undocumented migrants, and imported contract workers (braceros)—but which, as a whole, remained external to conventional definitions of the American working class and national body. I argue that that this transnational Mexican labor force, and especially its bracero and "wetback" constituents, constituted a kind of "imported colonialism" that was a legacy of the nineteenth-century American conquest of Mexico's northern territories. Modern, imported colonialism produced new social relations based on the subordination of racialized foreign bodies who worked in the United States but who remained excluded from the polity by both law and by social custom. I do not mean to suggest a formal structure or model of colonialism in the classical sense. Rather, imported colonialism is better described as a de facto socio-legal condition embedded in formally noncolonial relationships and spaces, in which free citizens of Mexico, an independent nation-state, voluntarily contracted to putatively free, waged labor, within the United States proper.

The chapter first discusses the formation of the Mexican migratory agricultural workforce from the 1920s to World War II. It then discusses the bracero program (1942–1964), America's largest experiment with a "guest worker program," today's euphemism for the federally sponsored importation of contract labor. Third, I discuss the problem of illegal immigration, the so-called wetback problem that emerged simultaneously, and in intimate relationship with, the bracero program, and the enforcement measures taken by the INS. Finally, the chapter examines the liberal critique of bracero and wetback labor by Mexican American civil rights groups and organized labor, and considers how the opposition was shaped and limited by its own understandings of and commitments to nation-state boundaries.

The Creation of the Mexican Agricultural Proletariat in the United States

From the turn of the century to World War I, labor flowed more or less freely from Mexico into the United States. Mexican workers provided the human labor power for the region's agricultural revolution and laid the infrastructure for the modern Southwest's economy: they laid railroad tracks that connected the region to the national market, cleared ranch lands for farming, and dug irrigation canals.[9] By 1914 Mexicans had become a noticeable presence in the burgeoning agricultural regions of south Texas and California.[10] Agricultural production in the Southwest expanded rapidly after World War I. By 1929 California, Arizona, and Texas accounted for 47 percent of the nation's large-scale cotton farms, and California alone contained 37 percent of all the large-scale farms in the United States.[11] Between 1920

4.1 Mexican Americans and immigrants cleared land in Texas during the 1910s and 1920s, making way for large-scale industrial-agricultural production. (By permission of the Robert Runyon Photograph Collection, E/VN03435, Center for American History, University of Texas at Austin.)

and 1930 the population of south Texas doubled, to 322,000, and the California farm labor force grew to some 200,000. The ethnic Mexican population in the United States more than doubled during the same decade, to over 1.4 million.[12]

More important than quantitative growth was a structural transformation of agriculture and the farm labor market. In Texas the mode of farming shifted from small- and medium-sized, family-owned and operated farms and sharecropping to large farms owned by banks, lawyers, and merchant investors. Moreover, the organization of the labor force shifted. Mexicans who entered south Texas in the 1900s and 1910s could still find year-round employment on farms and ranches, which still carried the marks of the traditional *patrón-peon* relationship. Others settled in small rural hamlets and began to raise families in the United States, even as they continued to travel frequently to Mexico. In the 1920s, however, the agricultural labor market assumed a distinctive migratory character. Migrant streams of landless laborers, including families, now followed the seasons of cotton, fruit, and vegetable crops on a year-long search for work at wages as low as $1.50 a day. The shift overwhelmed and displaced older patterns of work and settlement. The migratory agricultural workforce drew large numbers of new immigrants from Mexico—an average of 62,000 legal and an estimated 100,000 undocumented entries a year during the 1920s[13]—and swept more established immigrants and Mexican Americans into its embrace as well. Mexican Americans, old immigrants, and new immigrants alike worked the two major intrastate migrant streams in Texas and California; at the same time, smaller streams followed the cotton crops in Arizona and New Mexico, and reached northward to the sugar-beet fields of Colorado, Michigan, and Montana.[14]

The formation of the migratory agricultural workforce was perhaps the central element in the broader process of modern Mexican racial formation in the United States. Agribusiness desired large numbers of Mexican laborers, but the economic and social segregation and isolation of Mexicans was necessary to insure continued Euro-American control and domination. A settled resident workforce would have encouraged both labor organization and more stable communities, and all that they imply—higher wages, education, political participation, growth of a middle class. Such trends were not, in fact, entirely absent in the Southwest. Mexican American communities were established in Los Angeles and El Paso in the early decades of the century. But the structure of the agricultural labor market that emerged in the 1920s mitigated such development.[15]

Immigration policy and practices powerfully influenced the economic and spatial reorganization of the Southwest. Whereas before World War I the absence of a practical border policy bespoke frontier-like qualities like expansiveness, possibility, and lawlessness, by the 1920s the frontier gave way to a new spatiality marked by large commercial farms and hardened borders.[16] As discussed in chapter 2, restrictive policies created Mexican illegal aliens—migrants who were "undocumented" because they crossed the border without going through formal entry and inspection and therefore lacked the requisite papers: visas, head-tax receipts, border-crossing cards, inspection certificates, bathing certificates, and the like. Moreover, the new emphasis on formal status and the complexity of the deportation statutes generated confusion in an area long characterized by informal crossings. The possibility of sweeps, detainment, interrogation, and deportation was ubiquitous. It spread apprehension among Mexicans and loomed as perhaps the single greatest indication that Mexicans did not belong. Thus, even when deportations created labor shortages and drove up wages or temporarily disrupted production, restrictive immigration policies ultimately served the interests of agribusiness by creating a vulnerable "alien" workforce.

Euro-Americans perceived Mexicans as foreigners even though the majority of the Anglos themselves had also migrated to the Southwest during the same period. "Foreignness" was a racialized concept that adhered to all Mexicans, including those born in the United States, and carried the opprobrium of illegitimacy and inferiority. American citizenship, whether by native-birth or by naturalization, accrued few benefits. Throughout the Southwest, and especially in Texas, all Mexicans suffered from a system of segregation that mimicked the Jim Crow practices of the South. Mexican Americans and immigrants alike lived in segregated *colonías*, were denied service in restaurants and drug stores that were patronized by whites, and were seated in separate sections in movie theaters. In Texas, poll taxes and, in some south Texas counties, all-white primaries effectively kept Mexican Americans outside the polity.[17]

The construction of "Mexican" into a one-dimensional "commodity function and utility" devalued nearly everything that held meaning to Mexicans—the individual self, the family, culture, and political experience. Mexican workers coming to the United States were not, in fact, all unskilled and unschooled. Quite a few had experience in mining and farming; many had participated in the Mexican Revolution or in Mexican trade unions. Moreover, the injection of foreignness into the commodity-identity rendered Mexican labor *disposable*, in addition to being cheap. Equating Mexican culture with seasonal stoop labor was central to creating a negative referent, making Mexicans, as anthropologist Carlos Vélez-Ibáñez has described, "not only strangers in their own land but strangers to themselves."[18]

The creation of the Mexican migrant farm workforce might be understood as a modern solution to an old colonial problem. Since the seventeenth century, labor shortages loomed large in Euro-American colonial projects, whether the extraction of raw materials or the production of cash crops. Colonized native populations typically either numbered too few to meet the labor needs of colonial production (having been decimated by wars of conquest or disease) or proved too intractable to provide a stable workforce. Thus colonialists resorted either to the enslavement of natives, as in the Spanish conquest of the Americas, or to imported labor, including slaves, coolies, and convicts, as in the Anglo-American tradition. In the nineteenth century, imported colonial labor was characteristically racialized and unfree, as in the case of Asian Indian coolies sent to the English sugar colonies after the abolition of slavery. Imported colonial labor occupied a transitional site between chattel slavery and free labor. Comprising illegitimate subjects outside the polity (colored races displaced from other colonial spaces or, in other cases, convicts), imported bound-labor appeared acceptable during a time when free labor triumphed in the Anglo-American world as the hallmark of liberal citizenship.

Mexican migrant labor was, similarly, constructed as an imported workforce, which Euro-Americans defined and situated wholly in terms of the latter's labor needs. Casting Mexicans as foreign *distanced* them both from Euro-Americans culturally and from the Southwest as a spatial referent: it stripped Mexicans of the claim of belonging that they had had as natives, even as conquered natives. That is also why segregated communities formed in tandem with the reorganization of the labor force. The act of distancing was one way by which the "other" was constructed, out of what Tzvetan Todorov called the failure (or refusal) to identify the self in the other. It differed from the colonial stance toward native subjects, in which the other is a ward to be converted, civilized, and otherwise remolded in the colonialist's image. No such sense of responsibility inhered in the colonialists' relationship to imported labor.[19]

At the same time, Mexican labor differed from colonial imported labor in several important respects. In the 1920s Mexican labor was not unfree but free, waged labor. The destruction of semifeudal relationships of mutual obligation on the ranches and the shift to wage labor was, in fact, necessary to create the agricultural proletariat that modern agribusiness needed. Economic relations between absentee owners and migrant laborers were impersonal. Said one grower: "The relations between Mexican laborers and American employers are fine, and are regulated under economic, not personal[,] pressure."[20]

The modern economic relationship was a double-edged sword, however, which made a complete realization of imported colonial labor difficult. Commercial agriculture required seasonal wage-labor, but that also meant that the market determined wages and that Mexicans derived a certain leverage from their status as waged workers. To be sure, an overabundance of labor kept wages down, but the growers' dependence upon Mexican labor also gave workers some room to negotiate. A potato farmer in Colorado said, "First they [Mexicans] worked by the sack. Then they wanted a contact by the acre. The rascals struck for their own rates."[21] Spontaneous strikes for improved wages broke out during the 1920s and 1930s in south Texas and southern California. Farmers complained that "they will all sit down in the field, and not work if they hear somebody is paying a couple of cents more." After investigating a labor strike in the Imperial Valley in 1928, federal officials concluded that Mexican workers were neither "docile" nor "contented." Rather, investigators said, "many [Mexicans] do not favor any peonage attitude toward their race."[22]

Moreover, as free labor, Mexican workers exercised the right to quit. The potato farmer continued, "They will quit a job if they don't like the treatment even if they haven't food for the day and no other job in sight." A Texas onion grower said similarly, "The Mexicans' only protection is that they are the only labor available and you can't treat them too badly and hold them."[23]

Freedom of movement operated both at the level of the individual

4.2 Contrary to conventional belief, Mexican agricultural workers settled and raised families in the United States. This family lived in a three-room house without indoor plumbing in San Diego, 1941. (Courtesy of Russell Lee, FSA/OWI Collection, Library of Congress.)

worker's freedom to quit and at the level of collective migration and settlement. Through the 1930s Mexican migration comprised families: women worked in the fields, along with men, as well as in packinghouses and canneries. The longer Mexicans stayed in the United States the more they tended to move northward, as wages rose in direct relationship to distance from the border. The migrant labor force that worked sugar beets in Colorado comprised older immigrant and Mexican American families from New Mexico and Texas; sugar companies in Michigan and Ohio recruited workers from San Antonio every year, almost all of whom were Texas-born Mexican Americans.[24] From there, some migrated to Detroit, Chicago, and other northern cities, where they filled a demand for industrial labor created by the cutoff in European immigration. Moreover, increasing numbers of Mexican immigrants settled permanently, in both cities and rural towns, even as they continued to participate in seasonal migrant agricultural work.[25]

The economic structure of migratory wage-labor produced other contradictions, as well. Growers wanted not only seasonal workers. They also wanted a labor *surplus* so they could obtain workers on demand, at low wages, and in plentiful supply to pick their crops early and quickly. Herein lay the truth of the growers' perennial complaint of labor shortages. The rush to market not only encouraged an oversupply of labor, which depressed wages, but also flooded the market, which depressed prices. These trends were the ruin of Anglo small farmers and sharecroppers. A large onion grower admitted, "There is no scarcity of labor here. The little man is being crowded off the map. The market demands 100 cars of onions a day and we ship 300. The big farmer beats the little fellow because he ships quicker. The present situation will ruin us. The farmers would be better off here if we did not have so many Mexicans." Many farmers compared their plight to that of small white farmers in the South "injured by the Negro slavery system before the Civil War."[26]

These tensions and contradictions lent instability to the agricultural industry and frustrated growers' efforts to secure a cheap, disposable labor force entirely under their control. Labor militancy and permanent settlement in particular belied important assumptions that Euro-Americans held about Mexican workers and upon which agribusiness relied—that they were tractable and returned to Mexico after each season.

The repatriation of over 400,000 Mexicans and Mexican Americans during the early 1930s created a temporary labor shortage that agricultural workers used to their advantage to press for higher wages. Throughout the 1930s labor unrest attended southwestern and western agriculture. In 1933 and 1934 in Texas, Mexican onion setters and shed workers in the Lower Rio Grande Valley and pecan shellers in San Antonio organized unions and strikes. Strikes were especially prevalent in California. In 1933 a wave of strikes involved two-thirds of the value of the state's crops.[27]

In 1933 and 1934, Mexican workers in the Imperial and San Joaquin Valleys staged over fifty strikes, many of which were attended by vigilante violence. The 1933 strike of 18,000 cotton pickers in the San Joaquin Valley saw three workers killed and thirteen wounded in confrontations involving hundreds of strikers and vigilantes. Cotton pickers in Kern County struck in 1938 and again in 1939. Paul Taylor and Clark Kerr noted there were more than forty agricultural labor unions affiliated with the American Federation of Labor, mostly in the South and Southwest, in addition to the left-wing Cannery and Agricultural Workers Union. The Berkeley economists said the "uprisings" on the farms were the inevitable result of the "rise of intensive agriculture [that] has given us, almost unnoticed, a rural proletariat." They asked, "Is it a matter for surprise that proletarians strike?"[28]

In general, New Deal farm policy did not support agricultural workers. The central farm program of the New Deal, the Agricultural Adjustment Act (AAA), assisted the largest farmers and encouraged the further consolidation of landholdings through programs that accelerated mechanization and paid benefits to farmers to restrict production.[29] The political calculus in Congress, moreover, led northern Democrats to acquiesce to conservative southerners' demands to exclude agricultural workers from social and labor legislation. Agricultural workers were thus not covered by the National Labor Relations Act of 1935, the Social Security Act of 1935, or the Fair Labor Standards Act of 1938, which recognized the right to organize and bargain collectively, provided for social insurance for the elderly, and established a minimum wage, respectively. The exclusion of the agricultural proletariat from the legal definition of "worker," at least within the meaning of basic federal labor and social welfare legislation, was perhaps the single greatest guarantee that agribusiness would continue to have free rein over its workforce and that the South and Southwest would remain racialized, colonial-type backwaters of the nation.

One small program of the AAA, the Resettlement Administration, and its successor, the Farm Security Administration (FSA), attempted to address the plight of migrant farmworkers by constructing labor camps for migratory workers. The camps aimed to provide "minimum facilities" for health and safety, hot and cold running water, laundry, recreational activities, democratically elected self-government, health care, and liaisons with local schools. Ironically, Mexicans and Filipinos, the foundational agricultural workforce with a compelling interest and desire to raise agricultural labor standards, remained virtually untouched by the FSA camp experiment. Mexican workers tended to live in rural colonías, and Filipinos lived almost entirely in labor camps operated by their co-ethnics.[30] In the main, Dust Bowl refugees and transients populated the FSA camps. In some respects they were the neediest migrants because they had no local communities of their own. But they also had few stakes in the long-term prospects of agricultural wage-labor. Formerly independent farmers and tenants, they carried a conservative reputation and moved to urban areas when industrial war-production jobs became available in the late 1930s. In fact, the FSA chose white migrants for its social experiments in part because they presented a conservative, docile image to the public. Dorothea Lange's iconic photograph "Migrant Mother" delivered the FSA's preferred message that migratory workers were white, pathetically poor, singular, and passive.[31]

New Deal policy did little, then, to resolve the problems of agricultural labor. Against the backdrop of instability and conflict, growers increasingly called for the government to import Mexican nationals as contract laborers.

In 1936 growers in the Texas counties of Mercedes and Welasco pressed the state labor commissioner, their representatives in Congress, and the Department of Labor to declare an emergency labor situation. However, the Immigration Service reported that 50 percent of the cotton crop had already been picked and that no emergency existed. The director of the WPA in Texas stated flatly that labor existed if "reasonable wages" were paid.[32]

Again in 1937 the INS rejected growers' claims of a labor shortage, pointing out that cotton wages were higher in Arizona and even in Mexico than in Texas. In 1941 and 1942 growers of cotton, sugar beets, fruits, and vegetables flooded the Department of Labor with formal applications requesting exemption from the immigration laws prohibiting foreign contract labor. Although a labor shortage did exist in the nation, caused by the enlistment of 15 million men and women into the armed forces and the demands of war production, the INS continued to report that no emergency labor situation existed in southwestern agriculture. In Texas the WPA population numbered 32,000, but growers were willing to pay only half the rate of WPA wages, which were 40¢ an hour. The Bay City, Texas, Chamber of Commerce "flatly declined to even consider" hiring 3,000 unemployed laborers congregated in federal camps at Harlingen and Raymondville. In fact, growers did not want Mexican American workers. Whereas during the 1920s white Americans typically viewed Mexican Americans and immigrants without distinction, growers concluded from the labor unrest of the late 1920s and early 1930s that Mexican Americans demanded too much.[33]

While field reports from INS, Employment Service, and WPA district offices argued that the labor shortage was artificial, the resolve of their superiors in Washington began to collapse under pressure from members of Congress representing southwestern districts. On April 30 and May 4, 1942, the Department of Agriculture convened an interagency conference with the Farm Security Administration, the INS, the Department of Labor Employment Service, the Board of Economic Welfare, the Bureau of Inter-American Affairs of the State Department, the Office of Agricultural War Relations, the House Committee on National Defense Migration, the War Relocation Authority, and the War Production Board. The putative agricultural labor shortage trumped the Labor Department's concerns over wages and standards and the INS's warning that imported laborers would not return to Mexico upon the completion of their contracts. Preparations were made. In late May the U.S. Employment Service (USES) certified the need to import six thousand workers as contract laborers.[34]

The decision to use foreign contract labor was a momentous break with past policy and practice. The United States had outlawed foreign contract labor in 1885.[35] Since the time of the Civil War, Americans had believed that contract labor, like slavery, was the antithesis of free labor, upon which democracy depended. Like the slave, the contract laborer was not free to bargain over wages or working conditions, either individually or collectively. He did not have the right to choose his employer or to quit. Although, by the late nineteenth century, industry and monopoly had eroded the independence of craft workers and undermined the attributes of free labor, the incipient trade-union movement drew an absolute line against contract labor because the latter was unambiguously unfree. Americans' rejection of contract labor was so embedded in the national political culture that its practice in Hawai'i was terminated in 1898, when the United States formally annexed the islands. Nor was contract labor ever instituted in the Philippines or Puerto Rico, which in the same year came under American colonial rule.[36] That decades later, and in the mainland United States, Americans would turn to a colonial labor practice that they had rejected in their own colonies is explicable only in part as a response to a perceived war emergency. It was also an expression of the legacies of slavery and conquest. The old plantation class and its modern cousins in agribusiness in the South and Southwest succeeded in molding the modern agricultural workforce into modes of racialized labor that had more in common with nineteenth-century colonial practices than with modern industrial relations. As African American sharecroppers and tenant farmers in the South continued to bear the marks of race slavery, Mexican workers in the Southwest and California were racialized as a foreign people, an "alien race" not legitimately present or intended for inclusion in the polity.

The Bracero Program

The bracero program was not the only instance of imported contract-labor in the United States in the mid-twentieth century. During the same period, contract workers came from the British West Indies to perform farm labor in the Southeast and along the Atlantic seaboard. Puerto Ricans, who were American citizens, also migrated under the island government's auspices for migratory seasonal agricultural work in the northeastern United States. But the bracero program was by far the largest project, involving some 4.6 million workers.[37]

Mexico agreed to the program despite its concern that its nationals were treated poorly in the United States during the First World War. The project was proposed as an alternative to Mexican participation in the Allied armed forces. Some scholars have also argued that Mexico had come to the conclusion that if it could not prevent mass emigration, it would try to regulate or manage it. The United States admitted the first braceros on September 27, 1942, in time for the sugar-beet harvest. Under the wartime agreement (which was extended to 1947),[38] the United States imported some 215,000 Mexican nationals to work as agricultural laborers and 75,000 to work for the Southern Pacific and some twenty other railroads for maintenance of way and track work.[39]

From 1948 to 1964, the United States imported, on average, 200,000 braceros a year. Braceros worked in twenty-six states, the vast majority in California, Texas, and other southwestern states, and dominated crops such as cotton, citrus fruits, melons, lettuce, and truck vegetables. Only 2 percent of American farm operators employed braceros, but they were the wealthiest ones, the largest "industrial" farms. Braceros and other contracted foreign workers comprised a relatively small sector of the total U.S. farm labor force of 10 million, about 2 percent, but they were one-fifth of all migratory waged farmworkers.[40]

During the 1950s government economists spoke of the nation's "long-term dependence on foreign agricultural labor," citing the sectoral shift from small, tenant-operated farms to large commercial farms and the latter's need for large numbers of "off farm" temporary workers. Postwar liberals did not view foreign contract labor as a form of imported colonialism but, rather, as a statist solution to various economic and political problems. The Truman commission on migratory farm labor argued that government-sponsored contract labor would eliminate illegal migration, bring order to the farm labor market, and protect foreign nationals from abuse. The belief that braceros were the "legal successors to the illegal 'wetbacks'" was particularly widespread.[41]

In fact, the continued use of imported contract-labor long after the end of the war signaled the consolidation of industrial farm production as a low-wage enterprise beyond the reach of federal labor standards and workers' rights. In 1955 farm wages in the United States were 36.1 percent of manufacturing wages, a decline from 47.9 percent in 1946. That downward trend in large part resulted from the semicolonial use of foreign contract and undocumented laborers—workers who had no legal standing in the society in which they worked.[42]

Two elements born of wartime politics—direct contracting of foreign labor by the U.S. government and binational sponsorship and management—defined the wartime program and continued to undergird the program's myriad contradictions and conflicts after the war. In 1951 Congress passed Public Law 78, which, along with a diplomatic agreement negotiated with Mexico known as the Migrant Labor Agreement, governed the program until its completion in 1964. To facilitate the importation of Mexican agricultural labor, Congress lifted the ban against contract labor that had been law since 1885.[43]

The Migrant Labor Agreement stipulated that Mexican contract workers would not be used to replace domestic workers or to depress domestic farm wages. Braceros were guaranteed transportation, housing, food, and repatriation, and were exempt from American military service. Wages were set at the domestic prevailing rate and in no case less than an established minimum (30¢ an hour during the war and 50¢ throughout most of the 1950s), and workers were guaranteed work for 75 percent of the contract period. These were elementary provisions, but some growers complained that they were excessive, even "socialistic," pointing out that such guarantees and benefits were not available to domestic agricultural workers.[44]

The agreement also provided that braceros would not be subject to discrimination, such as exclusion from "white" areas of segregated public accommodations. Mexico had unilateral power to blacklist states, counties, or employers that were found to discriminate, until that power was curbed in 1954. At Mexico's insistence, recruitment centers were situated in the interior of Mexico. Mexico believed this was essential to its ability to control emigration. It worried that border recruitment would encourage a labor depletion from northern Mexican states, deny the privilege of participation to its citizens in other regions, and draw migration to the border for illegal entry into the United States.[45]

The agreement stipulated that reports of contract violations would be jointly investigated and determined by representatives of both governments. A provision added in 1951 gave braceros the right to select representatives from their own ranks to "communicate" with employers, but not for purposes of collective bargaining or altering the terms of the contract.

Finally, the international agreement designated the two parties to each "Individual Work Contract" as the individual Mexican national as the "worker" and the United States government as the "employer." These terms reflected Mexico's desire to protect each national it sent abroad. It worried that Americans would not respect each bracero as an individual person. (Indeed, there were some growers who wanted to merely contract large numbers of braceros without bothering to take their names.) Mexico also knew it had no leverage with individual employers. Thus the federal government assumed the role of labor contractor, responsible for contracting and delivering agricultural workers to American growers.[46] The Farm Security Administration of the Department of Agriculture served as the lead administrative agency for the program until 1949, when that responsibility transferred to the U.S. Employment Service in the Department of Labor. The INS was responsible for admitting and repatriating workers.

In May 1955, forty-four men from Aguacaliente de Garate, a small town in the state of Sinaloa, Mexico, entered the United States as contract agricultural workers. Earlier that spring, the bracero program had been the talk of Aguacaliente. Ricardo Velasquez recalled first hearing about it in a radio broadcast from Mazatlán; others read about it in the newspaper. As news spread quickly throughout town, the mayor circulated a paper for those interested to enlist. Many were family men; Velasquez, for example, was thirty-four years old, married, and had five children. As farm laborers, they earned 8 pesos a day, or 65¢ (U.S.). They heard that wages for braceros in Texas were 50¢ an hour and thus regarded the program as an opportunity to "make a lot of money."[47]

Their migration to Texas was neither easy nor cost free. First, the men had to pay for one of their group to take the papers to the state capital, Culiacan, and then to Mexico City for approval. This may have included the payment of *mordidas*, or bribes, to officials. They then journeyed to the contracting center in Monterrey, Nuevo Leon, where they waited for ten days before being processed. The cost for the initial authorization and subsistence in Monterrey to each man was 300 to 400 pesos. After finally being processed at Monterrey, Velasquez and five other Aguacaliente men were taken to a depot, fed lunch, and put on a train. They arrived at Reynosa, near the border, at 4:00 A.M., and then transferred to the U.S.-INS reception center at Hidalgo, Texas. There, they received breakfast and a routing slip, with which they proceeded, along with hundreds of other men, to be interviewed, photographed, and fingerprinted. They received a brief medical examination, a chest x-ray to detect tuberculosis, and fumigation for hoof-and-mouth disease. The INS reception centers processed from several hundred to several thousand incoming braceros a day. The maximum pace was set by the capacity of the x-ray machines, which each handled 175 braceros per hour.[48] The operation assumed the character of "batch processing" that alienated individual braceros and also strained INS personnel, who complained of a shortage of staff and equipment, long hours, temperatures from 108 to 117 degrees, and a "stench of sweaty, unwashed human bodies."[49]

The six men left Hidalgo at noon, each with a work card and a contract with the Valley Farmers Cooperative Harvesting Association. The contract provided for employment in Hidalgo, Willacy, or Starr County, from May 11 to June 8, 1955, as "harvest hands, Veg.—50¢ per hour" and, for "sustenance," a daily payment of $1.15 for provisions to furnish their own meals.[50]

An employee of the Valley Farmers Cooperative drove the men to a tomato- and melon-packing shed in Edinburg, Texas, and later that evening to a house that Velasquez said "didn't have a lock on it." Aureliano Ocampo said it was "in poor condition and very dirty. We didn't have a chance to clean it as we arrived after dark." The foreman, Eduardo Morales, delivered $3.19 worth of groceries for the six men. Ocampo added, "We didn't sleep good because of the condition of the cots."[51]

The next morning they traveled for two hours to the field in a truck with six or seven other men, who were "specials"—formerly undocumented workers who had been legalized as braceros. These men told the new arrivals that wages in the valley were 30¢ an hour, corroborating what the latter had heard from compatriots in Reynosa. When they arrived at the melon field,

4.3 Braceros contracted to work in the United States are processed for admission, 1957. (Courtesy of U.S.-INS Historical Reference Library.)

the foreman Morales gave each man a sack and showed them how to wear it over the shoulder. Pedro Cardozo recalled that Morales then told them that "he paid only thirty cents an hour, no more, and that if we did not want to work for thirty cents that we could leave."[52]

Like the six men from Aguacaliente, many braceros were assigned to employers who paid them wages and subsistence less than the amount stipulated in the contract. In general, work was hard and conditions were poor. But, a bracero contract promised a greater income than one could earn in rural Mexico. Braceros were therefore willing to endure difficult conditions for a short period of time in order to get their families ahead. During the 1950s braceros sent some $30 million a year home in remittance, making the bracero program the third largest "industry" in Mexico. However, many braceros did not earn enough to truly help their families, on account of debts they incurred to pay a mordida or, on occasion, from gambling in the labor camps.[53]

In practice, the bracero program fell far short of the terms stipulated in the Migrant Labor Agreement. The fundamental principle of the program, that braceros would not be used to undermine domestic wages or to displace domestic workers, was a fiction. The Department of Labor determined the "prevailing wage" by calling local meetings of growers, grower associations, and farm organizations. It made no independent investigation of the labor market and took no input from domestic workers, labor unions, or independent organizations. The prevailing wage was thus whatever growers decided it to be. The effect of imported contract labor on domestic wages was unmistakable. Over a ten-year period, the wages for tomato-picking in the San Joaquin Valley in California dropped 40 percent, during which time the proportion of braceros hired to pick them rose by 90 percent. Between 1953 and 1959, overall farm wages in the nation rose by 14 percent but remained frozen in areas that used bracero labor.[54]

The displacement of domestic farmworkers was both specific and deliberate, as in cases where domestic workers were fired and replaced with braceros, and generalized, as evidenced in the wholesale outmigration of Mexican American workers from south Texas each year during the harvest period. Over ten thousand union jobs in the Imperial and Salinas Valleys in California and in Arizona were lost in 1953 when growers abolished the packing sheds and moved packing operations to the field, where the work was done by braceros.[55]

Braceros had the right to file complaints if they believed the employer violated the contract. Data for the entire program are incomplete, but available evidence suggests that workers registered upwards of several thousand formal complaints a year. According to a Bureau of Employment Service official, braceros filed some eleven thousand formal complaints from 1954 to 1956, involving one to several hundred workers in each instance. Violations were found in roughly half the cases. Underpayment was the most common cause for complaint. Others concerned housing, subsistence, illegal deductions, threats, mistreatment, and occupational risks.[56]

The complaints made by braceros provide evidence of the working and living conditions experienced by many workers. Of course, not all employers violated the contract and the number of formal complaints was small compared to the total number of contracts—perhaps 5 percent. But contemporary observers consistently reported widespread contract violations and noted that many braceros were afraid to complain. Moreover, the labor-intensive character of commercial agriculture made the industry sensitive to wage competition, so that efforts by some growers to cut labor costs easily spread to other employers. Bernando Blanco, the Mexican consul at McAllen, Texas, estimated that over 50 percent of the contract workers in the Lower Rio Grande Valley were underpaid. Blanco received six to seven complaints a day from braceros about wages; most commonly, employers made braceros sign blank receipts and paid them 30–35¢ an hour instead of the contract rate of 50¢ an hour.[57]

Housing violations were common. USES routinely found deficiencies in one-third to one-half of its housing inspections. Workers hated the food. They complained about poor quality, lack of variety, and scant servings. A committee of braceros contracted to the Sunkist camp at Escondido, California, visited the Mexican consul in San Diego to complain about "tacos served [to] them . . . in a state of decomposition" and of workers taking ill en masse.[58]

Rarely did the government terminate an employer's contract. Most violators merely received a warning. In 1956, for example, only 50 out of 1,631 employers determined to have violated the contract were removed from the program, about 3 percent. Termination seems to have been reserved for extreme cases involving physical abuse, as in the case of N. A. Dugan, a grower in Muleshoe, Texas, who struck Miguel de Jesus Castañeda in the face because he left the field to get a drink of water.[59]

Contract enforcement was lax in part because federal agencies lacked adequate resources to do the job. In southern California, where fifty thousand braceros worked, the Department of Labor had six enforcement officers on staff.[60] Perhaps more problematic was the department's decentralized monitoring system, which was grounded in the close relationship between local branches of state employment and farm-placement services and growers' associations. An internal investigation conducted by the Solicitor's Office of the Labor Department in 1959 found a widespread practice of compliance personnel accepting gratuities (crates of fruits and vegetables), clerical assistance, and other favors from association offices. The largest growers dominated the associations and, in a perverse use of power, disciplined small growers who complied with the contract by subjecting them to an "abnormal number of investigations." Mariano Arevalo quit his job as a federal compliance officer. "I got sick of it," he said. "Pressure was always applied by the growers and I was often instructed [by Labor Department superiors] to take it easy."[61]

In addition to providing evidence of work conditions, the record of complaints belies the conventional view held by contemporaries as well as by scholars today that braceros were docile or ignorant of the terms of their contracts.[62] Undoubtedly many braceros could not read the contract or the message from the minister of foreign relations, Manuel Tello, that came attached to each one. The "special introductory message" praised the braceros' "intention of working diligently and showing . . . the good qualities of our race and the prestige of our nationality." It urged them to "fulfill then all your obligations and demand also that the employers fulfill exactly all the clauses of the contract they have signed . . . and immediately advise the Mexican Consulate of violations and irregularities." But even though many braceros could not read or write, the entire process of recruitment and migration was a crucible they experienced collectively, and within that collective process knowledge was diffused by word of mouth through family and village networks. In an essay about a prototypical bracero, a journalist described Rafael Tamayo as having had "only three years of schooling," but stressed that "he is no fool. . . . [H]e is fairly well informed about the problems he faces before and after becoming a bracero. . . . He gets all this from talking to his friends who have already been in the program and returned [to Mexico]."[63]

On rare occasions braceros took direct action. For example, Mexican nationals who were contracted to a lettuce grower in the Imperial Valley went on strike in November 1942, protesting low wages and other contract violations. Police forced them back to work while others reportedly "escaped" back to Mexico. The Pirus Citrus Company in southern California reported that braceros contracted to them lost "from one to three hours [of work] every morning while they bickered for wage rates." The workers objected as a group to the piece-rate because although the majority earned between five and six dollars a day, "some of them, no matter how hard they tried, could only earn around three dollars a day."[64]

More often, braceros complained to the nearest Mexican consul. One employer indicated just how important the consuls' role was. The contract, he said, "is just a piece of paper. If we get along with the men and are able to satisfy them and they don't go to the Mexican consul and kick, we get by." Indeed, it seemed that during the bracero program the consuls were the only ones who could get American officials to intervene against employers who abused workers or otherwise violated the contract.[65]

The INS believed that the consuls made an "international incident" out of every complaint and created a high volume of work for U.S. investigators. In the early 1950s American officials accused the consuls of "constant interruptions" in the operation of the program, "arbitrarily fixing minimum wage rates," and "unilaterally" raising subsistence rates.[66] In the summer of 1952 Mexican consuls stationed at the El Paso reception center refused to contract braceros to central Texas at the rate of $2.00 per hundredweight (cwt) for picking cotton, the rate set by the Labor Department, and insisted instead on $2.50 per hundred weight, which they argued was the equivalent of the stipulated minimum wage of 50¢ an hour. Mexican consuls at Harlingen and Eagle Pass refused to certify contracts with less than $1.50 a day for subsistence. Disputes like these persisted throughout the early 1950s. Mexican officials insisted that their "consuls have the right to 'represent' braceros as similar to 'minor wards' and would not renounce this right." The Americans argued that the consuls did not "represent" braceros and were not "bargaining agents" for them.[67]

The issues were finally resolved in amendments made to the Migrant Labor Agreement in March 1954. Mexico succeeded on a number of specific remunerative matters—raising the daily rate of subsistence, increasing insurance payments for work-related injuries, and adding nonoccupational insurance and burial expenses. Mexico also won an agreement on principle that the prevailing wage would not be affected by the presence of illegal labor. More important, however, the United States prevailed on questions of procedure. Mexico conceded that contracting would not stop on account of disputes over interpretations. It relinquished its right to unilaterally blacklist employers or counties, although an employer could be blackballed if the two nations jointly determined discrimination or physical abuse. With these two concessions Mexico lost the only practical leverage it had over the determination of wages and the treatment of braceros. Mexico also agreed to a liberal policy for recontracting braceros at the border, which effectively undermined whatever ability Mexico had to control the process of emigration.[68]

Why did Mexico make these concessions? In the immediate context, Mexico was under tremendous pressure. In 1954 growers continued to use illegal labor as leverage to change the bracero program to their liking. They also demanded a termination of the bilateral agreement in favor of a unilateral program of procuring Mexican agricultural labor. Illegal emigration and unilateral contracting potentially meant a total loss of control for Mexico. More generally, the ruling party in Mexico had moved to the right during World War II. The growth during the war of a Mexican industrial class with ties to American business and the postwar status of the United States as a world superpower informed this ideological and practical shift, notwithstanding the continued nationalist rhetoric expressed by the Mexican state.

While some workers filed complaints, others showed their dissatisfaction by simply leaving the farms. Within one month of the first 1,800 braceros' arrival in the United States, the INS reported 103 workers missing and repatriated 165 others at their own request—a "failure" rate of 15 percent. Workers who left farms in Arkansas and were apprehended by the INS in Indiana in 1949 explained why they deserted their contracts: "I left because I had not made much money and lost a lot of time because of rain. The company did not furnish me meals." "We were promised room and board but had to pay for it." "We could not see how much cotton we picked because they would not let us weigh it ourselves or see how much it weighed." "We stayed in a shack, the roof leaked, and there were bugs all over." "I wanted to come see my sister Amilia."[69]

Some skips said they would "rather go back to being a wetback than be a bracero." Carlos Morales cited paying a $48 mordida to get a contract in Mexico, only to come to the United States to find terrible conditions and to be cheated of wages. "As a wetback, alone, safely across the border," he said, "I may find a farmer who needs one man. He will pay me honestly, I think. But as a bracero, I am only a number on a paycheck . . . and I am treated like a number . . . not like a man."[70]

Some braceros deserted in groups that comprised kinfolk or friends from the same hometown in Mexico. When the six men from Aguacaliente found out the rate for picking melons was 30¢ an hour, they talked it over and decided to refuse the work and to return home. They walked for five hours before they caught a bus to McAllen, where the INS apprehended them. The men told the INS they wanted to return to Mexico. As Pedro Cardozo said, "We had bad luck."[71]

Other skips tried to improve their luck by finding jobs at farms where conditions were better, or by making their way to cities, where there were higher-paying factory jobs. A former bracero explained that he had earned only $28 a week in farm wages but $27 for two days of work in a factory. Officials also complained of "labor hijackers," contractors from southern states who came at night and lured braceros away with false promises of better pay. In the border area, many braceros simply went home after they had earned what they wanted or when their contracts ended, without formally checking out with the INS.[72]

The data on skips are scattered but suggestive. In 1951 the INS estimated a desertion rate of 10 percent. A sample survey of employer-reported skips in thirteen states in 1953 revealed an overall skip rate of 4.4 percent, but with rates from 14 to 30 percent in some counties. During the mid-1950s officials estimated the desertion rate in the Lower Rio Grande Valley at 20 to 35 percent.[73] Skipping was especially common in areas like Stockton and Salinas, where the wage structure was under continuous dispute, and in the sugar-beet region, where growers paid according to piece-rates. An INS official complained, "The laborer has absolutely no responsibility except to do as his own desires dictate." Another believed that, as a class, the braceros were "defiant." The INS despaired that the problem could be solved. Apprehension, said one official, "is impossible on a case basis because . . . there is no indication where the alien may have gone after he leaves the authorized employer."[74]

By deserting their contracts, of course, legal workers became illegal aliens. They joined an even larger population of undocumented Mexican migrants living and working in the Southwest.

The "Wetback Invasion"

The bracero program was supposed to be a solution to illegal immigration, but in fact it generated more illegal immigration. It was perhaps ironic that this began during the war as an unintended consequence of Mexico's exclusion of Texas, Arkansas, and Missouri employers from the bracero program on grounds of race discrimination. Mexico objected to segregation practices in these states, which refused Mexicans admittance to "white only" areas of public accommodations, movie theaters, restaurants, and the like. Growers in

4.4 The Office of War Information described these cotton pickers in Texas during World War II as "Mexicans workers who are doing a good turn for their American neighbors." Because the wartime bracero program recruited only men and because Texas was excluded from the program, this couple had most likely entered Texas illegally. (Courtesy of Howard Hollem, FSA/OWI Collection, Library of Congress.)

those states, ineligible to use braceros, increasingly resorted to illegal labor during the 1940s. But more broadly than the wartime exclusions, the bracero program itself encouraged illegal migration. More Mexicans wanted to become braceros than the Mexican government had spaces for. Rural poverty remained the biggest "push" factor in emigration, legal and illegal. On the "pull" side, some growers—especially in border areas like the Imperial Valley of California and the Lower Rio Grande Valley of Texas—preferred recruiting informally near the border to the formal process and cost of interior recruitment. "Wetback" wages, which a contemporary said were "highly standardized," were 25¢ an hour in the immediate postwar period, roughly two-thirds the domestic (and the putative bracero) rate.[75] The recruitment and use of braceros and undocumented workers thus took place in tandem.

In the years immediately after the war the recruitment and employment of undocumented labor soared. According to a Texas official, "There have always been wetbacks in Texas, but they didn't become a national and international problem until the Spring of 1947." Observers noted that in ten years the border towns on both sides of the line had "mushroomed" due to illegal traffic.[76]

Critics associated "wetbacks" with "misery, disease, crime, and many other evils." An INS official repeated the conventional view that illegal aliens were by definition criminal: Because the "wetback" starts out by violating a law, he said, "it is easier and sometimes appears even more necessary for him to break other laws since he considers himself to be an outcast, even an outlaw."[77]

The district attorney of Imperial County, California, said "wetbacks" were "criminal types from Mexico," including "destitute females from Mexico [who] cross the line and are transported by wildcat taxis and trucks to the various ranches . . . for purposes of prostitution." The association of the illegal entry of women with prostitution was common but not grounded in fact. A contemporary researcher found that, in southern California, prostitutes who plied the cantinas were often local women whom braceros had promised to marry but left stranded with child. Ostracized by the community, they turned to prostitution in order to support themselves. Another group comprised "older women" who traveled from town to town. The association of prostitution with illegal immigration reflected the assumption that illegal migrants were by nature criminal. It also constituted an erasure of the wives of illegal migrant farm laborers, who often worked as domestics, out of public view.[78]

The construction of the "wetback" as a dangerous and criminal social pathogen fed the general racial stereotype "Mexican." A 1951 study by Lyle Saunders and Olen Leonard, conducted as part of a project sponsored by the Mexican American social scientist and civil rights advocate George I. Sánchez, stated, "No careful distinctions are made between illegal aliens and local citizens of Mexican descent. They are lumped together as 'Mexicans' and the characteristics that are observed among the wetbacks are by extension assigned to the local people." Wetbacks, said one official, were "superficially indistinguishable from Mexicans legally in the United States."[79]

In fact, undocumented migrants were part of a heterogeneous ethno-racial Mexican community in the southwestern United States. More precisely, they represented that generation of newcomers that exists in nearly all immigrant groups, which is distinguished by its concentration in low-waged jobs, its lack of acculturation, and, simultaneously, by its settlement and assimilation into the resident ethnic community. Saunders and Leonard observed "a certain amount of integration of the wetback and the local Spanish-speaking population." The new arrivals gravitated to the "Mexican section of town" and shared with settled residents "common language and cultural traits." The undocumented included families as well, another indicator of settlement. In 1947 a Texas official reported that many undocumented Mexicans came with families and enrolled their children in valley schools. In July 1954, when the INS apprehended thirty illegal aliens on five Texas farms, more than half were women and children. In other cases, Saunders and Leonard noted, undocumented male migrants "court[ed] or marr[ied] the daughter of a [local] Spanish-speaking family." Saunders and Leonard concluded, "The longer [the undocumented migrant] stays, the more he becomes like the groups he lives among."

As they settled, undocumented Mexicans got nonagricultural jobs as city and county laborers, as school janitors, and as construction workers. A resident of Mission, Texas, claimed that "wetbacks" worked in "all kind of jobs . . . [as] carpenters, breaklayers [sic], painters, and laborers, restaurants, sheds, drug stores, bakers, housemaids, shineeboys, all wetbacks."[80] For some, the passage of time also involved spatial distancing from the border. The INS believed northern California attracted "illegal entrants from the entire border due to work opportunities, high salaries, and a large indigenous Spanish-speaking population." An undocumented migrant in Chicago working in a butcher shop earned $2.25 an hour—an entire day's wages in the Lower Rio Grande Valley. The INS believed that as "wetbacks" moved farther from the border they were "more difficult to apprehend."[81]

At the same time, undocumented migrants often pursued transnational lives. Some undocumented workers maintained family households in Mexico and traveled illegally to work in the United States. An immigration inspector observed that some "cross the river early in the morning, work all day on a farm adjacent to the river, and return to their homes in the evening." Others commuted weekly, monthly, or seasonally.[82]

The process of integration of undocumented workers into the ethnic Mexican community in the 1950s was complicated by a third element, the braceros. In Texas and California many growers routinely employed both "wetbacks" and imported contract-workers, in addition to Mexican Americans, who worked as shed workers or foremen. At times growers treated illegal and bracero workers equally; in other cases, undocumented workers earned less than braceros and had inferior living conditions. For example, Miguel Molina, who waded across the river near Brownsville, planted cotton seed for $2 a day. He slept in a shed with a canvas covering and ate food brought to him by a worker named Pancho, one of three braceros employed at the ranch.[83]

Braceros and "wetbacks" were sometimes members of the same family. Some illegal migrants were male relatives whom braceros recruited for their employers. José and Ricardo Adame were brothers who worked for the Gray Farm in Los Fresnos, Texas; José was a bracero and Ricardo was undocumented. Other braceros arranged for their conjugal families to migrate illegally so they could live and work together in the United States. In August 1955 the INS in southern California reported six cases of braceros "smuggling family" into the El Centro area. In other cases, braceros courted and married local Mexican American women. Braceros learned they could become legalized if they established families in the United States and some waited the requisite seven years to apply for a suspension of deportation and adjustment of their status to permanent resident. It is impossible to know how many braceros remained in the United States, although clearly the number was small relative to the total bracero population. But even if uncommon, the practice underscored a comingling of status categories within the family as well as in the realm of work.[84]

Five members of the Carmona-Velasquez family worked for the Wilson farm in south Texas. Their experience illustrates how the intertwining of bracero and illegal migration affected families. In June 1954 Ramón and Célia Carmona, a young couple in their early twenties from Nuevo Leon, Mexico, entered the United States illegally, wading across the Rio Grande at a point near the town of Santa Maria, Texas. They proceeded to the farm of Walter Wilson, where Célia's older brother, Pedro Velasquez, was employed as a bracero. Célia's father and twelve-year-old brother also worked illegally on the Wilson farm during the cotton harvest. Ramón and Célia picked cotton on the Santa Maria farm for about a month. In August, Wilson took them to Rio Hondo, where he owned additional acreage. There, Ramón worked in the field and Célia worked in the Wilson's house as a maid. Ramón and Pedro both earned $3 for a twelve-hour day and worked six or seven days a week. Célia received $5 for a five-day work-week.

Later that month the Border Patrol apprehended the Carmonas and returned them to Mexico. After a few days, the couple went back to the border in order to contact friends on the U.S. side, hoping they could retrieve the household items they left at the Wilson farm. Wilson sent word with Célia's father that Ramón should go to Rio Rico to meet Wilson's son, who would bring papers that legalized Ramón as a bracero. Ramón soon returned as a legal contract-worker to Wilson's farm at Rio Hondo, leaving Célia to live in Mexico with her father, who had returned from Texas.

Wilson, however, was not happy with the arrangement. He angrily asked Ramón why he had not brought his wife back with him, as he needed her to work in the house. Ramón had not done so in part because he knew that if she were caught he would lose his bracero contract but also because Célia had decided she wanted to stay in Mexico. But, Ramón recalled, "I saw that he was beginning to get mad, so I decided to . . . do whatever he said." Célia's little brother, Lupé, delivered a letter from Ramón across the river to Célia and then escorted Célia back across the river and to Santa Maria. Wilson met them with his pickup truck and drove Célia back to Rio Hondo. Lupé hung around the Santa Maria farm for a while before returning to his father in Mexico. Soon after, however, the Border Patrol apprehended and repatriated Ramón and Célia again.[85]

The experience of the Carmona-Velasquez family suggests how fluid was the line between "wetback" and bracero. The grower in this case appeared to prefer illegal to bracero labor, but was willing to contract braceros if necessary; whereas the workers seemed to prefer having a contract, probably for the security. There seems also to have been some confluence between workers' and growers' interests in hiring families. While young adult men comprised the backbone of the labor force, children, older men, and women worked illegally as supplemental labor. Women worked both in the field (though infrequently) and in the house. Célia Velasquez's experience does not appear to be atypical: throughout the Southwest private homes employed "wet" maids, who were likely the wives of braceros or illegal migrants working on nearby farms.[86] Finally, families had to decide whether it was better to stay together and risk deportation, or to live apart for safety and in order to secure steadier work.

INS Policy: Carrot and Stick

During the 1940s the INS continued the general policy that had evolved in the late 1920s—it attempted to apprehend smugglers and illegal entrants but pursued a policy of moderation with regard to undocumented workers on the farms. A government official described the INS's historical policy of control as "not rigid, [but] reasonable" with regard to the needs of the harvest. In 1948 the INS district director at El Paso advised his staff, "We do not have the personnel and means to prevent all these [Texas] farmers from using illegal labor; therefore, unless and until Texas farmers are given the privilege of legally importing farm laborers from Mexico, their farms should not be indiscriminately raided."[87]

Texas growers continued to use illegal labor after the state was removed from the blacklist in 1949. California growers also continued to employ illegal labor, especially in the Imperial Valley, even as they contracted braceros in the late 1940s and early 1950s. "Wetback" labor was cheaper and involved no bureaucratic delays. Some said braceros were "unsatisfactory" and that "wetbacks" were the "good workers." Defiant, the growers invoked their "right to hire and fire farm labor as we [see] fit."[88]

Growers further believed that too many federal agencies were involved in the program and specifically that the Department of Labor intruded upon the employment relationship. (They wanted the program placed under the Department of Agriculture.) They said the program was "too exacting of employers and too solicitous of the workers" and called the terms of the bracero contract "absurd and unworkable." They lodged "serious objections" to the principle of regulation by the federal government and lobbied for allowing Public Law 78 and the binational agreement to expire in 1955. They sought instead a unilateral program based on direct employer recruitment of temporary agricultural laborers from Mexico.[89]

With the growers restless and illegal immigration continuing unabated, it was increasingly difficult for the INS to continue its policy of selective enforcement. The INS felt pressured to control illegal migration, which depressed not only domestic wages but also bracero wages and destabilized the recruitment of legal contract-workers as well. Illegal immigration also seemed more glaring, more "illegal," when a "legal" method of procuring farm labor existed. Growers' reluctance to use braceros mocked the government's program.

During the early 1950s the INS made a greater effort to search farms for illegal workers. In February 1950 the Border Patrol increased its monthly apprehensions by 30 percent in Texas. The Los Angeles district of the INS mounted an aggressive campaign in 1953, in which it apprehended 175,000 undocumented workers during the three summer-harvest months. But these efforts provoked farmers into "open rebellion to our . . . whole enforcement operation." Critics accused the INS of using "Russian methods" and of acting like the "Gestapo." A national farm organization resolved, "We consider a man's farm much more analogous to his home than a factory, and it should be more secure from search."[90]

The INS was hamstrung not only because the growers had the sympathy of elected officials in Washington. It had also accommodated growers by legalizing their illegal workers on several occasions, some highly publicized, giving them little incentive to participate in the bracero program. This practice was called "drying out the wetbacks." In the famous "El Paso Incident" of October 1948, the INS (with the approval of the White House) opened the border at El Paso to allow the entry of some seven thousand migrants who had massed there and threatened to overrun the border. The INS "arrested" them and then paroled them to employers, explaining that this was a humanitarian gesture because both the laborers and farmers were "desperate." In 1949 the INS legalized four thousand illegal farm laborers for work in California and Arizona and eighty thousand in Texas. In 1953 the United States authorized bracero contracts to some five thousand illegal agricultural workers with who were longtime employees of American ranchers. The "specials" program was supposed to be for illegal workers who performed skilled labor, such as tractor driver or machine operator, but in practice employers used it to legalize unskilled farm hands as well.[91]

A second "border incident" took place in January 1954, when the INS orchestrated the legalization of several thousand farm workers by allowing them to effect a voluntary departure—in some cases stepping eighteen inches over the international boundary line—and then "enter" the United States under the Ninth Proviso. These included illegal workers whom the INS had previously apprehended and released at the border and those whom farmers "pushed back" over the line in order to have them legally reenter.[92]

Thus believing the INS would ultimately accede to their demands, growers

4.5 During the 1950s the INS legalized the status of undocumented agricultural workers by allowing them to "return" to Mexico by putting one foot onto Mexican soil and then to "reenter" through an official port of entry. Officials called the procedure "drying out wetbacks." (By permission of Loomis Dean/Timepix.)

continually clamored for the legalization of illegal workers. The Imperial Valley Farm Bureau Federation "respectfully and urgently recommend[ed] that all illegal entrants now gainfully employed in agriculture in the U.S. be legalized immediately." The [Lower Rio Grande] Valley Chamber of Commerce urged the creation of an "experimental free zone" in the border area, where "an alien laborer could come and go as he pleased" after passing nominal security and health checks. Others called for renewable temporary work permits or simplified contracts sanctioned by Mexico. The INS officially opposed all plans that "plac[ed] a premium upon illegal entry," but in fact the agency was already complicit in the practice.[93]

In 1954 federal officials still considered growers in the Lower Rio Grande Valley a "recalcitrant group" that would not convert to bracero labor. When Joseph M. Swing took over as commissioner general of the INS in March 1954, he was determined to solve the problem. Swing, a retired army general who had attended West Point with President Eisenhower, employed a carrot-and-stick method. In many respects it comprised the same elements of previous INS practices—raids and deportations on the one hand and the legalization of illegal workers on the other hand. But whereas previous INS policies had been haphazard and reactive, Swing rationalized them into a comprehensive whole and executed his program aggressively.[94]

Swing made the program more user-friendly by devising administrative methods to give growers what they had not been able to get the State Department to negotiate with Mexico: border recruitment, recontracting, and the legalization of illegal workers. He revamped the "specials" program, which legalized longtime illegal skilled workers, to create a larger system of "pre-designating" workers for return. The general declared, "Our policy will be to re-contract as many braceros as possible." He described the "ultimate objective" as "the creation of a reservoir of competent, security-screened farm workers who may be readmitted from time to time under a more efficient and satisfactory procedure." Also, by making recontracting contingent upon a satisfactory evaluation, Swing had found an innovative method of discipline against complaints, job actions, and skipping. While some employers chose to contract new braceros, "pre-designated return" became the preferred method of procuring labor.[95]

Swing's reforms effectively undermined the bracero program's official recruitment process of local selection and interior processing, which had aimed to regulate the distribution and flow of migration. During the spring of 1955, the recruitment center at Monterrey, Mexico, ceased processing braceros for lack of orders. The INS reception station at Hidalgo doubled, in effect, as the recruitment center for the entire valley. Mexican consul Bernando Blanco believed "specials" were merely "wetbacks with contracts," whose "legal" employment subverted the entire bracero program. In California, USES inspectors reported that upwards of 90 percent of the "specials" whom farmers called up had no record of prior contracts. By 1956 recontracting had increased by 43 percent from the previous year.[96]

If General Swing reasoned that growers would participate in the bracero program if it met their needs, he also believed they only convert if they were also deprived of illegal workers. "Operation Wetback" was a massive enforcement effort aimed at apprehending and deporting undocumented agricultural workers from the Southwest, especially south Texas and southern California. It was, in other words, the stick behind the carrot.

The project was conceived and executed as though it was a military operation. According to Swing, the "alarming, ever-increasing, flood tide" of undocumented migrants from Mexico constituted "an actual invasion of the United States." Operation Wetback commenced in June 1954 with a "direct attack . . . upon the hordes of aliens facing us across the border." The campaign involved approximately 750 immigration officers, Border Patrol officers, and investigators; 300 jeeps, cars, and buses; 7 airplanes, and "other equipment." The INS transferred personnel, vehicles, and radio equipment from northern and eastern districts to the Mexican border district.[97] This "full mobilization" of its forces and equipment was deployed in "direct action at the line." As Swing described, "Planes were used to locate wetbacks and to direct ground teams working in jeeps. Transport planes, trucks, and [buses] were used to convoy the arrested aliens to staging areas, and to discourage reentry, many of those apprehended were moved far into the interior of Mexico by train and ship." A "special mobile force" made "searches in the interior" and "seize[d] those who have illegally crossed the border." The operation extended to Los Angeles, San Francisco, and Chicago, where the undocumented had long settled and enjoyed a degree of prosperity.[98]

At the outset of the campaign, Operation Wetback apprehended 3,000 undocumented workers a day and some 170,000 during the first three months. The INS also reported an immediate increase of over 100 percent in the number of bracero contracts, both first-time contracts and renewals. In all, the INS apprehended 801,069 Mexican migrants from 1953 through 1955, more than twice the number of apprehensions made from 1947 through 1949. It returned them to Mexico by bus, train, and boat.[99] More than 25 percent were removed on hired cargo ships that ran from Port Isabel, Texas, to Vera Cruz, on the Mexican Gulf Coast; a congressional investigation likened one vessel (where a riot took place on board) to an "eighteenth century slave ship" and a "penal hell ship." The number of braceros admitted during the same period rose from 148,449 in 1954 to 245,162 in 1955 to 298,012 in 1956.[100]

Some observers were less than sanguine about Operation Wetback's success. An American labor official acknowledged that the INS had "performed a major task in clearing the border areas of literally hundreds of thousands of wetbacks" but added that Operation Wetback had "dumped" thousands of illegal workers over the border, creating problems on the Mexican side. In July 1955 "literally hundreds of thousands of braceros were roaming about the streets" of Mexicali, he reported. Some eighty-eight braceros died of sunstroke as a result of a round-up that had taken place in 112-degree heat, and he argued that more would have died had Red Cross not intervened. At the other end of the border, in Nuevo Laredo, a Mexican labor leader reported that "wetbacks" were "brought [into Mexico] like cows" on trucks and unloaded fifteen miles down the highway from the border, in the desert.[101]

Swing also wanted to build a chain-link fence along sections of the border in California and Arizona and towers at strategic locations. He argued that a fence would be particularly effective in deterring the illegal migration of "disease-ridden" women and children who he said comprised over 60 percent of those entering surreptitiously after Operation Wetback. The Mexican government and local labor and civil rights groups vehemently opposed the construction of a fence; the State Department envisioned photographs in the Moscow newspapers.[102]

In fact, the INS's enforcement campaigns could not "solve" the problem of illegal immigration. At best, Operation Wetback was a short-term success.

TABLE 4.1

Foreign Agricultural Laborers Contracted and Apprehended by INS, 1942–1964

Calendar year	Contracts, from Mexico	Contracts, Other	Total Contracts	Apprehensions, Mexicans
1942	4,203	—	4,203	NA[1]
1943	52,098	13,526	65,624	8,189
1944	62,170	22,249	84,419	26,689
1945	49,454	23,968	73,422	63,602
1946	32,043	19,304	51,347	91,456
1947	19,632	11,143	30,775	182,986
1948	35,345	9,571	44,916	179,385
1949	107,000	5,765	112,765	278,538
1950	67,500	9,025	76,525	458,215
1951	192,000	11,640	203,640	500,628
1952	197,100	13,110	210,210	534,538
1953	201,380	13,941	215,321	875,318
1954	309,033	11,704	320,737	1,075,168
1955	398,650	13,316	411,966	242,608
1956	445,197	14,653	459,850	72,442
1957	436,049	19,156	452,205	44,451
1958	432,857	14,656	447,513	37,242
1959	437,643	17,777	455,420	30,196
1960	315,846	18,883	334,729	29,651
1961	291,420	18,955	310,375	29,877
1962	194,978	22,032	217,010	30,272
1963	186,865	22,353	209,218	39,124
1964	177,736	22,286	200,022	48,844
Total	4,646,199	349,013	4,992,212	4,879,419

Source: Congress and the Nation, 1945–1964: A Review of Government and Politics in the Postwar Years (Washington, D.C.: Congressional Quarterly Service, 1965), 762.

[1]NA: Not available.

Illegal migration was curbed insofar as the INS legalized illegal workers and gave bracero contracts to erstwhile illegal workers whom employers recruited near the border. In fact, the "pre-designated return" program encouraged illegal migration, even as it rechanneled it. Officials knew that border recruitment was a "magnet for prospective wetbacks."[103]

Illegal migration continued even as the bracero program stabilized in the late 1950s. By 1961 the Border Patrol had an authorized force of 1,692 officers and pilots and 8 transport planes. Of those deported by train and air in 1960–1961, upwards of 20 percent were so-called repeaters. In six months in 1963 the INS apprehended over 17,000 aliens in the Southwest district, of which some 9,000 were Mexican adult males and 1,200 were adult females and children.[104] Although differences in enforcement effort make it difficult to compare apprehension and deportation data, it should be clear that, notwithstanding various programmatic and enforcement efforts made by the INS, bracero and illegal labor continued to coexist.

Critique and Opposition: Drawing the National Boundaries of Class

From the late 1940s through the 1950s, Mexican American civil rights advocates, trade unionists, and liberal elites tried to combat what they perceived were the pernicious effects of illegal and contract agricultural labor. The opposition had little success, however, until the early 1960s. Their problem was, perhaps, overdetermined. Mexican Americans and migratory farm workers had virtually no political standing in the face of powerful agricultural interests. When Congress finally terminated the bracero program in 1964, a more liberal mood had arrived in Washington. Just as important, growers' demands for a steady oversupply of cheap farm labor abated after the mechanization of cotton and sugar beets was achieved in the early 1960s.[105]

But while political and structural forces impeded reform, the opposition also suffered from its own internal contradictions. Its general problem might be described as a conflict of loyalties. Mexican Americans empathized with the plight of undocumented workers and braceros, with whom they shared a common ethno-racial identity. The Los Angeles journalist Rubén Salazar called Mexican Americans and braceros "racial brothers." Indeed, as we have seen, they were sometimes members of the same family. Moreover, Mexican Americans were tied to braceros through various economic relationships. The former worked as labor-camp managers, ran bars and other local establishments catering to braceros, and plied a petty trade servicing bracero labor camps on weekends, offering "clothes, soda pop, cigarettes and tobacco, illegal booze, personal items other sundries, and even prostitutes." Indeed, the bracero program stimulated the growth of an ethnic Mexican consumer market and a middle class of Mexican American entrepreneurs. In her study of Santa Paula, in Ventura County, California, Martha Menchaca found that "before the appearance of the braceros, the weekends were quiet and very few people visited the Mexican business zone . . . [which] had only one cafe, two grocery stores, and a *cantina*. Once the braceros settled in Santa Paula, Mexican entrepreneurs began opening more businesses. By the mid-1940s there were at least six *cantinas*, three grocery stores, one bakery, two cafes, and three boardinghouses."[106]

At the same time, Mexican Americans believed that "wetbacks" and braceros were the direct cause of their own social and economic problems. Mexican Americans considered braceros "scabs," who depressed wages and took jobs from locals. On occasion tensions broke out in fights over jobs or over the affections of Mexican American women. Braceros believed "the ones who treat us bad are the . . . Mexicans that are born [in the United States]. They felt resentment against us. They feel uncomfortable with us. . . . They try to take advantage of us. . . . They laugh [at] us."[107]

These dynamics were complex. Congressman Henry Gonzalez of Texas observed that the braceros, through no fault of their own, "used to bring the misery of a people in one country to further depress the misery of a people in another country."[108] A Mexican American activist elaborated the point:

> Naturally, we feel sorry for the braceros. We do what we can to see that they are exploited as little as possible up here. After all, our own parents were in pretty much the same position as the braceros a generation ago. . . . But look at what the program is doing to us. We're trying to climb our way up the social ladder. . . . It's a hard enough fight, at best. The braceros come along, and hang on to the tail of our shirts. We can't brush them off, because that wouldn't be human. But their weight is dragging us down.[109]

Mexican Americans, especially among the middle classes, also chafed at the racial degradation they believed illegal migrants brought upon them. One writer called the borderland a "twilight zone" where "wetbacks and even Spanish-speaking U.S. citizens will do work at wages that even Negroes and white trash refuse to do. . . . The Mexican peasantry," he said, "lives in near Asiatic poverty."[110] The comparison to "Asiatic poverty," of course, invoked the specter of the yellow peril. By situating the "Mexican peasantry" with "Asiatics" opposite (and below) "Negroes and white trash," the writer suggested that all Mexicans were not only foreign but as backward as the world's most dangerous backward race.

Mexican Americans tried to combat these associations and to forestall their own decline. They invoked their citizenship in order to distinguish themselves from undocumented workers and braceros. It seemed particularly outrageous to some that braceros, who were aliens, enjoyed privileges and guarantees that eluded domestic workers, who were citizens. A Mexican American from Lytle, Texas, wrote to President Eisenhower, "One glaring inequality which people cannot understand is why the United States will guarantee to an *alien* a specified wage and deny the same to its own citizens. Doesn't charity begin at home?"[111]

The League of United Latin-American Citizens, or LULAC, criticized the INS for "allowing an avalanche of illegal Mexican labor," which "signifies the lowering of wage standards almost to a peonage level and will force thousands of native born and naturalized Americans to uproot their families, suspend the education of their children and migrate to other states in search of a living wage." A group of Mexican American workers noted that the "annual Grapes-of-Wrath-with-a-Spanish-accent movement" coincided with the late-summer Texas primary elections and thus "deprived [them] of their prerogatives as voting citizens."[112]

The emphasis on citizenship remapped the lines of race loyalty. In a 1949 statement, LULAC leaders disentangled themselves from the "Mexican-Asiatic" axis by arguing that the Spanish-speaking person in the Southwest was "in the same position as the Negro." Both, they said, were "subject peoples" with a long history of discrimination. But that history was nothing compared to the problems caused by "wetbacks," who they felt were really dragging down Mexican Americans.[113] This was an interesting departure from LULAC's view during the 1920s and 1930s, which stressed that the "Latin American" or "Spanish-speaking" people in the Southwest were of Spanish descent, that is, that they were white. The shift perhaps reflected the influence of the post–World War II black civil rights movement. At the same time, locating Mexican Americans with black people seemed to say that even if they were both second-class citizens, they were citizens nonetheless and, therefore, still apart from and above the "wetback."

The "wetback's" illegal status seemed to be an irresistible hook for Mexican American civil rights leaders. The logic was normative: if illegal aliens were present, they should be removed. In 1948 LULAC sent telegrams to President Truman alleging that the illegal entry of laborers from Mexico constituted "a direct danger to our own citizens" and called for law enforcement to deport illegals. The American GI Forum, a civil rights organization, called for strengthening the Border Patrol.[114]

But the call to deport elided the fact that undocumented immigrants and Mexican Americans were part of a larger transnational community. When the INS actually made mass deportations, the consequences of the policy struck home. A Harlingen resident described the effects of a 1950 "drive by the Immigration Service to return Mexican families with their American-born children." He said, "Their home life was [abruptly] broken, they were compelled to sell homes [and] possessions at a great sacrifice; their incomes ended and they were picked up by the Border Patrol at night and 'dumped' on the other side of the river in numbers so great [that] Mexico's railways and bus lines could not move them into the interior fast enough. . . . [T]housands of these families were stranded along the border destitute without food or funds or employment." Similarly, Mexican Americans were of two minds about Operation Wetback. The Texas CIO's Latin American Committee praised the INS for "tightening up the border." But it opposed the INS's use of bloodhounds to track down illegal migrants and its proposed fence along the border, warning that the "militarization" of the Border Patrol would create an even "greater evil" than illegal immigration.[115]

Organized labor also wrestled with conflicting loyalties. Were braceros and "wetbacks" fellow workers, part of a single working class in the United States? Or were they a foreign element of unfree labor, whose introduction into the country brought only disaster to American workers?

In general, unions viewed illegal immigration as an unmitigated evil, a flooding of the domestic labor market with cheap labor. The National Agricultural Workers Union (NAWU, formerly the National Agricultural Laborers Union) of the AFL said illegal labor displaced local labor, especially Mexican Americans but also "colored [and] Okies," and called upon the INS to round up and deport all illegal aliens. In 1949 NAWU organized a demonstration of six thousand people in the Imperial Valley at the U.S.-Mexico border, protesting illegal migration. Union activists dramatically made "citizen's arrests" of alleged "wetbacks" and took them to the INS. The union's "anti-wetback" strike against lettuce growers in the valley in 1951 included picket lines at the border to dramatize opposition to illegal labor. U.S. and Mexican labor delegates meeting at an international trade union conference in 1953 resolved that the "wetback" was their number-one problem and agreed that the United States should enact legislation that imposed criminal sanctions on employers of illegal labor.[116]

At times, unions conflated illegal and contract labor, believing employers used both as a "stick" to keep wages down and unions out. NAWU organizer Ernesto Galarza said, "Braceros and 'wets' are the two sides of the same phony coin" that aimed to "cut down the wages of farm labor, to break strikes and to prevent [union] organization; to run American citizens off farm jobs, especially on the corporation ranches." Both were forms of unfree labor: the "wetback" was "legally a criminal in connivance by and with" the government, kept in "a position of peonage"; the contracted laborer likewise had no "civil rights." Each was "democracy in reverse." Contract labor was not compatible with a "system of free men," which included "freedom of mobility, association, [and] anything else meaningful." Braceros were "unassimilable, not by nature but by an act of Congress." Organized labor's opposition to contract labor was echoed by liberals: the bracero was a "legal slave," a "rented slave, "kept as if in [a] concentration camp."[117]

The use of slavery and concentration-camp metaphors emphasized the unfree nature of contract labor and aimed to evoke sympathy for the victimized braceros. Yet, that discourse also had the effect of constructing braceros as a foreign element entirely outside the American labor force and society, obscuring the many points of contact and integration that braceros had with other ethnic Mexicans in the United States and the transnational character of the agricultural workforce.

While unions opposed both illegal and contract labor on principle, their practical policies towards these two groups sometimes diverged. The NAWU consistently argued for enforcement (that is, deportation) as the solution to the "wetback problem" and did not try to organize illegal workers into the union, but it did try to recruit braceros. In the early 1950s in the Imperial Valley, Garlaza organized braceros as dues-paying union members. His effort dovetailed with ethnic-organizing strategies that he had already successfully deployed in the valley—using Spanish-language materials and creating

"Mexican committees" of the union that sponsored cultural activities and discussed the workers' specific concerns. His approach, as Stephen Pitti has argued, evinced a transnationalist sensibility to labor organizing. The number of braceros that joined the NAWU was never great, although one Labor Department official believed it might have been "substantial."[118]

The approach was supported by the U.S.-Mexico Joint Trade Union Committee, which resolved unanimously to "seek the full enjoyment of the right of Mexican braceros in the U.S. to organize and elect representatives as their bargaining agent." It decided that the *Confederación Trabajadores de Mexico* (CTM), the official trade union movement in Mexico, would issue leaflets in Mexico, urging braceros entering the United States to join NAWU, which would "accept the Mexican workers as members and seek to represent them in maintaining their contracts with employers." The CTM reportedly also planned to organize braceros in Mexico directly, by forming "committees in all of the work centers where camps of legally contracted laborers are situated." However, there is no evidence that these committees existed.[119]

NAWU's strategy was to interpret Article 21 of the Migrant Labor Agreement of 1951, which provided for braceros to select representatives to communicate with employers, to include union representation. When pressed, the Labor Department said that braceros could elect "anyone" to represent them but that the union would have to win a majority of workers of a unit, which was defined as the multigrower association, something clearly difficult if not impossible to achieve. Moreover, the department stated, the union, if elected, could only "present" grievances and could not bargain over wages or working conditions.[120]

There is scattered evidence that small organizations not related to the official Mexican labor movement attempted to organize braceros in Mexico. The *Alianza Naciónal de Braceros* (National Alliance of Braceros) was formed in 1948 or 1949 by former braceros in Mexico City. The *Alianza* wrote exposés of the bracero program in the Mexican press, especially the racketeering that went on both in Mexico and in the United States. It is not clear if it organized braceros directly. An organization called the League [for] Braceros Welfare reportedly recruited "agitators" in Guadalajara at 1,000 pesos a head to "infiltrate" the bracero program and "spread discontent" among braceros. Investigators found that one alleged agitator "invited [coworkers] to tell him their troubles" and "provoke[d] arguments" with field foremen. (He was repatriated.) In 1958 an INS investigator reported that an agitator at the Espalme, Sonora, recruitment center, was "talking to individuals and small groups, advising them to insist on their rights in their contract, and not to become victims of exploitation."[121]

Although these advisories probably made braceros more aware of their rights, neither U.S. nor Mexican efforts bore fruit organizationally. The employers were powerful, but more important, neither the U.S. nor Mexican government had an interest in seeing the braceros organized and neither country's labor federation put meaningful financial or political resources into it. NAWU leaders were particularly bitter about the AFL's meager support and by jurisdictional competition from the CIO's packinghouse workers union. Galarza challenged the AFL's leadership, "Will we protect the braceros and if so, how?"[122]

On the Mexico side, the CTM did not actually organize among the rural farming population that comprised the bracero constituency, as the Mexican state had severed the historical ties between industrial unions and peasant leagues in the 1930s as part of the process of forming an official labor movement.[123] The CTM's real role was to provide political support for the Mexican government and the ruling party's foreign policy interests in the binational venues established under the Migrant Labor Agreement. In truth, both the AFL-CIO and the CTM's support for organizing braceros remained in the realm of rhetoric.

The lack of federation support not only meant that the NAWU was unable to organize braceros; it also crippled its central mission, which was to unionize domestic farmworkers. Believing that bracero and illegal labor "doomed in advance" any effort to organize farmworkers, NAWU turned its attention to defeating the bracero program. During the 1950s Garlaza's work increasingly focused not on direct organizing but on researching and publicizing the negative effects of the bracero program on domestic farmworkers' wages and employment. Despite his transnational *cultural* sensibilities, Garlaza remained challenged by the *legal* distinctions between "domestic" and "foreign" farmworkers. While sympathetic to the plight of braceros, Garlaza ultimately identified with the interests of domestic workers against those of braceros and "wetbacks." The title of his 1956 exposé, *Strangers in Our Fields*, signaled this orientation.[124]

In the same vein, the unions tried to influence the terms of the Migrant Labor Agreement and pressured the Department to enforce the "no adverse effect" rule. For example, NAWU and the CTM argued that they should participate in the binational negotiations over revisions and extensions of the program. In 1955 the CIO proposed to the Department of Labor that it serve as an official "watchdog" for the bracero program, on grounds that it had a "third party interest" in the proper enforcement of the Migrant Labor Agreement. (The Labor Department rejected the proposal.) Making a pitch to the AFL-CIO for a major campaign to organize domestic farmworkers in 1956, NAWU emphasized, "Problems arising from the importation and employment of Mexican contract workers will have to be faced in the beginning. Provisions of Public Law 78 giving job preference for American workers over Mexican nationals will have to be enforced."[125] These efforts followed a logic, which reasoned that if the government enforced the "no adverse effects" rules, employers would find little advantage in using imported contract labor and the program would wither.

In 1959 the AFL-CIO made a renewed commitment to organizing domestic farmworkers that directly confronted bracero labor. The federation's new organizing project, the Agricultural Workers Organizing Committee (AWOC), took a different approach than previous efforts. It adopted a militant, "flying squadron" strategy, whereby a small number of domestic workers called strikes at farms and then demanded that the Labor Department remove braceros employed on those farms. The strategy was effective: in 1960–61 AWOC conducted some 150 strikes, mostly over wages, of which 90 percent the Labor Department certified as "bona fide" labor disputes.

This was a marked change from previous policy. Throughout most of the 1950s the Labor Department had construed Article 32 of the Migrant Labor Agreement, which barred use of braceros in strike situations, to mean that such action was required "only in such serious situations where the security of the Mexican worker and, in addition, friendly relations between the two governments are threatened, or jeopardized."[126] In 1959 Secretary of Labor Mitchell began to certify work stoppages and to remove braceros from strike situations. Under the Kennedy administration the Labor Department promoted the policy further. At the height of AWOC's strike activity in early 1961, when there were twenty-two strikes involving 379 striking domestic workers, the Labor Department removed 2,052 braceros from California farms, including 1,000 braceros from the Imperial Valley lettuce strike in February. Secretary of Labor Willard Wirtz also agreed to AWOC's demand for "gate hiring," which aimed to enforce the domestic-preference hiring rule. AWOC's militancy and the Labor Department's removal policy resulted in a serious disruption of the bracero program.[127]

The union's strategy also had a darker side: a growing hostility towards bracero workers. In August 1960, a group of fifty AWOC picketers at Tom Bowers's peach ranch in Gridley, California, charged into the orchard where braceros were working. The strikers shook the braceros' ladders and assaulted them with wooden staves from broken fruit crates. The Mexican consul demanded that the braceros be removed, citing concern for both their physical safety and their "subject[ion] to indignities."[128] AWOC also staged demonstrations at bracero housing camps, some of which degenerated into violent attacks, with union members beating braceros and, in one instance, setting fire to their barracks. The attack on the Corona bracero camp near El Centro during the 1961 lettuce strike by one hundred AWOC members resulted in the hospitalization of four braceros and the arrest of forty demonstrators. The union was badly damaged by negative publicity and lawsuits. AFL-CIO president George Meany cut support to AWOC within the year.[129]

AWOC's strategy also organized principally among disaffected transient white workers, the so-called fruit tramps, which got quick results but discouraged long-term organization. The union did not attempt to organize the more stable Mexican American and Filipino workers, and AWOC leaders rebuffed overtures from the Agricultural Workers Association, a group of farmworkers organized by the Catholic Church and community organizers, including César Chávez.[130] AWOC did not understand, as Chávez did, that organizing farm workers required a "social movement." That road was also considered but not taken in Texas. In 1960 the AFL-CIO ignored a proposal made by Jerry Holleman, head of the Texas AFL-CIO, for a community organizing strategy for Webb County in the Lower Rio Grande Valley. Holleman argued for an effort "directed at the entire community . . . to every person who works for wages in Laredo." Moreover, he noted, the "younger generation" of Mexican Americans wanted to fight race discrimination: "Many of the young Latin attorneys and community leaders have offered their assistance free in any organizing drive we wish to launch."[131]

The AFL-CIO's lack of interest reflected its general skepticism that farmworkers could be organized at all. Craft and industrial unionists in the United States historically viewed farmwork as a "feudal" vestige that would be eliminated by mechanization and other modern improvements in agricultural production. They also had a history of complicity with racism and segregation in the South; it fell there to socialists and communists to organize black and white tenant farmers and sharecroppers.[132] Trade unionism's ideological disposition against farm labor organizing was reproduced during the post–World War II period. In the 1950s and early 1960s, organized labor's priorities lay elsewhere, in negotiating high-wage packages that made their members in the northern primary labor market into middle-class consumers. The bracero program, illegal migration, and the displacement of domestic farm labor constituted a difficult and messy problem far removed from the federation's central concerns.

It might be argued that organized labor has been given too much credit for ending the bracero program. Its opposition, after all, amounted to little more than rhetoric. The liberal turn in public sentiment against the bracero program was no doubt in part influenced by the AFL-CIO's words, but it was also informed by the emergence of a broader political agenda of civil rights and civil liberties.[133] In this context a number of sensationalized stories about the conditions of migrant farm labor and the bracero program appeared during the late 1950s and early 1960s on television and in the press. For example, a CBS broadcast in August 1956, "Farm Labor Exposé," likened braceros' conditions to that of a "concentration camp." Ernesto Galarza's critique of the bracero program, *Strangers in Our Fields*, caused an uproar when it was published in 1956 and garnered additional publicity when the DiGiorgio Corporation, long the nemesis of farmworker unions, sued him for libel. Such negative publicity bruised postwar liberal sensibilities. Like the persistence of Jim Crow segregation in the South, the condition of American farmworkers blighted the nation's claim to be leader of the free world. In a time of postwar prosperity and national triumphalism, liberals were shocked by the impoverishment of migratory farmworkers. In this context, the bracero program could finally be understood as what Andrew Biemiller of the AFL-CIO called "imported colonialism."[134]

At the same time, American agribusiness found itself far less dependent upon imported contract labor. Cotton, the chief crop drawing braceros in Texas, Arizona, and parts of California, was mechanized by the early 1960s. The mechanization of sugar beets reduced demand for braceros in other western states. In California, where the majority of braceros were employed after 1961, growers felt increasingly inconvenienced by the Labor Department's tougher enforcement practices and anticipated the mechanization of tomato-harvesting, which was finally achieved in 1965.[135]

Terminating the bracero program, however, was only one part of the solution to imported colonialism. There remained the other side of the problem, the exploitation of undocumented labor, which, predictably, increased after 1964. The liberal opposition fell back on calls for greater border enforcement and immigration restrictions. They did not pursue more substantive strategies, such as reforming the nation's labor laws, even though they understood that establishing labor standards in agriculture was fundamental to any meaningful change.[136] Perhaps it would have been too much to expect that liberals, who were fighting southern racists over African American civil rights, would have simultaneously fought the same "solid South" on the matter of agricultural labor rights. But this lack, and the continued construction of Mexican migrant workers outside the American working class and outside the national body, meant that "imported colonialism" would in fact continue, through the ongoing, if informal, importation of undocumented Mexican migrants—a condition that has endured into the twenty-first century.

Part III

WAR, NATIONALISM, AND ALIEN CITIZENSHIP

WORLD WAR II was a watershed in the history of Asian Americans. Wartime politics had momentous consequences for the two largest Asian ethno-racial groups in the United States at the time, Chinese Americans and Japanese Americans: for the former, the repeal of Chinese exclusion in 1943, and for the latter, mass incarceration in U.S. concentration camps from 1942 to 1945. Each policy derived directly from the United States' wartime relationship with the home country: China, an ally; Japan, the enemy.[1]

The foregrounding of state relations in midcentury Asian immigration and race policy was a change from the past. From the late nineteenth century until World War II, Chinese and then Asiatic exclusion was driven not principally by foreign policy but by the politics of domestic racism and economic competition. Exclusion was a byproduct of manifest destiny, the nineteenth-century ideology that justified continental expansion as a divine project of Anglo-American Christianity, and the use of racialized foreign labor in western agriculture. To be sure, state relations informed immigration policy—the United States took advantage of China's weak, semicolonial status to explicitly exclude virtually all Chinese, whereas American concern over relations with Japan, an imperialist nation, mitigated the terms of restriction against Japanese immigration—but foreign policy was not the determining factor.[2]

World War II and the Cold War provided a new framework for defining Asian Americans' position in society, including the meaning of United States citizenship for the generation that was born in America. In the context of war—indeed, these extraordinary, "total" wars—the stakes of national security could not have been imagined higher. A half-century of exclusion policy had already legally and culturally construed Asian Americans as unalterably foreign; war, hot and cold, imbued that foreignness with political implications of an unprecedented nature. Japanese Americans' and Chinese Americans' affective ties, cultural identifications, and political sympathies with their native homelands assumed new meanings. Those meanings, moreover, shifted as U.S. political and military allegiances in East Asia shifted after World War II and through the Cold War—when the Chinese Revolution turned China into the enemy and a reconstructed Japan became America's ally.

The following two chapters examine the changing legal and cultural meanings of citizenship for Asian Americans from World War II through the late 1950s. Chapter 5 addresses the World War II internment of Japanese Americans in U.S. concentration camps and the conflicts over citizenship and nationalism that led some 5,500 Japanese Americans to renounce their U.S. citizenship. Chapter 6 examines the problem of illegal Chinese immigration during the 1950s and its imbrication in Cold War politics. This political crisis resulted in the Chinese Confession Program, a project of the U.S. Immigration and Naturalization Service that legalized the status of some 30,000 Chinese Americans who had since the turn of the century falsely claimed U.S. citizenship, the so-called "paper sons."

While very different in their particulars, both stories may be understood as conflicts over "alien citizenship"—that aspect of Asiatic exclusion that legally defined all Asians as racially unassimilable and hence ineligible to naturalized citizenship.[3] For Asian Americans born in the United States, birthright citizenship held certain tangible benefits (the right to be present, to own land, etc.) yet remained subject to enormous cultural denial by the mainstream of American society, which regarded "Asian" and "American citizen" as mutually exclusive concepts. World War II and the Cold War produced new iterations of alien citizenship, giving rise to a series of conflicts between Asian Americans and the U.S. government, as well as within the Chinese American and Japanese American communities.

The renunciation and confession cases reveal the malleability of citizenship as a legal-status category and as a political-subject identity. During World War II and the Cold War competing nationalisms, both real and imagined, put pressure upon Asian American alien citizens and generated a range of political uses and abuses of citizenship by Japanese Americans, Chinese Americans, and the United States government to serve their respective needs. Finally, I suggest that the tortuous trajectory of Asian American citizenship during the World War II–Cold War period gestured ultimately towards its rehabilitation. The postwar reconstruction of Asian American citizenship, along with the end of exclusion, signaled the beginnings of a major, if costly, transformation in the social and racial status of Asian Americans.

Migrants, Nationalism, and War

Migrant and disaporic communities have always sustained connections to political projects in and about their countries of origin, including both official state policies and non-state-based movements. We might call the politics generated by these connections "migrant nationalism." In the United States, for example, Irish immigrants and Irish Americans raised financial and political support for the Republican cause throughout the nineteenth and twentieth century. Similarly, American Jews have long been a mainstay of support for Zionism and the state of Israel. In the early twentieth century, Chinese republicanism, Korean independence, and Indian independence all found adherents amongst immigrants and exiled nationals in the United States.[4]

Like all nationalisms, migrant nationalism is neither monolithic nor stable. It is frequently the expressed outlook of educated elites and has varying degrees of support among other social and economic strata. In early-twentieth-century America, migrant nationalism often competed with (and at times combined with) Americanism, as well as with socialism and anarchism.[5] Nor is migrant nationalism a simple reproduction of nationalist ideology in the homeland state. Rather, it is produced from complex dynamic interactions between official and unofficial outreaches from the nation of origin and the various political and affective needs of people living in diaspora. For immigrant groups, nationalism is one of many elements that constitute ethnic identity in the country of settlement. Homeland movements or states may call for or inspire support, but local needs shape the content and propel the activities of migrant nationalism.[6]

In many instances Americans showed sympathy to immigrants' appeals for support for their countrymen's struggles, particularly when those movements sought freedom from European colonialisms or dynastic rule. Their appeals were particularly effective when they invoked American democratic principles and the trope of America as a haven for foreign victims of political persecution. Native white American elites worried more about alien radicalism among the immigrant laboring classes than they did about migrant nationalism.[7]

Except during wartime. The nation-state at war generates nationalism of the highest order in order to mobilize its citizens to arms and sacrifice. War nationalism is pervasive and demanding. Drawn in stark terms and heavily dependent upon symbol and ritual, it resists complexity and nuance. It is intolerant of dissent and leaves little, if any, room for competing ideologies.[8] Yet, from a different angle, wars have also provided opportunities for immigrants and racial minorities to demonstrate their loyalty and to win full acceptance and citizenship in the nation. German immigrants, for example, fought on both sides of the Civil War, and during World War I the U.S. Bureau of Naturalization naturalized tens of thousands of European immigrants serving in the U.S. armed forces. For African Americans, military service has always been a quintessential act of citizenship.[9]

At the start of World War I, when the United States was neutral and had not yet entered the fighting, there was widespread political debate about the merits of the war. Not surprisingly, migrant nationalists in Euro-American ethnic groups supported their native countries: Anglo-Americans supported England, whereas German Americans supported Germany. There was also a vigorous peace movement comprising reformers, pacifists, and socialists, which included German Americans and other ethnic minorities.[10] At the same time, the climate of war and war mobilization engendered a wave of nativist suspicion of the loyalty of "hyphenates." When the United States entered the fighting in 1917, anti-German sentiment swelled and played an important role in mobilizing support for the war among an otherwise apathetic public. American war patriotism targeted all things German—from renaming sauerkraut "liberty cabbage" to physical attacks against German Americans to shutting down German-language newspapers and schools. German Americans came under immense pressure to forsake all German language and cultural practices, which were conflated with support for the Kaiser. Most severely affected were the German religious denominations, whose identities had been forged through native language use and custom.[11] World War I nationalism forced a nearly complete assimilation of German Americans and promoted more generalized opposition towards the foreign-born, which led to the restrictive immigration laws of 1921 and 1924.

Like other immigrant groups in the United States in the early twentieth century, Chinese and Japanese maintained familial, cultural, and political ties with their native countries. These ties were especially enduring because the official policies of exclusion and ineligibility to citizenship afforded Chinese and Japanese virtually no opportunities to become American. Him Mark Lai has argued that racial exclusion and segregation nearly guaranteed that Chinese in America would remain interested in China politics and not American political affairs.[12] In both Chinese American and Japanese American communities, the ethnic presses featured homeland news and politics, and ethnic elites held power over their co-ethnics in part by maintaining both official and informal ties with their respective countries' consuls. The leaders of the Chinese Consolidated Benevolent Associations in the United States were usually members of the Kuomintang (Nationalist) Party. The Japanese Association of America, formed by the Japan consulate in San Francisco in 1908, registered Japanese immigrants' residence in and travel to and from the United States, according to requirements of the (U.S.-Japan) Gentleman's Agreement, which work provided the association with both income and a lever of social control.[13]

Migrant nationalism served local needs in complex ways. Historian Eiichiro Azuma has argued that Japanese Americans "conflated ethnic and state dimensions in their nationalism" in order to fashion an ethnic identity that they believed gave them an honorable place in the "narrative of modern Japanese history" and which facilitated their acceptance in America. When Japanese immigrant (*Issei*) farmers in California imagined they were "pioneers" in the "racial development" and "overseas expansion" of the Japanese empire, their nationalism was less about supporting Japanese imperialism than it was about situating and interpreting, one might even say aggrandizing, their agricultural expertise and predominance in California. Moreover, the Issei, whom Azuma states were "obsessed with how white elites perceived them," rehearsed Japanese theories of race superiority in order to position themselves favorably against other racialized minorities in California, notably Filipinos.[14]

The Sino-Japanese conflict during the 1930s intensified nationalist dis-

courses and activities in the Chinese American and Japanese American communities. The war inspired broad patriotic sentiments in each community.
In both Chinatowns and Little Tokyos, organizations sponsored mass rallies
and undertook vigorous fund-raising and propaganda work, with much of
the latter aimed at the American public. Consistent with other migrant nationalist movements, patriotic work became an arena of local political competition and contestation, as well.[15]

Members of both communities, especially among the American-born,
construed their nationalist work as complementary to their commitments to
assimilate into American life. The Japanese American Citizens League (JACL),
which is well known for its ardent assimilationism and American patriotism,
actively supported Japan's expansionism in Asia during the 1930s. The *Nisei*
(second generation) who led the JACL considered themselves a "bridge of
understanding" between two cultures and two states and believed their pro-
Japan work was patriotic to America because it contributed to healthy U.S.-
Japan relations.[16]

The United States was not directly involved in the conflict between China
and Japan, but American sympathies lay increasingly with China and by
1939–1940 U.S.-Japan relations had deteriorated rapidly. Chinese Americans'
dual loyalties mapped unproblematically upon American foreign policy interests but, as war between the United States and Japan loomed, Japanese
Americans knew that their dualism was no longer possible. They took practical measures, where they could, to protect their legal and physical safety.
Increasingly, for example, many Nisei with dual citizenship gave up their
Japanese citizenship. One-third of the Japanese Americans in Hawai'i relinquished their dual citizenship in the mid-1930s.[17]

Pro-Japan work shut down completely as both Issei and Nisei organizations turned about-face and professed exclusive loyalty to the United States.
In 1941 the Central Japanese Association of America produced a twenty-page
bilingual booklet, "Americanism," which declared, "We, the Japanese of
Southern California, have the utmost faith in America that has protected our
lives and wealth. . . . We strongly feel that it is also our duty and privilege to
join force with Americans in their effort to keep Americanism alive and
defend its ideals."[18]

JACL president Walter Tsukamoto declared in 1940, "[C]oursing through
the veins of the Nisei is a fervent love for the country of their birth equaling
that of any American and certainly surpassed by no American of whatever
racial origin." Indeed, the JACL went all out, its leaders cooperating with FBI
and military intelligence officers with information about allegedly disloyal
Issei and *Kibei-Nisei*, or Kibei (Nisei who were sent to Japan for schooling).[19]

The rhetoric of Issei and Nisei organizations probably exceeded the sentiments of the general Japanese American population. But, at the level of mass
political behavior, Japanese Americans' loyalty to the United States was evi-

denced in the fact that those called by the draft dutifully reported for military induction. Like other Americans they were law-abiding people who understood that military service was a responsibility of citizenship. Some probably went reluctantly, while others welcomed the draft as a chance to prove their loyalty; still others volunteered enthusiastically for service. And, as we now know, Japanese Americans committed no acts of sabotage or espionage against the United States. But Japanese Americans' loyalty to the United States was not necessarily free of conflict with their affective and cultural ties and even political sympathies with Japan. Loyalty as political behavior and nationalism as ideology were not necessarily coterminous, but neither were they necessarily contradictory. Conflation of these concepts would underwrite the evacuation and relocation of Japanese Americans after Pearl Harbor and haunt their internment.

Chapter Five

The World War II Internment of Japanese Americans and the Citizenship Renunciation Cases

War forced us from California
No ripples this day
on desert lake
  —Neiji Ozawa[1]

The internment of Japanese Americans during World War II stands as the most extreme case of the construction and consequences of alien citizenship in American history. The U.S. government never formally stripped Japanese Americans of their citizenship. But in effect it nullified their citizenship, exclusively on grounds of racial difference. Presuming all Japanese in America to be racially inclined to disloyalty, the United States removed 120,000 Japanese Americans—two-thirds of them citizens—from their homes on the Pacific Coast and interned them in ten concentration camps in the interior.[2] Military orders, posted on telephone poles throughout the western halves of California, Oregon, and Washington in early March 1942, called for the evacuation of "all persons of Japanese ancestry, both aliens and non-aliens"—"non-aliens" the rhetorical effacement of citizenship of some 80,000 Americans. Today we call this racial profiling. In 1942 it was said, "A Jap is a Jap."[3]

The government's wartime policy toward Japanese Americans diverged sharply from its views and treatment of persons of German and Italian descent, which was based on individual selection and investigation. This was apparent when the United States entered the war. Immediately after Japan's attack on Pearl Harbor and the United States' declaration of war, the Justice Department arrested 1,393 German and 264 Italian nationals, along with 2,192 Japanese, under authority of the Alien Enemy Act and presidential executive order. These persons had already been under surveillance by the FBI as potentially dangerous and were picked up within days and weeks of Pearl Harbor. The arrested aliens were sent to the regional detention facilities of the Immigration and Naturalization Service, where individual loyalty hearings were conducted. The Justice Department released most of the Germans and Italians.[4]

The 2,192 Japanese aliens arrested by the Justice Department in the days after Pearl Harbor comprised virtually the entire political, social, cultural, and business leadership of Japanese American communities—Buddhist priests, martial arts instructors, Japanese language teachers, members of theater companies, chamber-of-commerce leaders, employees of Japanese companies, and editors of the Japanese language press, as well as leaders of the Japanese Association of America and patriotic organizations. They either remained in detention or were "paroled" to the internment camps with the general Japanese American population.[5]

Earl Warren, then the attorney general of California, explained the difference in policy toward Germans and Italians on the one hand and towards Japanese on the other: "We believe that when we are dealing with the Caucasian race we have methods that will test the loyalty of them. . . . But when we deal with the Japanese we are in an entirely different field and cannot form any opinion that we believe to be sound."[6]

The legal basis for the mass evacuation of Japanese Americans lay in President Roosevelt's Executive Order 9066, issued on February 19, 1942, which authorized the secretary of war to define "military areas" from which persons without permission to enter or remain could be excluded as a "military necessity." General John L. DeWitt, commanding general of the Western Defense Command, had urged evacuation of all Japanese Americans from the West Coast on grounds of military danger, citing shore-to-ship signaling, arms and contraband found during FBI raids, and the location of Japanese farms near military installations. DeWitt argued that the "the Japanese race is an enemy race" and that even amongst the Americanized citizens, "the racial strains are undiluted."[7]

We now know that investigations by the Federal Communications Commission (FCC) and FBI found the charge of signaling to be entirely without substantiation. The FBI also discounted the arms and contraband in question as nonthreatening (for example, goods owned by a sporting goods store). The Office of Naval Intelligence (ONI) had, in fact, conducted an investigation of Japanese Americans in the fall of 1941 and concluded categorically that both Issei and Nisei were loyal to America. The ONI report was circulated at the highest levels of government and was seen by President Roosevelt in November 1941.[8] In effect, as Michi Weglyn observed, Executive Order 9066 "enabled the military, in absence of martial law, to circumvent the constitutional safeguards of over 70,000 American citizens and to treat the Nisei like aliens."[9]

The United States Supreme Court sanctioned this abridgment of civil rights in 1943 and 1944 in *Hirabayashi* and *Korematsu*, which upheld the curfew, exclusion, and evacuation of the Japanese American population on grounds of military necessity. Notably, *Korematsu* articulated the principle that classification and discrimination based on race is subject to "strict scrutiny" by the Court, but the Court ruled that such discrimination was justifiable when the military declared it to be necessary. It further ruled that the military's reasoning for such declaration was not subject to the Court's review.[10]

Citizenship nullification was not limited to the evacuation. The military also in effect canceled the citizenship of Japanese Americans serving in the U.S. armed forces, who numbered some five thousand in Hawai'i and on the mainland at the time of Pearl Harbor. After Pearl Harbor, Nisei soldiers on the mainland were dismissed with "honorable discharge" at the "convenience of the government." Local draft boards all but ceased to induct Japanese Americans. The Selective Service reclassified Nisei with I-A status (fit for duty) to IV-C (enemy alien). In June 1942 the Selective Service stated it would no longer induct Japanese Americans save for exceptional cases; in September it issued official regulations prohibiting their induction.[11]

Internment, Culture, and Loyalty

If internment rested on a foundation of simple racism—"a Jap is a Jap"— that racial logic was complicated by the administration of the camps by the War Relocation Authority (WRA). WRA officials in fact did not believe that all Japanese were racially inclined to disloyalty. Rather, they practiced a kind of benevolent assimilation, which used cultural assimilation to both measure and produce Japanese Americans' loyalty.

The conflation of culture and loyalty was not a new phenomenon in the United States. During World War I, American war nationalism pressured German Americans to forswear native language and religious cultural practices in order to demonstrate their loyalty to the United States. (Indeed, Earl Warren's assumptions about the loyalty of "Caucasians" elided the history of war-induced assimilation and the constructedness of Euro-Americans' ethnoracial identities.)[12] During World War II, Japanese Americans came under similar pressures to assimilate, but under radically different conditions of citizenship-nullification and internment.

The War Relocation Authority was a civilian agency under the Department of Interior. Its director, Milton Eisenhower, and his successor, Dillon Myer, were both New Deal liberals with backgrounds in the Department of Agriculture.[13] Unlike the unapologetic racists and nativists that wanted to rid the country of all Japanese Americans, these liberals considered themselves antiracist. Moreover, the New Dealers in charge of the WRA believed they had an opportunity to turn an unfortunate incidence of war into a positive social good. Ever optimistic about the potential of mass social engineering, they envisioned the camps as "planned communities" and "Americanizing projects" that would speed the assimilation of Japanese Americans through democratic self-government, schooling, work, and other rehabilitative activities. Comparing their own experiment with the Nazis' concentration camps,

WRA officials believed their "community building" project was "an 'ironic testimony' to the value of American democracy."[14] The greater irony, however, is that WRA's assimilationism led to the most disastrous and incendiary aspects of the internment experience—the loyalty questionnaire, segregation, and renunciation of citizenship.

Assimilationist thinking was inherently flawed by racist presumptions. The WRA viewed Japanese Americans as racial children in need of democratic tutelage, infantilizing them in much the same way that the government constructed Filipino colonial subjects and Native American Indians as dependent wards not yet fit for democratic citizenship.[15] Seen in this light, the nullification of Japanese Americans' citizenship was a constitutive element of the project.

As in the Philippines and on Indian reservations, the assimilationists in the WRA considered traditional cultures not conducive to liberal citizenship. They frowned upon the use of native language, kinship structures of leadership, and other manifestations of alleged cultural backwardness. In the Japanese case the pressure for cultural assimilation was freighted with the idea of loyalty. Liberals thus considered certain "types" of Japanese Americans particularly prone to disloyalty based on a cultural reading of their social status (for example, the Kibei, U.S.-born Japanese who had been sent to Japan for schooling, and "unassimilated" or "Japanesey" Nisei who practiced Buddhism).[16]

The conflation of culture and loyalty was not absolute and sometimes was contradictory. For example, while WRA policy embraced freedom of religion, officials suspected those who practiced Shintoism, which worshipped the Emperor.[17] WRA administrators also took a laissez-faire attitude toward recreational activities, allowing for both Japanese and American leisure practices. But in the areas deemed most important for citizenship construction—work, schooling, and self-government—WRA policy was pointedly assimilationist.[18]

Consistent with benevolent assimilation, the WRA seemed to believe that Japanese Americans would cooperate with, if not welcome, their reformation, unaware of its essentially coercive character. Other liberals, if not enthusiastic about internment, nevertheless believed that Japanese Americans proved their Americanness in the camps. Ansel Adams, for example, believed

5.1 (opposite page) Ansel Adams's *Born Free and Equal: Photographs of the Loyal Japanese Americans at Manzanar Relocation Center* was published in 1944 with the approval of the War Relocation Authority. Adams's photographs restored the humanity and dignity of Japanese Americans and praised their adjustment to internment. His photograph of high school students was captioned, "Manzanar is only a detour on the road to American citizenship." (Courtesy of Library of Congress, Prints & Photographs Division, Ansel Adams, photographer.)

that "out of the jostling, dusty confusion of the first bleak days in raw barracks they [Japanese Americans] have modulated to a democratic internal
society and a praiseworthy personal adjustment." The photographer also
read Manzanar's landscape as a site for democracy, believing that the "huge
vistas and the stern realities of sun and wind and space symbolize the im-
mensity and opportunity of America."[19]

Japanese Americans, of course, endured Manzanar and the other camps as
harsh and desolate, and never for a moment misunderstood that they were
deprived of their liberty. In fact the WRA's assimilationist programs were
sites of conflict within the camps. These conflicts suggest not only the limits
of racial paternalism and the improbability of a democratic concentration
camp. They also reveal the existence of Japanese nationalism and divided
loyalties among the internees. By nationalism, I mean both political support
for Japan and cultural nationalism, which emphasized cultural affinities with
the native country. Many more Japanese Americans were cultural nationalists
than were self-conscious political supporters of Japanese militarism. But cultural nationalism was also complicated because it sometimes suggested political aspects, such as reverence for the Emperor. At another level, support for
Japan was sometimes an expression of race pride or defiance of American
racism, not necessarily political conviction.

During the internment most Japanese Americans did not subscribe to the
WRA's assimilation program but took from it selectively those aspects that
they wanted, for example, schooling and work.[20] They ignored or resisted
programs that they considered not in their interest, such as surveys and
family counseling. Most notably, many rejected WRA's strategy of "self-government," which comprised "community councils" of elected block representatives. Internees regarded WRA's policies that only U.S. citizens could be
elected to the councils and that all meetings had to be held in English to be
affronts to the older generation. In some camps, internees boycotted elections. Those serving on the community council tended to be associated with
the JACL or were otherwise pro-assimilationist. Internees criticized them for
being pro-Administration and generally ostracized real and suspected in-
formers and collaborators as *inu* (dog). The Issei in turn asserted their authority by creating alternate bodies of leadership and self-governance.[21]

In a broad sense, everyday life in the camps involved both Japanese and
American culture and politics. Leisure and recreational activities were bicul-
tural, including such activities as flower arranging, sock hops, go tourna-
ments, cutting trees at Christmastime, and baseball games (played daily at
Tule Lake, even at the height of its troubles). Internees observed Lincoln's,
Washington's, and the Emperor's birthdays. They paid respects to fallen
American soldiers on Memorial Day and prayed for fallen Japanese soldiers
on the Emperor's birthday. These events undoubtedly drew different groups
of people, but some internees acknowledged or attended both. Internees also
gave farewell parties in the blocks whenever an individual or family departed

camp, whether to join the army, repatriate to Japan, resettle to Chicago, or relocate to Tule Lake (where "disloyals" were segregated). These patterns suggest not only that American and Japanese nationalisms coexisted in the camps but also that many internees were more invested in preserving ethnic solidarity than they were in politics per se. At another level, politically-minded internees on both sides criticized "fence-sitters." A pro-Japan nationalist said, "They are sitting on the fence waiting to see who is going to win the war. If the Americans win they are going to be Americans. If the Japanese win, they are going to be Japanese. . . . Such persons are no good for *any* country."[22]

Of course, internees' ability to self-organize was limited. For one, administrators did not have to negotiate with internees and ultimately had the backing of the army to enforce its authority. Second, internees had little power to enforce decisions made democratically amongst themselves. For example, in the early months of internment at Rohwer camp in Arkansas, Japanese Americans debated whether they should accept employment at a nearby factory that manufactured camouflage material for the army. The camp voted that they would work to produce food for the camp but not to assist the army. Nevertheless many internees took the jobs anyway.[23]

This example also illustrates a tension between politics and practicality. War talk and political debate in the camp were ubiquitous, especially among Issei men, for whom daily kibitzing was a major activity.[24] Yet even as internees obsessed over news and rumors from the outside, the import of political developments lay more in the practical realm of what they meant for their future. Many Japanese Americans believed that after the war they would be deported en masse or that even if they were not forcibly repatriated, it would be impossible to remain in the United States, where they were hated. These scenarios could be imagined no matter which side won the war. At the same time, many wished to stay in America—they regarded the United States as their adopted country and as the native homeland of their children. They had built a life in America and did not want to sacrifice their property. While some internees left the camps during the war to repatriate to Japan or to resettle in areas outside the West, most Japanese Americans wanted to remain in camp until the war ended. They preferred to await the peace and to keep their options open.[25] The pragmatic strategy required a certain balancing of dual nationalisms and dual allegiances. But that effort was thrown into crisis in early months of 1943, when the WRA required all adult internees to fill out a lengthy registration form to ascertain their loyalty to the United States.

The Loyalty Questionnaire

This famous intervention was officially called "Application for Leave Clearance." Its genesis lay in two initiatives that the War Department and the

WRA designed in order to promote Japanese Americans' citizenship and assimilation, the volunteer combat unit and resettlement, respectively.

It will be recalled that after Pearl Harbor the military ceased to induct Japanese Americans into service. Since the beginning of the war the JACL had vigorously lobbied the government for the Nisei's right to enlist, in order to prove their loyalty. As JACL leader Mike Masaoka explained, "We had to have a demonstration in blood." A few in the War Department began to argue for a reversal in the military's policy against Nisei military service, notably Assistant Secretary of War John McCloy and Director of the Office of War Information Elmer Davis. They believed the formation of a Nisei combat unit would rehabilitate Japanese Americans' citizenship and public image.[26] Davis explained:

> This matter is of great interest to OWI. Japanese propaganda to the Philippines, Burma, and elsewhere insists that this is a racial war. We can combat this effectively with counter propaganda only if our deeds permit us to tell the truth. Moreover, as citizens ourselves who believe deeply in the things for which we fight, we cannot help but be disturbed by the insistent public misunderstanding of the Nisei.[27]

In January 1943, after several months of debate, the War Department decided to proceed with the Nisei combat unit. The department stressed the importance of the volunteer nature of the project. According to McCloy's assistant, Colonel William Scobey, "[T]he advantage of the voluntary program to the Japanese Americans cannot be overemphasized. They must realize that a voluntary combat team constitutes a symbol of their loyalty which can be displayed to the American public and to those who oppose the Japanese Americans. Involuntary induction by means of the draft greatly detracts from that symbol." To make the symbol effective the War Department also deemed it necessary to create a segregated unit comprising only Nisei. To determine the loyalty of prospective volunteers and to effectuate their release from camp, it developed a questionnaire for male internees within the age range for military service and various investigative procedures.[28]

The WRA proposed that the loyalty questionnaire be extended to all internees over the age of seventeen. The WRA, committed to its assimilationist goal of returning Japanese Americans to the mainstream of American life, desired a mechanism to separate the truly disloyal from the loyal majority, in order to relocate the latter out of the camps. It was disappointed in the slow progress of its program of voluntary-leave clearance, by which internees determined to be loyal could move to an area outside the West Coast, provided they had personal sponsorship and an offer of employment or education. By the end of 1942 only 866 internees had relocated, mostly Nisei college students and young adults with ambition and without familial responsibilities. In the fall and winter of 1942 the WRA debated segregating the camp population by class—"Kibei, aliens, old bachelors, parolees, repatriates . . . although few people could agree on the same set of categories." The WRA decided that the loyalty questionnaire would "give us a basis for forming judgments as to an individual person's loyalty that may be reasonably sound."[29]

Registration, as it was called, was compulsory. The questionnaire was lengthy, comprising some eighty questions about religious affiliation, educational and occupational background, and the like. Many questions concerned cultural knowledge and practices, evincing the WRA's use of culture as an index of loyalty: "Will you conform to the customs and dress of your new home?" "Do you think you are 'losing face' by cooperating with the U.S. government?" and "Do you believe in the divine origin of the Japanese race?" There were also more direct questions about loyalty: "What would you do if you found a shortwave [radio] set . . . in your neighbor's apartment?" and "Give five references of people who can vouch for your conduct in the center other than members of your family. Include at least two representatives of the administration."

But the most incendiary questions were question 27, asked of all males of military age, "Are you willing to serve in the armed forces of the United States on combat duty, wherever ordered?" and question 28, asked of all adult internees, "Will you swear unqualified allegiance to the United States of America and faithfully defend the United States from any or all attack by foreign or domestic forces, and forswear any form of allegiance or obedience to the Japanese emperor, or any other foreign government, power or organization?"[30]

The registration program provoked widespread confusion, resentment, and opposition. The title of the questionnaire, "Application for Leave Clearance," suggested to many internees that they would be forcibly relocated to unfamiliar and hostile areas, without means and without their sons, whom many believed would now be drafted. Answering "yes" to question 28 would have made the Issei, who were barred from American citizenship, stateless persons. Moreover, expressing disloyalty to their country of birth connoted a lack of personal integrity. An Issei explained, "No Issei would disobey the laws of the United States. . . . In that sense they can be called loyal to the United States. On the other hand, none of them are disloyal to Japan."[31]

In every center there were mass meetings, some of them "extremely turbulent," where internees debated and argued over what to do. Family relations also strained. Some Issei parents pressured their children to answer "no" in order to keep the family together or to keep their sons out of the military. Some Nisei, having "seen their parents uprooted and humiliated . . . resolved to spare their elders any further worry and sadness, suppressed their own desires and voted 'no.'" Other Nisei militantly refused to register, contrary to their parents' wishes. Yamato Ichihashi noted that "the young people are very serious this time, and do not yield very easily. . . . Their parents are worried over the twenty year sentences" that they risked for refusing to register.[32]

Among the Nisei, including those who answered "yes," there was widespread opposition to the volunteer combat team. Ichihashi, who had thought that the Nisei would have done anything to get out of camp, wrote, "They began to grumble about the government's maltreatment accorded them since their evacuation, denying their rights of citizenship. . . . A number of Issei sympathized with the discontented Nisei." In fact, when his own son Woodrow considered volunteering, Ichihashi "vehemently opposed" the idea, arguing that if he were drafted he must not break the law, but he should not volunteer because the government had interned him.[33]

WRA administrators responded to the internees' resistance variously with persuasion and coercion. At Heart Mountain, Gila, and Tule Lake, administrators threatened recalcitrant internees with the Espionage Act, which made it a felony to obstruct the recruitment or enlistment of service to the United States. Of the 1,700 draft-eligible males at Heart Mountain, only 42 volunteered for service and over 400 answered "no." At Tule Lake, whole blocks vowed not to register and signed up, instead, for repatriation and expatriation. Despite mass arrests, as many as one-third of the residents at Tule Lake refused to register and the program was never actually completed.[34]

In all, 87 percent of the eligible internees gave an unqualified "yes" answer to the loyalty questions. (Issei "yes" answers improved when WRA reworded question 28: "Will you swear to abide by the laws of the United States and to take no action which would in any way interfere with the war effort of the United States?") Those who answered "yes" represented a range of motivation and belief. While many undoubtedly welcomed the opportunity to state their loyalty to the United States, others trod the path of least resistance and hoped that a "yes" answer would shield them from further accusations of disloyalty.[35]

Thirteen percent either refused to register or answered "no" to one or both questions. Fully 20 percent of Nisei males answered "no." Refusal to register or "no" answers were highest at Tule Lake (42 percent) and at Manzanar and Jerome (26 percent each). The War Department had hoped for 5,000 volunteers for the Nisei combat team, but fewer than 1,200 signed up. By contrast, over 3,000 internees applied for repatriation or expatriation during the registration period. (In Hawai'i, where there was no internment, 10,000 Nisei volunteered for combat service). The low rate of resettlement after the registration disappointed the WRA. During 1943 and 1944 about 15 percent of the total population left the camps each year on "indefinite leave" to resettle in the Midwest and East.[36]

Following registration, the WRA designated Tule Lake as a "segregation center" for disloyal Japanese Americans. The agency believed the disloyals were the source of "non-cooperation" and responsible for disturbances in the camps and now sought to remove and isolate the troublemakers. In the fall of 1943 the WRA transferred all disloyals to Tule Lake and sent loyal Tuleans to other camps, although the shift was not perfect because loyal family members accompanied disloyals to Tule Lake and some 1,100 loyal Tuleans simply refused to relocate. Segregation at Tule Lake applied to all those who refused to register or answered "no" to the loyalty questions (even if one later changed one's answer to "yes"), all those who had requested repatriation or expatriation (including those who answered "yes"), and any others with "adverse information" in their file. The registration segregants and prospective repatriates amounted to some 12,000 people. Another 4,000 people at Tule Lake comprised family members of segregrants. Although the WRA used specific criteria for segregation, it described disloyals and loyals in vague terms that reproduced the view that one's attitude towards assimilation was the key index of loyalty: the disloyals were "people who have indicated their desire to follow the Japanese way of life," and loyals were those "who wish to be American."[37]

The transfer of all disloyals to Tule Lake did not eliminate tension and conflict in the other camps. The loyal ranged from the superpatriotic JACL to those who continued to hold divided allegiances. The *inu* problem continued. Conflict actually *increased* at some centers when administrators responded to resistance to resettlement with "retrenchment" policies aimed at "making life [in camp] less easy-going." At Minidoka, relations between residents and administrators deteriorated after strikes by camp maintenance-workers, mail carriers, and construction workers and the director cancelled a popular experimental high school program.[38]

When in January 1944 the government resumed its policy of drafting Japanese Americans into the military, new conflicts arose. Some 2,800 Nisei were drafted out of the camps into a segregated infantry unit. While many went willingly, others believed the draft was yet another humiliation. Some Nisei tried to fail their physical examinations in order to avoid induction. Three hundred fifteen Nisei refused induction outright; 263 were convicted in federal courts and sent to prison.[39]

At Tule Lake, segregation produced new problems and conflicts. Officially, segregation was not considered punitive. But Tule Lake differed from other camps in that no one was allowed the privilege of leave clearance and there was no "self-government." American schooling was not compulsory; residents were allowed to establish Japanese-language schools, on grounds that they were returning to Japan. That logic also led the agency to allow "expressions of loyalty to Japan."[40]

In the fall of 1943 a series of events at Tule Lake led to mass demonstrations, violence, and martial law. In October, 800 farmworkers went on strike after a truck accident resulted in a worker's death. Internees held a mass public funeral in defiance of the camp director, Raymond Best, who had

prohibited it. Mass demonstrations protesting camp working and living conditions and Best's decision to bring in "loyal" farmworkers from other camps
as strikebreakers led to violent confrontations with WRA personnel. On November 4 the army entered the camp with guns and tanks, arrested 18 men,
and put 9 in the stockade. It declared martial law and occupied Tule Lake for
two months, during which time it continued to pick up suspected leaders,
often in the middle of the night. Ultimately some 350 were detained in the
stockade, some for as long as eight months, though no charges were ever
brought against any of them.[41]

The stockade became a "symbol of oppression to the entire colony." While
residents continued to protest with a partial strike and passive resistance,
administrators' efforts to create an alternate body of leadership comprising
"responsible men" failed. At the same time, factionalism among the internees
worsened, as a group of ardent pro-Japan nationalists demanded immediate
repatriation to Japan and "resegregation" to separate themselves from those
who they said were not "true disloyals" but were really loyal, *inu,* or "fence
sitters."[42]

In fact, most of the internees who had applied for repatriation and expatriation did not want to go to Japan immediately but wanted to see the
outcome of the war. Others had requested repatriation in order to avoid
resettlement or military service. A Tule Lake resident distinguished between
two groups of disloyals: those who "would not die for the United States yet
who would not surrender their American citizenship or do any acts against
the United States. Whereas another group would do anything in their power
to aid Japan and would not do any more than compelled to do for the
United States."[43]

The militant nationalists formed the *Sokuji Kikoku Hoshi Dan* (Organization to Return Immediately to the Homeland to Serve) and two subsidiaries,
Hokoku Seinen Dan (for young men) and *Hokoku Joshi Seinen Dan* (for
women and girls). The Hokoku Seinen Dan presented itself as a cultural, not
political, group, organized according to three principles:

> 1. To increase the appreciation of our racial heritage by a study of the
> incomparable culture of our mother country; 2. To abide by [WRA] reg-
> ulations and to refrain from any involvement in center politics; to be in-
> terested only in improving our moral life and in building our charac-
> ter; 3. To participate in physical exercises in order to keep ourselves in
> good health.[44]

In truth, the language classes and lectures on Japanese culture emphasized
Japan's war aims, and morning exercises became increasingly "exhibition-
istically militaristic." Nisei youth who were contemplating expatriation after
the war "flocked in droves" to the language and cultural programs, eager to
learn the "Japanese way of life," although many became uncomfortable with

the Hokoku Seinen Dan's extreme nationalism. The militants also became increasingly aggressive and coercive in promoting their program as the marker of racial authenticity, of the "true Japanese." They physically assaulted suspected *inu* and were implicated in the murder of one resident. Administrators, having conceded the disloyals' right to "prepare" for repatriation, did nothing to address the growing disorder.[45]

Renunciation of Citizenship

It was in this context that the renunciations of citizenship took place. Congress in July 1944 passed the Denationalization Act, which authorized citizens to make voluntary renunciation of citizenship provided that the attorney general did not find it detrimental to the interests of the United States. The act broke a long legal tradition prohibiting renunciation of citizenship on U.S. soil and during wartime, which aimed to prevent citizens from evading military service or aiding the enemy.[46]

Just as the loyalty questionnaire had aimed to facilitate assimilation through military service and resettlement, the renunciation act was similarly originally intended to promote Japanese Americans' citizenship and their reintegration into society. Attorney General Francis Biddle anticipated that the Supreme Court would find the internment of citizens not charged with any crime unconstitutional. He desired a way to release the great mass of internees but to detain at Tule Lake the "resegregationists," whom he believed were truly disloyal and should not be allowed to be "at large on the West Coast." Biddle thought that, given the opportunity, the pro-Japan nationalists would renounce their American citizenship, which would permit their continued detention. The attorney general also sought a more moderate course as a compromise to "punitive and constitutionally doubtful" bills introduced in Congress that called for mass repatriation and for revoking the citizenship of all Japanese Americans who answered "no" to the loyalty oath. As Rep. Clair Engle of California explained, "We don't want those Japs back in California and the more we can get rid of the better."[47]

In a sense, the attorney general's logic acknowledged that the loyalty oath was a failure. It had not distinguished loyal from disloyal Japanese Americans. Biddle did not think that Japanese Americans were, as a group, disloyal. In fact, he had been the only high-ranking member of the Roosevelt administration who opposed internment in the weeks following Pearl Harbor, even though in the end he acquiesced to the War Department. If the registration program had produced too many "false negatives," voluntary renunciation would, Biddle thought, allow authorities to identify and detain the truly disloyal and release everyone else, serving "the purposes both of national defense and of safeguarding civil liberties." All interests—

the loyal and the disloyal, the government, the Constitution—would thus be satisfied.[48]

It did not turn out that way. The citizenship renunciation program, like registration, was engulfed in confusion, resentment, and opposition, and produced far more renunciations than anyone expected. If renunciation became the new standard for disloyalty, WRA and Justice Department officials failed to recognize the perverse meanings that loyalty and disloyalty had acquired through registration and segregation. In effect, the government had merely ratcheted up the requirement for staying in camp.

In October 1944 the Department of Justice announced regulations for renunciation of citizenship. The procedure required the prospective renunciant to write to Washington for an application and an individual hearing to determine that the renunciation was both voluntary and not detrimental to the United States. The Hokuku Seinen Dan agitated for renunciation and widely distributed blank application forms, but by mid-December only 600 had applied to renounce their citizenship.[49] When Tule Lake officials received reports from informants that "several thousand Nisei and Kibei may apply" for renunciation, the solicitor's office of the WRA conceded there was a "considerable danger that potentially good Americans who are temporarily embittered by evacuation and detention may be stampeded into hasty action which they will regret for the rest of their lives." However, he instructed a passive course of action: "While we should not actively discourage evacuees from proceeding to renounce their citizenship, we should give them any information they request with respect to the legal consequences of renunciation."[50]

On December 18 the Supreme Court ruled in *Ex parte Endo* that protection from sabotage and espionage did not permit the government to detain citizens who it conceded were loyal. Two announcements directly flowed from *Endo*. First, the Western Defense Command rescinded the mass exclusion order and announced that it would exclude persons from the West Coast only on an individual basis. The army immediately sent officers to Tule Lake to conduct individual exclusion hearings. Second, the WRA announced it would close the camps within one year.[51]

One would think that Japanese Americans would welcome these announcements. In fact, the war was not yet over and many internees remained apprehensive about leaving the camps, even for California, where they feared mass hostility towards them still existed. By March 1945 only 1,500 Japanese Americans from all camps had returned to California. The situation was not helped by discouraging reports from those who had returned to California to find that their homes and farms had been stolen, destroyed, or ill cared for in their absence; that housing was scarce; and that the only employment available was menial labor. The WRA would spend months cajoling internees

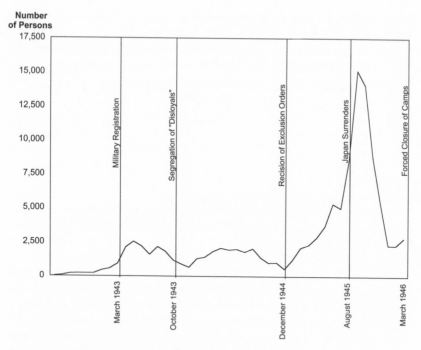

Number
of Persons

5.2 Outmigration from War Relocation Authority centers, by year. Outmigration includes indefinite leave and terminal departure for relocation, military service, institutions, internment camps, and repatriation to Japan. (Source: Dorothy Swaine Thomas, *The Salvage* [Berkeley, 1952], table 25, p. 615.)

to leave the camps, but most did not in fact leave until the war ended (see figure 5.2).[52]

At Tule Lake, administrators noted that the most "discernible evacuee reaction [to the rescission of the mass exclusion order] was opposed to relocation" and "passive resistance." Most troubling to internees, disloyalty no longer guaranteed that they would remain in camp. Worse yet, those given individual exclusion orders by the army (and it was unclear on what grounds these decisions were made) would have to resettle outside of the West Coast. Many drew the conclusion that renouncing citizenship was the now only way to remain in camp. At Tule Lake, internees reported that they were asked during individual exclusion hearings, "Do you want to go out or do you want to renounce your citizenship?"[53]

Between mid-December and the end of January some 5,500 internees applied to renounce their citizenship. At Tule Lake 85 percent of the citizens over the age of seventeen renounced their citizenship.[54] They justified their actions variously—to ensure repatriation, to avoid resettlement, to avoid the draft. A minority was militantly pro-Japan and sought immediate repatriation—those whom the Justice Department had originally targeted. For example, a Nisei woman who, with her husband, joined the resegregationist organizations explained that they had been loyal Americans but were angry that the government interned them and treated their citizenship as

> but scrap-papers that gave us no privileges what so ever. . . . Eventually it is true, that the questions and the discontentments of ours caused us to doubt and turn our mind. . . . Therefore thousands of us rose decisively to clarify our status by fulfilling our duties for a true sovereign. . . . We renounced our U.S.A. citizenships to clarify our status so that we would do our parts openly as Japanese whether in time of WAR or after the WAR. We offered our serimonious-bow [sic] to the Emperor of Japan every morning and prayed the Victory of Japan.[55]

Others would later state that they had been intimidated by the Hokoku Seinen Dan and renounced under pressure and in fear of reprisals.[56] But more commonly internees renounced their citizenship for considered, instrumental reasons. Many believed, for example, that only by renouncing citizenship could they avoid resettlement and remain in camp until the war ended. An Issei explained: "Put it this way. If you're a Hakujin [white American], you take this matter of soiling your loyalty record seriously and would never say anything to [soil] it. But if you're a Jap and nobody believes your loyalty in this country anyway, you'll think about your future and your family. . . . We're going to have [our children] renounce citizenship just to stay here."[57]

A Nisei said, "You know why the boys are renouncing? They are dodging the Army draft." In some families, the son renounced to avoid the draft but the daughter did not, so the family could keep one foot in America. Even among those who described themselves as "earnest" Japanese nationalists, there was a measure of instrumentalism: "We [want to] be on the priority list to be [repatriated] to Japan. We may change our feeling after the war, but for the time being, we must rely on the Emperor of Japan, not the U.S. government."[58]

At the same time, others were skeptical about renouncing their citizenship. One internee said, "[I]n a way you['re] just playing into these guys [the Justice Department's] hands. . . . As I see it, it's a frame up." Another stated, "I wasn't going to give them any weapon with my renunciation. . . . You've got everything to lose and nothing to gain." Still others expressed contempt for the Hokuku's campaign to renounce and repatriate, pointing out that many proponents were Kibei who had returned to the United States between 1935 and 1937 in order to avoid the draft in Japan. "Japan doesn't want those draft dodgers. Those fellows without citizenship will just become another International Problem," said one.[59]

John Burling, a special assistant to Attorney General Biddle, oversaw the individual renunciation hearings at Tule Lake. Burling was determined that the "super patriots be moved out of Tule Lake" and promised that "those who have renounced their citizenship, will without much warning be put on a train and sent out." Burling used a narrow definition of coercion—direct threat of immediate physical violence to oneself or a family member—to determine whether the renunciation was voluntary. The hearings proceeded with dispatch. Between March and May, the Justice Department approved 5,049 applications for renunciation of citizenship.[60]

Burling also considered the open pro-Japan activity in the camp a potential public relations disaster and did what the Tule Lake WRA administrators had been unwilling to do—he ordered that all activities promoting "Japanese nationalistic and anti-American activities and the disruption to the peace and security within the center" immediately cease. In January and February camp authorities raided the offices of Hokoku and Hoshi Dan, seizing Japanese flags, mimeograph machines, and documents, and arrested their leaders. Between December and May it sent 1,061 "renouncees and other aliens" to Justice Department detention centers in Santa Fe, New Mexico, and Bismarck, North Dakota. While the suppression of the nationalist organizations came as a relief to some, it also suggested that the WRA rewarded extreme disloyalty with detention while punishing all others with forced resettlement. Applications for renunciation continued to pour into the Justice Department through the end of February.[61]

Assistant Attorney General Herbert Weschler sent each renunciant a letter stating, "You are no longer a citizen of the United States . . . nor are you entitled to any of the rights and privileges of such citizenship." The Immigration and Naturalization Service further warned them, "Since you have renounced your United States citizenship, you are now considered to be aliens."[62]

Even before the attorney general approved the renunciations, some people began to change their minds. A few reconsidered and withdrew their application at their hearing; others regretted their action almost immediately afterwards. Beginning in late March, before the hearings were concluded, a number of renunciants wrote to the Justice Department asking to rescind their renunciations. They also asked the minister and project attorney at Tule Lake to help them. A number wrote to the ACLU. Their efforts were to no avail, even though the Justice Department was well aware that avoiding forced relocation was the principal reason for renouncing, not disloyalty.[63]

The Justice Department rebuffed all appeals from renunciants seeking to restore their citizenship, including those who wrote to withdraw their applications before they were acted upon. Edward Ennis of the Enemy Alien Control Unit told one renunciant who said he had been "confused" and "made a mistake" that, once approved, "loss of citizenship is complete." He added, "Since, as a person of the Japanese race, you are not eligible for naturaliza- tion, I can perceive no way by which your citizenship can be regained."[64]

Why did these renunciants change their minds? Some expressed regret that they had behaved without fully considering the implications of their actions. Wrote one, "I realize now that I should not have let [pressure] intimidate me and should have kept my citizenship. I should never have done anything so rash."[65] Minoru Kiyota, who had renounced his citizenship as "the one last thing I could do to express my fury toward the government of the United States," recalled that almost immediately after he submitted his application to renounce, it "dawned" on him,

> They got me! The American government threw me into a concentration camp, labeled me dangerous because I wouldn't declare my loyalty, intimi- dated me, and subjected me to extreme mental and physical stress. In fact, the government did such a good job of manipulating me that I just gave up my United States citizenship—voluntarily! Now they could deport me to Japan without any trouble at all, I realized.[66]

But, if most renunciants had acted out of a deliberate calculus to promote their individual or family's agenda, what happened to alter that calculus? The renunciants began to reconsider when they realized Japan was losing the war and they faced the prospect of deportation. Although the Hokoku Seinen Dan aggressively rehearsed Japanese war propaganda (received by short-wave radio) about Japan's military victories, there was, by the spring of 1945, enough news from other sources that suggested otherwise. After a visit to nearby Boise, a Kibei at Minidoka realized that his belief that Japan would win the war was unfounded. He became "resigned to staying in this country now. Japan's lost the war and there's no use in going back." At Tule Lake the internees learned that Germany surrendered in May and worriedly followed news about the fighting on Okinawa in June. Those who believed that "we Japanese should be talking of Japan winning the war" knew their talk was beginning to ring hollow.[67]

On July 14 President Truman issued Executive Order 2655, which declared that enemy aliens deemed "dangerous to the public peace and safety of the United States because they have adhered to . . . enemy governments . . . shall be subject upon order of the Attorney General to removal from the United States."[68] For the militant pro-Japan nationalists who wanted immediate re- patriation, this was good news. But most never actually wanted repatriation, only the *option* to repatriate, and in the present context they viewed the prospect of deportation with shock and dread. In renouncing their citizen- ship, most internees had acted according to a strategy of keeping their fami- lies together in camp and awaiting the peace to see where their better pros- pects lay. This strategy led them to make certain decisions to forestall one undesired consequence, only to constrain their future options in other ways. In fact, internees had never had much maneuverability or power. Despite Japanese Americans' efforts to resist the government's programs and to control their own fate, the forces that really determined their situation were the army, WRA, and Justice Department. Disloyalty, segregation, and renunciation in effect comprised a teleological journey that they understood only when they arrived at the penultimate point, the threshold of deportation to war-devastated Japan.

The dropping of atomic bombs on Hiroshima and Nagasaki on August 6 and 8 and Japan's surrender on August 14 created "major, mass emotional upheavals" at Tule Lake. The war was over, the army rescinded the individual exclusion orders, all were "free to leave whether they were Issei, Kibei, or Nisei, unless they were on the Department of Justice detention lists [i.e., renunciants]." Tule Lake project attorney Louis Noyes reported that a "large portion" of the camp population had "only been interested in staying in the center for the duration of the war" and was "caught off guard" by the sudden need to think concretely about resettlement. At the same time, the renunciants were "frozen," denied the right to leave and faced with the prospect of deportation. A member of Hokoku Seinen Dan wrote to the Justice Department: "After Japan surrender[ed] unconditionally, I am particularly sorry [to have renounced]." Another stated, "With the recent catastrophe in Hiroshima, it is doubtful if my husband's parents survived, so our plans have changed. Now I realize the mistake that I made and am thoroughly regretful of my action." Some, especially Nisei who "never desired to go to Japan before evacuation and have never been to Japan," became "confused, frightened, desperate and panicky." They pleaded with the Justice Department to cancel their renunciations of citizenship and, if that were not possible, respectfully asked "if you would allow us even to leave this center as aliens."[69]

A month before the war ended, Wayne Collins, a civil-rights attorney affiliated with the ACLU in San Francisco, visited Tule Lake and met with the parents of some renunciants who wanted to restore their citizenship. Collins was outraged that Japanese Americans had been induced to renounce their citizenship. He took on their cases in what became a thirteen-year-long legal battle to restore the citizenship of 5,000 Japanese Americans.

After Japan's surrender the renunciants remained detained at Tule Lake, while the other residents began leaving camp to return to the West Coast; 4,724 repatriated to Japan, far fewer than the 20,000 that had applied for repatriation during the war.[70] The Justice Department was determined to deport the renunciants, but opinion within the department was divided as to their legal status. The Enemy Alien Control Unit's view that they were Japanese enemy-aliens was legally questionable, in light of the renunciants' birth in the United States and the end of the war.[71] In October the Justice Depart-

5.3 Japanese Americans who renounced their citizenship in the winter of 1944–1945 tried to restore their citizenship when the war ended. These citizen renunciants lined up for mitigation hearings at Tule Lake in 1945 to protest the INS's decision to deport them to Japan. (Courtesy of National Archives [210-CL-S-14].)

ment informed the renunciants that they were "native American aliens," fingerprinted and photographed them, and announced that on November 15, all renunciants would be deported to Japan.

Efforts by Collins, other ACLU attorneys and leaders, and WRA director Dillon Myer to persuade the Justice Department to reopen the renunciant cases failed.[72] In November, Collins filed two lawsuits, a habeas corpus action to release the renunciants from detention and a mass equity suit to restore the renunciants' citizenship, and won a restraining order against the deportations. Not wishing to keep Tule Lake open indefinitely while the lawsuits were pending, the Justice Department held "mitigation hearings" for some 3,300 renunciants who requested release. It released all but 406, whom the department determined it would continue to detain for deportation. It sent them, and some family members, to internment centers in Crystal City, Texas, and Seabrook Farms in Bridgeton, New Jersey.[73]

The lawsuits in U.S. District Court in San Francisco came before Judge Louis E. Goodman. Judge Goodman was the son of German-Jewish immigrants and a liberal pluralist. He believed in "true Americanism" and opposed "intolerance as to a fellow citizen's origin or color or creed," and his own experiences with anti-Semitism may have made him sensitive to the plight of Japanese Americans. In 1944 Goodman presided over the case of twenty-seven Tule Lake draft resisters. In a bold move, Goodman dropped all charges against them, writing in his opinion that it was a "shock to the conscience that an American citizen be confined without authority and then, while so under duress and restraint, for his Government to accept from him a surrender of his constitutional heritage."[74]

Collins argued that the renunciations should be voided because the renunciants had not acted voluntarily. They had renounced under conditions of duress and coercion, beginning with their deprivation of liberty by the internment itself and ending in an atmosphere of fear and intimidation created by the resegregationists at Tule Lake. In each case, the renunciant was not

> a free agent in any sense of the words but . . . was unlawfully confined and restrained of his or her liberty and was held in duress by the United States government, its agents, servants and employees, as the jailor, custodian and guardian of plaintiffs, its wards, and by it and its agents . . . knowingly was permitted to be exposed and subjected to the duress, menace, fraud, and undue influence practiced upon and against each plaintiff by organized terroristic groups and gangs of persons, likewise there confined, who were fanatically pro-Japanese and committed to forsaking this country and who were engaged in and allowed to engage in a continuous campaign to engender, develop and promote loyalty to Japan among the internees.[75]

Collins also challenged the constitutionality of the Denationalization Act on grounds that it authorized treasonous acts by enabling renunciation and expatriation during wartime and because its sole intent and application to Japanese Americans violated the Fourteenth Amendment's guarantee of equal protection. He argued further that the government's position that the renunciants were Japanese nationals was spurious because the United States does not recognize dual citizenship and that the renunciants could not be enemy aliens because the war was over.[76]

In June 1947 Judge Goodman granted the writ of habeas corpus and ordered the Justice Department to release the renunciants at Crystal City and Seabrook Farms. In April 1948 the court ruled in the mass equity suit. Invoking his own decision in the Tule Lake draft-resisters case, Goodman cancelled the renunciations on grounds that they had been made involuntarily under conditions of duress and declared their citizenship restored.[77]

The case was set back on appeal, however. In January 1951 the Ninth Circuit Court of Appeals partially overturned Goodman's decision. The court let stand the cancellations of renunciation of 899 people because they were under the age of twenty-one when they renounced, 8 people who were declared mentally incompetent, and 58 people who had gone to Tule Lake to be with their family. But it ordered individual hearings for more than 3,000 plaintiffs to determine whether each one had in fact acted voluntarily. In October the U.S. Supreme Court refused to hear the case. To avoid the time and expense of several thousands of court hearings, the Justice Department agreed to a procedure of administrative clearance.[78]

Accordingly, the plaintiffs filed individual affidavits for the department to review. To organize the massive job, Collins relied on a group of renunciants who had formed a committee while still in Tule Lake to organize the lawsuit. As the case proceeded over the years, the Tule Lake Defense Committee did the yeomen's work of staying in contact with plaintiffs, who were dispersed throughout California, as well as in Japan; raising funds to support the suit by soliciting pledges of $100 minimum from each plaintiff and collecting payments; and assisting plaintiffs with writing their affidavits.[79]

By 1959 all cases were resolved. Of 5,409 requests for restoration of citizenship, 4,978 were granted, and 347 were denied owing to "reliable evidence of disloyalty." The restored citizens included a number of Nisei who had expatriated to Japan after the war but found it difficult to live there and wished to return to the United States.[80]

As each case settled, Wayne Collins sent a letter with a certified copy of the "Final Order, Judgment and Decree" in the mass equity suit that, he explained, "forever cancels your renunciation and declares you to be a native born citizen of the United States" and "end[s] the litigation" in the matter. He wrote:

> You are now free to exercise and enjoy all the rights, privileges and immunities of United States citizenship. You now may register as a voter and vote at elections. You can purchase and lease land and buildings, hold public office, obtain civil service positions and public employment on the same basis as any other citizen. You now can obtain licenses on the same basis and at the same rates as other citizens. You now can obtain a U.S. passport to travel abroad and to re-enter the United States. . . . In States where old age pension laws provide pensions only for citizens you will, in course of time, become eligible for such old age pensions because you are a citizen of the United States. You can be taxed only on the same basis as other citizens. You cannot be classed or treated as an alien. You cannot be required to register as an alien or to apply for an alien registration card. If you are in Japan you can apply to the nearest U.S. Consul for a U.S. passport.[81]

When in 1959 the Department of Justice announced that it had restored citizenship to all the renunciants, Edward Ennis, who as head of the Enemy Alien Control Unit had vigorously pursued deporting the renunciants, was pleased. "I think the [department] has responded magnificently to the problems presented by taking practically all the 'divorced' citizens back into the family of our American country," he said.[82]

Ennis's turnabout reflected the shift in political winds between the war and the mid-1950s. At the end of the war, deportation of disloyal elements was the order of the day. In 1951 Judge Goodman anticipated the liberalism of the Warren Court, still a few years away; the Ninth Circuit's decision ordering individual determinations was more representative of the McCarthy era's obsessive suspicion of alleged subversives. But the Cold War also required the reconstruction of Japan as the principal American ally in East Asia. Accordingly, the Immigration and Naturalization (McCarran-Walter) Act of 1952 repealed Japanese exclusion and the racial requirement for naturalization. By the middle and late 1950s, a general rehabilitation of Japanese Americans' citizenship was underway, which despite being based on dispersal, assimilation, and ethnic denial, created a space for the renunciants to reclaim their citizenship.[83]

The renunciation and restoration of citizenship by some 5,000 Japanese Americans has been a minor narrative in the history of internment. In part this is because the renunciants—like the draft resisters—remained a stigmatized group within the Japanese American community during the postwar period. A Nisei complained, "Japan has been crushed, they do not want to go back to Japan in the condition that [it is] now and it is a good chance for them to slide from under and again get out and make it tougher for the real loyal ones." At the JACL's first national convention after the war in 1946, delegates bitterly criticized the renunciants and draft resisters for confusing white Americans as to which Nisei were loyal and which were disloyal. Veterans of the Nisei battalions urged, "No sympathy whatsoever [should] be shown towards the Tulelake [sic] and other such groups." Some recommended that the "troublemakers" be deported; the convention voted to bar them from membership in the JACL.[84]

The renunciants' alleged disloyalty disrupted the JACL's ability to construct a narrative of the camps that emphasized the undivided loyalty of Japanese Americans, their endurance and patience during internment, and their valor in military service. Although such a collective memory is understandable, as the slightest hint at disloyalty or Japanese nationalism might imply that the internment was justified, the demands of suppressed and reconstructed memories have influenced the historiography of renunciation. The literature has emphasized that in rejecting their citizenship the renunciants acted neither rationally nor out of disloyalty. Rather, it is said, the renunciants were angry and disillusioned by their internment and intimidated by the fanatical "pressure groups." The argument was first made in *The Spoilage*, published in 1946 by the Japanese Evacuation and Resettlement Study (JERS), an inde-

pendent investigation of the camps led by Berkeley sociologist Dorothy
Swaine Thomas. *The Spoilage*, as the title connotes, viewed the renunciations
as a tragic ending in the internment experience for Nisei and Kibei. Renunciation completed a "cycle" that began with evacuation and proceeded
through registration and segregation, parental pressure and "ruthless tactics
of pressure groups," ending finally in the renunciation of "their irreparably
depreciated American citizenship."[85]

Michi Weglyn's *Years of Infamy* (1976), one of the first comprehensive
accounts of internment influenced by the civil rights and Asian American
movements of the 1960s and early 1970s, placed internment and renunciation in the context of a long history of racism and oppression of Japanese
Americans; her tone was that of outrage more than tragedy. According to
Weglyn, thousands of citizens renounced because they were in a state of
"mass delirium" that was induced by internment, bureaucratic malfeasance,
and pressure from pro-Japan factions, which held the "neutral majority . . .
in a reign of terror."[86] Weglyn suggests that the government deliberately encouraged renunciations in order to rid the country of Japanese Americans.
She asks, were "the authorities determined to make the people disloyal? Were
total spoilage and deportation a damnation conspired at?"[87]

The only book-length treatment of renunciation, *Native American Aliens*
(1985), by Donald Collins (no relation to Wayne Collins), similarly states
that renunciation of citizenship had nothing to do with loyalty or disloyalty,
but was a protest against the wartime treatment accorded them and the
result of "mass hysteria . . . verging on panic."[88]

In a sense the literature expresses incredulity that any American would
renounce citizenship unless he or she was in an abnormal state of mind. In
the same vein, the cancellation of the renunciations of citizenship is celebrated as evidence of democracy's capacity for self-correction. But I suggest
that some scholars have projected their own valorization of citizenship back
onto the renunciants. I believe the conventional thinking on renunciation
exaggerates the influence of the nationalists. In part this has resulted from an
insufficiently critical reading of the sources. For example, JERS field research
at Tule Lake, which comprised the evidence of *The Spoilage*, gave dispropor-
tionate attention to the views of certain pro-Japan loyalists who were the
ethnographer's informants.[89] Weglyn and Donald Collins both used *The
Spoilage* as a principal primary source. They were further influenced by the
legal strategy adopted by Wayne Collins in the mass equity suit. That strategy
emphasized the involuntary nature of the renunciants' acts because that was
the only statutory ground from which to attack the renunciations as null and
void.[90]

While this was proper legal strategy, it should not be mistaken for a transparent explanation of the renunciants' actions. In fact, Collins took pains to

present the renunciants' stories in a manner that would support and not hurt their case. He instructed renunciants to stop writing personal letters to the Justice Department lest they concede that they acted voluntarily. Renunciants were instructed to send a form letter instead. Collins and the Tule Lake Defense Committee helped plaintiffs prepare their affidavits carefully, providing them with a list of questions that framed the desired narrative. It was a difficult job, given the narrow legal grounds for cancellation and the multiplicity of reasons that had gone into each person's decision. A member of the committee wrote to a renunciant in Chicago, "I have noticed that many of the renunciants are having the same difficulties. They are forced to write their affidavits 3 to 4 times before it is a presentable document. If you were in Los Angeles, I could outline it for you; but this is very difficult to do over a mail."[91] Another letter instructed a renunciant to rewrite his affidavit according to the following questions:

14. Did your parents apply to be repatriated to Japan because they feared that they being aliens would never again be accepted in the U.S. and because they feared Caucasians were hostile to Japanese?

15. Did your parents pressure you to sign an application for repatriation to Japan so that you would not be separated from them?

16. What were the names of the older people who urged you to join the Hokoku Seinen Dan? . . .

17. Did you ever try to resign from the organization?

18. Were you afraid to resign? . . .

20. Did any person tell you what would happen to you if you tried? . . .

23. Did you fear to be relocated in the U.S. . . . because of danger from hostile Caucasians and because you had no funds and no place to go?[92]

The affidavits written in the mid-1950s thus read differently from the statements made by Japanese Americans in the winter of 1944–45, when they renounced, and the letters they wrote in spring and fall of 1945, when they sought to cancel their renunciations. The comparison is imperfect because the latter two sets of data are much smaller. Still, it is striking that intimidation and coercion by the ultranationalists were only occasionally offered as reasons for renunciation in the earlier statements. This is not to say that the affidavits contained false statements but that they were carefully constructed representations of the renunciants' experiences and sentiments. In fact, the affidavits are much like the applications for renunciation, which, as Collins and others pointed out, also showed evidence of coaching. Both the applications for renunciation and the affidavits to reclaim citizenship were carefully written to obtain a desired response from the authorities.

The problem with the overemphasis on intimidation and coercion is that it casts the renunciants as victims without individual agency. It constructs them as people whose actions were controlled by others, whether coercive parents or fanatical pressure groups. It also shifts the blame to other Japanese and reproduces stereotypes about Japanese culture as extremist, as manifested in patriarchal families and fanatical nationalism. Because the mass-delirium theory relieves renunciants of responsibility for their actions, it also leaves intact the belief that Japanese Americans were categorically not disloyal, which belief is critical to the collective memory of internment.

To be sure, the duress of internment, insensitivity and miscalculations by the WRA, parental pressures, and the coercive atmosphere created by the extreme nationalists were all factors that contributed to the renunciants' actions. But there is another factor, not acknowledged in the literature, that should make us more cautious about we how assess Japanese Americans' attitudes towards citizenship: the influence of dual nationalism. The renunciants were not exclusively patriotic citizens of the United States who were but temporarily confused. Rather, they held complicated, divided loyalties, a set of allegiances that sustained commitment to life in America alongside affective and cultural ties, even patriotic sympathies, with Japan. They may have considered the Hoshi Dan and Hokoku Seinen Dan to be extremists, but they did not necessarily believe it was abhorrent to support Japan. It may seem bizarre that people would fight to stay in a concentration camp, but Japanese Americans were not crazy to think that white Americans despised them. For otherwise loyal American citizens, repatriation to Japan was not unthinkable in the context of the war and internment.

At the same time, the history of the citizenship renunciations suggests that even if Japanese Americans sustained dual nationalisms, their patriotic ties to *both* the U.S. and Japanese nation-states were nevertheless weak. They were, above all, pragmatic people, who made pragmatic choices that were neither irrational nor primarily motivated by nationalist politics. In July 1945 the majority of citizen renunciants at Tule Lake did not so much awake from a mass delirium as realize that Japan was losing the war. They knew the liabilities of remaining in the United States without citizenship, as aliens or as stateless persons. Scholars have tended to shy away from this point—Donald Collins does not even mention Hiroshima—perhaps because it suggests opportunism. In fact this was a common charge that the superpatriots on *both* sides made against the nonideological majority.

But if the renunciants acted out of self-interest they were no different from most ordinary people, who are concerned more with their individual and family's well-being than with the interests of the nation-state. Their ethnic identity comprised many elements of historical experience and imagination, in which Japanese nationalism—an amalgam of signals from the homeland nation-state and the local interests of ethnic elites—was not necessarily the most central or even well formed. American nationalism was likewise weak, for the United States had constructed Japanese Americans as the despised racial other and consigned them to alien citizenship. The war put enormous pressure on these slender reeds of patriotisms, and Japanese Americans acted in myriad ways that were at once principled and pragmatic efforts to respond to an impossible choice.

Internment was a crisis of citizenship, in which citizenship was first nullified on grounds of race and then reconstructed by means of internment, forced cultural assimilation, and ethnic dispersal. The conflicts over the WRA's assimilation policies—camp governance, the loyalty oath, the volunteer combat unit, resettlement, segregation, and citizenship renunciation— might be read as conflicts over the cultural content of citizenship. But Japanese Americans also understood that citizenship is, in the first instance, a formal status with explicit legal rights and obligations, and that loyalty is a matter of political, not cultural, practice. Without that foundation, any effort by the government to impose a normative cultural citizenship could only have had perverse results.

Chapter Six

The Cold War Chinese Immigration Crisis and the Confession Cases

> The subpoenas in question can only be used for the obvious purpose of oppressing and intimidating the entire Chinese American community in San Francisco and, whether intentional or otherwise, they are having the effect of stigmatizing the social and family status of a respected community with criminal coloration.
> —Chinese Six Companies, 1956[1]

THE CHINESE have the dubious distinction of being the only group to be excluded from immigration into the United States explicitly by name. The Chinese exclusion laws, which barred all Chinese laborers from entry and prohibited Chinese from acquiring naturalized citizenship, generated the nation's first illegal aliens as well as the first alien citizens. Although the Supreme Court ruled in 1898 that Chinese born in the United States were citizens, the premises of exclusion—the alleged racial unassimilability of Chinese—powerfully influenced Americans' perceptions of Chinese Americans as permanent foreigners. Excluded from the polity and for the most part confined to Chinatown ghettoes and an ethnic economy, Chinese Americans remained marginalized from the mainstream of society well into the twentieth century.[2]

Chinese Americans' political and social standing in the United States rose and fell on multiple occasions from the 1930s to the 1960s, along with shifting American foreign policy and war interests. During the Sino-Japanese War in the 1930s, American sympathies lay with China. The United States was not a party to the conflict, but the Roosevelt administration sent arms to China and American missionaries' firsthand accounts of the war inspired widespread sympathy for the Chinese people. For example, Pearl S. Buck's *The Good Earth*, a humanist narrative of the Chinese peasantry, was one of the biggest best-sellers of the 1930s, according to one source second only to *Gone with the Wind*.[3] China had long been the "sick man of Asia," but Americans now read a noble pathos in its suffering, and Chinese Americans benefited from the association.

The Sino-Japanese War prompted widespread mobilization among Chinese Americans to support China. Chinatown communities hosted mass demonstrations, raised funds, and organized campaigns to stop the shipment of American scrap metal to Japan. Gender did the work of Chinese nationalism to particular effect, especially with the American public. The beautiful, Wellesley-educated Soong May Ling (Madame Chiang Kai-Shek) won the hearts of Americans in her tour of the United States. After Pearl Harbor and the American entrance into the Pacific war, China became a formal ally of the United States. Over twelve thousand Chinese American men and women served in the U.S. armed forces, and many construed their contribution to the war in terms of patriotism and national loyalty to both the United States *and* China.[4]

In 1943 Congress repealed the Chinese exclusion laws as a wartime measure to counter Japanese propaganda that held up Chinese exclusion as evidence of American's anti-Asiatic race policies.[5] But Congress's continued antipathy towards Chinese migration was evident in the annual Chinese quota of 105. This quota was unlike all other immigration quotas in that it was not for China but for all Chinese in the world, regardless of their country of birth or residence. The global Chinese race quota addressed the ways in which the Chinese diaspora mapped onto the system of national origins quotas. With the repeal of exclusion, Chinese in the British colony of Hong Kong would have had access to Britain's vast, mostly unused quota, and Chinese living in Cuba and other parts of the Western Hemisphere would have had unrestricted entrance. The global race quota was necessary to limit Chinese immigration.

Yet, the repeal of Chinese exclusion was an important democratic reform that ended a sixty-year-long racist policy. Exclusion's repeal legitimated Chinese immigration, allowed Chinese to naturalize as citizens, and opened the way for nonquota family migration. During the war Chinese Americans made other democratic gains as well: the war economy created opportunities for Chinese American employment outside of the Chinatown ethnic economy and the narrow occupational streams (Chinese hand-laundries and restaurants) that served white Americans. In the immediate postwar years a small number of Chinese intellectuals and professionals immigrated to the United States, as well as war brides and other family members of Chinese Americans. An expanded and reinvigorated Chinese American middle class began to live in suburbs and in university communities. In these ways Chinese began to move out of marginal, isolated Chinatown communities.[6]

Yet, the Chinese Revolution of 1949 and the advent of the Cold War attenuated and complicated the modest wartime progress that Chinese Americans had made in their legal standing and socioeconomic position. In a few short years the dominant image of Chinese lurched from despised oriental "other" to wartime ally to dangerous Communist threat. In the context of shifting

political winds both Chinese Americans and the U.S. government grappled
with the legacies of exclusion. In particular, exclusion had generated a widespread practice of illegal Chinese immigration. William Jack Chow, an immigration attorney, estimated that at least half of all Chinese immigrants during
the exclusion era entered the United States illegally. A conservative estimate,
based on a review of official data, indicates that at least 25 percent of the
Chinese American population in 1950 was unlawfully present in the United
States.[7] Most of the illegal immigrants comprised so-called paper sons—tens
of thousands of Chinese who entered the United States during the first half
of the twentieth century by posing as the sons of Chinese with American
citizenship by native birth.

While Chinese Americans sought to resolve this problem as part of a postexclusion trajectory toward legitimate migration and citizenship, the government felt during the Cold War a new urgency to eliminate illegal immigration. During the mid-1950s the United States Departments of State and
Justice waged a coordinated campaign to eliminate paper immigration, culminating in the Chinese Confession Program sponsored by the Immigration
and Naturalization Service. The INS pledged to help legalize Chinese who
confessed to their illegal status, and the vast majority of the thirty thousand
people who were involved in the program did in fact become legally resident
aliens or naturalized citizens. The benefits of legal status, however, did not
come without conflict or without cost. The politics of the Cold War and
McCarthyism shot through the government's campaign against illegal immigration and the Confession Program, shaping the government's perception of
Chinese immigration and impelling the process of negotiation by which Chinese Americans relocated their place in American society.

Exclusion and Paper Sons

The Chinese exclusion laws (1882–1943) barred all Chinese from entering
the United States save for merchants and their families, students, treaty
traders, and diplomats. Although not a few Chinese laborers entered the
United States by surreptitiously crossing the Mexican or Canadian borders,
many more gained entry by posing as persons who were legally admissible,
often with fraudulent certificates identifying them as merchants or by claiming to be American citizens by native birth or as the China-born sons of U.S.
citizens, known formally as derivative citizens.[8] Two Supreme Court rulings
during the 1890s encouraged a trend toward native-birth citizenship claims.
In 1895 the Court limited judicial review in cases where the customs collec-
tor rejected the prospective immigrants' claims to exempt status, making it
more difficult to enter with fake merchant papers. In 1898 the Court upheld
birthright citizenship for Chinese under the Fourteenth Amendment. Citi-

zenship claims were further encouraged by the San Francisco earthquake and fire of 1906. It has become nearly legendary that the destruction of the San Francisco Hall of Records enabled Chinese to assert native-birth citizenship because no records survived to contradict them. Thus, claiming derivative citizenship became the principal method of illegal immigration of Chinese laborers during the exclusion era. Between 1920 and 1940, 71,040 Chinese entered the United States as derivative citizens.[9]

Central to the problem of illegal Chinese immigration was the inability of the state to authenticate the identity of Chinese entering the United States. Typically, young Chinese men arriving in America during the first decades of the twentieth century claimed that they were born in the United States and taken back to China at a young age by their parents. When customs and immigration inspectors excluded Chinese entering without documentation, Chinese turned to the courts to overturn those decisions. Federal judges supported Chinese exclusion but felt obligated to hear habeas corpus cases, and once Chinese petitioners gained a hearing they found the courts inclined to accept uncontradicted oral testimony. Between 1891 and 1905 the United States District and Circuit Courts in San Francisco heard over 2,500 cases brought by Chinese petitioners and ruled favorably in over 60 percent of them.[10]

The courts' discharge papers in these cases *created* documentation of native-birth citizenship where none had previously existed. Chinese immigrants thus invented a system of illegal entry built entirely upon a paper trail derived from the state's efforts to enforce exclusion. In many instances, documentation supporting the identity of two or three generations of American citizens—including certificates of identity and citizenship, passports, and an ongoing registry of names of children born in China to American citizens—rested on a slender reed of evidence: an oral claim. Moreover, the authorities' interrogations of Chinese claimants and their witnesses about family history and the details of village life, which were originally devised to uncover fraud by finding discrepancies in testimonies, turned into something of its opposite by creating a record of facts that could be coached, memorized, and recited. The interrogations became increasingly elaborate over the years, but if that made the process of memorization and recitation more difficult, it did not solve the problem; it only enlarged the body of evidence. Thus the logic of enforcing exclusion compelled immigration officials to impose an upward spiral of evidentiary requirements upon Chinese immigrants; but, at the same time, the authorities mistrusted the entire register of documentary evidence that they had created. Captives of their bureaucratic procedures, immigration officials were indignant that they were mocked by impostors—the service frequently remarked that each Chinese woman residing in the United States before the 1906 earthquake would have had to have given birth to hundreds of sons to account for all the native-born citizens and despaired they could ever solve the problem of paper immigration. General Joseph Swing, the immigration commissioner during the Eisenhower administration, recalled, "Ever since the first Chinese came over here . . . the male Chinese went back . . . and he'd come back with a man child, and that went on, until there were ten, eleven children, all male, over the years. Well of course, it was a big fraud. . . . Going way back, the whole gang's illegal. They just had us spinning our wheels, trying to track these things down."[11]

The government and Chinese viewed paper immigration across a wide cultural divide. If the authorities believed Chinese were immoral because they knowingly broke the law, Chinese believed paper immigration was morally justified because it was one of the few ways to enter the United States when exclusion made legal immigration impossible. Chinese believed exclusion was immoral, even if it was legal. Testifying before a Congressional panel in 1952, Edward Hong of the New York Chinese Consolidated Benevolent Association explained the feelings of many Chinese Americans: "It is the fact that [Chinese Americans] do not have a chance to obtain and enjoy the freedoms of a democratic government in a legal manner that forces them to seek these privileges under any means whether legal or illegal."[12]

Legally, the authorities found paper immigration nearly impossible to eliminate, because it rested on documentation that was created by the state. Thus, just as oral testimony and interrogation helped create that body of evidence, "confession" became the only method of proving its fraudulent character. The question was: What would induce Chinese paper immigrants to confess?

The Cold War Immigration Crisis: Hong Kong

The impetus for solving the problem of paper immigration grew out of a crisis in Chinese immigration during the 1950s that reflected both the legacy of Chinese exclusion and Cold War politics. The roots of that crisis lay in part in the great increase in the number of Chinese seeking entry into the United States when unsettled conditions created by civil war and revolution in China prompted many Chinese to emigrate. Congress repealed the exclusion laws in 1943, but only a few could hope to enter the United States under the annual quota of 105. Most Chinese found alternative legal avenues for immigration as war brides and wives of citizens, refugees, and derivative citizens.[13]

After the Chinese Revolution in 1949, the American consulates in China closed, and several thousand visa and passport applications that had piled up during the war years were forwarded to the consulate at Hong Kong. In 1950, 117,000 Chinese American derivative citizens applied for passports at the United States Consulate at Hong Kong in order to join their families in

America, 67 percent more than had applied in 1940. Passport applicants were confronted with a four- to twelve-year wait for processing.[14]

In 1950 the Passport Division of the State Department issued special regulations for Chinese derivative citizens applying for passports. Applicants had to submit affidavits from the American father in triplicate, photographs from childhood onward, and other documentation difficult or impossible for many Chinese to acquire. Chinese without birth certificates had to produce "an identifying witness, preferably an American citizen, well and favorably known to the consular office." In 1951 the consulate began to use blood tests to determine paternity. It soon added bone x-rays to ascertain age. The scientific value of these tests was doubtful even at the time, but the courts upheld their use. Yet, even while demanding extraordinary forms of evidence, the consulate did not always accept them. An immigration attorney recalled, "Even if you passed the blood test, they might reject it if they felt they weren't fully satisfied. . . . Sometimes a marriage certificate was accepted by the passport office as documentation to show a child's legitimacy, but the same marriage certificate was rejected by the U.S. consular office in Hong Kong as documentation for the wife's visa."[15]

Investigators subjected applicants to severe interrogation, with questions even more numerous and detailed than in the past. They required applicants to answer eighty-one questions in writing (Question 22: "List all the people who lived within five houses on all sides of your last place of residence in China before you came to the U.S. and state their relationship to you if any") and then sit through one or more lengthy oral interviews. Discrepancies between declared statements and other testimony sometimes prompted investigators to visit the applicant's home, searching for incriminating evidence, such as family letters, a practice that the consulate knew infringed upon the subject's rights. The San Francisco paper *Chinese World* editorialized that the hurdles in the passport application process at Hong Kong were "so harsh and oppressive that even legitimate applicants cannot surmount them."[16]

Moreover, changes in immigration policy enacted in 1952 further restricted the rights of Chinese Americans by giving consular officials final authority to grant visas and by eliminating the right of judicial review in citizenship matters as provided by the Nationality Act of 1940. Between 1952 and the end of 1955, when the new provision went into effect, over twelve hundred Chinese American derivative citizens who were denied passports by the consulate in Hong Kong filed civil suits in United States District Courts in California, asking for declaratory judgment on their claims to citizenship.[17]

In 1955 the consulate still had over one thousand passport cases pending in which fraud was suspected. The State Department was determined to investigate "every single case" so that "we will not again be inundated with a flood of illegal Chinese." Representatives of the State Department conducting a site visit to the Hong Kong post in the spring of 1955 found the consular staff suffering from an "acute feeling of frustration" owing to the huge volume of cases and the "deviousness of all but a very few of the applicants they face." Morale at the post was so low that the visiting officials declared that Hong Kong was "without exaggeration . . . the worst of any Foreign Service post" they had ever seen.[18]

The consulate's fixation on fraud was imbued with the anti-Communist politics and anti-China policy of the time. By the mid-1950s the United States considered China its number one enemy; by 1954 the Korean War ended with the United States accepting a stalemate at the 38th parallel and the Americans were paying for 75 percent of the French military operation in Vietnam. The Eisenhower administration believed that the real threat in Vietnam, as in Korea, was China. During late 1954 and 1955, the United States came dangerously close to war with China over Jinmen and Mazu, tiny islands a few miles off the Chinese coast that had been seized by Chiang Kai-shek's forces when the deposed Nationalist government retreated to Taiwan in 1949.[19]

Relations between the United States and China during the mid-1950s thus seemed to rest on a hair trigger, and the implications were not lost on Chinese Americans and their relatives seeking entry to the United States. Framed by the Chinese Revolution, the issue of citizenship was not confined to Chinese Americans but was international, facing other overseas Chinese as well, especially in Southeast Asia, where 90 percent of all overseas Chinese resided. Eisenhower believed the twenty-two million overseas Chinese in Asia formed a fifth column for China. The Kuomintang also warned that Communist China would claim the citizenship of the overseas Chinese and, presumably, their loyalty. The warning was ironic, for the Kuomintang had been built with overseas Chinese support and funding, and had pursued an aggressive overseas Chinese policy based on the principle of *jus sanguinis*—that persons of Chinese blood, regardless of their country of birth, are citizens of China. When the Chinese Communist Party assumed power in 1949, it inherited an overseas Chinese "problem" that had evolved historically throughout Southeast Asia. Longstanding social and economic resentment towards the Chinese combined with fear of subversion. During the mid- and late 1950s, China attempted to reduce tensions with the countries of Southeast Asia by eliminating dual citizenship of overseas Chinese and distinguishing between Chinese nationals and citizens of local countries of Chinese descent.[20]

The central figure in the American campaign against immigration fraud in Hong Kong was the consul general, Everett F. Drumright. A former "China hand," Drumright was one of the few Foreign Service officers who did not come under attack during the early 1950s by McCarthy and Nixon for "losing China." The son of a midwestern farmer who struck oil in Oklahoma in 1902, he was the most politically conservative member in the Foreign Service in prewar China, a distinction that led his colleagues to sometimes call him

"Right Drum" and went a long way to place him above suspicion by the McCarthyites.[21]

Drumright led the American consulate at Hong Kong during the mid-1950s, at the height of the Cold War. An emphatic anti-Communist politics and racist suspicion of Chinese informed his approach to the immigration crisis. In December 1955, Drumright submitted an eighty-nine-page white paper to the State Department that directly linked the problem of fraud to Communist infiltration. The report alleged that Communist China was exploiting a widespread "criminal conspiracy," which included a fantastic multimillion-dollar black market operating in Hong Kong, San Francisco, and New York (complete with blood-type-matching services designed to thwart the new regulations). Drumright alleged there were 124 "citizenship brokerage houses" openly operating in Hong Kong, though he gave no evidence for the charge. He warned that China was sneaking espionage agents into the United States by purchasing false papers and that the Communists planned to organize the newcomers who are in the United States illegally and therefore are "open to blackmail." The passport fraud rings, Drumright warned, had to be "destroy[ed] . . . for once and for all, thus bringing to an end a unique history of illegal immigration and of resisting Americanization while buying and selling the rights of American citizenship before Communist China is able to bend that system to the service of her purposes alone."[22]

Drumright gave no evidence that China was sending spies into the United States, but he saw potential spies everywhere. The consulate believed a so-called smile campaign, conducted by the Communists towards overseas Chinese and their families in southern China during the mid-fifties (reclassifying families from "landlord" to "peasant" status, returning their houses, increasing rations, relaxing remittance procedures), was part of a Communist strategy to gain influence in the United States. By giving benefits to Chinese Americans' relatives in China, the consulate reasoned, the Communists would make Chinese Americans dependent upon them and therefore vulnerable to blackmail. It speculated that the Communists would gain further influence in the United States as the sons and paper sons of Chinese Americans, having been schooled in the Communist education system and served in the People's Liberation Army, emigrated to America. The consulate worried further about a Communist-backed "marriage racket." It alleged that the Communists sent "Chinese girls" into Hong Kong, where they married Chinese Americans and then sought entry into the United States with no other evidence of identity than their Hong Kong marriage certificate. The consulate despaired that it had "no way to even begin a security investigation" of such persons. In fact, the Communists' overseas Chinese policy was more complex than the fifth-column theory suggested. China was more concerned with keeping a smooth flow of remittance than exporting revolution.[23]

The Drumright report also betrayed racial hostility and suspicion towards the Chinese reminiscent of exclusion-era rhetoric. Drumright offered a crude analysis of Chinese culture, citing adoptions, plural marriages, multiple naming, and preference for male children as a "common cultural occurrence" that becomes "a perfect alibi" for illegal activity. Moreover, he alleged that Chinese were culturally inclined to fraud and perjury since they "lack a concept equivalent to the Western concept of an oath." In the final analysis, Drumright simply did not want to see so many Chinese immigrating into the United States. He recalled the late-nineteenth-century vision of the Chinese yellow peril and raised the specter of race riots and exclusion. Noting that 99 percent of Chinese immigration from Hong Kong was on a nonquota basis, Drumright suggested that the nonquota immigrants were somehow cheating the quota system that had, after all, been designed to limit Chinese immigration. He compared the 1940s, when the Chinese population of the United States increased by over 50 percent, to the 1870s, "when an increase of 67 percent so alarmed the West that Exclusion was enacted within a few years."[24]

However, Drumright opposed the State Department's decision to increase the investigative staff at Hong Kong and argued with his colleagues in Washington about it for over a year. Drumright believed it would be an impossible expense to investigate every case. He doubted there were enough competent and loyal local Chinese whom the consulate could hire for an expanded investigative staff. He also complained that the Hong Kong police would not give the consulate access to its files or issue search warrants for "home visits," making consular investigations more difficult. Drumright argued that direct investigation was not necessary except in unusual cases. He advocated instead a much easier method: if an applicant failed to meet the consulate's standards of evidence, passports and visas could be denied on the simple grounds of "identity not established."[25]

Since the consulate had erected nearly insurmountable barriers to proving identity and suspected every applicant of fraud, Drumright's method would have denied passports and visas to virtually all applicants. State Department officials regarded Drumright's views and practices with unease. A formal review of Drumright's report and recommendations concluded that denying passports and visas on the basis of mere suspicion, without investigation, was arbitrary and probably violated due process. Some officials also believed the standards of evidence imposed at Hong Kong were unreasonable.[26]

But Drumright continued to frustrate and embarrass the department, especially in visa cases, where he had final authority. He suspended hundreds of cases indefinitely—including those where evidence had already been submitted and the petition already approved by the INS—rather than grant the visa. He refused to respond to inquiries from members of Congress about specific cases.[27] The consul general believed the State Department should not bend to "bureaucratic pressure" from congressmen who were manipulated by Chinese American "pushers." In fact, the latter were wealthy Chinese American supporters of the Republican Party and the Kuomintang whom both Congress and the State Department were reluctant to offend.[28]

Drumright's position was actually the logical extension of the government's historical policies for authenticating the identity of Chinese immigrants. Drumright understood that Chinese determined to enter the United States could thwart nearly any requirement imposed by the government. Caught in an upward spiral, Drumright advocated policies that were so extreme as to lapse into farce. For example, when blood tests were first imposed in the early fifties, a negative result was considered proof that the claimed relationship was false. In 1956 Drumright wanted to also reject applicants who tested positive because he believed impostors had learned to match their blood types before making their claims—begging the question of what purpose a blood test served if any result was grounds for denial. Drumright wanted to fingerprint applicants, subject suspected impostors to polygraph tests, and install hidden microphones in interrogation rooms to monitor the consulate's Chinese interpreters, whom he did not trust. He deemed "worthless" and wanted to reject out of hand as inconclusive old certificates of identity, tax statements, remittances to family members other than the applicant, and letters without postmarked envelopes. He even suspected that Chinese made fake confessions after investigators produced evidence of fraud. "If an immigration family claims six sons and one is shown to be a blood fraud," he said, ". . . the family will . . . decide to 'confess everything.' The new family history will, however, continue to show all of the other five sons." While continuing to raise the standards of evidence, Drumright offered what he believed was the only way out of the spiral: just say no.[29]

Consistent with the premises of Chinese exclusion, Drumright believed Chinese immigration could not be addressed within existing law but was a special problem requiring special solutions that is, arbitrary power to deny Chinese entry to America. The State Department, whose standards of evidence for Chinese derivative citizens were already above and beyond those required of other derivative citizens, nevertheless argued that its policies and procedures should apply globally. Within that framework, it believed fraud could be uncovered only by directly investigating each case that came under suspicion.[30]

This is not to say that the State Department was any less committed to the anti-China, anti-Communist agenda. Drumright had strong support within the Far Eastern Bureau in the department. Scott McLeod oversaw the State Department's programs and divisions dealing with visas, passports, consular affairs, refugee admissions, as well as personnel and internal investigation—a massive "security" portfolio that critics claimed he directed as "Big Brother" and with "savage tactics." But the conflicts between Drumright and the State Department did reflect tensions in Washington over both immigration and foreign policy. While Drumright guarded the gate in Hong Kong with single-minded anti-Communist and anti-China determination, the State Department, while sharing the same fundamental position, also had to navigate foreign policy with the Nationalists in Taipei and the British colonial authorities in Hong Kong. The department worried that criticism of its policy and actions from those quarters would embarrass the United States. It was sensitive to charges of racial discrimination, knowing that such charges damaged the international image of the United States, and may have felt particularly vulnerable to criticism of the Chinese quota, which was based on race, not national origin.[31] Although nativists in Congress, led by Francis E. Walter, the cosponsor of the 1952 Immigration and Nationality Act, blocked immigration reform throughout the 1950s, the Eisenhower administration advocated reforming the quota system and viewed such reform as part of the United States' ability to present itself as the leader of the free world.[32]

Despite their differences, the consul general and State Department officials in Washington generally agreed that nearly all, if not all, Chinese passport and visa applicants at Hong Kong were impostors and that decisive action was needed to keep them from entering the United States. By September 1956 the department had assigned twenty-three additional investigative teams to Hong Kong. And, if Drumright lost the immediate battle over passport and visa procedures, he did not suffer politically from it. In 1957 he was named United States Ambassador to Nationalist China.[33]

The Cold War Immigration Crisis: Chinatown USA

The Department of Justice carried out the domestic component of the government's campaign against illegal Chinese immigration. In February 1956 the United States attorneys in San Francisco and New York impaneled grand juries to investigate fraudulent entry by Chinese. Whereas the enforcement of immigration policy in matters of admission and deportation was an administrative procedure, the Justice Department's action exposed Chinese paper sons to felony charges of fraud, perjury, and conspiracy.

The grand jury in San Francisco subpoenaed the officers of Chinese family and district associations, as well as the "lists, rolls, or other records of membership of the association during the entire period of the association's existence, all records of dues, assessments, contributions, and other income of the association, and all photographs of the membership or any portion thereof." The Justice Department believed that Chinese joined their true family association, not the association of their paper name. It therefore believed that the family associations' files contained "independent, accurate records of Chinese family relationships" that could be used to challenge the legitimacy of citizenship claims in the cases pending in District Court. The

U.S. attorney assembled a task force that included five investigators from the State Department Office of Security, eight investigators from the INS, and three United States marshals. Teams from the U.S. Attorney's office and the district office of the INS fanned out throughout Chinatown on the morning of February 29 and served the subpoenas on thirty-four family and district associations. The order gave twenty-four hours to comply.[34]

On March 1 the grand jury began proceedings at the Post Office building in San Francisco. Some fifty Chinatown residents and family associations leaders appeared, many armed with "pasteboard boxes full of papers and photographs." Jack Chow, an officer of the Gee Tuck Sam Tuck Family Association and an assistant district attorney under Edmund Brown, and Earl Louie, president of the Louie Fong Association and a member of the Central Committee of the California Republican Party, were among those present. In a dramatic move, the San Francisco Chinese Six Companies, the original and preeminent Chinese benevolent association in America, challenged the subpoena. The family associations refused to turn over their records, charging the subpoena was so vague as to constitute unlawful search.[35]

The grand jury investigation frightened and outraged the community. Lim P. Lee, the head of the Cathay Post of the American Legion, who later became the postmaster general of San Francisco, recalled, "Chinatown was hit like an A-bomb fell. Streets were deserted. Restaurants dropped income. Shoppers avoided Chinatown, and for three weeks it was a ghost town." Rumors circulated that Chinese would be rounded up en masse and deported, or, alternatively, put into "concentration camps."[36]

The state's attack on the Six Companies was ironic, since the local Kuomintang, which overlapped with the Six Companies leadership, had colluded with the FBI and INS to harass and deport Chinatown leftists during the early 1950s. Chinatown politics had enjoyed a period of popular-front unity during the 1930s and 1940s, but that situation changed after the Chinese Revolution and the advent of the Cold War. By 1956 organizations of the Chinese American left, such as the Chinese Hand Laundry Alliance and *China Daily News* in New York and the Chinese Workers Mutual Aid Association and the Chinese American Democratic Youth League in San Francisco, were crippled by state repression and local Kuomintang opposition.[37] When immigration politics reached into the community at large, Chinatown politics were severely fractured and the leadership of the community's resistance fell largely to the Chinese Six Companies.

The Six Companies' role in the immigration crisis recalled its historical position in the Chinese community dating back to the late nineteenth century. An associative council comprising all the family and district associations and led by the Chinese merchant elite, the Six Companies was an instrument of social and labor control within the community as well as its representative to mainstream society and voice of protest to the government.

During the exclusion era, when Chinese were ineligible for citizenship and excluded from the polity, the Six Companies carved out a narrow legal space within which it fought for the interests of Chinese in America. It used the federal courts adroitly to challenge Chinese immigration policy, taking many cases as far as the U.S. Supreme Court. Although the Chinese lost more cases than not, they achieved some significant victories, such as the ruling in *Wong Kim Ark* (1898), which upheld birthright citizenship under the Fourteenth Amendment for Chinese born in America.[38]

In response to the immigration crisis in the 1950s, Chinese again relied on legal means to protect themselves. But after World War II, Chinese Americans began to develop some political influence, owing to the repeal of the exclusion laws, a loosening of immigration restrictions, and the maturation of a generation of American-born Chinese, especially in California.[39] Candidates running for political office in San Francisco courted the Chinatown vote, and Chinese who were aligned with the Kuomintang supported the Republican Party in the belief that the latter was the strongest ally of the Nationalist government. These developments enlarged the space within which Chinese could organize their resistance.

When the grand jury subpoenas were served on the family associations, the Six Companies mustered a legal challenge literally overnight. It then moved to mobilize public support. On March 16 the Six Companies held a press conference where it said it would cooperate with the authorities in any investigation of Chinese that was a "legitimate and proper avenue of inquiry" but condemned the blanket subpoena in harsh language that reflected its essentially nationalist world view, claiming the subpoena was being used for the "obvious purpose of oppressing and intimidating the entire Chinese American community in San Francisco and, whether intentional or otherwise, they are having the effect of stigmatizing the social and family status of a respected community with criminal coloration."[40]

Several community organizations participated in the press conference, including the conservative Chinese Chamber of Commerce and Chinese American War Veterans Association, the more moderate Cathay Post, and the liberal Chinese American Citizens Alliance. The leadership of this united front was clearly in the hands of the Six Companies, which had the added moral authority derived from being the victim of an injustice. At the same time, the left was absent from the meeting as well as from any collective protection organized by the Six Companies.[41]

Chinese in New York watched with alarm as the situation unfolded in San Francisco. In response to reports that the INS had raided the Chinese New Year celebrations of numerous family associations in San Francisco, New York's Chinese Consolidated Benevolent Association (CCBA, the counterpart of the Six Companies) ordered all New Year banquets in New York canceled. The CCBA also retained a lawyer and, in an open letter printed in the China-

THE CHINESE NATIONALIST DAILY

6.1 During World War II and the Cold War, the U.S. government promoted a positive image of Chinese Americans who were aligned with the Chinese nationalist government. This merchant lived in Brooklyn, New York, 1942. (Courtesy of Marjorie Collins, FSA/OWI Collection, Library of Congress.)

town press, advised Chinese organizations and individuals "molested without cause" to report the matter to the CCBA, which would "assume its responsibility . . . to make preparations to protest . . . for their legislative rights according to law and according to justice." CCBA leaders also appealed to the Nationalist Chinese government to protest the Grand Jury actions.[42]

The grand jury proceedings met a storm of protest in the Chinese press. One paper deplored the "blunderbluss" tactics of the government that "failed to distinguish between racketeers and the long-established, reputable family associations." The press obtained a copy of the Drumright report from the U.S. Attorney's Office, adding fuel to the fire in Chinese press in both the United States and Hong Kong. The *World Journal* published a pamphlet with a lengthy critique.[43] Dai Ming Lee, editor of the *Chinese World*, polemicized against the Drumright report every day for two weeks. He criticized Drumright for ignoring Chinese immigrants' contributions to building the American West and "cast[ing] the antecedents of the Chinese in America in the role of criminals." Lee suggested that "methods that might have been taken out of the communist manual are being used upon children of Chinese Americans applying for a passport in Hong Kong." The *Hong Kong Tiger Standard* called the Drumright report "too fantastic for words" and said it was designed to "stir up the American public, which is given to hysteria on the slightest provocation."[44]

On March 20 Judge Carter granted the motion of the family associations to quash the subpoenas, agreeing that the blanket nature of the subpoena violated their Fourth Amendment rights. Carter said the subpoenas were "oppressive," "unreasonable," and "had the effect of a 'dragnet.'" The United States Attorney's Office, while still alleging "suspicion of fraud involving every family association," said it would conduct a "more limited probe."[45]

In fact, investigations in both the United States and Hong Kong continued. The State Department's Office of Security, the INS, and the FBI assigned additional investigators to assist the U.S. attorneys, especially in San Francisco, where the investigation was "bogging down" due to a lack of manpower.[46] Having lost in the matter of the mass subpoena, the U.S. attorney subpoenaed specific family association records in connection with specific individuals under investigation. In June the Welfare Committee of the Chinese Six Companies announced it had agreed to cooperate with the INS in the questioning of the officials of certain associations. But Chinese continued to resist in a number of ways. The CCBA in Boston, New York, and Washington instructed local family associations to relocate the names of paper sons from the records of their true family associations to the association to which the paper name belonged.[47]

Individual Chinese who were called before the grand jury were not entirely cooperative. A field report submitted to the State Department Office of Security, summarizing thirty cases heard by the San Francisco grand jury during the month of April 1956, shows that in four cases Chinese refused to cooperate outright, two by invoking the Fifth Amendment and two by failing to appear. In eighteen cases, more than half, Chinese dropped their suits and withdrew their applications for passports pending in Hong Kong; in exchange the U.S. attorney dropped criminal charges. In five cases Chinese maintained they were true sons or daughters while admitting to paper names. In only three cases did Chinese admit to creating or using false immigration "slots." The Justice Department was sufficiently frustrated that it considered filing charges against the CCBA for obstruction of justice for advising Chinese to not cooperate with the investigations.[48]

In Hong Kong, too, Chinese resisted by refusing to cooperate with investigators. Many witnesses "disappear[ed] rather than be interviewed" and many subjects "refused to respond to questioning or cooperation in any way." Although the task was more difficult, the consulate nonetheless completed the investigation of fifty cases by the end of July. The consulate reported indications of fraud in all fifty cases, but it obtained direct confessions only in twenty-six cases, of which half were confessions by true sons or daughters using paper names. Only one case revealed an exchange of money for papers. In fourteen cases the subjects either disappeared or refused to incriminate themselves.[49]

The high incidence of Chinese who were true family members using paper names suggests paper immigration had become a burden for many Chinese Americans. Once the paper trail had started in the early twentieth century, Chinese Americans using paper names had no choice but to perpetuate the false lineage in order bring their true family members into the United States. The high percentage of direct confessions by true family members using paper names suggests that they did not believe they had really committed a crime, even if they knew they had technically broken the law. Those Chinese confessed believing, perhaps, that the authorities would recognize their moral innocence and not prosecute them. At the same time, Chinese who asked that their civil suits be dismissed or refused to testify understood that without confession the prosecutors would not have enough evidence to obtain a conviction. Ironically, the U.S. attorney pursued criminal charges against Chinese who confessed to being true sons using paper names while it declined to prosecute cases stipulated for dismissal, even though the latter were more likely to involve the use of paper names by people of no relation or the sale of false immigration slots for profit.[50]

As a result of the coordinated investigations the district court dismissed some two hundred civil suits and the grand juries in New York and San Francisco handed up thirty-eight indictments. The authorities exposed only one "racket," operated by a prominent New York Chinatown businessman who owned two restaurants and a travel agency. Prosecutors said the latter was a "front" for an illegal immigration operation with connections to doctors who certified blood types and lawyers who handled the applications. They claimed that he filed sixty-five actions for more than one hundred applicants between 1949 and 1952, although they tried and convicted him in connection with only five cases. The trial also revealed that he made a profit of $23,000 in two years from selling false papers, a substantial sum but far less than the $3 million a year originally alleged by the government.[51]

Indeed, the actual cases involving fraud that were brought by the government hardly matched up to the sensational charges made by Drumright and the Justice Department. While paper citizenship was widespread, the result of sixty years of exclusion, contemporaries believed that the practice of buying false papers had ceased by the early 1950s because it had become widely known that the American consulate at Hong Kong was blocking most citizen-claimant applications. Observers also wondered why Communist China would try to sneak spies into the United States by what had become the most ineffective means of illegal entry, when agents could, for example, simply pose as seamen and jump ship.[52] The problem was not Communist infiltration or multimillion-dollar rackets, but the existence of tens of thousands of ordinary Chinese Americans who were related in some way to a paper citizen.

The INS Chinese Confession Program

In March 1957 the CCBA called a nationwide Chinese American conference on immigration reform in Washington, D.C. It was an unprecedented gathering, drawing 124 delegates from thirty-four cities from all regions of the country, including such unlikely places as Savannah, Minneapolis, Cleveland, and Houston. Howard Pyle, a White House assistant to President Eisenhower, addressed the conference. Delegates passed fourteen resolutions, mostly concerned with increasing Chinese immigration and reforming the discriminatory aspects of American immigration policy. A resolution to admit Chinese refugees to work as agricultural laborers, similar to Mexican braceros, recalled the CCBA's historical role as a labor contractor.[53]

The conference reflected some subtle shifts in the CCBA's perceptions of its role in community politics and evinced a growing sophistication in political lobbying. Significantly, the conference promoted an image of the Chinese as solid *American* citizens, not overseas Chinese. The issue of China was absent from the conference call and agenda. Conference delegates challenged the notion that the Chinese were not American in resolutions and statements that pronounced their commitment to being "good citizens" of the United States.[54]

Following the conference, the CCBA continued to lobby for reform. CCBA leaders held private discussions with the INS to promote legislative reforms, discourage immigration raids into the community, and find ways to adjust the status of the paper immigrants. Toward achieving the latter goal, CCBA leaders agreed to promote the service's Chinese Confession Program.[55]

The San Francisco district office of the INS started the Chinese Confession Program in 1956. The program was a procedure for an administrative adjustment of status. If Chinese who had entered the country by fraudulent means made voluntary disclosure of their false status, the service said it would assist confessors, "if at all possible under the law," to adjust their status. Under existing law, persons who were in the country illegally were eligible for a suspension of deportation and permanent resident status if they had resided in the United States continually for seven years. Aliens who served in the armed forces for ninety days were eligible for naturalized citizenship.[56]

According to an internal INS report, the service organized the confession program as a result of its experience in a case involving the Leong family of San Francisco. Leong Bok Yin had established himself as a native-born citizen in 1902 by means of a habeas corpus proceeding. In 1955 the American consulate at Hong Kong received information suggesting that Leong was not in fact a citizen and that therefore thirty-four people who claimed to be his descendants, including seventeen who had already immigrated into the United States, were also not citizens. However, the service only had sufficient evidence to deport three of them. Upon learning that ten of Leong's alleged descendants were either veterans or active members of the armed forces, the INS interviewed the veterans and explained that if they confessed they would be eligible for naturalized citizenship under their real names. After extensive family consultations, the entire family confessed. The service had thus discovered a method of exposing an entire family tree.[57]

In June 1956 Bruce Barber, the San Francisco district director of the INS, spoke before a meeting of the Cathay Post of the American Legion in San Francisco's Chinatown, recruiting veterans to confess in exchange for naturalized citizenship. By November the district had exposed 113 Chinese Americans holding false claims of citizenship and voided claims to citizenship of 73 others still in Hong Kong and China. In February 1957 the INS central office approved expansion of the program to the rest of the country. Instructions emphasized that no promises of immunity from prosecution should be made but that "every medium [should be] used to advise Chinese in the United States regarding the possibilities of adjustment under the law." The INS conducted the confession program with a great deal of discretionary authority. No statute governed the program, nor was there provision for general amnesty. Immigration Commissioner Joseph Swing and Congressman Francis E. Walter decided that the program did not need or warrant legislation.[58]

The INS's approach to confession derived from traditional law enforcement technique, in which confession and testimony against others are exchanged for immunity from prosecution. Recognizing that the INS successfully prosecuted cases of fraud only when investigators obtained confessions, Ralph Stanley, an INS investigator, urged that the agency give "every possible sympathetic consideration" to adjusting the status of confessors who appeared at trials as government witnesses. Stanley believed Chinese would cooperate because they understood that the failure to cooperate might "ultimately involve themselves and members of their immediate families in criminal action."[59] Given the atmosphere of anti-Communism, grand jury investigations, and rumors of mass deportations, it is not surprising that Chinese under investigation found reason to confess.

The confession program aimed to correct limitations in the investigations conducted by the Departments of State and Justice in Hong Kong and the United States. As reports of those investigations indicate, painstaking investigative work led to direct confessions in only about 50 percent of the cases. It was just as likely as not that the authorities would produce only inconclusive evidence of fraud. Even when Chinese were induced to confess, the authorities solved only individual cases, which did little to eliminate the *system* of paper immigration.

The INS thus hoped that the confession program would eliminate that system. It believed it could foreclose future illegal immigration by securing the confessions of entire families. As the Leong family case demonstrates, exposure of an entire family tree included the disclosure, and therefore the elimination, of false "slots" that were still unused. The INS held out the possibility (never the promise) of relief only to confessors who named all names. Investigator Stanley explained, "If this program is to be of value to this Service, it is imperative that full information concerning all family members be obtained and that the Chinese not be permitted to testify solely concerning his own individual identity and nationality."[60]

INS investigators worked patiently and persistently to get the confessions of whole families. Stanley noted that it could take as long as a year to obtain an entire family's cooperation and explained the need to "save face" for true family members who were caught in the web of illegality of their kin. An immigration attorney who handled confession cases in New York's Chinatown similarly recalled that service investigators often seemed like "social workers," who assisted families with their confessions.[61]

Yet, the process of individual and family confession was not always smooth. Many families divided over whether or not to confess, sometimes quite bitterly. And, although service publications described the confession program as a benefit for which Chinese could voluntarily apply without fear of prosecution, the program was not entirely voluntary or free from the taint of criminality. It began in 1956 when the grand jury and Hong Kong investigations were still taking place, blurring the line between voluntary confession and criminal proceedings. Moreover, the INS aggressively sought to induce confessions from people whose names surfaced in investigative leads from anonymous telephone calls, letters, and coaching material seized by the service. In many such cases, INS investigators called Chinese in for "informal interviews," where they would confront them with some evidence that suggested fraud or news that a paper brother living in another city had confessed. The Chinese often upheld their original story but then returned a few weeks later with an attorney and confessed.[62]

Confession entailed a formal interview with INS officials. After several years the program became somewhat routinized. Confessors answered questions according to a standardized form, confessing their fraudulent claim to citizenship and listing the names of their true family and paper family members, including their whereabouts. They were asked if they had ever been convicted of a crime, voted in an election, served in the armed forces, belonged to the Communist Party or believed in "communistic aims." Moreover, confessors had to turn over all documents of citizenship and write in their own hand, "I hereby surrender my passport" (or certificate of identity). At the conclusion of the hearing, INS officers required confessors to state that they were "amenable for deportation" and then instructed them to apply for a suspension of deportation and for permanent resident status or naturalized citizenship, depending on their eligibility. A memorandum was then referred to the INS board of special inquiry, where a hearing officer ruled on the confessor's status.[63]

The vast majority of confessors successfully received legal status, but some were found ineligible for relief. Of those, a relatively small number were deported; others remained in the United States because the U.S. attorney declined to prosecute and the INS shelved their cases—a mixed blessing, since they were left with no status at all. Sometimes an unsympathetic hearing officer simply denied relief to confessors even if they were eligible for adjusted status. In one case, a seaman who had jumped ship was advised by his attorney to confess; he was denied a suspension of deportation because the hearing officer did not believe it would be "unconscionable" to deport him. The seeming arbitrariness of the service's rulings and the lack of statutory or even published guidelines led immigration attorneys to complain that they could not properly advise prospective confessors. Not surprisingly, many Chinese immigrants mistrusted the program, especially in the beginning, and the INS considered the cooperation of the CCBA essential to giving credibility to the program.[64]

According to published statistics on the confession program in the INS's *Annual Reports* from 1957 to 1965, at least 11,336 Chinese Americans confessed to having entered the United States under false claim of citizenship. Another 19,124 people were implicated as holding false citizenship by the confessions of others. Finally, some 5,800 "slots"—names of nonexistent persons not yet used for illegal entry—were closed (table 6.1).[65]

If the confession program offered a resolution to the problem of paper immigration, the INS consistently denied that benefit to Chinese American leftists. The INS kept copies of the subscription list of the left-wing *China Daily News* and membership lists of groups like the Chinese Hand Laundry Alliance and the Chinese Workers Mutual Aid Association dating back to the 1930s and continued using those lists to determine eligibility for relief. Typically, in denying an application, the INS would refer to "confidential information the disclosure of which would be prejudicial to public interest," which was understood to mean "communist."[66]

During the early 1960s left-wing activists whom immigration and FBI agents had harassed over the years became subject to deportation and criminal proceedings once their false status was revealed by the confessions of others. In New York, Louie Pon of the Hand Laundry Alliance and Yee Sun Jok, an employee of the *China Daily News*, were deported in 1964 and 1966, respectively, after each was exposed as a paper son.[67]

TABLE 6.1
INS Chinese Confession Program, 1957–1965

Year(s)	Confessed[a]	Implicated[b]	Slots Closed[c]
1957, 1958, 1959	1,700	NA[1]	NA
1960 (Northeast only)	151	158	327
1961	1,248	2,235	1,187
1962	1,419	3,003	1,391
1963	2,241	4,233	NA
1964	2,579	5,911	1,192
1965	1,998	3,564	1,192
Total	11,336	19,124	5,800

Source: INS Annual Reports, 1957–1965.
[a]Number of persons who made direct confession of illegal status.
[b]Number of persons named by confessors as illegal, but no direct confession.
[c]Number of future illegal entries eliminated.
[1]NA: Not available.

In San Francisco, the owners of the World Theater, Karl Fung and Lawrence Lowe, were charged with fraudulent citizenship. Several members of the Chinese American Democratic Youth League, familiarly known as *Min Qing* (Democratic Youth), were arrested on criminal charges of fraud related to their alleged illegal entry into the United States. In August 1962 a federal grand jury in Tacoma, Washington, indicted Maurice Chuck for procuring a certificate of citizenship in 1954 as a result of "false and fraudulent statements." Chuck had come to the United States in 1948 at the age of fifteen to join his father, who was a paper son. He soon joined the Min Qing and wrote articles for *China Daily News*.[68]

Chuck's father, Hwong Jack Hong, had participated in the confession program and was subpoenaed to testify against his own son. During the trial, father and son stayed in the same hotel room. Their relationship had never been easy: Maurice Chuck had grown up in China without knowing his father, and when he came to the United States, they clashed over Maurice's radicalism. In Tacoma, the elder Chuck cried every night over the government's forcing him to testify against his son. The court found Chuck guilty and stripped him of his citizenship. He served three months of a five-year prison term.[69]

In 1961 Kai G. Dear, also of the Min Qing, was tried on criminal charges of conspiracy for entering the United States as a paper son in 1933 at the age of ten, falsely representing himself as a citizen by voting in elections, and serving as a witness at his wife's naturalization hearing in 1956. The case against Dear was based on the confession of his aunt. Dear's defense attempted to show that the INS had a secret list of Chinese American organizations, including the Min Qing, the members of which were to be denied the benefits of the confession program, but the court quashed the subpoena issued by Dear's lawyers for the INS. Dear too was convicted and stripped of his citizenship.[70]

The confession trials served not only to punish Chinese American leftists but as a public counterpart to the loyalty statement each confessor was required to make. The price of disloyalty was high: the accused faced charges that were often abusive and frivolous, involving crimes allegedly committed when they were children, as well as possible deportation or imprisonment. Their families suffered humiliation and anguish as their relatives were subpoenaed to testify against them, even though the INS had assured the community that confessors and their families would not be prosecuted.

The confession program served as a means of renegotiating the terms of Chinese Americans' citizenship. Although Chinese Americans and the INS approached that negotiation from asymmetrical positions of power, Chinese Americans resisted the state's efforts to criminalize the entire community. The Six Companies and CCBA successfully mobilized both legal and mass opposition to the grand jury's mass subpoenas and offered legal counsel and community support, which also made individual acts of resistance possible. They also utilized their connections within the Republican Party and the Kuomintang to lobby the State Department. The CCBA, of course, also benefited from the government's use of the confession program to further weaken the Chinese American left and strengthened its own political position in the community in the process.

The resistance offered by Chinese was not without effect. Whereas the Hong Kong investigations and grand jury proceedings granted no reward for admitting fraud, the confession program afforded benefits to both Chinese Americans and the state. The bargain at the core of confession—legalized status for those already settled in America in exchange for closing off future paper immigration—settled, for the most part, the legacy of illegal immigration from the exclusion era.

Yet, if confession follows sin and redemption follows confession, the community could not entirely redeem its virtue. Cold War politics and the sensationalized investigations against fraud reproduced racialized perceptions that all Chinese immigrants were illegal and dangerous. Confession legalized Chinese paper immigrants, but it did not necessarily bring them social legitimacy. The official history that racialized Chinese as unalterably foreign and unassimilable remained unchallenged. Dai-Ming Lee called for the government to recognize the "human aspect" of illegal immigration and suggested that public officials could "foster respect for the law by careful observance of the spirit as well as the letter of the law." To "condemn an entire racial group," he said, was "repugnant to the spirit of American justice."[71]

An official amnesty program might have resolved the problem, because amnesty is based on forgiveness, removes the stigma of wrongdoing, and suspends the letter of the law in the interest of justice. President Roosevelt's statement in 1943 that Chinese exclusion was a "historic mistake" and an "injustice to our friends,"[72] provided a basis for amnesty. Although the confession program fell short of such a resolution, it nevertheless stabilized the grounds upon which Chinese Americans would continue to strive for racial equality and the full rights of citizenship in the latter half of the twentieth century.

Part IV _____

PLURALISM AND NATIONALISM IN
POST–WORLD WAR II IMMIGRATION REFORM

Chapter Seven

The Liberal Critique and Reform of Immigration Policy

[D]emands for a change would not long be put off.
What neither Senator McCarran nor Congressman
Walter realized was that they had brought to light
the unlovely residue of outworn prejudices that
now stand in the way of our own national interest.
—OSCAR HANDLIN, 1953[1]

HISTORY BOOKS record the Civil Rights Act of 1964 and the Voting Rights and Immigration Acts of 1965 as watershed legislation of the Kennedy-Johnson era. The laws overturned longstanding legal traditions of race discrimination in America and broke the entrenched power of conservative sectional interests in Congress. As such, the legislative triad has been canonized in history and social science literature as the apotheosis of postwar liberalism, cultural pluralism, and democratic political mobilization: the "climactic achievements of the approach that had emphasized universalist principles" and the "high-water mark in the national consensus of egalitarianism."[2]

The Immigration Act of 1965 repealed the system of national origins quotas, replacing it with a new system of quotas that were at once global (applying to all countries) and evenly distributed (20,000 per country). It raised the ceiling on admissions to 300,000 a year and established preferences for family and occupationally based immigration. Its signal achievement was that it ended the policy of admitting immigrants according to a hierarchy of racial desirability and established the principle of formal equality in immigration. It increased the possibilities for migration for peoples from eastern and southern Europe and from Asia. As a result of immigration reform (as well as other developments in the world), patterns of migration to the United States changed tremendously in the last decades of the twentieth century. To paraphrase historian David Reimers, after 1965 the third world came to America.[3]

But in other, perhaps paradoxical ways the Immigration Act of 1965 did not "open" immigration, for it continued and, indeed, extended the reach of numerical restriction, a policy that would reproduce the problem of illegal immigration, especially from Mexico, to the present day. Increasingly in the post–World War II period, reformers regarded the national origins quotas as an illiberal deviation from American democratic traditions, yet they simultaneously viewed numerical restriction as a normative feature of immigration policy. In fact, both had been enacted for the first time in 1924, as part of a single thrust aimed at restricting immigration from southern and eastern Europe. Why, then, did post–World War II liberals attack one part of that proposition and naturalize the other?

To answer this question it shall be necessary to modify the conventional understanding of postwar immigration reform. That story has been told mainly as one about a growing political support for cultural pluralism, the idea that America comprises a diversity of ethno-racial groups. In this vision, democracy respects and depends upon all ethnic groups' contributions to society and the equal rights of all individuals, regardless of their national origin. Central to this narrative of reform are the ethnic European Americans who had, by World War II, become visible and vocal constituents of the New Deal political order, gaining important influence in urban politics, industrial unionism, and liberal Democratic Party circles. Their quest for immigration reform derived from critical opposition to the badge of inferior status that the quota laws had imposed upon them as well as by practical desire to admit more immigrants from their countries of origin. Thus American Jews, Italian Americans, Greek Americans, and other groups demanded their equal place in American society.[4]

In important respects immigration reform was very much akin to civil rights and desegregation. Both movements against racial discrimination were animated by mass democratic mobilization, and both received support for their causes among liberal white elites, who in the context of the world war against fascism had found America's race policies falling short of its democratic ideals. During the Cold War liberals felt it even more urgent to project a democratic image of the nation to the world. Sociologist Robert Amundson connected immigration and civil rights reforms in a way common amongst liberals in the 1950s. Making reference to Gunnar Myrdal's famous 1944 study of race discrimination, Amundson said, "An interesting extension of the American dilemma can be found in the field of immigration legislation. . . . Certainly most Americans must experience a sense of moral embarrassment when asked to justify our present immigration laws in light of the democratic concept of 'equal rights and justice for all.'"[5]

That immigration reform and civil rights were cut from the same cloth of democratic reform in the same historical moment seems undeniable. Immigration reformers were deeply influenced by the civil rights movement, both by its broad appeals for social justice and human freedom and by its more specific conception of formal equal rights, as articulated by the leading civil rights organizations and the Supreme Court's decision in *Brown v. Board of Education*. Yet the strong similarities have perhaps obscured important differences. One difference concerns race: whereas the civil rights movement targeted the legacies of racial slavery, immigration reform in the 1940s to 1960s addressed, for the most part, discriminations faced by ethnic Euro-Americans who were racialized as white.[6]

Another difference turns on the question of citizenship. The civil rights movement was incontrovertibly about winning full and equal citizenship for African Americans, but citizenship occupied a more ambiguous and problematic position in immigration policy and reform discourse. Immigrants are aliens, not citizens—a fundamental distinction in legal status that bears on the scope of rights held by each class of persons, beginning with the right to be territorially present. Insofar as immigrants were understood as assimilating subjects, reforming the quota system democratized access to citizenship. Still, citizenship remained for immigrants only a possibility. In fact, when immigration reformers spoke of "rights," they referred not to the rights of migrants but the rights of existing American citizens, the ethnic Euro-Americans who believed immigration policy was a proxy for their status. This was an important elision that would have consequences for how immigration reform was conceptualized. Indeed, the persistence of numerical restriction in the postwar period, with its emphasis on territoriality, border control, and deportation of illegal aliens, suggests that in some respects immigration reform only hardened the distinction between citizen and alien.

It might be, as well, that liberals' valorization of citizenship in the postwar period constructed alienage as a lack, as citizenship's opposite. It will be recalled that Supreme Court chief justice Earl Warren, one of the era's greatest champions of liberal citizenship, called citizenship "man's basic right." The full passage in Chief Justice Warren's dissent in *Perez v. Brownell* spoke of citizenship in direct contrast with alienage:

> Citizenship *is* man's basic right for it is nothing less than the right to have rights. Remove this priceless possession and there remains a stateless person, disgraced and degraded in the eyes of his countrymen. He has no lawful claim to protection from any nation, and no nation may assert rights on his behalf. His very existence is at the sufferance of the state within whose borders he happens to be. In this country the expatriate will presumably enjoy, at most, only the limited rights and privileges of aliens, and like the alien he might even be subject to deportation and thereby deprived of the right to assert any rights.[7]

Constitutional scholar Charles L. Black, Jr., saw in the work of the Warren Court "an affirmation—the strongest, by a very long interval, in our whole history—of the positive content and worth of American citizenship," a tripartite concept comprising the rights to participate in public affairs, to be treated fairly by government, and to lead a "private life"—rights, moreover, "to be enjoyed in all its parts without respect to race."[8] Writing in 1970,

Black added that emphasizing the importance of "the concept of citizenship need not result in neglect of the rights of aliens among us," noting that the Constitution spoke of persons and not only of citizens; but he considered the problem "part of the unfinished business of the Warren Court." More recently, legal scholar Peter Schuck also considered it anomalous that the Warren Court checked "governmental authorities on behalf of politically vulnerable groups [but] was abjectly deferential in the context of immigration law."[9]

The reason for this discrepancy is not transparent in the record of liberal discourse or the legislative history of immigration reform, for within the archive the alien's lack is asserted in large part by means of indirection or in silences. But if the alien lurked as the citizen's silent double, nationalism was the ground upon which this duality was produced. That nationalism had multiple, overlapping dimensions. At one level it was manifest in the explicit politics of the Cold War, which framed nearly every political issue at the time. Cold War politics suspected the foreign-born and judged migrants and refugees from the vantage point of U.S. geopolitical interests. The idea of national interest also included protecting a position of economic privilege within the global capitalist economy. Nationalism was articulated, as well, more subtly in normative constructions of nation-state territoriality that dominated immigration policy since World War I.

This chapter argues that the thinking that impelled immigration reform in the decades following World War II developed along a trajectory that combined liberal pluralism and nationalism. These views emerged in the historical specificities of postwar domestic race and class relations and the political economy of the United States' position as a world superpower. Post–World War II liberal nationalism conjoined a pluralist view of American domestic group relations and a nationalist privileging of the U.S. nation-state's geopolitical and economic position in the world. Elucidating the ways in which various strains of nationalism inflected liberal pluralism and the reformation of immigration policy helps us understand both the inclusionary and exclusionary features in the Immigration Act of 1965.

Cultural Pluralism

The post–World War II pluralist critique of the national origins quota system had its roots in a late-Progressive-era discourse of cultural pluralism. But, while the midcentury vision echoed some of the ideas and language of its antecedents, the two visions were substantially different. The trajectory from the earlier period was also not linear or predetermined. In order to understand the postwar critique of immigration restriction, it will be useful to review briefly the career of pluralism in the first half of the twentieth century.

In the 1910s and 1920s cultural pluralism arose as a critique to both race-based nativism and homogenizing assimilation. Although nativism and Americanization took opposing approaches to the so-called new immigrants who teemed into the country in the first decades of century, they were both articulations of old-line Anglo-American elites. By contrast, cultural pluralism was, to a great extent, an immigrant intervention. It articulated the new immigrant groups' own efforts to find a way to simultaneously retain their ethnic identity and be American.[10]

The term "cultural pluralism" may be credited to philosopher Horace Kallen. In a 1915 article, "Democracy versus the Melting Pot," Kallen argued that nationality groups in America should not be robbed of their cultural identities and coercively Americanized. He famously described America not as a melting pot but more like an "orchestra," in which "every type of instrument has its specific timbre and tonality . . . as every type has its appropriate theme and melody, and the harmony and dissonances and discords of them all make the symphony of civilization." Kallen's vision of America was that of a "federation" or a "democracy of nationalities."[11]

During the 1920s new ideas about race and culture in the social sciences also encouraged pluralist politics. In anthropology, the work of Franz Boas and his students at Columbia University (notably Ruth Benedict and Margaret Mead) severed race from culture, discrediting the premises of racial hierarchy that had underpinned physical anthropology since the late nineteenth century. At the University of Chicago, sociologist Robert E. Park and his colleagues used Chicago as an urban laboratory to study immigration and immigrant adaptation. Park advanced a theory of cultural assimilation that argued that all ethnic and racial groups coming into contact with each other in modern society go through stages of antagonism, accommodation, and, finally, assimilation. Although Park did not directly address the politics of pluralism, his work legitimated ethnic difference as an integral part of the American experience. The Chicago school's emphasis, however, positioned pluralism as a means to assimilation rather than an end in itself.[12]

These views were by no means monolithic and were also susceptible to a range of criticism; Kallen, for example, was criticized for reifying difference even as he celebrated it. But they shared a common outlook of antiracism and cultural relativism. Some advocates of pluralism also evinced a cosmopolitan sensibility, the idea that each person should be "a member of his own group of national origin and also a member of international society." Pluralism was seen less as a prescription for state intervention than as an ideal, the outcome of an organic process of modern society. Moreover, some intellectuals embraced both European immigrants and black Americans, creating an important conceptual linkage that was virtually without precedent in prior iterations of American democratic pluralism.[13]

Cultural pluralism was but a small voice in the late-Progressive-era conversation about race, culture, and national identity, which in the early 1920s was all but drowned out by the choruses of postwar reaction. Its fortunes began to change during the 1930s. The New Deal's general attitude of empathy for the common person created more space for cultural pluralism, although it might be said that New Deal liberalism was animated more by statist quests for economic stability than by concern with race and ethnic relations. During the New Deal the social-democratic and communist left-wing also viewed group conflict more as a problem of working-class unity than it did a problem of national unity.[14]

In the late thirties the spread of fascism and war in Europe more directly impelled American liberals to critically examine the condition of U.S. domestic group relations and, moreover, to see that problem inextricably connected to world events. Ruth Benedict's writings in the late 1930s on culture were inspired by both her research as an anthropologist and by her abhorrence of the racialist theories of European fascism. In 1938 the U.S. Department of Education sponsored a radio broadcast series, "Americans All, Immigrants All," to promote national unity.[15]

Evincing the same impulse in 1939, the Foreign Language Information Service, an immigrant advocacy and service organization established during World War I, reinvented itself as the Common Council for American Unity. Influenced in great part by the writer Louis Adamic, whose celebratory autobiography and other writings popularized the idea that America was a "nation of nations," the council promoted a radical view of national unity that combined common citizenship and cultural diversity, including "the freedom to be different."[16]

In the context of World War II these views became more urgent. Liberals envisioned domestic group conflict as a national weak point that fascism could potentially exploit. In a 1940 article that received much attention Adamic wrote, "[M]ere anti-fascism . . . is insufficient" to meet the crisis at hand. The nation, he said, needed a proactive program of national unity, based not on antialienism and Americanization, as during World War I, but a unity based on full "inclusion" and in recognition of the nation's ethnic diversity.[17]

Similarly, Carey McWilliams wrote:

It is pre-eminently our assignment to demonstrate to the world that peoples of diverse racial and national origins, of different backgrounds, and many cultures, can live and work together in a modern democracy. As a nation of nations we alone are in a position to exercise real political leadership. At the same time, however, the divisive forces that have brought disaster to the world also threaten our national unity. Our unique position constitutes both our strength and our weakness. If we fail in the world, we fail at home; if we fail at home, we are not likely to succeed in the world.[18]

If liberals clearly saw the war as an opportunity for advancing cultural pluralism, a more subtle process advocating a nationalist claim to superiority and world leadership is also visible. "Greatness," which a half-century earlier comprised Anglo-Saxon race superiority, now inhered in the American pluralist ethos, which was envisioned paradoxically as universal and unique to the U.S. nation-state. Adamic located American democracy at an advanced point in civilization's long teleology. He imagined the United States as a nation that lay beyond the historical category of nations:

> The United States is great. . . . [I]ts greatness consists of two elements: the idea it brought into government—that all men are created equal and have a voice in how they are governed—and the variegated texture of its makeup. . . . [S]uch an interplay was in line with the major direction in which the world has been moving—from the clan through the tribe, through the nation and race towards denationalization, Americanism (democracy), internationalism, humanity.[19]

Wartime nationalism was indeterminate, however, and as a vision for the postwar world order it was ambivalent and contested. Not all Americans were comfortable with Henry Luce's 1942 call for an "American Century" based on foreign investment, exports, and cultural and military hegemony. As Nikhil Singh has described, Henry Wallace redubbed Luce's idea as a "People's Century"; which in turn was pushed to further democratic ground by Ralph Ellison and Angelo Herndon, editors of the *Negro Quarterly*, with the "peoples' century." They and other champions of black liberation like W.E.B. Du Bois and Paul Robeson not only believed in the "Double V"— victory against fascism abroad and for civil rights at home—but also that victory should end colonialism and "bring in its train the liberation of all peoples."[20]

The potential promised in that extraordinary historical crossroad was realized during and immediately after the war in momentous if partial ways— from the desegregation of the U.S. armed forces and major league baseball to decolonization in Africa and Asia. The exigencies of war also led Congress to repeal Chinese exclusion in 1943, in order to stanch Japanese war propaganda in Asia that criticized U.S. policy as racist. The repeal of the exclusion laws was an important democratic reform that ended a sixty-one-year-long policy of explicit racial exclusion.[21] In the immediate postwar years Congress further weakened Asiatic exclusion by repealing the exclusion of Indians and Filipinos. Additional legislation granted nonquota admission to Chinese alien wives and children of U.S. citizens in 1946 and to Japanese war brides in 1947. These reforms were particularly significant because they laid the basis for Asian family immigration, which had been a near-impossibility under the exclusion laws.[22]

The democratic and internationalist spirit influenced even immigration officials. After briefly suspending the "pre-examination" program for adjusting the status of illegal aliens as a wartime precaution in 1941, the Justice Department reinstituted and routinized it, so that by the war's end it was granting permanent-resident status to thousands of aliens with illegal or temporary status, many of them refugees who had fled European fascism in the late 1930s. Indeed, the refugee crisis loomed as the greatest challenge for postwar migration policy. In 1944 Immigration Commissioner Earl G. Harrison suggested, "It might be well to consider the possibility of adopting a more flexible type of quota regulations which would enable us to meet situations of an urgent nature." The next commissioner, Ugo Carusi, inspired by the formation of the United Nations in 1945, called for extending the "new concept of international cooperation" to the nation's immigration policy.[23]

The advent of the Cold War in the late 1940s, however, quickly eclipsed and stemmed these trends, resituating them in a bipolar world order in which United States liberal capitalist democracy was defined as the "good" of the world and its best hope against the "evil" of Soviet Communism. American social democracy as articulated in the popular front politics of the thirties and forties became delegitimized as communistic and un-American. The rightward lurch redrew the boundaries of acceptable discourse, claiming as victim, for example, the idealism promoted by the Common Council for American Unity. Readers began to criticize the council's publication *Common Ground* for printing "too many sweetness and light articles" and "too much on the race question—Negroes and Jews."[24]

Cold War liberalism diminished the cultural aspect of cultural pluralism. Pluralism was now less about ethnic identity (much less identity politics) than it was a means for ethnic participation in politics. Pluralism conceived of ethnicity as a legitimate "interest" in a political world of interest groups. In this sense it was assimilationist, a strategy that recognized difference in order to efface it within the universality of liberal democratic politics. Moreover, the softer versions of wartime and postwar liberal nationalism, which mixed ideas about American world leadership with international cooperation, gave way to the Cold War liberalism of the "NATO intellectuals," who were interested not just in leadership but in hegemonism.[25] Like nearly everything else in American politics, pluralism became framed in the context of Cold War nationalism.

Postwar Immigration Legislation, 1948–1952

As noted, the refugee crisis posed perhaps the greatest challenge for immigration policy after the war. World War I had also created millions of refugees in Europe, but in the United States, where anti-alien animus ran high and where the Senate rejected membership in the League of Nations, there was virtually no support for doing anything for refugees. In fact the restrictive immigration laws of the 1920s were aimed at stemming migration from war-torn Europe.

The outlook prevailed throughout the 1930s, when Congress resisted calls to assist refugees fleeing from fascism's spread in Europe. The national origins quotas and the rigidities of the immigration law generally served well the interests of isolationism and anti-Semitism. President Franklin D. Roosevelt, not willing to challenge conservative sectional interests in Congress over immigration policy, granted special nonquota admission only to prominent persons—scientists, scholars, and artists—whose work and lives were at risk and otherwise publicly supported the quota system. In 1938 the Roosevelt administration resorted to administrative devices to assist some 15,000 Jewish refugees and exiles, mostly from Germany and Austria, who had already managed to enter the United States on tourist visas. The week after the *Kristalnacht*, Roosevelt announced that the State Department would grant six-month visa extensions to the "visitors" until the persecution stopped. But nothing was done to open the doors for those still in Europe.[26]

Some critics believed the United States' indifference to the refugees and victims of fascism was a profound moral failure of the nation. Looking back on Roosevelt's policy of the late 1930s, Freda Kirchwey wrote in 1943, "If we had behaved like humane and generous people instead of complacent, cowardly ones, the 2 million Jews lying today in the earth of Poland and Hitler's other crowded graveyards would be alive and safe. We had in our power to rescue this doomed people and we did not lift a hand to do it—or perhaps it would be fairer to say that we lifted just one cautious hand, encased in a tight-fitting glove of quotas and visas and affidavits, and a thick layer of prejudice." Indeed, the most generous estimates put Jewish refugee immigration to the United States from 1933 to 1944 at about 250,000, a trifling number compared to the magnitude of the Holocaust and total population of the United States.[27]

After the war the issue could not be ignored. At the end of 1945 there were 8 million displaced persons in Austria, Italy, and Germany, including 1 million in refugee camps, awaiting repatriation or resettlement. As the United States assumed the mantle of world leadership and a direct interest in the postwar reconstruction of Europe, addressing the European refugee crisis became a geopolitical imperative. (No consideration was given to the refugee problem in Asia, however.) Under President Truman's directive, the United States admitted 38,056 displaced persons as quota immigrants, mainly from Poland and Germany, between 1945 and 1948, while Congress debated legislation on the matter.[28]

The controversies surrounding refugee policy foreshadowed the major lines of argument that would define immigration debates throughout the 1950s and early 1960s. Foreign policy interests dictated that the United States take some responsibility for resettling war refugees. But conservative forces, opposed to any liberalization of the existing system and suspicious that refugees were Communists, job-takers, and other undesirables, determined to make refugee policy as narrow and stingy as possible. The Displaced Persons Act of 1948 provided for the admission of 202,000 European refugees over two years and stipulated that they all be charged, or "mortgaged," to future quotas of their countries of origin—a drastic reduction from the original bill, which called for 400,000 nonquota admissions.[29] The act defined a "displaced person" as a person who entered Germany, Austria, or Italy on or before December 22, 1945, a provision that critics charged was a deliberate attempt to render ineligible 100,000 Jews who entered the displaced persons camps in 1946 and early 1947.

Moreover, the law required that 30 percent of the refugees comprise agricultural workers (which also disadvantaged Jews, who were not farmers) and that second preference should be given to professional or highly skilled persons. This was an important move that introduced into immigration policy the idea that American economic preferences should determine the selection of immigrants—an idea that seems in retrospect ungenerous when applied to people rendered homeless and stateless by war but which idea quickly became naturalized as an assumption of immigration policy.[30]

Truman signed the Displaced Persons Act "with very great reluctance," noting that it "flagrantly" discriminated against Jews and Catholics and that he believed refugees should be admitted on a nonquota basis. Congress amended the act in 1950, enlarging the number of refugee admissions to 414,744 and extending the program to 1951. It redefined displaced persons as those entering Germany, Austria, or Italy before January 1, 1949, which aimed at admitting more Jews and Catholics. But Congress would not change the quota restriction.[31]

In the postwar period, human rights emerged as a salient principle for international law and for refugee policy, in particular, as indicated in the Universal Declaration of Human Rights of 1948. However, the United States continued to resist formulating a specific policy for refugees and admitted refugees and "escapees" from Communist countries on an ad hoc basis throughout the 1950s and early 1960s. It would not be until 1980 that Congress passed legislation that defined refugees in the same terms as international law defined them, that is, as persons unable or unwilling to return to their native country because of persecution or a well-founded fear of persecution.[32]

In 1947, in the midst of debate over war-refugee policy and in large measure in response to that crisis, the Senate authorized a subcommittee of the Judiciary Committee to conduct a comprehensive study of the nation's immigration policy, the first since the Dillingham Commission of 1907–1910.[33] The subcommittee, under the chairmanship of Senator Chapman Revercomb, devoted its attention to the refugee problem for a year, but after the

1948 elections Senator Pat McCarran took over the chair and generalized the work of the subcommittee. McCarran, a conservative and a devout Catholic from Nevada, was a dedicated anti-Communist and Cold War warrior. The 900-page report submitted by the subcommittee and the accompanying 250-page draft omnibus bill introduced by McCarran in 1950[34]—and the legislation that Congress ultimately passed in 1952—have been considered most notable for their preservation of the national origins quota system. To be sure, McCarran did represent conservative and sectional forces that were committed to the national origins system. But preserving the national origins quotas was not the central motivation for the bill—maintaining the status quo hardly required such major review and revision of the code. Rather, McCarran saw revision of the nation's immigration laws as a tool in the United States' urgent battle against Communism.

McCarran viewed immigration policy a matter of "internal security." The Senate subcommittee's report rehearsed the well-worn charge that "the Communist movement in the United States is an alien movement, sustained, augmented, and controlled by European Communists and the Soviet Union." McCarran stressed the need to "bring our immigration system into line with the realities of Communist tactics." In 1950 the Senate Judiciary Committee, believing the matter too urgent to wait for the general revision of the immigration law, included provisions for the exclusion, deportation, and denaturalization of Communists in the Internal Security Act.[35]

In 1952 Congress passed the omnibus Immigration and Naturalization Act, also known as the McCarran-Walter Act, which combined the McCarran bill with the House bill sponsored by Francis Walter. In typical Cold War language, McCarran described the law as a necessary weapon to preserve "this Nation, the last hope of Western civilization." He added, "If this oasis of the world shall be overrun, perverted, contaminated, or destroyed, then the last flickering light of humanity will be extinguished."[36]

The McCarran-Walter Act replaced the Immigration Act of 1917 as the nation's foundational immigration law (and it remains so today, as amended). The 1952 act brought the many fragments of the nation's immigration and naturalization laws under a single code, but it was less an overhaul than a hardening of existing policy, with a few reforms and innovations. The law retained the numerical ceiling of 155,000 quota-immigrants per year based on the national origins formula of 1924, which was numerically more restrictive than previous policy in light of increase in the nation's population since 1924. There were no specific provisions for admitting refugees. The law's sponsors stated there was no claim to "any theory of Nordic superiority," only concern for "similarity of cultural background." But the retention of the national origins quotas reflected that logic which cast the native-born as the most loyal Americans, especially whites of British and north European descent, and the foreign-born as subversive, especially Jews, who were imagined as Bolsheviks, and Italians, who were viewed as anarchists.[37]

While also preserving nonquota immigration from countries of the Western Hemisphere, it imposed quotas on the former British colonies in the Caribbean, a move that was designed to limit the migration of black people into the United States The law's Asiatic policy contained both progressive and reactionary elements. The law eliminated the racial bar to citizenship, which finally ended Japanese and Korean exclusion and made policy consistent with the recent repeals of Chinese, Indian, and Filipino exclusion. It was arguably the most important reform of the McCarran-Walter Act, as it established, for the first time, the general principle of color-blind citizenship. But the law also created an "Asia Pacific Triangle," which was a global race quota aimed at restricting Asian immigration into the United States. Persons of Asian descent born or residing anywhere in the world could immigrate only under the Asia-Pacific quotas of one hundred per country.[38]

Asian immigration policy thus articulated, on the one hand, American geopolitical interests in postwar Asia, which required a semblance of fairness to cement the loyalties of the "good Asians" (Republican Chinese, South Korea, and a reconstructed Japan) against the "bad Asians" (Chinese and other Communists). Secretary of State Dean Acheson supported the McCarran-Walter Act because its elimination of the racial bar to citizenship promised to resolve a "serious irritant of long standing in U.S.-Japanese relations." On the other hand, the prospect of mass Asiatic immigration to the United States remained anathema to the vast majority in Congress. Reformers believed the Asian race quota was a politically necessary "element of discrimination" to achieve formal color-blind naturalization policy.[39]

In addition to updating the law's index of racial desirability, the McCarran-Walter Act made other modifications in the structure of restriction. Most important, it introduced into the quotas a new concept of occupational "preferences" designed to further narrow and refine the immigrant stream. The law required at least one-half of each country's quota to go to persons with specialized skills deemed in short supply in the United States. The second and third preferences were for parents of adult U.S. citizens (30 percent) and spouses and children of permanent resident aliens (20 percent), respectively. Others could come only if quotas under the first three preferences were not filled. The policy thus established a new set of norms of desirability based on educational level, skill, and familial ties to Americans.

The move was of tremendous importance. As one observer remarked, "[T]he country could select the alien instead of the alien selecting the country."[40] Yet despite the innovation there was little discussion of the policy. Few shared the concern of Robert F. Wagner, then the borough president of Manhattan, who criticized the occupational preferences for excluding the "ordinary people [who] are the backbone of America." Liberals aimed their fire at the national origins quotas and may not, in fact, have been adverse to the premises of economic nationalism that undergirded the preference system.[41]

The exclusion and expulsion provisions of the McCarran-Walter Act were severe. It added six excludable classes, making a total of thirty-one. It stiffened deportation policy in ways that arguably violated Constitutional norms, making aliens deportable for acts that were not grounds for deportation at the time they were committed, eliminating the statute of limitations for nearly all deportable offenses, and narrowing the grounds of eligibility for a suspension of deportation. The law reenacted provisions in the Internal Security Act for the expulsion of aliens whose activities the attorney general deemed "prejudicial to the public interest."[42]

At the same time, the law conceded some elements of due process to aliens in deportation hearings—notice, representation by counsel, and the right of cross-examination. It also codified new conditions for relief from deportation, providing statutory, that is, mandatory relief for aliens who entered with fraudulent documents or by lying to inspectors if they had long-term residence and immediate family in the United States, although it narrowed the grounds for suspension of deportation in other ways. The law thus juggled the perceived needs of "internal security" with reforms made in the 1930s and 1940s that recognized certain (mostly European) illegal aliens' claims of belonging.[43]

Finally, the McCarran-Walter Act stiffened the requirements for naturalized citizenship, and provided for the denaturalization of naturalized citizens if within ten years of naturalization one was cited for contempt for refusing to testify about subversive activity. One could also lose one's citizenship if one became a member of a subversive organization, voted in a foreign election, deserted the military, or was found guilty of treason.[44]

Congress passed the McCarran-Walter Act over President Truman's veto. Truman opposed the law, principally for its racist features. "In no other realm of our national life are we so hampered and stultified by the dead hand of the past, as we are in this field of immigration," Truman said. He called the continuation of the national origins quotas "a slur on the patriotism, the capacity, and the decency of a large part of our citizenry." Indeed, that "part of our citizenry" sent the president some eleven thousand telegrams, letters, and cards urging him to veto the bill, compared to five hundred in support of the bill. Voicing what would emerge as a central rationale for reform throughout the period, Truman emphasized the need for an immigration policy that would be "a fitting instrument for our foreign policy and a true reflection of the ideals we stand for, at home and abroad."[45]

The Liberal Critique of National Origins Quotas

After Congress passed the McCarran-Walter Act over his veto, Truman established a Commission on Immigration and Naturalization to evaluate and

recommend immigration policy. The commission's hearings and report, issued in 1953, gave liberals a venue for airing their criticisms and for organizing for reform, an effort that would continue for thirteen years before finally
succeeding in 1965.[46]

The liberal reform effort comprised a coalition of interests, with liberal
religious and ethnic elements at the core and with Jewish organizations playing a particularly central role. Added to the coalition was a roster of native-
stock elites, which gave the project an aura of national legitimacy, and organized labor, which had emerged in the postwar period as a serious political
player. Many came directly from the postwar movement to admit displaced
persons and supported the movement for black civil rights.[47]

The immigration reform movement was an exemplar of postwar interest-
group political mobilization. It was a disciplined coalition that executed a
remarkably well-coordinated mass educational and lobbying campaign. Reformers circulated broadsides, pamphlets, and petitions; published op-ed
pieces and aired radio commentaries; and held meetings, conferences, and
forums. Liberal intellectuals, who saw in the immigration issue occasion to
promote a pluralist vision of American society, provided the movement with
arguments that were large, structured, and grounded in historical perspective
and sociological detail. Harvard historian Oscar Handlin, the most important immigration scholar at midcentury, was an active public intellectual
who wrote commentaries and short books aimed at a general audience.[48]
Handlin also served as consultant to Truman's immigration commission (he
drafted the commission's critique of national origins quotas) and to New
York senator Herbert Lehman. When John Higham, then a young assistant
professor, published his history of American nativism, *Strangers in the Land*,
in 1955, reform organizations and legislators immediately took note. Handlin and other academics churned out work for the Anti-Defamation League
of B'nai B'rith's "Freedom" pamphlet series and "One Nation Library" on
pluralism, religious tolerance, and antiracism, including *A Nation of Immigrants*, which was published under John F. Kennedy's name.[49]

In terms of legislative change the reform movement of the 1950s was a
failure. Francis Walter held a tight grip on the House immigration committee until his death in 1963. Throughout the fifties Walter constrained the
initiative of liberal lawmakers and Presidents Eisenhower and Kennedy, negotiating limited ad hoc legislation on refugee admissions and other issues in
exchange for leaving the national origins quotas untouched.[50] But despite its
legislative failures throughout the 1950s, liberal intellectuals and activists
worked out the ideological foundations and programmatic elements for policy proposals that would eventually be articulated in the Immigration Act of
1965.

Most notably, the reform movement pushed liberal politicians from tepid
proposals made in the early 1950s, which sought only to "pool" unused

quotas from undersubscribed countries (Great Britain, for example, used only 5 percent of its quota) for use by those with oversubscribed quotas, to full opposition to quota system. Opponents of the McCarran-Walter Act in Congress believed that the national origins system was so entrenched that it could not be eliminated overnight. But liberal activists like Will Maslow of the American Jewish Congress opposed "half way" measures such as pooling unused quotas. Others criticized congressional liberals for proposing legislation that "lacked boldness and vision." Oscar Handlin said congressional reform-proposals were "extremely cautious" measures that "compromised with the quota system," and he urged a "frontal attack upon the quota system." By 1953 the chief sponsor of reform legislation, Senator Herbert H. Lehman of New York, agreed to call for elimination of the national origins quotas.[51]

Herbert Lehman was perhaps the most prominent figure in the immigration reform movement during the 1950s. Lehman had a long history in liberal politics—he had been governor of New York and before that Franklin D. Roosevelt's lieutenant governor—and a reputation as the "conscience of the Senate." Lehman came from an august family of German-Jewish immigrants. His father was a cotton factor in Montgomery, Alabama, before the Civil War, and founded the cotton exchange in New York City and then the investment house bearing the family's name. Herbert's older brother, Irving, was a distinguished judge who sat on the Second Circuit Court of Appeals with Learned Hand and Benjamin Cardozo. During the 1950s Herbert Lehman not only took the lead in drafting and sponsoring alternate immigration legislation, his office was instrumental in organizing various civic coalitions that led the reform movement. The senator personally bankrolled much of the civic effort as well.[52]

Lehman expressed well the liberal nationalist outlook that suffused the immigration reform movement. He believed the McCarran-Walter Act was a racist law made worse by an excessive zeal against Communism, which was at that time operating at full throttle in the House Committee on Un-American Activities. Although Lehman was less cowed by the right wing than were many of his liberal colleagues (he was one of only seven senators who voted against the Internal Security Act) he did not stand outside of the postwar nationalist consensus. He believed in the U.S. nation-state's global projections of American universality and that "freedom loving people throughout the world look to the United States as the focal point of democracy and moral leadership." Even as Lehman criticized McCarthy for using "the evil countenance of Communism as a hobgoblin for his own purposes," he believed nonetheless that Communism was an "evil and frightening thing" that fomented dissent in Europe (Italy, Greece) and turned nationalist revolutions (China, Egypt) into "desperate dangers to world peace and security."[53]

That perspective framed his view of immigration policy. Testifying before the Truman immigration commission, Lehman said the national origins quota system

> is based on the same discredited racial theories from which Adolph Hitler developed the infamous Nuremberg laws. This System is based on the hypothesis that persons of Anglo-Saxon birth are superior to other nationalities and therefore better qualified to be admitted into the United States, and to become Americans. . . . According to this theory a man named Pastore is less qualified to become a good American than a man named Smith. . . . I need not tell you gentlemen how utterly repugnant such a theory is to every concept we call American. It is the complete denial of Americanism. . . . To defend ourselves against the evil implications of this concept, we recently fought a great war and expended billions of our wealth and sacrificed hundreds of thousands of American lives, including untold numbers whose names were not Smith, Brown, or Jones. Let those who defend the National Origins Quota System be forced to read aloud the names of the winners of the Congressional Medal of Honor, or to recite the daily casualty lists coming out of Korea—and then let them dare to say that those of one national origin are less fit to be Americans, less fit to live and die for America, than those of another national origin."[54]

In this passage fascism served a double calling. First, it highlighted the odious racism of the quota system. No doubt comparing the quotas to Hitlerism was done for calculated shock value, which value derived from the understanding widespread among Americans that their principles were the opposite of Hitler's. While undoubtedly the case, that understanding was nonetheless built on a concept of American democracy and racial equality more abstract than historical. Lehman pointed to an uncomfortable truth about American racism, yet the intention of his statement should not be read as an actual comparison of American policy to fascism but, rather, as an attempt to emphasize the opposite, to distinguish democracy from fascism. The point was to posit the national origins quotas as an anomalous interruption in the national narrative, a teleology that entailed "the mixture and molding of many cultures and blood strains, and the fusing of these streams, in a climate of freedom and opportunity." This had become a common rhetorical move, part of a broader conception of race equality that emerged in the postwar period, which Nikhil Pal Singh has aptly described as something "paradoxically always already accomplished and something that is never quite complete."[55]

Second, Lehman's reference to Hitlerism invoked the patriotism of American soldiers of all ethnic backgrounds who died in the war against it, which patriotism held even more currency when applied to the Cold War. His quick step from World War II to the Korean War articulated the commonplace notion that fascism and communism were commensurate evils joined under the general rubric of "totalitarianism." The fervor of Lehman's remarks indicate, as well, the felt need of liberals to perform their nationalist credentials in the tense and suspicious environment of McCarthyism and to argue their proposals for reform as a Cold War imperative.

Indeed, the Cold War overdetermined both international and domestic politics; it invaded debate on nearly every issue and prompted opposing sides to each assume the posture of anti-communism.[56] While immigration restrictionists warned against opening the floodgates to subversive aliens, reformers argued that the national origins quota system damaged the nation's reputation abroad. Emanuel Celler of New York City, one of the staunchest opponents of the national origins system in Congress, called immigration policy an important site in the U.S.–Soviet "race for the minds of men." Phrases like "It is intolerable that we should continue to maintain our own Iron Curtain—against visitors and alien immigrants alike—while criticizing the Iron Curtain abroad" were the stock of reform discourse throughout the postwar period.[57]

The political imperatives of the Cold War encouraged some to oppose the national origins quotas who might not have otherwise. The case of organized labor is illustrative. In general, throughout the 1950s organized labor did not pay much attention to immigration policy. The American Federation of Labor had a long tradition of nativism and the Congress of Industrial Organizations' large eastern and southern European–American membership led it to oppose the national origins quotas. But the low levels of immigration since the 1930s and the prosperity of the postwar years had made the issue unimportant to them.[58] Nevertheless, organized labor ardently supported American Cold War aims, and immigration reform was part of the Democratic Party's foreign affairs platform. After the AFL-CIO merged in 1955, it called for modifying the McCarran-Walter Act, framing its position in terms of U.S. foreign policy interests: "America needs a basic immigration law, which befits the present-day America as the leader of the free world." AFL-CIO president George Meany, a Cold War social democrat, was particularly committed to this view. Meany acknowledged organized labor's traditional worry that immigration could threaten American workers' jobs, but he emphasized that "part of our total program to combat world Communism must be a willingness to welcome a reasonable number to our own shores. In the long run it will enrich us." Cold War politics underwrote organized labor's strategic shift from nativism to reform.[59]

But in many ways Cold War politics narrowed and constrained cultural pluralism. For one thing, McCarthyism's assault on the left—from popular-front social democrats to the Communist Party—silenced anticolonial and internationalist politics. Liberal nationalism faced little if any opposition from alternate views of immigration policy; for example, views that approached policy from the vantage of international human rights or the non-

7.1 After World War II, opposition to the national origins quota system increased. This 1952 cartoon by the Congress of Industrial Organizations put the McCarran-Walter Act in historical perspective. (By permission of Tony Spina Collection, Walter P. Reuther Library, Wayne State University.)

aligned movement. If the politics of the reform movement seemed remarkably cohesive, that was in part because liberal nationalism was hegemonic
discourse.

Second, Cold War liberalism's emphasis on America's image abroad narrowed the concept of immigration reform to a question of formal equality.
In this regard immigration reform paralleled the trajectory of the civil rights
movement. As Mary Dudziak has shown, Cold War liberals believed formal
equality for African Americans was important for America's standing in the
third world, but foreign policy required no greater commitment from such
liberals to actually end racial subordination.[60] In the immigration context,
liberals formulated a policy of formal equality that put all countries on the
same footing and favored no national group over another. They believed the
nation's democratic image would be served by a policy that welcomed immigrants from all nations equally, regardless of race or nationality. But arguably
that policy was substantively unequal, because it failed to consider differences
in size and needs among countries or the particular historical relations between some countries and the United States. The racism of the national
origins quotas lay not in the differential distribution of the quotas per se but
rather in its racial hierarchy, which valued some nationalities over others. An
equal distribution of quotas was not the only or necessarily the best alternative.

Liberals' commitment to a policy of formal equality derived also from
their belief that treating nations equally represented equal treatment of all
American ethnic groups. They considered the distribution of quotas an expression of domestic group relations. Thus when reformers raised the issue
of equal rights, the subjects about whom they spoke were not migrants but
Americans. Specifically, they referred to the rights of ethnic Americans to be
treated as full members of American society. Writing in *Commentary*, Oscar
Handlin asked,

> Upon whom do the quotas cast the slur of inferiority? Upon all those
> whose grandfathers would not have been reckoned fit, under these laws,
> for admission to the United States. Whose grandfathers? . . . the grand-
> fathers of millions of Poles and Italians and Jews, and of hundreds of
> thousands of others who, by their contributions to American life, have
> earned the right to be counted the equals of the descendants of the Pil-
> grims. . . . [T]he descendants of immigrants have a right to be heard. . . .
> The Italian American has the right to be heard on these matters precisely
> *as* an Italian American. The quotas implicitly pass a judgment upon his
> own place in the United States.[61]

Handlin's view that ethnic Americans could contribute, as ethnics, to the
body politic articulated pluralism's melding with postwar interest-group politics. Yet liberals' emphasis on immigration reform as a means of redressing

domestic social discrimination, while understandable, encouraged the tendency to consider immigration policy in abstract and formal terms as well as from the exclusive vantage point of the U.S. nation-state.

Like most pluralists of his generation, Handlin imagined "the descendents of immigrants" as white Euro-Americans. In the same vein, John F. Kennedy's *A Nation of Immigrants* devoted all of two paragraphs to Asian and Latino immigration to the United States. Pluralism's Euro-American emphasis had important consequences. Asian Americans and Mexican Americans had virtually no presence in the immigration reform movement, notwithstanding their grandfathers' "contributions to American life."[62] The absence of non-European ethno-racial groups in the reform movement meant that liberals tended to view immigration policy for Asia, Mexico, and the Caribbean abstractly, disconnected from those immigrant communities in the United States and without the benefit of their experiences and perspectives.

More to the point, many liberals were ambivalent about immigration from the third world. On the one hand, liberals believed strongly that the Asia Pacific Triangle, with its global race quotas, was racist policy that damaged America's reputation and interests in Asia. There was little doubt that it should be eliminated. On the other hand, eliminating the Asia Pacific Triangle meant that large numbers of Chinese would be able to enter the United States from Western Hemisphere countries—theoretically an unlimited number as long as Western Hemisphere immigration remained outside the quotas—and from the British colony of Hong Kong, where they would have access to Great Britain's vast unused quota. Conservatives like Francis Walter made no secret of their hostility towards Asiatic immigration. In a 1961 interview, for example, Walter flatly declared his commitment to preventing a horde of Asiatics from overrunning the United States. To allay the conservatives' (and possibly their own) fears, liberals argued that opening Asiatic immigration in principle would not mean opening it in practice, at least not significantly. In 1963 State Department officials told Congress that the administration's proposal to eliminate the Asia Pacific Triangle would "not alter to any significant extent the present pattern of immigration." After canvassing U.S. consuls abroad, it projected an increase in Chinese immigration of approximately 5,000 to 6,000 from the Western Hemisphere and Great Britain.[63]

During the 1950s immigration reformers paid relatively little attention to Western Hemisphere immigration policy. There was little if any debate over Western Hemisphere quotas or about undocumented Mexican agricultural labor, even though the latter issue had come to national attention in the early 1950s. That issue remained curiously cabined in another realm of discussion, outside the mainstream of immigration policy.[64] Throughout much of the decade, supporters and opponents of reform generally agreed in maintaining the status quo policy of nonquota immigration for Western Hemisphere countries.

But if there was little discussion of Western Hemisphere policy in the 1950s, the Mexican migrant appeared symbolically in the discourse of immigration reform, as the racialized specter of the illegal alien. The "wetback" stood at the nation's back door, as a foil for the putatively legal, desirable, and freedom-loving European seeking entrance through the main gate. According to Lehman, the McCarran-Walter Act "permits 'undesirable aliens' by the thousands to stream across the Mexican and Canadian borders without any surveillance whatever, while making the alien who enters the United States legally run a series of completely unnecessary and onerous ordeals."[65]

Julius Edelstein, Lehman's executive assistant and chief architect of the National Committee on Immigration and Citizenship, wrote to a colleague, "Real Communists can get in very easily, either by outright lying or just by coming across the Mexican and Canadian borders. This Mexican-Canadian business should be hammered again and again and again. It is the unanswerable answer to the McCarran Walter claim that the law keeps Communists out." While Lehman and Edelstein referred generally to both Mexico and Canada, they made specific references only to illegal immigration across the southern border, which highlighted the problem as a Mexican one. Edelstein never gave details of illegal entry from Canada, but he always had data on illegal entry from Mexico, citing, in one instance, "an official figure of 4 million illegal immigrants across the Mexican border." He further observed that the lack of quota limitations on the Western Hemisphere meant that "theoretically, millions of undesirables might come in from Latin America including, I suppose, Communists from Guatemala."[66] On another occasion he told an audience of social workers,

> [W]hile ponderous controls are maintained on legal immigration, illegal immigration across the Mexican and Canadian borders thrives almost unimpeded. The *New York Times* estimated that in 1953, 1,500,000 illegal immigrants—mostly wetbacks—streamed across the Mexican border, without so much as a How-do-you-do to an American immigration inspector. We stand triple guard, at the front door, bayonets at the ready, to repel legal immigration, while illegal immigration swarms in at the back door and through the windows.[67]

What is noteworthy here is not only the ease with which Cold War imperatives were woven into every angle of debate but the normative assumptions about legal and illegal immigration and territoriality that undergirded the discussion. The Mexican "wetback" stood opposite the European immigrant in a binary construct that defined desirability in conflated terms of race, politics, and legal status. In fact, casting Europeans as legal and Mexicans as illegal was disingenuous, because the legal status of each was utterly contingent. The Europeans described by Lehman and Edelstein were not in fact "legal immigrants" but aliens denied legal entry either by the quota laws or by qualitative requirements. Using familiar tropes, Edelstein deplored the situation in which a "loaf of bread stolen to feed a starving family, a ration regulation violated out of ignorance or urgent need, a police state law violated out of defiance to the regime . . . can forever bar an alien from entering the United States." The grounds for exclusion may have been unjust or unduly harsh, but the law cannot, by definition, exclude legal immigrants—if they are legal, they cannot be excluded. The juxtaposition of "European" and "Mexican" obscured this slippage, the deserving claims of the former legitimized by the naturalized illegal image of the latter. Lehman and Edelstein decried the definition of "crimes of moral turpitude" that excluded European aliens who stole bread or firewood for their families' welfare. But they accepted without question the premises of nation-state territoriality—crossing the border "without as much as a How-do-you-do to an American immigration inspector"—that constructed Mexicans seeking work, also for their families' welfare, as illegal aliens. Indeed, Lehman seems to have imbibed the stereotype that Mexican illegal aliens were criminals. He told the Senate, "Theft, murder, and drug traffic are all plaguing the law enforcement officers of the . . . Southwest, where the uncontrolled human wave of wetbacks washes most of its flotsam and jetsam."[68]

It would not be until 1965, when the issue was forced in the final legislative negotiations over the immigration reform bills, that liberals had to come to terms with Western Hemisphere immigration policy. As we will see, liberals' acceptance of the naturalized condition of the illegal Mexican immigrant would have important consequences for how they responded in those negotiations.

Economic Nationalism and Immigration Reform

While some scholars have characterized the postwar immigration debate as one between "restrictionists" and "anti-restrictionists," the latter appellation is, at best, imprecise.[69] Liberals objected to many principles espoused by old-line restrictionists, but "restriction" was not one of them. The postwar immigration debate was never over whether to restrict, but by how much and according to what criteria. In this vein, reformers invariably coupled their calls to abolish the national origins system with statements like "immigration in limited and practicable amounts is good for our country" and proposals for "the orderly admission, with all proper safeguards, of a reasonable number of aliens."[70] Similarly, after advocating "greater freedom of movement [within] the North Atlantic Community," an American diplomat hastened to add, "This does not mean that we should remove all barriers and throw our gates open to all and sundry, without control or limits." When he was in the Senate, John F. Kennedy proposed reforming the quota system but emphasized, "Obviously, there must be a limit upon immigration."[71] These statements were in part a defensive response to conservatives' claims that reformers wanted to recklessly abandon all controls on immigration. But in fact liberals sought to open the doors but a crack.

What actually constituted a "reasonable number" of immigrants? One proposal, made in 1951 by Chester Bowles, former governor of Connecticut and head of the federal Office of Price Control during World War II, suggested an annual admission of 600,000 new immigrants. Bowles calculated that number by adjusting the ceiling from the 1924 act to the 1950 population and adding to it the cumulative backlog of 2.5 million unused quota slots since 1924, spread over six years. After six years, Bowles recommended an annual ceiling of four-tenths of one percent (with no quotas on the Western Hemisphere), or 640,000 a year. As that number was only half the actual number absorbed in the years before World War I, when the population was one-third smaller, Bowles considered his proposal quite moderate. Edward Corsi, former immigration commission at Ellis Island, argued for an annual admission of 500,000 immigrants. In 1952 the CIO suggested that the maximum number be set between 300,000 and 600,000. In the early 1950s Herbert Lehman proposed a ceiling of 300,000 to 350,000.[72]

The number that reformers came to agree upon was 250,000 a year. Their explanation was that 250,000 represented an application of the same formula used in 1924—one-sixth of one percent of the total U.S. population—updated to the 1950 Census, which formula, they claimed, determined the number of immigrants the nation could economically absorb. The "one-sixth of one percent" formula became the mantra of reformers, achieving the status of what Aristide Zolberg has called "numerological magic." It was adopted throughout the reform movement, by diverse groups such as the Massachusetts Congregational Christian Conference and the order Sons of Italy in America. In 1959 Senator John F. Kennedy articulated the consensus view that raising the ceiling to 250,000 "will authorize a substantial number of immigrants without having any adverse effects on our economy." The number appeared in virtually every reform bill introduced in Congress during the 1950s and early 1960s.[73]

The stated origins of the formula and its putative rationale about economic absorption, however, are suspect. Some proponents gave credit for the formula to organized labor and to studies by demographers and economists, no doubt to invoke these groups' authority on the subject. But reformers never cited specific studies, and I found none in their archives.[74] The claim that the architects of the Immigration Act of 1924 used the "one-sixth of one percent" formula as an index of reasonable economic absorption was false. In fact, the 155,000 ceiling established in the Johnson Act was derived from the formula of 2 percent of the foreign-born counted in the 1890 census. Ultimately Congress kept that ceiling but redistributed the quotas according to the "national origins" of the 1920 white population. The calculus of numerical restriction in the 1920s was aimed at engineering the racial composition of the nation; it had nothing to do with the economics of absorption. Postwar reformers read the 1924 ceiling backwards—the "one-sixth of one percent" did not determine the level of immigration but was derived after the fact.[75]

Reformers gave various reasons for increasing immigration. Most prominent was the argument that it was good for the expanding postwar American economy. The National Council of the Churches of Christ wrote that the nation needed more immigrants as "producers and consumers." Lehman argued that "an increase in immigration would . . . provide a stimulus to our expanding economy," as did Robert F. Kennedy, who claimed that under the legislation proposed by the Johnson Administration in 1964 "our economy will get three consumers for every worker that is admitted," presumably a reference to the nuclear family headed by a male breadwinner as the prototypical immigration unit.[76]

Oscar Handlin said immigrants would perform "useful tasks that Americans find unattractive," like agricultural and domestic labor. Moreover, he added, as consumers, immigrants would further expand the domestic market. The AFL-CIO was won over to this view, stating that immigrants were not just potential competitors for jobs but were "customers . . . [who] are buying shoes and milk and television sets and are going to the movies and eating in restaurants and sending their laundry out."[77]

Sometimes the economic argument assumed an urgent tone. In the context of the Cold War, more "manpower" was needed to shore up the nation's body count. Handlin warned that predictions of a declining birth rate pointed to a manpower shortage that threatened "our national survival." A report by the Bureau of Labor Statistics declared: "In comparison with countries found within the Soviet Orbit, our greatest relative shortage is in manpower resources. Our national self-interest requires that every consideration of our situation, including immigration policies, recognize this paramount fact."[78]

Yet an increase to 250,000 a year would not have gone terribly far in fulfilling the needs listed by reformers. In 1964 Secretary of Labor Willard Wirtz told the House Judiciary Committee that raising the ceiling to 250,000 would yield an addition of 23,750 quota immigrants to the labor force.*

---

* Wirtz's math appears to be based on the difference between the existing and proposed ceilings (250,000 − 155,000 = 95,000) and an assumption that only one out of four immigrants would actually enter the workforce (one-fourth of 95,000 = 23,750). The others were presumably nonworking spouses, children, or parents of employed male heads of households.

"Measured against a projected total work force of 79 million," Wirtz concluded with great understatement, "it becomes apparent the impact from the additional number will be insignificant."[79]

If the reformers seemed to want to have it both ways, economists more consistently advocated increases in immigration by greater margins. Staff economists working for Truman's immigration commission in 1952 concluded that the United States could readily absorb "several times" the existing quota limitation, pointing out that in the decade 1940–1950, northern and western cities drew two million African Americans from the South as well as Puerto Ricans to meet the demand for labor. Not only was the United States not overpopulated, they stated, it suffered from demographic imbalances—a declining population of young adults of working age and a female-male sex imbalance—that immigration might help to redress. Harold Moulton, an economist at the Brookings Institution, said in 1949 that if the nation's population doubled in the next one hundred years, its standard of living would be eight times as high.[80]

In the most comprehensive study of the economics of immigration published in the postwar years, British economist Julian Isaac argued that the optimum rate of population growth for "new countries"—defined as those with a carrying capacity far greater than actual population, like the United States, Canada, and Australia—was shown historically to be 2 percent per year. Immigration, he suggested, should be the difference between 2 percent of the total population plus emigration and native natural population growth. In the United States in 1950, that formula would have produced an annual immigration target of 722,000.[81]

Isaac explained that classical economic theory considered migration a kind of market corrective to "disharmonious population growth" among countries. In this view, overpopulated countries and countries with declining birthrates benefited from emigration and immigration, respectively. But Isaac pointed out that the latter countries were likely to view such a strategy as a "counsel of despair." He cited a British study's conclusion that "to rely chiefly on the encouragement of immigration as a means of redressing Britain's demographic balance would be an admission of national defeat."[82]

More to the point, Isaac stated, "So long as the control of migration is the prerogative of sovereign states, receiving countries will object to a volume of immigration which might lower the standard of living of the native population even if it should raise aggregate real income for the receiving and sending country taken together. The same reaction must be expected if it is not the general standard of living but that of political influential elements of the population (e.g., unskilled labor) which is adversely affected by immigration."[83]

Organized labor expressed this view. Testifying before Congress in 1955, AFL spokesman Walter Mason supported a "reasonable increase" of annual immigration to 250,000 but emphasized that the AFL "cannot permit a tidal wave of immigration [that] would threaten the employment opportunities of American workers or undermine established standards of wages and working conditions." The *Christian Science Monitor* questioned "the humanity of seeking to open the gates to large numbers of persons with greater or lesser skills . . . while large numbers of Negroes and Puerto Ricans are either unemployed or underemployed." A constituent wrote to Emanuel Celler, "It would not be fair to let better-educated Europeans compete with the poorly-educated young people of this country."[84]

But economist Melvin Reder pointed out the contradiction inherent to restricting immigration in order to protect society's lower wage earners:

[T]o restrict immigration in order to benefit poorer natives is to promote internal distributional equality by increasing *international* inequality in distribution . . . [A] concern for distributional equality, were it unalloyed with national bias, would suggest weaker rather than stronger barriers to immigration. But nationalism, that is, socio-political selfishness, does enter the picture. . . . We [the United States] have used part of the fruits of economic progress to create a national island of relatively homogenous and comfortable people.[85]

Isaac and Reder believed nationalist politics hindered the operation of a free market immigration policy, but they were resigned to nationalism's forceful influence. Given the history of American exceptionalism, it is perhaps not surprising that Americans rarely acknowledged that their prosperity was linked to the conditions of others in the world. Most Americans were blind to the causative connections between U.S. economic and political policies abroad and migration. Nor were they interested in a global redistribution of wealth.

Economic nationalism was expressed not only in numerical limits but in terms of occupational preferences as well. Throughout the 1950s reformers considered various plans, but in general they upheld the principle established in the Walter-McCarran Act that first preference should be given to professionals and highly skilled workers deemed in short supply domestically. Between 1952 and 1965 only 1 percent of all immigrants came as first-preference workers, mainly from advanced European countries. During the 1950s and 1960s scientists and technical workers from less developed countries also emigrated to the advanced nations in the West in increasing numbers, in large measure a consequence of post–World War II decolonization; but before 1965 the developing "brain drain" to the United States from the Third World comprised mainly nonreturning students, not regularly admitted immigrants.[86]

Not all subscribed to the nationalist orientation of immigration policy. In a speech delivered to the American Immigration Conference in 1959, the

Reverend Paul Empie of the National Lutheran Council resituated American "national interest" on the terrain of "international understanding, well-being, and peace." Empie considered the conventional view that restricting immigration was an exercise of national sovereignty to be "ultimately an appeal not to reason nor to morality but to *force* as the decisive factor in our policy." He noted the long history of Americans' "use of force . . . in obtaining various parts of this nation from the Indians, the British, the Mexicans. Having thus inherited the continent their descendents continued to use force to keep most other people out."[87]

Empie advocated a position of "secular morality" and called on policymakers to "resist the insistent pressure of groups of our citizens for a quick increase in their standard of living without regard to our relations to a world society." He stated, "Were the United States to base her immigration policies solely on considerations of material gain for her own citizens and a search for a higher standard of living which would increasingly widen the economic gap now existing between them and three-fourths of the earth's population, she would jeopardize the allegiance of even some of her closest allies."[88]

Like other liberals, Empie linked immigration reform to U.S. foreign policy interests, but his formulation is noteworthy because it went beyond considerations of image, reputation, and formal equality. He called for a policy that recognized "the interlocking and mutual interests of all nations with regard to the immigration of peoples, the interaction of culture, and the respect of universal human rights." Empie did not advocate eliminating all controls on immigration. He did not consider unlimited immigration in the best interests of either receiving or sending nations. Empie thought immigration from the needier countries of the world should be supplemented with "using . . . our resources in such as way as to help such persons in the countries where they are." He was sensitive to the United States' position—and responsibilities—in a world characterized by extreme disparities in wealth and power. Along the same lines, a coalition of Jewish organizations pointed out that "those areas of the world whose peoples are most urgently in need of resettlement and most deserving of assistance have among the lowest of the quotas."[89]

In 1962 and 1963 Senator Philip Hart of Michigan introduced legislation that captured some of these concerns. Hart also proposed the same ceiling of 250,000 on annual admissions, but rather than distribute quotas equally to all countries, the bill devised a formula that took into account the needs of refugees and emigrating countries. It allocated 20 percent of the total, 50,000, for refugees; distributed 80,000 among countries in proportion to the size of their population, with a maximum of 3,000 per country; and assigned 120,000 to countries in proportion to their emigration to the United States during the previous fifteen years. No country would receive fewer than 200 or more than 25,000. The quotas would be updated every five years. Countries of the Western Hemisphere would remain outside the quotas. Under Hart's plan, the only country that would receive a smaller quota would be Great Britain.[90]

Thirty-five senators and fourteen representatives cosponsored Hart's bill, not a small showing of support. But Kennedy's staff opposed it and pressured Hart to introduce the administration's more moderate bill.[91] More broadly, the view that the nation's interests could be considered in conjunction with the interests of other nations failed to rally mass support. The more popular position was for equal quotas for all, perhaps because of its simplicity, but perhaps also because its central rationale—that it stood for the equal rights of ethnic Americans—and its underlying premise of economic protectionism more strongly resonated with the liberal nationalist tenor of the time. Formal equality, numerical restriction, and family and occupational preferences were all linked in a single definition of national interest.

Western Hemisphere Quotas

While the reform movement opposed the national origins principle consistently and made it the centerpiece of their efforts, liberals' approach to Western Hemisphere policy was confused. Liberals, especially those in the Northeast who dominated the reform movement, had little or no direct experience with Mexican immigration or with Mexican Americans. They understood illegal immigration, and the so-called wetback problem in particular, more abstractly than they did concretely. Reformers' lack of experience with Mexican migration meant that their views on Western Hemisphere policy evolved on uncertain terrain. And on that terrain all the major lines of liberal thinking on immigration interacted and collided—formal equality, nation-state territoriality, numerical limits on immigration, and Cold War politics.

Before examining the evolution of liberal thinking on Western Hemisphere policy, it will be useful to briefly rehearse the history of it. The Immigration Acts of 1924 and 1952 did not impose numerical restrictions on immigration from countries of the Western Hemisphere. The policy had been justified as an expression of Pan-American and Good Neighbor policies promoted by the U.S. State Department. Foreign policy interests valued good relations with America's contiguous and hemispheric neighbors and in the context of the Cold War, a secure "backyard" was especially important. American business interests were also at stake. This included, of course, southwestern agribusiness's insatiable demand for cheap Mexican labor, but an open immigration policy also gave American businessmen easy access into Mexico and Caribbean and other Latin American countries. State Department officials understood that, even in a world of weak and strong nations, immigration policy was reciprocal. That is why the State Department historically opposed demands from hard-line race nativists to impose quotas on Mexican immigration.

In 1929 the State Department acceded to nativist demands but preserved its foreign policy prerogatives by restricting Mexican immigration by administrative means, using the public-charge provision to deny visas to nearly all Mexican laborers seeking legal admission to the United States. The McCarran-Walter Act continued the policy of formal nonquota immigration and administrative control on grounds that quotas were incompatible with good neighbor policy as well as the belief that it was "almost impossible" to protect the land borders from illegal entries.[92]

But, as we have seen, administrative restriction curtailed only legal immigration from Mexico to the United States. It did little to stop, and in fact it further generated, illegal immigration. Conservatives in Congress, from their strongholds in the West and Southwest, actually had few problems with illegal Mexican immigration. The Senate Judiciary Committee's 1950 report on immigration devoted two pages (out of nine hundred) to Western Hemisphere immigration and completely ignored the matter of illegal Mexican immigration. Senator Pat McCarran preferred illegal over bracero labor on grounds that "a farmer can get a wetback and he does not have go through that red tape." He explained, "We might just as well face this thing realistically. The agricultural people, the farmers . . . want this help. They want this farm labor. They just cannot get along without it."[93]

By the early 1950s Mexican Americans and organized labor opposed both bracero and illegal labor on grounds that they depressed American wage standards, displaced domestic workers, including U.S. citizens of Mexican descent, and suffered pitiful exploitation by growers. They criticized the hard-line restrictionists for hypocritically supporting restrictions on European migration while condoning illegal migration from Mexico. But their criticism of the conservatives' paradoxical position challenged their own traditional support for nonquota immigration for countries of the Western Hemisphere. The abstract and formal approach to reform undercut Pan-Americanism, as proposals to the replace the national origins quotas with a system of equal quotas for all countries begged application to the Western Hemisphere on grounds of consistency in principle. As early as 1953 Oscar Handlin advised Julius Edelstein, "Elimination of the Western Hemisphere [exemption from quota restriction] would be desirable. The argument of consistency, from our point of view, is so strong that none of the objections I have heard raised seem to me to have weight against it."[94]

The Lehman-Humphrey bill introduced in 1953 provided numerical quotas for the Western Hemisphere, but it was reversed in later legislation that they proposed. Nonquota status for the Western Hemisphere was consistently upheld in legislation introduced by Kennedy, Celler, and Hart from the late 1950s through 1965 as well.[95] Proponents of the nonquota tradition in the Western Hemisphere argued that a policy favoring neighboring countries was not discriminatory but beneficent. A lawyer from Miami, Florida, wrote Senator Lehman, "I doubt whether anyone will accuse us of being discriminatory simply because we have decided to continue a policy of preference to our neighbors with whom we are closely tied by economic, political and cultural bonds of long standing." Handlin's argument for a global policy of formal equality seemed less compelling to liberal members of Congress when it was unmoored from Euro-American ethnics' demands for equality and respect and even less compelling in the context of regional geopolitics.[96]

But the problem nagged, not because any one seriously objected to Pan-Americanism but, rather, on account of predictions that migration from Latin America and the Caribbean would increase. Sociologists and demographers told Congress that Latin America experienced a 15 percent increase in population from 1955 to 1964, which was paralleled by increases in immigration. A conservative broadside predicted that the population of Latin America would triple in forty-five years and asked, "How many can the United States accept without being swamped?" The *New York Times* warned that the nonquota policy would lead to a "sudden flood" of migrants from Latin America and the Caribbean "in the not-so-distant future." Noting opposition to nonwhite Commonwealth migration to Great Britain, the *Times* saw Western Hemispheric quotas as a prophylactic measure against a potentially "ugly situation" in the United States in the future.[97]

Still, reformers opposed extending quotas to the Western Hemisphere. When pressed, they argued that quotas were unnecessary because the government would continue to control immigration by administrative means. Norbert Schlei, the assistant attorney general in the Johnson administration, predicted that nonquota Western Hemisphere immigration would remain at the same level, approximately 200,000 a year, but stressed that "the real limitation on immigration from the Western Hemisphere is the power of the Secretary of Labor and the Immigration and Naturalization Service to confine immigrants to those who can find a place in our employment picture in the U.S."[98]

Leaders in the immigration reform movement similarly advised that, even with a rise in immigration from Western Hemisphere countries, "no ceiling is needed now. . . . [T]here are controlling features in our immigration law, of a qualitative nature, which safeguard against any future excess of such immigration, e.g., the exclusion of persons likely to become public charges, and the power of the Secretary of Labor to exclude immigrants who might injure the situation of American workers."[99]

White House aides to President Johnson went so far as to argue that administrative control was the functional equivalent of a numerical quota. They also dismissed concerns that immigration from Jamaica, Trinidad, and

Tobago might add ten to twenty thousand immigrants a year, arguing that "very few people in these areas can afford to travel to the United States. More important, fewer still can satisfy the stringent tests that apply to all immigrants."[100]

In retrospect, officials' confidence in the qualitative barriers to entry seems disingenuous or, at best, a naive understanding about the historical practice of administrative controls on migration from Mexico. As the bracero program wound down between 1961 and its final termination in 1964, illegal immigration (as expressed in apprehension statistics) increased yearly.[101] Yet most liberals failed to understand—or refused to admit—that illegal migration would rise as legal avenues for immigration were shut off. They focused on the problem of labor supply without addressing the conditions of demand. Economist Eleanor Hadley, for example, was pessimistic about the prospects for labor law reform and concluded that the condition of farmworkers could be improved by ending "unlimited entry from [the Western] hemisphere" and intensified enforcement efforts to control the border.[102]

Organized labor took the same approach. It continued to oppose illegal migration and also tried to end the practice of legal-alien commuting. Commuters were aliens who lived in Mexico (or Canada) but held jobs in the United States. Counted as legal immigrants, commuters entered and left the country with a simple border-crossing card. In 1961 some thirty thousand Mexican alien commuters earned $40 million and spent $290 billion purchasing goods in the United States. But Texas unions called commuters "legalized wetbacks," who worked for "starvation wages" and depressed Americans' living standards.[103] The American consul at Nuevo Laredo was sympathetic to the feelings of white American residents in the border area. "While I know that the [State] department objects to a quota," he wrote, "I feel that Americans are being pushed back from the border by Mexicans to such an extent that in the Laredo area an Anglo-Saxon hardly has a chance to make a living, especially if he doesn't speak Spanish. This is getting worse every year as we issue more and more immigration visas."[104]

Liberals' commitment to abstract notions of formal equality and border control led them to collapse on the question of Western Hemisphere quotas during the final negotiations over the Hart-Celler bill in 1965. Both the Kennedy and Johnson administration bills introduced in Congress in 1963 and 1964–65 had exempted Western Hemisphere immigration from numerical quotas, continuing past policy. However, a group of moderates in Congress intervened in the final moments of negotiation over the legislation in 1965. In the Senate immigration subcommittee, Sam Ervin and Everett Dirksen held repeal of the national origins quotas hostage to Western Hemisphere quotas, citing "fairness" and a "worldwide population explosion."

Quotas on Western Hemisphere immigration would also limit immigration of Asians from Latin America and the Caribbean, it was pointed out. In the House, Ohio Democrat Michael Feighan, who assumed leadership of the House immigration subcommittee after Francis Walter died in 1963, had also wanted a ceiling on Western Hemisphere immigration. He had initially backed down under pressure from the White House, but after the Senate bill was reported it was clear that the position would ultimately prevail. The Johnson White House conceded the point in order to pass the legislation. Said Jacob Javits, "We all understand that the bill is a package deal."[105]

The vote in Congress followed sectional political lines, with the industrial and urban Northeast and Midwest providing most of the support and the South and Southwest most of the opposition. The vote reflected the liberal character of the Congress that was elected on Johnson's coattails in 1964 (which some believed was the most liberal Congress elected since 1936) and the central political preoccupation over the national origins quotas.[106] The overall numerical ceiling, the eleventh-hour inclusion of the Western Hemisphere within that ceiling, and the preference for professional and skilled labor were conservative measures that allowed groups traditionally opposed to reform, like the American Legion, to support the bill's passage. Business and industry had said virtually nothing during the immigration debates either for or against reform, probably because it was generally understood that the projected increases in immigration were so small as to make little difference in the economy.

The Hart-Celler Act of 1965 and the Limits of Liberal Reform

The Immigration Act of 1965 raised the annual ceiling on immigration to 290,000, a slight rounding up of the "one-sixth of one percent" formula. As in the past, immediate family members of citizens—with parents added to spouses and unmarried minor children—could enter as nonquota immigrants. The law allocated 170,000 quota slots to the countries of the Eastern Hemisphere (that is, Europe, Asia, and Africa), according to a hierarchy of preferences for family members (80 percent) and occupations (20 percent) and with a maximum of 20,000 per country.[107] Six percent of Eastern Hemisphere quota admissions were provided for refugees. The Western Hemisphere received an annual quota of 120,000, without country-specific numerical limits and without preferences. The more flexible plan reflected the fact that Mexico and Canada comprised one-half to two-thirds of Western Hemisphere immigration.[108]

Finally, as a concession to organized labor, the law required more rigorous controls to ensure that immigrants would not threaten domestic employment and wages. Immigrants from Eastern Hemisphere countries not entering as family members and all immigrants from the Western Hemisphere had to be certified by the Department of Labor that there were not enough

7.2 President Lyndon B. Johnson at the Statue of Liberty, October 3, 1965, at a ceremony where he signed into law the Hart-Celler Immigration Act. (Courtesy of Yoichi Okamoto, LBJ Library.)

U.S. workers "able, qualified, willing, and available" to perform the jobs they sought and that their employment would not adversely affect prevailing wages and working conditions. Only those migrants whose professions were listed on a Department of Labor schedule of occupations deemed to be in short supply nationally (among them doctors, nurses, and engineers) could enter without a specific job offer.[109]

On October 3, 1965, President Johnson signed the Hart-Celler Act into law at a ceremony staged at the foot of the Statue of Liberty in New York harbor. Abolishing the national origins quotas, he said, "repair[s] a very deep and painful flaw in the fabric of American justice. It corrects a cruel and enduring wrong in the conduct of the American Nation." In place of national origins, Johnson said, the new law "says simply that from this day forth those wishing to immigrate to America shall be admitted on the basis of their skills and their close relationship to those already here." The new policy, he added, was consistent with the nation's democratic tradition that "values and rewards each man on the basis of his merit as a man."[110]

The abolition of the national origins quota system garnered the most attention and defined the law as a progressive measure. Sixty-three religious, labor, ethnic, and charitable organizations congratulated President Johnson and "hail[ed] the passage of the bill to abolish the national origins quota system," which they said "finally established an immigration policy consistent with our national philosophy that all men are entitled to equal opportunity regardless of race or place of birth." The *New York Times* called it a "major reform," comparing it to the McCarran-Walter Act, which it said was "restrictive." The 1965 act, it continued, put all countries on an "equal footing with preferences based on skills and other rational standards rather than race."[111] These statements correctly appraised the significance of abolishing the national origins quotas. But by limiting the meaning of "restriction" to the national origins system, they obscured from view the law's other restrictive provisions: the numerical ceiling (which, as we have seen, was judged severe by economists and demographers) and the imposition of quotas on Western Hemisphere immigration.

One organization that did understand the broader nature of restriction was the American Legion. Long one of the most restrictionist organizations in the country, the Legion supported the 1965 act precisely because it was not radical legislation but, rather, because it was a "moderate bill, based on common sense." It praised Michael Feighan for "disarming the camps of extremists who had been exploiting the inequities in the McCarran-Walter Act as an excuse to put immigration outside of legal control." The Legion estimated that the law's numerical quotas would permit a total immigration of "something less than the immigration to this country in 1850" and that its preference for professionals and scientists "well may add significantly to the wealth and power of the United States."[112]

The American Legion miscalculated the level of immigration after 1965, but it correctly predicted the acceleration of the post–World War II "brain drain" of scientific, technical, and professional migrants from less developed countries to the United States. By 1972, 86 percent of the scientists and engineers and 90 percent of the physicians and surgeons coming to the United States immigrated from less developed countries. But while the Legion lauded this trend for strengthening American power, critics said the West was "simply stealing talent, and stealing it from countries that can least afford it." The *Christian Science Monitor* noted, "With one hand the United States is giving [foreign] countries millions to develop themselves. And with the other it is casually taking away the seed corn of future leaders in natural science, health, and technical knowledge. These are even more precious to the country than food or machinery." The representative of Dahomey to the United Nations bluntly called the brain drain "an odious bleeding" of Africa and a continuation of the slave trade.[113]

The overall numerical limits set in 1965 must be assessed as a conservative measure. In fact, they was even more restrictive than the "one-sixth of one percent" formula that reformers had invoked, because that formula had, in the past, allowed for Western Hemispheric immigration above the quota ceiling. The new ceiling of 120,000 on annual immigration from the Western Hemisphere went into effect in 1968 over the objections of a congressional select commission that the 1965 act had mandated to study the matter. The commission, citing familiar Pan-Americanist arguments, had recommended labor certification as a "more flexible tool" for controlling Western Hemisphere immigration and, in the event of numerical restrictions, urged a quota of 40,000 per country. It also noted that a law aimed at ending the discriminatory national origins quotas should not make the "retrogressive step" of establishing nation-based quotas where none had existed before.[114]

But, it was too late, and the results were severe. The 120,000 hemispheric quota represented a 40-percent reduction from pre-1965 levels. In 1976 Congress completed the logic of formal equality by imposing country quotas of 20,000 on the Western Hemisphere. Again, that step put the greatest pressure on Mexico and Canada, the largest sending countries in the hemisphere. The 1976 amendments also closed an important loophole in the law that had allowed undocumented Mexican immigrants with children born in the United States to legalize their status.[115]

The imposition of a 20,000 annual quota on Mexico recast Mexican migration as "illegal." When one considers that in the early 1960s annual "legal" Mexican migration comprised some 200,000 braceros and 35,000 regular admissions for permanent residency, the transfer of migration to "illegal" form should have surprised no one. The number of deportations of undocumented Mexicans increased by 40 percent in 1968, to 151,000. The figure continued to rise: in 1976, when the 20,000 per country quota was imposed, the INS expelled 781,000 Mexicans from the United States. Meanwhile, the total number of apprehensions for all others in the world, *combined*, remained below 100,000 a year. As Nicholas DeGenova has noted, the INS's "enforcement proclivities and prerogatives, and the statistics they produce, have made an extraordinary contribution to the commonplace fallacy insinuating that Mexicans account for virtually all 'illegal aliens,' have served to stage the U.S.-Mexico border as the theatre of an enforcement 'crisis,' and have rendered 'Mexican' as the distinctive national/racialized name for migrant 'illegality'."[116]

The family and occupational preferences were used by different nationalities to meet their particular needs, often in ways that Congress did not anticipate. From 1965 through the mid-1970s, Italy, for example, used nearly all its 20,000 annual visas for brothers and sisters of American citizens (fifth preference). Asians used the preference system to quickly build a base for continued family migration. For example, a Korean war bride brought as a nonquota immigrant by her U.S.-citizen husband could become a naturalized citizen in three years and then bring her parents as nonquota immigrants and her siblings under the fifth preference. In turn, they could bring their spouses and children as second-preference immigrants. Similarly, a student from Taiwan who entered for postgraduate studies as a nonimmigrant could, with labor certification, apply for permanent resident status and, from there, bring over relatives under the second preference.[117]

Congress had not understood that the system of formal equality would have the practical result of continuously producing new chains of migration. As part of their abstract, formalist approach, reformers viewed the quotas statically, as a fixed number of admissions a year. They had not understood that each quota immigrant admitted into the country could open a path for nonquota family migration, as well as for additional family migration in other quota-preference categories. Speaking of the increased use of second- and fifth-preference immigration, in 1968 an elected official observed, "Don't we see now with the operation of this law that immigration *per se* begets immigration?"[118]

Thus the immigration of Asians and the Asian American population grew phenomenally in the last decades of the twentieth century. Between 1968 and 1980 the number of nonquota immediate family members from Asia more than quadrupled, and the use of second- and fifth-preference immigration increased more than sevenfold.[119] In 1965 immigrants from Europe outnumbered those from Asia by more than five to one; by 1971, more Asians migrated to the United States than did Europeans, and four of the top six sending nations in the Eastern Hemisphere were Asian, with the Philippines as number one. The population of Asian Americans grew from less than 1.2 million in 1965 to some 10.9 million in 2000.[120]

Notably, a significant proportion of new Asian immigrants entered under the occupational category for professionals (third preference). Political instability and a relative lack of opportunities for professional advancement in many Asian countries during the 1960s and 1970s encouraged those of the professional and technical classes to emigrate. In 1969 immigrants entering under occupational preferences comprised 20.8 percent of China's (Taiwan) total, 45 percent of India's, 23.2 percent of South Korea's, and 42.3 percent of the Philippines'. In 1971 Asians accounted for two-thirds of the physicians admitted as immigrants into the United States. On the demand side, an expanding scientific-industrial infrastructure and a shortage of health-care personnel in inner-city institutions provided ready markets for foreign-trained professionals. In South Korea and the Philippines, specialized professional training, particularly in medicine and nursing, became a national export industry.[121]

By the mid-1980s occupational migration from Asia decreased relative to migration under the family preference categories, but family-based immigration of the first brain-drain generation replicated its class composition. By the end of the century, some Asian ethnic groups would boast a large professional and business stratum (48 percent of the South Asian community), while others would develop bifurcated class structures weighted in both professional and low-wage service occupations (notably Chinese and Koreans).[122]

The Immigration Act of 1965, then, comprised a complex of measures that promoted both greater inclusions and greater exclusions. The chief gain on the inclusionary side of the register was, of course, the abolition of the national origins quota system. Eastern and southern Europeans, the principal objects of exclusion in the Immigration Act of 1924, could now enter the United States in equal numbers as northern and western Europeans. This was an important political victory for Euro-American ethnic groups. Acting from new urban and industrial bases of electoral influences after World War II, they rode the wave of liberal pluralism and leveraged Cold War foreign policy interests to overturn the last vestige of law that expressed their social subordination.

But, as we have seen, the new law was not inclusionary towards all. By extending the system of formal equality in admissions to all countries, the new law affected immigration from the Third World differently—creating greater opportunities for migration from Asia and Africa but severely restricting it from Mexico, the Caribbean, and Latin America.[123]

The merger of history and policy was an important factor in both the process and narration of reform. Historians were not dispassionate interpreters of the past; rather, they intervened in the pressing politics of their day, shaping political discourse and policy. Moreover, they wrote the history of reform in the very moment of its making, as a milestone in the telos of American liberal pluralism.

But while the Immigration Act of 1965 signaled the political arrival of Euro-American ethnic groups, non-European immigrant communities and intellectuals had virtually no agency in the reform movement. It would not be until the 1970s that Asian Americans, Mexican Americans and other non-European ethno-racial groups would find their own usable pasts to challenge their continued marginalization from the mainstream of society. Significantly, their efforts were inspired more by the African American civil rights and black power movements than by the liberal nationalism of Handlin's generation. Asian American, Chicano, and Latino Studies directly challenged the nationalist narrative of assimilation and proposed, instead, to read immigration and ethnic history through the lenses of race, conquest, and colonialism. Moreover, the advent of postmodernist and cultural studies in the 1980s and 1990s broadly challenged the premises of liberal pluralism, universal citizenship, and assimilation.[124]

But if post–World War II liberalism lost much of its currency in the last decades of the twentieth century, it has continued to inform historical judgment of the Immigration Act of 1965. That is, I believe, because liberal nationalism has had pernicious effects that extended beyond the problem of

Eurocentrism and which multiculturalism alone could not solve. The Hart-Celler Act furthered the trend begun in the 1920s that placed questions of territoriality, border control, and abstract categories of status at the center of immigration law. That shift in the law's center of gravity naturalized the construction of "illegal aliens" and, increasingly, of illegal aliens as "Mexican." Narrating Western Hemispheric restriction as an expression of the liberal principle of fairness reinforced the notion that illegal immigration was a problem that could be blamed on the Mexican migrant (or on Mexico) and, moreover, one that could be solved with enforcement.

Similarly, unquestioned assumptions about national interest, both economic and geopolitical, have entrenched a nationalist orientation in immigration policy. That nationalism resists humanitarianism and remains blind to the causal connections between the United States' global projections and the conditions abroad that impel emigration. In the globalized world of the early twenty-first century, when national borders have softened to encourage the movement of capital, information, manufactured goods, and cultural products, the persistence of hardened nationalist immigration policy would seem to demand our attention and critique.

Epilogue

IF THE JOHNSON-REED ACT ushered in the most restrictionist era in American immigration law, the Hart-Celler Act, which ended that period, altered and refined but in no way overturned the regime of restriction. Certainly, patterns of immigration changed dramatically in the period after 1965, as the abolition of quotas based on national origin opened the way for increased immigration from the third world. Yet Hart-Celler's continued commitment to numerical restriction, especially its imposition of quotas on Western Hemisphere countries, ensured that illegal immigration would continue and, in fact, increase. During the late twentieth century, illegal immigration became perceived as the central and singularly intractable problem of immigration policy and became a lightning rod in domestic national politics generally. Moreover, legal reform in the area of aliens' rights of due process was decidedly uneven over the past thirty years. Together, these trends have contributed to yet another ethno-racial remapping of the nation.

Notwithstanding the Hart-Celler Act's intentions to keep migration at modest levels, legal immigration into the United States has climbed steadily since 1965. Immigration rose sharply after 1990, when Congress raised the numerical ceiling on immigration by 35 percent in response to the 1980s boom in the U.S. economy and concomitant demands for labor in low-wage sectors and in some high ones as well. By the mid-1990s immigration approached one million a year. Refugee admissions also increased in the mid- and late 1970s from Southeast Asia in the wake of the Vietnam War and in the early 1990s from Russia and former Soviet-bloc countries. Just as important, if not more so, since 1980 Europeans have accounted for only 10 percent of annual legal admissions; Mexico and Caribbean nations account for half the new immigrants and Asia for 40 percent.[1]

Paralleling the increase in legal admission, illegal immigration also increased dramatically after 1965. As discussed in chapter 7, unauthorized migration increased radically in the late 1960s and mid-1970s as a direct result of the imposition of quotas on Western Hemisphere countries, especially Mexico. New illegal-migrant streams also emerged, comprising undocumented migrants displaced from war-torn countries in Central America and from the instabilities of economic transition in China. During the 1990s removals increased 40 percent from the previous decade; by the turn of the twenty-first century the INS was removing some 1.8 million illegal aliens a year. Yet the INS estimates that the illegal population still accretes by 275,000 persons a year.[2]

During the 1980s and 1990s Americans manifested a schizophrenic attitude towards illegal immigration. On the one hand, undocumented workers provided labor for low-wage agricultural, manufacturing, and service industries, as well as in the informal economy of domestic work, housing construction, and other services that support the lifestyle of not just the prosperous but many middle-class Americans. On the other hand, critics worried that the nation had lost control of its borders and was being overrun by undesirable illegal aliens; estimates of the illegal population in the early 1980s ranged from 2 to 8 million. After much contentious debate, Congress passed the Immigration Reform and Control Act of 1986. IRCA provided amnesty for some 2.7 million undocumented immigrants and sought, unsuccessfully, to curb future illegal entries by imposing sanctions against employers who knowingly hire illegal workers and by greater enforcement efforts.[3]

A stunning militarization of the U.S.-Mexico border was accomplished during the 1990s. Congress authorized a doubling of the Border Patrol's force, the erection of fences and walls, and the deployment of all manner of high-tech surveillance on land and by air. Enforcement at the southwest border now costs taxpayers $2 billion a year. The militarization of the border has not stopped illegal entry, but it has made it more difficult and dangerous. The INS's Operation Gatekeeper, initiated in 1994, pushed illegal entries from the San Diego–Tijuana border area to remote desert sections of California and Arizona, which has increased the likelihood that migrants will die of exposure before reaching safety. Others succumb as a result of desperate attempts to enter in the sealed holds of ships, trucks, and boxcars. Many pay thousands of dollars to smugglers or guides to make these dangerous journeys, and those who survive the trip then often remain indentured for years in sweatshops before they can pay their debts. Illegal aliens are at once familiar and invisible to middle-class Americans: their labor is desired but the difficulties of their lives for the most part go unnoticed. The INS now estimates there are at least 5 million undocumented immigrants residing in the United States—of which over half are from Mexico—and debate rages on about what to do about it.[4]

All told, net annual immigration (legal and illegal immigration less emigration) over the last decade averaged about 700,000. At less than one-half of 1 percent of the total U.S. population that is not a terribly large number, but the rate of increase and the shift to third-world immigration have had considerable consequence. The foreign-born now account for nearly 10 percent of the population, which is much greater than in 1970, when they were less than 5 percent, but still less than the historical high of 14 percent before World War I. And, while concentrated in six states, immigrants live and work in every region of the country and are thus a visible presence throughout the United States.[5]

The new demographics have both enhanced the politics of diversity and multiculturalism and provoked nativist sentiment and campaigns, like California's Proposition 187 and the English-only movement, suggesting that Asians and Latinos continue to be constructed as foreign racial others, even as their positions in the American racial landscape have changed.[6] In the last quarter of the twentieth century, Latinos and Latinas and Asian Americans were the fastest growing ethno-racial groups in the United States. The 2000 Census counted 32.8 million Latinos and Latinas in the United States; these diverse communities—Mexican, Cuban, Puerto Rican, Dominican, Salvadoran—collectively account for 12 percent of the total U.S. population. Because Mexicans and Central Americans make up the vast majority of undocumented immigrants today, they experience persistently high levels of poverty and disfranchisement and embody the stereotypical illegal alien. The growth of a dynamic transborder economy and culture in the Southwest has engendered new, hybrid cultures and identities, complicating ideas about national difference and belonging. At the same time, some Latinos and Latinas have achieved a measure of structural assimilation into the mainstream of American society. The business and professional classes (particularly among Cuban Americans and Mexican Americans) have garnered considerable political influence, particularly in Texas and Florida; and Latinos and Latinas such as Ricky Martin, Jennifer Lopez, and Cameron Diaz have broken into the top echelons of the entertainment industry.[7]

The end of Asiatic exclusion, the post-1965 influx of Asian immigrant professionals and, more recently, the arrival of wealthy elites from Hong Kong, South Korea, and Singapore have repositioned Asian Americans as "model minorities." While Asian Americans have in many ways overcome the status of alien citizenship that defined them during exclusion era—through access to naturalized citizenship and occupational and residential mobility—the model minority stereotype elides the existence of large numbers of working-class immigrants, undocumented workers, and refugees. Moreover, the model minority idea reproduces Asian Americans' foreignness. Critics contend it is a new, pernicious form of "yellow peril" that rests on essentialized notions of Asian culture and breeds new forms of race discrimination (occupational segregation and glass ceilings, reverse quotas against Asians in college admissions).[8]

The growth in the size of Asian and Latino and Latina populations has made it manifestly clear that the question of race in the United States is not just about the status of African Americans or black-white relations. Yet, in an important sense, contemporary multiracial politics remain informed by the historically dominant black-white paradigm, and are also implicated in reproducing it. For example, for Afro-Caribbean and African immigrants, foreignness becomes subsumed by racial "blackness," as these immigrants join, variegate, and complicate established African American communities.[9]

Social scientists, journalists, and politicians have used both Asian and Latino and Latina immigrant success narratives to discipline African Americans. Using cultural stereotypes to occlude economic structures, the strategy deploys immigrant exemplars of hard work, thrift, and self-reliance against an alleged "culture of poverty" among native-born minorities (African Americans as well as Puerto Ricans) to explain the persistence of unemployment and poverty among the latter. In a twist to this argument, some liberals blame immigrants for undercutting native-born workers' wages and for displacing African Americans from jobs in the lower strata of the workforce. While economists debate the costs and benefits of immigrant labor to the economy, the more troubling aspect of the new liberal restrictionism is that it posits minority groups in a zero-sum calculus and regards immigrants as outsiders whose claims on society are less deserving than those of citizens.[10]

While the number of legal admissions and illegal entries steadily increased since 1970, the trajectory of law in areas of aliens' rights of due process has been uneven. During the 1970s and 1980s, Congress, the courts, and the INS liberalized immigration law in some important respects. The Supreme Court affirmed the right of aliens to equal protection in rulings recognizing the right of undocumented children to public education (*Plyler v. Doe*, 1982) and the right of aliens to receive state welfare benefits (*Graham v. Richardson*, 1971). Other decisions expanded the rights of aliens to due process in matters of deportation and detention. The INS also regularized the practice of granting administrative relief in deportation cases by establishing a balance of equities (length of residence in the country, family ties, employment, evidence of rehabilitation in criminal cases, etc.). These reforms, as well as the 1986 IRCA amnesty and the liberalization of refugee law, reflected, albeit modestly, the influence of the "rights revolution" and human rights in law and of Latino populations in politics.[11]

Yet, the Supreme Court also ruled that Congress could withhold benefits to aliens as part of its power to regulate immigration (*Mathews v. Diaz*, 1976). Indeed, even as the courts slowly and spottily expanded aliens' rights of due process, they remained unwilling to challenge the doctrine of plenary power, so that Congress retains virtually unfettered authority to enact whatever immigration legislation it chooses. Responding to a growth in nativist sentiment in the 1990s (most dramatically expressed in California's Proposition 187), Congress passed legislation in 1996 that placed severe restrictions on aliens' rights, even as immigration into the country remained high.[12] The 1996 laws terminated welfare benefits for legal aliens, made removal mandatory for a broad range of offenses, and further curtailed judicial review and virtually eliminated administrative discretion in deportation cases. Legal permanent residents now remain in a condition of permanent probation because they may be deported for certain offenses regardless of how long they have lived in the country. In effect, the legislation of the 1990s reconfigured the line between legal and illegal alienage, enlarging the grounds that turn legal immigrants into illegal aliens and making it nearly impossible for illegal aliens to legalize their status.[13] In the aftermath of terrorist attacks on the United States on September 11, 2001, the Department of Justice used immigration laws to arrest and detain over 1,100 aliens, many without charge and in secret; Arabs and Muslims are now the most visible and feared racialized aliens, illegal aliens, and alien citizens.[14] Thus, even as immigrants have become a larger and more visible part of American society, alienage remains a conspicuous category of legal, cultural, and political difference.

What do these trends portend for the central figure of this study, the illegal alien? As in the mid-twentieth century, illegal immigration today results from the confluence of two conditions: macroeconomic structures that push and pull migration from developing countries to low-wage sectors of the United States, and positive domestic law, which sets qualitative terms and quantitative limits on immigration. The first dynamic is also what makes enforcement of the second difficult and is why enforcement alone has never been a solution for illegal immigration.

It may be that illegal immigration will persist as long as the world remains divided into sovereign nation-states and as long as there remains an unequal distribution of wealth among them. Yet, this is not to say that no solutions exist short of open borders, on the one hand, or a totalitarian police state, on the other. We might consider, instead, strategies aimed at altering the push-and-pull dynamics of migration from the developing world to the United States. Trade and investment policies that strengthen the economies of sending nations would lessen pressures on emigration. Raising the numerical ceiling on legal migration, reestablishing a statute of limitations on deportation, enforcing wage and hour standards, and facilitating collective bargaining for workers in agriculture and low-wage industries would counter the reproduction of undocumented workers as an exploited underclass.

Amnesty for undocumented immigrants has diverse political support, including from the presidents of the United States and Mexico, business and organized labor, and human rights activists. Amnesty is a humane gesture that recognizes the claims to legitimate membership that come with settlement. Still, it is a limited reform that addresses only past illegal migration. Some advocates of amnesty (now called "regularization") propose to curb future unlawful entries by channeling would-be illegal migrants into legal, temporary guest-worker programs. But guest-worker programs pose the moral problem of creating a caste of second-class persons that we exploit economically but deny full membership to in the polity. Historical experience also suggests that guest workers do not all quietly return home when their services are no longer needed. Many remain, and in so doing become illegal aliens.[15]

Some legal scholars propose eliminating or vastly lowering restrictions on migration from Mexico and Canada, a plan that has antecedents in the pre-1965 policy of Pan-Americanism. They argue for extending the North American Free Trade Agreement, which has already lowered national barriers in the hemisphere to ease the flow of capital and products, to migration, citing the European Union as a more comprehensive model of integrated regionalism. In fact, some critics believe NAFTA's one-sided emphasis on free trade will lead to greater pressures on illegal migration. Some observers fear that the elimination of tariffs on American agricultural products entering Mexico in 2003 threatens to "crush the ability of millions of Mexican farmers to survive and drive them north."[16]

Indeed, while the hardened nationalism that characterized the world order for so much of the last century has dramatically relaxed in many realms of economic and cultural exchange, it remains in force in other fields, notably politics. Nation-states remain committed to restrictive immigration policies, so that states' regulation of the transnational movement of bodies differs greatly from that of capital, goods, and information. The principle of universal human rights—that there is a moral code higher than positive domestic law—has grown in prominence over the last half-century and has been key to recognizing the claims of refugees and asylum-seekers, particularly in a number of European states. Yet human rights as an international or multinational legal regime carries little authority over sovereign nation-states. As Seyla Benhabib wrote, "There are still no global courts of justice with the jurisdiction to punish sovereign states for the way that they treat refugees, foreigners, and aliens." In fact, notwithstanding the European Convention on Human Rights, the European Union appears to be shifting emphasis to joint border operations against illegal migrants and unwanted asylum-seekers.[17]

Thus, even as migration patterns change according to new global conditions, they remain shaped by asymmetrical relations of economic and political power between nation-states. The endurance of "crustacean" immigration policies may not, in fact, be eccentric to twenty-first-century globalization but a constituent element of it, aimed at maintaining the privileged position of the most powerful countries. Transnational migrants today move about in a very different world than that of the mid-twentieth century, navigating faster and more dangerous circuits in pursuit of work and safety, but their journeys reprise past crossings in important ways. They travel with the ghosts of migrants past as they, too, traverse boundaries, negotiate with states over the terms of their inclusion, and alter the future histories of nations and the history of our world.

Appendix ————————————————————————

DATA USED IN FIGURES

TABLE A1

Immigration to the United States, 1820–2000

Year	Number	Year	Number	Year	Number	Year	Number	Year
1820–2000	66,089,431							
1820	8,385							
1821–30	143,439	1831–40	599,125	1841–50	1,713,251	1851–60	2,598,214	1861–70
1821	9,127	1831	22,633	1841	80,289	1851	379,466	1861
1822	6,911	1832	60,482	1842	104,565	1852	371,603	1862
1823	6,354	1833	58,640	1843	52,496	1853	368,645	1863
1824	7,912	1834	65,365	1844	78,615	1854	427,833	1864
1825	10,199	1835	45,374	1845	114,371	1855	200,877	1865
1826	10,837	1836	76,242	1846	154,416	1856	200,436	1866
1827	18,875	1837	79,340	1847	234,968	1857	251,306	1867
1828	27,382	1838	38,914	1848	226,527	1858	123,126	1868
1829	22,520	1839	68,069	1849	297,024	1859	121,282	1869
1830	23,322	1840	84,066	1850	369,980	1860	153,640	1870
1911–20	5,735,811	1921–30	4,107,209	1931–40	528,431	1941–50	1,035,039	1951–60
1911	878,587	1921	805,228	1931	97,139	1941	51,776	1951
1912	838,172	1922	309,556	1932	35,576	1942	28,781	1952
1913	1,197,892	1923	522,919	1933	23,068	1943	23,725	1953
1914	1,218,480	1924	706,896	1934	29,470	1944	28,551	1954
1915	326,700	1925	294,314	1935	34,956	1945	38,119	1955
1916	298,826	1926	304,488	1936	36,329	1946	108,721	1956
1917	295,403	1927	335,175	1937	50,244	1947	147,292	1957
1918	110,618	1928	307,255	1938	67,895	1948	170,570	1958
1919	141,132	1929	279,678	1939	82,998	1949	188,317	1959
1920	430,001	1930	241,700	1940	70,756	1950	249,187	1960

Source: U.S.-INS, *2000 Statistical Yearbook*, table 1.

Note: Data used in figure 1.1. The numbers shown are as follows: from 1820 to 1867, figures represent alien passengers arrived at seaports; from 1868 to 1892 and 1895 to 1897, immigrant aliens arrived; from 1892 to 1894 and 1898 to 1999, immigrant aliens admitted for permanent residence. From 1892 to 1903, aliens entering by cabin class were not counted as immigrants. Land arrivals were not completely enumerated.

[1]Transition quarter, July 1 through September 30, 1976.

Number	Year	Number	Year	Number	Year	Number	Year	Number
2,314,824	1871–80	2,812,191	1881–90	5,246,613	1891–1900	3,687,564	1901–10	8,795,386
91,918	1871	321,350	1881	669,431	1891	560,319	1901	487,918
91,985	1872	404,806	1882	788,992	1892	579,663	1902	648,743
176,282	1873	459,803	1883	603,322	1893	439,730	1903	857,046
193,418	1874	313,339	1884	518,592	1894	285,631	1904	812,870
248,120	1875	227,498	1885	395,346	1895	258,536	1905	1,026,499
318,568	1876	169,986	1886	334,203	1896	343,267	1906	1,100,735
315,722	1877	141,857	1887	490,109	1897	230,832	1907	1,285,349
138,840	1878	138,469	1888	546,889	1898	229,299	1908	782,870
352,768	1879	177,826	1889	444,427	1899	311,715	1909	751,786
387,203	1880	457,257	1890	455,302	1900	448,572	1910	1,041,570
2,515,479	1961–70	3,321,677	1971–80	4,493,314	1981–90	7,338,062	1991–2000	9,095,417
205,717	1961	271,344	1971	370,478	1981	596,600	1991	1,827,167
265,520	1962	283,763	1972	384,685	1982	594,131	1992	973,977
170,434	1963	306,260	1973	400,063	1983	559,763	1993	904,292
208,177	1964	292,248	1974	394,861	1984	543,903	1994	804,416
237,790	1965	296,697	1975	386,194	1985	570,009	1995	720,461
321,625	1966	323,040	1976	398,613	1986	601,708	1996	915,900
326,867	1967	361,972	1976,TQ[1]	103,676	1987	601,516	1997	798,378
253,265	1968	454,448	1977	462,315	1988	643,025	1998	654,451
260,686	1969	358,579	1978	601,442	1989	1,090,924	1999	646,568
265,398	1970	373,326	1979	460,348	1990	1,536,483	2000	849,807
			1980	530,639				

TABLE A2
Aliens Expelled, 1892–2000

Year	Formal Removals[1]	Voluntary Departures[2]	Total
1892–2000	2,616,514	37,650,483	40,266,997
1892–1900	25,642	NA[3]	25,642
1901–10	119,769	NA	119,769
1911–20	206,021	NA	206,021
1921–30	281,464	72,233	353,697
1931–40	185,303	93,330	278,633
1941–50	141,112	1,470,925	1,612,037
1951–60	150,472	3,883,660	4,034,132
1961–70	101,205	1,334,528	1,435,733
1971–80	240,217	7,246,812	7,487,029
1981–90	232,830	9,961,812	10,194,642
1991–00	932,479	13,587,183	14,519,662

Source: U.S.-INS, *2000 Statistical Yearbook*, table 63.
Note: Data used in unnumbered figure in Introduction.
[1]Formal removals include deportations, exclusions, and removals.
[2]Voluntary departures includes aliens under docket control required to depart and voluntary departures not under docket control; first recorded in 1927.
[3]NA: Not applicable.

TABLE A3
Net Increase in "Indefinite" and "Terminal" Departures (number of persons)

Month	1942	1943	1944	1945	1946
January	—	431	1,278	1,200	2,277
February	—	552	1,384	2,076	2,258
March	—	906	1,813	2,316	2,806
April	—	2,114	2,066	2,860	—
May	—	2,537	1,943	3,702	—
June	—	2,183	1,987	5,331	—
July	18	1,591	1,766	5,013	—
August	67	2,160	2,033	8,547	—
September	188	1,824	1,355	15,126	—
October	206	1,160	976	14,053	—
November	193	877	1,009	8,792	—
December	194	643	535	5,348	—
Total	866	16,978	18,145	74,364	7,341

Source: D. Thomas, *The Salvage* (Berkeley: University of California Press, 1952), 615.
Note: Data used for figure 5.2.

Notes

Note on Language and Terminology

1. Kevin R. Johnson, "'Aliens' and the U.S. Immigration Laws: The Social and Legal Construction of Nonpersons," *Inter-American Law Review* 28 (1996–97): 263–92.
2. Walter Lippmann, *Public Opinion* (New York: Macmillan, 1949), 68–69. I thank Michael Stamm for bringing this essay to my attention.
3. *Oxford English Dictionary*, vol. 1 (New York: Oxford University Press, 1971), 218.
4. Ewa Morawska and Willfried Spohn, "Moving Europeans in the Globalizing World: Contemporary Migrations in a Historical-Comparative Perspective," in *Global Histories and Migrations*, ed. Wang Gungwu (Boulder, CO: Westview Press, 1963), 23.

Introduction
Illegal Aliens

1. "Immigrant Ex-Cons Fight Deportation," *Houston Chronicle*, May 6, 2001, sec. A, 1. Illegal Immigration Reform and Immigrant Responsibility Act of 1996 (Division C of Public Law 104-208, 110 Stat. 3009); Antiterrorism and Effective Death Penalty Act of 1996 (Public Law 104-132, 110 Stat. 1214). Since 1996, immigration law no longer refers to deportation but calls the procedure removal. I use deportation for purposes of historical continuity. In June 2001 the U.S. Supreme Court overturned the IIRIRA's provisions that applied deportation retroactively to crimes that were not deportable offenses when they were committed. *INS v. St. Cyr*, 121 S. Ct. 2271 (2001).
2. Letter, James Houghterling to Sen. James Lewis, April 20, 1938, file 55819/402B, box 75, accession 58A734, U.S. Immigration and Naturalization Service, RG (Record Group) 85, National Archives, Washington, DC. On Perkins's intervention and the origins of administrative discretion in deportation policy, see chapter 2.
3. William Flores and Rina Benmayor, eds., *Latino Cultural Citizenship: Claiming Identity, Space, and Rights* (Boston: Beacon Press, 1996), 267. For other perspectives on cultural citizenship, see Aihwa Ong, "Cultural Citizenship as Subject Making: Immigrants Negotiate Racial and Cultural Boundaries in the United States," *Current Anthropology* 35 (1996): 737–62; Aihwa Ong and Donald Nonini, eds., *Ungrounded Empires: The Cultural Politics of Modern Transnationalism* (New York: Routledge, 1997); Lok Siu, "Diasporic Cultural Citizenship: Chineseness and Belonging in Panama and Central America," *Social Text* 69, no. 19 (Winter 2001): 7–28. On transnational communities, see, for example, Linda Basch, Nina Glick Schiller, and Christina Blanc, *Nations Unbound: Transnational Projects, Postcolonial Predicaments and Deterritorialized Nation-States* (Langhorne, PA: Gordon and Breach, 1993); Robert C. Smith, "Transnational Localities: Community, Technology and the Politics of Membership within the Context of Mexico and U.S. Migration," in *Transnationalism from*

Below, ed. Michael Peter Smith and Luis Eduardo Guarnizo, (New Brunswick, NJ: Transaction, 1998).

4. Act of May 25, 1924 (43 Stat. 153); named for its sponsors, Rep. Albert Johnson (R-Wash.) and Sen. David Reed (R-Penn.).

5. Thomas Archdeacon, *Becoming American: An Ethnic History* (New York: Free Press, 1988); Philip Gleason, "American Identity and Americanization," in *Harvard Encyclopedia of American Ethnic Groups*, ed. Stephen Therstrom (Cambridge, MA: Harvard University Press, 1980), 31–58; Kathleen Neils Conzen, et al., "The Invention of Ethnicity: A Perspective from the USA," *Journal of American Ethnic History* 12 (Fall 1992): 3–41; Russell Kazal, "Revisiting Assimilation: The Rise, Fall and Reappraisal of a Concept in American History," *American Historical Review* 100, no. 2 (April 1995): 437–71; Gary Gerstle, *Working-Class Americanism: The Politics of Labor in a Textile City, 1914–1960* (Princeton: Princeton University Press, 2002 [1989]); James Barrett, "Americanization from the Bottom Up: Immigration and the Remaking of the Working Class in the U.S., 1880–1930," *Journal of American History* 79, no. 3 (December 1992): 996–1020; Lizabeth Cohen, *Making a New Deal: Industrial Workers in Chicago, 1919–1930* (New York: Cambridge University Press, 1990).

6. Keith Fitzgerald, *The Face of the Nation: Immigration, the State, and National Identity* (Stanford: Stanford University Press, 1996); Desmond King, *Making Americans: Immigration, Race, and the Origins of Diverse Democracy* (Cambridge, MA: Harvard University Press, 2000); Aristide Zolberg, *A Nation by Design? Immigration Policy in the Fashioning of America* (Cambridge, MA: Harvard University Press and Russell Sage Foundation, 2004).

7. Rogers Brubaker, "Citizenship and Naturalization: Politics and Policies," in *Immigration and the Politics of Citizenship in Liberal Democratic Societies*, ed. Rogers Brubaker (Lanham, MD: University Press of America, 1989), 121; Lisa Lowe, *Immigrant Acts: On Asian American Cultural Politics* (Durham: Duke University Press, 1996), 6–7, 13–14.

8. Bonnie Honig, *Democracy and the Foreigner* (Princeton: Princeton University Press, 2001), 75.

9. The residency requirement for naturalization varied during the first years of the republic; the five-year period was set by the Naturalization Act of 1802. See James Kettner, *The Development of American Citizenship, 1608–1870* (Chapel Hill: University of North Carolina Press, 1978), 245–46. However, eligibility for citizenship was limited to "free white persons" (Nationality Act of 1790) and to "persons of African nativity and descent" (Nationality Act of 1870) until the McCarran-Walter Immigration and Naturalization Act of 1952 repealed all racial requirements for citizenship. National citizenship to all those born in the United States was granted by the Fourteenth Amendment and upheld in *United States v. Wong Kim Ark*, 169 U.S. 649 (1898); equal protection for all persons was upheld in *Yick Wo v. Hopkins*, 118 U.S. 356 (1886).

10. Hiroshi Motomura, "The Curious Evolution of Immigration Law: Procedural Surrogates for Substantive Constitutional Rights," *Columbia Law Review* 92 (1992): 1625–1704; Linda Bosniak, "Membership, Equality, and the Difference That Alienage Makes," *New York University Law Review* 69 (1994): 1047–1149; Alexander Bickel, *The Morality of Consent* (New Haven: Yale University Press, 1975), 54; Peter Schuck, "Membership in the Liberal Polity: The Devaluation of American Citizenship," in

Brubaker, *Immigration and the Politics of Citizenship in Liberal Democratic Societies*, 62–63.

11. Brubaker, "Citizenship and Naturalization," 99, 109.

12. Linda Bosniak, "Universal Citizenship and the Problem of Alienage," *Northwestern University Law Review* 94 (2000): 963–1147. On citizenship scholarship, see, for example, Michael Walzer, *Spheres of Justice: A Defense of Pluralism and Equality* (New York: Basic Books, 1983); Iris Marion Young, *Justice and the Politics of Difference* (Princeton: Princeton University Press, 1990); Will Kymlicka, *Multicultural Citizenship: A Liberal Theory of Minority Rights* (New York: Oxford University Press, 1995); Nancy Fraser and Linda Gordon, "Civil Citizenship against Social Citizenship?: On the Ideology of Contract-versus-Charity," in *The Condition of Citizenship*, ed. Bart van Steenbergen (London: Sage, 1994), 90–107; David Hollinger, *Postethnic America: Beyond Muliculturalism* (New York: Basic Books, 1995); Lauren Berlant, *The Queen of America Goes to Washington City: Essays on Sex and Citizenship* (Durham: Duke University Press, 1997); Yasemin Soysal, *Limits of Citizenship: Migrants and Post-national Membership in Europe* (Chicago: University of Chicago Press, 1994). See also Will Kymlicka and Wayne Norman, "Return of the Citizen: A Survey of Recent Work on Citizenship Theory," *Ethics* 104 (1994): 352–81. On achievement of universal citizenship, see Judith Shklar, *American Citizenship: The Quest for Inclusion* (Cambridge, MA: Harvard University Press, 1991); Rogers M. Smith, *Civic Ideals: Conflicting Visions of Citizenship in U.S. History* (New Haven: Yale University Press, 1997); Charles Kesler, "The Promise of American Citizenship," in *Immigration and Citizenship in the Twenty-First Century*, ed. Noah M. J. Pickus (Lanham, MD: University Press of America, 1998), 3–39.

13. Bosniak, "Universal Citizenship," 965.

14. Paul Gilroy, "One Nation under a Groove: The Cultural Politics of 'Race' and Racism in Britain," in *The Anatomy of Racism*, ed. David Theo Goldberg (New York: Routledge, 1990), 265.

15. *Ozawa v. United States*, 260 U.S. 178 (1922), and *United States v. Thind*, 261 U.S. 204 (1923). Related cases in 1923 upheld state laws proscribing agricultural land ownership by aliens ineligible to citizenship (*Terrance v. Thompson*, 263 U.S. 197; *Porterfield v. Webb*, 263 U.S. 225; *Webb v. O'Brien*, 263 U.S. 313; and *Frick v. Webb*, 263 U.S. 326); also in this period *Gong Lum v. Rice*, 275 U.S. 78 (1927) upheld a Mississippi law that deemed Chinese ineligible to attend white schools.

16. Ian Haney-López, *White by Law: The Legal Construction of Race* (New York: New York University Press, 1995).

17. David Montenajo, *Anglos and Mexicans in the Making of Texas, 1836–1986* (Austin: University of Texas Press, 1987); David Gutiérrez, *Walls and Mirrors: Mexican Americans, Mexican Immigrants, and the Politics of Ethnicity* (Berkeley: University of California Press, 1995). The "Mexican" race category in the census was short lived. See chapter 1 for more discussion.

18. Lowe, *Immigrant Acts*, 26; George Sánchez, "Race, Nation and Culture in Recent Immigration Studies," *Journal of American Ethnic History* (Summer 1999): 66–83. U.S. relations with Japan were not colonial but, rather, relations of competing colonialisms. I discuss this further in chapters 1 and 5.

19. For discussion on racialization of Asian Americans in law, see also Neil T. Gotanda, "Citizenship Nullification and the Impossibility of Asian American Politics,"

in *Asian Americans and Politics: Perspectives, Experiences, Prospects*, ed. Gordon H. Chang (Washington, DC: Woodrow Wilson Center Press, and Stanford: Stanford University Press, 2001); Robert S. Chang, *Disoriented* (New York: New York University Press, 1999).

20. Michael Omi and Howard Winant, *Racial Formation in the United States from the 1960s to the 1990s* (New York: Routledge, 1994), 55. The United States Supreme Court would not sanction de jure segregation in the North, but it did legitimate de facto segregation based on free market principles in *Corrigan v. Buckley*, which upheld the use of racial covenants in real property. *Buchanan v. Warley*, 245 U.S. 60 (1917), *Corrigan v. Buckley*, 271 U.S. 323 (1926). See Gilbert Orofsky, *Harlem, the Making of a Ghetto: Negro New York, 1890–1930* (New York, 1968); Donald Massey and Nancy Denton, *American Apartheid: Segregation and the Making of the Underclass* (Cambridge, MA: Harvard University Press, 1993). The Indian Citizenship Act of 1924, which declared all Native American Indians to be American citizens, completed the process of "assimilation" that stripped Native American Indians of their sovereignty. Citizenship in the case of Indians, however, was circumscribed by their continued status as wards, a legal status that codified their presumed racial backwardness. Act of June 2, 1924 (43 Stat. 253). See Frederick Hoxie, *A Final Promise: The Campaign to Assimilate the Indians, 1880–1920* (Cambridge: Cambridge University Press, 1995 [1984]), 236–37.

21. Paul Gilroy, *The Black Atlantic* (Cambridge, MA: Harvard University Press, 1992), 9–11. See also John Haller, *Outcasts from Evolution: Scientific Attitudes towards Racial Inferiority, 1859–1900* (Urbana: University of Illinois Press, 1971).

22. *Civil Rights Cases*, 109 U.S. 3 (1883); *Plessy v. Ferguson*, 163 U.S. 537 (1896); Neil Gotanda, "A Critique of 'Our Constitution Is Color-Blind,'" *Stanford Law Review* 44 (1991): 1–68.

23. Benedict Anderson, *Imagined Communities: Reflections on the Origin and Spread of Nationalism*, rev. ed. (London: Verso, 1991 [1983]); Eric Hobsbawm, *Nations and Nationalism since 1780: Programme, Myth, Reality*, 2d ed. (Cambridge: Cambridge University Press, 1992); Eric Hobsbawm and Terence Ranger, eds., *The Invention of Tradition* (Cambridge: Cambridge University Press, 1983); Geoff Ely and Ronald Suny, eds., *Becoming National* (New York: Oxford University Press, 1996); Prasenjit Duara, *Rescuing History from the Nation: Questioning Narratives of Modern China* (Chicago: University of Chicago Press, 1995); Partha Chatterjee, *The Nation and Its Fragments: Colonial and Postcolonial Histories* (Princeton: Princeton University Press, 1993); Ian Tyrell, "Making Nations/Making States: American Historians in Context of Empire," *Journal of American History* 86 (1999): 1015–44; Donna R. Gabaccia, "Liberty, Coercion, and the Making of Immigration Historians," *Journal of American History* 84 (1997): 570–75; Michael Geyer and Charles Bright, "Where in the World Is America? The History of the United States in the Global Age," in *Rethinking American History in a Global Age*, ed. Thomas Bender (Berkeley: University of California Press, 2002): 63–99.

24. Ewa Morawska and Willfried Spohn, "Moving Europeans in the Globalizing World": Contemporary Migrations in a Historical-Comparative Perspective," *Global Histories and Migrations*, ed. Wang Gungwu (Boulder: Westview Press, 1996): 23–61; Madeline Hsu, *Dreaming of Gold, Dreaming of Home: Transnationalism and Migration between the United States and South China, 1882–1943* (Stanford: Stanford University

Press, 2000); Adam McKeown, *Chinese Migrant Networks and Cultural Change: Peru, Chicago, Hawaii, 1900–1936* (Chicago: University of Chicago Press, 2001); Shirley Fitzgerald, *Red Tape, Gold Scissors: The Story of Sydney's Chinese* (Sydney: State Library of New South Wales Press, 1997); Jung-fang Tsai, *Hong Kong in Chinese History: Community and Social Unrest in the British Colony* (New York: Columbia University Press, 1993); Aristide Zolberg, "The Great Wall against China: Responses to the First Immigration Crisis, 1885–1925," in *Migration, Migration History, History: Old Paradigms and New Perspectives*, ed. Jan Lucassen and Leo Lucassen (New York: Peter Lang, 1997): 291–315; Joseph H. Carens, "Nationalism and Exclusion of Immigrants: Lessons from Australian Immigration Policy," in *Open Borders? Closed Societies? The Ethnical and Political Issues*, ed. Mark Gibney (Westport, CT: Greenwood, 1988).

25. John Higham, *Strangers in the Land: Patterns of American Nativism, 1860–1925* (New Brunswick, NJ: Rutgers University Press, 1992 [1955]), 131–57, 194–222.

26. John Torpey, *The Invention of the Passport: Surveillance, Citizenship, and the State* (New York: Cambridge University Press, 2000), 93–103, 116–21; Saskia Sassen, *Guests and Aliens* (New York: New Press, 1999), 135; Aristide Zolberg, "The Dawn of Cosmopolitan Denizenship," *Indiana Journal of Global Legal Studies* 7 (Spring 2000): 511–18. On Westaphalian sovereignty as a specific type, see Stephen D. Krasner, *Sovereignty: Organized Hypocrisy* (Princeton: Princeton University Press, 1999), 20–25.

27. Hannah Arendt, *Origins of Totalitarianism* (New York: Harcourt Brace, 1979 [1951]), chapter 5; *Perez v. Brownell*, 365 U.S. 44, 64–65 (1958) (C.J. Warren, dissenting). See also Giorgio Agamben, *Homo Sacer: Sovereignty and Bare Life*, trans. Daniel Heller-Roazen (Stanford: Stanford University Press, 1999), 130–32. According to Agamben, the war displaced 1.5 million White Russians, 700,000 Armenians, 500,000 Bulgarians, 1.0 million Greeks, and hundreds of thousands of Germans, Hungarians, and Rumanians. After the war France, Belgium, Italy, and Austria passed denationalization and denaturalization laws, culminating in the Nuremburg laws of the Third Reich.

28. Dipesh Chakrabarty, *Provincializing Europe: Postcolonial Thought and Historical Difference* (Princeton: Princeton Unversity Press, 2000); Sassen, *Guests and Aliens*, 135–37.

29. *Chinese Exclusion Case (Chae Chan Ping v. United States)*, 130 U.S. 518, 631 (1889).

30. For example, in Vattel's *Law of Nations* (1797): "Every nation has the right to refuse to admit a foreigner into the country. . . . What it owes to itself, the care of its own safety, gives it this right; and in virtue of its natural liberty, it belongs to the nation to judge whether the circumstances will or will not justify the admission of the foreigner." Cited in *Fong Yue Ting v. United States*, 149 U.S. 698, 707 (1893).

31. *Fong Yue Ting v. United States*, 149 U.S. at 706. Similarly: "If [the government] could not exclude aliens it would be to that extent subject to the control of another power" (*Chinese Exclusion Case*, 130 U.S. at 604). The same argument was made nearly one hundred years later when a federal court suggested that the influx of illegal Haitian migrants was a plot by the Duvalier regime to export undesirables to the United States. *Jean v. Nelson*, 727 F. 2d 957, 975 (11th Cir. 1984). See John Scanlan and O. T. Kent, "The Force of Moral Arguments for a Just Immigration Policy in a Hobbesian Universe," in *Open Borders? Closed Societies?* ed. Mark Gibney, 69.

32. Indeed, in the late nineteenth century the Qing government established consulates abroad to protect its subjects as part of its increasing awareness of, and imbrication in, a world of competitive nation-states. The Qing lifted its ban on emigration in 1893. See Wang Gungwu, *The Chinese Overseas: From Earthbound China to the Quest for Autonomy* (Cambridge, MA: Harvard University Press, 2000), 66.

33. Sassen, *Guests and Aliens*, 136–37; Scanlon and Kent, "Force of Moral Arguments," 69–70; Joseph Carens, "Aliens and Citizens: The Case for Open Borders," in *The Immigration Reader: America in Multidisciplinary Perspective*, ed. David Jacobson (Malden, MA: Blackwell, 1998), 365.

34. *Mathews v. Diaz*, 426 U.S. 67, 80 (1976); Linda Bosniak, "Membership, Equality, and the Difference That Alienage Makes," 1059–81; Peter Schuck, "The Transformation of Immigration Law," *Columbia Law Review* 84 (1984): 1–87, at 12–21; T. Alexander Aleinikoff, "Federal Regulation of Aliens and the Constitution," *American Journal of International Law* 83 (1989): 862–71.

35. Scanlon and Kent, "Force of Moral Arguments"; Bruce Ackerman, *Social Justice in the Liberal State* (New Haven: Yale University Press, 1980), 89–95; Carens, "Aliens and Citizens." Others argue that liberal societies require a sense of shared history and character in order to cohere, and hence the principle of exclusion is unavoidable. See Walzer, *Spheres of Justice*, 62; Schuck, "Transformation of Immigration Law," 85–87; David Miller, *On Nationality* (New York: Clarendon Press, 1995). See also Judith Lichtenberg, "How Liberal Can Nationalism Be?" *Philosophical Forum* 28 (Fall-Winter 1996–97): 53–72; Sanford Levinson, "Is Liberal Nationalism an Oxymoron? An Essay for Judith Shklar," *Ethics* 105 (Apr. 1995): 626–45; Kwame Anthony Appiah, "Citizenship in Theory and Practice: A Response to Charles Kesler," in Pickus, *Immigration and Citizenship in the Twenty-First Century*, 41.

36. Seyla Benhabib, *The Claims of Culture: Equality and Diversity in a Global Age* (Princeton: Princeton University Press, 2002), 173.

37. Robert W. Gordon, "Critical Legal Histories," *Stanford Law Review* 36 (1984): 57–125, at 125. See also Pierre Bourdieu, "The Force of Law: Toward a Sociology of the Juridical Field," *Hastings Law Journal* 38 (1987): 805–13; Alan Hunt, *Explorations in Law and Society: Towards a Constitutive Theory of Law* (New York: Routledge, 1993); Alan Hunt and Peter Fitzpatrick, eds., *Critical Legal Studies* (London: Basil Blackwell Ltd., 1987).

38. Homi Bhabha, *The Location of Culture* (New York: Routledge, 1994), 169–70.

Part I
The Regime of Quotas and Papers

1. John Torpey, *The Invention of the Passport: Surveillance, Citizenship, and the State* (New York: Cambridge University Press, 2000), 93–105, 117–21; Gerald Neuman, *Strangers to the Constitution: Immigrants, Borders, and Fundamental Law* (Princeton: Princeton University Press, 1996), 19–43; David Montgomery, *Citizen Worker: The Experience of Workers in the United States with Democracy and the Free Market during the Nineteenth Century* (New York: Cambridge University Press, 1993), 13–16.

2. Aristide Zolberg, "Global Movements, Global Walls: Responses to Migration, 1885–1925," in *Global History and Migrations*, ed. Wang Gungwu (Boulder, CO:

Westview Press, 1996), 279–307; John Bodnar, *The Transplanted: A History of Immigration in Urban America* (Bloomington: Indiana University Press, 1985), chapter 1; David Montgomery, *Fall of the House of Labor: The Workplace, the State, and American Labor Activism, 1865–1925* (Cambridge: Cambridge University Press, 1985), 70; June Mei, "Socioeconomic Origins of Emigration, Guangdong to California, 1850–1882," *Modern China* 5, no. 4 (October 1979): 463–501. In 1849 the Supreme Court invalidated state laws imposing taxes on incoming passenger ships (*Smith v. Turner*, 48 U.S. 283), but it was not until after the Civil War that the Court clearly asserted the notion that immigrants were "articles of commerce" and that immigration fell under the commerce clause of the Constitution (*Henderson v. Mayor of New York*, 92 U.S. 259 [1875], and *Chy Lung v. Freeman*, 92 U.S. 275 [1875]). Mary Sarah Bilder, "The Struggle over Immigration: Indentured Servants, Slaves, and Articles of Commerce," *Missouri Law Review* 61 (1996): 743–824.

3. Bill Ong Hing, *Making and Remaking Asian America through Immigration Policy* (Stanford: Stanford University Press, 1990); Alexander Saxton, *The Indispensable Enemy: Labor and the Anti-Chinese Movement* (Berkeley: University of California Press, 1971); Aristide Zolberg, "The Great Wall against China: Responses to the First Immigration Crisis, 1885–1925," in *Migration, Migration History, History: Old Paradigms and New Perspectives*, ed. Jan Lucassen and Leo Lucassen (New York: Peter Lang, 1997). On exclusion from citizenship, see chapter 1.

4. *Chan Chae Ping v. United States*, 130 U.S. 581, 606 (1889); *Fong Yue Ting v. United States*, 149 U.S. 698, 910 (1893). On the influence of Chinese exclusion cases on American immigration policy, see Lucy Salyer, *Laws Harsh as Tigers: Chinese Immigrants and the Shaping of Modern Immigration Law, 1882–1924* (Chapel Hill: University of North Carolina Press, 1995).

5. Page Law (18 Stat. 477 [1875]); Immigration Act of 1882 (22 Stat. 214); Alien Contract Labor Act (23 Stat. 332 [1885]); Immigration Act of 1891 (26 Stat. 1084); Immigration Act of 1903 (32 Stat. 1213); Chinese Exclusion Act (22 Stat. 58 [1882]).

6. Thomas Archdeacon, *Becoming American: An Ethnic History* (New York: Free Press, 1983), 146; Montgomery, *Fall of the House of Labor*, chapter 2; John Higham, *Strangers in the Land: Patterns of American Nativism, 1860–1925* (New Brunswick, NJ: Rutgers University Press, 1998 [1955]), 62–63, 80–87.

7. Higham, *Strangers in The Land*, 103–5, 191–92, 195–233.

8. Immigration Act of February 5, 1917 (39 Stat. 874); Edward Hutchinson, *Legislative History of American Immigration Policy, 1798–1965* (Philadelphia: University of Pennsylvania Press, 1981), 163–68; Higham, *Strangers in the Land*, 103–5, 191–92; Robert Divine, *American Immigration Policy, 1924–1952* (New Haven: Yale University Press, 1957), 3–5; William Preston, Jr., *Aliens and Dissenters: Federal Suppression of Radicals, 1903–1933* (Cambridge: Harvard University Press, 1963).

9. Montgomery, *Fall of the House of Labor*, 457–58.

10. Torpey, *Invention of the Passport*, 111–24; Act of May 25, 1924, Sec. 2(a).

11. Higham, *Strangers in the Land*, 308; Commissioner General of Immigration to the Secretary of Labor, *Annual Report*, 1923 (Washington, DC: GPO, 1923), 3–4.

12. "Temporary Suspension of Immigration," House Report 1109, 66th Congress, 3d Session (Washington, DC: GPO, 1920), appendix A.

13. Act of May 19, 1921 (42 Stat. 5).

Chapter One
The Johnson-Reed Act of 1924 and the Reconstruction of
Race in Immigration Law

1. John Higham, *Strangers in the Land: Patterns of American Nativism, 1860–1925* (New Brunswick, NJ: Rutgers Univ. Press, 1988 [1955]), 330.

2. Robert Divine, *American Immigration Policy, 1924–1952* (New Haven: Yale University Press, 1957), 5–6, 17.

3. "Restriction of Immigration," Hearings before the House Committee on Immigration and Naturalization (hereafter "House immigration committee"), 68th Congress, 1st Session (Washington, DC: GPO, 1924), 42–46, 293, 302, 1041–45.

4. John Trevor, "Immigration Problem," March 5, 1924, file 16, box 2, Reports, correspondence, and other records relating to immigration quota laws and national origins statistics, ca. 1920–1936, NN-374-63, Population Division, Records of the Census Bureau, RG 29, National Archives, Washington, DC (hereafter "Quota Board Papers"); idem, "Preliminary Study of Population," House Report 350, 68th Congress, 1st Session (Washington, DC: GPO, 1924), 26–29. See also "Europe as an Emigrant Exporting Continent," Hearings, House immigration committee, Mar. 8, 1924, 68th Congress, 1st Session, Appendix, tables 2 and 3.

5. Act of May 26, 1924 (43 Stat. 153).

6. Carl Degler, *In Search of Human Nature: The Decline and Revival of Darwinism in American Social Thought* (New York: Oxford University Press, 1991), 20–22; George Stocking, Jr., *Race, Culture, and Evolution: Essays in the History of Anthropology* (Chicago: University of Chicago Press, 1982 [1968]), 234–69.

7. Divine, *American Immigration Policy*, 14; Degler, *In Search of Human Nature*, 41–44.

8. Degler, *In Search of Human Nature*, 43.

9. For example, see Harry H. Laughlin, "Analysis of the Metal and Dross in America's Melting Pot," Hearings, House immigration committee, Nov. 21, 1922, 67th Congress, 3d Session (Washington, DC: GPO, 1923), and "American History in Terms of Human Migration," Hearings, House immigration committee, Mar. 7, 1928, 70th Congress 1st Session (Washington, DC: GPO, 1928). On army tests, see Degler, *In Search of Human Nature*, 51; Higham, *Strangers in the Land*, 275; *Stephen Jay Gould, The Mismeasure of Man*, rev. ed. (New York: Norton, 1996 [1981]), 227. The tests were highly flawed in the cultural assumptions of the questions and in the way they were administered. See Gould, 229–64.

10. Higham, *Strangers in the Land*, 270–77, 303, 313–15; John Higham, *Send These to Me, Immigrants in Urban America*, rev. ed. (Baltimore: Johns Hopkins University Press, 1984 [1975]), 44–47; Divine, *American Immigration Policy*, 45–49; Desmond King, *Making Americans: Immigration, Race, and the Origins of Diverse Democracy* (Cambridge, MA: Harvard University Press, 2000).

11. John S. Haller, *Outcasts from Evolution: Scientific Attitudes of Racial Inferiority, 1859–1900* (Urbana: University of Illinois Press, 1971), 124–28, 148–51. Stoddard quoted in Walter Benn Michaels, *Our America: Nativism, Modernism, and Pluralism* (Durham: Duke University Press, 1995), 65; see also Elazar Barkan, *The Retreat of*

Scientific Racism: Changing Concepts of Race in Britain and the United States between the World Wars (New York: Cambridge University Press, 1992), 104.

12. LaVerne Beales, "Distribution of White Population as Enumerated in 1920 according to Country of Origin," Oct. 16, 1924, file 16, box 2, Quota Board Papers; Minutes of Quota Board meeting, May 25, 1926, file 19, ibid. The taxonomy of "races and peoples" used by the Immigration Bureau was not consistent with the modern understanding of nation-states. For example, the schedule differentiated "Polish" from "Polish (Hebrew)," distinguished "Italy (north)" from "Italy (south)," and listed Indians as "Hindu" or "Hindoo."

13. Joseph A. Hill, "The Problem of Determining the National Origin of the American People," address at the Social Science Conference, Hanover, NH (August 25, 1926), 7, file 17, box 2, Quota Board Papers.

14. Sec. 12(a).

15. Sec. 11(d).

16. The Census Bureau was well aware that contemporary anthropological and race theories classified "Hindu" as a "Caucasian" race. The 1910 census population schedule included a note with the table on race explaining that, anthropology notwithstanding, the Census Bureau considered Hindus to be a colored race. Joan Jensen, *Passage From India* (New Haven: Yale University Press, 1988), 252.

17. The discrepancy was noted by Boggs but not corrected. Memorandum, S. W. Boggs to W. W. Husband, Nov. 11, 1926, 3, file 30, box 3, Quota Board Papers.

18. Congress granted a limited form of citizenship to Puerto Ricans in 1917. Jones Act, ch. 190 (39 Stat. 951 [1917]); *Balzac v. Porto Rico*, 258 U.S. 298 (1922).

19. John Trevor, "An Analysis of the American Immigration Act of 1924," *International Conciliation* 202 (September 1924): 428–29.

20. Hill, "The Problem of Determining the National Origin of the American People," 3.

21. Melissa Nobles, *Shades of Citizenship: Race and the Census in Modern Politics* (Stanford: Stanford University Press, 2000); David Theo Goldberg, *Racial Subjects: Writing on Race in America* (New York: Routledge, 1997), 34; Vaile quoted by Margo Anderson, *The American Census: A Social History* (New Haven: Yale University Press, 1988), 147.

22. Anderson, *The American Census*, 133–34.

23. Francis A. Walker, "Restriction of Immigration," *Atlantic Monthly* (June 1896): 828.

24. Higham, *Strangers in the Land*, 143; Francis A. Walker, "The Great Count of 1890," *Forum* (June 1891): 406–18; see also Walker, "Immigration and Degradation," *Forum* (August 1891): 634–44. Of course, there is more than one way to interpret census data. Urban families tend to have fewer children than do farm families, and families of the middle classes are usually smaller than are those in the laboring population.

25. Horace Kallen, *Culture and Democracy in the United States: Studies in the Group Psychology of the American Peoples* (New York: Boni and Liveright, 1924), 98.

26. William Peterson, *The Politics of Population* (New York: Doubleday, 1964), 198–200. Francis Walker quoted from "Our Population in 1900," *Atlantic Monthly* 32, no. 192 (Oct. 1873): 487–95.

27. Madison Grant, *The Passing of the Great Race* (New York: 1918), 104; Edward

Lewis, *Nation or Confusion? A Study of Our Immigration Problems* (New York: Galton Pub. Co., 1928), 79; Madison Grant and Charles Stewart Davison, eds., *The Alien in Our Midst, or "Selling our Birthright for a Mess of Pottage"* (New York: Galton Pub. Co., 1930), 15; "Immigration and Population," *Transactions of the Commonwealth Club of California* 17 (Oct. 1922), 1, file Immigration, California, box 2, Paul Scharrenberg Papers, (Bancroft Library, University of California, Berkeley (hereafter "Scharrenberg Papers").

28. *New York Herald Tribune*, Dec. 13, 1939, Career and Funeral file, box 3, Correspondence of Joseph Hill, Records of the Assistant Director of Statistical Standards, Records of the Chief Statistician, Administrative Records of the Census Bureau, RG 29, National Archives, Washington, DC (hereafter cited as "Joseph Hill Papers"); U.S. Congress, Senate, *Reports of the Immigration Commission*, "Occupations of the First and Second Generations of Immigrants in the U.S. and Fecundity of Immigrant Women," Jan. 12, 1910, 61st Congress, 2d Session.

29. Joseph Hill, "Some Results of the 1920 Population Census," paper delivered at the annual meeting of the American Statistical Association, Pittsburgh, Dec. 1921; idem, "Composition and Characteristics of Population," typescript [1920], file C-22, box 146, Memoranda and Notes, Joseph Hill Papers; idem, "Scope of the Fourteenth Census," typescript [1917–1919], file Papers Written by Dr. Hill, box 4, Misc. Records, ibid.

30. Hill, "The Problem of Determining the National Origin of the American People," 2–3.

31. Nancy Stepan, *The Idea of Race in Science: Great Britain, 1800–1960* (Hamden, CT: Arcon Books, 1992) xvi.

32. Minutes, Quota Board meeting of June 23, 1926, file 19, box 1, Quota Board Papers; Joseph Hill, Memorandum for the Secretary, June 21, 1926, 3, file 15, box 1, Memoranda and Notes, 1906–1940, Joseph Hill Papers; Joseph Hill, "Notes on Prof. Jameson's Paper on 'American Blood in 1775,'" typescript [1924–1925], file 20, box 2, Quota Board Papers.

33. "National Origin Provision of the Immigration Act of 1924," Dec. 16, 1926, Senate Document no. 192, 69th Congress, 2d Session; "Immigration Quotas on the Basis of National Origins," Feb. 25, 1928, Senate Document no. 65, 70th Congress, 1st Session.

34. Hill, Memorandum for the Secretary, June 21, 1926, 3; American Council of Learned Societies, "Report of Committee on Linguistic and National Stocks in the Population of the United States," *Annual Report of the American Historical Association* (Washington, DC, 1931), 1:124. See also Anderson, *American Census*, 148–49.

35. Hill, "The Problem of Determining the National Origin of the American People," 5–6.

36. Werner Sollors, ed., *The Invention of Ethnicity* (New York: Oxford University Press, 1989), xiv-xvi.

37. On the persistent denial of the existence and scale of interracial marriage in the United States, see Gary Nash, "The Hidden History of Mestizo America," *Journal of American History* 82 (Dec. 1995): 941–64; see also Joel Williamson, *New People, Miscegenation and Mulattos in the U.S.* (New York: New York University Press, 1984); Peggy Pascoe, "Miscegenation Law, Court Cases, and the Ideology Race in Twentieth Century America," *Journal of American History* 83 (June 1996): 44–69.

38. Hill, Memorandum for the Secretary, June 21, 1926, 2; Minutes, meeting of the Quota Board, May 25, 1926, 3, file 19, box 2, Quota Board Papers; Joseph Hill to Secretary of State, Secretary of Commerce, Secretary of Labor, Feb. 15, 1928, in "Immigration Quotas on the Basis of National Origins," Feb. 28, 1929, Senate Document no. 65, 70 Congress, 1st session, 9; LaVerne Beales, "Committee on Distribution of Population by National Origin," typescript, Dec. 1, 1924, file 16, box 2, Quota Board Papers.

39. Hill, Memorandum for the Secretary, 2; Minutes, Quota Board meeting, May 25, 1926, 3, file 19, box 2, Quota Board Papers; Hill, "Problem of Determining the National Origin of the American People," 21; Hill to Secretary of State, Secretary of Commerce, Secretary of Labor, Feb. 15, 1928, in "Immigration Quotas on the Basis of National Origin," 7.

40. Sen. 70A-J17, box 179, Records of the United States Senate, RG 46, National Archives, Washington, DC (hereafter "Senate records").

41. Divine, *American Immigration Policy*, 37–40; U.S. Congress, Senate, "National Origin Provision of the Immigration Act of 1924," Dec. 16, 1926, 69th Congress, 2d session; U.S. Congress, Senate, "Immigration Quotas on the Basis of National Origins," Feb. 25, 1929, 70th Congress, 1st session; petitions in support of S.J. Res. 122 and H.R.J. Res. 233-234, from YMCA, YWCA, League of Women Voters, and Kiwanis Club of Milwaukee, Sen. 70A-J17, box 179, Senate records.

42. Sen. 70A-J17, box 179, Senate records; *Washington Post* [Feb. 18, 1929], Feb. 23, 1929.

43. Statement by St. Brendan Society of Boston, n.d.; petition, Anti-National Origins Clause League, n.d., Sen. 71-A-J32, box 171-172, Senate records.

44. "National Origins Provision of the Immigration Law," Hearings before the Senate Committee on Immigration, Feb. 4, 1929, 70th Congress, 2d Session (Washington, DC: GPO, 1929), 16, 18.

45. Frank Kellogg, William Whiting, and James Davis, to the President, Feb. 26, 1929, Senate Document no. 259, 70th Congress, 2d Session; "Proclamation by the President of the United States of America," March 22, 1929.

46. Vicente Rafael, "White Love: Surveillance and Nationalist Resistance in the U.S. Colonization of the Philippines," in *Cultures of United States Imperialism*, ed. Amy Kaplan and Donald Pease (Durham: Duke University Press, 1993), 188.

47. Torpey, *The Invention of the Passport* 13; Partha Chatterjee, *The Nation and Its Fragments, Colonial and Postcolonial Histories* (Princeton: Princeton University Press, 1993), 19, 238.

48. Joseph Hill, "Composition of the American Population by Race and Country of Origin," *Annals of the American Academy of Political and Social Science* (Philadelphia, PA), November 1936: 1, 7–8.

49. Act of May 26, 1924 (43 Stat. 152), Sec. 13(c); Paul Scharrenberg, "America's Immigration Problem," December 1926, 4, file "Immigration Quotas," box 2, Scharrenberg Papers.

50. Act of May 6, 1882 (22 Stat. 58); Act of May 5, 1892 (27 Stat. 25); Act of April 29, 1902 (32 Stat. 176); Act of April 27, 1904 (33 Stat. 428).

51. Act of February 5, 1917 (39 Stat. 874). The barred zone included parts of Arabia, Afghanistan, India, Burma, Thailand, Indochina, the Malay States, the East Indian Islands, Asiatic Russia, and the Polynesian Islands.

52. Yuji Ichioka, *The Issei: The World of First Generation Japanese Immigrants, 1880–1924* (New York: Free Press, 1988), 71–72, 251–54; Bill Ong Hing, *Making and Remaking Asian America through Immigration Policy, 1850–1990* (Stanford: Stanford University Press, 1993), 29.

53. Act of March 6, 1790 (1 Stat. 103); Immigration and Naturalization Act of 1952 (66 Stat. 163).

54. Act of July 14, 1870 (16 Stat. 25); Stanford Lyman, "The Race Question and Liberalism: Casuistries in American Constitutional Law," *International Journal of Politics, Culture, and Society* 5, no. 2 (1991): 231.

55. U.S. Dept. of Commerce, Bureau of Census, *Historical Statistics of the United States from Colonial Times to 1970* (Washington, DC: GPO, 1975), 114–15. Although nativists commonly referred to southern and eastern Europeans as "undesirable races," their eligibility to citizenship as "white persons" was never challenged and the legality of naturalizing European immigrants never an issue in public and political discourse.

56. Brief for the Petitioner, 48, *Takao Ozawa v. United States*, 160 U.S. 178 (1922).

57. *Takao Ozawa v. United States*, 160 U.S. 178 (1922); *United States v. Bhagat Singh Thind*, 261 U.S. 204 (1923).

58. Ichioka, *The Issei*, 51–53, 59, 148–52, 191. On the pioneer Japanese agricultural colony at Cortez, see Valerie Matsumoto, *Farming the Home Place: A Japanese American Community in California, 1919–1982* (Ithaca: Cornell University Press, 1993).

59. "Japanese Immigration," Hearings, House immigration committee, 66th Congress, 2d Session (Washington, DC: GPO, 1921), 20.

60. James Thomson, Jr., Peter Stanley, and John Curtis Perry, *Sentimental Imperialists: The American Experience in East Asia* (New York: Harper and Row, 1981), 140, 147; W. G. Beasley, *Japanese Imperialism, 1894–1945* (Oxford: Oxford University Press, 1992, [1987]), 99–100,122; Roger Daniels, *The Politics of Prejudice: The Anti-Japanese Movement in California and the Struggle for Japanese Exclusion* (Berkeley: University of California Press, 1977 [1962]), 33–35, 37–41; Sydney Giffard, *Japan among the Powers, 1890–1990* (New Haven: Yale University Press, 1994), 36; Ichioka, *The Issei*, 212–13.

61. Executive Order no. 589, March 14, 1907. The order banned immigration from American territories and the Canal Zone by persons holding passports not issued for the mainland United States. See also Daniels, *The Politics of Prejudice*, 43–44. On Gentleman's Agreement, see Ichioka, *The Issei*, 214.

62. By 1913 Japanese had challenged their designation as ineligible to citizenship four times in federal court, losing each time. *In re Saito*, 62 F. 126 (C.C.D. Mass. 1894); *In re Yamashita*, 30 Wash. 234, 70 F. 482 (1902); *In re Buntaro Kumagai*, 163 F. 922 (W.D. Wash. 1908); *Bessho v. United States*, 178 F. 245 (4th Cir. 1910). Other cases ruled that persons who were half European and half or one-quarter Japanese were not white. *In re Knight*, 171 F. 299 (E.D. N.Y. 1909), *In re Young*, 195 F. 645 and 198 F. 715, (W.D. Wash. 1912).

63. Ichioka, *The Issei*, 153; Milton Konvitz, *The Alien and the Asiatic in American Law* (Ithaca: Cornell University Press, 1946), 161, 187–89. Eight states restricted or prohibited aliens ineligible to citizenship from taking or holding real estate: Arizona, California, Idaho, Kansas, Louisiana, Montana, New Mexico, and Oregon.

64. In 1913 Japan had only six shipyards, in 1921 it had twenty-seven; 32 percent of Japan's national budget went to the navy, a level of spending ominously compared to the German military budget in 1914. *New York Herald*, Sept. 28, 1921, in HR71A-F16.4, Records of the U.S. House of Representatives, RG 233, National Archives, Washington, DC (hereafter "House records").

65. Uchimura Kanzo, quoted in James Thomson et al., *Sentimental Imperialists*, 143. Roger Daniels argues that through much of the first two decades of the century the anti-Asiatic movement in California had little influence outside the state, and in fact was regarded on the East Coast as composed of political hysterics who might plunge the nation into war with Japan. But anxiety over Japan's power gave the California nativists a more receptive audience nationwide. *The Politics of Prejudice*, 65.

66. Daniels, *The Politics of Prejudice*, 83; ibid., 21.

67. William Stephens to Bainbridge Colby, June 19, 1920; "Japanese Immigration," Hearings, House immigration committee, July 1920, 66th Congress, 2d Session (Washington, DC: GPO, 1921), 72.

68. Joan Jensen, *Passage from India: Asian Indian Immigrants in North America* (New Haven: Yale University Press, 1988), 42–58, 94. See also "Hindu Immigration," Hearings, House immigration committee, 63rd Congress, 2d Session (Washington, DC: GPO, 1914). On Asian exclusion in Australia, see Brian Murphy, *The Other Australia: Experiences of Migration* (Cambridge: Cambridge University Press, 1993), 30–31; Myra Willard, *History of the White Australia Policy to 1920* (London: Frank Cass and Co., 1967 [1923]), 18.

69. Bonaparte quoted in Jensen, *Passage from India*, 247; Ichioka, *The Issei*, 211.

70. *People v. Hall*, 4 Cal. 399 (1854); Jensen, *Passage from India*, 12–14; Ian Haney-López, *White by Law: The Legal Construction of Race* (New York: New York University Press, 1996), 51–52.

71. Konvitz, *The Alien and the Asiatic in American Law*, 93.

72. Takao Ozawa, "Naturalization of a Japanese Subject," n.d., in Ichioka, *The Issei*, 219.

73. "Bhagat Singh Thind's Statement regarding His Race," December 9, 1918, Respondent's Brief, 49, *United States v. Thind*, 261 U.S. 204 (1923); Jensen, *Passage from India*, 256; *In re Bhagat Singh Thind*, 268 F. 683 (1920).

74. *Dred Scott v. Sandford*, 60 U.S. 393 (1857); Haney-López, *White by Law*, 39–40, 42; Peter Schuck and Rogers Smith, *Citizenship without Consent: Illegal Aliens in the American Polity* (New Haven: Yale University Press, 1985), 67–68, 73. See also Gerald Neuman, *Strangers to the Constitution: Immigrants, Borders, and Fundamental Law* (Princeton: Princeton University Press, 1996); Reginald Horsman, *Race and Manifest Destiny: The Origins of American Racial Anglo-Saxonism* (Cambridge, MA: Harvard University Press, 1981), 208–9.

75. Kelly Miller, "Who is White?" *Nation*, April 23, 1924; Brief for the Petitioner, 62–65, *Ozawa v. United States*, 160 U.S. 178 (1922).

76. *In re Najour*, 174 F. 735 (N.D. Ga. 1909). See also Haney-López, *White by Law*, 67–72.

77. Haney-López, *White by Law*, 72–73.

78. Brief for the Petitioner, 62, 67, *Ozawa v. United States*, 160 U.S. 178 (1922).

79. Ibid., 77–79.

80. Ibid., 64–65.

81. *Ozawa v. United States*, 160 U.S. 178, 197–98 (1922).

82. Ibid., 194.

83. Brief of Respondent, 10, 36, *United States v. Thind*, 261 U.S. 204 (1923).

84. Brief for the United States, 16, 19, *United States v. Thind*, 261 U.S. 204 (1923).

85. *United States v. Thind*, 261 US 204, 209–10 (1923).

86. Ibid., 213–14.

87. Haney-López, *White by Law*, 94.

88. *United States v. Thind*, 261 U.S. 204 (1923), 214.

89. Jeff Lesser, "Always 'Outsiders': Asians, Naturalization, and the Supreme Court," *Amerasia Journal* 12, no. 1 (1985): 83–100.

90. *United States v. Thind*, 261 U.S. at 215.

91. *Truax v. Corrigan*, 257 U.S. 312 (1920), cited in *Terrace v. Thompson*, 263 U.S. 197 (1923) at 218; *Terrace v. Thompson*, at 221.

92. V. S. McClatchy, "California Joint Immigration Committee, Its History and Achievements," CJIC no. 479, February 18, 1937, Press Releases and Statements, box 1, Papers of the California Joint Immigration Committee, Bancroft Library, University of California, Berkeley (hereafter "CJIC Papers"); Daniels, *The Politics of Prejudice*, 91.

93. "Japanese Immigration Legislation," Hearings before the Senate Committee on Immigration, 68th Congress, 1st Session, 9, 11, 135.

94. Ibid., 59.

95. Masanao Hanihara to Charles Evan Hughes, cited in Daniels, *The Politics of Prejudice*, 101–2.

96. Charles Evans Hughes to Sen. Colt, March 11, 1924, cited in "Japanese Immigration Legislation," 54.

97. In 1913 Johnson bragged before the House committee of his participation in the Bellingham riots. Permdatta Varma, "The Asian Indian Community's Struggle for Legal Equality in the U.S.," (Ph.D. dissertation, University of Cincinnati, 1989), 78.

98. V. S. McClatchy, address to convention of California State Federation of Labor, September 18, 1928, press releases and statements, box 1, CJIC Papers; Ichioka, *The Issei*, 245; Daniels, *The Politics of Prejudice*, 101–2.

99. Ichioka, *The Issei*, 247; *Tacoma News Tribune*, May 28, 1925, HR71A-F16.3, House records; McClatchy, address to California State Federation of Labor, September 18, 1928. On efforts for a Japanese quota in the late 1920s and 1930s, see Izumi Hirobe, *Japanese Pride, American Prejudice: Modifying the Exclusion Clause of the 1924 Immigration Act* (Stanford: Stanford University Press, 2001).

100. *Shin Sekai* (San Francisco), Jan. 1, 1928, HR71A-F16.3, House records.

101. Jensen, *Passage from India*, 261–64.

102. W. W. Hubbard, quoted in Hearings on S.J. Res. 128, Senate Committee on Immigration, 69th Congress, 2d Session (Washington, DC: GPO, 1927); Albert Johnson to McClatchy, Dec. 22, 1926, HR71A-F16.3, House records.

103. Divine, *American Immigration Policy*, 52.

104. David Gutiérrez, *Walls and Mirrors: Mexican Americans, Mexican Immigrants, and the Politics of Ethnicity* (Berkeley: University of California Press, 1995), 13–20; Horsman, *Race and Manifest Destiny*, 210.

105. Carey McWilliams, *North from Mexico: the Spanish-Speaking People of the U.S.* (New York: Greenwood Press, 1968, [1948]), 51–52. The treaty also included provi-

sions that the United States would respect the property of the inhabitants, including the original Spanish land grants, as well as their language and religion, provisions that the Americans trampled over time. On ascriptive citizenship based on territoriality, see Schuck and Smith, *Citizenship without Consent,* 40.

106. General Provisions, Section 10, Constitution of the Republic of Texas (1936); *Boyd v. Nebraska,* 135 U.S. 169 (1892).

107. Tomás Almaguer, *Racial Fault Lines: The Historical Origins of White Supremacy in California* (Berkeley: University of California Press, 1993), 55–56. With the vote, *Californios* from southern California elected statewide representatives between 1850 and 1870, although the influx of white settlers into the state soon rendered their influence marginal.

108. By the late nineteenth century, Anglo-Americans in the Southwest had created a romantic identity with the region's Spanish cultural roots, monumentalized in buildings and festivals, and increasingly divorced from the realities of life for the conquered Mexican population. Carey McWilliams points out the Spanish "fantasy heritage" was not even Spanish, but Mexican throughout—in cuisine, dance, music, and architecture. *North From Mexico,* 35–45. See also Chris Wilson, *The Myth of Sante Fe: Creating a Modern Regional Tradition* (Albuquerque: University of New Mexico Press, 1997).

109. Douglas Monroy, *Thrown among Strangers: The Making of Mexican Culture in Frontier California* (Berkeley: University of California Press, 1990), 106–7. Historians Gerald Poyo and Gilberto Hinojosa suggest that a scarcity of Spaniards on the eighteenth-century Texas frontier "may explain the concurrent phenomena of exogamy and racial bias." See "Spanish Texas and Borderlands Historiography in Transition: Implications for United States History," *Journal of American History* 75 (1988): 411; Nash, "The Hidden History of Mestizo America," 951.

110. McWilliams, *North from Mexico,* 115–32; David Montejano, *Anglos and Mexicans in the Making of Texas, 1836–1986* (Austin: University of Texas Press, 1987), 88–89; Almaguer, *Racial Fault Lines,* 58–59, 66. See also Richard Peterson, "Manifest Destiny in the Mines, a Cultural Interpretation of Anti-Mexican Nativism in California, 1848–1853," unpublished manuscript, n.d., Bancroft Library, University of California, Berkeley; David Langum, *Law and Community on the Mexican California Frontier: Anglo-American Expatriates and the Clash of Legal Traditions, 1821–1846* (Norman, OK: University of Oklahoma Press, 1987).

111. Almaguer, *Racial Fault Lines,* 59, 66.

112. Lawrence Cardoso, *Mexican Emigration to the United States, 1897–1931* (Tucson: University of Arizona Press, 1980), 37.

113. Ibid., 52–53.

114. Montejano, *Anglos and Mexicans in the Making of Texas,* 113–15.

115. Congressman John Box, who sponsored legislation for Mexican restriction, came from East Texas, an area predominated by Anglo small farmers. Montejano, *Anglos and Mexicans in the Making of Texas,* 186.

116. Editorial, "Time to Put up the Bars," *Saturday Evening Post,* November 24, 1928.

117. Edward Hanna to Sen. Shortridge, February 24, 1926, HR70A-F14.3, House records.

118. California State Department of Public Health, Bureau of Tuberculosis, "A

Statistical Study of Sickness among the Mexicans in the LA County Hospital," July 1, 1922 to June 30, 1924 (Sacramento, CA: California State Printing Office, 1928), 2–3; Edythe Thompson to Albert Johnson, January 17, 1928; Thompson to Johnson, February 18, 1930, HR70A-F14.3, House records; "Cost of Mexican Labor Not Cheap," unidentified newspaper clipping from San Bernardino County, HR70A-F14.3, House records; "Immigration from the Countries of the Western Hemisphere," Hearings, House immigration committee, 70th Congress, 1st Session, 2–3, 9; California Joint Committee on Immigration, press release no. 253, "California Editors on Mexican Immigration," February 7, 1930, Press releases and statements, CJIC Papers.

119. James Davis to Albert Johnson, February 14, 1929, HR71A-F16.1, House records.

120. *In re Rodriguez*, 81 Fed. 337, 337–38 (W.D. Tex. 1897).

121. Ibid., 338.

122. Ibid., 349, 352, 354–55.

123. Ibid., 337.

124. Davis to Johnson, February 14, 1929, 5.

125. Joseph A. Hill, "Composition of the American Population by Race and Country of Origin," 1. The census also counted only first and second generation Mexicans as a separate race and continued to count additional generations of Mexican Americans as simply "white." Paul Taylor estimated 200,000 "Spanish Americans" in Colorado who were counted as white and not Mexican in the 1930 census. See Paul Taylor, "Mexican Labor in the U.S.: Migration Statistics 4," *University of California Publications in Economics* 12, no. 3 (1934): 27–28. The "Mexican" race category in the census did not last, owing to protests by Mexico. Paul A. Schor, "Census Day 2000: Observations on Race and the Census," paper presented at Organization of American Historians, St. Louis, April 1, 2000, 13 (in possession of author).

126. Divine, *American Immigration Policy*, 62–68; United States Department of State, "Latest Statistics on Immigration from Mexico," May 12, 1930, HR71-F16.4, House records.

Chapter Two
Deportation Policy and the Making and Unmaking of Illegal Aliens

1. *U.S. ex rel. Klonis v. Davis*, 13 F.2d 630 (C.C.A. 2nd 1926).

2. Transcript, testimony before Executive Session of the House immigration committee, January 15, 1930, file 55688/876-1, entry 9, U.S. Immigration and Naturalization Service, RG 85, National Archives, Washington, DC (hereafter "INS").

3. Ibid.; the Congressional order cited by Harris is the Appropriations Act of February 27, 1925 (43 Stat. 1049). The bureau's policy was an expansive interpretation of a 1916 federal court ruling, *Lew Moy et al. v. United States* (237 Fed. 50). In that case the court upheld the arrest of Chinese aliens two hundred miles north of the Mexican border on the grounds that the alleged act of conspiracy to smuggle had not yet been completed. Commissioner General of Immigration to the Secretary of Labor, *Annual Report* (hereafter *INS Annual Report*), fiscal year ending June 30, 1930, 36; "Immigration Border Patrol," (preliminary hearing, unrevised), March 5, 1928, Hearings,

House immigration committee, 70th Congress, 1st Session (Washington, DC: GPO, 1930), 11.

4. *Chae Chan Ping v. United States*, 130 U.S. 581 (1889); *Nishimura Eiku v. United States*, 142 U.S. 652, 659 (1892); *Fong Yue Ting v. United States*, 149 U.S. 698, 706, 723 (1893). See also Linda S. Bosniak, "Membership, Equality, and the Difference That Alienage Makes," *New York University Law Review* 69 (December 1994): 1047–149.

5. The official record is not without problems. Data on apprehensions and deportations do not represent all unlawful entries and are further skewed by policy decisions to police certain areas or populations and not others. On methodologies employed, see U.S. Immigration and Naturalization Service, *Statistical Yearbook of the Immigration and Naturalization Service, 1998* (Washington, DC: GPO, 2000), 199–205, 238–42; see also Barry Edmonston, Jeffrey Passel, and Frank Bean, *Undocumented Migration to the United States: IRCA and the Experience of the 1980s* (Santa Monica, CA: Rand Corporation, 1990), 16–18, 27. I thank Neil Gotanda for suggesting that the racial concept of "passing" may be applied to illegal immigrants.

6. Gerald L. Neuman, *Strangers to the Constitution: Immigrants, Borders, and Fundamental Law* (Princeton: Princeton University Press, 1996), 19–43; Kunal Parker, "From Poor Law to Immigration Law: Changing Visions of Territorial Community in Antebellum Massachusetts," *Historical Geography* 28 (2000): 61–85. On migration and nineteenth-century economic development, see David Montgomery, *The Fall of the House of Labor: The Workplace, the State, and American Labor Activism, 1865–1925* (New York: Cambridge University Press, 1987), 70–74; John Bodnar, *The Transplanted* (Bloomington: Indiana University Press, 1985), xviii–xix; Aristide Zolberg, "Global Movements, Global Walls: Responses to Migration, 1885–1925," in *Global History and Migrations*, ed. Wang Gungwu (Boulder, CO: Westview Press, 1997), 279. On transition from state to federal regulation of immigration, see Mary Sarah Bilder, "The Struggle over Immigration: Indentured Servants, Slaves, and Articles of Commerce," *Missouri Law Review* 61 (1996): 744–824.

7. Edward Hutchinson, *Legislative History of American Immigration Law, 1798–1965* (Philadelphia: University of Pennsylvania Press, 1981), 163–68; 22 Stat. 58 (first Chinese exclusion law, 1882); 22 Stat. 214 (Immigration Act of 1882); 23 Stat. 332 (Alien Contract Labor Law, 1885). On "cultural pre-suppositions" in application of "likely to become a public charge" provision, see Patricia Russell Evans, "'Likely to Become a Public Charge': Immigration in the Backwaters of Administrative Law, 1882–1933" (Ph.D. dissertation, George Washington University, 1989). On criminal anthropology, anti-Chinese coolieism, and late-nineteenth-century anti-modernism, see Colleen Lye, "Model Modernity: The Making of Asiatic Racial Form, 1882–1943" (Ph.D. dissertation, Columbia University, 1999).

8. Hutchinson, *Legislative History*, 447.

9. Congress extended the statute of limitations for deportation to two years from time of entry in 1903 (32 Stat. 1213) and to three years in 1907 (34 Stat. 898). On Palmer Raids, see William Preston, Jr., *Aliens and Dissenters: Federal Suppression of Radicals, 1903–1933* (Cambridge, MA: Harvard University Press, 1963).

10. *Historical Statistics of the US from Colonial Times to 1970* (Washington, DC: GPO, 1975), 105, 113–15; *INS Annual Report*, 1921, 14–15; William Van Vleck, *The*

Administrative Control of Aliens: A Study in Administrative Law and Procedure (New York: Commonwealth Fund, 1932), 20. See also Jane Perry Clark, *Deportation of Aliens from the U.S. to Europe* (New York: Columbia University Press, 1931), 275.

11. Immigration Act of May 26, 1924, Sec. 14. Those who entered before 1924 continued to be subject to deportation according to the terms of the Immigration Act of 1917.

12. Act of February 27, 1925 (43 Stat. 1049); Act of March 4, 1929 (45 Stat. 1551).

13. *Fong Yue Ting v. United States,* at 708; *Wong Wing v. United States,* 163 U.S. 228 (1896); *Flora v. Rustad,* 8 F.2d 335 (C.C.A. 8th 1925).

14. Between 1930 and 1936 the service brought over 40,000 criminal cases against unlawful entrants, winning convictions in some 36,000, or 90 percent, of them. *INS Annual Reports,* 1929–32; Secretary of Labor, *Annual Reports,* 1933–36. However, in 1933 the Secretary of Labor reported that criminal prosecution did not have the expected deterrent effect. Judges tended to order imprisonment for time the alien already spent in detention awaiting trial. Secretary of Labor, *Annual Report,* 1933, 45.

15. Van Vleck, *Administrative Control,* 21; *INS Annual Report,* 1925, 9; White testimony in "Lack of Funds for Deportations," Hearings on H.R. 3, H.R. 5673, H.R. 6069, January 5, 1928, House immigration committee, 70th Congress, 1st Session. (Washington, DC: GPO, 1928), 10 (hereafter "1928 House Immigration Hearings").

16. *Historical Statistics,* 114. Figures include deportation under formal warrant and voluntary departures.

17. *INS Annual Report,* 1931, 255–56.

18. I am grateful to Kunal Parker for suggesting this illustrative formulation.

19. Act of May 24, 1924, Sec. 7(b), (d).

20. *INS Annual Report,* 1925, 12–13, emphasis added.

21. Editorial, *Los Angeles Evening Express,* December 6, 1930, HR71A-F16.2, House records; Madison Grant, "America for the Americans," *Forum,* September 1925, 354; Flora Lasker, "Backstairs Legislation," *Survey,* March 15, 1929, 796.

22. Department of Labor Solicitor, "In Re Whether Aliens Who Violate Any of the Provisions of the Prohibition Laws Are Subject to Deportation," September 17, 1924, box 3229, file 54933/351-10, [entry 9], INS; V. S. McClatchy and James Fisk to Hiram Johnson, December 4, 1930, HR71A-F16.4, House records. It is worth noting that bootlegging itself was not a deportable offense. As vague as the term "crimes of moral turpitude" was, the Labor Department did not so classify violation of the Volstead Act.

23. Interview of Edwin M. Reeves by Robert H. Novak, June 25, 1974, transcript, tape no. 135, 5, Institute of Oral History, University of Texas, El Paso (microfilm) (hereafter "Edwin Reeves Oral History File"); *National Republic,* May 1929, cited in California Joint Immigration Committee, "Deportable Aliens," release no. 251, Jan. 24, 1930, Press releases and statements, CJIC Papers.

24. *INS Annual Report,* 1927, 15–16, emphasis added.

25. Organized labor, which was generally restrictionist, opposed alien registration on grounds that such information could be used against union activists. See sundry correspondence from union leaders to congressmen, HR69A-H3.5, box 404, House records.

26. I. F. Wixon, "Lack of Funds for Deportations," 1928 House Immigration Hearings, 22–23.

27. Chinese were the first illegal aliens (and continued to be racially constructed as unalterably foreign) but do not appear in deportation statistics or discourse because Chinese illegal immigrants mostly comprised persons who claimed to be U.S. citizens by native birth or descendants of those citizens. Deportation was exceedingly difficult because the fraudulent papers were actually official documents issued by the Immigration Service. See chapter 6. See also Madeline Y. Hsu, *Dreaming of Gold, Dreaming of Home: Transnational Migration from South China to the U.S. 1882–1943* (Stanford: Stanford University Press, 2000), chapter 3; Erika Lee, "Enforcing and Challenging Exclusion in San Francisco: U.S. Immigration Official an Chinese Immigrants, 1882–1905," *Chinese America: History and Perspectives* 11 (1997).

28. Mary Kidder Rak, *Border Patrol* (Boston: Houghton Mifflin, 1938), 17.

29. I. F. Wixon, "Mission of the Border Patrol," lecture no. 7, March 19, 1934, U.S. Department of Labor, INS (Washington, DC: GPO, 1934), 2.

30. The Chinese Division was also called the Outside Division, because it operated separately from the main Immigration Service. In general the Outside Division was understaffed and "not overloaded with talent." Clifford Perkins, *Border Patrol: With the U.S. Immigration Service on the Mexican Boundary, 1910–1954* (El Paso: Texas Western Press, 1978), 9, 75.

31. George Sánchez, *Becoming Mexican American: Ethnicity, Culture, and Identity in Chicano Los Angeles, 1900–1945* (New York: Oxford University Press, 1993), 52–53; *INS Annual Report*, 1919, 24–25, 61; *INS Annual Report*, 1923, 16.

32. Marian Smith, "The INS at the U.S.–Canadian Border, 1893–1933: An Overview of Issues and Topics," *Michigan Hisorical Review* 26 (Fall 2000): 127–47; *INS Annual Report*, 1934, 96; see also Bruno Ramirez, *Crossing the 49th Parallel* (Ithaca: Cornell University Press, 2001), chapters 1–3; Thomas A. Klug, "The Detroit Labor Movement and the United States-Canada Border, 1885–1930," *Mid-America: An Historical Review* 80 (Fall 1998): 209–34; Gary Gerstle, *Working-Class Americanism: The Politics of Labor in a Textile City, 1914–1960* (New York: Cambridge University Press, 1989).

33. Testimony of T. G. Gallagher, representative of Continental Sugar Co., Toledo, in "Immigration from Countries of Western Hemisphere," Hearings, House immigration committee, February 21–April 5, 1928, 70th Congress, 1st Session, 555–57; oral history interview with Rudolfo M. Andres by Helen Hatcher, June 27, 1981, file BA/NC81-Fil-004-HMH-1, Demonstration Project for Asian Americans (Seattle, WA).

34. "The Eclipse of Ellis Island," *Survey*, January 19, 1929, 480.

35. Walter Elcarr to Commissioner General, January 11, 1924, file 53990/160A, box 792, accession 60A600, INS; W.J. Egan to John H. Clark, March 25, 1924, ibid.; John Clark to Commissioner General, March 27, 1924, ibid.; FBI Report filed by W. F. Blackman, "Smuggling of Aliens across the Canadian Border," January 21, 1925, file 53990/160C, ibid.; *INS Annual Report*, 1923, 16.

36. *INS Annual Report*, 1925, 9, 18; *INS Annual Report*, 1929, 7; *INS Annual Report*, 1930, 13; *INS Annual Report*, 1931, 24; *INS Annual Report*, 1932, 17.

37. Ibid., 1927, 12.

38. Ibid., 1924–1932.

39. Ibid., 1925, 17–18. See Smith, "The INS at the U.S.-Canadian Border."

40. *INS Annual Report*, 1925, 19.

41. After 1927 expulsions include both formal deportations under warrant and voluntary departures. *INS Annual Report,* 1928–1932; Secretary of Labor, *Annual Report,* 1933–1938.

42. Leon Metz, *Border: The U.S.-Mexico Line* (El Paso: Mangan Books, 1989), 20–40; Oscar Martínez, *Troublesome Border* (Tucson: University of Arizona Press, 1988), 17–21, 87. See also Americo Paredes, "The Texas Rangers," n.d., file Paredes, box 66, Papers of Juan Samora, Bensen Latin American Library, University of Texas, Austin.

43. Speech of John Farr Simmons, Chief of Visa Office, State Department, at Conference on Immigration, Williamstown, MA [1930], 7–9, file Sen71A-F11, box 93, Senate records; Sánchez, *Becoming Mexican American,* 61, 59.

44. Irving McNeil to J. W. Tappan, U.S. Public Health Service, December 22, 1923; Inspector in charge to Supervising Inspector, El Paso, December 13, 1923, file 52903/29, entry 9, INS. See also "Immigration Border Patrol," 31–32; Alexandra Minna Stern, "Buildings, Boundaries, and Blood: Medicalization and Nation-Building on the U.S.-Mexico Border, 1910–1930," *Hispanic American Historical Review* 79, no. 1 (1999). Chinese immigrants landing at Angel Island were subjected to rigorous medical inspection and prolonged interrogation, but not mass bathing and delousing. On Chinese inspection procedures, see Erika Lee, "At America's Gates: Chinese Immigration during the Exclusion Era" (Ph.D. dissertation, University of California, Berkeley, 1999).

45. *INS Annual Report,* 1925, 14–15.

46. Ibid.; Sánchez, *Becoming Mexican American,* 59; David Blackwell to S.W. Regional Commissioner, "Border Patrol 50th Anniversary," January 19, 1954, in Edwin Reeves Oral History File; Perkins, *Border Patrol,* 95–6, 102; Nick Collaer, serial no. 58, February 14, 1927, file 55494/25, box 3, accession 58A734, INS.

47. Perkins, *Border Patrol,* 96; Edwin Reeves interview, 5; David Blackwell to S.W. Regional Commissioner, "Border Patrol 50th Anniversary"; *INS Annual Report,* 1930, 37. El Paso district circulars by G. C. Wilmoth, on going to Mexico to drink alcohol, on and off duty, serial no. 2274, September 2, 1924, reissued February 16, 1928; on careless and reckless driving and failure to maintain vehicles, serial no. 4073, April 3, 1929; on reading or "entertaining friends by relating stories or jokes" while on duty, serial no. 4136, November 21, 1929; on engaging in "useless and harmful talk to outsiders," serial no 4133, November 19, 1929; on taking gratuities from aliens, serial no. 4127, Oct. 1, 1929, file 55494/25-A, box 3, accession 58A734, INS.

48. Testimony of Henry Hull before House immigration committee, January 15, 1930; *INS Annual Report,* 1930, 41.

49. *Bisbee (Arizona) Review,* Feb. 1, 1927; G. C. Wilmoth to Chief Patrol Inspectors, June 7, 1929, file 55494/25-A, box 3, accession 58A734, INS; U.S. Dept. of Labor, Bureau of Immigration, *Problems of the Immigration Service: Papers Presented at a Conference of Commissioners and District Directors of Immigration,* January 1929 (Washington, DC: GPO, 1929); D. W. MacCormack, "The Spirit of the Service," Lecture 1, February 12, 1934, U.S. Dept. of Labor, INS (Washington, DC: GPO, 1934), 4.

50. "Immigration Border Patrol," 30. According to Douglas Foley, the federal government "left [the] southern labor force to work out their own problems with local Texas Rangers, the Border Patrol, and hostile Anglos." Foley, *From Peones to Politicos: Class and Ethnicity in a South Texas Town, 1900–1987* (Austin: University of Texas Press, 1988 [1977]), 18.

51. Perkins, *Border Patrol*, 116; "Expulsions of Mexicans," *La Opinión*, January 29, 1929, 1 (trans. from Spanish). In 1932 the INS counted 3,812 apprehensions along the Canadian border and 19,072 along the Mexican border. *INS Annual Report*, 1932, 44. The INS did not report comparable data in other years.

52. R. M. Cousar, Inspector in Charge at Nogales, circular, May 19, 1928, HR70A-F14.3, box 236, House records; on commuter classification, see *Karnuth v. United States*, 279 U.S. 231 (1929); *INS Annual Report*, 1930, 16; Lawrence Herzog, "Border Commuter Workers and Transfrontier Metropolitan Structure along the U.S.-Mexico Border," in *U.S.-Mexico Borderlands: Historical and Contemporary Perspectives*, ed. Oscar Martínez (Wilmington, DE: Scholarly Resources Books, 1996), 179; on bath requirement, see José Cruz Burciaga interview by Oscar Martínez, February 16, 1972, transcript of tape 148, Institute of Oral History, University of Texas-El Paso, 20–22.

53. "Immigration Border Patrol," 18; Lawrence Cardoso, *Mexican Emigration to the United States, 1897–1931* (Tucson: University of Arizona Press, 1980), 94; Paul Taylor, "Mexican Labor in the United States: Migration Statistics," *University of California Publications in Economics* 6, no. 3 (1929): 244–45.

54. Paul Taylor, "Migratory Farm Labor in the United States," United States Department of Labor, Bureau of Labor Statistics, *Monthly Labor Review*, Ser. No. R530 (March 1937), reprinted in Taylor, *Labor on the Land, Collected Writings 1930–1970* (New York: Arno, 1981), 101; *Denver Post*, May 16, 1935; Thomas Fowle to M. F. Lence, May 14, 1936, file 55854/100, INS.

55. Oscar Martínez, Jr., "Prohibition and Depression in Ciudad Juárez–El Paso," in Martinez, *U.S.-Mexico Borderlands*, 155–56; Edward Shaughnessy to Harry Coffee, June 4, 1935, file 55854/100, INS.

56. John Zurbrick to Commissioner General, May 9, 1935, file 55854/100, INS. The labor agent, Jesse Bejar of San Antonio, had been instructed by sugar companies to recruit only legal immigrants.

57. Thomas Fowle to M. F. Lence, May 14, 1936; Lence to Commissioner General, April 22 and May 16, 1936; Grover Wilmoth to I. F. Wixon, April 27, 1936, Shaughnessy to Coffee, June 4, 1935, file 555854/100, INS.

58. Manuel García y Griego, "The Importation of Mexican Contract Laborers to the United States, 1942–1964: Antecedents, Operation, and Legacy," in *The Border That Joins: Mexican Migrants and U.S. Responsibility*, ed. Peter Brown and Henry Shue (Totowa, NJ: Rowman and Littlefield, 1983), 2–3, 52. See also Rudolfo Acuña, *Occupied America: The Chicano's Struggle toward Liberation* (San Francisco: Canfield Press, 1972), 190.

59. On the Depression-era repatriations, see Abraham Hoffman, *Unwanted Mexican Americans in the Great Depression: Repatriation Pressures, 1929–1939* (Tucson: University of Arizona Press, 1974); Paul Taylor, "Mexican Labor in the United States: Migration Statistics 4," *University of California Publications in Economics* 12, no. 3 (1934), 23–50; Sánchez, *Becoming Mexican American*, 209–26; Camille Guerin-Gonzalez, *Mexican Workers and American Dreams: Immigration, Repatriation and California Farm Labor, 1900–1939* (New Brunswick, NJ: Rutgers University Press, 1994); Francisco E. Balderrama and Raymond Rodriguez, *Decade of Betrayal: Mexican Repatriation in the 1930s* (Albuquerque: University of New Mexico Press, 1995).

60. Hoffman, *Unwanted Mexican Americans*, 86–87. The Mexican government paid for the repatriates' transportation from the border to the interior and offered

incentives for resettlement in agricultural colonies, although these had little success. Ibid., 138–42, 95. See also George Clements to H. E. Drobish, Februrary 27, 1936, in Documents re: migrant laborers and establishment of camps, 1936–1937, Irving Wood Papers, Bancroft Library, University of California, Berkeley.

61. Balderrama, *Decade of Betrayal,* 56–60.

62. Hoffman, *Unwanted Mexican Americans,* 65. Visel and other proponents of removal often made the contradictory claims that Mexicans took jobs from Americans while simultaneously crowding the relief rolls.

63. Ibid., 128–29.

64. Mexican revolutionaries like Rivera, concerned that Mexico was losing its population through emigration, supported repatriation. In Detroit, Rivera (there painting an epic mural of autoworkers) helped found the League of Workers and Peasants of Mexico, which actively urged Mexicans to return home. Later, disillusioned by the experience of repatriated Mexicans, Rivera urged Mexican workers to make their claims as workers in Detroit. Zaragosa Vargas, *Proletarians of the North: A History of Mexican Industrial Workers in Detroit and the Midwest, 1917–1933* (Berkeley: University of California Press, 1993), 182–83, 185–86.

65. Balderrama, *Decade of Betrayal,* 84.

66. Hoffman, *Unwanted Mexican Americans,* 91, 113–14; Sánchez, *Becoming Mexican American,* 220–23.

67. Paul Taylor, *An American-Mexican Frontier, Nueces County, Texas* (Chapel Hill: University of North Carolina Press, 1934), 316.

68. Taylor, "Migration Statistics 4," 26–27. The third (or greater) generation population ranged from a low of 7.9 percent in California to a high of 57.1 percent in Colorado. Other scholars have made similar estimates. See Hoffman, *Unwanted Mexican Americans,* 119–20; David Gutiérrez, *Walls and Mirrors: Mexican Americans, Mexican Immigrants, and the Politics of Ethnicity* (Berkeley: University of California Press, 1995), 93, 67.

69. *LULAC News,* vol. 1, no. 9 (April 1932), 7; *LULAC News,* vol. 1, no. 8 (March 1932), 3. A full-page notice launched a campaign against venereal disease: "Cleanliness is next to godliness" and "We must learn the truth about these diseases, how to avoid them and how to eliminate them. Until then, diseased citizens will be an unbearable burden to those who are endeavoring to carry the colors of their people." *LULAC News,* vol. 6, no. 8 (August 1939), 43. On LULAC, see Mario García, *Mexican Americans: Leadership, Ideology, and Identity, 1930–1960* (New Haven: Yale University Press, 1989), 29–61; Gutiérrez, *Walls and Mirrors,* 74–87.

70. Cardoso, *Mexican Emigration,* 94. Mexican nationalism also betrayed anti-Asiatic sentiments. Ernesto Galarza believed that Mexican emigration created a labor vacuum in Mexico that was filled by Chinese and Japanese, which threatened to create a "serious Asiatic problem" in Mexico. Telegram, Sacramento Church Federation to Albert Johnson, Februrary 29, 1928, HR70A-F14.3, box 237, House records.

71. Hoffman, *Unwanted Mexican Americans,* 90.

72. See file 55957/456, box 1224, accession 85-58A734, INS; Balderrama, *Decade of Betrayal,* 57–192; Hoffman, *Unwanted Mexican Americans,* 138–42.

73. Sánchez, *Becoming Mexican American,* 224–25; *San Francisco News,* February 20, 1936, clipping file, Irving Wood Papers.

74. U.S. Senate, Committee on Immigration, "Deportation of Criminals, Preservation of Family Units, Permit Noncriminal Aliens to Legalize Their Status," February 29, 1936, 74th Congress, 2d Session, 122.

75. *Fong Yue Ting v. United States*, at 743, 737.

76. "Deportation of Aliens (Notes)," *Columbia Law Review* 20 (June 1920): 683.

77. Jane Perry Clark, *Deportation of Aliens*; U.S. National Commission on Law Observance and Enforcement, *Report on the Enforcement of the Deportation Laws of the United States* (Washington, DC: GPO, 1931) (hereafter "Wickersham Report"); William Van Vleck, *Administrative Control.*

78. Lucy Salyer, *Laws Harsh as Tigers: Chinese Immigrants and the Shaping of Modern Immigration Law* (Chapel Hill: University of North Carolina Press, 1995), 172–83; *Japanese Immigrant Case* (*Yamataya v. Fisher*), 189 U.S. 86 (1903); Wickersham Report, 27.

79. Van Vleck, *Administrative Control*, 26, 90–95; Wickersham Report, 65, 157–58, 170–71.

80. Van Vleck, *Administrative Control*, 99–100, 107; Clark, *Deportation of Aliens*, 324–25; Kohler, *Immigration and Aliens in the United States* (New York: Bloch Publishing Company, 1936), 413; Wickersham Report, 107–8. On immigration lawyers in New York, see Louis Anthes, "Bohemian Justice: The Path of the Law in New York, 1870–1940" (Ph.D. dissertation, New York University, 2000).

81. Clark, *Deportation of Aliens*, 72–103, quote at 79; Van Vleck, *Administrative Control*, 97–98, 119–25.

82. *INS Annual Report*, 1928–1932; Secretary of Labor, *Annual Report*, 1933–1936.

83. Morton Horwitz, *The Transformation of American Law: The Critique of Legal Orthodoxy, 1870–1960* (New York: Oxford University Press, 1992), 189, 199; *Nation*, April 29, 1931, 463; "Statutory Construction in Deportation Cases," *Yale Law Journal* 40 (1931): 1284–97. On proposed legislation to further restrict or to suspend immigration during the Depression, see Hutchinson, *Legislative History*, 215, 221–22, 229.

84. Van Vleck, *Administrative Control*, 126–27, 135–37.

85. Ibid., 119, 125, 236.

86. Ibid., 124–25.

87. Ibid., 124. A district immigration director told Clark that a majority of deportation cases stemmed from so-called "spite cases" or "grudge reports." Clark, *Deportation of Aliens*, 324.

88. Van Vleck, *Administrative Control*, 29; Kohler, *Immigration and Aliens*, 38; *Meyer v. State of Nebraska*, 262 U.S. 390 (1923); *Griswold v. Connecticut*, 381 U.S. 479 (1965). In *Commissioner of Immigration of Port of N.Y. v. Gottleib*, 265 U.S. 310 (1924), the Court rejected the argument that family unification could override the quota law. However, Congress acknowledged the primacy of family unity by giving nonquota status to the wives and minor children of U.S. citizens in the Immigration Act of 1924. On the Supreme Court's use of *Meyer* to invent a tradition in support of family rights, see Martha Minow, "We the Family: Constitutional Rights and American Families," *Journal of American History* 74 (December 1987): 959–83.

89. "Statutory Construction in Deportation Cases," 1285, 1289; Emma Wold, "Alien Women vs. the Immigration Bureau," *Survey*, November 15, 1927, 217; *INS Annual Reports*, 1925–1932.

90. *Browne v. Zurbrick*, 45 F.2d 931 (C.C.A. 6th 1930); *Iorio v. Day*, 34 F.2d 920

(C.C.A. 2nd 1929); see also *Lisotta v. U.S.*, 3 F.2d 108 (C.C.A. 5th 1924); *U.S. ex rel. Klonis v. Davis*, 13 F.2d 630 (C.C.A. 2nd 1926).

91. See "Pardons, Commutations, and Reprieves," in *Public Papers of Governor Herbert S. Lehman, 1933–1942* (Albany, NY: J. B. Lyon and Company, 1935–1947).

92. *INS Annual Report*, 1931, 12–13.

93. Secretary of Labor, *Annual Report*, 1934, 53.

94. Morton Keller, *Regulating a New Society: Public Policy and Social Change in America, 1900–1933* (Cambridge: Harvard University Press, 1994), chapters 3–4; Addams quoted in Mary Ross and Paul Kellogg, "New Beacons in Boston: The Fifty-Seventh National Congress of Social Work," *Survey*, July 15, 1930, 347; "A Mistake Congress Should Correct," *Interpreter*, vol. 8, no. 5 (April 1929): 76.

95. "Frequent Deportation of Mexicans," *La Opinión*, January 30, 1929, 2 (trans. from Spanish).

96. *INS Annual Report*, 1925, 12–13; Act of March 2, 1929 (45 Stat. 1512); *INS Annual Report*, 1930–1932; Secretary of Labor, *Annual Report*, 1933–1940; Paul Taylor, "Mexican Labor in the United States: Dimmit County, Winter Garden District, South Texas," *University of California Publications in Economics* 6, no. 5 (1930): 322.

97. Secretary of Labor, *Annual Report*, 1934, 50. On Perkins, see George Martin, *Madam Secretary, Frances Perkins* (Boston: Houghton Mifflin, 1976). MacCormack came from an elite New York family. He was a cousin of Eleanor Roosevelt, a banker, and a former diplomat. I am grateful to Marian Smith for biographical information on MacCormack.

98. *Report of the Ellis Island Committee* (New York, [n.p.], 1934), 77, 87.

99. Secretary of Labor, *Annual Report*, 1934, 50–53.

100. D. W. MacCormack, "The Spirit of the Service," lecture 1, February 12, 1934, U.S. Department of Labor, INS (Washington, DC: GPO, 1934), 2, 4. See also in ibid., MacCormack, "The Lecture Course of Study for the Immigration and Naturalization Personnel—Retrospect and Prospect," lecture 20, June 18, 1934; W. H. Wagner, "Personnel and Fiscal Administration," lecture 2, February 19, 1934; Rosa Fisher, "Visa Petitions," lecture 5, March 12, 1934; H. L. Volker, "Naturalization Requirements concerning Race, Education, Residence, Moral Character, and Attachment to the Constitution," lecture 8, March 26, 1934; Robert Ludwig, "Time Limitations for Deportation," lecture 16, May 21, 1934; Henry Hazard, "Where and How to Find the Law (Legal Research)," lecture 19, June 11, 1934; Howard Ebey, "Chinese Exclusion and Immigration Laws as Applied to Chinese," lectures 32–33, January 21 and 28, 1935; L. E. Crone, "Citizenship Status of Inhabitants of the Territories and Outlying Possessions: Hawai'i, Alaska, Puerto Rico, Virgin Islands, Philippine Islands, Guam, Samoa, and Panama Canal Zone," lecture 35, February 11, 1935.

101. D. W. MacCormack, "Memorandum of the Commissioner of Immigration and Naturalization to the Committee on Immigration of the Senate and the Committee of Immigration and Naturalization of the House of Representatives, Relative to Certain Proposed Changes in the Immigration Law," April 24, 1934, 2; U.S. Senate, Committee on Immigration, "Deportation of Criminals," Feb. 24, 29, and March 3, 11, 1934, 16, 198.

102. "Deportation of Criminals," 218–19.

103. Immigration Act of 1917 (39 Stat. 874). The 1917 act included twelve provisos, or exceptions, to the law's rules of exclusion. See Senate Report 352, 64th

Congress, 1st session, 6, on Seventh Proviso as a hardship clause. See also Letter, Frances Perkins to Rep. Dave Satterfield, Jr., September 17, 1940, file Immigration, General, 1940, box 66, Secretary's General Subject Files, Records of the Department of Labor, RG 174, National Archives, College Park, MD (hereafter "Perkins Papers").

104. Perkins to Satterfield, September 17, 1940; memorandum, Attorney General to Rufus Holman, January 4, 1943, 4, file 55819/ box 75, accession 58A734, INS.

105. Memoranda, A. M. Doig, Acting District Director, Detroit to Commissioner General, Sept. 7, 1933; MacCormack to District Directors, Newport [VT], Buffalo, NY, Detroit, Grand Forks [ND], and Seattle, December 18, 1933, file 55819/402, box 75, accession 58A734, INS. Pre-examination as described here is distinguished from the INS policy of "pre-inspection," which refers to inspection abroad before emigration.

106. Department of Immigration and Colonization [Canada], Official Circular no. 31, February 23, 1935; MacCormack to A. L. Jolliffee, Commissioner of Immigration [Canada], October 21, 1935, file 55819/402, box 75, accession 58A734, INS.

107. Letter, Perkins to Mrs. Roosevelt, January 27, 1939, file Immigration-Deportations 1939, box 69, Perkins Papers.

108. 8 CFR pt. 142.

109. Letter, James Houghterling to Sen. James Lewis, April 20, 1938, file 55819/ 402B, box 75, accession 58A734, INS; I. F. Wixon to Secretary of State, November 8, 1937, file 55819/402A, ibid.

110. Sen. Robert Reynolds to James Houghterling, April 4, 1938, file 55819/402B, box 75, accession 58A734, INS; "Seven Hundred Deportable Aliens Sheltered by U.S. Labor Department," *Congressional Record*, October 10, 1940, 20424–28; Perkins to Satterfield, September 17, 1940, file Immigration, General, 1940, box 66, Perkins Papers.

111. Attorney General to Sen. Rufus C. Holman, January 4, 1943, file 55819/402D, INS; I. F. Wixon to Secretary of State, November 8, 1937; "Summary of cases listed on page 47 of the State Dept. Appropriation Bill, 1939, with particular reference to the nature of the crimes involving moral turpitude in connection with which the Seventh Proviso to Section 3 of the 1917 Act was invoked by the Secretary of Labor," file 55819/402A, box 75, accession 58A734, INS; "Seven Hundred Deportable Aliens Sheltered by U.S. Labor Department."

112. Five or more years of residence was required for those without citizen or legally-resident alien spouse, parent, or minor child; one year of residence was required of the latter. Memorandum, Joseph Savoretti to A. R. Mackey, March 27, 1946, file 55819/402D, INS.

113. Perkins apparently wished to help Asians, but the law tied her hands. For example, see the case of Ramkrishana Sakharan Jivotode, in letter, Perkins to Josephus Daniels, April 22, 1940, file Immigration-Deportation, 1940, box 67, Perkins Papers.

114. Memoranda, G. C. Wilmoth to Commissioner General, Nov. 3, 1938; William Blocker to Secretary of State, November 3, 1938; Wilmoth to Commissioner General, November 29, 1938, file 55819/402C, box 75, accession 58A734, INS.

115. MacCormack died suddenly in 1937. It is possible that had he lived he would have fought for a universal application of the pre-examination program, although of course we cannot know.

116. G.C. Wilmoth to all inspectors in charge and chief patrol inspectors, El Paso

District (draft) [1938], file 55819/402C, box 75, accession 58A734, INS, emphasis in original; formal application form [1942] and Part 142 of Immigration Regulations, 1943, file 55819/402D; Ugo Carusi to Tom Clark, October 15, 1945, ibid.; U.S. Senate, Report of Committee of the Judiciary, "Immigration and Naturalization Systems of the U.S.," Senate Report 1515, April 20, 1950, 81st Congress, 2d Session (hereafter "Senate Report 1515"), 604.

117. Common Council for American Unity, "An Immigration Summary: Outstanding Facts about the Admission, Exclusion, and Deportation of Aliens," June 1941, 20–21; Henry L. Feingold, *The Politics of Rescue: The Roosevelt Administration and the Holocaust, 1938–1945* (New Brunswick, NJ: Rutgers University Press, 1970), 15–20; Robert Divine, *American Immigration Policy, 1924–1952* (New Haven: Yale University Press, 1957), 103–4.

118. For pre-examination data, see *INS Annual Reports*, 1942–1959; see also Senate Report 1515. Pre-examination was suspended in 1940 for about one year as a wartime "internal security" precaution. See Attorney General to Sen. Rufus C. Holman, January 4, 1943. It was reinstituted but then discontinued in 1952 because the McCarran-Walter Act (66 Stat. 163) provided statutory relief for illegal aliens who entered by way of fraud or misrepresentation, who were otherwise admissible, and who had immediate family in the United States. Sec. 241(f), amended 71 Stat. 640 (1957). Pre-examination was reinstituted again in 1955 as a remedy to the flood of private legislation brought on behalf of illegal aliens whom the INS denied relief under 241(f). However, Congress imposed narrower grounds for pre-examination, limiting it to persons who had acquired eligibility for nonquota status as the spouse or child of a U.S. citizen. See *INS Annual Report*, 1955. Since 1961, relief in fraud cases has been at the attorney general's discretion. 75 Stat. 657 (Act of September 26, 1961), now 8 USC 1182(i) (2000).

119. Act of June 28, 1940 (54 Stat. 670). For discussion on "good moral character" in suspension of deportation cases, see Senate Report 1515, 596–97.

120. Published data for 1941–1960 indicate a total of 34,632 suspensions of deportation, see *INS Annual Reports*, 1941–1960; memorandum, Helen F. Eckerson, Statistical Unit, to L. Paul Winings, General Counsel, March 12, 1946, file 55819/402D, box 75, accession 58A734, INS.

121. Transcript of speech by Marshall Dimock, "Security Within," delivered to Veterans of Foreign Wars, Los Angeles, August 27, 1940, file Immigration-Naturalization, box 66, Perkins Papers.

122. The basic terms of the Seventh Proviso were incorporated into Sec. 212(c) of the Immigration and Naturalization Act of 1952 (66 Stat. 163). It remained in the law until 1996, when it was eliminated. Suspension of deportation was incorporated into Sec. 244(a) of the INA. It remains in law, although the grounds for it are now very narrow.

123. Administrative Procedures Act, Act of June 11, 1946 (60 Stat. 237); *Wong Yang Sung v. McGrath*, 339 U.S. 33, 1950; Marion Bennett, *American Immigration Policies: A History* (Washington, DC: Public Affairs Press, 1963), 90–94; Act of September 27, 1950 (64 Stat. 1044). Congress repealed the exemption in 1952 and wrote provisions into the McCarran-Walter omnibus immigration act to effect the same results. On the "unmistakable purpose to exempt immigration hearings from the procedural requirements of the Administrative Procedures Act," see President's Commission on Immigration and Naturalization, *Whom We Shall Welcome* (Washington, DC: GPO, 1953), 159.

124. See, generally, Matthew Jacobson, *Whiteness of a Different Color: European Immigrants and the Alchemy of Race* (Cambridge: Harvard University Press, 1998); James Barrett and David Roediger, "In-between People: Race, Nationality, and the 'New Immigrant' Working Class," *Journal of American Ethnic History* 16, no. 3 (Spring 1997): 3–44; Ian Haney-López, *White by Law: The Legal Construction of Race* (New York: New York University Press, 1995).

Part II
Migrants at the Margins of Law and Nation

1. Richard Hofstadter, *The Age of Reform: From Bryan to FDR* (New York: Alfred A. Knopf, 1955), 41–42; Carey McWilliams, *Ill Fares the Land* (New York: Barnes and Noble, 1941), 307–14.

2. Carey McWilliams, *Factories in the Field* (Santa Barbara: Peregrine, 1971 [1935]), 11–27, 103–33; Kevin Starr, *Endangered Dreams: The Great Depression in California* (New York: Oxford University Press, 1996), 63–64. But see Victoria Saker Woeste, "Land Monopoly, Agribusiness, and the State: Discovering the Family Farm in Twentieth-Century California," in *The Countryside in the Age of the Modern State: Political Histories of Rural America*, ed. Catherine McNicol Stock and Robert D. Johnson (Ithaca: Cornell University Press, 2001).

3. I distinguish the concept of imported colonialism from internal colonialism, which some scholars have used to describe the subordination of ethnic Mexicans in the territory ceded from Mexico in 1848. The internal colonialism theory has many merits, in particular its emphasis on the history of conquest and the structural subordination of ethnic Mexicans in land ownership, the polity, and other realms in the Southwest, although political and social conditions varied considerably throughout the region. I use imported colonialism more narrowly to describe colonial-like relations in agricultural labor in-migration. On internal colonialism, see Laura Gomez, "Race Mattered: Racial Formation and the Politics of Crime in Territorial New Mexico," *UCLA Law Review* 49, no. 5 (June 2002): 1395–1416; Tómas Almaguer, "Toward the Study of Chicano Colonialism," *Aztlan* 2, no. 1 (Spring 1971): 7–20; Tómas Almaguer, *Racial Fault Lines: The Historical Origins of White Supremacy in California* (Berkeley: University of California Press, 1994); Cardell Jacobson, "Internal Colonialism and Native Americans: Indian Labor in the United States from 1871 to World War II," *Social Science Quarterly* 65, no. 1 (March 1984): 158–71; Norma Beatriz Chalout and Yves Chalout, "The Internal Colonialism Concept: Methodological Considerations," *Social and Economic Studies* 28 (December 1979): 85–99; and Joseph Love, "Modeling Internal Colonialism: History and Prospect," *World Development* 17 (June 1989): 905–22. See also Linda Gordon, *The Great Arizona Orphan Abduction* (Cambridge: Harvard University Press, 1999), 178–85.

Chapter Three
From Colonial Subject to Undesirable Alien

1. Carlos Bulosan, *America is in the Heart* (Seattle: University of Washington Press, 1993 [1943]), 124, 126.

2. San Francisco district INS, manifest of departing repatriates, Feb. 6, 1937, file 5883/412-D, INS. According to the manifest, Rodesillas was married, but there is no indication as to the identity or whereabouts of his wife. Of the repatriates traveling with children, not a few were men without wives. They may have been separated or divorced.

3. Public Law No. 202 (July 10, 1935), 74th Congress; 48 Stat. 456 (March 22, 24, 1934).

4. 48 Stat. 456, Sec. 8 (1), (4).

5. Arnold H. Leibowitz, *Defining Status: A Comprehensive Analysis of U.S. Territorial Relations* (Boston: Academic Publishers, 1989), 6.

6. Stuart Creighton Miller, *"Benevolent Assimilation": The American Conquest of the Philippines, 1899–1903* (New Haven: Yale University Press, 1982), 3; Lodge quoted in David Healy, *U.S. Expansionism: The Imperialist Urge in the 1890s* (Madison: University of Wisconsin Press, 1970), 51; see also 50–57, 91; Walter LaFeber, *The New Empire: An Interpretation of American Expansionism 1860–1898* (Ithaca: Cornell University Press, 1963), 3–5.

7. "Exclusion of Immigration from the Philippine Islands," Hearings on H.R. 8708, House immigration committee, April 10, 1930, 71st Congress, 2d Session, 119.

8. LaFeber, *New Empire*, 73–75, 98–99.

9. Schurman quoted by Sandra Treadway, *"Terra Incognita*: the Philippine Islands and the Establishment of American Colonial Policy, 1898–1904," (Ph.D. dissertation, University of Virginia, 1978), 114; Richard Welch, *Response to Imperialism: The United States and the Philippine-American War, 1899–1902* (Chapel Hill: Univesity of North Carolina Press, 1979), 67; Thomas Gossett, *Race: The History of an Idea in America* (New York: Schocken, 1965), 333; Miller, "Benevolent Assimilation," 1.

10. Oscar Campomanes, "The New Empire's Forgetful and Forgotten Citizens: Unrepresentability and Unassimilability in Filipino-American Postcolonialities," *Critical Mass* 2, no. 2 (Spring 1995): 145–200, at 152–53; McKinley cited in Welch, *Response to Imperialism*, 163–64 n. 30.

11. Welch, *Response to Imperialism*, 35, 42.

12. The *Insular Cases* comprise nine rulings handed down in 1901: *De Lima v. Bidwell*, 182 U.S. 1; *Goetze v. United States*, 182 U.S. 221; *Grossman v. United States*, 182 U.S. 221; *Dooley v. United States*, 182 U.S. 222; *Armstrong v. United States*, 182 U.S. 243; *Downes v. Bidwell*, 182 U.S. 244; *Huus v. New York and Porto Rico Steamship Company*, 182 U.S. 392; *Dooley v. United States*, 183 U.S. 151; and *Fourteen Diamond Rings v. United States*, 183 U.S. 176. For discussion of these and related cases, see Efrén Rivera Ramos, "The Legal Construction of American Colonialism: The Insular Cases (1901–1922)," *Revista Juridica Universidad de Puerto Rico* 65 (1996): 225–328.

13. *Downes v. Bidwell*, 182 U.S., at 341–2. On the matter of tariffs, *Downes* upheld the Foraker Act of 1900 (31 Stat. 77), by which Congress established a civilian government in Puerto Rico and set duties on imports from Puerto Rico. Defining Puerto Rico as "foreign to the United States in a domestic sense," the Court ruled that the Uniformity Clause of the Constitution did not apply.

14. Christina Burnett and Burke Marshall, "Between the Foreign and the Domestic: The Doctrine of Territorial Incorporation, Invented and Reinvented," in *Foreign in a Domestic Sense: Puerto Rico, American Expansion, and the Constitution*, ed. Burnett and Marshall (Durham: Duke University Press, 2001), 13. On similarities in

immigration and colonial doctrines, see T. Alexander Aleinikoff, "The Canon(s) of Constitutional Law: Sovereignty Studies in Constitutional Law: A Comment," *Constitutional Commentary* 17 (2000): 197–203.

15. Jones Act, ch. 190 (39 Stat. 951 [1917]); *Balzac v. Porto Rico*, 258 U.S. 298 (1922); Ramos, "Legal Construction of American Colonialism," 164–272.

16. These were typical arguments of southern white Democrats and organized labor, respectively. See Welch, *Response to Imperialism*, 62, 87.

17. Gossett, *Race: The History of an Idea*, 337–38.

18. The first Filipinos who came to the United States seem to have been deserting seamen from Spanish galleon ships. A community of "Manilamen" settled in Louisiana during the late eighteenth century. Fred Cordova, *Filipinos: Forgotten Americans* (Seattle: Demonstration Project for Asian Americans, 1983), 1–7; Yen Le Espiritu, *Filipino American Lives* (Philadelphia: Temple University Press, 1995), 3–4; Barbara Posades and Roland Guyotte, "Unintentional Immigrants: Chicago's Filipino Foreign Students Become Permanent Settlers, 1900–1941," *Journal of American Ethnic History* 9 (Spring 1990): 26–47.

19. Gary Okihiro, *Cane Fires: The Anti-Japanese Movement in Hawaii, 1865–1945* (Philadelphia: Temple University Press, 1991), 49–51.

20. Bruno Lasker, *Filipino Immigration to Continental U.S. and to Hawaii* (Chicago: University of Chicago Press, 1931), 31, 164–65, 207. By the mid-1920s emigration had become so popular that the HSPA stopped targeted recruitment and paying for transportation in 1926.

21. Telegram, Frank Helm to Brig. General McIntire [*sic*]; May 11, 1917, *Philadelphia Inquirer* April 22, 1917; telegram, F. S. Cairns to McIntyre, June 2, 1917; McIntyre to Cairns, n.d., file 26671/5–8, box 1103, General Classified Files, 1914–1945, Records of the Bureau of Insular Affairs, RG 350, National Archives, College Park, MD (hereafter "BIA").

22. Lasker, *Filipino Immigration*, 21; telegram, Florencio Tamesis to Francisco Verona, March 20, 1921, file 22671/33, box 1103, BIA.

23. Memorandum, Francisco Varona to Governor General, March 26, 1921, file 26672/38; memorandum, W. C. Carpenter to Director General, USES, June 18, 1921, file 22671/44A, box 1103; letter, Varona to Pablo Manlapit, April 14, 1921, file 22671/42, box 1103, BIA.

24. Letter, McIntyre to Wood, August 6, 1924, file 22671/54, box 1027, BIA; *Free Press*, September 20, 1924, file 22671/55–56, box 1103, BIA.

25. Lasker, *Filipino Immigration*, 1, 31, 347–48.

26. Ibid., 73–75.

27. Filipino Oral History Project, Inc., *Voices, A Filipino American Oral History* (Stockton, CA: Filipino Oral History Project, 1984), n.p.

28. Interview with Trinidad Rojo, by Carolina Koslosky, February 18–19, 1975, 3–9, FIL-KNG75-17ck, Washington State Oral/Aural History Project, 1972–1977, Washington State Archive, Olympia, WA (hereafter "WSOAHP").

29. H. Brett Melendy, "Filipinos in the United States," *Pacific Historical Review* 43 (1974): 520–47; "Facts about Filipino Immigration into California," special bulletin no. 3 (San Francisco: California Dept. of Industrial Relations, April 1930), 11–13, 66; Lasker, *Filipino Immigration*, 128.

30. Lasker, *Filipino Immigration*, 21, 53–54. Melendy found the annual return mi-

gration rate to be 16 to 50 percent of arrivals between 1920 to 1934—a wide range that tended to be higher in the later years. "Filipinos in the U.S.," 526.

31. Howard DeWitt, *Anti-Filipino Movements in California* (San Francisco: R&E Associates, 1976), 31–32; *Washington Star,* November 12, 1927, box 1103, BIA.

32. File 22671/68, 72, 73, box 1103, BIA; Lasker, *Filipino Immigration,* 365–66.

33. Lasker, *Filipino Immigration,* 6.

34. "Facts about Filipino Immigration into California," 12–13; Lasker, *Filipino Immigration,* 43–65; Charles Franks, "Filipino Labor Situation," December 17, 1928, file 22671/80, box 1103, BIA.

35. Manuel Buaken, *I Have Lived with the American People* (Caldwell, ID: Caxton Printers, 1948), 61.

36. James Woods, field notes, 23, 32, 35, 48, 50, file 2:16 box 2, James W. Woods Papers, Bancroft Library, University of California, Berkeley (microfilm; hereafter "James Woods Papers" and "James Woods field notes"); ibid., file 2:18, 2–5.

37. "Facts about Filipino Immigration into California," 72.

38. Lasker, *Filipino Immigration,* 55–57; "Facts about Filipino Immigration into California," 72–73; Oral history interview with Roman and Hazel Simbe, by DeeAnn Dixon and Nancy Koslosky, January 18, 1981, Aberdeen, Washington, 9–10, PNW82-Fil-030ad/nk, Demonstration Project for Asian Americans, Seattle, WA (hereafter "DPAA").

39. Letter, Filipino Workers Delegation to Asparagus Growers, [February 1928], reprinted in *Stockton (CA) Philippine Advertiser,* February 29, 1928, file 26671/61, box 1103, BIA; Lasker, *Filipino Immigration,* 18–19; James Woods field notes, file 2:16, 27; "Martin's Ten Points Warn Contractors, Laborers," *Stockton Philippine Advertiser,* February 29, 1928. See also Howard DeWitt, *Violence in the Fields: California Filipino Farm Labor Unionization during the Great Depression* (Saratoga, CA: Century Twenty One Publishing, 1980), 14; Melendy, "Filipinos in the U.S.," 527–28.

40. Letter, Filipino Workers Delegation to Asparagus Growers, BIA; James Woods field notes, file 2:16, 27, 34–35.

41. Lasker counted twenty-six incidents of racial conflict (including three which involved Japanese or Mexicans); James Woods recorded an additional half dozen incidents. Lasker, *Filipino Immigration,* 13–20; James Woods field notes, file 2:16, 19–22, 42, 50.

42. Lasker, *Filipino Immigration,* 13–14; James Woods field notes, 19–21; Howard DeWitt, *Anti-Filipino Movements in California,* 34–36; "Testimony, Statements, Etc. Relating to Filipinos in California," in folder 2:18, box 2, James Woods Papers.

43. Lasker, *Filipino Immigration,* 18; James Woods field notes, file 2:16, 22, 34–35.

44. James Woods field notes, file 2:16, 22, 32.

45. *Salinas Torch* no. 2, January 1930, file 3:5, box 3, James Woods Papers.

46. Lasker, *Filipino Immigration,* 15, 35.

47. Alexander Saxton, *The Indispensable Enemy: Labor and the Anti-Chinese Movement in California* (Berkeley: University of California Press, 1995 [1974]).

48. Homi Bhabha, "Of Mimicry and Man: The Ambivalence of Colonial Discourse," in *The Location of Culture* (London: Routledge, 1994); Patrick Wolfe, "History and Imperialism: A Century of Theory, from Marx to Postcolonialism," *American Historical Review* 102 (April 1997): 415–16.

49. Rydell, *All the World's a Fair,* 176–77. The racism towards Filipinos and in American society generally shocked a delegation of the Federalist Party of the Philip-

pines that visited the Louisiana Purchase Exposition. The Federalists represented the most conservative comprador elements in Philippine society; they had, of course, taken American promises of benevolent assimilation seriously. Upon their return to the Philippines the Federalists reconsidered the party's position for U.S. statehood and rewrote its platform for national independence at its 1906 convention.

50. Paul Cressey, *The Taxi Dance Hall: A Sociological Study in Commercialized Recreation and City Life* (Chicago: University of Chicago Press, 1932), chapter 7; Linda Maram, "Negotiating Identity: Youth, Gender, and Popular Culture in Los Angeles' Little Manila, 1920s–1940s" (Ph.D. dissertation, U.C.L.A., 1996).

51. Lasker, *Filipino Immigration*, 98–99; Carey McWilliams, *Brothers under the Skin* (Boston: Little, Brown and Company, 1943), 237. For reasons unknown, McWilliams excised this sentence from the 1951 edition of *Brothers under the Skin*.

52. Trinidad Rojo, "Social Maladjustment among Filipinos in the U.S.," *Sociology and Social Research* 21, no. 5 (May–June 1937): 447–57, at 447; Buaken, *I Have Lived with the American People*, 134–35. On Chicago Sociology's training of native informants as sociologists, see Henry Yu, *Thinking Orientals* (New York: Oxford University Press, 2000).

53. Donald Elliot Anthony, "Filipino Labor in Central California," *Sociology and Social Research* 16, no. 3 (January-February 1932): 149–56, at 153.

54. Benecio Catapusan, "The Social Adjustment of Filipinos in the U.S.," (Master's Thesis, University of Southern California, 1940), 76. On difficulties in Filipino-white marriages, see also Cressey, *Taxi Dance Hall*, 147–48, 167–74.

55. Robert G. Lee, *Orientals: Asian Americans in Popular Culture* (Philadelphia: Temple University Press, 1999), 83–87.

56. James Woods field notes, file 2:16, 35–37; Catapusan, "The Social Adjustment of Filipinos in the U.S.," 49. On feminization of Filipinos, see also Charles V. Hawley, "'Savage Gentlemen': Filipinos and Colonial Subjectivity in the United States" (Ph.D. Dissertation, University of Iowa, 1999), 10.

57. Lasker, *Filipino Immigration*, 360–61; Buaken, *I Have Lived with the American People*, 169.

58. Buaken, *I Have Lived with the American People*, 170; DeWitt, *Anti-Filipino Violence*, 50. See also Lasker, *Filipino Immigration*, 99.

59. DeWitt, *Anti-Filipino Violence*, 46–51; Michael Showalter, "The Watsonville Anti-Filipino Riot of 1930: A Reconsideration of Fermin Tobera's Murder," *Southern California Quarterly* 71, no. 4 (Winter 1989): 341–48.

60. Lasker, *Filipino Immigration*, 14–15; Reports of Riots, file 22671/114, box 1104, BIA; Carey McWilliams, *Factories in the Field* (Santa Barbara: Peregrine Publishers, 1971 [1935]), 138.

61. *San Francisco Philippine Advocate*, July 1, 1931; interview with Felix Zamora, n.d., PNW81-Fil-011PA, DPAA, 13; James Woods field notes, file 2:16, 42.

62. Roman and Hazel Simbe, interview by DeeAnn Dixon and Nancy Kosolosky, January 18, 1981 and January 22, 1982, 14, PNW82-Fil030ad/nk, DPAA; *San Francisco Philippine Advocate*, July 1, 1931, 4.

63. *Salvador Roldan v. Los Angeles County*, 129 Cal. App. 267 (1933); California Civil Code, Sec. 60 (1906) (amended 1937, repealed 1959). See Leti Volpp, "American Mestizo: Filipinos and Antimiscegenation Laws in California," *U.C. Davis Law Review* 33 (Summer 2000): 795–835.

64. Lasker, *Filipino Immigration*, v, 34–35, 299.

65. H.R. 13799, 70th Congress, 1st Session; H.R. 8708, 70th Congress, 2d Session.

66. "Exclusion of Immigration from the Philippine Islands," Hearings, House immigration committee, April 10, 1930, 71st Congress, 2d Session, 6, 27.

67. Ibid., 6, 92, 131.

68. Lasker, *Filipino Immigration*, 37.

69. "Exclusion of Immigration from the Philippine Islands," 174–77, 4, 59, 34–37.

70. *New York Herald Tribune*, March 12, 1930; "Philippine Independence," Hearings before the Senate Committee on Territories and Insular Affairs, Report 781, May 21, 1930, 71st Congress, 2d Session, 10–11.

71. Stanley, *A Nation in the Making*, 203–11; Benedict Anderson, "Cacique Democracy in the Philippines," in *Discrepant Histories: Translocal Essays on Filipino Cultures*, ed. Vicente Rafael (Philadelphia: Temple University Press, 1995), 12; "Philippine Independence," 13.

72. "Philippine Independence," 5–7. See also Brands, *Bound to Empire*, 149–51.

73. Anderson, "Cacique Democracy in the Philippines," 14–15.

74. Ibid., 13; Stanley, *Nation in the Making*, 213; *New York Filipino American*, vol. 1, no. 3 (Sept. 1929); *Herald* cited in *Stockton Three Stars*, vol. 2, no. 19 (June 15, 1930), in Filipino American Experience Research Project, Filipino American National Historical Society (Seattle) (hereafter "FAERP").

75. *San Francisco Philippine Advertiser*, February 29, 1928; Brands, *Bound to Empire*, 147; "The Filipino Federation of America Today," *Filipino Nation*, December 1928, file 3:5, box 3, James Woods Papers.

76. *Stockton Three Stars*, April–May, 1932, FAERP.

77. Act of March 22, 24, 1934 (48 Stat. 456); Brands, *Bound to Empire*, 156–57.

78. Maximo Manzon, *The Strange Case of the Filipino in the United States* (New York: American Committee for the Protection of the Foreign Born, 1938), 16; "It Is Your Patriotic Duty to Reject the McDuffie-Tydings Filipino Independence Bill," *Salinas Philippines Mail*, April 30, 1934, FAERP.

79. DeWitt, *Violence in the Fields*; Chris Friday, *Organizing Asian American Labor: The Pacific Coast Canned-Salmon Industry, 1870–1942* (Philadelphia: Temple University Press, 1994), 125–48.

80. Robert Acelar to D. W. MacCormack, November 30, 1934; E. W. Cummings to D. W. MacCormack, n.d., file 55883/412, INS. Samuel Dickstein also received inquiries from or on behalf of indigent Filipinos wishing to return home. See Casiano Pagdilao Coloma, "A Study of the Filipino Repatriation Movement" (Master's Thesis, University of Southern California, 1939; reprint, San Francisco: R&E Research Assoc., 1974), 33.

81. Samuel Dickstein, "Return Unemployed Fiipinos to Philippine Islands," House immigration committee, report accompanying H.R.J. Res. 577, January 27, 1933, 2–3; Coloma, "A Study of the Filipino Repatriation Movement," 32–35.

82. Act of July 10, 1935 (49 Stat. 478); "Memorandum in re Repatriation of Filipinos," July 2, 1935 (unsigned), file 55883/412, INS.

83. Cahill to MacCormack, July 20 and August 10, 1935, file 55883/412, INS; Coloma, "A Study of the Filipino Repatriation Movement," 38.

84. Coloma, "A Study of the Filipino Repatriation Movement," 43–45, 47–48.

85. Unsigned memorandum, "Filipino Repatriation Acts," August 24, 1940, file 55883/412-C, INS. The Filipino Repatriation Acts, Act of July 10, 1935 (49 Stat. 478),

extended June 4, 1936 (49 Stat. 1462), May 14, 1937 (50 Stat. 165), and July 27, 1939 (53 Stat. 1133).

86. See passenger manifests, file 55853/412-A, INS. See also "Statistics regarding Filipino Repatriates," attachment to Cahill to Wagner, January 27, 1938, file 55883/412-B, INS.

87. Mexican repatriation followed a similar pattern. Contemporaries observed among the first Mexican repatriates families traveling in cars laden with household furnishings. In the later years, repatriates tended to be poorer, suggesting that they decided to return only after their struggle to survive in the United States had failed. See Abraham Hoffman, *Unwanted Mexican Americans in the Great Depression: Repatriation Pressures, 1929–1939* (Tucson: University of Arizona Press, 1974), 128–29.

88. SERA was remarkably flexible. When authorities realized that the legislation stipulated funds for transport to Manila, SERA paid for the repatriates' transportation from Manila to their home towns, at least for Filipinos who were California residents. See Cahill to Wagner, December 3, 1937, file 55883/412-B, INS.

89. Edward J. Shaughnessy, INS circular letter, Oct. 26, 1935; radiogram, Murphy to Secretary of War, April 6, 1936, file 55883/412, INS.

90. Cahill to E. M. Kline, August 23, 1937, file 55883/412-B, INS.

91. Memorandum for the Commissioner, "Summary of file 55874/464," November 30, 1937, file 55883/412-B; Edward Shaughnessy, INS circular letter, October 26, 1935, file 55883/412; manifests, file 55883/412-A, INS.

92. Paul McNutt to Frank Merriam, November 19, 1937, file 55883/4120-B, INS.

93. Cahill to Wagner, July 5, 1935, file 55883/412, INS; Coloma, "A Study of the Filipino Repatriation Movement," 48.

94. Coloma, "A Study of the Filipino Repatriation Movement," 50; Benicio T. Catapusan, "Filipino Repatriates in the Philippines," *Sociology and Social Research*, 21, no. 1 (September–October 1936): 72–77.

95. Friday, *Organizing Asian American Labor*, 149–92.

96. Act of July 2, 1946 (60 Stat. 416).

Chapter Four
Braceros, "Wetbacks," and the National Boundaries of Class

1. Maria Herrera-Sobek, *The Bracero Experience: Elitelore versus Folklore* (Los Angeles: UCLA Latin American Center Publications, 1979), 79.

2. Cited by José David Salvidar, "Américo Paredes and Decolonization," in *Cultures of United States Imperialism*, ed. Amy Kaplan and Donald Pease (Durham: Duke University Press, 1993), 304.

3. *Perez v. Brownell*, 356 U.S. 44 (1958); Sec. 401(e), (j), Nationality Act of 1940 (54 Stat. 1137). The subject should be properly called Martínez, according to the Mexican custom that gives primary recognition to the paternal surname.

4. *Perez v. Brownell*, 356 U.S. at 64 (C.J. Warren, dissenting); *Afroyim v. Rusk*, 387 U.S. 254 (1967).

5. *Perez v. Brownell*, Brief for Petitioners, 13–45. *Perez* was the first case to address revocation of birthright citizenship. During the World War II and postwar period the Court also ruled on several cases involving denaturalization, mostly on anti-Commu-

nist grounds. See, for example, *Schneiderman v. United States*, 320 U.S. 118 (1943); *Knauer v. United States*, 328 U.S. 654 (1947).

6. *Perez v. Brownell*, 356 U.S. at 46.

7. *Perez v. Brownell*, 235 F.2d 364 (C.C.A. 9th 1956).

8. Martínez's case was not unique. See *Perez v. Brownell*, Brief of *Amicus Curiae* (Francisco Mendoza-Martinez).

9. Lawrence Cardoso, *Mexican Emigration to the United States* (Tucson: University of Arizona Press, 1980), 24–28; David Gutiérrez, *Walls and Mirrors: Mexican Americans, Mexican Immigrants, and the Politics of Ethnicity* (Berkeley: University of California Press, 1995), 45; David Montejano, *Anglos and Mexicans in the Making of Texas* (Austin: University of Texas Press, 1987), 109–10.

10. See chapter 2.

11. Paul Taylor, "Migratory Farm Labor in the United States," United States Department of Labor, Bureau of Labor Statistics, *Monthly Labor Review*, serial no. R530 (1937), reprinted in Taylor, *Labor on the Land, Collected Works* (New York: Arno Press, 1980), 94; Mark Reisler, *By the Sweat of Their Brow: Mexican Immigrant Labor in the U.S., 1900–1940* (Westport, CT: Greenwood Press, 1976), 79. According to Reisler, the Departments of Commerce and Agriculture defined "large scale" as any farm with an annual production valued at $30,000 or more.

12. Montejano, *Anglos and Mexicans*, 110; Carey McWilliams, *Factories in the Field* (Santa Barbara: Peregrine, 1971 [1935]), 125; Cardoso, *Mexican Emigration*, 91.

13. Douglas Foley, *From Peones to Politicos, Class and Ethnicity in a South Texas Town, 1900–1987* (Austin: University of Texas Press, 1988 [1977]), 5–6. Figures include immigrants and legal nonimmigrants (including temporary, or seasonal, entrants). See Manuel García y Griego, "The Importation of Mexican Contract Laborers to the U.S., 1942–1964: Antecedents, Operation and Legacy," in *The Border That Joins: Mexican Migrants and U.S. Responsibility*, ed. Peter Brown and Henry Shue (Totowa, NJ: Rowman and Littlefield, 1983), 50.

14. Paul Taylor, "Mexican Labor in the United States: Valley of the South Platte, Colorado," *University of California Publications in Economics* 6, no. 2 (1929): 93–235, at 105–6, 119–23; idem, "Mexican Labor in the United States: Migration Statistics 2," *University of California Publications in Economics* 12, no. 1 (1933): 1–10; idem, "Mexican Labor in the United States: Migration Statistics 3," *University of California Publications in Economics* 12, no. 2 (1933): 11–22.

15. On Chicano community formation in Los Angeles, see George Sánchez, *Becoming Mexican American*; on El Paso, see Mario T. García, *Desert Immigrants: The Mexicans of El Paso, 1880–1920* (New Haven: Yale University Press, 1981).

16. Sánchez, *Becoming Mexican American*, 38, 57–62.

17. Paul Taylor, "Mexican Labor in the United States: Dimmit County, Winter Garden District, South Texas," *University of California Publications in Economics* 6, no. 5 (1930): 293–464, at 432–57, esp. 436, 442–43.

18. Carlos Vélez-Ibáñez, *Border Visions: Mexican Cultures of the Southwest United States* (Tucson: University of Arizona Press, 1996), 65, 72. See also Mark Reisler on the fusion of "Mexican" and "peon" in *By the Sweat of Their Brow*, 143. On political and military experience of immigrants in the Mexican Revolution, see John Mason Hart, "The Evolution of the Mexican and Mexican American Working Classes," in *Border Crossings: Mexican and Mexican-American Workers*, ed. John Mason Hart

(Wilmington, DE: Scholarly Resources, 1998), 17–18; Devra A. Weber, *Dark Sweat, White Gold: California Farm Workers, Cotton, and the New Deal* (Berkeley: University of California Press, 1994), 57–58, 84–85. Camille Guerin-Gonzales has pointed out that the stereotype of the Mexican seasonal laborer rendered women and families invisible. Guerin-Gonzales, *Mexican Workers, American Dreams: Immigration, Repatriation and California Farm Labor, 1900–1939* (New Brunswick, NJ: Rutgers University Press, 1994).

19. Tzvetan Todorov, *The Conquest of America: The Question of the Other*, trans. Richard Howard (New York: Harper Perennial, 1992 [1984]), 157, 185, and passim. Patrick Wolfe discusses how differences in colonial labor structures have resulted in a heterogeneity of colonial discourses in "History and Imperialism: A Century of Theory, From Marx to Postcolonialism," *American Historical Review* 102 (April 1997): 418–20.

20. Quoted in Taylor, "Mexican Labor in the United States: Dimmit County," 448.

21. Taylor, "Mexican Labor in the United States: Valley of the South Platte," 153. Growers also complained that Mexican American labor contractors tended to negotiate wages up. At other times, however, contractors underbid each other for work or cheated workers of their wages. Taylor, "Mexican Labor in the United States: Dimmit County," 346, 351–53, 453.

22. Taylor, "Mexican Labor in the United States: Dimmit County," 346; "Report to National Labor Board by Special Commission," Federal Release no. 3325, February 11, 1934, 7, file Documents re: Migrant Laborers and Establishment of Labor Camps, 1934–May 1935, Irving Wood Papers, Bancroft Library, University of Califiornia, Berkeley (hereafter "Migrant Labor file").

23. Taylor, "Mexican Labor in the United States: Valley of the South Platte," 153; idem, "Mexican Labor in the United States: Dimmit County," 448.

24. Rosalinda M. González, "Chicanas and Mexican Immigrant Families 1920–1940: Women's Subordination and Family Exploitation," in *Decades of Discontent*, ed. Lois Scharf and Joan Jensen (Westport, CT: Greenwood Press, 1983); Taylor, "Mexican Labor in the United States: Valley of the South Platte," 105; T. G. Gallagher, Continental Sugar Company, "Immigration from Countries of the Western Hemisphere," Hearings, House immigration committee, 70th Congress, 1st Session (Washington, DC: GPO, 1929), 556–57.

25. Paul Taylor, "Mexican Labor in the United States: Chicago and the Calumet Region," *University of California Publications in Economics* 7, no. 2 (1932): 25–284, at 25–28. Taylor noted an additional pattern of "leapfrog migration" whereby Mexicans from central Mexico migrated directly to the industrial North. The movement of Mexican workers northward alarmed Texas growers, who feared labor shortages would result. Texas passed the Emigrant Labor Agency Laws of 1929 to restrict labor agents from recruiting for northern sugar companies. See Montejano, *Anglos and Mexicans in the Making of Texas*, 190, 210–13. In some cases growers and local sheriffs colluded to apply vagrancy laws to keep Mexicans in a state of peonage. Paul Taylor, *An American-Mexican Frontier: Nueces County, Texas* (Chapel Hill: University of North Carolina Press, 1934), 325–29. On permanent settlement, see Taylor, "Mexican Labor in the United States: Migration Statistics 3," 18–19; Sánchez, *Becoming Mexican American*, 198; Selden C. Menefee, "Mexican Migratory Workers in South Texas: Crystal City, 1938," in *U.S.-Mexico Borderlands, Historical and Contemporary*

Perspectives, ed. Oscar Martínez (Wilmington, DE: Scholarly Resources Books: 1996), 171.

26. Taylor, "Mexican Labor in the United States: Dimmit County," 448. On the relativity of labor shortages, see David Montejano, *Anglos and Mexicans in the Making of Texas,* 177; Devra Weber, *Dark Sweat, White Gold,* 37–38. H. H. Hagerty to Albert Johnson, November 24, 1928. HR70A-F14.3, box 236, House records. The analogy to the American South was, in fact, apt. Not only did the large growers squeeze smaller farmers, the former's complaints about labor shortages echoed those of southern cotton planters in the aftermath of the Civil War. Eric Foner has pointed out that while freedpeople worked fewer hours than they had as slaves, the labor shortage was as much a question of power as it was one of hours. Foner, *Reconstruction: America's Unfinished Revolution* (New York: Harper and Row, 1988), 140.

27. U.S. Department of Labor, Bureau of Labor Statistics, "Labor Unionism in American Agriculture," Bureau of Labor Statistics Bulletin no. 836 (Washington, DC: GPO, 1945), 270–81; Weber, *Dark Sweat, White Gold,* 79; Kevin Starr, *Endangered Dreams: The Great Depression in California* (New York: Oxford University Press, 1996), 61–83; Don Mitchell, *The Lie of the Land: Migrant Workers and the California Landscape* (Minneapolis: University of Minnesota Press, 1996), chapter 6.

28. Taylor, "Mexican Labor in the United States: Imperial Valley," 45–54; idem, "Migratory Farm Labor in the United States," 102; Weber, *Dark Sweat, White Gold,* 79–111, 180–99; Vicki Ruiz, *Cannery Women, Cannery Lives: Mexican Women, Unionization, and the California Food Processing Industry, 1930–1950* (Albuquerque: University of New Mexico Press, 1984), 41–85; Linda Majka and Theo Majka, *Farm Workers, Agribusiness, and the State* (Philadelphia: Temple University Press, 1982), 128; Paul Taylor and Clark Kerr, "Uprisings on the Farms," *Survey Graphic* 24 (January 1934): 19–44, quote at 19.

29. Majka and Majka, *Farm Workers, Agribusiness, and the State,* 103–4.

30. Letter, Pelham Glassford to Imperial County Board of Supervisors, June 23, 1934, file Copies of Materials re: Laborers in Imperial Valley, 1934, Irving Wood Papers; Irving Wood, "Instructions to Camp Managers, Confidential," August 1, 1935, Migrant Labor file, 1936–1937, Irving Wood Papers; Irving Wood, "Social and Economic Justification [for Labor Camps]," n.d., Documents, Migrant Labor File, 1936–1937, Irving Wood Papers; Otey Scruggs, "Evolution of the Mexican Farm Labor Agreement," *Agricultural History* 36 (1966): 143 n. 18; Majka and Majka, *Farm Workers, Agribusiness, and the State,* 111–12. See also Sidney Baldwin, *Poverty and Politics: The Rise and Decline of the Farm Security Administration* (Chapel Hill: University of North Carolina Pares, 1968), 222, 270–71. The absence of Mexicans and Filipinos in the FSA camps is evident in weekly camp census reports. See file Marysville Reports, 1935–1936, and Arvin Migratory Labor Camp, weekly reports, 1935–1936, Irving Wood Papers. Devra Weber found that Mexicans were "generally unwelcome and stayed away" from FSA camps. Weber, *Dark Sweat, White Gold,* 135.

31. Byron Darnton, "Migrants' Dream of Owning Land Makes Them a Conservative Lot," *New York Times,* March 6, 1940, 25. For a discussion on the cultural "whitening" of California farm labor, see Colleen Lye, "Model Modernity: The Making of Asiatic Racial Form" (Ph.D. dissertation, Columbia University, 1999), 204–97. Lange, who had been trained in the 1920s as a society portrait photographer, applied these techniques to her migratory worker series. Julia C. Ballerini, "Political Propaganda/

Autobiography: Dorothea Lange's Farm Service Administration Mothers," paper presented at Women and Society Seminar, Columbia University, September 25, 2000.

32. Telegrams, C. G. MacCormack to Fred Nichols, Texas state commissioner of labor; William Whalen to MacCormack; H. P. Drought, state WPA, to Nels Anderson, WPA; D. W. Brewster to Whalen; all August 6, 1936, file 55854/100, entry 9, INS.

33. Memorandum, Whalen to Commissioner General, August 13, 1937; memorandum, Wilmoth to Commissioner General, Oct. 29, 1937, file 55854/100-A; sundry applications, file 55854/100-E; Lemuel Schofield, Memo for file in re Mexican Labor, May 19, 1942, file 55854/100-E, entry 9, INS.

34. Scruggs, "Evolution of the Mexican Farm Labor Agreement of 1942," 141, 145; Conference notes, April 30 and May 4, 1942, file 55854/100-E, entry 9, INS.

35. Anti-Alien Contract Labor Law of 1885 (23 Stat. 332).

36. The prohibition of contract labor in Hawai'i after 1898 should not be underestimated. Although sugar and other plantation owners in Hawai'i continued to import farmworkers from Japan and the Philippines, the lack of formal contracts meant that many workers quit the plantations and sought better paying work in towns or on the Pacific Coast of the mainland United States. President Roosevelt curbed Japanese migration from Hawai'i to the mainland in 1907 by executive order but not Filipinos, who were not aliens but "nationals," and who were therefore not restricted by the immigration laws. Executive Order 589 (1907). See also Ronald Takaki, *Raising Cane: The World of Plantation Hawai'i* (New York: Chelsea House, 1994); Gary Y. Okhiro, *Cane Fires: The Anti-Japanese Movement in Hawaii* (Philadelphia: Temple University Press, 1991), 57–61; Ronald Takaki, *Pau Hana: Plantation Life and Labor in Hawai'i* (Honolulu: University of Hawai'i Press, 1983). On ideological contestation over the meanings of free labor and contract labor, see Gunther Peck, *Reinventing Free Labor: Padrones and Immigrant Workers in the North American West, 1880–1930* (New York: Cambridge University Press, 2000).

37. On migratory farm labor and imported contract workers in the Southeast, see Cindy Hahamovitch, *The Fruits of Their Labor: Atlantic Coast Farmworkers and the Making of Migrant Poverty* (Chapel Hill: University of North Carolina Press, 1997); and idem, "'In America Life is Given Away': Jamaican Farmworkers and the Making of Agricultural Immigration Policy," in *The Countryside in the Age of the Modern State: Political Histories of Rural America*, ed. Catherine McNicol Stock and Robert D. Johnson (Ithaca: Cornell University Press, 2001).

38. Scruggs, "Evolution of the Mexican Farm Labor Agreement of 1942," 143, 146; Garcia y Griego, "Importation of Mexican Contract Workers," 60. The extensions were 59 Stat. 645 (1945) and 61 Stat. 55 (1946). On continuation of war emergency, see Kitty Calavita, *Inside the State: The Bracero Program, Immigration, and the INS* (New York and London: Routledge, 1992), 25–30.

39. Memorandum, L. M. Brody to Adjudications Branch, INS, November 30, 1942, file 55854/100-G, entry 9, INS; memorandum, J. O. Walker to Allen Devaney, December 28, 1942, ibid.; Majka and Majka, *Farm Workers, Agribusiness, and the State*, 145; Richard Craig, *The Bracero Program: Interest Groups and Foreign Policy* (Austin: University of Texas Press), 43. During the war, 100,000 agricultural workers were also imported from the Bahamas, Barbados, Jamaica, Canada, and Newfoundland. For more discussion on railroad workers during the war, see Joseph Savoretti, "Memorandum for the Immigration Bd. of Appeals, in re: application of War Man-

power Commission for permission to import additional 25,000 unskilled Mexican railway laborers," March 9, 1945, file 56135/227, box 2515, accession 58A734, INS.

40. Andrew Biemiller, Statement before House Subcommittee on Equipment, Supplies, and Manpower, Committee on Agriculture, March 25, 1960, file 9, box 19, RG 1–027, Records of the AFL-CIO, George Meany Memorial-Labor Archives, Silver Spring, MD (hereafter "AFL-CIO"); "Migratory Labor in American Agriculture," Report of the President's Commission on Migratory Labor (Washington, DC: GPO, 1951), 6–7.

41. Typescript, Louis Levine, "Long Range Trends in Farm Labor Demand and the Outlook for the Coming Year," May 3, 1954, 14–15, file 56321/448E, box 3299, accession 58A734, INS; "Migratory Labor in American Agriculture," 178; "A New Deal for the Mexican Worker," Look 23, no. 20 (September 29, 1959): 54–56, at 54.

42. Paul Taylor, "Migratory Farm labor and the Body Politic," February 20, 1951, file staff studies, President's Commission on Migratory Labor (hereafter "PCML"), Harry S. Truman Presidential Library, Independence, MO (hereafter "HST").

43. 65 Stat. 119 (1951). Public Law 78 was incorporated as Title V into the Agricultural Act of 1949. In 1943 Congress lifted the ban on imported contract-labor, which had been law since 1885. Public Law 45 (57 Stat. 70 [1943]). Public Law 78 contained a similar provision that allowed imported contract-labor in case of domestic labor shortage and where such imported labor did not "adversely affect the wages and working conditions" of workers in the United States similarly employed (Public Law 78, Sec. 503). The Immigration and Nationality Act of 1952 allowed for the importation of temporary labor at the discretion of the attorney general. See Immigration and Nationality Act, Public Law 414 (66 Stat. 163 [1952]). The section giving the attorney general discretion is 214(c), at 66 Stat. 189.

44. USES, "Letter of Agreement and Regulations," July 23, 1942, file 55854/100-F, entry 9, INS. On guaranteed wages and work as "socialistic," see Scruggs, "The Evolution of the Mexican Farm Labor Agreement of 1942," 149.

45. Calavita, Inside the State, 29–30, 45–46. During the war, recruitment took place in Mexico City. During the postwar phase, recruitment centers (also called migratory stations) were established in Monterrey, Nuevo Leon; Irapuato, Guanajuato; Guadalajara; Durango; and Chihuahua. Monterrey, 146 miles west of Harlingen, Texas, was closest to the border; others were from 500 to 1400 miles away. U.S. "reception centers" were set up in Harlingen, Eagle Pass, and El Paso, Texas; Nuevo Laredo, New Mexico; and El Centro, California. Additional migratory stations were later established in Mexicali and additional reception centers at Calexico, California, and Hidalgo, Texas. In 1952 Mexico temporarily closed the station at Monterrey after the governor of Nuevo Leon complained that it "had created an adverse economic and social situation . . . due to the almost continuous existence of thousands of laborers in the city . . . hoping to be contracted for work in the U.S. . . . They are ordinarily without funds and loaf about the city, sleeping at the railway station, the city hall, public parks, or wherever they can find a place to rest. They also steal and beg." Most migratory stations opened and closed amid similar scenes at various times owing to a lack of orders or lack of men. See Department of State telegraph no. 150, to Neal from Blocker, July 22, 1952, file 56321.448C, box 3298, accession 58A734, INS.

46. Letter, E. Dewitt Marshall to Lic. Gustavo Diaz Ordaz, September 10, 1954, file 56321/448G, box 3299, accession 58A734, INS. During a brief interregnum from 1948 to 1949, a government-to-government agreement authorized the program but employers directly recruited and contracted braceros. However, growers complained of the burden and cost of recruiting in the interior of Mexico, and Mexico complained that without formal responsibility for each contract American enforcement became even more lax. A new agreement in 1949 restored the U.S. government's role as the "employer." For more discussion on the "laissez faire" phase, see Calavita, *Inside the State*, 42–44.

47. Transcripts, sworn statements of R.V.L. to N. Thomas Sherfy and P.C.S. to Sherfy, May 14, 1955, file 56364/42.34 part 1, box 87, accession 59A2038, INS. Names in text are pseudonyms. The exchange rate in 1955 was 12.5 pesos to the dollar. International Monetary Fund, *International Financial Statistics Yearbook* (Washington, DC: IMF, 1979), 294–95.

48. Statements of R.V.L. and P.C.S. For a description of INS processing, see M. R. Toole to G. C. Wilmoth, re: processing of Mexican agricultural laborers, May 22, 1948, file 56246/339A, box 3055, accession 58A734, INS; Fred Eldridge, "Helping Hands from Mexico," *Saturday Evening Post* 230, no. 6 (August 10, 1957): 28–29, 63–64. According to Eldridge, less than one-half of one percent of 450,000 bracero applicants were rejected for any reason in 1956.

49. C. R. Porter to District Director Los Angeles, workload report, Calexico, October 3, 1951, file 56321/448A, box 3298, accession 58A734, INS. See also memorandum, Joseph Minton to A. C. Devaney, June 3, 1953, file 56321/448D, ibid. Minton remarked that there was only one immigration officer at Iraputo, and that it was "physically impossible for him to continue examining 500 braceros a day."

50. Statement of R.V.L.

51. Ibid.; transcript, sworn statement of A.O.G. to N. Thomas Sherfy, May 14, 1955, file 56364/42.34 part 1, box 87, accession 59A2038, INS.

52. Statements of R.V.L., A.O.G., P.C.S.

53. American GI Forum of Texas, *What Price Wetbacks?* (Austin: Texas State Federation of Labor, [1954]), 73. According to one critic, the average debt for a mordida and subsistence while waiting to be contracted was $85, plus interest. The typical bracero working on a thirteen-week contract earned $19 a week, of which $10 went to pay off his debt, $4 towards living expenses, and $5 remitted home. That amount of remittance was in fact less than braceros said their families needed. Henry P. Anderson, Statement Relative to the Proposed Extension of PL 78, February 27, 1961, file 10, box 19, RG 1-027, AFL-CIO.

54. Fay Bennett, "The Condition of Farm Workers in 1958," 3, file Migrants, box 33, George I. Sánchez Papers, Bensen Latin American Collection, University of Texas, Austin (hereafter "Sánchez Papers"); Calavita, *Inside the State*, 22–23, 70–71.

55. For example, in March 1952 three major fruit growers in the Imperial Valley fired two hundred local workers and replaced them with braceros. Domestic workers were driven out of melon picking, considered the only crop in the valley that farm workers could make enough to subsist. See letter, Ernesto Galarza to William Green, June 2, 1952, file 52, box 47, RG 1-023, AFL-CIO. On out-migration from South Texas, Lyle Saunders and Olen Leonard, *The Wetback in the Lower Rio Grande Valley of Texas* (Austin: University of Texas Press, 1951), 44–45; Eleanor Hadley, "A Critical

Analysis of the Wetback Problem," *Law and Contemporary Problems* 21 (Spring 1956): 334–357, at 344. Hadley reported ninety thousand "Texas Mexicans" displaced in 1949. On loss of union jobs, memorandum, Bud Simonson to John Henning, February 15, 1963, file ES 2-6-1, box 75, Records of the Secretary of Labor, Department of Labor, RG 174, National Archives, College Park, MD (hereafter "Secretary of Labor files"). See also Fay Bennett, "The Condition of Farm Workers in 1958," 3.

56. Memorandum, Robert Goodwin to Frank Noakes, September 26, 1956, file Mexican Labor Program, General Correspondence, 1954–60, part 1, box 3, coded administrative files, 1942–1947, War Food Administration and Production and Marketing Administration, United States Department of Agriculture, Farmers Home Administration, RG 96, National Archives, Pacific Region, San Francisco (hereafter "FHA"). For additional statistics on complaints and violations found, see United States Department of Labor, Bureau of Employment Service, Farm Labor Service, "Report of Operations of Mexican Farm Labor Program Made Pursuant to Conference Report 1449, House of Representatives, 84th Congress, 1st Session," (hereafter "BES, Report of Operations"), July 1–December 31, 1960, file ES 2-6-1, box 55, Secretary of Labor files. For statistical analysis of complaints, see, for example, "Contracting of Mexican National Agricultural Workers, 1949 Season," [August 1950], PCML/HST; Appendix to Regional Foreign Labor Operations Advisory Committee, meeting no. 10, May 17, 1956, file BES/FLOAC 1954–58, part 4, box 2, FHA. See also sundry file, "Joint Determinations," box 4, Office of the Solicitor, Region 9, Records of the Department of Labor, RG 174, National Archives, Pacific Region, San Francisco (hereafter "DOL Solicitor's files").

57. Ernesto Galarza, *Merchants of Labor: The Mexican Bracero Story* (Charlotte and Santa Barbara: McNally and Loftin, 1967), 183; Fay Bennett, "The Condition of Farm Workers in 1955," [1956], file Wetbacks, 1955–1956, box 45, Sánchez papers; M. Mason, Inspection Report, Agricultural Program, for week of May 9, 1955, file 563664/42 part 1, box 87, accession 59A2038, INS; letter, Bernando Blanco to Ed McDonald, May 9, 1955, ibid.

58. For example, in 1959, 3,642 housing inspections found 1,364 violations. BES, Report of Operations, 1960, 1. On food complaints, FSA Ventura office, farm visit report, Fillmore Lemon Association at Fillmore, August 21, 1943; idem, farm visit report, Tapo Citrus Association at Simi, August 24, 1943, file 8-G16, box 71, FHA; letter, E. Ruiz Russek to Earl Williams, August 5, 1943, file 7.3, box 70, FHA.

59. Final Joint Determination, M. de J. C., October 5, 1959, file Joint Determinations 1959, box 4, FHA; memorandum, William Tolbert to William Anglim, October 8, 1943, file 8-G16, box 71, FHA; BES, "Report on Operations." See also handwritten note, "no contracts terminated this year [1955] due to contract violations in connection with underpayment," in M. Mason, "Inspection Report Agricultural Labor Program," file 56364/42.43, part 1, box 87, accession 59A2038, INS.

60. Memorandum, H. R. Zamora to A. J. Norton re: televised news report on Mexican National Labor Program, August 10, 1956, attachment no. 1 to "A Report on Strangers in Our Fields," file *Ernesto Galarza v. DiGiorgio Corp.*, box 13, DOL Solicitor's Office files.

61. Calavita, *Inside the State*, 117–18; memorandum, Charles Kelley to Harold Nystrom, "Investigation of Mexican Labor Program," November 20, 1959, 3, 12, file Federal Investigation of Mexican Farm Labor Program, 1959–1960, box 9, DOL So-

licitor's Office files; Arevalo quoted in Rubén Salazar, *Border Correspondent: Selected Writings 1955–1970* (Berkeley: University of California Press, 1995), 140.

62. Erasmo Gamboa, for example, wrote, "In spite of the fact that the contract was explained to [the braceros] before they affixed their signatures, most of the men did not have a rudimentary understanding of the terms and conditions. The whole idea that a young person from a tiny community in [Mexico] could comprehend the meaning was farfetched." Cited by Calavita, *Inside the State*, 20.

63. "Introductory statement" with seal of Ministry of Foreign Relations, dated August 22, 1952, (translated from Spanish), file 56321/448C, box 3298, accession 58A734, INS; Deborah Cohen, "Masculine Sweat, Stoop-Labor Modernity: Gender, Race, and Nation in Mid-Twentieth-Century Mexico and the U.S." (Ph.D. dissertation, University of Chicago, 2001), 241–92; Eldridge, "Helping Hands from Mexico," 63.

64. Clipping of article from *La Prensa*, November 14, 1942 (translation), in file 55854/100-I, INS; FSA farm visit report, Fillmore Lemon Association camp, August 21, 1943.

65. "Migratory Labor in American Agriculture," 45; sundry correspondence, William Tolbert to William Anglim, [1943], file 8-G16, box 71, FHA. According to some scholars, the consuls did not always defend the interests of Mexican migrants in the United States. For example, during the 1930s consular officials encouraged repatriation and at times intervened in labor disputes in order to undermine local unionizing efforts by Mexican Americans. See Gilbert Gonzalez, *Mexican Consuls and Labor Organizing: Imperial Politics in the American Southwest* (Austin: University of Texas Press, 1999), passim; Weber, *Black Sweat, White Gold*, 148, 210; for a more positive account, see Francisco Balderrama, *In Defense of La Raza: The Los Angeles Mexican Consulate and the Mexican Community 1929–1936* (Tucson: University of Arizona Press, 1982). The mixed record of the consuls is understandable in the context of their general function as representatives of the Mexican national state, its ruling party, and its policy and organizational interests.

66. Robert C. Jones, "Mexico–United States Agricultural Labor Recruitment Program and Its Operation, Staff Study no. 1," December 15, 1950, PCML/HST; [United States Department of State], memorandum of conversation, "Bracero Agreement Preparations," August 28, 1952, file Mexican Labor, folder 2, Papers of David Stowe, HST; letter, Michael Gavin to Undersecretary of State, July 11, 1952, ibid.; memorandum of conversation, [United States Ambassador to Mexico] O'Dwyer, Paul Culbertson, and Thomas Mann, August 19, 1952, ibid.

67. State Department telegram no. 1855, for Mann and Neal from Blocker, June 27, 1952, file 56321/448C, ibid.; telegram no. 228, for [William] Belton from Blocker, July 31, 1952, Ibid; United States Department of State telegram no. 513, White to Secretary of State, November 5, 1953, file 56321/448D, ibid.

68. Amendments and Joint Interpretations of the Migrant Labor Agreement of 1951, as amended, approved by the United States and Mexico, March 10, 1954, file 5636443.38, part 2, box 98, accession 59A2038, INS; telegram, Robert Goodwin to Regional Directors BES, March 10, 1954, file Mexican farm labor program, box 1, FHA; W. K. Aishlie, "Braceros: Mexico Desires That American Employers Be Discouraged from Coming to Mexico to Recruit Agricultural Workers," State Department Dispatch no. 1711, February 6, 1953, file 56321/448C, box 3298, accession 58A734,

INS. On recontracting as permanent emigration, see I. F. Shrode, memorandum for file, May 1, 1956, file 56364/43.38, part 2, box 98, accession 59A2038, INS. On Mexico's construction of braceros as ambassadors of modernity, see Deborah Cohen, "Masculine Sweat and Stoop Labor Modernity," passim.

69. Sundry reports by Clyde Cross to officer in charge, New Orleans, LA, 1949, file 56246/339D, box 3055 and file 56246/339F, box 3056, accession 58A734, INS.

70. "U.S. Farms Breed Wetbacks," *Washington Daily News*, November 19, 1956, file Mexican Labor Program, 1956, box 140, Secretary of Labor files.

71. Statements of R.V.L., A.O.G., P.C.S.

72. Letter, Matias Covarrubias to Susano Sota, censorship report, October 29, 1942, file 55854/100-H, entry 9, INS; I. F. Wixon to Assistant Commissioner for Inspection, February 25, 1943, file 55854/100-I, ibid; letter, John M. McCollough to John Lehmann, February 8, 1954, file 56353/110, box 3387, accession 58A734, INS; memorandum, J. W. Holland to A. C. Devaney, December 12, 1953, file 56353/110, box 3387, accession 58A734, INS.

73. Typescript, "Agricultural Labor Program," April 4, 1951, file 56321/448, box 3298, accession 58A734, INS. According to these estimates, of 93,340 braceros imported, some 9,220 deserted. Desertion rates were highest in the Los Angeles district (11.9 percent) and in El Paso (9.5 percent). Typescript, "Sample Survey of Skips Reported by Employers, July 1, 1951 to July 1, 1953," file 56353/110, box 3387, accession 58A734, INS; typescript, "CC Discussion," [n.a.], August 13, 1954, file 56364/43.38, part 1, box 98, accession 59A2038, INS; memorandum, E. DeWitt Marshall to William P. Snow, September 1, 1954, ibid.; letter, E. DeWitt Marshall to Lic. Gustavo Diaz Ordaz, September 10, 1954, file 56321/448G, box 3299, accession 58A734, INS. For example, the president of the American Agricultural Council told an embassy official, "McAllen Fruit and Vegetable Co. lost 31 out of 100 within 20 days; Mr. W. of Raymondville 24 out of 50 left within a few days; C. J., Lyford, 24 out of 30 left 'right away'," and so on. See Marshall to Snow, September 1, 1954.

74. Memorandum, District Director, Los Angeles, to INS Commissioner, Washington, D.C., November 2, 1953, file 56353/110, box 3387, accession 58A734, INS; memorandum, Jackson to District Director, San Francisco, February 2, 1943, file 55854/100-I, entry 9, INS; memorandum, District Director, Los Angeles, to INS Commissioner, Washington, D.C., November 2, 1953, file 56353/110, box 3387, accession 58A734, INS.

75. Saunders and Leonard, *The Wetback in the Lower Rio Grande Valley*, 42–44.

76. Pauline Kibbe, "Report to Good Neighbor Commission of Texas," in Nellie W. Kingrea, *History of the First Ten Years of the Texas Good Neighbor Commission* (Fort Worth, TX: Texas Christian University Press, 1954), 68; typescript, "Report on [INS–State Department] Meeting on Mexican Laborers," August 13, 1954, 5, file 56321/448F, box 3299, accession 58A734, INS.

77. Report, Willard Kelly, "The Wetback Issue," 2, December 15, 1953, file 56321/448D, box 3298, accession 58A734, INS; memorandum, Marcus T. Neelly to A. C. Devaney, August 24, 1954, file 56321/448F, box 3299, accession 58A734, INS.

78. Typescript report, Don C. Bitler to Herbert Brownell, Jr., "re: Wetback Mexican Problems in California," August 27, 1953, file 56364/45.7, box 104, accession 59A2048, INS; Henry P. Anderson, *A Harvest of Loneliness: An Inquiry into a Social Problem* (Berkeley: Citizens for Farm Labor, 1964), 301–2; Guerin Gonzalez, *Mexican Workers and American Dreams*, 135–36.

79. Saunders and Leonard, *The Wetback in the Lower Rio Grande Valley*, 70; "Mexicans Convert Border into Sieve," *New York Times*, March 27, 1950, 11.

80. Saunders and Leonard, *The Wetback in the Lower Rio Grande Valley*, 34, 61; Kibbe, "Report to Good Neighbor Commission of Texas;" memorandum, Marcus Neelly to Frank Patridge, July 8, 1954, file 56321/448F, box 3299, accession 58A734, INS. Saunders and Leonard, *The Wetback in the Lower Rio Grande Valley*, 61, 57; letter, Jesus Clemente to Harry S. Truman, June 15, 1950, Official File (hereafter OF/HST).

81. Memorandum, David Carnahan to Assistant Commissioner, Examinations Division, "re: Extensions of Bracero Contracts and Form I-100 Contracts," February 27, 1957, file 56364/42.43, part 1, box 87, accession 59A2038, INS; memorandum, Oran Pugh to Charles Kirk, October 27, 1954, file 56364/43.36, part 1, box 39, ibid.; N. D. Collaer to Watson Miller, January 12, 1949, file 56246/339D, box 3055, ibid.

82. Memorandum, Joseph Minton to A. C. Devaney, April 13, 1953, file 56321/448C, box 3298, accession 58A734, INS.

83. Transcript, interview with M.M.A. by Joseph Hunt, April 16, 1955; file 56364/42.43, part 1, box 87, accession 59A2038, INS; report, Joseph Hunt, "Apprehension of Wetbacks on C—— Farm, Rio Hondo, Texas," April 21, 1955, ibid. Names here and in following paragraphs are pseudonyms.

84. Untitled report, Buck West, April 12, 1955, file 56364/42.43, part 1, box 87, accession 59A2038, INS; memorandum, John Swanson to Harlon B. Carter, August 12, 1955, file 56364/42.43, part 2, ibid.; Robert C. Jones, "Mexico-United States Agricultural Labor Recruitment and its Operation, Staff Study No. 1," December 15, 1950, file staff studies, PCML, HST; "County Bar Unit Will Study Rights of Illegal Aliens," *Sacremento Bee*, April 8, 1954, in file 56364/43.38, part 1, box 98, accession 59A2038, INS. On braceros' relationships with local Mexican American women and the anxieties these generated within the community, see Matt García, *A World of Its Own: Race, Labor, and Citrus in the Making of Greater Los Angeles, 1900–1970* (Chapel Hill: University of North Carolina Press, 2001), chapter 6. The difficulty in gauging the prevalence of family migration and settlement among braceros is compounded by the braceros' own silence. Most did not want to call attention to their former status as braceros, in order to avoid deportation and also because the braceros remained stigmatized in the Mexican American community. Nevertheless a few scholars have located and interviewed former braceros living in the United States. See Maria Herrera-Sobek, *The Bracero Experience*; Matt García, *A World of Its Own*; Ronald L. Mize, "The Invisible Workers: Articulations of Race and Class in the Life Histories of Braceros," (Ph.D. dissertation, University of Wisconsin-Madison, 2000).

85. Transcripts of INS interviews with R.C.G., January 30, 1955, file 56364/42.34, part 1, box 87, accession 59A2038, INS; C.V.deC., January 31, 1955, ibid.; P.V.R., January 31, 1955, ibid. Neither Ramón nor Célia was literate; Ramón dictated the letter to a friend, and another friend read it to Célia.

86. These "wet" maids were of no small concern to the INS, and the agency worked extensively to track them down. One memo reported eighteen "illegal alien maids" arrested in one neighborhood in El Centro, CA. See memorandum for file, re: Complaint of W.H.R., January 17, 1956, file 56346/41.11, part 2, box 85, accession 59A2038, INS. It should be noted that the complaint by W. R. that led to this memo asserted that zealous INS agents had, while nobody in his house was home, come onto his property and interrogated his maid, who lived in a detached structure in the

back. The maid, as the INS discovered, was a native Californian, who had "proper identification papers with her at all times." This did not deter a different set of INS agents from returning the next month on the same errand. See W.H.R. to Attorney General Herbert Brownell, January, 1956, ibid.

87. Memorandum, James Sundquist to Roger Jones, March 30, 1950, OF/HST; circular, District Director El Paso, "Service Policy in the Matter of Handling Deportable Alien Farm Laborers This Year," April 12, 1948, file 56246/339A, box 3055, accession 58A734, INS. On deportation policy in the 1920s and 1930s, see chapter 2.

88. For example, see memorandum, A. J. Norton to Anthony Figueroa, "Imperial Valley Farmers, Apprehensions of Illegal Aliens," January 21, 1953, file Mexican Labor Program, General Correspondence, 1950–54, box 2, FHA; letter, Sen. Clinton P. Anderson to Harry S. Truman, August 24, 1949, OF/HST; memorandum, E. DeWitt Marshall to William P. Snow, September 1, 1954, file 56364/43.38, part 1, box 98, accession 59A2038, INS; "Petition for 120-Day Moratorium on Deportation of Cotton-Picking Mexican Laborers," June 21, 1951, OF/HST.

89. Report, "Future of Program," November 1954, 4–5, file 56321/448H, box 3299, accession 58A734, INS; Sen. Clinton P. Anderson to Harry S. Truman, Aug. 24, 1949; "Employers Input to Policy," September 20, 1954, file 56321/448G, box 3299, accession 58A734, INS; memorandum, L. W. Williams to R. L. Williams and Paul Lindsay, November 15, 1954, file 56321/448H, ibid.

90. Calavita, *Inside the State*, 35; typescript, "Administrative Reforms in the Immigration and Naturalization Service," n.a., [1956], 4, file CO659P, Subject Files of U.S.-I.N.S., United States Immigration and Naturalization Service, Central Office, Washington, D.C. (hereafter "INS-CO"); memorandum of telephone conversation with [Willard] Kelly, July 11, 1951, file 56321/448, box 3298, accession 58A734, INS; "The Russian Method!" *Gilroy (California) Dispatch*, September 17, 1953, file 56346/41.11, box 85, accession 59A2038, INS; letter, Noel Carroll to INS, July 29, 1953, ibid.; Resolution, House of Delegates, American Farm Federation, December 13, 1951, file 56321/448A, box 3298, accession 58A34, INS.

91. David K. Niles, memorandum for the president, June 8, 1949, file 407-D, OF/HST; Calavita, *Inside the State*, 28–30; memorandum, R. H. Robinson to A. R. Mackey, July 25, 1949 file 56246/339F, box 3056, accession 58A734, INS; on legalization of workers in Texas, see Robert C. Jones, "Mexico-U.S. Agricultural Labor Recruitment and Its Operation, Staff Study No. 1," December 15, 1950, PCML/HST; Garcia y Griego, "Importation of Mexican Contract Workers," 65; telegraph, W. K. Aishlie, State Deptartment dispatch no. 1711, February 6, 1953, file 56321/448C, box 3298, accession 58A734, INS.

92. Memorandum, A. J. Norton to Glenn Brockway, January 28, 1954, file Mexican Farm Labor Program 1954, box 1, FHA. On 1948 and 1954 border incidents, see also Calavita, *Inside the State*, 29–30; Garcia y Griego, "Importation of Mexican Contract Workers to the U.S.," 68–73.

93. Telegram, Baxter Loveland to INS, September 10, 1953, file 56321/448D, box 3298, accession 58A734, INS; "Valley Chamber Moves to Legalize Workers," *San Antonio Express*, May 7, 1949; "Labor Free Zone Called Solution on Wetbacks," *San Antonio Evening News*, July 2, 1949, both clippings in file 56246/339F, box 3056, accession 58A734, INS; letter, Charles Leicester to Argyle Mackey, September 1953, file 56321/448D, box 3298, accession 58A734, INS; W. A. Carmichael to Officer in

Charge, San Diego, July 15, 1949, file 56246/339F, box 3056, accession 58A734, INS; R. H. Robinson to A. R. Mackey, July 25, 1949, ibid.

94. Memorandum, E. DeWitt Marshall to William P. Snow, September 1, 1954, file 56364/43.38, part 1, box 98, accession 59A2038, INS. On Swing's background, see interview with Joseph Swing by Ed Edwin, June 21, 1964, Eisenhower Administration Oral History Project, Columbia University.

95. Minutes, meeting of Joint Migratory Labor Commission, September 16, 1954, file 56321/448G, box 3299, acccession 58A734, INS; letter, Joseph Swing to Joe M. Kilgore, May 24, 1955, file 56321/448I, ibid.; typescript, "Notes of Discussion at [INS] Conference Relating to Braceros," n.a., May 17, 1955, file 56364/42.43, part 1, box 87, accession 59A2038, INS; report, Joseph Swing to Harold Cooley, [March] 1956, file 56364/42.43, part 2, box 87, accession 59A2038, INS; Kelley to Nystrom, "Investigation of Mexican Labor Program," 10; typescript, Regional Foreign Labor Operators Advisory Committee, meeting no. 9, March 22, 1956, file BES/FLOAC 1954–58, part 4, box 2, FHA.

96. Regional Foreign Labor Operators Advisory Committee, March 22, 1956. In May 1955 USES rejected ninety out of ninety-three "returning" workers at Calexico and thirty-nine out of forty-three "specials" whom farmers had called up at San Diego. When USES ceased screening specials, the INS "began screaming" and took over the contract process itself. Memorandum, L. E. Gowen to Mr. Hennessy, June 7, 1955, file 56321/448I, box 3299, accession 58A734, INS; BES, Report on Operations.

97. "Administrative Reforms in the Immigration and Naturalization Service," 4; typescript, Joseph Swing, Report to the American Section of the Joint Commission on Mexican Migrant Labor, September 3, 1954, 3, file CO629P, INS-CO; typescript, "Notes on [INS–State Department] Meeting on Mexican Laborers," August 13, 1954, 2, file 56321/448F, box 3299, accession 58A734, INS. Harlon Carter, chief of the Border Patrol, reported that the Canadian border was left with only a "sustaining force."

98. "Administrative Reforms in the Immigration and Naturalization Service," 4–5; Oran Pugh to Charles Kirk, October 27, 1954, file 56364/43.36, part 1, box 39, accession 59A32038, INS; Thomas C. Langham, "Federal Regulation of Border Labor: Operation Wetback and the Wetback Bills," *Journal of Borderlands Studies* 7 no. 1 (Spring 1992): 81–91. A Mexican newspaper reported that a group of eight hundred deportees arriving in Vera Cruz from the "central part of the U.S." were well dressed and prosperous, bringing with them ten tons of baggage and $17,500 cash (250,000 pesos). *El Dictamen* (Vera Cruz), October 12, 1954 (translation), file 56364/43.36, part 1, box 98, accession 59A2038, INS.

99. "Administrative Reforms in the Immigration and Naturalization Service," 4–5; minutes, meeting of American section, Joint Migratory Labor Commission, September 10–11, 1954, file 56321/448G, box 3299, accession 58A734, INS. Apprehensions for 1947, 1948, and 1949 totaled 337,328. Memorandum, N. D. Collaer to W. B. Miller, "Aliens Apprehended by Border Patrol," January 11, 1949, file 56246/339D, box 3055, accession 58A734, INS.

100. Joseph Swing to Harold Cooley, [March] 1956, file 56364/42.43, part 2, box 87, accession 59A2038, INS. The INS said it could not find a shipping line with cargo ships equipped with bunks or hammocks for eight hundred to one thousand passengers. It also considered using a Landing Ship Tank, in mothballs since World War II, and a naval

training ship, but neither was appropriate for the task. Typescript report, n.a., [November 1956]. See memoranda, R. A. Vielhaber to James Hennessey, November 2, 1956; R. W. Doerner to E. A. Loughran, March 11, 1957, file 56364/46.36, part 2, box 98, accession 59A2038, INS; on "operation boatlift," see typescript, n.a., August 28, 1956, and memorandum, Swing to Attorney General, [1956], ibid. Swing stopped using the *Mercurio*, but he defended the INS's practices, claiming that all the ships it used were seaworthy and inspected to the satisfaction of Mexican consuls.

101. Testimony of Milton Plumb before House Committee on Agriculture, March 22, 1955, file Wetbacks, 1948–49, box 45, Sánchez Papers.

102. "Administrative Reforms in the Immigration and Naturalization Service," 6; minutes, Meeting of Joint Migratory Labor Commission, September 16, 1954, file 56321/448G, box 3299, accession 58A734, INS; Texas CIO, Report of Committee on Latin American Affairs, September 17, 1955, Sánchez Papers; notes on [INS–State Department] meeting on Mexican laborers, August 13, 1954, 3, file 56321/448F, box 3299, accession 58A734, INS.

103. "Report on [INS-State Department] Meeting on Mexican Laborers," August 13, 1954, 5.

104. Typescript, Border Patrol Program Data, February 13, 1961, file CO659P, part 2, INS-CO; mimeographed circular, Enforcement Division, Central Office, "Operating Procedures," March 30, 1962, ibid.; report, Louis Cates, "Analysis, Control of the Borders, First Half FY 1963," file CO659P, part 3, INS-CO.

105. Eight percent of cotton was harvested mechanically in 1951, compared to 78 percent in 1964. See Calavita, *Inside the State*, 143–44.

106. Salazar, *Border Correspondent*, 139; Saunders and Leonard, *The Wetback in the Rio Grande Valley*, 61–64; José Angel Gutiérrez, *The Making of a Chicano Militant: Lessons from Cristal* (Madison: University of Wisconsin Press, 1998), 22; Martha Menchaca, *The Mexican Outsiders: A Community History of Marginalization and Discrimination in California* (Austin: University of Texas Press, 1998), 98. See also Henry P. Anderson, *A Harvest of Loneliness*, 293–94.

107. Garcia, *A World of Its Own*, 177–82; Maria Herrera-Sobek, "An Oral History Interview with a Composite Bracero," in *The Bracero Experience*, 65.

108. Gonzalez cited by Salazar, *Border Correspondent*, 134.

109. Interview with president of Community Service Organization, June 28, 1957, cited in Henry P. Anderson, *A Harvest of Loneliness*, 662.

110. Memorandum, Byron Mitchell to J. Otis Garber, "Immigration from Mexico," December 31, 1948, file Mexican Labor, David Stowe Papers, HST.

111. Letter, Ernest Zepeda to Pres. Eisenhower, Senators Lyndon Johnson, William Knowland, Wayne Morse, and Rep. Paul Kilday, April 6, 1955, file 56321/448-I, box 3299, accession 58A734, INS. Emphasis in original. See also Salazar, "Braceros Guaranteed More than Domestics" (October 22, 1963), in *Border Correspondent*, 136–38.

112. LULAC telegram to President Truman, Attorney General Tom Clark, and Rep. Dennis Chavez, cited in circular to LULAC Councils, October 18, 1948, file LULAC, correspondence, 1941–43, box 31, Sánchez Papers; "Memorandum from a Committee Representing the Workers of the Lower Rio Grande Valley of Texas," [November 1949], file Wetbacks, Philleo Nash Papers, HST.

113. R. A. Cortez, Gus Garcia, and George I. Sánchez, "The 'Wetback' Problem of the Southwest," January 27, 1949, file Wetbacks, Philleo Nash Papers, HST.

114. Telegram, LULAC Council 160 to Harry S. Truman, October 22, 1948, file 407-D, OF/HST; American GI Forum of Texas, *What Price Wetbacks?* 38.

115. Typescript testimony, F. Ferree, "Mexican Alien Families with American-born Children," August 1, 1950, PCML/HST; report, Texas CIO Committee on Latin American Affairs, September 17, 1955, file Wetbacks, 1955–1956, box 45, Sánchez Papers.

116. Hank Hasiwar, "Report on the Imperial Valley," January 30, 1950, 7, file 407-D, OF/HST; mimeograph, "The Voice of the Disinherited," [1959], file 10, box 54, RG 28-002, AFL-CIO; memorandum, National Farm Labor Union AFL, "The Wetback Strike," [1951], file 2, box 1, RG 1-027, AFL-CIO; International Conference of Trade Unions of Mexico and the United States, Resolutions, December 14–16, 1953, file Mexican Labor, box 54, Secretary of Labor files; "The Problem of the Wetback," *El Diario* (Nuevo Laredo, Mexico) (translation), December 14, 1953, in file 56321/448C, box 3298, accession 58A734, INS.

117. Memorandum, Byron Mitchell to J. Otis Garber, December 31, 1948; letter, Ernesto Galarza to Serafino Romualdi, May 9, 1955, file 6, box 1, RG 1-027, AFL-CIO; Henry P. Anderson, "Statement relative to the proposed extension of PL 78," February 27, 1961, file 10, box 19, ibid.; "U.S. Farms Breed Wetbacks," *Washington Daily News*, November 19, 1956, file Mexican Labor Program 1956, box 140, Secretary of Labor files; Arnold Mayer, "Grapes of Wrath, Vintage 1961," *Reporter*, February 2, 1961; CBS television broadcast, "Farm Labor Exposé," cited H. R. Zamora to A. J. Norton, August 10, 1956, file *Galarza v. DiGiorgio*, box 13, DOL Solicitor's files. See also Truman Moore, *The Slaves We Rent* (New York: Random House, 1965).

118. Letter, Ernesto Galarza to Anthony Figueroa, [1953], file Mexican Labor Program, General Correspondence 1950–1954, box 2, FHA; letter, Walter Simcich to Glenn Brockway, re: CIO proposals to USES on bracero program, February 2, 1955, file Mexican Labor Program, General Correspondence 1954–1960/1, box 3, FHA; Stephen Pitti, *The Devil in Silicon Valley: Northern California, Race, and Mexican Americans* (Princeton: Princeton University Press, 2003), 141–44.

119. Memoranda, T. L. Ball to Charles Kirk, October 1, 1954, file 56354/43.48, part 1, box 98, accession 59A2038, INS; S. Romualdi to George Meany, June 28, 1954, file 5, box 1, RG 1-027, AFL-CIO.

120. Ernesto Galarza to Anthony Figueroa, [1953]; Walter Simcich to Glenn Brockway, February 2, 1955; letter, Lloyd Mashburn to William Knowland, May 20, 1953, file Special Problems 1953–60, Interpretation of Article 21, box 9, DOL Solicitor's files; Kenneth Robertson to Albert Misler, June 10, 1953, ibid.

121. Memoranda, Edwin Hoard to Edward Rudnick, September 4, 1956, file 56364/42.43, part 1, box 87, accession 59A2038, INS; Ernesto Galarza to Serafino Romualdi, May 9, 1955; John Barnes, INS Report of Investigation, August 22, 1956, file 56364/42.43, part 1, box 87, accession 59A2038, INS; memorandum, F. C. Chenaldt to Commissioner, October 12, 1958, ibid. Galarza communicated with the *Alianza*, but the collaboration came to little, reflecting both parties' organizational weaknesses. Pitti, *The Devil in Silicon Valley,* 144.

122. Memorandum, Ernesto Galarza to Serafino Romualdi, May 9, 1955. The conflict between the CIO and NAWU had a long history, which dated back to Southern Tenant Farmers Union's withdrawal from the CIO in 1939 after disputes between Mitchell, a Socialist Party member, and Communist Party sympathizers in the

CIO leadership. See "The Voice of the Disinherited, a Brief History of the Agricultural Workers Union, 1934–1959," [1959], file 10, box 54, Organizing Department Records, RG 1–028, AFL-CIO.

123. Kevin J. Middlebrook, *The Paradox of Revolution: Labor, the State, and Authoritarianism in Mexico* (Baltimore: Johns Hopkins University Press, 1995), 91–92.

124. Ernesto Galarza, *Strangers in Our Fields* (Washington, DC: Fund for the Republic, 1956); idem, *Merchants of Labor*. On NAWU's "single-minded" pursuit to terminate the bracero program, see Majka and Majka, *Farm Workers, Agribusinrss, and the State*, 149.

125. Unsigned typescript, "Meeting among Fidel Velazquez, General Secretary of CTM, H. L. Mitchell, Pres. NAWU, and Serafino Romualdi, Latin Amererican Rep. AFL," August 3, 1953, file 6, box 1, RG 1-027, AFL-CIO; International Conference of Trade Unions of Mexico and the U.S., Resolutions, December 14–16, 1953, file Mexican Labor Program, Miscellaneous 1954, box 54, Secretary of Labor files; memorandum, Walter Simcich to Glenn Brockway, February 2, 1955; memorandum, National Agricultural Workers Union to Executive Council, AFL-CIO, "An Organizing Campaign in Agriculture," [1956], 2, file 6, box 1, RG 1-027, AFL-CIO.

126. J. Craig Jenkins, *The Politics of Insurgency: The Farm Worker Movement in the 1960s* (New York: Columbia University Press, 1985), 120; DOL Solicitor William S. Tyson, cited in memorandum, V. H. Blocker to State Department, May 25, 1951, file Mexican Labor Program 1951, box 83, Secretary of Labor files. During the 1951 NAWU strike in the Imperial Valley, Tyson warned against acceding to strike demands for removal of braceros. Farms could be disrupted everywhere if USES moved braceros each time a local group protested, he wrote.

127. "Labor," *Fortune* 60, no. 5 (November 1959): 274–75, at 275; table, "1961 California Agricultural Labor Disputes (as of March 1)," file *Crosetti v. Brockway*, box 17, DOL Solicitor's files; "California: Tossed Salad," *Newsweek*, February 20, 1961, 26. AWOC took credit for reducing the number of braceros in California by twenty thousand, but this included more than strike-related removals. See pamphlet, "AWOC and You," [1961], file ES 2-6-1, box 55, Secretary of Labor files; Jenkins, *Politics of Insurgency*, 126. See also Calavita, *Inside the State*, 122–26.

128. "Call from Merle Grimm to M. P. McCaffrey," August 1, 1960, file *DiGiorgio Fruit Corp. v. California Department of Employment*, box 3, DOL Solicitor's files; "Judge Balks at Ordering Bracero Use," *San Francisco Chronicle*, August 7, 1960, file State Courts-Tom Bowers, part 1, box 9, DOL Solicitor's files.

129. Jenkins, *Politics of Insurgency*, 125–27; *Newsweek*, February 20, 1961, 26. On demonstrations at housing camps, file 1961 Labor Disputes, box 14, FHA.

130. Jenkins, *Politics of Insurgency*, 118–19, 128–30.

131. Letter, Jerry Holleman to Jack Livingston, February 2, 1960, file 11, box 18, RG 1-27, AFL-CIO.

132. William P. Jones, "Race, Proletarianization, the Industrial Unionism in the Southern Lumber Industry, 1929–1938," paper presented at Newberry Labor History Seminar, Chicago, October 11, 2002; Nell Irvin Painter, *The Narrative of Hosea Hudson: His Life as a Negro Communist in the South* (Cambridge, MA: Harvard University Press, 1979). On H. L. Mitchell's roots in the Southern Tenant Farmers Union and Socialist Party, see Robin D. G. Kelley, *Hammer and Hoe: Alabama Communists during the Great Depression* (Chapel Hill: University of North Carolina Press, 1990), 164, 169–70, 187–88.

133. Majka and Majka, *Farm Workers, Agribusiness, and the State*, 159.

134. Memorandum, H. R. Zamora to A. N. Norton, re: Televised News Report on Mexican National Labor Program, August 10, 1956, file *Ernesto Galarza v. DiGiorgio Corp.*, box 13, DOL Solicitor's Office Files; Region X, BES, "A Report on 'Strangers in Our Fields,'" ibid.; Andrew Biemiller, Statement before House Subcommittee on Equipment, Supplies, and Manpower, March 24, 1960, 3, file 9, box 19, RG 1-027, AFL-CIO. On the DiGiorgio strike, see Ernesto Galarza, *Spiders in the House and Workers in the Field* (Notre Dame: University of Notre Dame Press, 1970).

135. Calavita, *Inside the State*, 143–44; "Machines Take Over 'Bracero' Job," *Business Week*, January 8, 1966, 108–10.

136. For example, the President's Commission on Migratory Labor recommended minimum-wage legislation for farmworkers in 1950. "Migratory Labor in American Agriculture," 182. The commission also considered, but did not ultimately recommend, additional reforms to improve the condition of migratory farmworkers, including coverage under the Social Security Act, collective bargaining rights, housing and transportation standards, licensing of labor contractors, prohibition on use of child labor, occupational training, public relief, and education, civil rights, and recreational programs. See Notes of Executive Session of the President's Commission on Migratory Labor, Detroit, September 14–16, 1950, file Records of Executive Sessions, August to December 1950, PCML/HST. Similarly the National Sharecroppers Fund's legislative program included extending the Fair Labor Standards Act to farm workers and the right to organize. See Bennett, "The Condition of Farm Workers in 1955." The AFL-CIO was also on record as supporting labor and social legislation for farmworkers. See statements by James Carey, William Schnitzler, and Katherine Ellickson, Public Hearings on Farm Labor, Conference of National Advisory Committee on Farm Labor, February 5, 1959, file BES National Conference on Farm Labor Services, box 2, FHA.

Part III
War, Nationalism, and Alien Citizenship

1. On the importance of U.S. wars in East Asia and the Pacific for the legal and social construction of Asian Americans as a racial other, see Lisa Lowe, *Immigrant Acts: On Asian American Cultural Politics* (Durham: Duke University Press 1996), 4–6.

2. On Chinese and Japanese exclusion, see, generally, Sucheng Chan, ed., *Entry Denied: Exclusion and the Chinese Community in America, 1882–1943* (Philadelphia: Temple University Press, 1991); Alexander Saxton, *The Indispensable Enemy: Labor and the Anti-Chinese Movement in California* (Berkeley: University of California Press, 1971), and idem, *The Rise and Fall of the White Republic: Class Politics and Mass Culture in Nineteenth-Century America* (New York: Verso, 1990); Roger Daniels, *The Politics of Prejudice: The Anti-Japanese Movement and Japanese Exclusion* (Berkeley: University of California Press, 1962); Yuji Ichioka, *The Issei: The World of First Generation Japanese Immigrants* (New York: Free Press, 1988), 176–254.

3. See chapter 1.

4. For example, see Matthew Jacobson, *Special Sorrows: The Diasporic Imagination of Irish, Polish, and Jewish Immigrants in the United States* (Cambridge, MA, Harvard University Press, 1995); Judy Yung, *Unbound Feet: A Social History of Chinese Women*

in San Francisco (Berkeley: University of California Press, 1995); Wayne Patterson, *The Korean Frontier in America: Immigration to Hawai'i* (Honolulu: University of Hawai'i Press, 1988); Joan Jensen, *Passage from India: Asian Indian Immigrants in North America* (New Haven: Yale University Press, 1988).

5. David Montgomery, "Nationalism, American Patriotism, and Class Consciousness among Immigrant Workers in the U.S. in the Epoch of World War I," in *Struggle a Hard Battle: Essays on Working Class Immigrants*, ed. Dirk Hoerder (DeKalb, IL: Northern Illinois University Press, 1986), 327–51; see also Jacobson, *Special Sorrows*, 41–52.

6. Jacobson, *Special Sorrows*, 217–43; Benedict Anderson, *Imagined Communities: Reflections on the Origin and Spread of Nationalism* (London: Verso, 1991 [1983]), 187–99. See also Wei-Ming Tu, ed., *The Living Tree: The Changing Meaning of Being Chinese Today* (Stanford: Stanford University Press, 1994); Aihwa Ong, *Flexible Citizenship: The Cultural Logics of Transnationality* (Durham: Duke University Press, 1999); 55–57.

7. William Preston, Jr., *Aliens and Dissenters: Federal Suppression of Radicals 1903–1933* (Cambridge: Harvard University Press, 1963); Kevin Kenny, *Making Sense of the Molly Maguires* (New York: Oxford University Press, 1998); Melvin Dubofsky, *We Shall Be All: A History of the Industrial Workers of the World* (Urbana, IL: University of Illinois Press, 1988).

8. Anderson, *Imagined Communities*, 141–54. See also John Dower, *War without Mercy: Race and Power in the Pacific War* (New York: Pantheon, 1986).

9. Jack Foner, *Blacks and the Military in American History* (New York: Praeger, 1974); Phillip McGuire, *Taps for Jim Crow: Letters from Black Soldiers in World War II* (Santa Barbara, CA: ABC-Clio, 1983).

10. Frederick C. Luebke, *Bonds of Loyalty: German-Americans and World War I* (DeKalb, IL: Northern Illinois University Press, 1971), 204–5.

11. John Higham, *Strangers in the Land: Patterns of American Nativism, 1850–1924* (New Brunswick, NJ: Rutgers University Press, 1985 [1955]), 207–17; Luebke, *Bonds of Loyalty*, 83–111, 267, 311.

12. Him Mark Lai, "To Bring Forth a New China, to Build a Better America: The Chinese Marxist Left in America to the 1960s," *Chinese America: History and Perspectives* 8 (1992). See also Adam McKeown, *Chinese Migrant Networks and Cultural Change* (Chicago: University of Chicago Press, 2001), 92–97.

13. Him Mark Lai, "The Kuomintang in Chinese American Communities Before World War II," in Chan, *Entry Denied*, 185–88; Ichioka, *The Issei*, 157–63; Brian Hayashi, "Transcending Nationalism: Koreans and Japanese in California during World War II," paper presented to the Asian American Historians Symposium, Japanese American National Museum, Los Angeles, May 18, 2002, 12–14.

14. Eiichiro Azuma, "Racial Struggle, Immigrant Nationalism, and Ethnic Identity: Japanese and Filipinos in the California Delta," *Pacific Historical Review* 67 (1998): 166–68, 178.

15. Renqui Yu, *To Save China, To Save Ourselves: The Chinese Hand Laundry Alliance of New York* (Philadelphia: Temple University Press, 1992), 165; Yuji Ichioka, "Japanese Immigrant Nationalism: The Issei and the Sino-Japanese War, 1937–1941," *California History* (Fall 1990): 260–75; Eiichiro Azuma, "Interstitial Lives: Race, Community, and History among Japanese Immigrants Caught between Japan and the U.S., 1885–1941" (Ph.D. dissertation, UCLA, 2000), 319.

16. Azuma, "Interstitial Lives," chapter 7; Yuji Ichioka, "A Study in Dualism: James Yoshinori Sakamoto and the *Japanese American Courier*, 1928–1942," *Amerasia Journal* 13, no. 2 (1986–87): 49–81.

17. California Joint Immigration Committee, statement no. 448, "Statehood for Hawai'i," April 22, 1936, California Joint Immigration Committee, Bancroft Library, University of California, Berkeley. Japan automatically conferred citizenship upon those born in America to Japanese parents before 1924 and upon those born thereafter if the parents registered them with the Japan consul within fourteen days of birth. The United States does not recognize dual citizenship and as a practical matter it meant little to Nisei until the 1930s. In 1939–1940 the Hawai'ian-Japanese Civic Association gathered thirty thousand signatures on petitions to the U.S. State Department, asking it to negotiate with Japan easier procedures to relinquish the Japanese citizenship of dual citizens. I am grateful to Brian Niiya for bringing my attention to the petition campaign.

18. Azuma, "Interstitial Lives," 349.

19. Ichioka, "Study in Dualism," 70, 72–73.

Chapter Five
The World War II Internment of Japanese Americans and the Citizenship Renunciation Cases

1. Violet Kazue Matsuda De Christoforo, "There Is Always Tomorrow: An Anthology of Wartime Haiku," *Amerasia Journal* 19 (1993): 100.

2. In Hawai'i the government imposed martial law but did not evacuate Japanese Americans, owing to the large size of the Japanese American population and its centrality to the local labor force. However it sent 1,875 "dangerous" Japanese aliens and citizens to Department of Justice and WRA camps on the mainland. U.S. Commission on Wartime Evacuation and Relocation of Civilians, *Personal Justice Denied: Report of the Commission on Wartime Relocation and Internment of Civilians: Report for the Committee on Interior and Insular Affairs* (Washington, DC: GPO, 1983; reprint, Seattle: Civil Liberties Public Education Fund and University of Washington Press, 1997), 268–77.

3. In fact, as with all race classifications, it was not so easy to determine who was a person of "Japanese ancestry." A Catholic priest who ran an orphanage in Los Angeles inquired which children he should send—for he had under his charge some who were "half Japanese, others one-fourth or less"—and was told by Colonel Karl Bendesten, "If they have one drop of Japanese blood in them, they must go to camp." Father Hugh Lavery, quoted by Michi Weglyn, *Years of Infamy: The Untold Story of America's Concentration Camps* (New York: William Morrow, 1976), 76–77.

For general histories of internment, see *Personal Justice Denied*; Weglyn, *Years of Infamy*; Roger Daniels, *The Decision to Relocate Japanese Americans* (New York: Lippincott, 1975; idem, *Concentration Camps USA: Japanese Americans and World War II* (New York: Holt, Rinehart, and Winston, 1972).

4. Alien Enemy Act of 1798 (1 Stat. 577); *Personal Justice Denied*, 54–55, 286–88. In 1942 Attorney General Francis Biddle declassified Italians as "aliens of enemy nationality." German nationals were also deemed not to be a threat, despite the fact that as late as February 1939 the American Bund, which claimed 200,000 members, sponsored a pro-Hitler rally with 20,000 people in Madison Square Garden.

5. *Personal Justice Denied*, 60–63; Bob Kumamoto, "The Search for Spies: American Counterintelligence and the Japanese American Community, 1931–1942," *Amerasia Journal* 6, no. 2 (1979): 70–72.

6. Warren testimony at House Select Committee Investigating National Defense Migration hearings (Tolan Committee), quoted by David O'Brien and Stephen Fugita, *The Japanese American Experience* (Bloomington: University of Indiana Press, 1991), 47. As historian John Dower has shown, different racial policies also marked the United States' portrayal of the Axis enemies throughout the war: the government was careful to condemn the Nazi government and fascism and not the German people but made no such distinctions about "Japs." See John Dower, *War Without Mercy: Race and Power in the Pacific War* (New York: Pantheon, 1986), 8–11, 34–41.

7. *Personal Justice Denied*, 6, 85–88.

8. *Personal Justice Denied*, 87–88; Weglyn, *Years of Infamy*, 40–44. See also Greg Robinson, *By Order of the President: FDR and the Internment of Japanese Americans* (Cambridge, MA: Harvard University Press, 2001). The ONI report is widely cited as the principal evidence that the government knew that Japanese Americans were not disloyal. The report, however, is not without problems. Its conclusions derived in part from the lack of evidence of subversive activity but also from stereotypes about Japanese, i.e., that the Issei were passive, unsophisticated people and that the Nisei were pathetic, overly eager Americanizers.

9. Weglyn, *Years of Infamy*, 69. On citizens rights in the absence of martial law, see *Ex parte Milligan*, 71 U.S. 2 (1866). Some forty years after the internment, the U.S. government officially acknowledged that Executive Order 9066 "was not justified by military necessity and the decisions which followed from it . . . were not driven by analysis of military conditions. The broad historical causes which shaped these decisions were race prejudice, war hysteria and a failure of political leadership." Quoted in *Personal Justice Denied*, 18.

10. *Hirabayashi v. United States*, 320 U.S. 81 (1943); *Korematsu v. United States*, 323 U.S. 214 (1944). In 1987 federal courts vacated Hirabayashi and Korematsu's convictions in *corum nobis* decisions, after it came to light that the Justice Department was fully aware of reports contraindicating military necessity and deliberately covered up its knowledge when it prepared briefs for the cases in 1943. However, the courts did not redress the constitutionality of the curfew, exclusion, and evacuation held in the original decisions. See Peter Irons, *Justice at War* (New York: Oxford University Press, 1983) and idem, *Justice Delayed: The Record of Japanese American Internment Cases* (Middleton, CT: Wesleyan University Press, 1989).

11. *Personal Justice Denied*, 187. Two thousand Nisei serving in two infantry units in Hawai'i were not discharged but put in a segregated unit, even though they had defended Pearl Harbor. The segregated unit, the 100th Infantry Battalion, was transferred to mainland bases and eventually sent to fight in North Africa and Italy. Ibid., 187, 265. To add insult to injury, many of those honorably discharged did not receive their mustering-out pay. See Louis Noyes to Edwin Ferguson, [Tule Lake] Project Attorney's Weekly Report, November 21, 1933, Japanese American Evacuation and Resettlement Study Papers, Bancroft Library, University of California, Berkeley (hereafter "JERS"), microfilm reel 161, frame 298.

12. Frederick C. Luebke, *Bonds of Loyalty: German-Americans and World War I* (DeKalb, IL: Northern Illinois University Press, 1971). See also Matthew Jacobson,

Whiteness of a Different Color: European Immigrants and the Alchemy of Race (Cambridge, MA: Harvard University Press, 1998).

13. Richard Drinnon, *Keeper of the Concentration Camps: Dillon S. Myer and American Racism* (Berkeley: University of California Press, 1987).

14. Orin Starn, "Engineering Internment: Anthropologists and the War Relocation Authority," *American Ethnologist* 14 (1986): 700–720, at 709, 715. On camps as "community building" projects, see Thomas and Nishimoto, *The Spoilage*, 57. On liberalism and the internment, see also Gordon H. Chang, "'Superman Is About to Visit the Relocation Centers' and the Limits of Wartime Liberalism," *Amerasia Journal* 19, no. 1 (1993): 37–60; Colleen Lye, "Model Modernity: The Making of Asiatic Racial Form, 1882–1945" (Ph.D. dissertation, Columbia University, 1999), 281.

15. In fact, WRA officials included the former superintendent of the Navajo Indian reservation and the head of the Navajo school system. See Thomas James, *Exile Within: The Schooling of Japanese Americans, 1942–45* (Cambridge, MA: Harvard University Press, 1987), 36–38; Raymond Okamura, "'The Great White Father': Dillon Myer and Internal Colonialism," *Amerasia Journal* 13, no. 2 (1986–87): 155–60.

16. James Sakoda, "'The Residue': The Unresettled Minidokans, 1943–1945," in *Views from Within: The Japanese American Evacuation and Resettlement Study*, ed. Yuji Ichioka (Los Angeles: UCLA Asian American Studies Center, 1989), 249.

17. *Rabbit in the Moon*, dir. Emiko Omori (Public Broadcasting System: Point of View, 1999).

18. James, *Exile Within*; John Provinse and Solon Kimball, "Building New Communities during War Time," *American Sociological Review* 11, no. 4 (August 1946): 396–409; Thomas and Nishimoto, *The Spoilage*, 33–40.

19. Ansel Adams, *Born Free and Equal: Photographs of Japanese Americans at Manzanar Relocation Center, Inyo County, California* (New York: U.S. Camera, 1944), 9.

20. For firsthand accounts of camps and camp life, see Mine Okubo, *Citizen 10366* (New York: Columbia University Press, 1946); Gordon H. Chang, ed., *Morning Glory, Evening Shadow: Yamato Ichihashi and His Internment Writings* (Stanford: Stanford University Press, 1997) (hereafter "Ichihashi diary"); Takeo Kaneshiro, ed., *Internees: War Relocation Memoirs and Diaries* (New York: Vantage Press, 1976) (hereafter "Kaneshiro diary"). Okubo's annotated drawings, Ichihashi's writings, and Kaneshiro's diary are among the few contemporaneous accounts of the internment experience. For memoirs, see, for example, Yoshiko Uchida, *Desert Exile: The Uprooting of a Japanese American Family* (Seattle: University of Washington Press, 1982); Minoru Kiyota, *Beyond Loyalty: The Story of a Kibei* (Seattle: University of Washington Press, 1997); John Modell, ed., *The Kikuchi Diary: Chronicle from an American Concentration Camp, The Tanforan Journals of Charles Kikuchi* (Urbana, IL: University of Illinois Press, 1973).

21. James, *Exile Within*, 104; Provinse and Kimball, "Building New Communities," 407; Ichihashi diary, 180, 239; Arthur Hansen and David Hacker, "The Manzanar Revolt," *Amerasia Journal* 2, no. 2 (1974): 112–57, at 133–34; John Embree, "Resistance to Freedom: An Administrative Problem," *Applied Anthropology* 2, no. 4 (1943): 10–14, at 12; Lon Kurashige, *Japanese American Celebration and Conflict: Ethnicity and Festival in Los Angeles, 1934–1990* (Berkeley: University of California Press, 2001), 75–118.

22. Ichihashi diary, 202; Kanehiro diary, 38, 47–48, 69, 80; "Summary of Monthly

Reports [Tule Lake]," December 1944, JERS R161/F448; Rosalie Hankey, field notes, November 20, 1943, JERS 93/265 (hereafter "Hankey field notes").

23. Kaneshiro diary, 22–23.

24. Kaneshiro describes "boiler room conferences" of Issei men that took place daily in his block. Kaneshiro diary, 71, 79–80. See also Ichihashi diary, 188–93.

25. Embree, "Resistance to Freedom," 14; Thomas and Nishimoto, *The Spoilage*, 184–220; Sadoka, "The 'Residue,'" 254.

26. Weglyn, *Years of Infamy*, 140; *Personal Justice Denied*, 187–88.

27. Elmer Davis, quoted in *Personal Justice Denied*, 189.

28. *Personal Justice Denied*, 189–90; Scobey quoted in Muller, *Free to Die for Their Country*, 55.

29. *Personal Justice Denied*, 190–91; Dorothy Swaine Thomas, *The Salvage* (Berkeley: University of California Press, 1952), 615; Memo from Director WRA to Secretary of War, March 12, 1943, cited in [Morton Grodzins], "Segregation: Development of the Policy," [October 1943], JERS 93/164. Not only did the WRA conflate assimilation and loyalty, Mike Masaoka of the JACL recommended that the WRA should segregate "Kibei who had studied in Japan five or more years, all or part of that time falling after 1930 or all or part experienced after the age of 12." Ibid., 93/160.

30. Questions 27 and 28, Thomas and Nishimoto, *The Spoilage*, 57–58; the rest of the questionnaire is reprinted in Weglyn, *Years of Infamy*, 196–99.

31. Thomas and Nishimoto, *The Spoilage*, 65–71, 100–1, quote at 100.

32. Edward Spicer, "The Use of Social Scientists by the War Relocation Authority," *Applied Anthropology* 5, no. 2 (1946): 16–36, at 22; Ichihashi diary, 190. The Espionage Act made it a felony to interfere with military recruitment or induction, punishable by up to 20 years in prison and a $10,000 fine.

33. Ichihashi diary, 220, 176.

34. Thomas and Nishimoto, *The Spoilage*, 60–63; Muller, *Free to Die for Their Country*, 55–57.

35. Kurashige, *Japanese American Celebration and Conflict*, 104.

36. *Personal Justice Denied*, 195–97, 203; Thomas and Nishimoto, *The Spoilage*, 61. On resettlement, see Thomas, *The Salvage*; Charles Kikuchi diary; Charlotte Brooks, "In the Twilight Zone between Black and White: Japanese American Resettlement and Community in Chicago, 1942–1945," *Journal of American History* 86, no. 4 (March 2000): 1655–87.

37. *Personal Justice Denied*, 208–9; Tule Lake census in Hankey field notes, July 29, 1944, JERS 93/493; Thomas and Nishimoto, *The Spoilage*, 86–87; Spicer, "Use of Social Scientists," 24.

38. Sadoka, "The 'Residue,'" 262–64.

39. *Personal Justice Denied*, 246–47. For a detailed treatment of Japanese American draft resistance during the war, see Muller, *Free to Die for Their Country*.

40. Myer quoted in "FBI Investigation of Tule Lake Relocation Center," November 12–December 10, 1943, 460 (hereafter "FBI report on Tule Lake"), folder 1.4, box 14, Japanese American Internment Case Files, Records of the United States Attorneys, RG 118, National Archives, Pacific Region, San Francisco (hereafter "Internment files"); Thomas and Nishimoto, *The Spoilage*, 87; Edward Spicer, quoted in Weglyn, *Years of Infamy*, 233.

41. For details on the Tule Lake disturbances and martial law, see Thomas and

Nishimoto, *The Spoilage*, chapters 5–7; Weglyn, *Years of Infamy*, 160–65; *Personal Justice Denied*, 247.

42. Irvin Lechliter to Philip Glick, [Tule Lake] Project Attorney's Weekly Report, May 5, 1944, JERS 161/221–24. Lechliter reported, "There was virtually no response to our overture." See also Hankey field notes, May 13 and 20, 1944, JERS 93/393, 409; Thomas and Nishimoto, *The Spoilage*, 261–82.

43. FBI Report on Tule Lake, 18.

44. Thomas and Nishimoto, *The Spoilage*, 312.

45. Weglyn, *Years of Infamy*, 231; *Personal Justice Denied*, 248.

46. Act of July 1, 1944, Public Law 405 (58 Stat. 677) (repealed 1947). As recently as December 1943 the State Department had rejected a request by "truly disloyal Nisei" that they be given the status of Japanese nationals on grounds that renunciation was legally not possible. See Thomas and Nishimoto, *The Spoilage*, 309.

47. Letter, Edward Ennis to Ernest Besig, August 22, 1945, Papers of Wayne Collins, Bancroft Library, University of California, Berkeley (hereafter "Collins Papers"), microfilm, reel 26, frame 341–45; Donald Collins, *Native American Aliens: Disloyalty and the Renunciation of Citizenship by Japanese Americans during World War II* (Westport, CT: Greenwood Press, 1985), 70–74; Engle quoted by Weglyn, *Years of Infamy*, 229.

48. Ennis to Besig, August 22, 1945.

49. Collins, *Native American Aliens*, 85, 91–93.

50. Louis Noyes to Edwin Ferguson, [Tule lake] Project Attorney's Weekly Report, November 21, 1944, JERS 161/298; Ferguson to Noyes, December 6, 1944, JERS 161/300.

51. *Ex Parte Endo*, 323 U.S. 283 (1944); Collins, *Native American Aliens*, 91.

52. *Personal Justice Denied*, 241; James Wolfe, "The Dawn of a New Day," address to the residents of Topaz Relocation Center, March 10, 1945, JERS 23/627; Robert C. L. George, "Our Japanese Americans Now," *Survey* (November 1946): 291–94; Sadoka, "The 'Residue,'" 264–67.

53. [Tule Lake] WRA Reports Office, Monthly Reports Summary, December 1944, JERS 161/448, and February 1945, JERS 161/457; Collins, *Native American Aliens*, 91.

54. [Tule Lake] Project Attorney's Weekly Report, March 8, 1945, JERS 161/312–15.

55. Letter, Mrs. Y. to War Relocation Authority, Oct. 23, 1945, JERS 172/578–79.

56. See below.

57. Quoted in Thomas and Nishimoto, *The Spoilage*, 339.

58. Ibid., 345, 326; Hankey field notes, May 21, 1944, JERS 93/411.

59. Hankey field notes, January 30, 1945, JERS 93/165, March 16, 1945, JERS 94/231; Dec. 18, 1944, 6–7, JERS 94/32.

60. Hankey field notes, December 13, 1944, JERS 94/26; Collins, *Native American Aliens*, 92–109; Noyes to Ferguson, March 8, 1945, JERS 161/312–15.

61. Thomas and Nishimoto, *The Spoilage*, 357; Noyes to Ferguson, Project Attorney's Weekly Report, March 8, 1945, JERS 161/312–15.

62. Collins, *Native American Aliens*, 109; memorandum, Ivan Williams to "All Japanese Renunciants, Tule Lake Center," n.d., Collins Papers 26/362.

63. Collins, *Native American Aliens*, 109; Noyes to Ferguson, Project Attorney's Weekly Report, March 14, 1945, JERS 161/316; letter, Edward Ennis to Clifford For-

ster, July 23, 1945, Collins Papers 26/336. In fact, Burling blamed the WRA decision to close the camps and forcibly resettle the reluctant camp population before the end of the war for causing so many renunciations of citizenship. Dillon Myer opposed Burling's proposal to keep Tule Lake open through the end of the war because he feared that by doing so "pressure to remain in camp will increase in the nine other centers and Myer would have 9 Tule Lakes on his hands." Hankey field notes, February 16, 1945, JERS 94/188, and January 20, 1945, JERS 94/153.

64. Letter, Edward Ennis to Y. T., July 27, 1945, Collins Papers 26/336.

65. Letter, M.R.W. to Edward Ennis, August 24, 1945, JERS 172/604.

66. Kiyota, *Beyond Loyalty*, 111–12.

67. Hankey field notes, August 23, 1944, JERS 93/537; Kaneshiro diary, 77–80; Sadoka, "'The Residue,'" 268.

68. Quoted in Collins, *Native American Aliens*, 110.

69. Project Attorney's Weekly Report, September 8, 1945, JERS 161/354; letter, T. Y. to Edward Ennis, August 25, 1945, JERS 172/604; letter, M. Y. to Edward Ennis, August 24, 1945, JERS 172/603; [Tule Lake] Project Attorney's Weekly Report, September 8, 1945, JERS 161/312–15; letter, M. Y. and C. Y. to Edward Ennis, August 22, 1945, JERS 172/595.

70. *Personal Justice Denied*, 251–52. Of those repatriating to Japan, approximately 2,000 were renunciants. Collins, *Native American Aliens*, 121.

71. Clifford Foster, "Department of Justice Policies after Signing of Surrender," August 28, 1945, Collins Papers 26/346.

72. They argued that the renunciants were stateless, not aliens, as there could be no presumption of Japanese citizenship in view of their birth in the United States; that renunciation was not grounds for deportation; that renunciants had acted under duress. The Justice Department remained adamant that the renunciants had acted voluntarily. Ennis insisted, "I am satisfied that in substantially every case the renunciation was accomplished as an exercise of the renunciant's free will." See [Roger Baldwin] to Ernest Besig, September 17, 1956, Collins Papers 26/346; Dillon Myer to Roger Baldwin, n.d., JERS 26/337; Herbert Weschler to Ernest Besig, August 21, 1945, JERS 26/338; Ernest Besig to Alexander Meiklejohn, September 4, 1945, JERS 26/349–50; Edward Ennis to Ernest Besig, August 22, 1945, JERS 26/341–45.

73. Here, Collins parted company with the national office of the ACLU, which had recommended bringing only a test case, "even though the prospects are poor," to restrain the deportations of persons who had attempted to withdraw their renunciations. The ACLU wanted to select a plaintiff who it believed would present well to the public and whose reputation was vouched by the JACL. Collins was not interested in publicity but wanted a class-action suit to restore the citizenship of every renunciant who desired it. He also worked for the renunciants as a private attorney, keeping only informal relations with the northern California branch of the ACLU, so that he could make a range of legal arguments not limited to constitutional issues. See "Report of [ACLU] Committee on Japanese American Cases," October 3, 1945, Collins Papers 26/362; Collins, *Native American Aliens*, 115–19, 132–33.

74. Muller, *Free to Die for Their Country*, 133–34, 178. *United States v. Massaki Kuwabara*, 56 F. Supp 716 (1944).

75. Complaint to Rescind Renunciation of Nationality, to Declare Nationality, for Declaratory Judgment and for Injunction, *Abo v. Clark*, Nov. 5, 1945; file 25294-S, 4/4, *Abo v. Clark*, Internment files.

76. Brief for Plaintiffs, *Application for a Writ of Habeas Corpus by Abo et al.*, 23–23, 30–31, file Tule Lake Briefs and Affidavits for Plaintiffs and Petitioners, box 9, Internment Files; Brief for Plaintiffs, *Abo v. Clark*, 51, ibid.

77. *Abo v. Clark*, 77 F. Supp. 806 (1947); Collins, *Native American Aliens*, 129–30.

78. Collins, *Native American Aliens*, 137–40.

79. For example, form letter of November 1, 1948, Collins Papers 3/224.

80. Collins, *Native American Aliens*, 142; Every major city in Japan except for Kyoto was devastated by conventional or atomic bombing. Many Japanese Americans originated from Hiroshima prefecture, but returning there was impossible. In general, food and jobs were scarce. A number of Nisei got jobs with the American occupation force, but these were all cancelled in September 1947. See Collins, *Native American Aliens*, 121–22; Muller, *Free to Die for Their Country*, 177–78.

81. Form letter, December 1956, Collins Papers 4/21–23.

82. Weglyn, *Years of Infamy*, 263.

83. McCarran-Walter Act, June 27, 1952 (66 Stat. 163). Less than one-half of the Japanese Americans interned during the war returned to the evacuated areas on the Pacific Coast. *Personal Justice Denied*, 150. On assimilationism and the racial repositioning of Japanese Americans in the 1950s, see Caroline Chung Simpson, *An Absent Presence: Japanese Americans in Postwar American Culture, 1945–1960* (Durham: Duke University Press, 2001).

84. Letter, T. Y. to [Raymond] Best, Oct. 7, 1945, JERS 160/14; Muller, *Free to Die for Their Country*, 179–80; Nakanishi, "The Enduring Legacy of Executive Order 9066," 14.

85. Thomas and Nishimoto, *The Spoilage*, 361. Unlike the anthropologists whom the WRA employed as community analysts, JERS sociologists did not work for the government and had a policy of not giving their findings to the WRA. This did not entirely relieve them of the *inu* problem, however. See Yuji Ichioka, "JERS Revisited: Introduction," in *View from Within*, 3–27.

86. Weglyn, *Years of Infamy*, 240–47, quotes at 246, 240.

87. Ibid., 234.

88. Collins, *Native American Aliens*, 34, 91–92.

89. For discussion of controversy over JERS and Rosalie Hankey, see Frank S. Miyamoto, "Dorothy Swaine Thomas as Director of JERS: Some Personal Observations," in *View from Within*.

90. In fact, Collins was a pragmatist who was determined to use any and all arguments he thought would help win his case, including "the kitchen sink" if need be. Collins, *Native American Aliens*, 115, 123, 132–34.

91. "Resumé of meeting with Mr. Collins," October 8, 1945, 6, Collins Papers 1/56; notes from follow-up meeting, n.d., 4, Collins Papers 1/59; letter to R. N. (Chicago), Nov. 29, 1954, Collins Papers 3/62.

92. Letter, Wayne Collins to K. Y., January 5, 1955, Collins Papers 3/70.

Chapter Six
The Cold War Chinese Immigration Crisis and the Confession Cases

1. "Six Companies Protest Calumny Heaped on Entire Chinese Community," *Chinese World*, March 16, 1956, 1.

2. Chinese exclusion was first enacted in 1882 for a period of ten years (Act of May 6, 1882 [22 Stat. 58]), renewed twice, extended indefinitely in 1904 (Act of April 27, 1904 [33 Stat. 428]), and repealed in 1943 (Act of December 17, 1943 [57 Stat. 600]). Birthright citizenship was upheld in *United States v. Wong Kim Ark*, 169 U.S. 649 (1898). On early Chinese American history, see Sucheng Chan, *This Bittersweet Soil: The Chinese in California Agriculture, 1860–1910* (Berkeley: University of California Press, 1986); Brett DeBarry Nee and Victor Nee, *Longtime Californ': A Documentary Study of an American Chinatown* (Stanford: Stanford University Press, 1986); Madeline Y. Hsu, *Dreaming of Gold, Dreaming of Home: Transnationalism and Migration between the United States and South China, 1882–1943* (Stanford: Stanford University Press, 2000); Yong Chen, *Chinese San Francisco, 1850–1943: A Trans-Pacific Community* (Stanford: Stanford University Press, 2000); John Kuo-Wei Tchen, *New York before Chinatown: Orientalism and the Shaping of American Culture, 1776–1882* (Baltimore: Johns Hopkins University Press, 1999).

3. Peter Conn, *Pearl S. Buck: A Cultural Biography* (New York: Cambridge University Press, 1996), 402, n. 26.

4. Renqui Yu, *To Save China, to Save Ourselves: The Chinese Hand Laundry Alliance of New York* (Philadelphia: Temple University Press, 1993); Judy Yung, *Unbound Feet: A Social History of Chinese Women in San Francisco* (Berkeley: University of California Press, 1995), 240, 253; Karen Leong, "The China Mystique: Mayling Soong, Pearl S. Buck, and Anna May Wong in the American Imagination" (Ph.D. dissertation, University of California, Berkeley, 1999); Peter Kwong, *Chinatown New York: Labor and Politics, 1933–1950* (New York: Monthly Review Press, 1979).

5. Act of December 17, 1943 (57 Stat. 600).

6. Fred Riggs, *Pressures on Congress: A Study of the Repeal of Chinese Exclusion* (New York: Columbia University Press, 1950); Bill Ong Hing, *Making and Remaking Asian America through Immigration Policy, 1850–1990* (Stanford: Stanford University Press, 1990), 36; K. Scott Wong, "War Comes to Chinatown: Social Transformation and the Chinese of California," in *The Way We Really Were: The Golden in The Second Great War*, ed. Roger Lotchin (Urbana: University of Illinois Press, 2000); Xiaojian Zhao, *Re-Making Chinese America: Immigration, Family, and Community* (Philadelphia: Temple University Press, 2002).

7. William Jack Chow, cited by Serena Chen, "A Look Back on the Chinese Confession Program," *East/West News* 21 (April 23, 1987): 1, 7–9. INS annual reports from 1957 to 1965 indicate 30,460 Chinese whose claims to American citizenship were revealed as fraudulent, amounting to 25.8 percent of the 117,629 Chinese counted in the 1950 U.S. census.

8. Under Section 6 of the exclusion law, persons of the exempt classes were admissible with certificates issued by the Chinese government attesting to their status. The Nationality Act of 1870 (16 Stat. 2254) granted "derivative citizenship" to children born abroad of American citizens. The Immigration Service treated Chinese American derivative citizens entering the United States for the first time as though they were immigrants, subjecting them to immigration inspection. On illegal border crossings by Chinese, see Erika Lee, "Enforcing the Borders: Chinese Exclusion Along the U.S. Borders with Canada and Mexico," *Journal of American History* 89, no. 1 (June 2002): 54–86.

9. *Lem Moon Sing* (158 U.S. 538 [1895]); *Wong Kim Ark* (169 U.S. 649 [1898]);

Timothy Malloy, "A Century of Chinese Immigration: A Brief Review," *INS Monthly Review,* December 1947, 73.

10. Lucy Salyer, *Laws Harsh as Tigers: Chinese Immigrants and the Shaping of Modern Immigration Law* (Chapel Hill: University of North Carolina Press, 1995), 69–93.

11. U.S. Department of Labor, *Annual Report of the Commissioner General of Immigration to the Secretary of Labor,* 1925 (hereafter *"INS Annual Report"*), 22–23; *INS Annual Report,* 1928, 8; Joseph Swing interview with Ed Edwin, June 21, 1964, 54, Eisenhower Administration Oral History Project, Columbia University. Chinese immigrants were overwhelmingly male, owing to the practice of sending men to labor for remittance and the inadmissibility of Chinese alien wives of American citizens; hence the term "paper sons." There were some "paper daughters," but they were relatively few. See Sucheng Chan, "Exclusion of Chinese Women, 1870–1943," in *Entry Denied: Exclusion and the Chinese Community in America, 1882–1943,* ed. S. Chan (Philadelplia: Temple University Press, 1991), 130. Chinese women immigrants at the turn of the century mostly comprised wives of merchants and prostitutes, the latter often brought in under the guise of servants, daughters, or wives of merchants. See Yung, *Unbound Feet.*

12. U.S. Congress, House of Representatives, *Hearings before the President's Commission on Immigration and Naturalization,* September 30, 1952 et seq., 1812.

13. Between 1944 and 1960, 42,935 Chinese immigrants entered the United States. Of these, nearly two-thirds were either wives (16,985) or refugees (10,376). Since refugees with relatives in America were given preference, postwar immigration significantly contributed to family reunification. On postwar nonquota immigration, see Roger Daniels and Harvey Kitano, *Asian Americans: Emerging Minorities* (Upper Saddle River, NJ: Prentice-Hall, 2001 [1988]), 15–16. On Refugee Relief Act, see "The Refugee Relief Act of 1953: What It Is—And How It Works," *I&N Reporter,* 3, no. 1 (July 1954): 23, 25. For more discussion on refugee policy, see chapter 7.

14. Timothy Malloy, "A Century of Chinese Immigration," 73; LeMont Eaton, "Inspections and Examinations Work of the Service," *INS Monthly Bulletin* (September 1950): 31.

15. U.S. Department of State, Passport Division, "Procedures for Documentation of Persons of Chinese Origin Who Claim American Citizenship for the First Time," August 4, 1950, in United States Congress, House of Representatives, *Hearings before the President's Commission on Immigration and Naturalization,* 422–23. A federal district judge found the use of blood tests by the INS to be discriminatory because they were applied only to Chinese cases (*Lee Kum Hoy et al. v. Shaughnessey,* 133 F. Supp. 850 [1955]), but the Supreme Court ruled their use was legitimate as long as the INS agreed to apply blood tests to all citizenship claimants without regular documentation such as birth certificates (*Hoy v. Shaughnessey,* on certiorari [1957]). Some Chinese opposed the blood test as a form of "self-incrimination," since it could only disprove, and not prove, paternity. See "U.S. Citizens of Chinese Ancestry Face Blood Test Demand to Get Passports," *Chinese World,* November 8, 1955, 1; Benjamin Gim interview with author, February 19, 1993.

16. Editorial, "How to Win Enemies and Antagonize People," *Chinese World,* April 25, 1956, 1; editorial, "Drumright's Version of a "Five-Anti's Campaign," *Chinese World,* April 27, 1956, 1; Office of Security, "Staff Study on Hong Kong Police Liaison," May 21, 1956, file 1-C/4, Declassified Decimal Files, 1953–1960, Lot File 62-

D-256, Records of the Bureau of Security and Consular Affairs, General Records of the Department of State, Record Group 59, National Archives, College Park, MD (hereafter "SCA, Dept. of State"); editorial, "Revision of the Refugee Relief Act," *Chinese World,* April 26, 1956.

17. Section 503 of the Nationality Act of 1940 (54 Stat. 1148), at 1171–72; Everett F. Drumright, "Report on the Problem of Passport Fraud at Hong Kong," Foreign Service Dispatch 931, 9 December 1955, 19–20, 46, file 122.4732/12–955, Central Files, Dept. of State.

18. Jack Minor to Dennis Flinn, July 13, 1955; Basil Capella to Everett Drumright, November 15, 1955; Jack Minor and Halleck Rose, "Report on Survey of Investigative Section and Refugee Relief Program at the Consulate General in Hong Kong," July 14, 1955, and Jack Minor and Halleck Rose to Scott McLeod, July 14, 1955, file 1-C/4, SCA.

19. John Lewis Gaddis, *Strategies of Containment: A Critical Appraisal of Postwar American National Security Policy* (New York: Oxford University Press, 1982), 115–16, 169–71; Gordon H. Chang, *Friends and Enemies, the United States, China, and the Soviet Union, 1948–1972* (Stanford: Stanford University Press, 1991), 165–69.

20. The Kuomintang's policy was consistent with the racialized Chinese immigration laws of the United States, which also defined Chinese on a global, racial basis. The racial basis of Chinese exclusion and postexclusion immigration quotas reinforced the Chinese concept *huaqiao* (overseas Chinese). On Communist China's policy, see Stephen Fitzgerald, *China and the Overseas Chinese: A Study in Peking's Changing Policy* (Cambridge: Cambridge University Press, 1972), 5–11, 79, 104–10. However, some of the Southeast Asian countries that were aligned with the United States adopted hostile policies towards overseas Chinese. In 1955 the Philippine government forbade aliens from bequeathing property; in 1956 South Vietnam issued a forced naturalization decree and barred aliens from owning businesses. See "Chinese in Philippines Face Harsh Measures," *Chinese World,* August 18, 1955; "Involuntary Citizenship in South Vietnam," *Chinese World,* May 2, 1957.

21. E. J. Kahn, *The China Hands: America's Foreign Service Officers and What Befell Them* (New York: Viking Press, 1975 [1972]), 1, 9, 37. See also Earl Newsom, *Drumright! The Glory Days of a Boom Town* (Perkins, OK: Evans Publishers, 1985), 7–10.

22. Drumright, "Report on the Problem of Passport Fraud at Hong Kong," 1–3, 28, 79–81.

23. Maurice Rice, "Recent Communist Chinese Policy toward American-Chinese," Foreign Service Dispatch 1485, June 5, 1956, 2, 34, file 1-C/4, SCA. Rice stated that Communist propaganda aimed at youth was so successful that "occasional American-Chinese visiting Hong Kong have informed the Consulate General that they do not wish to apply for their sons or grandsons to go to the U.S. since the Communists have 'ruined their minds.'" Fitzgerald, *China and the Overseas Chinese,* 1–2, 33–34.

24. Drumright, "Report on the Problem of Passport Fraud," 49–52, 25–26.

25. Drumright to Basil Capella, October 18, 1955; State Department Office of Security, "Staff Study on Hong Kong Police Liaison," May 21, 1956; Everett F. Drumright, "Proposals to Better Cope with the Problem of Fraud at Hong Kong," Foreign Service Dispatch 942, December 13, 1955, file 1-C/4, SCA.

26. Report by committee representing Far Eastern Affairs, Office of Passport, Visa Office, Office of Security, and Office of Special Consular Services, Jack Minor, Chair, January 4, 1956, 4, file 1-C/4, SCA (hereafter cited as "Minor Report").

27. Frances Knight, Passport Office, to Haywood P. Martin, Exec. Director, SCA, December 5, 1955, and Rolland Welch, Visa Office, to Martin, December 15, 1955, file 1-C/4, SCA.

28. Drumright to Capella, October 18, 1955; Minor Report, 6. See also Drumright, "Proposals to Better Cope with the Problem of Fraud."

29. Drumright, "Proposals to Better Cope with the Problem of Fraud;" Drumright to Scott McLeod, May 4, 1956, file 1-C/4, SCA. On fraudulent confessions, see Drumright, "Report on Problem of Passport Fraud at Hong Kong," 37.

30. Drumright to McLeod, June 21, and July 25, 1956, file 1-C/4, SCA. Drumright appears to have dodged the policies of the Passport and Visa Offices for as long as he did because he had personal and political support in the department's Bureau of Far Eastern Affairs. He was also stubborn and ill tempered. See H. P. Martin to Scott McLeod, Jan. 25, 1956, and Jack Minor and Halleck Rose to Scott McLeod, July 14, 1955, file 1-C/4, SCA.

31. William Haren Hale, "'Big Brother' in Foggy Bottom," *Reporter*, August 17, 1954, 10–17; "Celler Assails Refugee Relief," *New York Times*, December 13, 1954, 37, 39; Scott McLeod to Drumright, September 14, 1956, file 1-C/4, SCA. The department authorized Drumright's request to fingerprint visa and passport applicants but insisted that provisions for fingerprinting be applied globally to preempt charges of racial discrimination. Minor Report, 8.

32. U.S. President's Commission on Immigration and Naturalization, *Whom We Shall Welcome* (Washington, DC: GPO, 1953); Stephen Wagner, "The Lingering Death of the National Origins Quota System: A Political History of U.S. Immigration Policy, 1952–1965" (Ph.D. dissertation, Harvard University, 1986); Robert Divine, *American Immigration Policy, 1924–1952* (New Haven: Yale University Press, 1957), 189; John Higham, "The Politics of Immigration Restriction," in *Send These to Me: Immigrants in Urban America* (Baltimore: Johns Hopkins University Press, 1984 [1975]), 63. See also discussion in chapter 7.

33. Robert Cartwright to Walter Yeagley, September 18, 1956, file 1-C/4, SCA; Kahn, *The China Hands*, 277.

34. "Federal Grand Jury Probes Chinatown Associations," *Chinese World*, March 3, 1956; Office of Security, "Federal Court Actions in Chinese Passport Cases," n.d., file 1-C/3.1, SCA; Dennis Flinn to Scott McLeod, "Chinese Fraud Cases, San Francisco," March 1, 1956, ibid.; Bruce Barber to Commissioner, Central Office, March 5, 1956, file 56364/51.6, Subject files of the U.S. Immigration and Naturalization Service, Central Office, Washington, DC (hereafter "INS-CO")

35. Unidentified newspaper clipping, March 2, 1956, in file 56341/51.6, INS-CO; "U.S. Probe of Illegal Entries Spreads to H.K.," *Chinese World*, March 3, 1956, 1.

36. Lim P. Lee, quoted in Serena Chen, "A Look Back at the Chinese Confession Program," 8; Maurice Chuck interview with author, January 24, 1993; see also Franklin Woo interview in Nee and Nee, *Longtime Californ'*, 216; Him Mark Lai et al., *The Chinese in America, 1785–1980: An Illustrated History* (San Francisco: Chinese Culture Foundation, 1980), 73.

37. Mae M. Ngai, "The Politics of Immigration: the Cold War, McCarthyism, and the Chinese in America" (Master's thesis, Columbia University, 1993). See also Peter Kwong, *Chinatown, New York: Labor and Politics 1930–1950* (New York: Monthly Review Press, 1979); Yu, *To Save China;* Him Mark Lai, "Historical Survey of the Organizations of the Left among Chinese in America," *Bulletin of Concerned Asian*

Scholars 4 (Fall 1972): 13–15. On relations between the CCBA and Kuomintang in the United States, see Nee and Nee, *Longtime Californ'*; and idem, "The Kuomintang in Chinatown," in *Counterpoint: Perspectives on Asian America,* ed. Emma Gee (Los Angeles: UCLA Asian American Studies Center, 1976), 146–51; Him Mark Lai, "The Kuomintang in Chinese American Communities before World War II," in Chan, *Entry Denied,* 170–212.

38. On Six Companies and CCBA historical role in Chinese communities, see Him Mark Lai, "Historical Development of the CCBA/Huiguan System," *Chinese America: History and Perspectives* (1992): 13–51; Salyer, *Laws Harsh as Tigers;* Charles McClain, *In Search of Equality: The Chinese Struggle against Discrimination in Nineteenth-Century America* (Berkeley: University of California Press, 1994); *United States v. Wong Kim Ark,* 169 U.S. 649 (1898).

39. On the experience of Chinese Americans in the post–World War II period, see Roger Daniels, *Asian America: The Chinese and the Japanese in the U.S. since 1850* (Seattle: University of Washington Press, 1988); S. W. Kung, *Chinese in American Life: Some Aspects of Their History, Status, Problems, and Contributions* (Seattle: University of Washington Press, 1962); and especially Rose Hum Lee, *The Chinese in the United States of America* (Hong Kong: Hong Kong University Press, 1960), the most comprehensive contemporary study of the postwar period. Lee believed the growth of the American-born Chinese population would lead to the decline of the CCBA.

40. "Six Companies Protests Calumny Heaped on Entire Chinese Community," *Chinese World,* March 16, 1956, 1.

41. Leftists who were called before the grand jury were by this time too isolated to resist on their own. On March 6 Happy Lim, the secretary of the Chinese Mutual Aid Workers Association, responded to an order to appear and testified before the grand jury. Lim told the grand jury that the association had been a clearinghouse for Chinese salmon-cannery workers in Alaska during the 1940s but that the organization was now defunct. "Arguments Due on Chinatown," *San Francisco News,* March 7, 1956, 9.

42. *New York Chinese Journal,* March 7 and 8, 1956 (translation), cited in J. Edgar Hoover to Dennis Flynn, "Movement of Communist Chinese, Internal Security-CH," May 22, 1956, file 1-C/3.1, SCA; Shing Tai Liang interview with author, January 14, 1993; Memorandum of Conversation, Wellington Koo, Mr. Sebald, Mr. McConoughy, "U.S. Grand Jury Investigations of Chinese Passport Fraud Cases," March 13, 1956, file 1-C/4, SCA; State Department to Chinese Embassy, *Aide-Memoire,* March 27, 1956, file 1-C/3.1, SCA.

43. "Buring Down the Barn to Catch a Few Rats," *Chinese World,* March 7, 1956; Li Ta-ming, "A Critique of the Report of the Consul General in Hong Kong," *World Journal,* [n.d.] I thank Adam McKeown for this reference.

44. Dai-Ming Lee, "Fifty Years after the Fire and the Quake," *Chinese World,* April 18, 1956, 1; idem, "Drumright's Amazing Charges," *Chinese World,* April 20, 1956, 1; idem, "Drumright Stoops to 'Third-Degree' Methods," *Chinese World,* April 21, 1956, 1; *Hong Kong Tiger Standard,* March 3, 1956, cited in "Hong Kong Press and Governmental Reaction to Consular Fraud Problems at Hong Kong," Foreign Service Dispatch 1330, April 14, 1956, file 1-C/4, SCA.

45. Oliver J. Carter, U.S. district judge, "In the Matter of the Application of the Presidents, Secretaries, Treasurers, and Custodians of Records of Certain Chinese

Family Benevolent and District Associations to quash Grand Jury subpoenas duces tecum," Misc. No. 8016, Memorandum and Order, U.S. District Court for the Northern District of California, Southern Division, March 20, 1956, 1, 4; "Judge Carter Stays Execution of Subpoena Order," *Chinese World*, March 27, 1956, 1.

46. Dennis Flinn to Scott McLeod and Edward Crouch, "San Francisco Passport and Immigration Frauds, Grand Jury Investigation (staff paper)," April 25, 1956, file 1-C/3.1, SCA. In San Francisco the State Department and INS fought over jurisdiction and control of the investigations. Flinn believed the INS's participation in passport investigations was part of INS commissioner Swing's plan to get "his own Foreign Service."

47. "Immigration Service Probes Chinese Family Associations," *Chinese World*, June 14, 1956, 1; Dai-Ming Lee, "Right of Privacy Abridged," *Chinese World*, June 22, 1956, 1; William Bartley to Edwin Howard, October 24, 1956, SE 80/62.1, INS-CO; Scott McLeod to Herbert Brownell, April 12, 1956, file 1-C/3.1, SCA.

48. James Cavanaugh, "San Francisco Chinese Passport and Immigration Frauds, Grand Jury Investigation, Summary Report," June 12, 1956, file 1-C/3.1, SCA; George Spoth, "New York Chinese Passport and Immigration Frauds, Grand Jury Investigation, Composite Report," March 28, 1956, ibid.

49. Aaron Coleman to Dennis Flinn, May 15, 1956; Coleman, "Report on Civil Action Cases to Be Investigated in Hong Kong," Foreign Service Dispatch 102, August 7, 1956, file 1-C/4, SCA.

50. Cavanaugh, "San Francisco Chinese Passport and Immigration Frauds."

51. Scott McLeod to Loy Henderson, "Summary of Accomplishments in Passport Investigation Field from May 1, 1955 to July 31, 1956," September 14, 1956, file 1-C/4, SCA; Dai-Ming Lee, "Mr. Drumright Displays Amazing Naiveté," *Chinese World*, May 1, 1956, 4; "N.Y. Grand Jury Indicts Travel Agent for Fraud," *Chinese World*, May 4, 1956, 1; "Chinese Leader Is Indicted Here," *New York Times*, May 4, 1956, 1, 16; "Chinese Is Guilty in Passport Plot," *New York Times*, February 20 1957, 13.

52. Benjamin Gim interview.

53. *National Conference of Chinese Communities in America, March 5–7, 1957*, Washington, DC, Report and Proceedings, 16, 42–43, 29–36 (in possession of author).

54. The conveners clarified to the press that the conference proceedings would have "no international significance," and the Nationalist embassy in Washington announced it would play no role. Dai-Ming Lee, "The Chinese Conference in Washington," *Chinese World*, March 7, 1957, 1; idem, "A Conference on Chinese Affairs," *Chinese World*, February 9, 1957, 1; idem, "The Organization of a Chinese Welfare Council," *Chinese World*, March 20, 1957, 1; *National Conference of Chinese Communities in the America*, 14–15.

55. Shing Tai Liang interview.

56. *Annual Report of the Attorney General of the United States*, 1957 (Washington, DC: United States Department of Justice), 442. See also "Chinese Confession Program Highlights Year-End Report," *INS Information Bulletin*, January 8, 1960, 2.

57. Ralph Stanley to Ralph Harris, December 19, 1956, file 56364/51.6, INS-CO, 2–3. Leong is a pseudonym.

58. Ibid., 15; INS Southwest Region Investigations Monthly Activity Report, Janu-

ary 14, 1957, and Raymond F. Farrell to Regional Commissioners, February 6, 1957, file 56364/51.6, INS-CO; Joseph Swing interview, 54; Benjamin Gim to author, March 4, 1993. The September 1957 act, Public Law 85-316 (71 Stat. 639), has been mistakenly construed as the legal statute governing the confession program. However, the INS would not apply the 1957 law to paper sons; according to the service, Congress intended that law to assist Mexican immigrant families who would suffer hardship if an illegal family member were deported. The service reasoned that Chinese paper sons were ineligible for relief under the 1957 amendment because they had entered as citizens, not as aliens, and had therefore not gone through immigrant inspection—a specious argument since the INS had ruled on the admissibility of derivative citizens since the 1890s. In 1972 the Ninth Circuit Court of Appeals ruled that confessed paper sons were eligible for relief under the 1957 act. By that time, however, the confession program no longer existed. See *Lee Fook Chuey v. Immigration and Naturalization Service*, 439 F.2d 244.

59. Stanley to Harris, December 19, 1956, 1–2.

60. Ibid., 4.

61. Ibid.; Benjamin Gim interview.

62. Benjamin Gim interview; Maurice Chuck interview; Stanley to Harris, December 19, 1956, 3.

63. Sundry documentation of confessions in Segregated Chinese Files, U.S.-INS, RG 85, National Archives, Pacific Region, San Francisco, and Northeast Region, New York.

64. Benjamin Gim interview; Matter of C——, in Deportation Proceedings, 7 INS Administrative Decision 608, 611 (1957); Elmer Freed, "Immigration and Nationality Law," *New York University Law Review* 35 (1960): 191; interview with Francis Leo, Chinese interpreter for the INS in San Francisco, by Serena Chen, in "A Look Back at the Chinese Confession Program," 1, 4.

65. The INS never publicly announced an official termination of the confession program, but unpublished INS documents reported the end of the program variously as December 1965 and February 1966. "A History of Chinese Immigration," December 31, 1972, 14; "Chinese Confession Program," n.d., 3.

66. Benjamin Gim interview. J. Edgar Hoover also took a direct interest in the confession program. Raymond Farrell, Asst. Commissioner, Investigations Division, Central Office, to Regional Commissioner, Southeast Region, March 22, 1956, file 56364/51.6 Inv., INS-CO.

67. *INS Annual Report*, 1965, 11, *INS Annual Report*, 1966, 16.

68. Him Mark Lai, "To Bring Forth a New China, To Build a Better America: The Chinese Marxist Left in the America to the 1960s," *Chinese America: History and Perspectives* 8 (1992): 51–52; Maurice Chuck interview.

69. Maurice Chuck interview; *United States v. Chung Man Hwong*, Case 16869, U.S. District Court, Western District of Washington, Southern Division, Tacoma.

70. *United States v. Dear Wing Jung, aka Dear Kai Gay*, No. 37681, Reporter's Transcript Proceedings on Trial, Oct. 16, 1961 et seq.: 92–96, 137, 143, 188–92, 212; Order of Proof, Oct. 19, 1961; Proceedings on Sentence, Reporter's Transcript, Dec. 15, 1961: 7–8; *Dear Wing Jung v. United States*, 312 F.2d 73 (1962).

71. Dai-Ming Lee, "The Sins of Fathers and Grandfathers," *Chinese World*, April 19, 1956, 1.

72. "Message from the President of the United States Favoring the Repeal of the Chinese Exclusion Laws," Oct. 11, 1943, reprinted in Fred Riggs, *Pressures on Congress: A Study of the Repeal of Chinese Exclusion* (New York: Columbia University Press, 1950), 210.

Chapter Seven
The Liberal Critique and Reform of Immigration Policy

1. Oscar Handlin, "We Need More Immigrants," *Atlantic Monthly* (May 1953): 27–31, quote at 27.

2. Philip Gleason, "American Identity and Americanization," *Harvard Encyclopedia of American Ethnic Groups*, ed. Stephen Threnstrom (Cambridge, MA: Harvard University Press, 1980), 52; Roger Daniels, *Coming to America* (New York: Harper Collins, 1990), 338.

3. Immigration and Nationality Act of 1965 (79 Stat. 911); David Reimers, *Still the Golden Door: The Third World Comes to America* (New York: Columbia University Press, 1985).

4. Reimers, *Still the Golden Door*, 83–84; John Higham, *Send These to Me: Immigrants in Urban America* (Baltimore: Johns Hopkins University Press, 1975), 58–64.

5. Robert H. Amundson, "The McCarran-Walter Act," *America*, July 20, 1957, 423–35; Gunnar Myrdal, *An American Dilemma: The Negro Problem and American Democracy* (New York: Harper and Brothers, 1944).

6. For example, see David Roediger, *The Wages of Whiteness: Race and the Making of the American Working Class* (New York: Verso, 1991); James Barrett and David Roediger, "In-between Peoples: Race, Nationality, and the 'New' Immigrant Working Class," *Journal of American Ethnic History* 16 (Summer 1997): 40–65; Matthew Jacobson, *Whiteness of a Different Color: European Immigrants and the Alchemy of Race* (Cambridge, MA: Harvard University Press, 1998); Gary Gerstle, *American Crucible: Race and Nation in the Twentieth Century* (Princeton: Princeton University Press, 2001).

7. *Perez v. Brownell*, 356 U.S. 44, 64–65 (1958) (Warren, C.J., dissenting), emphasis in original. It should be noted that alienage was not always the principal imagined opposite of citizen. In late-eighteenth and early-nineteenth-century America, citizenship comprised a range of status positions, with property-holding white men at the apex and the slave its most definitive opposite.

8. Charles L. Black, Jr., "The Unfinished Business of the Warren Court," *Washington Law Review* 46 (1970): 3–46, at 8–9.

9. Ibid., 10; Peter Schuck, "The Transformation of American Immigration Law," *Columbia Law Review* 84 (1984): 1–90, at 16.

10. Not all late Progressive pluralists were immigrants. See Alain Locke, *Race Contacts and Interracial Relations: Lectures on the Theory and Practice of Race* (Washington, DC: Howard University Press, 1992); Randolph Bourne, "Transnational America," *Atlantic Monthly* 118 (July 1916): 86–97.

11. Horace Kallen, "Democracy versus the Melting Pot," *The Nation* 100 (Feb. 18 and 25, 1915): 190–94, 217–220, quote at 200; idem, *Culture and Democracy in the United States* (New Brunswick, NJ: 1988 [1924]), 124. Kallen first used the term "cultural pluralism" in the latter publication.

12. Boas also participated in the debate over immigration restriction. He debated the eugenicist pop theorist Madison Grant in "That Nordic Nonsense," *Forum* 75 (October 1925): 502–11. Ruth Benedict, *Patterns of Culture* (Boston: Houghton Mifflin, 1934); Margaret Mead, *Coming of Age in Samoa: A Psychological Study of Primitive Youth for Western Civilization* (New York: W. Morrow and Company, 1928); Robert E. Park, *Race and Culture* (New York: Free Press, 1964 [1950]). On cultural pluralism understood variously as means to assimilation and cultural diversity as an end in itself, see James Henry Powell, "The Concept of Cultural Pluralism in American Social Thought, 1915–1965" (Ph.D. dissertation, University of Notre Dame, 1971), 79–80, 114.

13. For critiques of Kallen, see Higham, *Send These to Me*, 210; Werner Sollors, *Beyond Ethnicity: Consent and Descent in American Culture* (New York: Oxford University Press, 1986); Walter Benn Michael, *Our America* (Durham: Duke University Press, 1995). Boas never entirely abandoned the idea of race but argued, rather, that racial differences did not account for differences in culture or intelligence. See Vernon Williams, *Rethinking Race: Franz Boas and His Contemporaries* (Lexington: University of Kentucky Press, 1996). Quote by Carl H. Grabo, "Americanizing the Immigrant," *Dial*, 66 (1919). Here, pluralism and cosmopolitanism do not function as mutually exclusive concepts, as David Hollinger argues in *Post-Ethnic America* (New York: Basic Books, 1995), 85–86. On organicism in American social science, see Dorothy Ross, *The Origins of American Social Science* (New York: Cambridge University Press, 1991), 347–49, 375. Robert Park's studies of the Negro "caste" problem, European immigrants, and Orientals denote his efforts to theorize assimilation at the most general level. See Henry Yu, *Thinking Orientals* (New York: Oxford University Press, 2000), 35–47. Not all late-Progressivists were as inclusivist as the Chicago sociologists. Political opponents to the national origins act argued for the inclusion of east and south Europeans in part by emphasizing their support for Asiatic exclusion. See Gerstle, *American Crucible*, 94–97.

14. John Dewey's rewriting of liberal political theory from Lockean individualism to statist economic intervention stressed economic security as the predicate of liberty. Dewey, *Liberalism and Social Action* (New York: Putnam, 1935). Similarly, Herbert Lehman in the 1950s retrospectively located New Deal liberalism's inattention to civil rights in a mistaken belief that economic prosperity was the key to freedom. Lehman, "Liberalism, A Personal Journey: A Survey and Prospect of American Liberalism," Gino Spiranza Lecture, Columbia University, April 1958, file C259, Articles, Papers of Herbert H. Lehman, Herbert H. Lehman Suite and Library, Columbia University (hereafter "HHL"). See also Alan Brinkley, *The End of Reform* (New York: Vintage, 1995); Gary Gestle, "The Protean Character of American Liberalism," *American Historical Review* 99 (1994): 1043–73, at 1044.

15. Ruth Benedict, *Race and Racism* (London: G. Routledge and Sons, 1942); Barbara Savage, *Broadcasting Freedom: Radio, War, and the Politics of Race, 1938–1948* (Chapel Hill: University of North Carolina Press, 1999), 59.

16. Program of Common Council of American Unity, reprinted in Louis Adamic, *From Many Lands* (New York: Harper and Bros., 1939), 347. Adamic borrowed from Walt Whitman's introduction to the 1855 edition of *Leaves of Grass*: "Here is not merely a nation but a teeming nation of nations."

17. Louis Adamic, "The Crisis is an Opportunity," *Common Ground* 1 (Autumn 1940): 62–73, at 63.

18. Carey McWilliams, *Brothers under the Skin* (Boston: Little, Brown and Company, 1943), 4. For an excellent discussion of this universalizing impulse, see Nikhil Pal Singh, "Culture/Wars: Recoding Empire in an Age of Democracy," *American Quarterly* 50 (1998): 471–522.

19. Louis Adamic, *A Nation of Nations* (New York, Harper, 1945), 12–13.

20. Singh, "Culture/Wars," 479–81; Roi Ottley, cited ibid., 481–82. See also Penny Von Eschen, *Race against Empire: African Americans and Anti-Colonial Politics, 1937–1957* (Ithaca: Cornell University Press, 1997).

21. Truman's Executive Order 9981 (1948) desegregated the armed forces; Jackie Robinson's signing with the Brooklyn Dodgers in 1947 integrated major league baseball. Other major events in World War II–era civil rights include FDR's Executive Order 8802 (1941), establishing the Fair Employment Practices Committee; the U.S. Supreme Court's rejection of racial covenants in real estate (*Shelley v. Kraemer* 344 U.S. 1 [1948]) and of state laws proscribing alien land-ownership (*Oyama v. California* 332 U.S. 633 [1947]); and numerous decisions and laws in northern states desegregating public accommodations. Chinese repealer, Act of Dec. 17, 1943 (57 Stat. 600). While repealing Chinese exclusion, Congress did not intend to allow Chinese immigration in any substantial way. It set an annual quota of 105, which was applicable to all persons of Chinese descent regardless of country of birth. This made the Chinese quota a racial one, unlike the national origins quotas.

22. Repeal of Filipino and Indian exclusion and ineligibility to citizenship, Act of July 2, 1946 (60 Stat. 416); nonquota admission for Chinese alien spouses of citizens, Act of Aug. 9, 1946 (60 Stat. 975); nonquota admission of war brides otherwise racially ineligible for admission, Act of July 22, 1947 (61 Stat. 401). Despite the repeal of Chinese, Indian, and Filipino exclusion, Japanese and Koreans remained excluded on grounds of ineligibility to citizenship under the terms of the Immigration Act of 1924. That provision would not be repealed until 1952 (see discussion below). For more on Chinese exclusion and its repeal, see chapter 6.

23. Harrison and Carusi quoted by Divine, *American Immigration Policy*, 157. Harrison had also ordered the elimination of "Hebrew" as a race category from the INS classificatory scheme of "races and peoples," which category had long been criticized by Jewish organizations as racist. Patrick Weil, "Races at the Gate: A Century of Racial Distinctions in American Immigration Policies, 1865–1965," *Georgetown Immigration Law Review* 15 (Summer 2001): 625–48; Marion T. Bennett, *American Immigration Policies* (New York: Public Affairs Press, 1963), 78. For more discussion on pre-examination program, see chapter 2.

24. The criticisms of *Common Ground* were reported in a 1947 report by David Truman prepared for the Carnegie Corporation, the council's major funder. File 13, box 75, Records of the American Council for Nationality Services, Immigration History Research Center, University of Minnesota (Minneapolis).

25. "NATO Intellectuals," by C. Wright Mills, cited by Ira K. Katznelson, *Liberalism's Crooked Circle* (Princeton: Princeton University Press, 1999), 8.

26. Henry L. Feingold, *The Politics of Rescue: The Roosevelt Administration and the Holocaust, 1938–1945* (New Brunswick, NJ: Rutgers University Press, 1970), 17; Divine, *American Immigration Policy*, 92–104.

27. Freda Kirchwey, "While the Jews Die," *Nation*, March 13, 1943, 366; Divine, *American Immigration Policy*, 104. A study conducted in 1944 by the Committee for

the Study of Recent Immigration from Europe reported that 243,800 refugees entered the United States from Europe between 1933 and 1944, of whom two-thirds were Jews. *Survey*, January 1946.

28. Bennett, *American Immigration Policies*, 89.

29. Act of June 25, 1948 (62 Stat. 1009). The mortgaging of quotas meant that some countries' quotas were "filled" for dozens if not scores of years—for Yugoslavia, 90 years; Greece, 78 years, Rumania, 108 years. Memorandum, George Steuart, Jr., to Harry Rosenfield, Nov. 19, 1952, State Dept./Special file, Papers of the President's Commission on Immigration and Naturalization, Harry S. Truman Library, Independence, MO (hereafter "HST"). On displaced persons as undesirables, see memorandum, Attorney General's office to Steelman, "Comments on the Revercomb Report," Feb. 2, 1947, file 127, Official File, HST (hereafter "OF/HST").

30. On criticisms of discrimination against Jews, see also *New Republic*, June 14, 1948.

31. Act of June 16, 1950 (64 Stat. 219). Liberals succeeded in passing the amendment by abandoning the demand for nonquota refugee admissions. See Divine, *American Immigration Policy*, 143. According to an official report made in 1952, 16 percent of the displaced persons admitted to the United States were Jews and 47 percent were Catholic. *Memo to America: The DP Story, Final Report of the U.S. Displaced Persons Commission* (Washington, DC: G.P.O., 1952), 248. Congress lifted the mortgaged quotas in the Act of Sept. 11, 1957 (71 Stat. 639).

32. Universal Declaration of Human Rights, UN General Assembly Resolution 217 (a) III, Dec. 10, 1948. The Refugee Relief Act of 1953 admitted over 189,000 non-quota refugees and "escapees" from Communist countries. In 1956, President Eisenhower paroled some 40,000 Hungarian refugees into the United States. During the 1960s and early 1970s, some 650,000 Cubans entered the United States. Thomas Archdeacon, *Becoming American* (New York: Free Press, 1989), 209; Refugee Act of 1980 (94 Stat. 102).

33. S. Res. 137, 80th Congress, 1st Session, 1947.

34. Senate Report 1515 and S. 1832, April 20, 1950, 81st Congress, 2d Session.

35. Divine, *American Immigration Policy*, 161–62; Act of Sept. 22, 1950 (64 Stat. 987). Passed over Truman's veto, that law also required the Communist Party, its members, and its "subsidiary" organizations to register with the government. Truman said the Internal Security Act put the government in the "thought control business." Not surprisingly, no organization ever registered under the terms of the law. The Supreme Court ruled in 1965 that the registration requirement violated the Fifth Amendment's protection against self-incrimination. *Aptheker v. Secretary of State*, 378 U.S. 500 (1964); *Albertson v. Subversive Activities Control Board*, 382 U.S. 70 (1965). See also David Caute, *The Great Fear: The Anti-Communist Purge under Truman and Eisenhower* (New York: Simon and Schuster, 1978), 38–39; Ellen Schrecker, *Many Are the Crimes: McCarthyism in America* (Boston: Little, Brown and Company, 1998), 141.

36. McCarran bill S. 2550, 82nd Congress, 2d Session, Walter bill H.R. 5678, 82nd Congress, 2d Session; Immigration and Nationality Act of June 27, 1952 (66 Stat. 163); Divine, *American Immigration Policy*, 179.

37. Divine, *American Immigration Policy*, 167.

38. There was also an overall Asian-Pacific quota of 2,000. The total did not in-

clude the Chinese quota of 105 or the Japanese quota of 185, however. On racial eligibility to citizenship, see chapter 1.

39. Letter, Dean Acheson to Harry S. Truman, April 14, 1952, file "Immigration, Memos and Letters/4," David Lloyd files, HST; typescript, Robert McCullom, "Considerations affecting CEN [Committee for Equality in Naturalization] policy concerning immigration," [1950], file Naturalization Bill, Philleo Nash files, HST. Commenting on Acheson's position, Truman's budget director Frederick Lawton reminded the president that the "bill takes away at least as much as it appears to give." Memorandum, Lawton to Truman, May 9, 1952, ibid.

40. Sec. 203. Of unused quotas, 25 percent was to go to a fourth preference comprising brothers, sisters, and adult children of U.S. citizens. Quote by Bennett, *American Immigration Policies*, 152. The law also eliminated nonquota status for students, making them nonimmigrants and therefore subject to deportation if they overstayed their visas, and for professors and ministers, forcing them to compete for precious quota slots. It did strike a note for gender equality by allowing for the nonquota admission of citizens' spouses (previously, only wives were eligible). See Sec. 202(a)(2) and Sec. 203(a)(3).

41. Letter, Robert F. Wagner to Harry S. Truman, June 18, 1952, file McCarran-Walter Bill—Con, OF/HST. On lack of debate over economic preferences, see Aristide Zolberg, "The Back Door and the Main Gate," draft manuscript chapter (in author's possession), *A Nation by Design? Immigration Policy in the Fashioning of America* (Cambridge, MA: Harvard University Press and Russell Sage, 2004).

42. Sec. 212(a). The new excludable classes were aliens convicted of two or more offenses, whether or not involving moral turpitude, if aggregate possible confinement exceeded five years; those who practiced fraud or lied to procure documents or to attempt entry; narcotics-law violators; smugglers of aliens; and anyone "coming to the U.S. solely, principally, or incidentally to engage in any immoral act." At the same time, Sec. 212(c) exempted from deportation fraud cases if the alien had immediate family relatives in the U.S. Bennett, *American Immigration Policies*, 117, 149. See also chapter 2.

43. Sec. 235, Sec. 273(d), Sec. 242(f), Sec. 212(c); Sec. 244 (a), (b), (c); Senate Report 1515, 600. In line with the spirit of the law, the INS in 1956 closed Ellis Island and ceased detaining aliens awaiting deportation hearings, save for cases inimical to the public interest. See typescript report, Joseph Swing, "Administrative Reforms in the INS," file CO-659P, Part 1, Subject Files of the U.S.–I.N.S.

44. Sec. 349.

45. Truman, "Veto of Bill to Review the Laws Relating to Immigration, Naturalization, and Nationality," June 25, 1952, *Public Papers of the Presidents, Harry S. Truman, 1952* (Washington, DC: GPO, 1956), 441–47; memorandum, William J. Hopkins to Harry S. Truman, June 20, 1952, file McCarran-Walter Bill–Pro, OF/HST. On Truman and civil rights, see also William Berman, *The Politics of Civil Rights in the Truman Administration* (Columbus, OH: Ohio State University Press, 1970); Richard Dalfiume, *Desegregation of the U.S. Armed Forces: Fighting on Two Fronts* (Columbia, MO: University of Missouri Press, 1969); Michael Gardner, *Harry Truman and Civil Rights: Moral Courage and Political Risks* (Carbondale, IL: Southern Illinois University Press, 2002).

46. Executive Order 10392, Sept. 4, 1952. The commission's final report, *Whom We Shall Welcome*, was issued in 1953.

47. Key organizations of the National Committee on Citizenship and Immigration were the American Jewish Congress, American Jewish Committee, National Catholic Welfare Council, United Auto Workers, and AFL-CIO. Officers included Philip Perlman, former solicitor general and chairman of the Truman immigration commission, Msgr. John O'Grady of the National Catholic Charities, and Spyros Skouras, a prominent businessman. Its advisors included Earl Harrison, the former immigration commissioner who had served on Truman's commission on displaced persons, and historian Oscar Handlin.

48. Handlin's *Boston's Immigrants: A Study in Acculturation* (Cambridge, MA: Harvard University Press, 1941) and *The Uprooted: The Epic Story of the Great Migrations that Made the American People* (New York: Grossett and Dunlap, 1951) were seminal works that established and legitimated the field of immigration history. His popular works included *Danger in Discord: Origins of Anti-Semitism in the U.S.* (New York: Anti-Defamation League of B'nai B'rith, 1948); *Race and Nationality in American Life* (Boston: Little, Brown and Company, 1957 [1950]); *Newcomers, Negroes, and Puerto Ricans in a Changing Metropolis* (Cambridge, MA: Harvard University Press, 1951); *American Jews: Their Story* (New York: Anti-Defamation League of B'nai B'rith, 1958); *Out of Many: A Study Guide to Cultural Pluralism in the U.S.* (New York: Anti-Defamation League of B'nai B'rith, 1964). See also Harry Rosenfield, "National Origins, Handlin" [Oct. 1952], President's Commission on Immigration and Naturalization, Subject File, National Origins, Harry Rosenfield Papers, HST (hereafter "Rosenfield/HST"). Handlin was retained as a consultant at $35 a day during the month of October 1952. See Budget file, ibid.

49. Higham, *Strangers in the Land*, 331. B'nai B'rith's publications included Handlin's *Danger in Discord, American Jews,* and *Out of Many,* as well as Edward Corsi, *Paths to the New World* (1956), John F. Kennedy, *A Nation of Immigrants* (New York 1959), Clarence Senior, *Strangers Then Neighbors* (1961); William Mack, *Patterns of Minority Relations* (1964). The B'nai B'rith proposed the *Nation of Immigrants* project to Kennedy, contributing an outline prepared by historian Arthur Mann for Kennedy's writers. The book, published in 1959, was intended for high school students and was reissued in an enlarged edition in 1963, after the president's assassination, by Harper and Row for a general audience. Typescript, Arthur Mann, "Immigrants All," n.d.; letter, William Korey to Ralph Dungan, April 29, 1958, file Immigration, box 767, Senate files, Pre-Presidential Papers, John F. Kennedy Library, Boston (hereafter "JFK").

50. Refugee Relief Act of August 7, 1953 (67 Stat. 400). Stephen T. Wagner, "The Lingering Death of the National Origins System: A Political History of U.S. Immigration Policy" (Ph.D. dissertation, Harvard University, 1986), 237–87; Meg Greenfield, "The Melting Pot of Francis E. Walter," *New York Reporter*, Oct. 26, 1961. Greenfield described members of Congress as reluctant to offend Walter because they depended on him to steer private legislation admitting or preventing deportation of immigrants, considered a necessary last resort in individual cases as long as the Walter-McCarran Act remained on the books.

51. Typescript, Will Maslow, "Suggestions for a Model Immigration Bill," Dec. 18, 1952, personal correspondence file, Rosenfield/HST; Joachim Prinz to Kennedy, Feb.

8, 1963, file LE/IM 1, box 483, White House Central Subject File, JFK (hereafter "WHCF"); Oscar Handlin, "The Immigration Fight Has Only Begun," *Commentary* 14 (July 1952): 1–7, at 6. Julius Edelstein credited Dean Jefferson Fordham of the University of Pennsylvania Law School, who helped draft the alternative omnibus bill in 1953, for convincing Lehman and Humphrey to "make a fresh start" and eliminate the national origins quotas. Author interview with Julius Edelstein, Nov. 22, 2000, New York. See also Wagner, "The Lingering Death of the National Origins System," 25–86.

52. Unidentified clipping, Milton Friedman, "Herbert Lehman: Conscience of the Senate," [1958], file, Articles, HHL. Lehman's biographer called him a "lonely independent" in the Senate, though lacking both charisma and "distinguished force of mind." Allan Nevins, *Herbert H. Lehman and His Era* (New York: Charles Scribner's Sons, 1963), 4–14, 153–54, 352, 404. In 1956 Lehman contributed over $12,000 of the National Citizens Committee for Immigration and Citizenship's total income of $20,754. Memorandum from Tom Burke to Walter Reuther, re: National Committee on Immigration and Citizenship, Nov. 15, 1956, folder 16, box 507, Papers of Walter Reuther, Records of the United Auto Workers, Wayne State University Archives of Labor and Urban Affairs, Detroit (hereafter "UAW").

53. Herbert H. Lehman, Statement in support of H.R. 2910 [Displaced Persons Act], before the House Subcommittee on Immigration and Naturalization, June 1947, 4, file Immigration H.R. 2910, Special Subject File, HHL (hereafter "SSF/HHL"); Remarks by Herbert H. Lehman at National Conference of Christians and Jews, Feb. 23, 1953, SSF/HHL; Lehman, "Liberalism: A Personal Journey, a Survey and Prospect of American Liberalism," 20, 28.

54. Press release of Herbert H. Lehman's statement before the President's Commission on Immigration and Naturalization, Sept. 30, 1952, 2, file Immigration, McCarran-Walter Act, SSF/HHL.

55. Lehman, "Judaism and Liberalism," 9, Singh, "Culture/Wars," 487. As Singh notes, the exemplar of this view is Gunnar Myrdal's *The American Dilemma* (1944).

56. This was particularly evident in the civil rights movement. The Cold War cleaved African American politics deeply, with figures like Bayard Rustin and A. Philip Randolph ascending to leadership through anti-communist realignments that exiled, both literally and figuratively, progressives like W.E.B. DuBois and Paul Robeson. On anti-communism and civil rights, see Mary Dudziak, *Cold War Civil Rights: Race and the Image of American Democracy* (Princeton: Princeton University Press, 2000); Von Eschen, *Race against Empire*; Rene Romano, "No Diplomatic Immunity: African Diplomats, the State Department, and Civil Rights, 1961–1964," *Journal of American History* 87 (Sept. 2000): 546–70.

57. Newsletter, "Washington Pro and Con," [1954], file Immigration, box 478, Papers of Emanuel Celler, Manuscripts Division, Library of Congress (Washington, DC) (hereafter "Celler Papers"); mimeographed statement, Emanuel Celler, "The Consequences of Our Immigration Policy," Dec. 5, 1955, 1, file Immigration, box 478, ibid.; Statement by twenty Democratic sponsors of the Humphrey-Lehman immigration bill, press release from the office of Herbert H. Lehman, Feb. 25, 1955, SSF/HHL. Celler used the same metaphor: "Is the way to destroy an iron curtain . . . to erect an iron curtain of our own?" Celler, "The Consequences of Our Immigration Policy," 2. See also Alex Brooks, "McCarran's Iron Curtain," *Nation*, Mar. 29, 1952, 299.

58. In 1952 the AFL tepidly endorsed the McCarran-Walter Act. EC minutes, May 19–22, 1952, file 19, box 27, Legislative Dept., RG 27-001, AFL-CIO. For summary of AFL and CIO policies on immigration at the time of the federation merger, see memorandum, Stanley Ruttenberg to Thomas Harris, Jan. 20, 1956, file 17, box 27, ibid. The Executive Council of the AFL-CIO discussed immigration policy only when the issue was prominent in Congress. That it took its cues from the Democratic Party is evident in the federation's legislative staff urging that the EC not to "lag behind the [Johnson] administration in this field." Memorandum, Kenneth Meiklejohn to Andrew Biemiller, Nov. 23, 1964, file 31, box 27, ibid.

59. "Statement by AFL-CIO Executive Council on Immigration Reform," EC minutes, Feb. 4, 1957, 157–58, file 19, box 27, ibid.; letter, Meany to Eli Jesberg, Feb. 19, 1957, ibid. On labor's commitment to Truman and Eisenhower administrations' Cold War aims, see, for example, Robert H. Zieger, *The CIO: 1935–1955* (Chapel Hill: University of North Carolina Press, 1995), 296, 328–30.

60. Dudziak, *Cold War Civil Rights,* 11–17.

61. Handlin, "The Immigration Fight Has Only Begun," 6, emphasis in original.

62. Kennedy, *A Nation of Immigrants,* 62–63. On the Eurocentrism of cultural pluralism, see Higham, *Send These to Me,* 202–14. The Eurocentrist orientation is also evident in Louis Adamic's works on cultural diversity. *From Many Lands* (1939) comprised chapters on the life stories of Croatian, Bohemian, Finnish, Polish, Greeks, Armenian, and Dutch immigrants, and one chapter on the marriage of a Mexican American and a native-born white American. *A Nation of Nations* (1945) elaborated a theme of "Americans from"—from Italy, France, Holland, Sweden, Russia, Germany, Yugoslavia, Norway, Greece, Poland, and Ireland, as well as "from Spain and Mexico" and "Negro Americans." Adamic, like Handlin, considered Mexicans to be white. The exception to this trend was Carey McWilliams's *Brothers under the Skin* (1943), no doubt because the writer was from California. Not one Asian American or Mexican American is listed among the founding individuals or officers of the National Committee on Immigration and Citizenship, an otherwise studiously diverse group. Typescript, "Meeting of Preparatory Group for Revision of McCarran-Walter Act," Nov. 5, 1953, file Immigration, McCarran-Walter Act, 1953–55, SSF/HHL; typescript, "Memorandum on National Committee on Immigration and Citizenship," n.d., file 224-695, General Personal Correspondence 1958, HHL (hereafter "GPC/HHL"). Only one Asian American, Mike Masaoka of the JACL, and one Mexican American, George I. Sánchez of the University of Texas, were listed among over one hundred names on the letterhead of the American Immigration and Citizenship Conference. File 232-1279, GPC 1963, HHL.

63. Greenfield, "The Melting Pot of Francis E. Walter"; typescript, State Department Bureau of Consular and Security Affairs, "Principal Provisions of State Dept.'s Tentative Proposal for Immigration Legislation," May 27, 1963, file LE/IM FG105, box 482, WHCF, JFK. The study estimated an increase in Asiatic immigration from nonquota Western Hemisphere countries to be about 6,000, including 1,000 from Bolivia, 2,500 from Mexico, 400 from British Guyana, as well as 1,000 from Great Britain. The same study projected increases in European immigration according to a proposed redistribution of unused quotas without regard to national origin: 15,043 from Italy, 1,288 from Portugal, 12,976 from Poland. See also testimony of Abba Schwartz, in "Immigration," hearings before the House Judiciary Committee on H.R.

7700, Part 2, July 2, 1964 et seq., 88th Congress, 2d session, 532 (hereafter "Immigration").

On liberal avoidance of Chinese Americans during the early 1940s, see Fred Riggs, *Pressures on Congress* (New York: Columbia University Press, 1950); Renqiu Yu, "Little Heard Voices: The Chinese Hand Laundry Alliance and *China Daily News'* Appeal for Repeal of the Chinese Exclusion Act in 1943," *Chinese America: History and Perspectives* (1990): 21–35.

64. Julius Edelstein told me that Lehman simply did not impute much importance to the so-called wetback problem. Edelstein interview, Nov. 22, 2000.

65. Letter, Herbert Lehman to Norman R. Sturgis, Jr., March 5, 1954, file C75-34, Legislative files, HHL (hereafter "LF/HHL").

66. Letter, Julius Edelstein to Jules Cohen, June 22, 1954, file C75-35, LF/HHL. On rhetorical elision of differences between U.S.–Mexico and U.S.–Canada borders, see chapter 2.

67. Transcript of Remarks by Julius Edelstein before National Federation of Settlements, March 1, 1954, 8, file C75-34, LF/HHL.

68. Ibid. Similarly, in 1954 Emanuel Celler read into the Congressional Record nine cases of Europeans refused admission on grounds that they had committed crimes of moral turpitude. As in the 1930s and 1940s, Celler made the case for reform by invoking cases like that of Helga Josefa Wiley, who took firewood from the forest in Bremen, Germany, for fuel and was fined the equivalent of five cents. File Immigration, box 478, Celler Papers. Lehman quoted in Congressional Record, June 14, 1954, 8182, cited by Rick Olguin, "Defining the Foreign: Wetbacks, Braceros, and Subversives in the 1950s," in *Chicano Discourse: Selected Conference Proceedings of the National Assoc. for Chicano Studies*, ed. Tatcho Mindiola, Jr., and Emilio Zamora (Houston: Mexican American Studies Program, University of Houston, 1992), 94.

69. See, for example, Higham, *Send These to Me*; Divine, *American Immigration Policy*.

70. Press release, office of Hubert Humphrey, March 12, 1952, file C76-4, LF/HHL; transcript of statement by Herbert H. Lehman, Jan 2, 1959, file 225-859, GPC/HHL.

71. Statement of William H. Draper to the President's Commission on Immigration and Naturalization, Nov. 19, 1952, 2, C76-11, LF/HHL; press release, "Senator Kennedy Announces Seven-Point Immigration Bill," Feb. 19, 1959, file 86th-1st Immigration, box 630, Senate files, Pre-Presidential Papers, JFK.

72. Chester Bowles, "Call for a New Immigration Policy," *Survey* (November 1951): 463–65; Edward Corsi, *Paths to the New World: American Immigration—Yesterday, Today, and Tomorrow* (New York: Anti-Defamation League of B'nai B'rith, 1956), 20; "McCarran Immigration Law Violates American Traditions," *Economic Outlook* 13 (November 1952): 80; transcript of statement of Herbert H. Lehman to the President's Commission on Immigration and Naturalization, Sept. 30, 1952, SSF/HHL.

73. Zolberg, "The Main Gate and the Back Door"; sundry correspondence to Herbert Lehman in C75-51, C75-21, LF/HHL; press release, "Sen. Kennedy Introduces Three-Point Immigration Program," May 18, 1959, file 86th-1st, Immigration, general, box 630, Pre-Presidential Papers, JFK.

74. I found no such studies among the papers and records of the AFL-CIO, INS, Labor Department, State Department, House and Senate committees on immigration, Herbert Lehman, Emmanuel Celler, Harry S. Truman, John F. Kennedy, or Lyn-

don B. Johnson, or in contemporary periodical or academic literature. Edelstein recalled the figure came from the AFL-CIO, but never saw a study. Edelstein interview.

75. The formulas used in 1921 and initially for the 1924 act originated in the Dillingham Commission's 1912 proposal to limit immigration to 10 percent of number of aliens counted in the 1910 census, a rough approximation of contemporary demographics. The 1921 temporary act arbitrarily set the figure at 3 percent in order to achieve a greater degree of restriction than Dillingham's 10 percent. Albert Johnson, chair of the Houses immigration committee, liked the concept of "percentage restriction" and came up with a "2 percent/1890 census" formula because it "almost exactly divides the population as between the two great groups [Nordics and Mediterraneans] in accordance with the origins of the people of the United States." Johnson cited by Desmond King, *Making Americans* (Cambridge: Harvard University Press, 2000), 204. Restrictionists toyed with various other formulas after being criticized that using 1890 as the baseline census discriminated against southern and eastern Europeans. John Trevor compared one-fifth of one percent of the population enumerated in the 1920 census (192,792); *pi* of one percent (239,165); H.R. 6540 (169,083); Act of 1921 (357,803). Appendix A, "Preliminary Study of Population," House Report 350, H.R. 7995, May 24, 1924, 68th Congress, 1st Session. Trevor and Sen. David Reed, who cosponsored the 1924 act with Johnson, finally came up with the method of determining quotas based on the "national origin" of the entire U.S. population in 1920—which conveniently yielded the same results as the 2-percent formula, giving 85 percent of the quotas to Great Britain, Ireland, and Germany. The final quotas determined in 1929 reduced those countries' share to 65 percent. See chapter 1.

76. Newsletter, Information Service of the National Council of the Churches of Christ in the USA, "Give Me Your Tired . . . ," April 4, 1953, 6, file C76-19, LF/HHL; letter, Herbert Lehman to Mrs. John Pendleton, March 14, 1955, file C75-44, LF/HHL; testimony of Robert Kennedy in "Immigration," 417.

77. Oscar Handlin, "We Need More Immigrants," *Atlantic Monthly* (May 1953): 27–31, quote at 29; typescript, Hyman Bookbinder, "The World's Refugees: A Challenge to America," March 30, 1960, file 18, box 27, RG 27-001, AFL-CIO.

78. Oscar Handlin, "The Immigration Fight Has Only Begun," 1; BLS statement cited in typescript, "Does America Need More People?" [1952], 3, Population Studies, Special Files, President's Commission on Immigration and Naturalization, Rosenfield/ HST. On declining birthrate and comparisons to the Soviet population, see also Corsi, *Paths to the New World*, 19–20.

79. Testimony of Willard Wirtz, "Immigration," 440. See also "Should the Gates Be Opened Wider?" *Business Week*, October 17, 1964; testimony of Nicholas Katzenbach before Immigration Subcommittee, Senate Judiciary Committee, Feb. 10, 1965, 9, file Road to Final Passage, part 2, box 1, Legislative Background, Immigration Law-1965, Lyndon Baines Johnson Presidential Library, Austin, TX (hereafter "LBJ").

80. "Does America Need More People?" 2; typescript, Dudley Kirk, "Demographic Absorbtive Capacity for Immigration, Conclusions," Oct. 31, 1952, 1–2, Population studies, subject files, Presidential Commission on Immigration and Naturalization, Rosenfield/HST; Moulton quoted in typescript report, Harry Flannery, "Labor and Immigration: "Is the McCarran-Walter Act Strangling the Nation's Economy?" [1955], 3, file 15, box 27, RG 27-001, AFL-CIO.

81. Julian Isaac, *Economics of Migration* (London: Paul Kegan, 1947), 111–12. The U.S. population enumerated in the 1950 census was 154 million; emigration averaged 42,000 a year for the decade 1951–1960; native population growth was 2.5 million a year. 3,180,000 (2 percent of total population) + 42,000 (emigration) − 2,500,000 (native growth) = 722,000.

82. Isaac, *Economics of Migration*, 96.

83. Ibid., 103.

84. Testimony of Walter Mason before immigration subcommittee, Senate Judiciary Committee, Nov. 21, 1955, file 16, box 27, RG 27-001, AFL-CIO; "Pres. Johnson's Immigration Proposals," [February 1965], 4, file Immigration, box 482, Frederick Panzer files, LBJ; typescript, "Analysis of Letters Opposing the Immigration Bills H.R. 2580, S. 500," n.d., file Immigration, box 480, Celler Papers.

85. Melvin W. Reder, "The Economic Consequences of Increased Immigration," *Review of Economics and Statistics* 45 (August 1963): 221–230, at 229, emphasis in original.

86. Vernon M. Briggs, Jr., *Immigration Policy and the American Labor Force* (Baltimore: Johns Hopkins University Press, 1984), 59. According to a survey by the House Committee on Foreign Affairs, 70 percent of the 102,000 foreign students enrolled in U.S. colleges and universities in 1967 came from less developed countries, with an estimated nonreturn rate of 15 to 25 percent. Library of Congress, Foreign Affairs Division, *Brain Drain: A Study of the Persistent Issue of International Scientific Mobility: Prepared for the Subcommittee on National Security Policy and Scientific Developments, House Committee on Foreign Affairs* (Washington, DC: GPO, 1974), 33–35 (hereafter *Brain Drain*).

87. Transcript of speech by Paul C. Empie, "Immigration Legislation: Moral Issues and the National Interest," Oct. 16, 1959, 2, file 10, box 30, Washington office/Jacobs-Sifton, UAW, emphasis in original (hereafter "Jacobs-Sifton/UAW").

88. Ibid., 3, 5.

89. Ibid., 2, 4–5; mimeograph, National Community Relations Advisory Council, "A Statement of Principles regarding American Immigration and Naturalization Policies," March 15, 1955, 7–8, file 7, box 30, Jacobs-Sifton/UAW.

90. S. 3043, 87th Congress, 2d Session, 1962; reintroduced S. 747, 88th Congress, 1st Session, 1963. For more discussion of the original Hart bill, see Zolberg, "Main Gate and Back Door"; Wagner, "The Lingering Death of the National Origins Quota System," 475.

91. David Reimers, *Still the Golden Door*, 64–68.

92. Senate Report 1515, 25–26, 630–32. On administrative exclusion, see chapter 2.

93. McCarran quoted by Eleanor Hadley, "A Critical Analysis of the Wetback Problem," *Law and Contemporary Problems* 21 (1956): 334–57, at 337.

94. Letter, Oscar Handlin to Julius Edelstein, July 17, 1953, file C76-18, LF/HHL.

95. S. 2585, 83rd Congress, 1st session, 1953 (Lehman); S. 1206, 84th Congress, 1st Session, 1955 (Lehman); H.R. 3364, 85th Congress, 1st Session, 1957 (Celler); S. 3043, 87th Congress 2d Session, 1962 (Hart); S. 747, 88th Congress, 1st Session, 1963 (Hart); S. 747, 88th Congress, 1st Session, 1963 (Hart); S. 1932/H.R. 7700, 88th Congress, 1st Session, 1963 (Hart-Celler, Kennedy administration bill); S. 500/H.R. 2580, 89th Congress, 1st Session, 1965 (Hart-Celler, Johnson administration bill). See

also memorandum, Department of State, Bureau of Consular and Security Affairs, "Principal Provisions of State Dept.'s Tentative Proposal for Immigration Legislation," May 27, 1963, file LE/IM FG 105, box 482, WHCF, JFK.

96. Letter, Ralph Aguilera to Herbert Lehman, April 11, 1955, file Immigration C75-46, HHL; typescript, Gladys Uhl, "Confidential background information on McGregor and Gilberg amendments," n.d., file 32, box 27, RG 27-001, AFL-CIO.

97. William Stern, "An Abstract of HR 2580, the Immigration and Nationality Amendments of 1965: A Case Study" (Ph.D. dissertation, New York University, 1970), 112; American Committee on Immigration Policies, "Our Immigration Laws—Protect You, Your Job, and Your Freedom" (1964), in file Immigration Legislation 1958, 1963–69, box 7, Abba Schwartz Papers, JFK; editorials, New York Times, July 17, 1965, 24, col. 1, and September 24, 1954 (International edition), 4, col. 1.

98. Testimony of Norbert Schlei, in "Immigration," 481.

99. Uhl, "Confidential background information."

100. "Questions and Answers," [1965], 4–5, file Road to Final Passage, part 3, box 1, Immigration Law-1965, Legislative Background files, LBJ.

101. See chapter 4, table 4.1.

102. Hadley, "A Critical Analysis of the Wetback Problem," 357.

103. Texas State AFL-CIO v. Robert F. Kennedy et al., civil action no. 3468-61, U.S. District Court, District of Columbia, in file 210.91, box 11, lot 64D363, Records relating to Mexico, 1938–1963, Bureau of Inter-American Affairs. U.S. Dept. of State, RG 59, National Archives, College Park, MD (hereafter "BIA"). In 1963 the Labor Department tightened control over issuing visas for commuter workers by requiring that employers requesting such visas receive clearance from the department. See letter, John Henning to George Meany, Nov. 12, 1963, file ES 2-4-1, box 74, Secretary of Labor files, General Records of the U.S. Dept. of Labor, RG 174, National Archives, College Park, MD.

104. Memorandum, Ben Zweig to Rolland Welch, July 5, 1961, file 210.91, box 11, Records relating to Mexico, 1938–63, BIA.

105. Stern, "An Abstract of HR 2580," 176, 322; Abba Schwartz, The Open Society (W. Morrow, 1968), 124; New York Times, September 30, 1965 (International edition), 2, col. 5.

106. Wagner, "The Lingering Death of the National Origins Quota System," 419.

107. Immigration Act of 1965 (Public Law 89-236, 79 Stat. 911). The preferences went, first, to unmarried adult children of citizens (no more than 20 percent of 170,000); second, to spouses and unmarried children of lawfully resident aliens (20 percent); third, to professionals, scientists, and artists of "exceptional ability" (10 percent); fourth, to married adult children of citizens (10 percent); fifth, to brothers and sisters of citizens (24 percent); sixth, to skilled and unskilled workers deemed in short supply in the United States (10 percent); and seventh, to refugees (6 percent). Within countries, undersubscribed higher family categories could "kick down" visas to lower categories, ending finally with a final, "nonpreference" category, which benefited unskilled workers without family ties in the United States. See Sec. 203.

108. Report of the Select Commission on Western Hemisphere Immigration, Jan. 1968, 12.

109. Sec. 203(a). Nonquota immediate family immigrants and refugees were not subject to labor certification.

110. "Remarks at the Signing of the Immigration Bill, Liberty Island, New York," Oct. 3, 1965, *Public Papers of the Presidents, Lyndon B. Johnson, 1965*, (Washington, D.C.: GPO, 1965), 1038.

111. Letter to President Johnson, Sept. 30, 1965, transmitted by Edward Ennis, Sept. 30, 1965, file LE/IM 9/21/65 to 12/2/65, box 74, WHCF, LBJ. Of the sixty-three organizations signing the letter, there were only two Asian American organizations (the JACL and the National Chinese Welfare Council) and no Mexican Americans. Editorial, *New York Times*, September 24, 1965, 4, col. 1.

112. Deane and David Heller, "Our New Immigration Law," *American Legion Magazine*, February 1966, 6–8. The Legion went as far as to conclude that the new law promoted a "naturally-operating national origins system." "Four of the preferences favor the admission of immediate family members of people who are already here, while the other three are either highly selective or, indeed, restrictive," it said. On the American Legion's lack of opposition to the bill in 1964–65, see also Reimers, *Still the Golden Door*, 71, and Stern, "An Abstract of HR 2580," 239–44.

113. *Brain Drain*, 70, 2, 7. Brain drain flowed not only to the United States but to Great Britain, Canada, and Australia.

114. *Report of the Select Commission*, 9, 12.

115. Public Law 94–571, 90 Stat. 2703.

116. Nicholas DeGenova, "Migrant 'Illegality' and Deportability in Everyday Life," *Annual Review of Anthropology* 31 (2002); 419–47, at 436.

117. Elliot Abrams and Frank S. Abrams, "Immigration Policy: Who Gets in and Why?" *Public Interest* [1974]: 9–11; Bill Ong Hing, *Making and Remaking Asian America through Immigration Policy, 1850–1990* (Stanford: Stanford University Press, 1993), 199; Reimers, *Still the Golden Door*, 95–96.

118. Cited by Abrams and Abrams, "Immigration Policy," 12. See also "Questions and Answers" [1965], 3.

119. Reimers, *Still the Golden Door*, 109.

120. Stern, "An Abstract of H.R. 2580," 341–43. Of the top sending nations in the Eastern Hemisphere in 1971, the Philippines was first (28,471), China (including Taiwan) ranked fourth (14,417), India ranked fifth (14,310), and Korea ranked sixth (14,297). The second and third were Italy (22,137) and Greece (15,939), respectively. On population of Asian Americans, see Hing, *Making and Remaking Asian America*, 81, 118; http:www.census.gov/population/socdemo/race/api/ppl-146/tab01.xls.

121. Hing, *Making and Remaking Asian America*, 99; *Brain Drain*, 80. See also Catherine Ceniza Choy, "The Usual Subjects: Medicine, Nursing, and American Colonialism in the Philippines," *Hitting Critical Mass*, 5 (Fall 1998).

122. Hing, *Making and Remaking Asian America*, 85, 99, 104.

123. Immigration from Africa did not increase substantially until the 1980s.

124. George Sánchez, "Race, Nation and Culture in Recent Immigration Studies," *Journal of American Ethnic History* (Summer 1999): 66–83; Lisa Lowe, *Immigrant Acts: On Asian American Cultural Politics* (Durham: Duke University Press 1996); Avery Gordon and Christopher Newfield, eds., *Mapping Multiculturalism* (Minneapolis: University of Minnesota Press, 1996); Stuart Hall and Paul Gilroy, eds., *Questions of Cultural Identity* (London: Sage, 1996); Michael Moon and Cathy Davidson, eds., *Subjects and Citizens: Nation, Race, and Gender from Oroonoko to Anita Hill* (Durham: Duke University Press, 1995); John Rajchman, ed., *The Identity in Question*

(New York: Routledge, 1995); Neil Smelser and Jeffrey Alexander, eds., *Diversity and Its Discontents: Cultural Conflict and Common Ground in Contemporary American Society* (Princeton: Princeton University Press, 1999); Priscilla Wald, *Constituting Americans: Cultural Anxiety and Narrative Form* (Durham: Duke University Press, 1995); Homi Bhabha, ed., *Nation and Narration* (London: Routledge, 1990); Paul Gilroy, *The Black Atlantic: Modernity and Double Consciousness* (Cambridge, MA: Harvard University Press, 1993); Paul Gilroy, *Against Race: Imagining Political Culture beyond the Color Line* (Cambridge: Belknap, 2000); Arjun Appadurai, *Modernity at Large: Cultural Dimensions of Globalization* (Minneapolis: University of Minnesota Press, 1996); Lauren Berlant, *The Queen of America Goes to Washington City: Essays on Sex and Citizenship* (Durham: Duke University Press, 1997); Iris Marion Young, *Justice and the Politics of Difference* (Princeton: Princeton University Press, 1990).

Epilogue

1. U.S.-INS, *2000 Statistical Yearbook*, table 1, Immigration to the U.S., fiscal years 1820–2000; Immigration and Naturalization Act of 1990 (Public Law 101-649, 104 Stat. 4978). See also David M. Reimers, *Unwelcome Strangers: American Identity and the Turn against Immigration* (New York: Columbia University Press, 1998), 27–28, 154. Refugee admissions also increased as a result of the Refugee Act of 1980 (94 Stat. 102), which adopted the internationally recognized definition of a refugee as a person unable or unwilling to return to their homeland because of persecution or fear of persecution. See also Bill Ong Hing, *Making and Remaking Asian America through Immigration Policy* (Stanford: Stanford University Press, 1990), chapter 4; Reimers, *Unwelcome Strangers*, 110.

2. Total removals, including formal deportations and voluntary departures, numbered 14,519,622 for the 1990s, compared to 10,194,742 for the 1980s. U.S.-INS, *2000 Statistical Yearbook*, table 63, Aliens expelled from the U.S., fiscal years 1820–2000; and ibid., "Estimates," 3.

3. Immigration Reform and Control Act of 1986 (Public Law 99-603, 100 Stat. 3359); Frank Bean, Barry Edmonston, and Jeffrey Passel, *Migration to the U.S.: IRCA and the Experience of the 1980s* (Santa Monica, CA: Rand Corporation, 1990), 16–18, 27.

4. Joseph Nevins, *Operation Gatekeeper: The Rise of the 'Illegal Alien' and the Making of the U.S.-Mexico Boundary* (New York: Routledge, 2001); "Illegal Immigrant Death Rate Rises Sharply in Barren Areas," *New York Times*, August 6, 2002, sec. A, 1, 12; "Mexico Fears Migrant Deaths Will Increase with Despair," *New York Times*, October 20, 2002, sec. A, 4; Ko-lin Chin, *Smuggled Chinese: Clandestine Immigration into the United States* Philadelphia: Temple University Press, 1998); U.S.-INS, *2000 Statistical Yearbook*, "Estimates," 3–6.

5. U.S.-INS, *2000 Statistical Yearbook*, table 1. Immigrants are concentrated in California, Texas, New York, Florida, New Jersey, and Illinois. See also Reimers, *Unwelcome Strangers*, 27–28.

6. Reimers, *Unwelcome Strangers*, 31–33, 119–29. Proposition 187, approved by a 59 to 41 percent margin by the California electorate in 1994, barred undocumented children from public schools, excluded all undocumented immigrants from state-

funded nonemergency medical services, and required social service providers to report suspected undocumented aliens to the INS. The provisions were enjoined and never implemented. *LULAC v. Wilson*, 908 F. Supp. 775 (C.D. Calif. 1995). On the English-only campaign, see also Raymond Tatlovich, *Nativism Reborn? The Official English Language Movement and the American States* (Lexington: University of Kentucky Press, 1995).

On the effects of late-twentieth-century immigration on American life, see also Charles Hirschmann, Philip Kasinitz, and Josh DeWind, *The Handbook of International Migration: The American Experience* (New York: Russell Sage, 1999); U.S. Commission on Immigration Reform, *1997 Report to Congress: Becoming an American: Immigration and Immigrant Policy* (Washington, DC: GPO, 1997); James P. Smith and Barry Edmonston, eds., *The New Americans: Economic, Demographic, and Fiscal Effects of Immigration* (Washington, DC: National Academy Press, 1997); Peter Brimelow, *Alien Nation: Common Sense about America's Immigration Disaster* (New York: Random House, 1995); Daniel James, *Illegal Immigration: An Unfolding Crisis* (Lanham, MD: University Press of America, 1991); George Borjas, *Heaven's Door: Immigration Policy and the American Economy* (Princeton: Princeton University Press, 1999).

7. U.S. Bureau of Census, "The Hispanic Population in the United States: Population Characteristics," March, 2000; Alejandro Portes, "Making Sense of Diversity: Recent Research on Hispanic Minorities in the United States," *American Review of Sociology* 13 (1987): 359–85; Alejandro Portes and Alex Stepick, *City on the Edge: The Transformation of Miami* (Berkeley: University of California Press, 1993); Suzanne Oboler, *Ethnic Labels, Latino Lives: Identity and the Politics of (Re)presentation in the United States* (Minneapolis: University of Minnesota Press, 1995); Douglas S. Massey, Jorge Durand, and Nolan J. Malone, *Beyond Smoke and Mirrors: Mexican Immigration in an Era of Economic Integration* (New York: Russell Sage, 2002); Gloria Anzaldúa, *Borderlands: The New Mestiza = La Frontera* (San Francisco: Spinsters/Aunt Lute, 1987); Carlos Vélez-Ibáñez, *Border Visions: Mexican Cultures of the Southwestern U.S.* (Tuscon: University of Arizona Press, 1996).

8. Hing, *Making and Remaking Asian America*; Aihwa Ong, *Flexible Citizenship: The Cultural Logics of Transnationality* (Durham: Duke University Press, 1999); Grace Yun, ed., *A Look beyond the Model Minority Image: Critical Issues in Asian America* (New York: Minority Rights Groups, 1989); Robert G. Lee, *Orientals: Asian Americans in Popular Culture* (Philadelphia: Temple University Press, 1999); Mia Tuan, *Forever Foreigners or Honorary Whites? The Asian Ethnic Experience Today* (New Brunswick, NJ: Rutgers University Press, 1998).

9. On Afro-Caribbean migration, see Mary C. Waters, *Black Identities: West Indian Immigrant Dreams and American Realities* (Cambridge, MA: Harvard University Press, 1999); Milton Vickerman, *Crosscurrents: West Indian Immigrants and Race* (New York: Oxford University Press, 1999).

10. Susan Carter and Richard Sutch argue that the question of whether immigrants help or hurt the economy is never completely objective but depends on the questions asked and methodologies employed. Carter and Sutch, "Historical Background to Current Immigration Issues," in *The New Americans*, 318–19. See also Franklin Mixon, "Friends of Strangers: Examining the Theoretical and Empirical Evidence on Immigration," *International Journal of Social Economics* 20 (1993): 47, 48.

For an example of liberal neorestrictionism, see Christopher Jencks, "Who Should Get In?" *New York Review of Books*, November 29, 2001, 57–63, and "Who Should Get In? Part 2," *New York Review of Books*, December 20, 2001, 94–102.

11. *Plyler v. Doe*, 457 U.S. 202 (1982) (undocumented aliens are "persons within the jurisdiction" of the state and therefore have the right to equal protection); *Graham v. Richardson*, 235 U.S. 365 (1971) (states cannot deny economic benefits on grounds of alienage); *Bolanos v. Kiley*, 509 F.2d 1023 (2d Cir. 1975) (aliens, including illegal aliens, have the right to sue); *Landon v. Plasencia*, 459 U.S. 21 (1982) (the right to procedural due process for a returning alien in an exclusion hearing); *Almedia-Sanchez v. U.S.*, 413 U.S. 266 (1973) (Fourth Amendment protection); *Matter of Marin*, 16 I.&N. Dec. 581 (1978) (balance of equities in determining relief from deportation). For different views on the import of these reforms, see Peter Schuck, "The Transformation of Immigration Law," *Columbia Law Review* 84 (1984): 1–90; Hiroshi Motomura, "The Curious Evolution of Immigration Law: Procedural Surrogates for Substantive Constitutional Rights," *Columbia Law Review* 92 (1992): 1625–1703; Linda Bosniak, "Membership, Equality, and the Difference That Alienage Makes," *NYU Law Review* 69 (1994): 1047–49.

12. *Mathews v. Diaz*, 426 U.S. 67 (1976) (Congress may deny federal benefits to aliens as part of its authority to regulate immigration).

13. Personal Responsibility and Work Opportunity Reconciliation Act of 1996 (Public Law 104-193, 110 Stat. 2105); Anti-Terrorism and Effective Death Penalty Act of 1996 (Public Law No. 104-132, 110 Stat. 1214); Illegal Immigration Reform and Immigrant Responsibility Act of 1996 (Public Law 104-208, div. C, 110 Stat. 3009-546). In 2001 the Supreme Court overturned two aspects of the 1996 laws, indefinite detention in cases where there is no country to receive a deportable alien (*Zadvydas v. Davis*, 121 S.Ct. 249) and retroactive application of mandatory removal for crimes committed before 1996 (*INS v. St. Cyr*, 121 S.Ct. 2271). On 1996 laws, see Daniel Kanstroom, "Deportation, Social Control, and Punishment: Some Thoughts on Why Hard Laws Make Bad Cases," *Harvard Law Review* 113 (June 2000): 1889–1935; Nancy Morawetz, "Understanding the Impact of the 1996 Deportation Laws and the Limited Scope of Proposed Reforms," *Harvard Law Review* 113 (2000): 1936–62; Paul B. Hunker III, "Cancellation of Removal or Cancellation of Relief? The IIRIRA Amendments: A Review and Critique of Section 240(A)(A) of the INA," *Georgetown Immigration Law Journal* 15 (2000): 1–46; Stephen Legomsky, "Immigration Fear and Loathing in Congress and the Courts: Immigration and Judicial Review," *Texas Law Review* 78 (2000): 1615–42.

14. The number of aliens detained after September 11, 2001, is not known beyond 1,147 disclosed on Nov. 8, 2001, the government's last announcement of a cumulative total. Leti Volpp, "The Citizen and the Terrorist," *UCLA Law Review* 49 (2002): 1575–99.

15. "Bush Panel Backs Legalizing Status for Some Migrants," *New York Times*, July 24, 2001, sec. A, 1; "AFL-CIO Calls for Amnesty for Illegal U.S. Workers," *Los Angeles Times*, Feb. 17, 2000, sec. A, 1. For discussion comparing modern guest workers with the *metic* class in ancient Greece, see Michael Walzer, *Spheres of Justice: A Defense of Pluralism and Equality* (New York: Basic Books, 1983), 53–62.

16. *New York Times*, "Mexico Fears Migrant Deaths"; T. Alexander Aleinikoff, "Legal Immigration Reform: Towards Rationality and Equity," in *Blueprints for an Ideal*

Legal Immigration Policy, ed. Richard D. Lamm and Alan Simpson (Washington, DC: Center for Immigration Studies, 2001); Kevin R. Johnson, "Legal Immigration in the Twenty-First Century," ibid. The European Union model is not without problems. Free migration attains only to citizens of member EU states; North African, Turkish, and other non-European migrants in Europe lack both national and EU rights. See Jacqueline Bhabha, "'Get Back to Where You Once Belonged': Identity, Citizenship, and Exclusion in Europe," *Human Rights Quarterly* 20 (1998): 592–627; *New York Times,* "Europeans Move Cautiously on Illegal Immigration Issue," June 23, 2002, sec. A, 6.

17. Richard Primus, *The American Language of Rights* (New York: Cambridge University Press, 1999), chapter 5; "Europeans Move Cautiously On Illegal Immigration Issue," *New York Times;* "How Immigrants Are Transforming the Politics of Europe," *New York Times,* November 30, 2002, sec. A, 30; Seyla Benhabib, *The Claims of Culture: Equality and Diversity in the Global Age* (Princeton: Princeton University Press, 2002), 177. For different assessments of the impact of globalization and human rights law on national sovereignty and immigration restriction, see Bhabha, "'Get Back to Where You Once Belonged'"; David Jacobson, *Rights across Borders: Immigration and the Decline of Citizenship* (Baltimore: Johns Hopkins University Press, 1996); Saskia Sassen, *Losing Control? Sovereignty in the Age of Globalization* (New York: Columbia University Press, 1996), 59–99; Christian Joppke, "Immigration Challenges the Nation State," in *Challenge to the Nation State: Immigration in Western Europe and the U.S.,* ed. Christian Joppke (New York: Oxford University Press, 1998).

Archival and Other Primary Sources

Manuscript Collections

Columbia University, New York

Herbert H. Lehman Papers, Lehman Library
Oral History Collection, Butler Library

Filipino American National Historical Society, Seattle

Demonstration Project for Asian Americans
Filipino American Oral History Project
Filipino American Experience Research Project

Library of Congress, Washington, DC

Emanuel Celler Papers

George Meany Memorial Labor Archives, Silver Spring, MD

Records of the AFL-CIO

United States Immigration and Naturalization Service, Central Office, Washington, DC

Subject Files of the U.S.-INS

United States National Archives and Records Administration

Lyndon Baines Johnson Library, Austin, TX
John F. Kennedy Library, Boston
Harry S. Truman Library, Independence, MO
U.S. Attorneys, Record Group 118, Pacific Region, San Francisco
U.S. Bureau of the Census, Record Group 29, Washington, DC
U.S. Bureau of Insular Affairs, Record Group 350, College Park, MD
U.S. Congress, House of Representatives, Record Group 233, Washington, DC
U.S. Congress, Senate, Record Group 46, Washington, DC
U.S. Department of Labor, Record Group 174, College Park, MD, and Pacific Region, San Francisco
U.S. Department of State, Record Group 59, College Park, MD
U.S. District Courts, Record Group 21, Pacific Region, San Francisco
U.S. Farmers Home Administration, Record Group 96, Pacific Region, San Francisco
U.S. Immigration and Naturalization Service, Record Group 85

Subject Correspondence Files, Washington, DC
Segregated Chinese Files, Northeast Region, New York; and Pacific Region, San
Francisco

University of California, Berkeley, Bancroft Library

California Joint Immigration Committee Papers
Wayne Collins Papers
Japanese American Evacuation and Resettlement Study Papers
Paul Scharrenberg Papers
Irving W. Wood Papers
James W. Woods Papers

University of Minnesota, Minneapolis, Immigration History Research Center

Records of the American Council for Nationality Services

University of Texas, Austin, Bensen Latin American Collection

Records of League of United Latin American Citizens
Records of Order Sons of America (Council 5)
George I. Sánchez Papers
Carlos Eduardo Castaneda Papers
Julian Samora Papers
Eustasio Cepeda Collection

University of Texas, El Paso, Institute of Oral History

Washington State Oral/Aural History Project, 1972–1977, Olympia

Wayne State University, Detroit, Walter P. Reuther Labor Archives of Labor and Urban Affairs

Records of Agricultural Workers Organizing Committee
Records of United Auto Workers

Interviews and Oral Histories

Andres, Rudolfo M. Interview by Helen Hatcher, June 27, 1981. Demonstration Project for Asian Americans, Seattle, WA.
Burciaga, José Cruz. Interview by Oscar Martínez, February 16, 1972. Institute of Oral History, University of Texas, El Paso.
Chuck, Maurice. Interview by the author, January 24, 1993, San Francisco.
Edelstein, Julius. Interview by the author, Nov. 22, 2000, New York.
Filipino Oral History Project, Inc. Voices, A Filipino American Oral History. Stockton, CA: Filipino Oral History Project, 1984.

Gim, Benjamin. Interview by the author, February 19, 1993, New York.

Liang, Shing Tai. Interview by the author, January 14, 1993, New York.

Reeves, Edwin M. Interview by Robert H. Novak, June 25, 1974. Institute of Oral History, Univ. of Texas, El Paso.

Rojo, Trinidad. Interview by Carolina Koslosky, February 18–19, 1975. Washington State Oral/Aural History Project, 1972–1977, Washington State Archive, Olympia, WA.

Simbe, Roman and Hazel. Interview by DeeAnn Dixon and Nancy Koslosky, January 18, 1981, Aberdeen, Washington. Demonstration Project for Asian Americans, Seattle, WA.

Swing, Joseph. Interview by Ed Edwin, June 21, 1964. Eisenhower Administration Oral History Project, Columbia University.

Zamora, Felix. [n.d.] Demonstration Project for Asian Americans, Seattle, WA.

Newspapers and Periodicals

America
Atlantic Monthly
Business Week
Chinese World (San Francisco)
Commentary
Common Ground
East/West News (San Francisco)
Fortune
Forum
Interpreter/Interpreter Releases
La Opinión (Los Angeles)
Los Angeles Times
Nation
National Republic
Newsweek
New Republic
New York Herald Tribune
New York Times
Public Interest
Reporter
San Francisco Chronicle
Saturday Evening Post
Survey/Survey Graphic
Washington Post

Government Serial Publications

Congressional Record
I&N Reporter
INS Information Bulletin
INS Monthly Review

U.S. Department of Justice, *Annual Report of the Attorney General of the United States*
U.S. Department of Justice, *Annual Report of the Commissioner General of Immigration*
U.S. Department of Justice, *Statistical Yearbook of the Immigration and Naturalization Service*
U.S. Department of Labor, *Annual Report of the Commissioner General of Immigration to the Secretary of Labor*
U.S. Department of Labor, *Annual Report of the Secretary of Labor*

Published Government Documents

California State Department of Public Health, Bureau of Tuberculosis. "A Statistical Study of Sickness among the Mexicans in the LA County Hospital" July 1, 1922 to June 30, 1924. Sacramento: California State Printing Office, 1928.
Dickstein, Samuel. "Return Unemployed Filipinos to Philippine Islands." House Committee on Immigration and Naturalization, Report accompanying H.J. Res. 577, January 27, 1933. Washington, DC: GPO, 1933.
"Facts about Filipino Immigration into California." Special Bulletin no. 3 San Francisco: California Department of Industrial Relations, April 1930.
Laughlin, Harry L. "Analysis of the Metal and Dross in America's Melting Pot." Hearings, House Committee on Immigration and Naturalization. Nov. 21, 1922, 67th Congress, 3d Session. Washington, DC: GPO, 1923.
———. "Biological Aspects of Immigration." Hearings, House Committee on Immigration and Naturalization, April 16–17, 1921, 66th Congress, 2d Session. Washington, DC: GPO, 1921.
MacCormack, D. W. "The Lecture Course of Study for the INS Personnel—Retrospect and Prospect." Lecture no. 20, June 18, 1934. Washington, DC: GPO, 1934.
———. "The Spirit of the Service." U.S. Department of Labor, Bureau of Immigration, *Problems of the Immigration Service: Papers Presented at a Conference of Commissioners and District Directors of Immigration*, January 1929. Washington, DC: GPO, 1929.
Smith, Darrell H., and H. Guy Herring. *The Bureau of Immigration: Its History, Activities, and Organization.* Institute for Government Research, Service Monographs of the U.S. Government, no. 30. Baltimore: Johns Hopkins University Press, 1924.
Taylor, Paul S. "Migratory Farm Labor in the United States." United States Department of Labor, Bureau of Labor Statistics, *Monthly Labor Review*, Ser. no. R530, March 1937. Washington, DC: GPO 1937.
Trevor, John. "Preliminary Study of Population." House Report 350, 68th Congress, 1st Session. Washington, DC: GPO, 1924.
U.S. Bureau of Census. "The Hispanic Population in the United States: Population Characteristics." March 2000.
U.S. Commission on Immigration. *Dictionary of Races or Peoples.* Washington, DC: GPO, 1911.
U.S. Commission on Wartime Evacuation and Relocation of Civilians. *Personal Justice Denied: Report of the Commission on Wartime Relocation and Internment of Civilians. Report for the Committee on Interior and Insular Affairs.* Washington, DC:

GPO, 1983. Reprint, Seattle: Civil Liberties Public Education Fund and University of Washington Press, 1997.

U.S. Congress. House. Committee on Immigration and Naturalization. "Hindu Immigration." Hearings, 63rd Congress, 2d Session. Washington, DC: GPO, 1914.

———. "Temporary Suspension of Immigration." Report, 66th Congress, 1st Session. Washington, DC: GPO, 1920.

———. "Japanese Immigration." Hearings, 66th Congress, 2d Session. Washington, DC: GPO, 1921.

———. "Proposed Restriction of Immigration." Hearings, 66th Congress, 2d Session. Washington, DC: GPO, 1921.

———. "Temporary Suspension of Immigration." House Report 1109, 66th Congress, 3d Session. Washington, DC: GPO, 1920.

———. "Europe as an Emigrant Exporting Continent." Hearings, 68th Congress, 1st Session. Washington, DC: GPO, 1924.

———. "Preliminary Study of Population." House Report 350, 68th Congress, 1st Session, H.R. 7995. Washington, DC: GPO, 1924.

———. "Restriction of Immigration." Hearings, 68th Congress, 1st Session Washington, DC: GPO, 1924.

———. "Restriction of Immigration." Hearings, 68th Congress, 2d Session. Washington, DC: GPO, 1925.

———. "Seasonal Agricultural Laborers from Mexico." Hearings, 69th Congress, 2d Session. Washington, DC: GPO, 1926.

———. "American History in Terms of Human Migration." Hearings, 70th Congress, 1st Session. Washington, DC: GPO, 1928.

———. Hearings on H.R. 3, H.R. 5673, H.R. 6069, 70th Congress, 1st Session. Washington, DC: GPO, 1928.

———. "Immigration from Countries of the Western Hemisphere." Hearings, United States House of Representatives, 70th Congress, 1st Session. Washington, DC: GPO, 1929.

———. "Immigration Border Patrol." Preliminary hearing, unrevised. Hearings, [1928], 70th Congress, 1st Session. Washington, DC: GPO, 1930.

———. "Lack of Funds for Deportations." Hearings, 70th Congress, 1st Session. Washington, DC: GPO, 1928.

———. "Immigration from Countries of the Western Hemisphere." Hearings, 71st Congress, 1st Session. Washington, DC: GPO, 1931.

———. "Exclusion of Immigration from the Philippine Islands." Hearings, 71st Congress, 2d Session. Washington, DC: GPO, 1930.

———. "Naturalization." Hearings, 71st Congress, 2d Session. Washington, DC: GPO, 1930.

———. Immigration from Mexico." Hearings, 71st Congress, 2d Session. Washington, DC: GPO, 1930.

———. "Restriction of Immigration." Report to accompany H.R.J. Res. 473, 71st Congress, 2d Session. Washington, DC: GPO, 1931.

———. "Restriction of Immigration." Report to accompany H.R.J. Res. 570, 71st Congress, 2d Session. Washington, DC: GPO, 1931.

———. "Temporary Restriction of Immigration." Report to accompany H.R.J. Res. 500, 71st Congress, 2d Session. Washington, DC: GPO, 1931.

———. "Western Hemisphere Immigration." Hearings, 71st Congress, 2d Session. Washington, DC: GPO, 1930.

———. "Restriction of Immigration." Report to accompany H.R. 10602, 72d Congress, 1st Session. Washington, DC: GPO, 1932.

———. "Return Unemployed Filipinos to Philippine Islands." Report to accompany H.R.J. Res. 577. Washington, DC: GPO, 1933.

———. "To Return Unemployed Filipinos to Philippine Islands." Hearings, 72d Congress, 2d Session. Washington, DC: GPO, 1933.

———. "Amendments to the Immigration Laws as Recommended by the Department of Labor and the Secretary's Ellis Island Committee." 73d Congress, 2d Session. Wasington, DC: GPO, 1934.

———. "To Exclude and Deport Alien Habitual Criminals." Hearings, 74th Congress, 1st Session. Washington, DC: GPO, 1935.

U.S. Congress, House. Committee on the Judiciary. "Hearings before the President's Commission on Immigration and Naturalization." 82d Congress, 2d Session. Washington, DC: GPO, 1952.

———. "Immigration." Hearings, 88th Congress, 2d Session. Washington, DC: GPO, 1964.

U.S. Congress. Senate. Committee on Immigration. *Reports of the Immigration Commission.* Senate Document no. 747, Two parts, 42 vols. 61st Congress, 3d Session. Washington, DC: GPO, 1911.

———. "Regulation and Restriction of Immigration." Senate Report 352, 64th Congress, 1st Session. Washington, DC: GPO, 1916.

———. "Emergency Immigration Legislation." Hearings, 66th Congress, 3d Session. Washington, DC: GPO, 1921.

———. "Japanese Immigration Legislation." Hearings, 68th Congress, 1st Session. Washington, DC: GPO, 1924.

———. "National Origins Provision of the Immigration Act of 1924." Senate Document no. 192, Dec. 16, 1926, 69th Congress, 2d Session. Washington, DC: GPO, 1927.

———. Hearings on S.J. Res. 128, 69th Congress, 2d Session. Washington, DC: GPO, 1927.

———. "Immigration Quotas on the Basis of National Origin." Senate Document no. 65, 70th Congress, 2d Session. Washington, DC: GPO, 1929.

———. Frank Kellogg, William Whiting, and James Davis to the President, Feb. 26, 1929. Senate Document no. 259, 70th Congress, 2d Session. Washington, DC: GPO, 1927.

———. "National Origins Provision of the Immigration Law." Hearings, 70th Congress, 2d Session. Washington, DC: GPO 1929.

———. "Amending the Immigration Act of 1924 Respecting Quota Preferences." Hearings, 71st Congress, 2d Session. Washington, DC: GPO, 1930.

———. "Deportation of Criminals, Preservation of Family Units, Permit Noncriminal Aliens to Legalize their Status." Hearings, 74th Congress, 2d Session. Washington, DC: GPO 1936.

U.S. Congress. Senate. Committee of the Judiciary. "Immigration and Naturalization Systems of the United States." Senate Report 1515, 81st Congress, 2d Session. Washington, DC: GPO, 1950.

————. "Immigration." Hearings on S.500, 89th Congress, 1st Session. 2 vols. Washington, DC: GPO, 1965.

U.S. Congress. Senate. Committee on Territories and Insular Affairs. "Philippine Independence." Senate Report 781, 71st Congress, 2d Session. Washington, DC: GPO, 1930.

U.S. Department of Commerce. Bureau of Census. *Historical Statistics of the United States from Colonial Times to 1970.* Washington, DC: GPO, 1975.

U.S. Department of Labor. Bureau of Employment Security. "Mexican Farm Labor Program, Consultants' Report." Washington, DC: GPO, 1959.

————. Bureau of Employment Service. Farm Labor Service. "Report of Operations of Mexican Farm Labor Program Made Pursuant to Conference Report 1449, House of Representatives, 84th Congress, 1st Session." Washington, DC: GPO, 1960.

————. Bureau of Immigration. "Problems of the Immigration Service: Papers presented at a conference of Commissioners and District Directors of Immigration." January 1929. Washington, DC: GPO, 1929.

————. Bureau of Labor Statistics. "Labor Unionism in American Agriculture." Bureau of Labor Statistics Bulletin no. 836. Washington, DC: GPO, 1945.

————. Immigration and Naturalization Service. *Information concerning Origin, Activities, Accomplishments, Organization, and Personnel of the Immigration Border Patrol.* Washington, DC: GPO, 1938.

————. Immigration and Naturalization Service. "Memorandum of the Commissioner of Immigration and Naturalization to the Committee on Immigration of the Senate and the Committee on Immigration and Naturalization of the House of Representatives Relative to Certain Proposed Changes in the Immigration Law." Washington, DC: GPO, 1934.

U.S. Displaced Persons Commission. *Memo to America: The DP Story, the Final Report.* Washington, DC: GPO, 1952.

U.S. National Commission on Law Observance and Enforcement. *Report on the Enforcement of the Deportation Laws of the United States.* Washington, DC: GPO, 1931.

U.S. President's Commission on Immigration and Naturalization. *Whom We Shall Welcome.* Washington, DC: GPO, 1953.

U.S. President's Commission on Migratory Labor. *Migratory Labor in American Agriculture: Report of the President's Commission on Migratory Labor.* Washington, DC: GPO, 1951.

U.S. Select Commission on Western Hemisphere Immigration. *Report.* January 1968. Washington, DC: GPO, 1968.

Wixon, I. F. "Mission of the Border Patrol." Lecture no. 7. U.S. Department of Labor, Immigration and Naturalization Service. Washington, DC: GPO, 1934.

Theses and Manuscripts

Anthes, Louis. "'Bohemian Justice': The Path of the Law in Immigrant New York, 1870–1940." Ph.D. dissertation, New York University, 2000.

Aquino, Valentin R. "The Filipino Community in Los Angeles." Master's thesis, University of Southern California, 1952. Reprint, San Francisco: R&E Assoc., 1974.

Ave, Mario. "Characteristics of Filipino Organizations in Los Angeles." Master's thesis, University of Southern California, 1956. Reprint, San Francisco: R&E Assoc., 1974.

Azuma, Eiichiro. "Intersitial Lives: Race, Community, and History among Japanese Immigrants Caught between Japan and the U.S., 1885–1941." Ph.D. dissertation, UCLA, 2000.

Ballerini, Julia C. "Political Propaganda/Autobiography: Dorothea Lange's Farm Service Administration Mothers." Paper presented at Women and Society Seminar, Columbia University, September 25, 2000.

Catapusan, Benecio. "The Social Adjustment of Filipinos in the US." Master's thesis, University of Southern California, 1940.

Cavanaugh, Francis P. "Immigration Restriction at Work Today: A Study of the Administration of Immigration Restriction by the United States." Ph.D. dissertation, Catholic University, 1928.

Cohen, Deborah. "Masculine Sweat, Stoop-Labor Modernity: Gender, Race, and Nation in Mid-Twentieth Century Mexico and the U.S." Ph.D. dissertation, University of Chicago, 2001.

Coloma, Casiano. "A Study of the Filipino Repatriation Movement." Master's thesis, University of Southern California, 1939. Reprint, San Francisco: R&E Assoc. 1974.

DeWitt, Howard. "Hiram Johnson and American Foreign Policy." Ph.D. dissertation, University of Arizona, 1972.

Evangelista, Susan P. "Carlos Bulosan and the Beginnings of Third World Consciousness." Ph.D. dissertaion, University of the Philippines, 1981.

Gilbert, James Carl. "A Field Study in Mexico of the Mexican Repatriation Movement." Master's thesis, University of Southern California, 1934.

Green, John Hawkes. "The Filipino in the US with Special Reference to California." Unpublished seminar papers, Dept of History, Occidental College, 1937.

Hawley, Charles Valencia. "'Savage Gentlemen': Filipinos and Colonial Subjectivity in the U.S., 1903–1946." Ph.D. dissertation, University of Iowa, 1999.

Hayashi, Brian. "Transcending Nationalism: Koreans and Japanese in California during World War II." Paper presented to the Asian American Historians Symposium, Japanese American National Museum, Los Angeles, May 18, 2002 (in author's possession).

Heyer, Virginia. "Patterns of Social Organization of New York City's Chinatown." Ph.D. dissertation, Columbia University, 1953.

Jones, William P. "Race, Proletarianization, the Industrial Unionism in the Southern Lumber Industry, 1929–1938." Paper presented at Newberry Labor History Seminar, Chicago, Oct. 11, 2002 (in author's possession).

Lapp, Michael. "Managing Migration: The Migration Division of Puerto Rico and Puerto Ricans in NYC, 1948–1968." Ph.D. dissertation, Johns Hopkins University, 1990.

Leader, Leonard. "Los Angeles and the Great Depression." Ph.D. dissertation, UCLA, 1972.

Lee, Erika. "At America's Gates: Chinese Immigration during the Exclusion Era." Ph.D. dissertation, University of California, Berkeley, 1999.

Leong, Karen. "The China Mystique: Mayling Soong, Pearl S. Buck, and Anna May Wong in the American Imagination." Ph.D. dissertation, University of California, Berkeley, 1999.

Lye, Colleen. "Model Modernity: The Making of Asiatic Racial Form, 1882–1943." Ph.D. dissertation, Columbia University, 1999.

Maram, Linda. "Negotiating Identity: Youth, Gender, and Popular Culture in Los Angeles's Little Manila, 1920s-1940s." Ph.D. dissertation, UCLA, 1996.

Mariano, Honorante. "The Filipino Immigrants in the US." Master's thesis, University of Oregon, 1933. Reprint, San Francisco: R&E Assoc., 1974.

Martínez, Oscar Jr. "The Border in the National Consciousness, 1848–1920: Historiographical Comments on Selected Themes." Paper presented at the International Conference on Border Relations, La Paz, Mexico. Feb. 28–29, 1980.

Ngai, Mae M. "The Politics of Immigration: the Cold War, McCarthyism, and the Chinese in America." Master's thesis, Columbia University, 1993.

Powell, James Henry. "The Concept of Cultural Pluralism in American Social Thought, 1915–1965." Ph.D. dissertation, University of Notre Dame, 1971.

Schor, Paul A. "Census Day 2000: Observations on Race and the Census." Paper presented at Organization of American Historians, St. Louis, April 1, 2000 (in possession of author).

Stern, William. "An Abstract of HR 2580, the Immigration and Nationality Amendments of 1965: A Case Study." Ph.D. dissertation, New York University, 1970.

Treadway, Sandra. "*Terra Incognita*: the Philippine Islands and the Establishment of American Colonial Policy, 1898–1904." Ph.D. dissertation, University of Virginia, 1978.

Varma, Permdatta. "The Asian Indian Community's Struggle for Legal Equality in the US." Ph.D. dissertation, University of Cincinnati, 1989.

Wagner, Stephen. "The Lingering Death of the National Origins Quota System: A Political History of U.S. Immigration Policy, 1952–1965." Ph.D. dissertation, Harvard University, 1986.

Published Books and Articles

Adamic, Louis, *From Many Lands*. New York: Harper, 1939.

———. *A Nation of Nations*. New York: Harper, 1945.

Adams, Ansel. *Born Free and Equal: Photographs of Japanese Americans at Manzanar Relocation Center, Inyo County, California*. New York: U.S. Camera, 1944.

American GI Forum of Texas. *What Price Wetbacks?* Austin: Texas State Federation of Labor, [1954].

Anderson, Henry P. *The Bracero Program in California, with Particular Reference to Health Status, Attitudes, and Practices*. School of Public Health. University of California, Berkeley. March 1961.

———. *A Harvest of Loneliness: An Inquiry into a Social Problem*. Berkeley: Citizens for Farm Labor, 1964.

Anthony, Donald Elliot. "Filipino Labor in Central California." *Sociology and Social Research* 16, no. 3 (January–February 1932): 149–56.

Arendt, Hannah. *Origins of Totalitarianism*. New York: Harcourt Brace, 1979 [1951].

Benedict, Ruth. *Patterns of Culture*. Boston: Houghton Mifflin, 1934.

———. *Race and Racism*. London, G. Routledge & Sons, 1942.

The Bracero Program and Its Aftermath: An Historical Summary. Prepared for the use of the Assembly Committee on Agriculture. 1965.

Buaken, Manuel. *I Have Lived with the American People.* Caldwell, ID: Caxton Printers, 1948.

Bulosan, Carlos. *America Is in the Heart.* Seattle: University of Washington Press, 1993 [1943].

Catapusan, Benicio T. "Filipino Repatriates in the Philippines." *Sociology and Social Research* 21, no. 1 (September–October 1936): 72–77.

Chang, Gordon H., ed. *Morning Glory Evening Shadow: Yamato Ichihashi and his Internment Writings.* Stanford: Stanford University Press, 1997.

Clark, Jane Perry. *Deportation of Aliens from the United States to Europe.* New York: Columbia University Press, 1931.

Corsi, Edward. *Paths to the New World: American Immigration—Yesterday, Today, and Tomorrow.* New York: Anti-Defamation League of B'Nai B'Rith, 1956.

Cressey, Paul. *The Taxi Dance Hall: A Sociological Study in Commercialized Recreation and City Life.* Chicago: University of Chicago Press, 1932.

"Crimes Involving Moral Turpitude." *Harvard Law Review* 43 (1929–30): 117–21.

"Deportation of Aliens." *Columbia Law Review* (June 1920): 680–85.

Dewey, John. *Liberalism and Social Action.* New York: Putnam, 1935.

Eckerson, Helen. "Immigration and National Origins." *Annals of the American Academy* (September 1966): 4–32.

Embree, John. "Resistance to Freedom: An Administrative Problem." *Applied Anthropology* 2, no. 4 (1943): 10–14.

Grant, Madison. *The Passing of the Great Race.* New York: Scribners, 1916.

Grant, Madison, and Charles Stewart Davison, eds. *The Alien in Our Midst, or "Selling our Birthright for a Mess of Pottage."* New York: Galton, 1930.

Hadley, Eleanor. "A Critical Analysis of the Wetback Problem." *Law and Contemporary Problems* 21 (1956): 334–57.

Handlin, Oscar. *Danger in Discord: The Origins of Anti-Semitism.* New York: Anti-Defamation League of B'nai B'rith, 1948.

———. *Immigration as a Factor in American History.* Englewood Cliffs, NJ: Prentice Hall, 1959.

———. "The Immigration Flight Has Just Begun." *Commentary* 14 (July 1952): 1–7.

———. *Out of Many: A Study Guide to Cultural Pluralism.* New York: Anti-Defamation League of B'nai B'rith, 1964.

———. "We Need More Immigrants." *Atlantic Monthly* (May 1953): 27–31.

Hill, Joseph. "Composition of the American Population by Race and Country of Origin." *Annals of the American Academy of Political and Social Science*, November 1936.

Isaac, Julian. *Economics of Migration.* London: Paul Kegan, 1947.

Kallen, Horace. *Culture and Democracy in the United States, Studies in the Group Psychology of the American Peoples.* New York: Boni and Liveright, 1924.

Kaneshiro, Takeo, ed. *Internees: War Relocation Memoirs and Diaries.* New York: Vantage Press, 1976.

Kennedy, John F. *A Nation of Immigrants.* New York: Anti-Defamation League of B'nai B'rith, 1959.

Kiyota, Minoru. *Beyond Loyalty: The Story of a Kibei.* Seattle: University of Washington Press, 1997.

Kohler, Max. *Immigration and Aliens in the United States.* New York: Bloch, 1936.

Lasker, Bruno. *Filipino Immigration to Continental United States and Hawaii.* Chicago: University of Chicago Press, 1931.

Lewis, Edward. *Nation or Confusion? A Study of Our Immigration Problems.* New York: Harper and Row, 1928.

Locke, Alain. *Race Contacts and Interracial Relations: Lectures on the Theory and Practice of Race.* Washington: Howard University Press, 1992.

Mack, William. *Patterns of Minority Relations.* New York: Anti-Defamation League of B'nai B'rith, 1964.

Manzon, Maximo. *The Strange Case of the Filipino in the United States.* New York: American Committee for the Protection of the Foreign Born, 1938.

McWilliams, Carey. *Brothers under the Skin.* Boston: Little, Brown, 1943.

Mead, Margaret. *Coming of Age in Samoa: A Psychological Study of Primitive Youth for Western Civilization.* New York: W. Morrow, 1928.

Modell, John, ed. *The Kikuchi Diary: Chronicle from an American Concentration Camp, The Tanforan Journals of Charles Kikuchi.* Urbana, IL: University of Illinois Press, 1973.

Moore, Truman. *The Slaves We Rent.* New York: Random House, 1965.

Myrdal, Gunnar. *An American Dilemma: The Negro Problem and American Democracy.* New York: Harper, 1944.

National Conference of Chinese Communities in America. Report and Proceedings. March 5–7, 1957, Washington, DC.

Okubo, Mine. *Citizen 10366.* New York: Columbia University Press, 1946.

Park, Robert E. "Race and Culture." *Collected Papers of Robert Ezra Park,* ed. Everett C. Hughes, et al. Glencoe, IL: Free Press, 1950.

Peterson, William. *The Politics of Population.* New York: Doubleday, 1964.

Provinse, John, and Solon Kimball. "Building New Communities During War Time." *American Sociological Review* 11, no. 4 (August 1946): 396–409.

Rak, Mary Kidder. *Border Patrol.* Boston: Houghton Mifflin, 1938.

Reder, Melvin W. "The Economic Consequences of Increased Immigration." *Review of Economics and Statistics* 45 (August 1963): 221–30.

Report of the Ellis Island Committee. New York: n.p., 1934.

Rojo, Trinidad. "Social Maladjustment Among Filipinos in the U.S." *Sociology and Social Research* 21, no. 5 (May–June 1937): 447–57.

Saunders, Lyle, and Olen Leonard. *The Wetback in the Lower Rio Grande Valley of Texas.* Austin: University of Texas Press, 1951.

Schmidt, Fred H. *After the Bracero: An Inquiry into the Problems of Farm Labor Recruitment.* Los Angeles: UCLA Institute of Industrial Relations, 1964.

Scruggs, Otey. "Evolution of the Mexican Farm Labor Agreement." *Agricultural History* 36 (1966): 140–49.

Senior, Clarence. *Strangers Then Neighbors: From Pilgrims to Puerto Ricans.* New York: Freedom Books, 1961.

Spicer, Edward. "The Use of Social Scientists by the War Relocation Authority." *Applied Anthropology* 5, no. 2 (1946): 16–36.

"Statutory Construction in Deportation Cases." *Yale Law Journal* 40 (1931): 1284–97.

Taylor, Paul S. *An American-Mexican Frontier, Nueces County, Texas.* Chapel Hill, University of North Carolina Press, 1934.

———. "Mexican Labor in the United States: Chicago and the Calumet Region." *University of California Publications in Economics* 7, no. 2 (1932): 25–28.

———. "Mexican Labor in the United States: Dimmit County, Winter Garden District, South Texas." University of California *Publications in Economics* 6, no. 5 (1930), 322.

———. "Mexican Labor in the United States: Migration Statistics." *University of California Publications in Economics* 6, no. 3 (1929): 244–45.

———. "Mexican Labor in the United States: Migration Statistics. II." *University of California Publications in Economics* 12, no. 1 (1933): 1–10.

———. "Mexican Labor in the United States: Migration Statistics. III." *University of California Publications in Economics* 12, no. 2 (1933): 11–22.

———. "Mexican Labor in the United States: Migration Statistics. IV." *University of California Publications in Economics* 12, no. 3 (1934): 23–50.

———. "Mexican Labor in the United States: Valley of the South Platte, Colorado." *University of California Publications in Economics* 6, no. 2 (1929): 105–6, 119–23.

Ten Broek, J., E. N. Barnhart, and F. W. Matson. *Prejudice, War, and the Constitution: Japanese American Evacuation and Resettlement.* Vol. 3. Berkeley: University of California Press, 1954.

Thomas, Dorothy Swaine. *The Salvage.* Berkeley: University of California Press, 1952.

Thomas, Dorothy Swaine, and Richard Nishimoto. *The Spoilage.* Berkeley: University of California Press, 1946.

Trevor, John. "An Analysis of the American Immigration Act of 1924." *International Conciliation* 202 (September 1924): 58–59.

Van Vleck, William. *The Administrative Control of Aliens: A Study in Administrative Law and Procedure.* New York: Commonwealth Fund, 1932.

Walker, Francis A. "Immigration and Degradation." *Forum* (August 1891): 634–44.

———. "Our Population in 1900." *Atlantic Monthly* 32, no. 192 (Oct. 1873): 487–95.

———. "Restriction of Immigration." *Atlantic Monthly* (June 1896): 822–29.

Index

Acheson, Dean, 238
Adamic, Louis, 232, 233, 346n.62
Adams, Ansel, 179
Adams, Brooks, 98
Adams, Henry, 31
Addams, Jane, 82
Administrative Procedures Act (60 Stat. 237, 1946), 88–89
admissibility, 3, 18, 57; literacy as measure of, 19–20. *See also* exclusion
AFL-CIO, 163–66, 243, 250. *See also* American Federation of Labor; Congress of Industrial Organizations
African Americans, 8–9, 24, 42–43, 110–11, 138, 171, 251, 267–68; and civil rights, 166, 229, 245; and quota laws, 26, 33–34, 36–38. *See also* Civil Rights movement
agribusiness, 93, 128–29, 135–36, 166
Agricultural Adjustment Act (48 Stat. 31, 1933), 136
agricultural labor, 13, 23, 50, 70–71, 128–30, 136; attempts to organize, 165; labor activism of, 161–64; racial composition of, 93–95, 103–4; shortages of, 135, 137. *See also* foreign contract labor
Agricultural Workers Association, 164
Agricultural Workers Organizing Committee, 164–65
Alaska, territory of, 26, 94, 97
Alien and Sedition Laws (1 Stat. 570, 1798; 1 Stat. 577, 1798; 1 Stat. 566, 1798; 1 Stat. 596, 1798), 58
"alien citizenship," 2, 8, 170, 175, 267, 269
Alien Contract Labor Law (23 Stat. 332, 1885), 138, 139, 281n.5, 291n.7, 311n.35
Alien Enemy Act (1 Stat. 577, 1798), 175
alien land laws, 40, 46–47, 49
Alien Registration Act (54 Stat. 670, 1940), 87
aliens and alienage, xix, 4, 6, 8, 57, 61, 79–80, 82; cases pertaining to, 38, 42, 44–49, 53–54, 76–77, 80, 81, 88, 214, 268; cultural understandings of, 3, 62
American Civil Liberties Union, 191, 193–94
American Coalition, 116

American Council of Learned Societies, 32
American Council of the Institute of Pacific Relations, 106
American Federation of Labor (AFL), 20, 116–17, 135, 161, 163, 243, 251–52
American GI Forum, 160
American Immigration Conference, 252
American Jewish Congress, 241
American Legion, 20, 35, 47, 114, 116, 219, 258, 260, 351n.112
American Protective Association, 19
Americanization, 177, 231, 232
anarchism and anarchists, 18, 59, 76, 237. *See also* subversion and subversives
Anglo-Saxonism, 18, 50, 94, 98, 233
Anti-Defamation League of B'nai B'rith, 240
Anti-Terrorism and Effective Death Penalty Act of 1996 (110 Stat. 1214, 1996), 1, 268, 275n.1, 354n.13
Arendt, Hannah, 10
Armenians, 38, 43
Asian American studies, 263
Asian Americans, 13, 169, 262
Asians, 8, 13, 50; exclusion of, 18, 37, 46, 238, 246; occupational migration of, 262–63, 267; as racial category, 7–8, 37, 44–46, 109
Asia-Pacific Triangle, 238, 246
Asiatic Exclusion League, 47
assimilation, 2, 22, 24, 38, 46, 49, 109
atomic bomb, 193
Australia, 18, 27
Austria, 30, 235

Barber, Bruce, 219
Barker, Howard, 32–33
Barrows, David, 110–11
Belgium, 27, 66
Benedict, Ruth, 231–32
Best, Raymond, 185–86
Beveridge, Alfred, Jr., 99, 101
Biddle, Francis, 187
Board of Economic Welfare, 137
Boas, Franz, 231
Bogardus, Emory, 111

POLITICS AND SOCIETY IN TWENTIETH-CENTURY AMERICA

Civil Defense Begins at Home: Militarization Meets Everyday Life in the Fifties, by Laura McEnaney

Cold War Civil Rights: Race and the Image of American Democracy, by Mary L. Dudziak

Divided We Stand: American Workers and the Struggle for Black Equality, by Bruce Nelson

Poverty Knowledge: Social Science, Social Policy, and the Poor in Twentieth-Century U.S. History, by Alice O'Connor

Suburban Warriors: The Origins of the New American Right, by Lisa McGirr

The Politics of Whiteness: Race, Workers, and Culture in the Modern South, by Michelle Brattain

State of the Union: A Century of American Labor, by Nelson Lichtenstein

Changing the World: American Progressives in War and Revolution, by Alan Dawley

Dead on Arrival: The Politics of Healthcare in Twentieth-Century America, by Colin Gordon

For All These Rights: Business, Labor, and the Shaping of America's Public-Private Welfare State, by Jennifer Klein

The Radical Middle Class: Populist Democracy and the Question of Capitalism in Progressive Era Portland, Oregon, by Robert D. Johnston

American Babylon: The Struggle for the Postwar City in Oakland and the East Bay, by Robert O. Self

The Other Women's Movement: Workplace Justice and Social Rights in Modern America, by Dorothy Sue Cobble

Impossible Subjects: Illegal Aliens and the Making of Modern America, by Mae M. Ngai